Dictionary of Literary Biography

Documentary Series

Yearbooks

Concise Series

Concise Dictionary of American Literary Biography, 6 volumes (1988-1989): *The New Consciousness, 1941-1968; Colonization to the American Renaissance, 1640-1865; Realism, Naturalism, and Local Color, 1865-1917; The Twenties, 1917-1929; The Age of Maturity, 1929-1941; Broadening Views, 1968-1988.*

Concise Dictionary of British Literary Biography, 8 volumes (1991-1992): *Writers of the Middle Ages and Renaissance Before 1660; Writers of the Restoration and Eighteenth Century, 1660-1789; Writers of the Romantic Period, 1789-1832; Victorian Writers, 1832-1890; Late Victorian and Edwardian Writers, 1890-1914; Modern Writers, 1914-1945; Writers After World War II, 1945-1960; Contemporary Writers, 1960 to Present.*

American Book Collectors
and Bibliographers
Second Series

Dictionary of Literary Biography® • Volume One Hundred Eighty-Seven

American Book Collectors and Bibliographers
Second Series

Edited by
Joseph Rosenblum
University of North Carolina at Greensboro

A Bruccoli Clark Layman Book
Gale Research
Detroit, Washington, D.C., London

The paper used in this publication meets the minimum requirements
of American National Standard for Information Sciences–Permanence
Paper for Printed Library Materials, ANSI Z39.48-1984. ○ ™

Library of Congress Cataloging-in-Publication Data

American book collectors and bibliographers. Second series / edited by Joseph Rosenblum.
  p. cm.–(Dictionary of literary biography; v. 187)
"A Bruccoli Clark Layman book."
Includes bibliographical references and index.
ISBN 0-7876-1842-X (alk. paper)
1. Bibliographers–United States–Bio-bibliography. 2. Book collectors–United States–
Bio-bibliography. I. Rosenblum, Joseph. II. Series.
Z1004.A49 1997
012'.092'273–dc21

97-39600
CIP

10 9 8 7 6 5 4 3 2 1

To Lily, for her many years of companionship

Contents

Plan of the Series

. . . Almost the most prodigious asset of a country, and perhaps its most precious possession, is its native literary product — when that product is fine and noble and enduring.

Mark Twain*

The advisory board, the editors, and the publisher of the *Dictionary of Literary Biography* are joined in endorsing Mark Twain's declaration. The literature of a nation provides an inexhaustible resource of permanent worth. We intend to make literature and its creators better understood and more accessible to students and the reading public, while satisfying the standards of teachers and scholars.

To meet these requirements, *literary biography* has been construed in terms of the author's achievement. The most important thing about a writer is his writing. Accordingly, the entries in *DLB* are career biographies, tracing the development of the author's canon and the evolution of his reputation.

The purpose of *DLB* is not only to provide reliable information in a convenient format but also to place the figures in the larger perspective of literary history and to offer appraisals of their accomplishments by qualified scholars.

The publication plan for *DLB* resulted from two years of preparation. The project was proposed to Bruccoli Clark by Frederick G. Ruffner, president of the Gale Research Company, in November 1975. After specimen entries were prepared and typeset, an advisory board was formed to refine the entry format and develop the series rationale. In meetings held during 1976, the publisher, series editors, and advisory board approved the scheme for a comprehensive biographical dictionary of persons who contributed to North American literature. Editorial work on the first volume began in January 1977, and it was published in 1978. In order to make *DLB* more than a reference tool and to compile volumes that individually have claim to status as literary history, it was decided to organize volumes by topic, period, or genre. Each of these freestanding volumes provides a biographical-bibliographical guide and overview for a particular area of literature. We are convinced that this organization—as opposed to a single alphabet method—constitutes a valuable innovation in the presentation of reference material. The volume plan necessarily requires many decisions for the placement and treatment of authors who might properly be included in two or three volumes. In some instances a major figure will be included in separate volumes, but with different entries emphasizing the aspect of his career appropriate to each volume. Ernest Hemingway, for example, is represented in *American Writers in Paris, 1920–1939* by an entry focusing on his expatriate apprenticeship; he is also in *American Novelists, 1910–1945* with an entry surveying his entire career, as well as in *American Short-Story Writers, 1910–1945, Second Series* with an entry concentrating on his short stories. Each volume includes a cumulative index of the subject authors and articles. Comprehensive indexes to the entire series are planned.

The series has been further augmented by the *DLB Yearbooks* (since 1981) which update published entries and add new entries to keep the *DLB* current with contemporary activity. There have also been *DLB Documentary Series* volumes which provide biographical and critical source materials for figures whose work is judged to have particular interest for students. One of these companion volumes is entirely devoted to Tennessee Williams.

We define literature as the *intellectual commerce of a nation:* not merely as belles lettres but as that ample and complex process by which ideas are generated, shaped, and transmitted. *DLB* entries are not limited to "creative writers" but extend to other figures who in their time and in their way influenced the mind of a people. Thus the series encompasses historians, journalists, publishers, book collectors, and screenwriters. By this means readers of *DLB* may be aided to perceive literature not as cult scripture in the keeping of intellectual high priests but firmly positioned at the center of a nation's life.

**From an unpublished section of Mark Twain's autobiography, copyright by the Mark Twain Company*

DLB includes the major writers appropriate to each volume and those standing in the ranks behind them. Scholarly and critical counsel has been sought in deciding which minor figures to include and how full their entries should be. Wherever possible, useful references are made to figures who do not warrant separate entries.

Each *DLB* volume has an expert volume editor responsible for planning the volume, selecting the figures for inclusion, and assigning the entries. Volume editors are also responsible for preparing, where appropriate, appendices surveying the major periodicals and literary and intellectual movements for their volumes, as well as lists of further readings. Work on the series as a whole is coordinated at the Bruccoli Clark Layman editorial center in Columbia, South Carolina, where the editorial staff is responsible for accuracy and utility of the published volumes.

One feature that distinguishes *DLB* is the illustration policy–its concern with the iconography of literature. Just as an author is influenced by his surroundings, so is the reader's understanding of the author enhanced by a knowledge of his environment. Therefore *DLB* volumes include not only drawings, paintings, and photographs of authors, often depicting them at various stages in their careers, but also illustrations of their families and places where they lived. Title pages are regularly reproduced in facsimile along with dust jackets for modern authors. The dust jackets are a special feature of *DLB* because they often document better than anything else the way in which an author's work was perceived in its own time. Specimens of the writers' manuscripts and letters are included when feasible.

Samuel Johnson rightly decreed that "The chief glory of every people arises from its authors." The purpose of the *Dictionary of Literary Biography* is to compile literary history in the surest way available to us–by accurate and comprehensive treatment of the lives and work of those who contributed to it.

The *DLB* Advisory Board

Introduction

Dictionary of Literary Biography volume 187, *American Book Collectors and Bibliographers,* Second Series, is a companion volume to *DLB 140, American Book Collectors and Bibliographers,* First Series. Like the earlier volume, the present one includes booksellers and librarians in addition to book collectors and bibliographers. The two volumes complement and interconnect with each other. For example, A. Edward Newton, who is covered in *DLB 140,* often drew on the stock and bibliographic knowledge of his fellow Philadelphian Charles Sessler, who is included in the present volume. Newton was also a close friend of Robert Borthwick Adam II, with whom he shared a love of Samuel Johnson and eighteenth-century British literature; the Adam entry appears in this volume. George Brinley Jr. bought many of his books, including his first major purchase, from Samuel Gardner Drake; Brinley is covered in *DLB 140,* Drake in *DLB 187.*

The introduction to *DLB 140* points out some of the ways in which collectors, booksellers, bibliographers, and librarians interact, and also how these categories blend into each other. These observations apply to the figures discussed in this volume as well. Stephen B. Weeks built his extensive collection of North Caroliniana to further his bibliographical studies of the state's literature and history. Bruce Cotten, who collected in the same area, drew on Weeks's knowledge and writings to pursue his avocation. Whereas Weeks collected for the purpose of compiling bibliographies, Irvin Kerlan's bibliographies were a by-product of his collecting. Kerlan's interest was in children's books published roughly between 1920 and 1960. Others had collected and documented children's literature published before 1900, but among the attractions of collecting more-recent works were the excitement of being a pioneer and the lack of strong competition. On the other hand, like any pioneer, Kerlan found few paths in this new territory: he could not turn to a reference book that would list all the works of a particular author or illustrator; no one had identified the "collectible" works, the classics (or future classics) in the field; nor had anyone determined whether a particular binding indicated a first or later printing of a book. If Kerlan wanted such information, he had to undertake the research himself. He did so, and he shared his discoveries in his publications. John

Work Garrett's collecting interest in Marylandia, especially of the seventeenth century, prompted his important article "Seventeenth Century Books Relating to Maryland" in the *Maryland Historical Magazine* in 1939. Thus, categories elide. The bibliographer becomes the collector; the collector becomes a bibliographer.

Collectors, bibliographers, booksellers, and librarians can enjoy symbiotic relationships. Garrett's collection—and his money—allowed his librarian, Elizabeth Baer, to publish *Seventeenth Century Maryland: A Bibliography* (1949). In the introduction to *The First Editions of the Writings of Charles Dickens and Their Values: A Bibliography* (1913) John C. Eckel thanks Harry B. Smith and Charles Sessler "for valuable assistance cheerfully rendered." John Cook Wyllie, librarian of the University of Virginia, shared his bibliographical knowledge with the collector Linton R. Massey. Frederick R. Goff of the Rare Book Division of the Library of Congress assisted Lessing J. Rosenwald in his pursuit of early illustrated books. Rosenwald also drew on the vast fund of knowledge of the bookseller A. S. W. Rosenbach (treated in *DLB 140*). These two *DLB* volumes on American bibliophiles exemplify such cooperation: many of those who have written the entries are themselves librarians, bibliographers, collectors, or booksellers, and these contributors have drawn on information in bibliographies or book catalogues generously supplied by other librarians, collectors, and booksellers.

Bibliophiles require books, but books also require bibliophiles. Twentieth-century literature would not have been the same without the collector John Quinn, whose purchases and sales helped fund such major modernists as William Butler Yeats, Ezra Pound, T. S. Eliot, James Joyce, and Joseph Conrad. Grateful for Quinn's interest and support when Yeats was still largely unknown in the United States, the Irish poet wrote to the New York lawyer on 18 March 1904, "I am facing the world with great hopes and strength and I owe it all to you and I thank you and shall always be grateful." In a letter of 19 February 1913 Conrad thanked Quinn for the financial support that allowed the writer to continue producing his novels: "The hundred pounds will pay last year's doctor bill and cover my overdraft at my bank. They save me from the necessity of stories for the magazines." Eliot also thanked Quinn for buying his manuscripts and securing American publication of his works, writing on 26 April 1923, "Perhaps I can only say that it is the greatest stimulus to me to commence the work I have in mind, which is more ambitious than anything I have ever done yet. And a stimulus to do my part to bring about the conditions which will make the work possible." The bookseller Frances Steloff guaranteed the survival of Cyril Connolly's *Horizon* by purchasing a thousand copies of each issue, and Charles Henri Ford was able to pay for the printing of *View,* an influential periodical devoted to Surrealism, because of Steloff's large orders. She employed Tennessee Williams, Allen Ginsberg, and LeRoi Jones and lent Anaïs Nin the money to buy the press on which the revised edition of Nin's *Winter of Artifice* (1942) and the first edition of *Under a Glass Bell* (1944) were printed. Kerlan was also a promoter of the works he collected: more than a third of his nine thousand volumes were inscribed copies, tributes to his many friendships. Through visits, letters, and publications he promoted and encouraged authors and illustrators.

The bibliophile's role in scholarship is equally—perhaps even more—significant. Many book lovers have themselves been scholars or made scholarly contributions. Hubert Howe Bancroft, Wilmarth Sheldon Lewis, Thomas Prince, and Rosenbach provide examples from *DLB 140*. Figures in the present volume demonstrate the same scholarly bent. Steloff organized the James Joyce Society to "introduce Joyce students to scholars, maintain a Joyce library, further the publication and distribution of his works, . . . and issue occasional bulletins." In *The Invention of Printing* (1876) Theodore Low De Vinne established, for the first time, Johannes Gutenberg's claim to being the first printer in Europe. Isaiah Thomas's *The History of Printing in America* (1810) has stood since its publication as the standard work on its subject.

The work of students and scholars would be impossible without the efforts of dealers and collectors who find books and bring them together, bibliographers who describe them, and librarians who organize them. George Birkbeck Hill, the biographer of Samuel Johnson, traveled from England to Buffalo to consult the books and manuscripts of Adam, who allowed Hill the use of the proof sheets for James Boswell's *The Life of Samuel Johnson, LL.D.* (1791). Hill later wrote, "May more old libraries . . . be carried across the Atlantic, provided that they come into the hands of citizens as enlightened and liberal as my friend Mr. R. B. Adam." William Wallace's edition of the correspondence of Robert Burns

and Frances Anna Wallace Dunlop (1898) was made possible by Adam, who owned most of their letters. Of another collector, the historian C. R. Boxer wrote: "No man [did] more to foster the study of Portuguese history, and especially Portuguese colonial history, than William B. Greenlee did founding the collection at the Newberry Library which bears his name." Rosenwald allowed eight of his copies of William Blake's rare illuminated books to be reproduced by Arnold Fawcus at the Trianon Press in Clairvaux, thus making the works accessible to a wider audience. The Library of Congress also published facsimiles of Rosenwald rarities, and he made the originals available to researchers at the library. Bruce Redford, editor of the letters of Samuel Johnson (1992–1994), relied heavily on the collection assembled by Donald and Mary Hyde and praised the latter for her "crucial role in the development of Johnsonian studies." Just as there would have been no Yale edition of the letters of Horace Walpole (1937–1983) without the efforts of Lewis, it is unlikely that Redford's edition of Johnson's letters would have been possible without the Hydes' Four Oaks Library.

The generosity of the bibliophiles treated in this volume—and of many others—continues beyond their deaths in the contributions they have made to public and academic libraries. Kerlan's nine-thousand-volume gift to the University of Minnesota served as the nucleus of a growing collection that is a major center for the study of juvenile literature. The Cotten and Weeks books are central to the North Caroliniana collection at Chapel Hill. William Andrews Clark Jr.'s gift of his books and a $1.5 million endowment to UCLA made the school an excellent resource for the study of eighteenth-century British literature and Oscar Wilde, and he also gave valuable Thomas Jefferson and Edgar Allan Poe material to the University of Virginia, his alma mater. The American Antiquarian Society is largely the result of the vision and generosity of Thomas, who gave his collection of early American imprints, newspapers, magazines, and pamphlets "to contribute to the advancement of the arts and sciences, and . . . to assist the researches of future historians of our country." Thomas also gave the land and $10,000 for the construction of the first Antiquarian Hall.

Even when collectors and booksellers have not donated or sold their books directly to libraries, they have assembled and preserved material that has later found its way into such institutions. The manuscript for Joyce's *Ulysses* (published in 1922) resides in the Rosenbach Museum and Library because Rosenbach was able to purchase the treasure at the sale of Quinn's library. The Berg Collection of the New York Public Library owns Eliot's draft of *The Waste Land* (published in 1922) annotated by Ezra Pound, another work preserved by Quinn. The Huntington, Newberry, and Morgan libraries secured important works at the 1911–1912 sale of Robert Hoe III's extensive collection. At the 1920 sale of the De Vinne collection dealing with the history of printing in 1920, the Newberry secured 250 important titles.

These two *DLB* volumes may be regarded as a history of book culture in America. The three most important collectors in the colonies are treated in *DLB 140:* William Byrd II of Virginia, James Logan of Philadelphia, and Cotton Mather of Massachusetts. The nature of their collections reveals much not only about the individuals who assembled them but also about the interests of their respective regions. History, law, and belles lettres comprised the majority of Byrd's books. He was not indifferent to science or religion: he owned the finest medical library in colonial Virginia and the largest collection of Anglican works in the British colonies. Still, his focus was not on these areas. Though Mather was, like Byrd, a polymath and a member of the Royal Society, religious works predominated in his collection, indicative not only of Mather's occupation of minister but also of the strong Puritan influence in New England. Situated between these two men geographically and intellectually, Logan concentrated on the sciences. His library highlighted the practical bent of the Middle Colonies that is exemplified by Logan's fellow Philadelphians Benjamin Franklin and John Bartram.

These collections were, by later standards, relatively small. Byrd's library held some thirty-five hundred volumes, Mather's probably about four thousand. Books were not readily available in the colonies; Byrd, who lived in rural Virginia, secured most of his from London. Even in Philadelphia, the second-largest city in the British Empire in the eighteenth century, or in Boston, book lovers turned to England for the majority of their purchases. Colonial libraries were also utilitarian, Mather collecting to support his ministry, Byrd for his legal interests, Logan for his scientific pursuits and classical translations. Even had American collectors of the Colonial era wanted to buy books as rarities, they would have found no Colonial bookseller with a similar interest.

The first American to seek rare books as such was William Mackenzie, who pursued beautifully printed and well-illustrated works: incunabula, color-plate books, English literature, and Americana. His pursuits were aided by his fellow Philadel-phian, the bookseller Nicholas Gouin Dufief. Dufief did not specialize in rare books; Drake was the first American bookseller to do so. In his store and auctions Dufief did, however, include rare books, some of them from the libraries of Byrd and Franklin.

Though still a cultural colony of Britain, America in the first decades of the nineteenth century was beginning to assert intellectual independence, as indicated by Noah Webster's American spelling books and Thomas's founding of the American Antiquarian Society in 1812. Thomas's presses helped make books more readily available, and his own collection of Americana served as the nucleus of an important library concerned with the history of the country and its books. Cultural nationalism is evident, too, in the collecting interests of Brinley and James Lenox (treated in *DLB 140*). To supply their needs they could turn to American booksellers such as Drake and Henry Stevens (treated in *DLB 140*). In 1845 Drake provided Brinley with his first major purchase, a collection of books dealing with Native Americans—a library that attests to Americans' growing interest in their land, their people, and their past. The formation of such collections is of a piece with James Fenimore Cooper's novels about American history and the prairie, Ralph Waldo Emerson's call for an American poet, and Walt Whitman's response to Emerson's summons.

The nineteenth century's westward migration is reflected in American book culture—and, hence, in these two *DLB* volumes. All of the figures included from before the Civil War hugged the East Coast, and with the exception of Byrd, all were northerners. In the later nineteenth century other book centers emerged. Chicago's significance is symbolized by Eugene Field (treated in *DLB 140*) and later by Vincent Starrett, whose collecting and writing are part of the Chicago Renaissance. The West Coast came to rival the East in bibliophily through the efforts of Bancroft, Ernest Dawson (treated in *DLB 140*), Clark, Warren Richardson Howell (treated in *DLB 140*), and David Magee. The progress of Charles Frederick Heartman from Europe to the East Coast and then to the Southwest replicates the pattern of American migration, as does the movement of the Hoe books from New York to the Huntington Library in San Marino, California.

Heartman found the South hungry for books, and he helped to fill this need. Others below the Mason-Dixon line also pursued bibliophilic interests. The collecting careers of Cotten, Weeks, and Massey coincide with the South's literary renaissance, just as Brinley's and Lenox's did with the American literary renaissance of the 1850s.

The emergence of America as a world power in the early twentieth century may be measured in many ways; one of those ways is through books. While Stevens championed American imprints, he did so from London. As important as Dufief and Drake were, they lacked the stature of their European counterparts. Dealers who came to the first Hoe sale in April 1911 scoffed at the idea of a major book auction in New York and expected little competition from their American counterparts. Even the Anderson Gallery, which undertook the sale, lacked confidence in its own auctioneer and imported Sidney Hodgson from London to sell the high spot of the collection, the Gutenberg Bible printed on vellum. The sale of that work symbolized the transfer of economic power from the Old World to the New as the American George D. Smith, backed by the deep pockets of Henry E. Huntington (both treated in *DLB 140*), routed the Englishman Bernard Quaritch. Overall, in the first series of Hoe sales Smith spent more than $500,000; Quaritch was a distant second at $90,000. As Matthew J. Bruccoli writes in *The Fortunes of Mitchell Kennerly, Bookman* (1986), "The Hoe sale made New York a serious contender for the position of rare book center of the world." In the 1920s Rosenbach and Sessler would continue the trend begun by George D. Smith, annually bringing millions of dollars worth of books back from England and the Continent. *Ubi libri, ibi potestas* (Where there are books, there is power).

The kinds of books collected and sold also reveal cultural transformations. In 1830 Sydney Smith, cofounder of the *Edinburgh Review,* scoffed, "Who reads an American book?" He might as easily have asked, "Who collects an American author?" The Romantic era's concern with the past combined with nationalism to inspire collections of Americana, but American literature lagged well behind as a field of bookselling or book collecting. In 1900 Stephen H. Wakeman began his library of American literature, concentrating on nine authors: Emerson, Poe, William Cullen Bryant, Nathaniel Hawthorne, Oliver Wendell Holmes, Henry Wadsworth Longfellow, James Russell Lowell, Henry David Thoreau, and John Greenleaf Whittier. That such a focus seems commonplace in the late twentieth century is due in large part to Wakeman. As Timothy D. Pyatt writes in the Wakeman entry in this volume, "The attention generated by the [1924] sale [of Wakeman's books], combined with the record prices received for Poe and Hawthorne items, attracted bibliophiles to this newly charted genre." Cambridge University Press had published its first history of American literature in 1917, and in 1927 Duke University became one of the first schools in the country to hire a professor–Jay B. Hubbell–to teach American literature.

Western Americana was another field that was of little interest to collectors, booksellers, and bibliographers before the Civil War. Among the pioneers in this field was Bancroft, whose library and the historical works that emerged from it document the Far West. Although Clark did not concentrate on Americana, in 1924 he paid $15,000 for Charles N. Kessler's collection dealing with Clark's native Montana and the Pacific Northwest. Like Bancroft, Henry R. Wagner (treated in *DLB 140*) collected western Americana to support his research, which in his case was bibliographical. Wagner's bibliography of Western travel narratives, *The Plains and the Rockies* (1920), helped stimulate collecting in this field, and among those who responded was Thomas Winthrop Streeter (treated in *DLB 140*). Streeter's bibliography of Texas, based largely on his own library, served as a guide to later collectors, and the seven-volume catalogue of the sale of his books (1966–1969) constitutes another important bibliography in the field. Just as the Wakeman sale highlighted the acceptance of American literature as a legitimate field for study and collecting, so the Streeter sale confirmed the significance of western Americana. Collectors are both mirrors and makers of manners.

What is collected and sold, and where these activities occur, serve as signs of political and cultural trends. Economics also affects the tides of taste and the techniques of collecting. Huntington, John Pierpont Morgan and John Pierpont Morgan Jr., J. K. Lilly Jr., and Carrie Estelle Doheny (all treated in *DLB 140*) had fortunes large enough to enable them to assemble wide-ranging collections, but increasingly the tendency has been to specialize, to find new subjects to collect, and to discover new ways to do so. Quinn and Kerlan, for example, cultivated authors and artists and secured material directly from them, and both concentrated on the then-unconsidered contemporary writer. The specialization that characterizes every other facet of twentieth-century life surfaces in book collecting and bookselling as well, whether in Rosenwald's pursuit of illustrated books, Gordon Norton Ray's (treated in *DLB 140*) concentration on English and French illustrated works of the eighteenth and nineteenth centuries, Lewis's focus on Horace Walpole, or Massey's interest in Faulkner.

To paraphrase Jacques Derrida, "Il n'y a pas hors de l'histoire du livre" (There is nothing outside the history of the book). The growth of America is reflected in the development of its private and public libraries and the increased prominence of its book dealers. Demographic and literary movements correspond to the appearance of bibliographies. The history of the book in America is also the history of America as seen through its books.

–Joseph Rosenblum

Acknowledgments

This book was produced by Bruccoli Clark Layman, Inc. Karen L. Rood is senior editor for the *Dictionary of Literary Biography* series. Philip B. Dematteis was the in-house editor. He was aided by Karen Rood, Denis Thomas, Sam Bruce, Tracy S. Bitonti, and Penelope M. Hope.

Administrative support was provided by Ann M. Cheschi and Brenda A. Gillie.

Bookkeeper is Joyce Fowler.

Copyediting supervisor is Jeff Miller. The copyediting staff includes Phyllis A. Avant, Patricia Coate, Christine Copeland, Thom Harman, and William L. Thomas Jr. Freelance copyeditors include Ron Aiken and Rebecca Mayo.

Editorial associate is L. Kay Webster.

Layout and graphics staff includes Marie L. Parker and Janet E. Hill.

Office manager is Kathy Lawler Merlette.

Photography editors are Margaret Meriwether and Paul Talbot. Photographic copy work was performed by Joseph M. Bruccoli.

Production manager is Samuel W. Bruce.

Systems manager is Chris Elmore.

Typesetting supervisor is Kathleen M. Flanagan. The typesetting staff includes Pamela D. Norton and Patricia Flanagan Salisbury. Freelance typesetters include Melody W. Clegg, Judith E. McCray, and Delores Plastow.

Walter W. Ross, Steven Gross, and Mark McEwan did library research. They were assisted by the following librarians at the Thomas Cooper Library of the University of South Carolina: Linda Holderfield and the interlibrary-loan staff; reference-department head Virginia Weathers; reference librarians Marilee Birchfield, Stefanie Buck, Stefanie DuBose, Rebecca Feind, Karen Joseph, Donna Lehman, Charlene Loope, Anthony McKissick, Jean Rhyne, and Kwamine Simpson; circulation-department head Caroline Taylor; and acquisitions-searching supervisor David Haggard.

Dictionary of Literary Biography® • Volume One Hundred Eighty-Seven

American Book Collectors
and Bibliographers
Second Series

Dictionary of Literary Biography

Robert Borthwick Adam II
(7 July 1863 – 11 April 1940)

William H. Loos
Buffalo and Erie County Public Library

BOOKS: *Johnsoniana in the Library of Robert B. Adam* (Buffalo, N.Y., 1895);

Catalogue of the Johnsonian Collection of R. B. Adam (Buffalo, N.Y.: Privately printed, 1921);

Printed Only for a Few Friends (Buffalo, N.Y.: Volksfreund Printing Co., 1925);

English Literature from the Library of Mr. R. B. Adam . . . To Be Sold by Auction . . . February Fifteenth, Sixteenth (New York: Anderson Galleries, 1926);

The R. B. Adam Library Relating to Dr. Samuel Johnson and His Era, 4 volumes (Buffalo, N.Y.: Printed for the author / London & New York: Oxford University Press, 1929–1930);

Works, Letters and Manuscripts of James Hogg, "The Ettrick Shepherd" (Buffalo, N.Y.: Privately printed, 1930).

The Robert Borthwick Adam collection of books and manuscripts by and about Dr. Samuel Johnson and his era was the result of the efforts of three generations of bibliophiles, all members of the same family. The three men all bore the same name. The first Robert Borthwick Adam began the formation of the famous collection devoted to Johnson; the second brought it to its greatest development; and the third, who at the age of four had been elected an honorary member of the Johnson Society of Lichfield, England, was ultimately obliged, whatever his personal feelings may have been, to preside over its sale.

Robert Borthwick Adam III died in September 1993 at the age of seventy-five. The family business that had given his father and grandfather the means and the leisure to build a great book collection was sold a few months after his death.

Robert Borthwick Adam II (Buffalo and Erie County Public Library)

The Johnsonian collection traces its origins to the efforts of the first Robert Borthwick Adam. He was born on 4 February 1833 in Peebles, Scotland, twenty-two miles south of Edinburgh. His father was the Reverend Thomas Adam, a Presbyterian clergyman and a graduate of Edinburgh University. The Adam family—there were at least five chil-

Robert Borthwick Adam I, who founded the Adam family's Samuel Johnson collection (Buffalo and Erie County Public Library)

Johnson, John Ruskin, and other British writers. A reporter from the *Buffalo Express* once asked Adam if it "was not rather strange that a Scotchman should take such a delight in collecting the relics of such a pronounced Scotch hater." Adam replied, "I don't know, a Scotchman wrote his best biography."

In only a few years Adam's collection had achieved international fame, and scholars began to travel to Buffalo to consult his books and manuscripts. The Englishman George Birkbeck Hill, biographer of Johnson, was one. In his 1894 essay on the proof sheets of James Boswell's *The Life of Samuel Johnson* (1791), which Adam willingly sent to Hill while he was working in Barnstable on Cape Cod, Hill states, "May more of our old libraries . . . be carried across the Atlantic, provided that they come into the hands of citizens as enlightened and liberal as my friend Mr. R. B. Adam." William Wallace, editor of the correspondence of Burns and Frances Anna Dunlop, also acknowledged his debt to Adam, as Adam had acquired the bulk of that correspondence and made it available to Wallace.

As a collector, Robert Borthwick Adam I followed one of the older collecting traditions of assembling letters, portraits, prints, and documents that were mounted and inserted into extended multivolume works. At his death his extraillustrated copies of six of Hill's octavo books on Johnson, including his 1887 edition of *The Life of Samuel Johnson* (Oxford: Clarendon Press), numbered about twenty-five volumes; when completed by his son (before 1909) the sixty-two thick folio volumes contained hundreds of letters, documents, portraits, and prints related to Johnson and his contemporaries. These, however, were only the most splendid of several extraillustrated books the first Robert Borthwick Adam assembled.

Robert Borthwick Adam I did not devote himself solely to his bibliophilic interests. After 1880 he also became active in the affairs of the Young Men's Christian Association. He was president at the time of his death and on two occasions was chairman of a committee for the construction of a new building for that flourishing organization. While Adam took no interest in politics, his younger brother, James Noble Adam, who came to Buffalo in 1881, served as mayor of Buffalo from 1906 to 1909.

Adam's greatest contribution to his community resulted from his chairmanship, beginning in 1888, of the Buffalo grade-crossing commission. Many lives were lost every year at the street-level crossings for the railroads that passed through Buffalo, the second-largest rail center in the United States. Between 1 January 1890 and 1 August 1892 fifty-five fatal accidents occurred. Over a period of a

dren—was not wealthy. Robert's formal education ended at age ten when he was apprenticed to a glove and hosiery merchant in Edinburgh.

In 1855 he married Grace Harriet Michie, and the couple immigrated to the United States. They arrived in Boston on 7 November 1857. After Adam had worked for ten years in the dry-goods business, his friend John Taylor, president of the Scots' Charitable Society of Boston (established in 1657), offered to set Adam up in business in any American city he wished. Adam had himself joined the Scots' Charitable Society in 1862 and had served as its secretary; he remained a lifelong member. The city Adam chose for his business was the growing metropolis on Lake Erie—Buffalo, New York. He, with several partners, opened a dry-goods store in 1867, and by the early 1880s the Adam, Meldrum and Anderson Company had become the largest retail department store in western New York.

With a flourishing business, Adam finally had the time and the means to follow his literary interests. He began to collect books and manuscripts by his fellow Scot Robert Burns, as well as those by

dozen years Adam and the commission fought the railroads and compelled them to construct viaducts and tunnels to reduce the slaughter. Chauncey M. Depew, head of the New York Central Railroad, was once quoted as saying, "I don't want to see Mr. Adam. He costs the New York Central $100,000 every time he comes to New York."

Adam and his wife were concerned that they had no children to carry on their name and their family's business. In 1879 they adopted a son and a daughter of his sister Jean Finlayson Adam and her husband John Scott, headmaster of the Corporation's Academy of Berwick-upon-Tweed. The nine-year-old boy, who had been named Robert Borthwick in honor of his uncle, assumed the Adam family name. He had been born on 7 July 1863 in Loughborough, Leicestershire, England.

Robert and his six-year-old sister, Margaret, traveled to America on the Cunard ship *Scotia,* the last ocean liner equipped with paddlewheels. Robert II was to have more formal education than his father. He graduated from Buffalo's Central High School and also attended a local private school, where he studied German. After high school, however, he devoted himself to the family business, not to earning a college degree. He began his career as a merchant by working for a year in the department store owned by his uncle, J. N. Adam. He learned all aspects of the family business by working for a time in each department in the store, and by 1902 he had become president of the company. In the years he had lived with his adoptive father, Robert II had acquired an appreciation for the literary and collecting interests of the older man. Robert I had joined the Grolier Club (an organization for bibliophiles) in New York City in 1892. Possibly that organization influenced the two men to compile and publish the first of three catalogues devoted to their Johnsonian collection. That catalogue, an edition of only twenty-one copies, appeared in 1895. The younger Adam was principally responsible for its publication.

In 1904 Robert I died, leaving his nationally known business and his internationally known collection to Robert II. In November 1909 Robert II lent ninety-seven volumes from the Johnson collection to Yale University for the two hundredth anniversary of Johnson's birth; this loan apparently marked the beginning of Adam's long relationship with the university. From 1925 to 1938 he also served as a trustee for the Grosvenor Library in Buffalo.

Until the Great Depression, Adam's enthusiasm for books and bookmen continued unabated.

Title page for the catalogue for the auction at which Robert Borthwick Adam II sold off the non-Johnsonian items in his collection (Bruccoli Collection)

His circle of friends and acquaintances in the book world included the eminent collector A. Edward Newton, the author Christopher Morley, Chauncey Brewster Tinker of Yale, Charles G. Osgood of Princeton, R. W. Chapman of Oxford, and the Philadelphia bookseller A. S. W. Rosenbach.

By 1926 his collecting interests had undergone a change. He resolved to divest himself of many of the collections that had grown since the 1870s and to concentrate on his Johnsoniana. The fame of his Johnson collection had already led to his election as the first American honorary member of the Johnson Club of London.

In the introduction to the Anderson auction catalogue of his English literature he refers to the catalogue he had published in 1921, describing the best of his collections, and notes that he had no intention at that time of ever disposing of any of them.

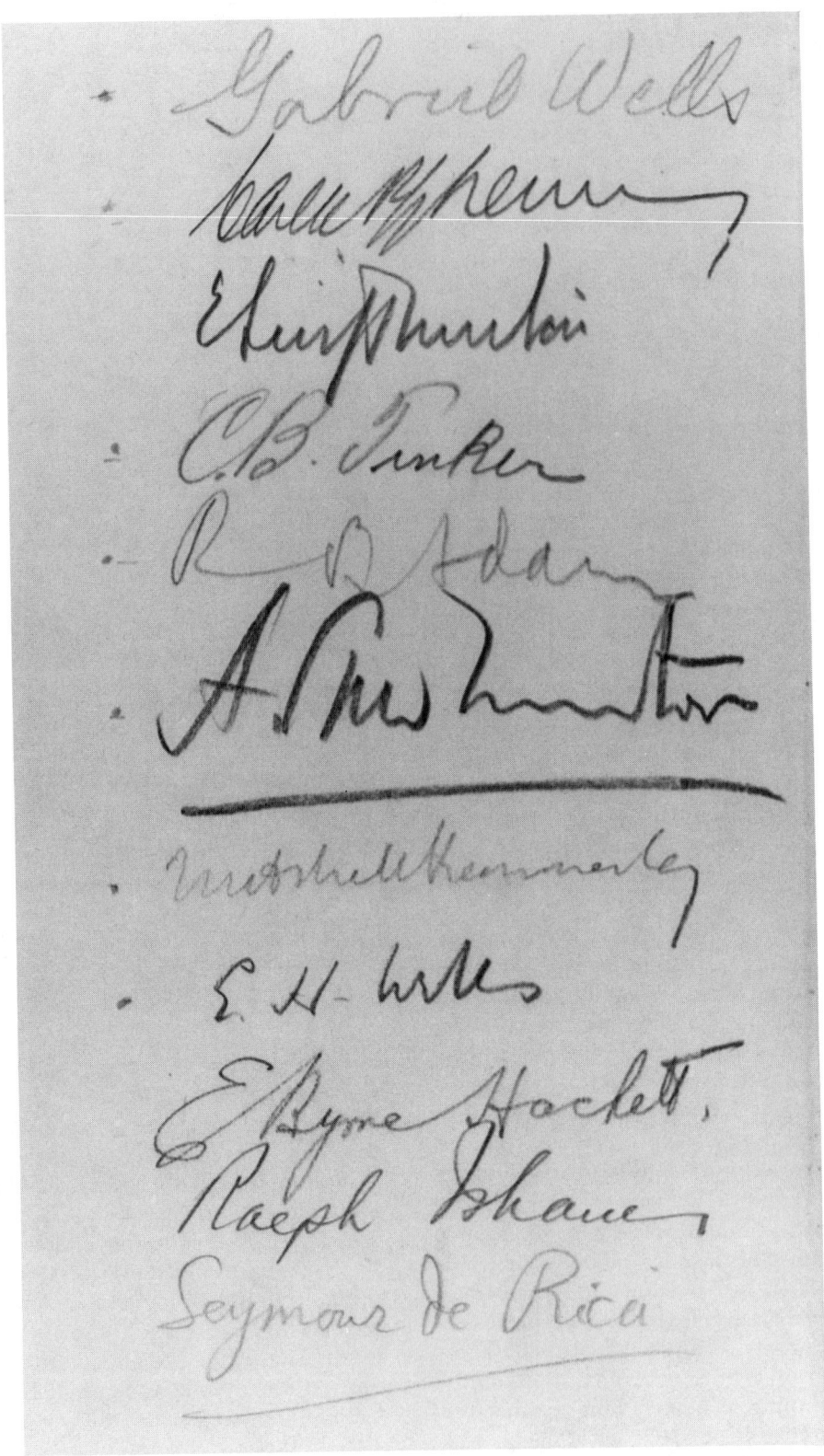

Endpapers of the 1926 auction catalogue, signed by eminent bookmen who attended the sale
(Bruccoli Collection)

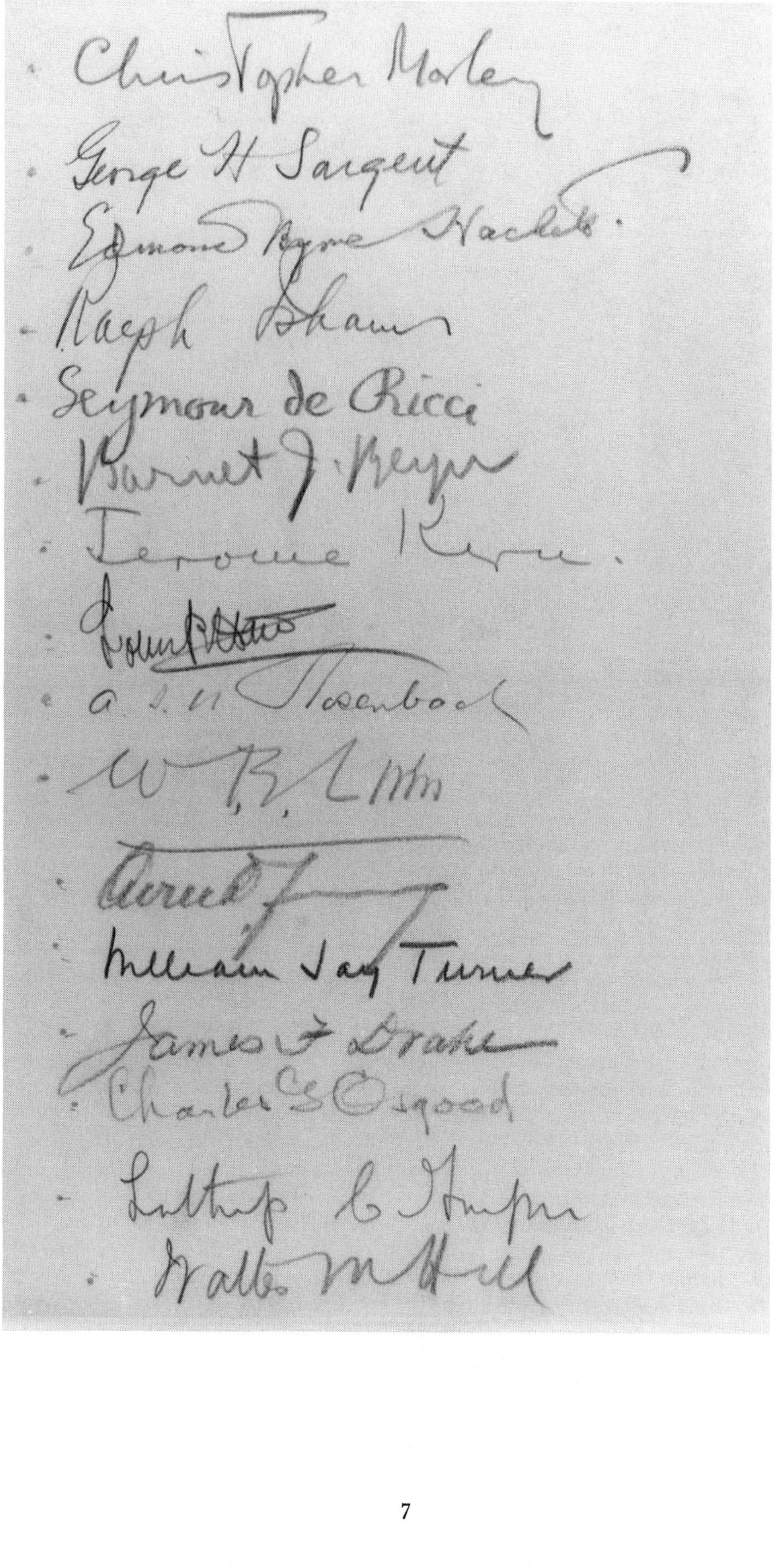

Christopher Morley

George H Sargent

Edmond Byrne Hackett

Ralph Shaw

Seymour de Ricci

Barnet J. Beyer

Jerome Kern

[signature]

A. S. W. Rosenbach

W. B. Littm

[signature]

William Jay Turner

James F Drake

Charles S Osgood

Lathrop C Harper

Walter M Hill

The "Johnson Corner" of Robert Borthwick Adam II's library in Buffalo, New York (Buffalo and Erie County Public Library)

He goes on to say, "Drinking, smoking, thinking, one evening in my library, I decided the time had come to separate my special, and some of my miscellaneous books, from that great period of literature, the eighteenth century, in which my chief interest endures and to give what I can spare of what remains to me of my days and nights to the study of the Johnsonian era."

Many prize books and manuscripts were included in the sale, even a few Johnson and Boswell titles. The copy of *The Life of Samuel Johnson* annotated by Johnson's friend Hester Lynch Piozzi was included among the books offered for sale. A group of first editions of the great eighteenth-century novels—for example, Samuel Richardson's *Clarissa* (London: Printed for A. Richardson, 1748), Henry Fielding's *Tom Jones* (London: A. Millar, 1749), Oliver Goldsmith's *The Vicar of Wakefield* (Salisbury: B. Collins for F. Newberry, 1766), Jonathan Swift's *Gulliver's Travels* (London: Benjamin Motte, 1726), and Laurence Sterne's *Tristram Shandy* (York and London: various publishers, 1760–1767)—were among the lots, as were a few incunabula and other

early printed books. Adam's copy of *The Pickwick Papers* (London: Chapman and Hall, 1836–1837) in parts, with all eleven points, brought a winning bid of $4,000 from Rosenbach. The star of the sale, however, was a first edition of John Milton's *Comus* (London: Humphrey Robinson, 1637), which went to Rosenbach for $11,500. In all, Adam realized $122,188 from the sale.

Once Adam had decided to concentrate on his Johnsonian collection, he continued to divest himself of other collections. His British sporting and other color prints were sold at auction, also at Anderson's, a month after the sale of his English literature. In February 1929, while still working on the first three volumes of his catalogue of the Johnsonian collection, he presented to Yale University his nearly complete collection of all the significant first and later editions of the writings of Ruskin, a collection begun by his adoptive father decades before. Only a few Ruskin high spots—those included in the 1926 auction—were lacking. Yale was sufficiently grateful for this gift to award Adam a master of arts degree in June 1930. Adam was so delighted with this honor that in 1931 he presented to Yale his collection of the writings of James Hogg, "the Ettrick Shepherd." In the formal catalogue of the Hogg collection, which he compiled and published in 1930, Adam used the M.A. after his name on the title page.

In those early days of the Great Depression, Adam also sold to Rosenbach the great collection of Burnsiana begun by his adoptive father. Rosenbach sold only a few choice items, so the bulk of the Burnsiana remains in the collection of the Rosenbach Foundation.

After the 1926 auction Adam spent a great deal of his time in preparing his monumental three-volume catalogue of the Johnsonian collection. It was published to critical acclaim in 1929 by Oxford University Press. As Adam wished to supervise the printers personally and was unable to leave his family business to work with the printers in Oxford, the photography, engraving, and printing were all done by craftsmen in Buffalo. When completed, the catalogue had a new preface by Adam's friend Newton and a reprint of Osgood's introduction from the 1921 catalogue. Five hundred copies of the boxed three-volume set were printed. They sold for $75 each, and some copies were offered for sale in the book department of the Adam, Meldrum and Anderson department store. Adam soon realized that the three volumes did not include all the material, primarily the non-Johnsonian manuscripts and letters, that he wished to document. He therefore published a fourth volume in 1930, but in a limited edition of 225 copies. In spite of the catalogue's size and importance, the four volumes present a challenge to those who consult them. The idiosyncratic arrangement of the four volumes, their lack of proper indexes, and their lack of continuous pagination make them difficult to use.

As the nation's financial problems worsened, Adam was forced to consider divesting himself of his greatest collection. In 1932 he even felt it necessary to resign his membership in the Grolier Club, which he had joined in 1918.

In a poignant letter, Adam asked whether Rosenbach would be willing to appraise the collection at $1.5 million. Rosenbach was unwilling to agree to so large a sum, but he did agree to $500,000. When no buyer came forward, Adam offered the collection as collateral for a loan, a step that helped to save the family's department store. After the collection had remained in a bank vault for a few years, its inaccessibility became a problem for scholars who wished to consult its treasures. By 1936 arrangements were made with the University of Rochester to deposit the collection there for five years—later renewed—so

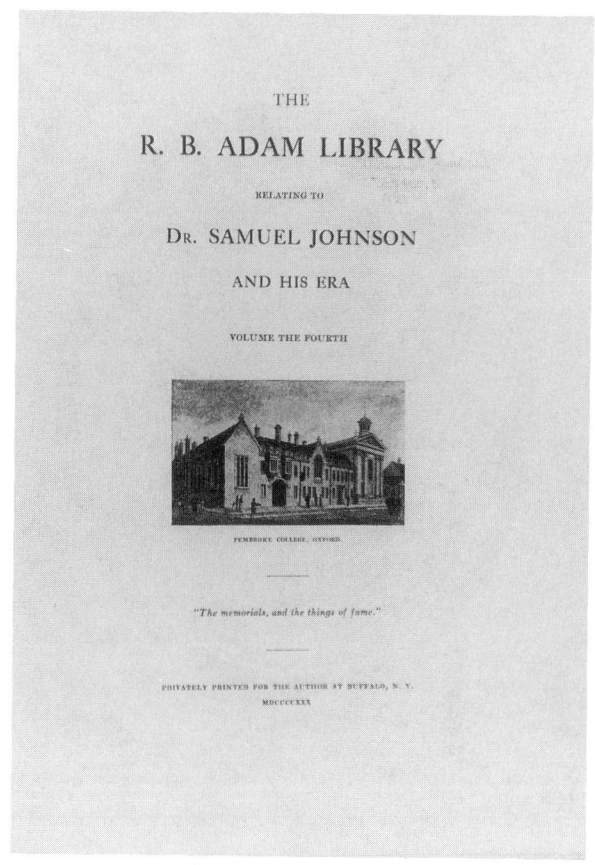

THE

R. B. ADAM LIBRARY

RELATING TO

Dr. SAMUEL JOHNSON

AND HIS ERA

VOLUME THE FOURTH

PEMBROKE COLLEGE, OXFORD.

"The memorials, and the things of fame."

PRIVATELY PRINTED FOR THE AUTHOR AT BUFFALO, N. Y.
MDCCCCXXX

Title page for the final volume of the catalogue

that it could once again become available. Adam himself frequently traveled the seventy miles to Rochester to consult his own collection. At this time there were more than 10,000 items, including 3,000 books. In 1938 the university bestowed on Adam the honorary degree of doctor of letters. Under the stewardship of Richard L. Greene and later under that of Robert F. Metzdorf, the collection remained on deposit at the University of Rochester for ten more years.

Adam died on 11 April 1940, after an illness that had lasted more than two years. In his will he left no clear instructions as to the disposition of his collection. The decision was left to his widow, Lena Adam, but she died less than a month after her husband. Twenty-one-year-old Robert Borthwick Adam III suddenly found himself responsible not only for the family business but also for his father's great book collection. Circumstances forced Adam to sell the family's mansion at 780 West Ferry Street, which was full of books and antiques. The sale took place through a local auction. Many fine books discovered throughout the house were sold for quite modest prices. The Grosvenor Library, the

Robert Borthwick Adam II's bookplate (Buffalo and Erie County Public Library)

Buffalo Public Library, and the library of Canisius College were among the buyers.

A local book collector, John Grenzebach, acquired a large group of titles (perhaps on consignment) and issued a catalogue (his first) with 339 lots, all from the Adam collection. At least one important Johnsonian title had been discovered in the basement, and Greene added it to the collection still on deposit at the University of Rochester. The book auction reportedly produced little more than $12,000.

The coming of World War II, during which Robert III served in the U.S. Army, caused the family to defer any final decision on the fate of the Johnsonian collection. When the war was over, Adam and his two older sisters decided to offer the collection for private sale. The University of Rochester was unwilling to purchase the collection, and Yale evidenced no interest.

Laurence Gomme of Brentano's Rare Book Department in New York City served as an agent for the sale of the collection; he had appraised the collection in November 1941 as having a market value of "from $500,000 to $550,000." His now rare nine-page pamphlet, *The Robert B. Adam Library Re-*

lating to Dr. Samuel Johnson and His Era, appeared in 1945 in an edition of 525 copies, apparently to publicize the still unsold collection.

In 1948 Donald and Mary Hyde, who had assembled a notable Johnsonian collection of their own, including much of A. Edward Newton's collection, learned of the availability of the Adam collection and contacted Metzdorf at the University of Rochester. While reluctant to part with the collection at first, Metzdorf realized that the Hydes were the ideal people to have it. The Adam family accepted the surprisingly low price of $75,000, and the collection was transported to the Hydes' secure and soon-to-be expanded library in Somerville, New Jersey.

Donald Hyde died in 1966. After years of uncertainty as to the ultimate fate of the greatest Johnsonian collection in the world, Mary Hyde (now the Viscountess Eccles) decided in the late 1970s that the most appropriate place for the collection would be the Houghton Library at Harvard University. Special quarters were constructed at the Houghton, which in time will receive the great Hyde-Adam Johnsonian collection. The "public misfortune" that Newton had feared might befall the Adam collection did not come to pass.

References:

William Harris Arnold, *Ventures in Book Collecting* (New York: Scribners, 1923);

Gabriel Austin, ed., *Four Oaks Library* (Somerville, N.J., 1967);

Carl L. Cannon, comp., "Robert B. Adam, 1863–1940," in *American Book Collectors and Collecting from Colonial Times to the Present* (New York: Wilson, 1941);

R. W. Chapman, "Hyde Collection of Johnsonian Manuscripts," *Times Literary Supplement,* 23 September 1949, p. 624;

Seymour De Ricci, "The Library of Robert Borthwick Adam, Buffalo, New York," in *Census of Medieval and Renaissance Manuscripts in the United States and Canada,* 2 volumes (New York: Wilson, 1937), II: 1215–1219;

Donald C. Dickinson, comp., "Adam, Robert B.," in *Dictionary of American Book Collectors* (New York: Greenwood Press, 1986);

Robert D. French, "The Robert B. Adam Collection of Ruskin," *Yale University Library Gazette,* 4 (July 1929): 1–7;

Laurence Gomme, *The Robert B. Adam Library Relating to Dr. Samuel Johnson and His Era, A Brief Study* (New York: Printed for private distribution, 1945);

John Grenzebach, *Catalogue No. 1—Books from the Library of the Late Robert Borthwick Adam II, of Buffalo* (Buffalo, N.Y., 1940);

George Birkbeck Hill, "Boswell's Proof-Sheets," *Atlantic Monthly,* 74 (November 1894): 657–668;

Donald and Mary Hyde, "Contemporary Collectors VI: The Hyde Collection," *Book Collector,* 4 (Autumn 1955): 208–216;

Mary Hyde, "The History of the Johnson Papers," *Papers of the Bibliographical Society of America,* 45 (Second Quarter 1951): 103–116;

In Memory of Robert B. Adam (Buffalo, N.Y., 1905);

Robert Frederic Metzdorf, "Robert Borthwick Adam, 1863–1940," in *Grolier 75: A Biographical Retrospective to Celebrate the Seventy-Fifth Anniversary of the Grolier Club in New York* (New York, 1959), pp. 121–123;

Frederick E. Pierce, "James Hogg: 'The Ettrick Shepherd,'" *Yale University Gazette,* 5 (January 1931): 39–41;

W. Roberts, "A Johnsonian Collection," *Times Literary Supplement,* 20 April 1922, p. 258;

Natalie Tarbet, "Doctor Johnson in Buffalo," *Buffalo Spree,* 13 (Fall 1979): 59–61, 109–110;

"Treasures in a Buffalo Library: Mr. Adam's Collections Famous Among Scholars on Both Sides of the World: Johnson, Burns, Ruskin," *Buffalo Express,* 3 July 1904, p. 25, cols. 3–4;

William Wallace, ed., *Robert Burns and Mrs. Dunlop, Correspondence Now Published in Full for the First Time,* 2 volumes (New York: Dodd, Mead, 1898);

Deshler Welch, "Johnsoniana: A Wonderful Collection in Buffalo—But Not Well Known Even There," *New York Times Saturday Review,* 30 December 1899, p. 908, cols. 1–3;

Edwin Wolf II and John F. Fleming, *Rosenbach: A Biography* (Cleveland: World, 1960).

Luther A. Brewer
(17 December 1858 – 6 May 1933)

Robert A. McCown
University of Iowa

BOOKS: *History of Linn County, Iowa, from Its Earliest Settlement to the Present Time* (Cedar Rapids, Iowa: Torch Press, 1911);

About a Great Book, with Some Literary Autographs (Cedar Rapids, Iowa: Privately printed for the friends of Luther Albertus and Elinore Taylor Brewer, 1914);

The Fascination of Prints, Another of Our Hobbies (Cedar Rapids, Iowa: Privately printed for the friends of Luther Albertus and Elinore Taylor Brewer, 1915);

Beside Our Reading Lamp (Cedar Rapids, Iowa: Privately printed for the friends of Luther Albertus Brewer and Elinore Taylor Brewer, 1916);

Beside Our Fireplace (Cedar Rapids, Iowa: Privately printed for the friends of Luther Albertus and Elinore Taylor Brewer, 1917);

Around the Library Table: An Evening with Leigh Hunt (Cedar Rapids, Iowa: Privately printed for the friends of Luther Albertus and Elinore Taylor Brewer, 1920);

Stevenson's Perfect Virtues, as Exemplified by Leigh Hunt (Cedar Rapids, Iowa: Privately printed for the friends of Luther Albertus and Elinore Taylor Brewer, 1922);

The Love of Books with a Reprint of Leigh Hunt's Essay on "My Books" (Cedar Rapids, Iowa: Privately printed for the friends of Luther Albertus and Elinore Taylor Brewer, 1923);

Some Lamb and Browning Letters to Leigh Hunt (Cedar Rapids, Iowa: Privately printed for the friends of Luther Albertus and Elinore Taylor Brewer, 1924);

Wanderings in London (Cedar Rapids, Iowa: Privately printed for the friends of Luther Albertus and Elinore Taylor Brewer, 1925);

Marginalia (Cedar Rapids, Iowa: Privately printed for the friends of Luther Albertus and Elinore Taylor Brewer, 1926);

Golden Days in France (Cedar Rapids, Iowa: Privately printed for the friends of Luther Albertus and Elinore Taylor Brewer, 1927);

Luther A. Brewer

The Joys and Sorrows of a Book Collector (Cedar Rapids, Iowa: Privately printed for the friends of Luther Albertus and Elinore Taylor Brewer, 1928);

Leigh Hunt and Charles Dickens; the Skimpole Caricature (Cedar Rapids, Iowa: Privately printed for the friends of Luther Albertus and Elinore Taylor Brewer, 1930);

Leaves from a Leigh Hunt Note-book (Cedar Rapids, Iowa: Privately printed for the friends of the Torch Press and of Luther Albertus and Elinore Taylor Brewer, 1932);

My Leigh Hunt Library, Collected and Described by Luther A. Brewer (Cedar Rapids, Iowa: Privately printed, 1932);

My Leigh Hunt Library: The Holograph Letters (Iowa City: University of Iowa Press, 1938).

OTHER: *A Record of a Useful and Beautiful Life,* edited by Brewer (Cedar Rapids, Iowa: Torch Press, 1907);

Some Letters from My Leigh Hunt Portfolio, with Brief Comment, edited by Brewer (Cedar Rapids, Iowa: Privately printed for the friends of Luther Albertus and Elinore Taylor Brewer, 1929).

SELECTED PERIODICAL PUBLICATIONS– UNCOLLECTED: "The Delights of a Hobby: Some Experiences in Book-Collecting," *The Nineteenth Year Book of The Bibliophile Society, Boston* (1920): 55–72;

"The First Edition of Leigh Hunt's *Sir Ralph Esher,*" *Bookman's Journal,* 17 (1930): 219–221;

"Leigh Hunt's Love of Books," *American Book Collector,* 2 (July 1932): 13–15.

The nineteenth-century poet and critic Leigh Hunt was an important figure in the Romantic era of English literature. His stature has been enhanced by the large collection of his books, manuscripts, and letters gathered early in the twentieth century by Luther A. Brewer, an Iowa bibliophile, printer, businessman, and political activist.

Luther Albertus Brewer was born on 17 December 1858 in Welsh Run, Pennsylvania, just north of Hagerstown, Maryland. At the age of eight he left the home of his parents, Jacob and Kate Brewer, to live with an aunt and uncle, first in Sharpsburg, Maryland, and then on a farm near Hagerstown. It was while he was a student in a Maryland grammar school that Brewer became a lover of books: after reading *The Pickwick Papers* (1836–1837) he began to buy inexpensive editions of the novels of Charles Dickens as they were published by the Seaside Library. Around the same time he acquired a paper-bound edition of the works of William Shakespeare. Coming across a sale catalogue from the New York auction house Bangs and Company, he was successful in bidding on an early edition of Thomas Paine's *Common Sense* (1776) and a seventeenth-century volume titled *Sermons on Death.*

Brewer received a bachelor's degree in 1883 from Pennsylvania College (now Gettysburg College), where he was a member of the Phi Gamma Delta fraternity. He seems to have spent the 1883–1884 school year in Boonsboro, Maryland, near Hager-

Brewer's bookplate, with a reproduction of an unfinished portrait of Leigh Hunt by Samuel Lawrence

stown, as principal of a grammar school. In 1884 he moved to Iowa–perhaps first to Spencer, in the northwest part of the state, and then to Cedar Rapids. In 1887 he became city editor of the *Cedar Rapids Daily Republican,* moving on to become assistant business manager, business manager, publisher, part owner, and finally owner of the paper. The paper's name was indicative of its political leanings: it was an ardent supporter of the Grand Old Party, and Brewer himself was active in Republican politics. From about October 1894 until June 1898 he served as state inspector of oils; he was appointed to the position by the governor after the death of his predecessor, L. S. Merchant, one of the owners of the *Daily Republican.* The major duty of the inspector and his deputies was to test the quality of illuminating oils, such as kerosene, offered for sale in the state. In 1898 Brewer married Elinore Taylor.

From about 1900 to 1907 Brewer commuted the twenty-eight miles south to Iowa City to lecture

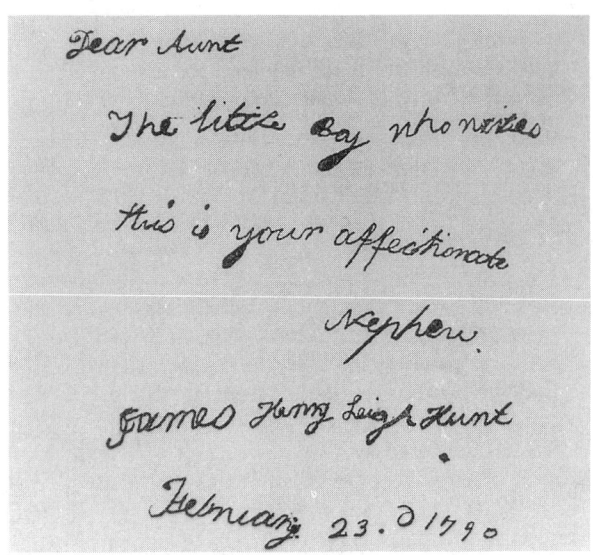

Note written by the five-year-old Hunt to his aunt, Lydia Shewell (from Brewer's My Leigh Hunt Library: The Holograph Letters, *1938)*

on journalism and printing in the English Department at the University of Iowa. From 1901 until 1905 Brewer also served as publisher for the university.

Around 1904 Brewer established the Torch Press, combining its operations with those of the Republican Printing Company in a new four-story building on the northeast corner of Fourth Avenue and Third Street S.E. Brewer was president of the firm. The Torch Press Bookshop, established in 1907, was run by William Harvey Miner; in July 1916 the William Harvey Miner Company was opened in Saint Louis as the successor to the Torch Press Bookshop. Brewer was vice president of the company.

The combined presses produced the *Daily Republican* and the *Cedar Rapids Evening Times* as well as the *Mississippi Valley Historical Review,* the predecessor of the *Journal of American History.* The Torch Press turned out books in limited editions for the Bookfellows of Chicago, the Bibliophile Society of Boston, the Rowfant Club of Cleveland, and the Chicago book dealer Walter M. Hill. In most years at Christmas, Brewer produced a limited-edition book for his own use; the title page would carry the notation "Privately printed for the friends of Luther Albertus and Elinore Taylor Brewer" or "Privately printed for the friends of the Torch Press and of Luther Albertus and Elinore Taylor Brewer." Each of the early Christmas books, from 1912 to 1917, had an illuminated initial created by Brewer's wife. The Torch Press also printed trade books for the University of Minnesota Press, Columbia University Press,

the Arthur H. Clark Company, and the State Historical Society of Iowa. Many of the historical books are impressive pieces of Americana.

Brewer was a delegate to several Republican state conventions and a delegate at large to the Republican National Conventions of 1912 and 1916. In 1912 he was the secretary and a member of the Advisory Committee of the Iowa League of Taft Clubs, and he was a strong supporter of William Howard Taft when Taft ran for reelection as president against the Democrat Woodrow Wilson and Theodore Roosevelt of the Progressive Party. Defeated by Wilson, Taft became Kent Professor of Constitutional Law at Yale University. Brewer sent Taft at least one of his Christmas books, *Beside Our Reading Lamp* (1916), and he arranged for Taft to give speeches in Iowa in 1917, 1918, and 1919; during these visits Taft was a guest in Brewer's home. In a 15 March 1929 letter to "My dear Luther," Taft, who was then chief justice of the United States Supreme Court, wrote, "I never think of the West or Iowa without thinking of that generous, hospitable home where I spent many hours."

In 1924, when the Republicans in Iowa nominated the liberal Smith W. Brookhart for the U.S. Senate, Brewer, saying that he wanted to give Republicans an opportunity to vote for a man whose Republicanism was unquestioned, took out nomination papers as an independent Republican. Later he withdrew and supported the Democratic candidate.

Brewer was a patron of the University of Iowa chapter of his old fraternity, Phi Gamma Delta; in 1923 he became national treasurer of the organization, retaining the position until his death and leaving $2,500 to the University of Iowa chapter in his will. He was president of the Cedar Rapids Art Association and head of the board of trustees of the public library. One of the founders of the Rotary Club branch in Cedar Rapids, he later served as president of the local club and then as district governor. He was treasurer of his Lutheran church, a director of the American Trust and Savings Bank, and a member of the board of directors of the Cedar Rapids Auditorium Company. Apparently on the basis of his early residence in Maryland, he was also secretary of the Society of the South, a group for people who had been born or had lived in the South.

Brewer's childhood interest in book collecting intensified during his adult years. He spoke and wrote often of his hobby of collecting books, autograph letters, and prints. At first his collecting interests were quite wide: books on printing and bookmaking, which were related to his profession; fine-press books; art monographs; and favorite authors (Dickens, Charles Lamb, Robert Louis Stevenson,

Thomas Moore, Robert Browning, and George Gordon, Lord Byron). At various times he tried to cease collecting, but he was unable to give up the pursuit. He was not interested in recent imprints but in older volumes bound in calf or vellum. He was fond of bookshops that allowed one to browse at leisure without interference from clerks; Maggs Brothers of London was a favorite.

Before World War I Brewer began to accumulate first editions and autograph letters by Leigh Hunt, and around 1920 he decided to make his Hunt collection as complete as possible. He chose Hunt because the author had lived during an exciting period of English literature and knew many of the great writers of his era; also, Hunt first editions and autographs were easier to find and much less expensive than those of Byron, Lamb, Percy Bysshe Shelley, or John Keats, and there were few competitors for them. He was assisted in his undertaking by Hill and by Ernest Maggs of Maggs Brothers. On 10 March 1925 he sold many of his non-Hunt items, including books on printing and bookmaking and fine-press editions from the Doves Press, in an American Art Association auction.

Many of the first editions of Hunt works that Brewer acquired were inscribed copies that had been presented to friends by the author. Most of the books were in their original bindings; recognizing the bibliographical importance of such copies, Brewer did not rebind them, and he placed some in protective cases. He also collected subsequent editions as well as autograph letters by and to Hunt and manuscripts of Hunt's writings; he had the letters bound in leather or paper wrappers and the manuscripts in leather. In addition he had copies of works by other authors in which Hunt had made marginal annotations. Copies of periodicals with which Hunt had been associated were also in the collection, as were books and manuscripts by writers such as Shelley, Dickens, Byron, Thomas Carlyle, and William Hazlitt, all of whom had connections to Hunt. Brewer was especially proud of presentation copies of Hunt's *The Descent of Liberty* (London: Printed for Gale, Curtis, and Fenner, 1815), inscribed to Byron, and Hunt's edition of *Wit and Humour* (London: Smith, Elder, 1846), inscribed to Mary Shelley. Brewer's Hunt collection included about 520 printed volumes of Hunt's works, 1,200 volumes on Hunt and his era, and 200 bound volumes of manuscripts, comprising about 3,000 pages.

Brewer retired from his positions with the Torch Press and the *Daily Republican* in 1929. By that time his collection was well known; researchers were coming to Cedar Rapids to use its riches, and

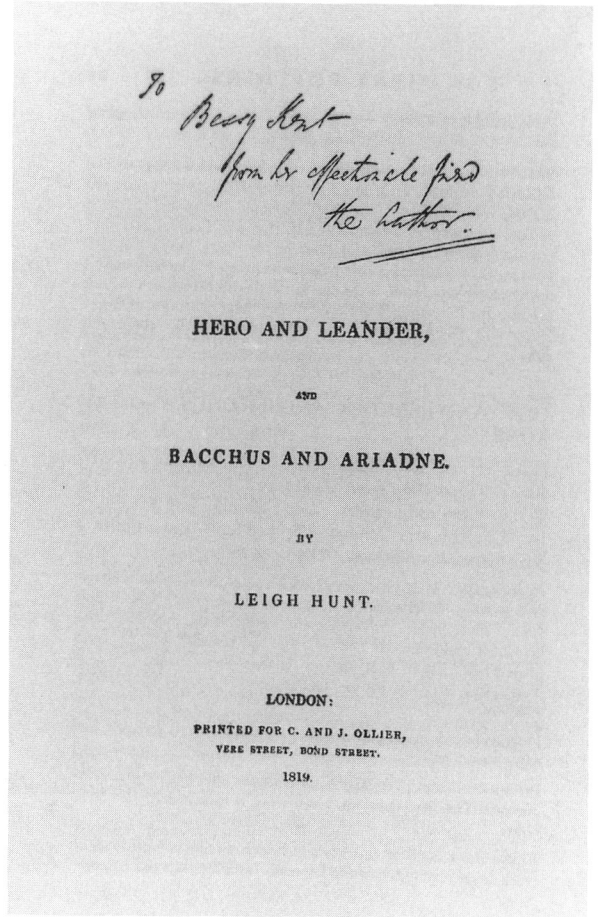

Title page of a work in Brewer's collection, inscribed by Hunt (from Brewer's My Leigh Hunt Library, 1932)

he was corresponding with others such as Edmund Blunden and Louis Landré, who were interested in Hunt. He finally decided to publish a three-part catalogue of his collection; the only part to appear during his lifetime was *My Leigh Hunt Library, Collected and Described by Luther A. Brewer* (1932), a descriptive bibliography of his Hunt first editions.

Elinore Brewer died on 10 March 1933; Luther Brewer followed her on 6 May. He left his Hunt collection to his niece, Katherine D. Connor, of Cedar Rapids. With the help of an anonymous donor the University of Iowa purchased the collection in 1934. Another volume of Brewer's catalogue of his collection, *My Leigh Hunt Library: The Holograph Letters,* appeared in 1938. A third volume, "Huntiana and Association Books," was in galley proofs at the time of Brewer's death but has never been published. The Torch Press continued to operate under the direction of Edward Misak until Misak's death in 1959.

Luther A. Brewer left a rich legacy. Torch Press imprints are sought by collectors; *My Leigh Hunt Li-*

Collection at the University of Iowa Libraries continues to grow.

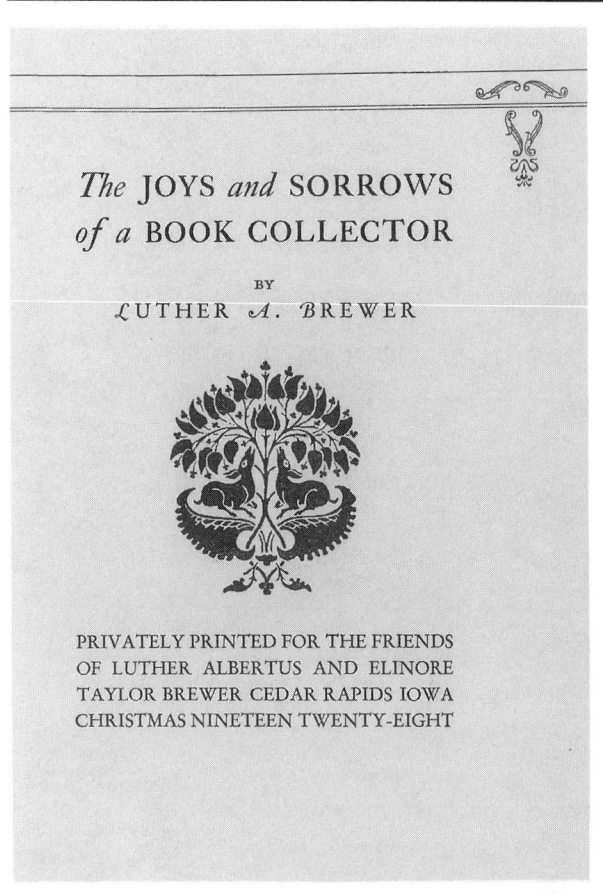

Title page for one of the limited editions Brewer produced for his friends each Christmas

brary, Collected and Described by Luther A. Brewer is still cited by book dealers, and the Brewer Leigh Hunt

References:

J. Christian Bay, *The Leigh Hunt Collection of Luther Albertus Brewer* (Cedar Rapids, Iowa: Privately printed for the friends of the Torch Press in memory of Luther Albertus and Elinore Taylor Brewer, 1933);

Thomas L. Carney and Joyce Crawford, "The Torch Press: A Preliminary History," *Books at Iowa*, 21 (November 1974): 3–25;

Frank S. Hanlin, "The Brewer–Leigh Hunt Collection at the State University of Iowa," *Keats-Shelley Journal*, 8 (Autumn 1959): 91–94;

Mike Maddigan, "The Torch Press: Addenda to a Checklist," *Books at Iowa*, 31 (November 1979): 35–54;

Robert A. Shaddy, "Around the Library Table with Luther A. Brewer: Annual Reflections on Collecting Leigh Hunt," *Books at Iowa*, 57 (November 1992): 17–34.

Papers:

Luther A. Brewer's business correspondence with the State Historical Society of Iowa is in the society's archives in Iowa City. The course of the Taft-Brewer friendship can be followed in the microfilm edition of the William Howard Taft Papers published by the Library of Congress. The Special Collections Department of the University of Iowa Libraries in Iowa City has letters by and to Brewer, photographs, and lecture notes for a course he taught at the university.

Pierce Butler
(19 December 1884 – 28 March 1953)

Jud H. Copeland
Emporia State University

BOOKS: *Checklist of Incunabula in the Newberry Library, Compiled for the Use of the Library Staff* (Chicago: Newberry Library, 1919);

Dante, His Work, His Time, and His Influence: A Selected List of Books Prepared in Connection with an Exhibit in Commemoration of the Six Hundredth Anniversary of the Poet's Death, 1321–1921 (Chicago: Newberry Library, 1921);

Check List of Books Printed During the Fifteenth Century (Chicago: Newberry Library, 1924);

The First Fifty Years of the Printed Book, 1450–1500: Notes Descriptive of an Exhibition (Chicago: Newberry Library, 1925);

Virgil: An Exhibition of Early Editions and Facsimiles of Manuscripts Commemorating the Two-Thousandth Anniversary of His Birth, 70 B.C.–1930 A.D. (Chicago: Newberry Library, 1930);

A Check List of Fifteenth Century Books in the Newberry Library and in Other Libraries of Chicago (Chicago: Newberry Library, 1933);

An Introduction to Library Science (Chicago: University of Chicago Press, 1933; Cambridge: Cambridge University Press, 1933);

The Literary History of Scholarship (Chicago: Chicago Classical Club, 1937);

The Origin of Printing in Europe (Chicago: University of Chicago Press, 1940; Cambridge: Cambridge University Press, 1941);

Scholarship and Civilization (Chicago: University of Chicago Press, 1944);

Ernst Frederick Detterer, 1888–1947, by Butler and R. Hunter Middleton, calligraphy by James Hayes (Chicago: Lakeside Press, 1948);

Culture and Communication, by Butler and Redmond A. Burke (Chicago: DePaul University Library, 1953).

Editions: *Introduction to Library Science,* introduction by Lester E. Asheim (Chicago: University of Chicago Press, 1961);

The Origin of Printing in Europe (Chicago: University of Chicago Press, 1966).

Pierce Butler

OTHER: Ernest Schulz, *Collections of Incunabula and Their Value for Scholars with Special Reference to the Vollbehr Collection,* translated by Powell Spring, foreword by Butler (New York: Rudge, 1927), pp. 117–128;

"The Venetian Masters" and "Book Illustration," in *The Golden Book; The Story of Fine Books and Bookmaking—Past and Present,* edited by Douglas C. McMurtrie (Chicago: Covici, 1927), pp. 117–128, 324–339;

The Last Will and Testament of the Late Nicolas Jenson, Who Departed This Life in the City of Venice in the Month of September, A.D. 1480, translated by

Butler (Chicago: Ludlow Typograph Co., 1928);

"Fifteenth Century Editions of Arabic Authors in Latin Translation," in *The MacDonald Presentation Volume; A Tribute to Duncan Black MacDonald,* edited by William G. Shellabear (Princeton: Princeton University Press, 1933), pp. 63–71;

"The Research Worker's Approach to Books–The Humanist," in *The Acquisition and Cataloging of Books,* edited by William M. Randall (Chicago: University of Chicago Press, 1940), pp. 270–283;

The Reference Function of the Library: Papers Presented before the Library Institute at the University of Chicago, June 29 to July 10, 1942, edited by Butler (Chicago: University of Chicago Press, 1943);

Books and Libraries in Wartime, edited by Butler (Chicago: University of Chicago Press, 1945);

"The Life of the Book," in *Librarians, Scholars and Booksellers at Mid-Century: Papers Presented before the Sixteenth Annual Conference of the Graduate Library School of the University of Chicago,* edited by Butler (Chicago: University of Chicago Press, 1954), pp. 1–7.

SELECTED PERIODICAL PUBLICATIONS–
UNCOLLECTED: "A Typographical Library: The John M. Wing Foundation of the Newberry Library," *Papers of the Bibliographical Society of America,* 15, part 2 (1921): 73–87;

"Bibliography and Scholarship," *Papers of the Bibliographical Society of America,* 16 (1922): 53–63;

"Chicago's Typographical Library–The Wing Foundation," *Typothetae Bulletin,* 29 (September 1924): 304;

"Incunabula Markets of Europe," *Publishers' Weekly,* 111 (5 March 1927): 1–5;

"Extending the Active Life of Books," *Publishers' Weekly,* 111 (2 April 1927): 1399–1401;

"The Library: A Laboratory or a Warehouse?," *Illinois Libraries,* 9 (October 1927): 49–52;

"The Dentition of *Equus Donatus,*" *Library Quarterly,* 1 (April 1931): 204–211;

"College Students' Reading," *Bulletin of the Association of American Colleges,* 19 (November 1933): 337–345;

"The Cultural Import of Typography," *Bulletin of the Louisiana Library Commission,* 3 (June 1940): 3–9;

"A Possible Field for Book Conservation," *Library Quarterly,* 12 (July 1942): 399–403;

"The Gutenberg Celebration of 1940: A Survey of the Literature," *Library Quarterly,* 13 (January 1943): 63–67;

"The Professor and the Campus Library," *School and Society,* 65 (19 April 1947): 273–276;

"Librarianship as a Profession," *Library Quarterly,* 21 (October 1951): 235–247;

"The 36-Line Bible," *Newberry Library Bulletin,* 7 (October 1951): 214–215;

"The Cultural Function of the Library," *Library Quarterly,* 22 (April 1952): 79–91;

"The Bibliographical Function of the Library," *Journal of Cataloging and Classification,* 9 (March 1953): 3–11.

Pierce Butler devoted most of his career to the service of the nation's librarians. His early professional disappointments and a physical disability shaped his keen sense of observation and his commitment to scholarly pursuits aimed at promoting, as John V. Richardson Jr. puts it in his 1992 biography of Butler, a "true understanding of human life in the past or in the present." Butler's work at the Wing Foundation of the Newberry Library prepared him for his seminal role as professor of bibliographical history at the University of Chicago's Graduate Library School. There Butler provided students with a cultural and historical context for understanding bibliography and rare-books librarianship that was unknown in other library schools at the time. He made a lasting impression on these fields not only through his publications but also through the students he influenced. He provided them with a guiding philosophy, a sense of "deep librarianship," that emphasized the preservation of cultural values and the promotion of wisdom.

Lee Pierce Butler was born in the Chicago suburb of Clarendon Hills to John Pierce Butler, a railroad clerk, and Evaline Content Whipple Butler, a station agent and postmistress. Although standard biographical sources give his birth year as 1886, his birth certificate and other early records indicate he was born on 19 December 1884. Infantile paralysis left Butler with scoliosis and a permanent limp, and a severe case of scarlet fever resulted in seriously impaired hearing.

In 1893 the family moved to rural Pittsfield, Massachusetts, where two spinster cousins of his father stimulated Butler's interest in nineteenth-century English history and literature. Another influence was a visit to his high school by Harlan Hoge Ballard, the librarian of the Berkshire Athenaeum, a member of the city's textbook committee and the translator of the first six books of Virgil's *Aeneid* (1902) for Houghton, Mifflin. In "Bibliography and Scholarship" (1922) Butler would acknowledge Ballard's "unfailing interest in our schoolboy readings and his unflagging efforts to stimulate our interest in the world of books which was a valuable educational factor." When Butler was a senior in high school, the family doctor recommended that he be sent to a less severe climate for the winter; as a result he spent a year at the University of Georgia as a special student, returning in 1903 to graduate from Pittsfield High. He then entered Dickinson College, a Methodist-related institution in Carlisle, Pennsylvania, selecting the Latin-scientific curriculum.

During summer vacations Butler read books recommended by his instructors and friends. He developed the habit of jotting down the titles in a notebook, and he would take the list to bookstores when he went to Boston or Springfield. When he graduated with a bachelor of philosophy degree in 1906, the yearbook noted that "perhaps no man in College is better read than he."

Butler secured an instructorship in German and Latin at the Locust Dale Academy in Madison County, Virginia, but on his arrival he discovered that, because a former staff member had resigned without notice, he was to teach science and mathematics instead. Citing overwork and ill health, he resigned in December and returned to his parents' home in Pittsfield. He spent the next two months recovering from pneumonia. In 1907 he entered Union Theological Seminary in New York City, where he studied Hebrew, Greek, and systematic theology. He also enrolled as a special student in the political science department at nearby Columbia University, where he took history courses taught by Carlton J. H. Hayes and James T. Shotwell and sociology courses taught by Franklin H. Giddings, who held the first professorship of sociology in the country.

To supplement his $200 scholarship Butler worked in the seminary's library; for a brief period he tended bar at a tavern on Eighth Street, where he was beaten and robbed one morning by four masked men. During the summers he worked as a preacher. In 1909, while serving at the First Methodist Church in Blossburg, Pennsylvania, he decided to switch from Union Theological Seminary to Hartford Theological Seminary. It was also at this time that he began signing his name Pierce Butler, dropping Lee. In March 1910 he received the bachelor of divinity degree with a thesis titled "Napoleon's Attitude to Christianity and to the Roman Catholic Church." The following month he was awarded a graduate fellowship to work on a master of sacred theology (S.T.M.) degree in church history. He also received the Turrentin Prize in Ecclesiastical Latin.

In June 1910 Butler earned his M.A. by examination from Dickinson College. During his two years at Hartford he commuted once a week to

Butler at the time he entered Union Theological Seminary

Berkeley Seminary at Middletown to work under the classicist and theologian Samuel Hart. He decided to pursue a Ph.D. in church history rather than an S.T.M. and submitted a dissertation on the church father Irenaeus. Butler was awarded the Ph.D. on 29 May 1912.

Unable to find a teaching position, Butler was ordained as a deacon in the Episcopal Church in June and was appointed to the staff of All Saints Cathedral in Indianapolis. His deafness, however, made it impossible for him to carry out the parish work he was assigned; moreover, having been educated in a liberal environment, he discovered that the Episcopalian orthodoxy no longer satisfied him. At the end of August he resigned his deaconship and returned to his parents' home in Clarendon Hills. He would resign from the Protestant Episcopal Church in 1922.

In June 1914 Butler started working as a clerk in the Burlington Railroad freight department, pro-

Butler's bookplate

cessing claims on damaged and late-arriving freight. He still wanted to find a place in the scholarly world, so in 1916 he applied for admission to the University of Illinois library school at Urbana; he was accepted and planned to start on 1 September. To help him financially the school offered him a clerkship at thirty dollars per month. While riding on a commuter train in early August, however, he happened to sit next to Dr. W. N. C. Carlton, librarian at the Newberry Library. During their conversation Carlton suggested that Butler apply for employment at the Newberry.

On 21 August 1916 Butler joined the Public Service Division of the Newberry Library as a reference assistant. He was initially on probation because of his hearing problem, but during the fall he acquired his first hearing aid. One of his main tasks was to make up lists of books to be purchased from British dealer catalogues. In September 1917 he was promoted to head of the Book Selection, Ordering, and Receipt Department.

Butler's first major scholarly effort, *Checklist of Incunabula in the Newberry Library, Compiled for the Use of the Library Staff,* was published in October 1919. Butler identified among the Newberry's holdings a total of 270 incunabula from 144 presses in thirty-four cities in seven countries. In December he was appointed custodian and bibliographer of the library's newly established John M. Wing Foundation on the History of Typography and the Printed Book.

Butler believed that the Wing Foundation should possess the greatest collection of fifteenth-century books in the Western Hemisphere and that the Newberry should become the best-known typographical library in the world. He intended to eclipse Harvard University, which owned 1,500 incunabula, as well as the Library of Congress, which held 1,220. His goal was not, however, to make the Newberry known solely for the number of rare books or incunabula it could obtain but to acquire textually important incunabula, especially exemplars from many different presses; he also proposed to acquire only incunabula that had aesthetic value. He discovered that the Newberry already owned most of the appropriate incunabula that were within its reach at current prices. Butler demonstated the rigor of his selection criteria when he reported at the end of 1919 that he had examined nearly 6,000 titles but had ordered only 687. He believed that rare books, or "collector's prizes," were sometimes needed by libraries such as the Newberry, but he never became involved in the "cult of the book."

Initially Butler relied on American booksellers, especially Walter M. Hill of Chicago, but in 1922 he began traveling abroad to acquire books. On that first trip he purchased at least twenty-six incunabula from Maurice Ettinghausen of Maggs Brothers in London; included in this transaction was Jacobus Magni's *Sophologium,* printed in Lyon in 1495 by Jean de Vingle; no other library in the United States held this title. In the summer of 1924 Butler purchased a seventy-seven-leaf fragment of Geoffrey Chaucer's *The Canterbury Tales,* printed in London in 1490 by Richard Pynson, for $125 from Seymour De Ricci of Paris. Printed in two different types, *The Canterbury Tales* may have been Pynson's first book. On his 1926 trip Butler purchased the two-volume *Epistolae* (Parma: Andrea Portilia, 1480) of Saint Jerome for sixty pounds from Robert A. Peddie of Grafton and Company in London. Also in 1926 Butler married Ruth Lapham, a member of the Newberry book-selection staff. Other European booksellers with whom Butler dealt included Ernst Goldschmidt of Vienna and Arthur Spaeth of Lugano.

In 1927 the Graduate Library School was founded at the University of Chicago. Professor James W. Thompson, a member of the founding committee who had written the foreword to Butler's

Butler at home in the late 1940s

exhibition catalogue *The First Fifty Years of the Printed Book, 1450–1500* (1925), recommended Butler for a teaching position there. Butler began as a part-time instructor in the summer of 1928, while continuing his full-time duties at the Wing Foundation. But he experienced several disappointments at the foundation. First, the Newberry failed to pursue an opportunity to acquire the Otto H. F. Vollbehr collection, which was unique in holding books in classical, as well as vernacular, languages. Another disappointment was the Newberry's inability to acquire a few leaves of the thirty-six-line Bible; Butler held the contrarian view that this Bible antedated Johann Gutenberg's forty-two-line Bible, and he believed that this monument of printing should be represented in the Wing collection. Finally, George B. Utley, the Newberry's librarian, refused to give adequate recognition to Butler and his staff for the contributions they were making to the foundation, and this situation ultimately led to a confrontation between the two men. Butler, therefore, left the foundation and accepted a full-time position at the Graduate Library School in the fall of 1931. By then he had obtained fifteenth-century books from eleven countries, ninety-five cities, and 516 printers; the Newberry's 1,850 incunabula constituted slightly more than 5 percent of all such works known to exist.

Butler developed an encyclopedic course for the 1931–1932 academic year titled "History of Scholarship (with Reference to Bibliographical Fac-

tors)." He hoped that his students would realize that the real purpose of libraries and librarianship was to promote scholarship—by which he meant "the total intellectual content of a culture"—and, ultimately, wisdom in the community. Whereas other professors in the Graduate Library School taught students how to be librarians, Butler taught them what librarianship could be.

In the early 1930s librarianship was experiencing a crisis in its intellectual foundations. Those who favored the traditional practices were led by C. Seymour Thompson, while Douglas Waples advocated the introduction into librarianship of the methods of social science. Butler entered the debate with his seminal *Introduction to Library Science* (1933), in which he holds that there is "ample scope for the application of sociological, psychological, and historical methods of research" in librarianship. Butler places the study of bibliography and rare books in the context of what he calls "the literary history of scholarship," or what is known today as intellectual history. His goal is to show researchers in seemingly disparate fields of librarianship that they are working toward a common goal, "with the assurance that the resultant science [would] take into account every phase of librarianship."

Butler's course "Origin and Development of the Printed Book" allowed him to pursue his thesis that the thirty-six-line Bible took priority over the Gutenberg forty-two-line Bible. A second edition, he argued, would be more compact and would employ a more refined typeface than a first edition, and both of these characteristics are found in the forty-two-line Bible; the type in the thirty-six-line Bible is thicker and cruder, as would be expected in a first edition. In *The Origin of Printing in Europe* (1940) Butler continued to argue for the priority of the thirty-six-line Bible. (Scholars today, however, ascribe the thirty-six-line Bible to Albrecht Pfister and date it around 1459–1460–five to ten years after Gutenberg's Bible.)

Butler was reinstated and restored to the Order of the Diaconate in March 1937. He was elevated to the priesthood on 18 December 1940 and served as the rector at Saint Paul's Church in Kenwood. He later was rector at Saint James's and Saint Chrysostom's, both in Chicago.

Butler's "Problems of Curatorship" course was based to a large extent on his experiences at the Newberry Library. It included the administration of archives, bibliographical museums, and rare-book rooms and the preservation and repair of rare books and manuscripts. Butler gave this course at least nine times, later changing its title to "Rare Book Room Administration." As he taught the course, he was collecting material for a book tentatively titled "Rare Books and Their Care," but it would remain unwritten at his death.

Butler retired from teaching in 1952. Two of his final writings were "The Cultural Function of the Library" (1952), in which he contends that "the library contributes not merely to the well-being of civilization but to its existence," and "The Bibliographical Function of the Library" (1953), where he argues that bibliographers are held in low esteem by other librarians because they lack understanding of their function in librarianship. In essence, bibliography is "the systematic process by which civilized man finds his way about in the world of books that he has created." It is the bibliographer's task to study the customs that civilization has developed in connection with books and the "intellectual routines to which civilized people are habituated." The bibliographer's work is just as scholarly and scientific as that of professionals in other disciplines, he says. Butler died on 28 March 1953 of injuries he received in an automobile accident.

Pierce Butler's goal was to develop a theory of professional librarianship that would, as Richardson puts it, "balance our science (the facts of librarianship), our technology (the skill to manipulate these facts), and our humanity (the study of the abstract principles of librarianship)." He wanted to recognize and interpret the social history of the library in terms that would validate it for the modern age. His life's work exemplified the mission of the modern librarian: the promotion of scholarship and wisdom in the individual and in the community.

Biographies:
Stanley M. Pargellis, "Pierce Butler—A Biographical Sketch," *Library Quarterly,* 22 (July 1952): 170–173;

John V. Richardson Jr., *The Gospel of Scholarship: Pierce Butler and a Critique of American Librarianship* (Metuchen, N.J. & London: Scarecrow Press, 1992).

References:
Lee Ash, "Tribute to Pierce Butler," *Library Journal,* 78 (15 May 1953): 826;

Bernard Iddings Bell, "Pierce Butler, Professor and Priest," *Library Quarterly,* 22 (July 1952): 174–176;

Fredson Thayer Bowers, "The Four Faces of Bibliography," in his *Essays in Bibliography, Text, and Editing* (Charlottesville: University Press of Virginia, 1975), pp. 94–108;

John V. Richardson Jr., *The Spirit of Inquiry: The Graduate Library School at Chicago, 1921–51* (Chicago: American Library Association, 1982), pp. 54–55, 76–86, 133–136, 152–156.

C. E. Frazer Clark Jr.

(26 August 1925 -)

Matthew J. Bruccoli
University of South Carolina

BOOKS: *The Merrill Checklist of Nathaniel Hawthorne* (Columbus, Ohio: Merrill, 1970);

Nathaniel Hawthorne, Consul of the United States of America, Liverpool, England, 1853–1857: An Exhibition, July 15–20, 1971, from the Collections of C. E. Frazer Clark, Jr. and the Liverpool City Libraries, Liverpool, England, 1971 (Bloomfield Hills, Mich.: Clark, 1971);

F. Scott Fitzgerald and Ernest M. Hemingway in Paris: An Exhibition at the Bibliothèque Benjamin Franklin in Conjunction with a Conference at the Institut d'Etudes Américaines, 23–24 June 1972 (Bloomfield Hills, Mich. & Columbia, S.C.: Bruccoli Clark, 1972);

Hawthorne's Hand: An Exhibition from the Collection of C. E. Frazer Clark, Jr., 31 October through 8 December, at The Grolier Club, New York, 1973 (Bloomfield Hills, Mich.: Clark, 1973);

Nathaniel Hawthorne: The American Experience. An Exhibition from the Collection of C. E. Frazer Clark, Jr. . . . William L. Clements Library, The University of Michigan (Bloomfield Hills, Mich.: Clark, 1974);

Nathaniel Hawthorne: The College Experience. An Exhibition from the Collection of C. E. Frazer Clark, Jr., 16 May through 21 June at The Kent State University with The Friends of the Kent State University Libraries (Kent, Ohio: Kent State University Libraries, 1974);

Nathaniel Hawthorne: A Descriptive Bibliography (Pittsburgh: University of Pittsburgh Press, 1978).

OTHER: *Longfellow, Hawthorne, and Evangeline: A Letter from Henry Wadsworth Longfellow, November 29, 1847, to Nathaniel Hawthorne,* edited by Clark (Brunswick, Maine: Bowdoin College, 1966);

Evangeline M. O'Connor, *An Analytical Index to the Works of Nathaniel Hawthorne,* introduction by Clark (Detroit: Gale, 1967);

Fitzgerald/Hemingway Annual, 11 volumes, edited by Clark and Matthew J. Bruccoli (Detroit: Bruccoli Clark/Gale, 1969–1979)–includes in volume 1 (1969), "Hemingway at Auction," by Clark, pp. 105–124; in volume 2 (1970), "The Beginnings of Dealer Interest in Hemingway," by Clark, pp. 191–194; in volume 3 (1971), "'Buying Commission Would Cut Out Waste': A Newly Discovered Hemingway Contribution to the *Toronto Daily Star,*" pp. 209–211, "The Crosby Copy of *In Our Time,*" pp. 237–238; in volume 4 (1972), "Hemingway in Advance," by Clark, pp. 197–206; in volume 5 (1974), "American Red Cross Reports on the Wounding of Lieutenant Ernest M. Hemingway–1918," by Clark, pp. 131–136; in volume 7 (1976), review of Hanneman, *Supplement to Ernest Hemingway: A Comprehensive Bibliography,* by Clark, pp. 277–279;

Nathaniel Hawthorne Journal, 8 volumes, edited by Clark (Detroit: Bruccoli Clark/Gale, 1971–1978)–includes in volume 2 (1972), "New Light on the Editing of the 1842 Edition of *Twice-Told Tales:* Discovery of a Family Copy of the 1833 Token Annotated by Hawthorne," by Clark, pp. 91–140, "An Exhibition Commemorating Nathaniel Hawthorne in England: Liverpool, England, 15–20 July 1971," by Clark, pp. 203–218; in volume 3 (1973), "Hawthorne's 'Moonlight': A Lost Manuscript," by Clark and Arthur Monke, pp. 27–34, "Distinguishing the First Printing of the Blithedale Romance," by Clark, pp. 172–176, "Census of Nathaniel Hawthorne Letters," by Clark, pp. 202–252;

"Hawthorne and the Pirates," in *Proof, the Yearbook of American Bibliographical and Textual Studies,* volume 1, edited by Joseph Katz (Columbia: University of South Carolina Press, 1971), pp. 90–121;

Letters of Hawthorne to William D. Ticknor, 1851–1865 (Carteret Book Club, 1910), foreword by Clark (Washington, D.C.: Bruccoli Clark / NCR Microcard Editions, 1972);

Love Letters of Nathaniel Hawthorne, 1839–1863 (William K. Bixby, Society of DOFABS, 1927), fore-

C. E. Frazer Clark Jr. in his library at Bloomfield Hills, Michigan

word by Clark (Washington, D.C.: Bruccoli Clark / NCR Microcard Editions, 1972);

Hawthorne at Auction, 1894–1971, edited by Clark (Detroit: Bruccoli Clark / Gale, 1972);

Hemingway at Auction, 1930–1973, edited by Clark and Bruccoli (Detroit: Bruccoli Clark / Gale, 1973);

Pages: The World of Books, Writers, and Writing, managing editor (Detroit: Bruccoli Clark / Gale, 1976);

First Printings of American Authors, volumes 1–4, managing editor (Detroit: Bruccoli Clark / Gale, 1977–1979);

Dictionary of Literary Biography, 248 volumes published, managing editor (Detroit: Bruccoli Clark Layman / Gale, 1978–).

SELECTED PERIODICAL PUBLICATIONS–
UNCOLLECTED: "Bulls, Bears, and Books," *Among Friends,* no. 52–54 (Fall–Winter 1968; Spring 1969): 5–8;
"Nathaniel Hawthorne . . . The College Experience," *Among Friends,* no. 68 (Winter 1975): 10–23.

C. E. Frazer Clark Jr.'s unparalleled collection of Nathaniel Hawthorne materials shows how much

can be achieved by a determined but not wealthy single-author collector. But Clark's activities on behalf of books extend far beyond his own library: he is a bibliographer, a friend of libraries, an enthusiastic lecturer, a generous producer of exhibitions, and a publisher of reference books.

Clark was born in Detroit on 26 August 1925 to C. E. Frazer Clark Sr., an educator, and Lucy Huffman Clark. During World War II he served in the Eighty-seventh Infantry Division and fought in the Battle of the Bulge. The skills that subsequently brought him so many bookish acquisitions were demonstrated when he persuaded the German who had captured him to surrender. He graduated in 1951 from Kenyon College, where he was introduced to Hawthorne's writings by Professor Denham Sutcliffe.

While Clark was writing his master's thesis–"Nathaniel Hawthorne, The Artist, A Self-Portrait"–at Wayne State University, he worked at Charles S. Boesen's antiquarian bookstore in Detroit. He was converted from a Hawthorne buff to a serious collector when he spotted Hawthorne's signature, which Boesen had missed, in a forty-five-dollar copy of *The Scarlet Letter* (Boston: Ticknor & Fields, 1850). Boesen allowed him to buy the book at the market price in weekly one-dollar payments. This experience established Clark's basic collecting rule: "Pay attention." He believed that other collectors missed important items because they did not concentrate on what they were doing. Clark became an account executive with Florez in Detroit in 1952. On 7 August 1953 he married Margaret Ann Swanson; they had two children, C. E. Frazer III and Douglas Alexander. He received his master of arts in 1956.

A hunch player, Clark enjoys taking bibliographical gambles. One such gamble occurred in 1962:

> One day my mail included a letter from a New Jersey dealer reporting that he had an old dispatch case in his attic which had belonged to Hawthorne's daughter. It seems she had resided in the house the dealer was occupying, and the case had been left behind when she moved. The dealer wrote that it had been some time since he had inspected the contents of the case, but as best he could remember the contents included some family papers, odd documents, and the like. He couldn't be bothered to get it out of the attic unless it was a sure sale. He had recently quoted it to a university but had not as yet heard from them. I could have dispatch and contents, sight unseen, for $150. My instinct told me I should buy the case, that it had all the characteristics of a "sleeper." I sent off a check, and in due course the dispatch case made its way to me. The case contained many treasures: a copy of the separate printing of Hawthorne's tale "The Gentle Boy" (Mary Peabody Mann's copy), letters from Rose Hawthorne and George Parsons Lathrop, the book sales and royalty statements from Ticknor and Fields (Hawthorne's publisher), and other family documents. Collectors have told me that often when they walk into a rare book store for the first time they can sense that there is something in the store for them, and it has proven true. I have found this to be true, and I have learned to trust my instinct.

As a collector, Clark never gave up. In 1963, learning that the stencil Hawthorne had used in the Salem Custom House had been sold in the 1927 Wakeman Sale, Clark tracked down the purchaser's grandson and courted him until the beleaguered man agreed to sell the stencil. Clark had the ability to persuade dealers to part with treasures they had hidden away to provide for their old age. He was particularly effective with English dealers, who were taken in by his naive-American routine.

From 1964 through 1966 Clark worked as an account executive with the Jam Handy Organization in Detroit. In 1967 he became a partner in his own consulting firm, Paramarketing, in the Detroit suburb of Bloomfield Hills. The business was successful, but determination and knowledge were more important than money in his Hawthorne

The stencil Nathaniel Hawthorne used when he worked in the Salem Custom House, acquired by Clark in 1963 (House of Seven Gables)

work. Clark formulated collecting policies on the basis of his experiences in competing successfully against larger purses:

> Most collectors keep score on their performance, and the resolute collectors quickly learn from sad experience that more determination in backing your own convictions is essential. Creeds concerning how to perform the act of auction faith develop. Two axioms regarding auction decisions have guided my own adventures in the gallery. The first axiom can be summarized as "things aren't as expensive as they seem"; and the second axiom, having to do with material you really need, is "buy it now and worry about how to pay for it later."

During the 1950s Clark was a high-spot collector; he became an in-depth or completist collector in the 1960s through his affiliation with *The Centenary Edition of the Works of Nathaniel Hawthorne* (1963–1969). His friendship with the supervisor of that project, Professor Matthew J. Bruccoli, then at Ohio State University, developed into a partnership that reshaped their lives. They began acquiring books for each other; some of Bruccoli's best twentieth-century American items were procured by Clark, whose book sense was not restricted to Hawthorne.

Clark decided to compile the standard descriptive bibliography of Hawthorne; for this purpose he determined to acquire every variant of every printing of every edition of each of Hawthorne's works. A serious bibliographer, he believes, needs the books at hand for rechecking and comparison. The process of finding books one at a time and integrating them into an organic collection teaches lessons that cannot be learned by using library books.

The Clark Collection became the most comprehensive research archive for Hawthorne ever assembled. He ultimately owned every separately published Hawthorne work (bibliography A-items), except for two newspaper carriers' addresses, *Time's Portraiture* and *The Sister Years*—and he has not

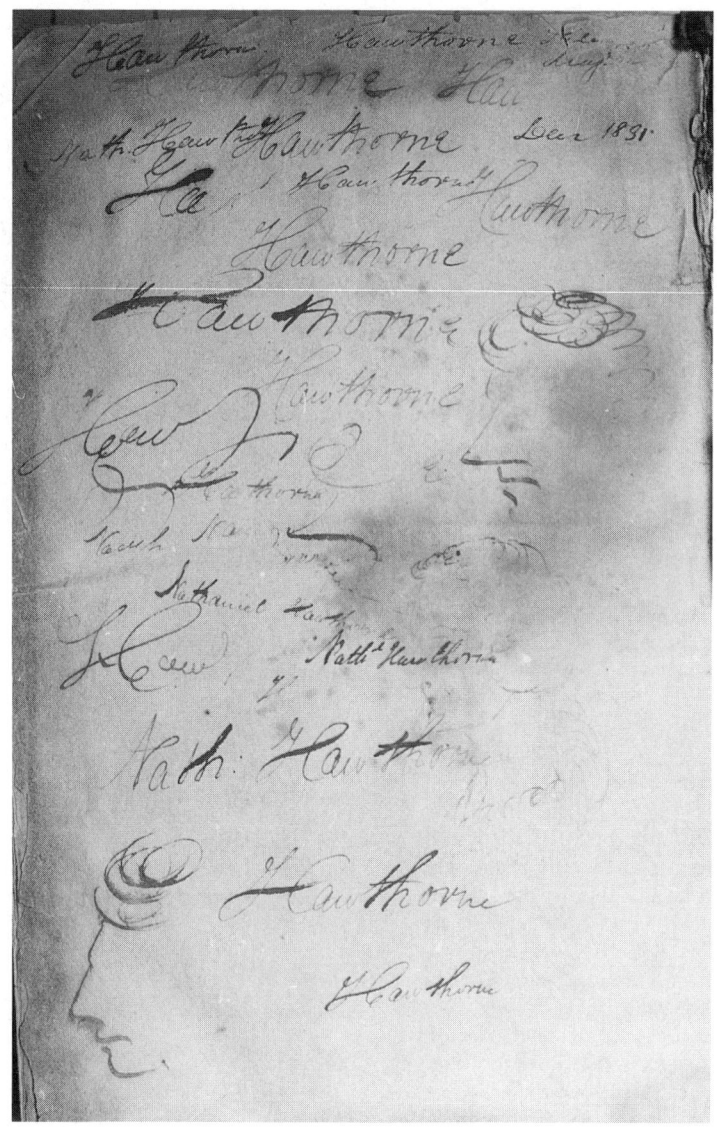

Rear flyleaf from Clark's copy of A New Critical Pronouncing
Dictionary of the English Language, *on which Hawthorne
experimented with various ways of signing his name and
sketched three profiles (Peabody Essex Museum)*

stopped searching for them. His *Fanshawe* (Boston: Marsh and Capen, 1828) is one of two extant presentation copies:

> Almost the first duty I had in my apprenticeship to Charles S. Boesen was to wrap a package for shipment to T. E. Hanley, the Bradford, Pennsylvania, collector. The order consisted of two items, Thomas à Becket's *The Comic History of England* and Nathaniel Hawthorne's *Fanshawe*. Hanley's *Fanshawe* was the copy owned by Hawthorne's aunt, Susan D. Manning, and had appeared in the 1929 Jerome Kern sale. Almost ten years to the day after I had first had the Hanley copy of *Fanshawe* in my hands, I had a telephone call from the rare books curator of an Eastern college reporting that he had been offered a copy of *Fanshawe* and could I tell him what I thought it was worth. Shortly thereafter I had a call from another curator of rare books at a different school with the same request. The two curators declined to get into a bidding contest, and the seller withdrew what later proved to be the Hanley copy from the market. After a proper period of time I secured permission to try to capture this *Fanshawe*. Three trips to Bradford later, I was successful.

By the time Clark became a major Hawthorne player there was little manuscript material outside of libraries. Nonetheless, he found more than forty letters and the manuscript for "Buds and Bird Voices." Clark took particular gratification from association material that personalized Hawthorne. A happy acquisition was *A New Critical Pronouncing Dictionary of the English Language* (Burlington, N.J.: D. Allinson, 1813), with twenty-two Hawthorne signatures in variant forms: like other apprentice authors, the young Hawthorne was experimenting with his byline.

Clark's most remarkable collecting coup was the purchase of the Essex Institute duplicates of the *Salem Gazette,* the *Salem Register,* the *Salem Observer,* the *Salem Mercury,* the *Salem Advertiser,* and the *Essex Mercury* from 1814 to 1860—some fifteen hundred newspapers altogether. He spent years studying them to identify possible unsigned Hawthorne contributions, confident that "if there was Hawthorne in those newspapers, I had the items in my collection." The papers provided considerable data about the Hawthorne and Manning families. Clark found twenty-eight previously unknown *Salem Gazette* advertisements for *Fanshawe,* establishing that Hawthorne had actively promoted the apprentice novel he later disavowed. Furthermore, comparison with the first appearances of Hawthorne's "twice-told tales" in the *Gazette* made it possible to identify the revisions the author made when he collected the stories for book publication.

Clark cofounded the Nathaniel Hawthorne Society in 1971, serving as president, and initiated the annual Hawthorne birthday celebration at the House of the Seven Gables in Salem, Massachusetts. He wrote bibliographical and biographical articles about Hawthorne; founded the *Nathaniel Hawthorne Journal* in 1971, editing the annual alone or with collaborators until 1978; and provided introductions for Hawthorne-related publications. He took particular pleasure in the catalogues of the Hawthorne exhibitions he mounted; the catalogues were usually designed by his wife. His *Nathaniel Hawthorne: A Descriptive Bibliography,* published by the University of Pittsburgh Press in 1978, supersedes all previous endeavors.

Their joint collecting activities led Clark and Bruccoli—who had moved to the University of South Carolina in 1969—to establish a firm to publish books about books. The Bruccoli Clark imprint (since 1987 Bruccoli Clark Layman), incorporated in 1971, began as a publisher of annuals and limited editions of previously unpublished writings by such authors as James Dickey, James Gould Cozzens, Robert Coover, and Reynolds Price. The early volumes were supervised by Bruccoli's cherished friend Vernon Sternberg, director of the Southern

THE NATHANIEL HAWTHORNE JOURNAL 1971

C. E. Frazer Clark, Jr., Editor

Consulting Editor: Matthew J. Bruccoli
University of South Carolina

NCR Microcard Editions

Title page for the first volume of the journal Clark founded in 1971. It was published until 1978.

Illinois University Press. These collectors' items terminated after Clark and Bruccoli decided to concentrate on reference books. Alliances were made with Gale Research and Omnigraphics, both of Detroit; NCR Microcard Editions Books of Washington, D.C.; and Facts on File of New York to produce reference works such as *First Printings of American Authors* (5 volumes, Gale, 1977–1987) and *Bibliography of American Fiction* (4 volumes, Facts on File, 1991–1994). Literary trade books, including Vladimir Nabokov's lectures (1980–1983) and letters (1989), were copublished with Harcourt Brace Jovanovich.

Clark and Frederick G. Ruffner, founder of the Gale Research reference-book empire, met through the Friends of the Detroit Public Library; both men served as presidents. Ruffner invited Clark and Bruccoli to develop bibliographical and biographical projects for Gale, of which the *Dictionary of Literary Biography* became the most comprehen-

*Title page for Clark's work that supersedes
previous bibliographies*

sive. The first *DLB* volume was published in 1978; the *DLB Yearbooks* and the *DLB Documentary Series* began in 1981 and 1982, respectively.

Clark and Bruccoli shared the conviction that producing facsimile editions of the manuscripts for great works of American literature would stimulate scholarship and an understanding of the writing process by getting the documents into the hands of people who would otherwise never have access to them. These facsimiles include Stephen Crane's *The Red Badge of Courage* (1895), published in 1972; F. Scott Fitzgerald's *The Great Gatsby* (1925) and *Ledger,* both in 1973; Mark Twain's *Huckleberry Finn* (1884) in 1983; and Ernest Hemingway's *The Sun Also Rises* (1926) in 1990. Scottie Fitzgerald Smith provided the necessary permissions for Bruccoli Clark to publish limited and trade editions of the writings of her father, F. Scott Fitzgerald. In 1977 the firm published facsimiles of the first editions of Hemingway's first Paris books, *Three Stories and Ten Poems*

(1923) and *in our time* (1924), again with the intention of providing students and serious readers with a sense of the real thing. Literary history, they believe, is book history.

A book collector needs to collect; no serious collector wants to leave a bookshop empty-handed. By the late 1960s there was not much Hawthorne left for Clark to acquire; therefore, to remain active, he began collecting Hemingway. He has explained that he chose Hemingway because Hemingway was usually shelved near Hawthorne, but the real reason was that it was still possible to find major Hemingway material. Since he was already scouting for Bruccoli's twentieth-century figures, it was convenient for Clark to add a modern author to his own library. In a short time he built a significant collection that included Hemingway's letters to Charles Poore and Caresse Crosby. The way he acquired Hemingway's family correspondence demonstrates Clark's technique: Hemingway's sister Sunny, who owned the family material, wanted a stained-glass window in memory of her brother for the Petoskey, Michigan, Episcopal Church; in 1969 Clark paid for the window in return for the letters. He also acquired the piano of Hemingway's mother, Grace, from the family's summer cottage at Walloon Lake, Michigan.

Clark's Hemingway activity led to his work with Bruccoli as coeditor of the *Fitzgerald/Hemingway Annual,* clothbound volumes that they published from 1969 to 1979 and for which Clark wrote dozens of bibliographical notes. In 1972 he organized a conference at the Institut d'Etudes Américaines in Paris to celebrate the fiftieth anniversary of the meeting of Fitzgerald and Hemingway; he was three years early, but he did not want to wait. The event brought together 1920s Paris hands and scholars to evaluate the expatriate experience. Clark mounted an exhibition at the Bibliothèque Benjamin Franklin featuring material from his and Bruccoli's collections and published an illustrated catalogue, *F. Scott Fitzgerald and Ernest M. Hemingway in Paris* (1972). Nevertheless, his true love was Hawthorne, and in 1975 he sold his Hemingway collection to the University of Maryland.

Clark enjoys participating in bookish organizations and their events. He cofounded the Book Club of Detroit in 1952 and serves on the Clements Library Associates Board of Governors at the University of Michigan. He has also been a member of the American Antiquarian Society, the Modern Language Society of America, the Society for Applied Anthropology, the Bibliographical Society of America, the Sons of the Whiskey Rebellion, the Grolier Club, the Pittsburgh Bibliophiles, the Friends of the

Leland Township Public Library, and the Prismatic Club.

Scholar-collectors are committed to maintaining the usability of their libraries, and Clark has always been generous about sharing his collections with scholars and students. When his health began to fail he endeavored to place his entire Hawthorne collection in a single institution for the use of researchers. Like many in-depth collectors, he was defeated by library-school-engendered neurosis about duplication; more great research collections have been vitiated by librarian opacity than by fire or flood. Clark grieved in 1983 when he was compelled to divide his thirty thousand Hawthorne items between the House of the Seven Gables and the Essex Institute in Salem, which merged with the Peabody Museum to form the Peabody Essex Museum in 1992.

Clark has applied the General Motors structural principle to his book activities: everything connects. He regards collecting, writing, editing, lecturing, and publishing as integrated aspects of a single vocation. Clark's work provides the proper response to outsiders' questions about the utility of book collecting; he has demonstrated the uses of what civilians call "mere collector's items." His rat-trap memory, by enabling him to make connections between seemingly trivial items, has led to significant discoveries:

> Collecting has its puzzles. After Hawthorne's death there was a growing demand for samples of his autograph. Hawthorne's wife, Sophia, received numerous requests for examples of her husband's signature, as did Sophia's sister, Elizabeth Peabody. It is common to find letters from Hawthorne lacking his signature. When the signatures ran out, specimens were cut from the bodies of the letters. Twenty-five years ago I bought a small clipping from a Hawthorne-to-Elizabeth Peabody letter. With the clipping was a covering letter from Elizabeth Peabody explaining that she was running out of samples of Hawthorne's autograph. The clipping was too small to reveal the substance of the letter. I filed away the scraps and didn't think about them much. Years later I bought another fragment of a Hawthorne letter and filed it away. In the middle of the night I woke up to see in my mind's eye the two fragments of the Hawthorne letters and I recognized the same blue letter paper favored by Hawthorne, the same color ink, the same size of the sheet. I retrieved the two letter fragments. I put them side by side, and the two clippings fit together like a perfect jigsaw puzzle. Whereas the two separate pieces offered little content, the matched pair revealed important bibliographical information.

American bibliography and American publishing were deprived of C. E. Frazer Clark's generosity, determination, and energy as the result of a debilitating illness that began in the early 1980s. Despite this too-early interruption, his place in the line of distinguished American bookmen is secure.

References:

William Dunn, "Limited Books, Limitless Authors," *New York Times,* 22 May 1977, III, p. 7;

"Those Who Leave No Tome Unturned," *Fortune,* 90 (November 1974): 79, 82, 86, 90, 94, 98, 102, 105;

Alden Whitman, "Zeal for 'Mr. Hawthorne' Leads to Labor of Love," *New York Times,* 27 January 1971, p. 30.

William Andrews Clark Jr.

(29 March 1877 – 14 June 1934)

Joseph Rosenblum

BOOK: *The Library of William Andrews Clark, Jr.,* 20 volumes, by Clark, Robert Ernest Cowan, Cora Edgerton Sanders, and Harrison Post (San Francisco: Printed by John Henry Nash, 1920–1931).

OTHER: Percy Bysshe Shelley, *Adonais, an Elegy on the Death of John Keats, by Percy Bysshe Shelley, in Commemoration of the Hundredth Anniversary of the Death of the Poet,* published by Clark (San Francisco: Printed for W. A. Clark Jr. by J. H. Nash, 1922);

Oliver Goldsmith, *The Deserted Village: A Poem,* published, with an introduction, by Clark (San Francisco: Printed for W. A. Clark Jr. by J. H. Nash, 1922);

Edgar Allan Poe, *Tamerlane and Other Poems,* published by Clark (San Francisco: Printed for W. A. Clark Jr. by J. H. Nash, 1923);

Some Letters from Oscar Wilde to Alfred Douglas, 1892–1897 (Hitherto Unpublished) with Illustrative Notes by Arthur C. Dennison, Jr., and Harrison Post, and an Essay by A. S. W. Rosenbach, Ph.D., published by Clark (San Francisco: Printed for W. A. Clark Jr. by J. H. Nash, 1924);

Thomas Gray, *An Elegy Written in a Country Churchyard,* published, with an introduction, by Clark (San Francisco: Printed for W. A. Clark Jr. by J. H. Nash, 1925);

Elizabeth Barrett Browning, *Sonnets from the Portuguese,* published, with notes, by Clark (San Francisco: Printed for W. A. Clark Jr. by J. H. Nash, 1927);

Alexander Pope, *An Essay on Criticism,* published by Clark (San Francisco: Printed for W. A. Clark Jr. by J. H. Nash, 1928);

John Dryden, *All for Love; or, The World Well Lost: A Tragedy,* published by Clark (San Francisco: Printed for W. A. Clark Jr. by J. H. Nash, 1929);

Robert Louis Stevenson, *Father Damien: An Open Letter to the Reverend Dr. Hyde of Honolulu, Dated February Twenty-fifth MDCCCXC,* published by

William Andrews Clark Jr.

Clark (San Francisco: Printed for W. A. Clark Jr. by J. H. Nash, 1930);

Christmas Greetings from William Andrews Clark, Jr., Mcmxxxii: The Lord's Prayer from the Sermon on the Mount, published by Clark (San Francisco: Printed for W. A. Clark Jr. by J. H. Nash, 1932);

Gray, *Ode on the Pleasure Arising from Vicissitude, Left Unfinished by Mr. Gray, and since Completed,* published by Clark (San Francisco: Printed for W. A. Clark Jr. by J. H. Nash, 1933).

William Andrews Clark Jr. devoted his inherited fortune to his literary and artistic interests, which focused on the seventeenth-century English poet and dramatist John Dryden and more generally on English culture from 1640 to 1750. He also secured an extensive collection of works by and about Oscar Wilde and lesser collections in a variety of areas, ranging from Elizabethan and Jacobean drama to western Americana. In 1926 he donated his books and the library he built for them to the University of California, Southern Branch (now UCLA); named for his father, it was the first important gift to that institution. Through his generosity Clark, in the words of William Andrews Clark Memorial Library director Lawrence Clark Powell, "joined the select company of American book-collectors whose bequests are among the glories of [America's] national library strength."

Clark was the fourth child and second son of William Andrews and Katherine Louise Stauffer Clark. His father had been a prospector in Colorado and the Montana Territory; when he was not panning for gold, he had passed the time reading one of his three books: the poems of Robert Burns, Edward Hitchcock's *Elementary Geology* (1840), and Theophilus Parsons's *The Law of Contracts* (1853–1855). William Andrews Clark Sr.'s sons would inherit not only his fortune but also his enjoyment of books. By the time Clark Jr. was born in Deer Lodge, Montana Territory, on 29 March 1877, Clark Sr. was Montana's leading capitalist, with interests in mining, smelting, and banking. In 1878 he took his family to Europe, and the young Clark spent his earliest years in Paris. He spoke French before English, and he would remain a lifelong Francophile. Toward the end of his life he would buy an apartment on the Left Bank in Paris, and in January 1930 he would write to his employee and later biographer William D. Mangum, "I am heartily sick of the U.S.–Montana and California. There is only one place to live & that is France." This sentiment would be reflected in his small but choice collection of French books and manuscripts.

In the summer of 1883 the Clarks settled in Garden City, New York, so that the children could attend school in the East while Clark Sr. shuttled between Butte and New York City. Clark Jr. attended the local public schools but also studied at the Drisler Academy in New York City and the public schools of Los Angeles, where his grandmother, Mary Andrews Clark, had settled in 1880. Clark evidently was admitted to law school without an undergraduate degree. He entered the University of Virginia School of Law in 1896, graduated with a bachelor of law degree in 1899, and returned to Los

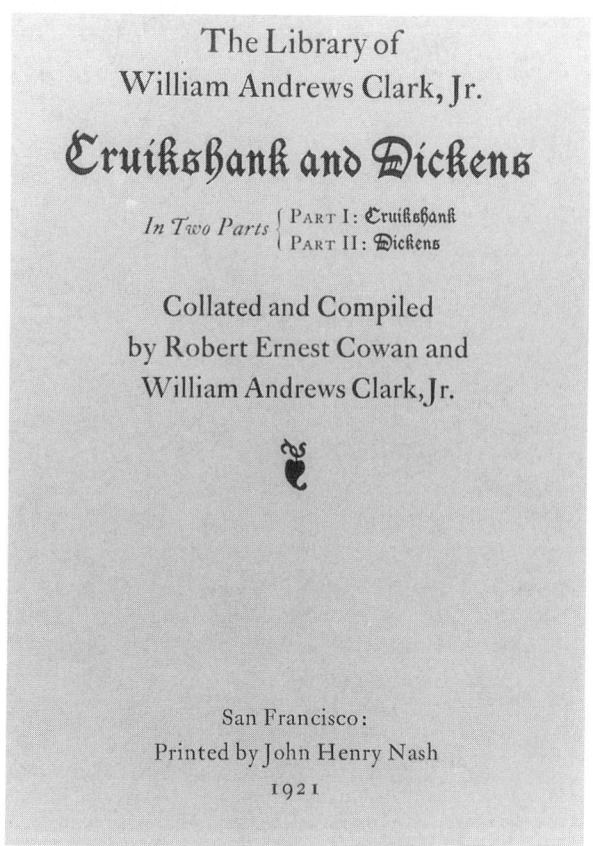

The Library of
William Andrews Clark, Jr.

Cruikshank and Dickens

In Two Parts { PART I: Cruikshank
                 PART II: Dickens

Collated and Compiled
by Robert Ernest Cowan and
William Andrews Clark, Jr.

San Francisco:
Printed by John Henry Nash
1921

Title page for one of the eighteen volumes of Clark's catalogue of his collection. There are also two index volumes.

Angeles to read law under Frank W. Burnett, a corporate lawyer. In 1900 he moved to Montana, where he was admitted to the bar and formed a parnership with Jesse B. Roote. (Roote's former partner, John B. Wellcome, had been disbarred for bribing members of the Montana legislature to elect Clark Sr. to the United States Senate.) Clark Jr. had an office in Butte and a branch office in the Van Nuys Hotel in Los Angeles, but after his marriage to Mabel Duffield Foster of Butte on 19 June 1901, he largely abandoned the practice of law to devote his time to the family's extensive copper interests.

Mabel Clark died a month after the birth of a son, Tertius, on 1 December 1902 (Tertius Clark would die in an airplane crash in 1932). On 7 May 1907 Clark married Alice McManus of Virginia City, Nevada, and shortly thereafter the family moved to Los Angeles. At first they leased a house in the 700 block of West Adams Street, but in 1910 Clark bought the McCan residence at 2205 West Adams. He eventually acquired the entire block, an area of about five acres; there he created an Italian sunken garden, an observatory, and a library.

Clark studied violin in Paris under the Belgian virtuoso Martin Marsick; in Los Angeles he studied

Clark in 1933; oil painting by Henrique Medina (University of Virginia School of Law)

under Florence Heinze and Edwin H. Clark (no relation). In 1911 the two Clarks organized the Saint-Saëns Quartet, which soon became a quintet; Edwin Clark played first violin, William Clark second violin. When the Los Angeles Symphony foundered in 1919, Clark organized the Los Angeles Philharmonic under the direction of Walter Henry Rothwell.

Clark had begun collecting books in 1909; he may have been introduced to bibliophily by his older brother, Charles, a collector of incunabula. (Though their father also enjoyed books, his main interest was in art; his collection would eventually fill a wing of the Corcoran Gallery in Washington, D.C.) As early as 1911 Clark was buying from E. Byron Hostetter of Boston. These purchases were unfocused: William E. Conway lists what he calls "a remarkable assortment of titles—books on tobacco and snuff and on the life of P. T. Barnum, various French works, a number of volumes obviously purchased for their decorative bindings, a run of American firsts by standard authors such as Longfellow, Lowell, E. C. Stedman, and Mark Twain." In May 1911 Clark bought one of the fourteen copies of Dante's *Lo inferno* (completed in 1321) printed on vellum in 1902 at St. John Hornby's Ashendene Press in London and one of the 160 copies of Lon-

gus's *Daphnis and Chloe* printed in New Rochelle, New York, by Clarke Conwell's Elston Press in 1904. He also bought from Hostetter first editions of works by Oscar Wilde, including *The Ballad of Reading Gaol* (London: L. Smithers, 1898). Wilde was Clark's first major collecting interest.

Charles Clark introduced his younger brother to his booksellers, George and Alice Millard of Pasadena and George D. Smith of New York City; most of William Clark's early purchases were made through these dealers. The Millards encouraged his interest in fine printing: in 1917 he bought from them seventeen titles from William Morris's Kelmscott Press in London; the following year they sold him thirty-two books from T. J. Cobden-Sanderson's Doves Press, also in London.

Most of Clark's purchases were made between 1920 and 1926, but by 1920 he already had eleven hundred volumes and had planned the first two volumes of a catalogue of his collection. Published between 1920 and 1931, the catalogue would comprise eighteen volumes plus two volumes of indexes. To assist him, in 1919 Clark had hired the distinguished bookseller, collector, and bibliographer Robert Ernest Cowan of San Francisco, who had been recommended by Charles Clark and the San Francisco printer John Henry Nash. Clark assumed that Cowan would remain for six months; he would stay for fourteen years. For the first seven years he spent alternate months at Clark's house in Los Angeles and in San Francisco, where he continued to sell books. Cowan strenthened Clark's reference collection, suggested purchases, and worked with Clark and Sanders on the catalogues, though Clark always made the final decisions.

After George Millard's death in 1918 Alice Millard continued to sell books to Clark, adding the 1896 Kelmscott Chaucer to his library in 1921. He would eventually own complete collections of the books printed by the Kelmscott and Doves presses as well as examples of works from the Ashendene, Beaumont, Cayme, Cranach, Cresset, Cuala, Daniel, Eragny, Essex House, Franfrolico, Fleuron, Florence, Fortune, Gaige, Grabhorn, Golden Cockerel, Gregynog, Halcyon, High House, Nonesuch, Oxford, Pear Tree, Riccardi, Bruce Rogers, Scholartis, Shakespeare Head, Taylor and Taylor, and Vale presses. Clark also had a virtually complete collection of books and ephemera produced in San Francisco by Nash. Besides some sixteen incunabula, Clark owned works from the presses of the noted early printers Wynkyn de Worde, Richard Pynson, John Day, Jacob Tonson the Elder, William Baskerville, Horace Walpole (the Strawberry Hill Press), William Pickering, Firmin Didot, and

*The William Andrews Clark Memorial Library of the University of California,
Los Angeles (photograph by Thelner Hoover)*

the Alduses, the Elzeviers, the Bodonis, and the Plantins.

The Millards were a source not only of private-press books but also of Wilde material, most of which Clark bought in the 1920s. The most important supplier of works by and about Wilde, however, was Christopher S. Millard, who was not related to George and Alice and who had published a bibliography of Wilde in 1914 under the pseudonym Stuart Mason. Millard was in an ideal position to catalogue and acquire Wilde material because he served as secretary to Robert Ross, Wilde's literary executor, and was a friend of Vyvyan Holland, Wilde's son. In 1923 Holland offered Clark two groups of letters from Wilde to Ross, the manuscript "The Duchess of Padua" (written in the early 1880s but not published until 1891, when it appeared as *Guido Ferranti*), two-thirds of the manuscript for "The Rise of Historical Criticism" (written

at Oxford in 1879 but not published in its entirety until 1909), and other papers for £12,000. Clark refused Holland's offer, reluctant to buy material en bloc. As he wrote to the Brick Row Book Shop in New Haven on 27 March 1926, declining a large Joseph Conrad collection: "The particular disinclination I have to purchase the collection is that I find more pleasure in picking up the books . . . item by item and not a collection en bloc. It gives me far more enjoyment and I can familiarize myself in this way more thoroughly with my books." In 1928, though, Dulau and Company of London offered these Wilde items, minus "The Duchess of Padua," as part of a larger collection of books and papers that had belonged to Holland, Ross, and Christopher Millard. Clark bought sixty-four lots for £5,000; he also bought fifty-eight volumes of ephemera relating to Wilde. ("The Duchess of Padua" would come to the William Andrews Clark

Memorial Library in 1949 from the Los Angeles bookseller Jake Zeitlin.)

Six of the eighteen catalogues of Clark's collection deal with Wilde; one of these is devoted to a previously unknown portrait Clark found in Chicago. His Wilde holdings numbered more than a thousand items and included drafts of poems, essays, lectures, letters, and notebooks. Clark privately printed the letters of Wilde to Lord Alfred Douglas in 1924; he had secured the letters in 1920 for $8,690 from the library of John B. Stetson. Other important Wilde letters in the William Andrews Clark Memorial Library are those written to Ross and to More Adey from prison. They offer background to *De Profundis* (1905) as well as *The Ballad of Reading Gaol*.

Smith probably encouraged Clark to buy works by Dryden and other British dramatists of the late seventeenth century because they could be purchased cheaply. By 1920 Clark owned 125 items relating to Dryden, most of them from the sale of the Winston H. Hagen library at the Anderson Galleries in New York City on 13 May 1918, and he decided to build a major Dryden collection. In 1921 he gave Alice Millard a want list of Dryden material, and in 1923 he sent Cora Edgerton Sanders to London with Millard to study the British Museum's Dryden holdings. Sanders was the niece of Wilbur Fiske Sanders, who, like Clark's father, served as United States senator from Montana. She had been secretary and companion to both of Clark's wives, and after the death of Alice Clark in 1918 she became Clark's official hostess and his first library assistant. She would remain at the Clark Library as librarian until her retirement on 31 December 1943. Clark enjoyed great success in his pursuit of Dryden. By 1928 he could write to Alan Devoe, "My Dryden collection . . . I think is the finest in the world." Conway notes that Clark held "First and most later editions to 1700 of the major works (often in multiple copies); many of the separate publications of the prologues and epilogues, and a few of the separate songs. To these printed works he added a few letters in Dryden's hand and an important group of ten items of correspondence and contracts between Dryden and his publisher, Jacob Tonson." These strong holdings would lead to publication by the University of California Press at Berkeley of the definitive scholarly edition of the entire Dryden corpus (1956–). Donald Wing's *Short-Title Catalogue of Books Printed in England, Scotland, Wales, and British America and of English Books Printed in Other Countries, 1641–1700* (1945–1951) includes 198 Dryden entries; in its *Report of the First Decade, 1934–1944* the William Andrews Clark Memorial Library noted that its collection contained 173 of these items, most of them acquired by Clark himself. With 828 volumes, Clark's Dryden holdings were surpassed in his lifetime by only one other private library, that of the British collector, bibliographer, and forger Thomas James Wise. Clark assembled the collection for the moderate sum of $42,000. Dryden led Clark to other Restoration dramatists and poets, and thence to late-seventeenth- and eighteenth-century British literature and culture in general. This area has become the William Andrews Clark Memorial Library's chief interest; its Augustan Reprint Society continues Clark's efforts to make the library's holdings accessible to a larger public by issuing reprints of rarities in the collection, conducting annual seminars, awarding fellowships, and, since 1969, endowing the Clark Library Professorships.

While Clark concentrated on Wilde, Dryden, and the seventeenth and eighteenth centuries, his interests ranged over the entire corpus of English and American literature. Dryden, who translated Chaucer and whose 1700 edition of *Fables* included one of the earliest printings of Chaucer in roman type, led Clark to acquire various important editions of this medieval poet. Of the first printed editions of Chaucer by William Caxton, de Worde, and Pynson, Clark had only one leaf of the 1478 Caxton *Canterbury Tales*, the work's first appearance in type. Clark did, however, acquire a complete run of sixteenth-century editions, beginning with that prepared by William Thynne in 1532 and including those published in 1542, 1550, 1561, and 1598 as well as those of 1602 and 1687. Clark also secured eighteenth-century translations and imitations of Chaucer by Alexander Pope, John Gay, Matthew Prior, and George Ogle. In the field of Elizabethan and Jacobean literature pride of place belongs to his Shakespeare folios. He owned a fine copy of the First Folio (London: Printed by Isaac Jaggard and Edward Blount, 1623); his most expensive acquisition, it was the William K. Bixby copy and came from the 1920 George D. Smith sale. He also owned six copies of the Second Folio (London: Printed by Thomas Cotes, 1623), two of the Third (London: Printed for Philip Chetwinde, one dated 1663, the other 1664), and three of the Fourth Folio (London: Printed for H. Herringman, E. Brewster, and R. Bentley, 1685). A 1946 census of Shakespeare quartos published between 1594 and 1709 ranked the William Andrews Clark Memorial Library as having the fourth-largest holdings in the United States; only Harvard, Yale, and the University of Pennsylvania had more. Among the Clark quartos are *The Merchant of Venice* (London: Printed by I. R. for Thomas Heyes, 1600); *Much Ado about Nothing* (London: Printed by

Drawing room of the William Andrews Clark Memorial Library, decorated by Allyn Cox (photograph by Thelner Hoover)

V. S. for Andrew Wise and William Aspley, 1600); and the first (London: Printed by Nicholas for Thomas Halkley, 1622), second (London: Printed by A. Mathewes for Richard Hawkins, 1630), third (London: Printed for W. Leak, 1655), and fourth (London: Richard Bentley, 1681) quartos of *Othello*. Charles Clark had paid A. S. W. Rosenbach $12,750 for *Much Ado about Nothing* and later gave the book to his brother. In 1922 William Clark stopped in New York on his way back to the West Coast from Paris and bought $23,950 worth of Shakespeare material that had belonged to Marsden J. Perry, who had sold his extensive Shakespeare holdings to Rosenbach in 1919. Altogether, Clark owned thirty volumes of Shakespeare rarities, for which he spent $126,000.

Clark had two copies of Ben Jonson's First Folio (London: Imprinted by W. Stansby, 1616), one of them printed on large paper; a large-paper copy of Jonson's Second Folio (London: Printed for Richard Meighem, 1640); and Lucy, Countess of Bedford's copy of *Fountaine of Self Love or Cynthia's Revels* (London: Walter Burre, 1601) with Jonson's dedication to the countess. Also in Clark's library were the Francis Beaumont and John Fletcher folios of 1647 (London: Printed for Humphrey Robinson at the Three Pidgeons, and for Humphrey Moseley at the

Princes Armes in St Pauls church-Yard) and 1679 (London: Printed by J. Macock, for John Martyn, Henry Herringman, [and] Richard Marriot) as well as twenty-six quarto editions of these playwrights' works published before 1700. The Beaumont and Fletcher items came chiefly from the libraries of Robert Hoe III and the dukes of Bridgewater. The latter collection had been begun by Sir Thomas Egerton around 1600 and had been sold to Henry E. Huntington in 1917; Huntington sold his duplicates, allowing collectors such as Clark to secure some of the Bridgewater treasures.

Of George Chapman's sixteen first editions, Clark had twelve. In addition he owned sixteen quartos of Philip Massinger's works and his *Three New Plays* (London: Humphrey Moseley, 1655), thirty-three quartos of James Shirley's works and his *Six New Plays* (London: Humphrey Robinson and Humphrey Moseley, 1653), seven Thomas Middleton quartos, four of Thomas Heywood's, and three of Thomas Dekker's, including a unique *Magnificent Entertainment Given to King James* (London: Thomas Man the Younger, 1604) with each page inlaid and with five plates added.

Four volumes of Clark's catalogues are devoted to early English literature; four others deal with modern English literature, another area where

The Dryden collection at the William Andrews Clark Memorial Library in 1946. Of the 173 items then in the collection, most were acquired by Clark himself (photograph by Thelner Hoover).

the collection is selective rather than comprehensive but nonetheless contains valuable and important works. Among the Romantics, George Gordon, Lord Byron; Shelley; John Keats; and Charles Lamb are well represented. Clark's Byron collection included *Poems on Various Occasions* (Newark: Printed for S. and J. Ridge, 1807). This is the rare second privately printed edition with twelve pieces that Byron omitted from the suppressed 1806 *Fugitive Pieces;* only one hundred copies were printed. Clark also owned *Hours of Idleness* (Newark: Printed for S. and J. Ridge, 1807), *Euthanasia* (London: Printed for the author, 1812), *Waltz* (London: Printed by S. Gosnell, 1813), and twenty-five other first editions, among them the two-page *Additional Stanzas of the First, Second and Third Editions of Beppo* (London: Privately printed by John Murray, 1818). In 1939 the only other known copies of this item would be one in the British Museum and two belonging to the estate of John A. Spoor.

The earliest Shelley item in the collection is *Queen Mab* (London: Printed by P. B. Shelley, 1813), of which 250 copies were printed; the poem was never officially published because of its radical political sentiments. Clark owned first editions of *Alas-*

tor (London: Printed for Baldwin, Cradock, and Joy and Carpenter and Son, by S. Hamilton, 1816); *Laon and Cythna* (London: Printed for Sherwood, Neely, and Jones and C. and J. Ollier, 1818), which was suppressed and altered to become *The Revolt of Islam* (London: Printed for C. and J. Ollier, 1818), also in the Clark collection; *Rosalind and Helen* (London: Printed for C. and J. Ollier, 1819); *The Cenci* (Italy: Printed for C. and J. Ollier, 1819); *Prometheus Unbound* (London: C. and J. Ollier, 1820); *Epipsychidion* (London: C. and J. Ollier, 1821); *Adonais* (Pisa, 1821), Shelley's moving pastoral elegy on the death of Keats; and the bitter political satire *The Masque of Anarchy* (London: Edward Moxon, 1832). Shelley's first book, the novel *Zastrozzi* (London: Printed for G. Wilkie and J. Robinson, 1810), was in the collection, as was his second novel, *St. Irvyne* (London: Printed for J. J. Stockdale, 1811); both works are rare.

Clark owned the three volumes of Keats's works published in the poet's lifetime; his copy of the *Poems* (London: C. and J. Ollier, 1817) had been presented by Keats to John Byng Gattie, the brother-in-law of the publisher Charles Ollier, with the inscription, "I hope your eyes will soon be well enough to read this with pleasure and ease." Lamb titles included the 1818 edition of the *Works* (London: Printed for C. and J. Ollier); the extremely rare *The King and Queen of Hearts* (London: Printed for Thomas Hodgkins, 1806); *Tales from Shakespear* (London: Printed for Thomas Hodgkins, 1807); *Specimens of English Dramatic Poets* (London: Printed for Longman, Hurst, Rees, and Orme, 1808), a pioneer effort in resurrecting Shakespeare's contemporaries; *The Adventures of Ulysses* (London: Printed by T. Davison, 1808); and the *Essays of Elia* (London: Printed for Taylor and Hessey, 1823), the work on which Lamb's fame chiefly rests.

Clark's holdings in the Victorian poets were limited but, again, choice. He had Alfred Tennyson's first book, *Poems by Two Brothers* (London: W. Simpkin and R. Marshall; Louth, J. and J. Jackson, 1827), and the important first collected edition of Tennyson's poems (London: Edward Moxon, 1842). He also owned corrected trial issue and proof sheets of *Idylls of the King* (London: Edward Moxon and Company, 1859), important for tracing the textual history of one of Tennyson's greatest poems. Most of Robert Browning's early and late works were present, though the middle period was ignored. Clark's copy of *Pauline* (London: Saunders and Otley, 1833), Browning's first book, came from Rosenbach in 1924 for $2,850 (Rosenbach had replaced Smith as one of Clark's chief booksellers after Smith died in 1920); it was one of about a dozen known copies. Elizabeth Barrett Browning was more fully represented, beginning with the scarce *The Battle of Marathon* (London: Printed for W. Lindsell, 1820). She wrote the poem when she was twelve or thirteen, and her father paid for the printing of fifty copies, of which about ten survive. It is the most elusive of her titles. Clark had *An Essay on Mind, with Other Poems* (London: J. Duncan, 1826), her second book, published when she was twenty; *Prometheus Bound* (London: Printed and published by A. J. Valpy, 1833), her translation of Aeschylus's play; *The Seraphim and Other Poems* (London: Saunders and Otley, 1838); the 1844, 1850, 1853, and 1856 editions of her *Poems* (all published in London by Chapman and Hall); the then-prized *Sonnets from the Portuguese* (Reading, 1847), which was later discovered to have been forged by Wise; *Casa Guidi Windows* (London: Chapman and Hall, 1851); *Aurora Leigh* (London: Chapman and Hall, 1857); *Poems before Congress* (London: Chapman and Hall, 1860); and *Last Poems* (London: Chapman and Hall, 1862).

In Victorian prose Clark's library included several important works. In 1917 he bought from Smith a fine copy of William Makepeace Thackeray's *Vanity Fair* (London: Bradbury and Evans, 1847–1848) in parts, together with three original Thackeray drawings and Charles Dickens's *Master Humphrey's Clock,* including *The Old Curiosity Shop* and *Barnaby Rudge* (London: Chapman and Hall, 1840–1841), in parts. One of Clark's catalogues was devoted to his prime copy of Dickens's *The Pickwick Papers* (London: Chapman and Hall, 1836–1837) in parts, acquired by Clark in 1917 for $4,500 at the Samuel H. Austin sale. Clark's extensive Dickens holdings also included *Dombey and Son* (London: Bradbury and Evans, 1846–1848), *David Copperfield* (London: Bradbury and Evans, 1849–1850), *Bleak House* (London: Bradbury and Evans, 1852–1853), *Little Dorrit* (London: Bradbury and Evans, 1855–1857), and *Our Mutual Friend* (London: Chapman and Hall, 1864–1865), and *Mystery of Edwin Drood* (London: Chapman and Hall, 1870), all in parts, as they were first published before they appeared in book form. Since the parts appeared in thin pamphlets, usually of thirty-two pages, they were more likely to be discarded, making them more elusive—and more expensive.

In 1924 Clark, acting on Cowan's advice, violated his rule against buying libraries en bloc by paying $15,000 for a collection of works dealing with Montana and the Northwest. The material had been assembled by Charles N. Kessler, the son of a Montana pioneer. The collection included 1,890 bound volumes; 2,832 pamphlets,

The Shakespeare collection at the William Andrews Clark Memorial Library in 1946. At that time the library was ranked as having the fourth-largest holding of Shakespeare quartos in the United States (photograph by Thelner Hoover).

magazines, articles, and documents; 225 maps; 123 pictures; 147 unbound newspapers; 4 volumes of clippings; 93 signatures of the members of the Montana Constitutional Convention (over which Clark Sr. had presided); Granville Stuart's manuscript vocabulary of the Snake Indian dialects; 26 editions of the journals of the Meriwether Lewis and William Clark expedition; Pacific Railroad reports rich in geographical and historical information; 131 volumes of Montana state documents; 63 editions of the Book of Mormon; a manuscript account of a 1775 Indian uprising in San Diego; and a report by the nineteenth-century Spanish governor of California, Jose Maria Echeandia, that is supposedly in the handwriting of California's first printer, Augustin Zamorano.

During his annual sojourns in Paris in the 1920s and 1930s Clark bought works of French literature directly from Seymour De Ricci and, through him, from Maggs Brothers of London. His French collection was small but contained the first edition of Michel de Montaigne's *Essais* (Bordeaux: S. Millanges, 1580), presentation copies of Emile Zola's works, and books by major French authors from the sixteenth through the eighteenth centuries, such as Pierre de Ronsard, Jean Racine, Pierre Corneille, Alain-René Le Sage, and Jean-Jacques Rousseau.

In 1921 Clark was the first recipient of the Los Angeles Realty Board's Service Watch for community service, and on 29 April 1922 seventeen Los Angeles clubs presented him with an illuminated parchment designating him the "Lorenzo de' Medici of this southwestern metropolis." A small fire in Clark's house in the summer of 1923 did no damage but prompted him to erect a separate fireproof building for his library. The architect Robert Farquhar patterned the building's exterior after Christopher Wren's late-seventeenth-century addition to Hampton Court Palace. Allyn Cox decorated the library; he would later execute murals for the United States Capitol in Washington, D.C. Flanking the marble hallway, with its painted ceiling, were book rooms modeled on the library of the Château de Chantilly outside Paris. The bookcases, balconies, and window frames were manufactured by the John Polachek Bronze and Iron Company of New York, using copper from Clark's mines. Construction began in early 1924 and was completed in 1926. That year Cowan moved into a house that Clark made available to him next to the library.

Also in 1926 Clark retired from business. On 4 June of that year he wrote to the board of regents of the University of California: "For some time it has been my intention to make a conditional gift of the library building, the books, manuscripts and equipment contained therein, and the real property, where I reside while I am in Los Angeles, California, so that the grounds may eventually be used as a park by the public, generally, and the library building and its contents by students for research." Clark stipulated that his collection should remain intact, that no books should leave the building, and that the title pages not be perforated or the books otherwise mutilated. He retained a life estate on the property and books. By that time he had spent more than $1.5 million on books and manuscripts, and another $1 million on the library building and its furnishings.

After 1926 Clark collected less vigorously and spent less time in California and more in his beloved France. In 1927 he gave a library building, also designed by Farquhar, to the University of Nevada at Reno in memory of his second wife. In 1928 the Clark family sold its copper interests in Montana, retaining the United Verde Mine in Arizona. Clark presented letters of the Montmorency and Condé families to the Musée Condé in Chantilly, and he donated more than two hundred letters of the Emperor Louis-Philippe and his family to the Bibliothèque Nationale. He gave a library to the Pacific Lodge Boys' Home for Wayward Youth and a room to the Pershing Hall in Paris dedicated to the memory of the graduates of the University of Virginia who died in World War I. He also contibuted $2 million for the relief of Belgians during and after the war.

Clark's generosity and contributions to culture were acknowledged by honorary degrees from Mills College and the University of San Francisco; he was also made an honorary member of Phi Beta Kappa. In 1932 the Los Angeles Philharmonic Orchestra erected a statue of Ludwig van Beethoven in Pershing Park in honor of its patron. Also in 1932 Clark presented the Clark Memorial Hall to the University of Virginia School of Law in memory of his first wife. To his alma mater he also gave manuscripts by Thomas Jefferson, including Jefferson's plans and specifications for the university, and Edgar Allan Poe material.

The Depression further curtailed Clark's book buying; on 16 January 1933 he wrote to Cowan from Paris, "Things have come to such a point that I have to drastically cut down my expenses or face bankruptcy. . . . I have bought no books for the Library and have spent very little on myself, but for two years and a half I have received no income of any kind." Clark told Cowan that his salary would be reduced beginning in March. On 6 July 1933 Clark wrote to ask Cowan to resign; Cowan did so on 18 July, the day he received Clark's letter. The two parted amicably.

Clark not only collected examples of fine printing but also created some. Between 1922 and 1933 he commissioned Nash to produce nine gift books based on his holdings. The series began with Shelley's *Adonais*. It was followed the next year by Poe's *Tamerlane and Other Poems;* Clark acquired the rare original (Boston: Printed by Calvin F. S. Thomas, 1827) from Rosenbach in 1923 for $9,500. Also in the series, in addition to the letters from Wilde to Douglas, was a 1927 reprinting of the forged *Sonnets from the Portuguese.* The series concluded with an edition of the offprint of Thomas Gray's *Ode on the Pleasure Arising from Vicissitude* that William Mason circulated before he published it in *The Poems of Mr. Gray* in 1775. Clark had secured the only known copy of this offprint from Rosenbach. Most striking of these works was the 1929 reprint of Dryden's *All for Love* (London: Printed by Thomas Newcomb for Henry Herringman, 1678), which reproduced Cox's paintings on the ceiling of the drawing room of Clark's library; the printing cost $37,500.

Clark died at his summer home on Salmon Lake, Montana, on 14 June 1934. At the time of his death his library contained 16,280 volumes. In his will Clark left $1.5 million to the university to support the collection and maintain the grounds. Clark's generosity to UCLA was almost matched by his patronage of the Los Angeles Philharmonic Orchestra, which he had supported from 1919 to 1934 with a total subvention of some $3 million. On 23 June 1934 Frank Harvey Colby wrote in the *Pacific Coast Musician,* "In the death of William A. Clark, Jr., Los Angeles has lost a benefactor who gave more to advance the musical culture of this city and this part of California than has been given by any other person in this country in the interest of musical art." The orchestral music Clark had purchased for the Philharmonic went to the Los Angeles Public Library, but his bequest to UCLA included musical reference books and fifty scores, together with letters by Franz Josef Haydn, Felix Mendelssohn, Franz Liszt, Richard Wagner, Hector Berlioz, Charles Gounod, and Camille Saint-Saëns. Conway aptly summarized Clark's significance: "The Clark copper, in the hands of William Andrews Clark, Jr., . . . has been transmuted into architectural, bibliothecal, and cultural gold."

Biography:

William D. Mangum, *The Clarks: An American Phenomenon* (New York: Silver Bow Press, 1941).

References:

William E. Conway and Robert Stevenson, *William Andrews Clark, Jr.: His Cultural Legacy* (Los Angeles: William Andrews Clark Memorial Library, 1985);

Historical Records Survey, California, *List of the Letters and Manuscripts of Musicians in the W. A. Clark Memorial Library* (Los Angeles: Southern California Historical Records Survey Project, 1940);

Lawrence Clark Powell, "From Private Collection to Public Institution: The William Andrews Clark Memorial Library," *Library Quarterly,* 20 (April 1950): 101–108;

University of California, Los Angeles, William Andrews Clark Memorial Library, *Report of the First Decade, 1934–1944* (Berkeley & Los Angeles: University of California Press, 1946).

Papers:

The Clark papers are housed at the William Andrews Clark Memorial Library, University of California, Los Angeles.

John L. Clawson
(17 March 1865 – 27 November 1933)

William H. Loos
Buffalo and Erie County Public Library

John L. Clawson of Buffalo, New York, achieved his wish to be recognized as a serious book collector when his collection of Elizabethan and early Stuart literature was sold in 1926 for $642,687–the second-largest sum realized at any American book auction to that time. But while the sale of Robert Hoe's huge collection in nine sessions in 1911 and 1912 had brought in $1,932,056, in some ways Clawson's achievement was more impressive. Hoe's library had consisted of 14,996 lots, Clawson's of only 926 lots; thus, while Hoe's collection was sixteen times the size of Clawson's, it sold for only three times as much. Furthermore, it had taken less than ten years for Clawson to put his collection together, while it had taken Hoe nearly thirty years. The first book Clawson purchased in what was to become his chief field of interest was a Fourth Folio of William Shakespeare's plays (London: H. Herringman, E. Brewster & R. Bentley, 1685), acquired in 1914; the last was Nicholas Breton's *The Pilgrimage to Paradise* (Oxford: Joseph Barnes, 1592), purchased in 1923. Clawson had the means, the persistence, and the foresight to acquire the extraordinary books in his chosen field as they came on the market during that remarkable period in book-collecting history that preceded the Great Depression.

John Lewis Clawson was born in Campbell, New York, on 17 March 1865. He moved to Buffalo with his bride, Frances Collier Phelps, in 1891. There he became a partner in the firm of Bean, La Due and Clawson, manufacturers of men's clothing. In 1897 he and his friend James P. Wilson established the wholesale dry goods firm of Clawson and Wilson. After being incorporated in 1903, the company quickly grew into what has been claimed to be the largest firm of its kind between New York City and Chicago. Clawson and Wilson established a branch in Cleveland; at its height the firm had offices in New York City; Belfast, Ireland; and Chemnitz, Germany. The firm also owned and operated two clothing factories.

It is not clear just when Clawson began to collect books, but it had to have been some years be-

John L. Clawson

fore he auctioned off part of his collection in 1915 at the Merwin-Clayton Sales Company in New York. His early interests seem to have been autographs, association copies, and seventeenth-century books. His second and third auction sales were held at Anderson Galleries in New York in January and March 1917.

Over the years Clawson acquired some Elizabethan and early Stuart literature, but he did not concentrate on that field until 1920. He selected this period in English literature at the suggestion of his son, Hamilton Phelps Clawson. In 1974, the year before his death at the age of eighty-two, H. Phelps Clawson told Thomas D. Mahoney, an antiquarian bookseller in Buffalo, that his father seldom read

40

any of the Elizabethan or Stuart books he acquired, but that he, H. Phelps, had read most of them. His father had built the collection, he said, as an intellectual and financial exercise, not out of any personal interest in that particular period of British literary history. He also told the bookseller that the most dramatic incident in his father's book-collecting career occurred on 4 March 1920, when father and son were visiting the shop of America's foremost antiquarian bookseller, George D. Smith, who had supplied the elder Clawson with many of his finest books (including the Shakespeare Fourth Folio). During a heated discussion in his private office with W. Lanier Washington, who had recently sold Smith and others some fraudulent George Washington association items, Smith died of a heart attack; he was only fifty years old. A. S. W. Rosenbach would shortly assume the mantle of America's foremost antiquarian bookseller, and John L. Clawson would be one of his clients.

In 1920 Clawson decided to dispose of many of the books and manuscripts he owned that were outside the scope of his chosen field: English plays, poetry, and fiction printed between 1560 and 1660. Anderson Galleries sold 534 lots for Clawson on 29 and 30 November, including first editions and autographs of Robert and Elizabeth Barrett Browning, John Keats, and Percy Bysshe Shelley; twenty-seven letters by Charles Dickens; eight letters from Samuel Johnson to Mrs. Hester Thrale; letters by Robert Louis Stevenson; and a collection of rarities by William Makepeace Thackeray. One lot consisted of a lock of Napoleon Bonaparte's hair. Clawson could not have been happy with the $71,500 the sale realized, as his annotated copy of the auction catalogue reveals that he had paid $76,803 for the items sold.

Clawson's wife had died in February 1919; in 1923 he married Jane Miller, a young actress from the South. About this time he decided to stop increasing his collection and to document what he had. Seymour De Ricci, an authority on English book collectors, was paid $7,000 to prepare a formal catalogue of Clawson's library. De Ricci refrained from repeating the collation statements that are found in other reference works, concentrating instead on descriptive notes and on the provenance and rarity of the more important volumes. The inclusion of 102 illustrations, nearly all of them reproductions of title pages, added to the value of the catalogue. In his introduction De Ricci describes his work on the catalogue as "a labour of love and a labour of joy." Two hundred numbered copies of the catalogue, which was dedicated to H. Phelps Clawson, appeared in 1924 under the imprint of the Rosenbach Company.

Cover of the catalogue for the 1920 sale of many items in Clawson's collection that did not relate to the Elizabethan and early Stuart period of English literature

Clawson and, at his direction, the Rosenbach Company, sent complimentary copies of the catalogue to famous bookmen and women. Thirty-eight of the thank-you letters have survived through the efforts of H. Phelps and his wife, the English silent-film actress Valiantina Venitskya, whom he married in London on 12 April 1924. The couple assembled the letters and nearly twenty newspaper and periodical reviews of the 1924 catalogue, plus a few articles on the 1926 sale, and had them bound into an album, apparently prepared as a surprise for the elder Clawson. Among the more eminent individuals acknowledging the gift are Henry E. Huntington, Henry C. Folger, William Andrews Clark Jr., Carl H. Pforzheimer, Belle da Costa Greene, Wilfred Partington, Thomas J. Wise, and Clawson's neighbor and fellow collector Robert Borthwick Adam II.

Title page for the illustrated catalogue of Clawson's collection

Clawson seems to have been content to allow the splendid De Ricci catalogue to serve as a permanent monument to his brief career as a book collector; the time had come to sell. What was to prove to be the second-greatest book auction in American history up to that time occurred on 20–21 and 24–25 May 1926 at the Anderson Galleries; the auction catalogue was based on De Ricci's catalogue. Of the works in the sale, 210 had been printed before 1600, the other 716 between 1600 and 1700. The highly publicized sale attracted many of the most important private and a few institutional collectors. The thirty-nine lots of Shakespeareana, including nineteen quartos and three folios (Clawson never acquired a First Folio), brought $121,250. Clawson's copy of the Fourth Folio—the first book he had purchased in what was to become his chosen period—sold for $750; he had paid $400 for it. His Third Folio brought $4,500, which was $1,000 more than it had cost him. The last book he purchased, Breton's *The Pilgrimage to Paradise*, also sold for $2,500, but it had cost Clawson $5,000. Most of

Clawson's Shakespeare quartos were later editions, but the three first editions did well at the sale. *Much Adoe about Nothing* (London: Printed by Valentine Simmes for Andrew Wise and William Aspley, 1600), the only quarto edition and the finest of all the known copies, according to De Ricci, sold for $21,000; it had cost Clawson $13,090. *The Historie of Troylus and Cresseida* (London: Printed by G. Eld for R. Borian and H. Walley, 1609), the second issue of the only quarto edition and the tallest of the eleven known copies, sold for $11,000; Clawson had paid $9,500 for it. *The Tragædy of Othello* (London: Printed by Nicholas Okes for Thomas Walkley, 1622), the excessively rare first edition and the finest copy known, sold for $10,700; it had cost $6,772.

The writings of John Milton were also well represented, with thirty-one lots. One of the finest copies known of the first edition of *Comus* (London: Printed for Humphrey Robinson, 1637) commanded the greatest amount of any single lot: $21,500. Clawson had paid $5,000 for it. His copy of the first edition of *Paradise Lost* (London: Printed and sold by Peter Parker, Robert Boulter, and Matthias Walker, 1667), with the first title page and all other first-issue points, sold for $2,950; the cost to Clawson had been $1,400. A perfect copy of John Gower's *Confessio Amantis* (Westminster: Printed by William Caxton, 1483) was sold to Rosenbach for the third-highest price paid at the auction: $20,000; Clawson had purchased it for $13,000. Long series of works by some of the lesser lights from Clawson's period, such as Philip Massinger (fourteen lots), George Wither (fifteen lots), James Shirley (twenty-eight lots), and the "Water Poet" John Taylor (forty-one lots), were also sold. Many of the books by these four authors went for less than $200 each and some for less than $100. Rosenbach acquired about a third of the lots; the $447,500 he paid, however, accounted for nearly two-thirds of the collection's total sales. Among the clients for whom he was buying were Huntington and Pforzheimer. Harvard University acquired 131 titles through the efforts of two Harvard graduates living in New York City.

Clawson's annotated copy of the catalogue indicates that he did little better than break even during the first two days of the sale. It was only with the second session that he made a profit, but not a large one. He estimated the total cost of purchasing and maintaining the collection at $525,171; after the expenses of the sale he netted $585,000, leaving him a modest profit of $59,829—a bit more than 10 percent.

A month after the sale Clawson told a *Buffalo Times* reporter that he had decided to sell his collection because he feared theft and fire. He had a small vault in his home, but as the collection grew in size and value he had transferred it to the vault of a local bank. Clawson also said that by 1924 "I had my catalogue prepared and printed [and] had achieved my goal in being recognized as a collector and owning one of the best libraries in private hands. After a catalogue is printed there isn't much incentive left for continuing the collection."

More than twenty titles from Clawson's collection found their way back to Buffalo. Thomas B. Lockwood, a lawyer and businessman and a neighbor of Clawson's, was assembling a gentleman's library and purchased some of the more famous high spots in the sale. Among the titles he acquired were Francis Beaumont and John Fletcher's *Comedies and Tragedies* (London: Humphrey Robinson and Humphrey Moseley, 1647), Robert Burton's *The Anatomy of Melancholy* (Oxford: Printed by John Lichfield and James Short for Henry Cripps, 1621), Robert Herrick's *Hesperides* (London: Printed for John Williams and Francis Eglesfield, 1648), John Donne's *Poems* (London: Printed by Miles Flesher for John Marriot, 1633), *The Workes of Benjamin Jonson* (London: Printed by William Stansby, 1616; London: Printed for Richard Meighen and Thomas Walkley, 1640), *Paradise Lost,* and Edmund Spenser's *The Faerie Queen* (London: Printed for William Ponsenbie, 1590). In 1935 Lockwood presented his collection to the University of Buffalo, which became part of the state university system in 1962; thus, many of the books that were formerly in Clawson's library are now in the Poetry/Rare Books Collection of the State University of New York at Buffalo.

During their last years in Buffalo the Clawsons lived in a mansion at 1109 Delaware Avenue, near the residences of two of Clawson's fellow book collectors: Adam lived around the corner at 780 West Ferry, Lockwood at 844 Delaware. A few years after the 1926 auction Clawson sold his interest in the Clawson and Wilson firm to his partner, Wilson. The company was dissolved in 1931, a victim of the Great Depression. Clawson's wife divorced him that same year. Around that time he moved to New York City, where he died at Doctors' Hospital on 27 November 1933 following an operation.

Although Clawson's book-collecting career was brief, he assembled an important library, and De Ricci's catalogue of it remains a useful bibliography. The sales of his books enriched other public and private collections, allowing scholars and bibliophiles to benefit from his efforts.

SALE NUMBER 2078
PUBLIC EXHIBITION FROM SATURDAY, MAY FIFTEENTH

THE
SPLENDID ELIZABETHAN &
EARLY STUART LIBRARY
OF
MR. JOHN L. CLAWSON
BUFFALO, N. Y.

PART TWO
THOMAS MAY — RICHARD ZOUCH

TO BE SOLD BY AUCTION
BY ORDER OF MR. CLAWSON
AT UNRESERVED PUBLIC SALE
MONDAY AFTERNOON & EVENING
& TUESDAY EVENING
MAY TWENTY-FOURTH, TWENTY-FIFTH
AT TWO-THIRTY & EIGHT-FIFTEEN

THE ANDERSON GALLERIES
[MITCHELL KENNERLEY, President]
489 PARK AVENUE AT FIFTY-NINTH STREET, NEW YORK
[REGENT 0250]

Title page for the catalogue for the second part of the 1926 sale of Clawson's Elizabethan and early Stuart collection—the second most remunerative American book auction to that time

References:

Robert J. Bertholf, *A Descriptive Catalog of the Private Library of Thomas B. Lockwood* (Buffalo: State University of New York, University Libraries, 1983), entries 20, 21, 27, 41, 108-A, 130, 170, 232, 233, 234, 258, 275, 392, 393, 394, 398, 407, 467, 468, 1288;

Carl L. Cannon, "John L. Clawson, 1865–1933," in *American Book Collectors and Collecting* (New York: Wilson, 1941), pp. 221–223;

"Clawson Lifts Silence Veil in Explaining Library Sale; Reveals Three Thrills; Great Responsibilities Lifted; Clawson Asserts, Feared Theft and Fire," *Buffalo Times,* 27 June 1926, pp. 65, 72;

THE
SECOND
and laſt part of Conny-catching.

With new additions containing many merry tales of all lawes worth the reading, becauſe they are worthy to be remembred.

Diſcourſing ſtrange cunning in Coofnage, which if you reade with-out laughing, Ile giue you my cap for a Noble.

Mallem men eſſe quam non prodeſſe patriæ.
R. G.

LONDON.
Printed by Iohn Wolfe for William Wright.
1 5 9 2.

[NUMBER 325]

Title page for a work by Robert Greene in the 1926 sale of Clawson's collection (Anderson Galleries, sale number 2078, 24–25 May 1926)

Seymour De Ricci, *A Catalogue of Early English Books in the Library of John L. Clawson, Buffalo* (Philadelphia & New York: Rosenbach, 1924);

Donald C. Dickinson, "Clawson, John L.," in *Dictionary of American Book Collectors* (New York: Greenwood Press, 1986), pp. 69–70;

Charles F. Heartman, *George D. Smith, G.D.S. 1870–1920* (Beauvoir Community, Miss., 1945);

William A. Jackson, "John L. Clawson's Early English Books," in *To Doctor R.: Essays Here Col-* lected and Published in Honor of the Seventieth Birthday of Dr. A. S. W. Rosenbach, July 22, 1946 (Philadelphia, 1946), pp. 97–119;

Later English Literature from the Library of John L. Clawson of Buffalo, New York . . . November 29, November 30, sale no. 1537 (New York: Anderson Galleries, 1920);

George L. McKay, comp., *American Book Auction Catalogues, 1713–1934: A Union List* (New York: New York Public Library, 1937), entries 7492, 7777, 7814, 8265, 8938, 8940;

George H. Sargent, "A Master Collector of Early English Books," *Boston Evening Transcript,* 27 September 1924;

The Splendid Elizabethan & Early Stuart Library of Mr. John L. Clawson, Buffalo, N.Y. . . . . To Be Sold by Auction by Order of Mr. Clawson at Unreserved Public Sale, May Twentieth, Twenty-First, May Twenty-Fourth, Twenty-Fifth, sale nos. 2077, 2078 (New York: Anderson Galleries, 1926);

George Parker Winship, "Library Values," *Harvard Alumni Bulletin,* 28 (10 July 1926): 1057–1038;

Edwin Wolf II and John H. Fleming, *Rosenbach: A Biography* (Cleveland: World, 1960).

Papers:

When John L. Clawson's son, Hamilton Phelps Clawson, died in 1975, a Buffalo antiquarian bookseller, Thomas D. Mahoney, acquired his library and discovered several items that directly related to the book-collecting career of John L. Clawson. Unwilling to sell or break up the small archive, Mahoney donated the materials to the Rare Book Room of the Buffalo and Erie County Public Library. The archive includes John L. Clawson's loose-leaf notebook, listing the mounting value of his books from 1915 to 1926; an annotated copy of the 1920 Anderson catalogue, with the prices Clawson paid (in his private code) and the prices realized; the album of thank-you letters from bookpeople who had been sent free copies of the Seymour De Ricci catalogue; an annotated copy of the 1926 Anderson catalogue with the prices Clawson paid (in code) and the prices realized; and a second album, in a fine binding produced by John F. Grabau of Buffalo in 1930, with newspaper and magazine clippings about Clawson's various sales.

Bruce Cotten
(3 March 1873 – 1 April 1954)

Eileen L. McGrath
University of North Carolina at Chapel Hill

BOOKS: *An Adventure in Alaska During the Gold Excitement of 1897–1898: A Personal Experience* (Baltimore: Sun Printing Office, 1922);

The Mirrors of Bensboro (Baltimore: Privately printed, 1925);

As We Were: A Personal Sketch of Family Life (Baltimore: Privately printed, 1935);

Housed on the Third Floor: Being a Collection of North Caroliniana formed by Bruce Cotten (Baltimore: Horn-Shafer, 1941);

The Cotten Family of North Carolina, edited by Elba Brown Cotten Wesson (Tucson, Ariz.: Privately printed, 1963).

Bruce Cotten was the preeminent twentieth-century collector of North Caroliniana. A North Carolina native who left the state as a young man, he collected almost two thousand titles that represent the cultural heritage of the state as a way to reconnect himself to his family and birthplace. He left this collection, and an endowment to support it, to the University of North Carolina Library, where it has strengthened the North Carolina Collection.

Bruce Cotten was born in Wilson, North Carolina, the fifth child of Robert Randolph Cotten and Sallie Southall Cotten. Robert Randolph Cotten, a native of Edgecombe County, North Carolina, was a prominent businessman, planter, and civic leader in eastern North Carolina for more than sixty years. Sallie Swepson Sims Southall was a native of Amelia County, Virginia. She spent her early childhood in Petersburg, Virginia, but at thirteen she was sent to live with relatives in Murfreesboro, North Carolina. She attended Wesleyan Female College in Murfreesboro and was graduated from Greensboro Female College in 1863. In the 1890s, after most of her children were grown, she began a public life as an advocate for women and children in North Carolina. She was one of the North Carolina "lady managers" for the 1893 Columbian Exposition in Chicago, an organizer of the North Carolina Federation of Women's Clubs, a participant in the

Bruce Cotten during his service in the U.S. Army (North Carolina Collection, University of North Carolina Library at Chapel Hill)

first National Congress of Mothers, and the author of many poems and essays. She was also the most important early influence in her son's life. He characterized her as a loving and devoted mother but also as unconventional and impatient with tradition, a good reader, and a romantic.

The Cottens resided first in Tarboro, then in Wilson and Falkland, North Carolina. In 1879 the family settled permanently at Cottendale, one of two Pitt County plantations owned by Robert Randolph Cotten. Isolation forced family members to depend on each other for entertainment, education, and emotional support. Bruce Cotten's early education therefore took place at home, where he and his brothers and older sister took instruction from a governess under their mother's direction. He later went to private primary and secondary schools in Warrenton and Oxford, North Carolina. He entered the University of North Carolina in 1891 but stayed only two years.

Robert Cotten's businesses had weathered many ups and downs in the years after the Civil War, but the 1890s were especially difficult. Prices for Cottendale's main agricultural product, cotton, were at a new low. Robert Cotten saw the need to find a new crop, but he unwisely made an expensive switch to tobacco just as the financial panic of 1893 occurred.

Bruce Cotten was little help in this family crisis. He went to Baltimore in search of employment, but he could not secure a position with any firm in the city. When gold was discovered in the Yukon Territory in 1896, Cotten became obsessed with the possibilities for wealth and adventure that Alaska might offer, and he left for Alaska in October 1897. Cotten's unpublished memoir of his later military experiences, "Drills, Raids, and Escapades," opens with this judgment of his Alaska experience: "This trip to Alaska had been an experience very excellent, hardening and educating; it had set me aright with myself and the world."

This air of derring-do and self-confidence is evident in Cotten's privately published chronicle of his Alaska trip, *An Adventure in Alaska During the Gold Excitement of 1897–1898* (1922). Cotten wrote this book at his parents' request, in response to their desire to learn something of his life in the years after he left North Carolina. He planned other volumes and wrote "Drills, Raids, and Escapades" in 1925, but only the Alaska volume was published.

On returning to Seattle in June 1898, without the wealth he had sought, Cotten joined a battalion of Washington State volunteers that was being organized to fight in the Spanish-American War. When he realized that his chances of seeing action would be greater in another unit, he resigned from this battalion and joined the regular army. He served in China in fall 1900 during the later stages of the Boxer Campaign and in the Philippines during the insurrection of 1901–1902. Shortly after receiving his commission as second lieutenant in 1902 he returned to the United States and was posted in the Pacific Northwest. In early 1907, while stationed at Fort Monroe, Virginia, Cotten met Edyth Johns Tyson, a wealthy widow. The couple were married on 4 August 1910 in England. Cotten had gone to Alaska, he said, "to win at one turn of the wheel, that fortune and affluence that is denied many deserving millions after a life of toil and labor." Winning Edyth Tyson's hand was Cotten's lucky turn at the wheel; after his marriage he never wanted for affection, status, or comfort. Cotten resigned from the service just prior to his marriage, but he reenlisted during World War I, serving as chief of G-2, the military intelligence division of the U.S. Army General Staff. He resigned at the Armistice and returned to Cylburn, the mansion that Jesse Tyson, Edyth's first husband, had built on a 180-acre estate in suburban Baltimore.

After his marriage Cotten, who found himself with time on his hands and money to spend, began collecting North Caroliniana in earnest. He traced the origin of this interest to his mother's experiences when she was trying to collect books about the state for the North Carolina exhibit for the 1893 Columbian Exposition. As she traveled the state, sometimes with Bruce accompanying her, she found that there were few libraries of North Caroliniana and no bibliography to guide her. After persistent searching the Cottens gathered only about twenty volumes. In *Housed on the Third Floor* (1941) Cotten noted that the experience "planted the germ and desire in me to know and to possess something of the books and literature that had been published in and about my native State." He began collecting for himself when he was in the army, frequenting used bookstores and curiosity shops. Although hindered by a lack of "both money and knowledge," he had amassed a collection of about two hundred volumes by the time of his marriage.

Shortly after his marriage Cotten called on the notable collector and bibliographer of North Caroliniana, Stephen B. Weeks, who was at that time working in Washington, D.C. The two men became friends, and as Cotten acknowledged in *Housed on the Third Floor,* Weeks "opened up to me vast new fields in book collecting: a study of the physical book itself, the causes of its publication, its influence, the press it came from, as well, of course, as its author and substance." His contact with Weeks also helped Cotten to focus his collection. Unlike Weeks, who collected comprehensively and who would acquire volumes that included only a section on North Carolina, Cotten intended his collection to be "a private, cleancut collection, purely North Carolina, embracing everything of major interest that has been published about our state in every field."

Caricature of Cotten by Jack Lambert (North Carolina Collection, University of North Carolina Library at Chapel Hill)

With leisure time, his wife's substantial wealth, and many contacts around the state, Cotten was in a particularly good position to develop his collection. Family members, particularly his mother, participated in the collecting process. Both his parents were active in civic and social affairs, and their travels around the state provided Cotten with contacts and information that enabled him to locate and acquire many obscure titles.

Cotten did not rely solely on family contacts. Like all collectors, he read dealers' catalogues. By the time he published *Housed on the Third Floor* he estimated that he had read over half a million pages of catalogues. He also used book dealers and book scouts in North Carolina and neighboring states, even publishing a newsletter that he mailed them. The few copies of these bulletins that still exist offer insight into Cotten's collection and his methods of operating. While he used the

HOUSED ON THE THIRD FLOOR

being

A Collection of North Caroliniana

※

formed by

BRUCE COTTEN

With some Facsimile Impressions of Titles

BALTIMORE · 1941

Title page for Cotten's catalogue of his library at Cylburn, his estate outside Baltimore (North Carolina Collection, University of North Carolina Library at Chapel Hill)

bulletins to inform "certain dealers, scouts, and friends of my Collection of North Caroliniana" about his most notable acquisitions, he also included pointed, but friendly, jabs to goad scouts into giving his interests more attention. Cotten professed that he had little success at auctions, but his address book shows that he maintained contact with at least one New York auction house; it also shows that he corresponded with librarians and other collectors.

The collection that Cotten amassed comprises almost two thousand titles. It includes books printed in North Carolina, books by North Carolinians, books about North Carolina, and a few associational volumes. Speeches, biographies, catechisms, college and secondary-school publications, genealogies, histories, memorial volumes, natural histories, novels, poetry, and religious tracts are all present. In *Housed on the Third Floor* Cotten states that limiting the scope of the collection was "the most perplexing problem that a collector has to deal with." He responded to this problem by letting his own preferences shape his collecting. Because politics was distasteful to him, he made little attempt to se-

cure political addresses and public documents. He collected only North Carolina laws made prior to 1800. He excluded items that rarely came as complete sets, such as newspapers, church minutes, and school catalogues. He was also "very partial to items of some interest large enough to stand in their own binding," so he rejected many pamphlets. The physical condition of an item was also important. He bought and sold (or gave away) progressively better copies of a work until he had a specimen that met his standards for condition. There is also evidence that Cotten rebound volumes for aesthetic purposes. For example, Cotten's copy of Patrick Nisbett Edgar's *The American Race-Turf Register, Sportsman's Herald and General Stud Book* (New York: Press of H. Mason, 1833) has been bound in full morocco by Joseph Ruzicka; the top and bottom edges are gilt, and Cotten's home, Cylburn, is portrayed in a gilt fore-edge painting.

Cotten was not a scholar, but he was knowledgeable about the history and publishing heritage of North Carolina, and he knew the important early titles that should be the basis of any collection of North Caroliniana. Yet despite his wealth and contacts abroad, he had difficulty acquiring first editions of European works on North Carolina. He had Thomas Hariot's *A Briefe and True Report of the New Found Land of Virginia* (New York: Dodd, Mead, 1903; facsimile of the London, 1588 edition), Mark Catesby's *The Natural History of Carolina, Florida and the Bahama Islands* (third edition, London: Printed for B. White, 1771), William Bartram's *Travels through North and South Carolina, Georgia, East and West Florida* (second London edition, Reprinted for J. Johnson, 1794), and John Lawson's *A New Voyage to Carolina* (London, 1709). Cotten felt a justifiable pride that among his few British first editions was Sir Walter Ralegh's *The History of the World* (London: Printed for Walter Burre, 1614). Cotten was far more successful at acquiring works published in North Carolina. He had forty-four eighteenth-century North Carolina imprints, including the sixth work published in the state, *A Collection of All the Public Acts of Assembly, of the Province of North-Carolina* (Newbern: Printed by James Davis, 1752). He also had seventy-one Confederate imprints, chiefly from North Carolina presses. Cotten was selective in acquiring twentieth-century works. The twentieth-century portion of the collection is heavily weighted toward materials on the eastern part of the state. Here Cotten's roots and his family connections resulted in a fine collection of histories, biographies, and genealogies relating to that region.

By the mid 1930s Cotten's collecting had reached the point where he was looking for particular books rather than all North Caroliniana. After his wife's death in 1942 he sold Cylburn and its gardens to the city of Baltimore and moved to smaller quarters. No longer was Cotten's collection "housed on the third floor." Edyth Cotten's death and Cotten's dissatisfaction with how his books were handled in the move from Cylburn prompted him to consider what would become of his books when he died. By the mid 1940s Cotten and the library staff at the University of North Carolina were engaged in a steady correspondence about Cotten's collection. In December 1948 Mary Lindsay Thornton, the librarian of the North Carolina Collection at the university, visited Cotten at his home to record Cotten's thoughts on specific volumes in his collection. The trip cemented the relationship between Cotten and the University of North Carolina Library. Cotten consulted John Sprunt Hill, a prominent benefactor of the university and someone Cotten much admired, about how his will should be amended to give his collection to the university. The university librarian, Charles E. Rush, made several suggestions, most of which became part of the final document. The main suggestion that Cotten rejected was that the collection be named for his mother. Although *Housed on the Third Floor* was dedicated to the memory of his mother, "who first proposed and always encouraged me in this gentle pastime," Cotten stipulated in his will that the collection be known as the Bruce Cotten Collection of North Caroliniana and that the name never be changed or amended. The will also specified that the collection be kept intact, that each volume, including additions to the collection, be marked with Cotten's own bookplate, and that the volumes could not be removed from the library without written approval of the library director. Remembering his displeasure with how his books were handled in the move from Cylburn, Cotten also stipulated that university staff must come to Baltimore to oversee the packing and transportation of the collection. Agreeing to these terms, the university was given Cotten's collection of North Caroliniana, Cotten's bookplate die, his notes on the collection, a general collection of about six hundred volumes, and whatever furnishing the university wished to use with the collection.

Cotten was revitalized by the successful conclusion of negotiations, and he remained active as a collector during the last few years of his life. In his correspondence with Mary Lindsay Thornton he

Bookplate for the collection Cotten donated to the University of North Carolina at Chapel Hill (North Carolina Collection, University of North Carolina Library at Chapel Hill)

began to address her as "My dear Partner." Correspondence between the two increased as they discussed additions to the collection, and Cotten urged Thornton to call him immediately if she learned of some choice work that the university could not afford. Cotten also began to rewrite his manuscript catalogue of the collection. In a 13 March 1950 letter to Robert B. House, the chancellor of the university, Cotten wrote that he "realized that I have a much finer collection here than I had remembered it to be." Yet because the collection still did not measure up to his ideal, he decided to leave the university money so that "the Library could in time build it up to be a really distinguished collection of its sort." A founding member of the Friends of the Library, Cotten was honored at the spring 1951 Friends of the Library dinner. Members of the library staff continued to visit and correspond with Cotten; his correspondence with Mary Lindsay Thornton was interrupted only by his frequent bouts of ill health. The last letter from Thornton reached Cotten just a week before his death on 1 April 1954.

After the first shipment of Cotten's books was received by the library, Mary Lindsey Thornton wrote Bruce Cotten's sister, Sallie Cotten Wiggins, on 8 July 1954: "The books that have come are in perfect condition. I knew his library would be that way. . . . I have a strange feeling of the survival of his personality in them." Thornton noted in her annual report for 1950–1951 that Cotten meant his collection to be a "'lengthening shadow' of a distinguished collector whose life has been devoted to the preservation of the history and literature of his naive state." The collection is evidence of Cotten's steady pursuit of both the obvious and the obscure in North Caroliniana, the power of his wealth and family connections, and his own delight in the fine and attractive. Because of the endowment that Cotten left for the collection, by 1995 it had grown to almost double its original size, and it adds luster to the North Carolina Collection at the University of North Carolina.

Papers:

The North Carolina Collection at the University of North Carolina at Chapel Hill owns "A Catalogue of the Tar-Heel Book-Shelves of Mr. Bruce Cotten," a four-volume annotated typescript inventory of Cotten's collection of North Caroliniana; "Drills, Raids, and Escapades," Cotten's memoir of his years in the U.S. Army; Cotten's address book; an inventory of his collection of general books; and miscellaneous volumes of notes. Letters from Bruce Cotten to officers of the University of North Carolina and their letters to him can be found in the archives of the University of North Carolina at Chapel Hill and the files of the North Carolina Collection at the university. The Sallie Southall Cotten Collection in the Manuscripts Department of the university library comprises chiefly Sallie Southall Cotten's correspondence to her son Bruce for the years 1902 to 1929; it also contains information on Cotten's collecting, including information on particular titles of interest to him and the ways in which family members assisted him in his pursuit.

Harvey Cushing

(9 April 1869 – 7 October 1939)

Harold N. Boyer
Florence County Library

BOOKS: *The Pituitary Body and Its Disorders: Clinical States Produced by Disorders of the Hypophysis Cerebri* (Philadelphia & London: Lippincott, 1912);

Realignments in Greater Medicine: Their Effect upon Surgery and the Influence of Surgery upon Them: General Address in Surgery Delivered to the XVIIth International Congress of Medicine, at Its Meeting in London on August 7, 1913 (London: Oxford University Press, 1914);

Tumors of the Nervus Acusticus and the Syndrome of the Cerebellopontile Angle (Philadelphia & London: Saunders, 1917);

The Story of U.S. Army Base Hospital No. 5, by a Member of the Unit, anonymous (Cambridge, Mass.: Harvard University Press, 1919);

The Life of Sir William Osler (2 volumes, Oxford: Clarendon Press, 1925; 1 volume, London & New York: Oxford University Press, 1940);

A Classification of the Tumors of the Glioma Group on a Histogenetic Basis with a Correlated Study of Prognosis, by Cushing and Percival Bailey (Philadelphia & London: Lippincott, 1926);

Studies in Intracranial Physiology and Surgery: The Third Circulation, the Hypophysics, the Gliomas (London: Oxford University Press, 1926);

The Meningiomas Arising from the Olfactory Groove and Their Removal by the Aid of Electro-Surgery (Glasgow: Jackson, Wylie, 1927);

The Pathological Findings in Four Autopsied Cases of Acromegaly, with a Discussion of Their Significance, by Cushing and Leo M. Davidoff (New York: Rockefeller Institute for Medical Research, 1927);

Tumors Arising from the Blood-Vessels of the Brain: Angiomatous Malformations and Hemangioblastomas, by Cushing and Bailey (Springfield, Ill. & Baltimore: Thomas, 1928; London: Baillière, Tindall & Cox, 1928);

Consecratio Medici, and Other Papers (Boston: Little, Brown, 1928);

Harvey Cushing in 1929 (photograph by Arnold Carl Klebs)

The Medical Career: An Address on "The Ideals, Opportunities, and Difficulties of the Medical Profession" Containing a Tribute to Dr. Nathan Smith, Founder of the Dartmouth Medical School, Delivered at Dartmouth College, November 20, 1928 (Hanover, N.H.: Dartmouth College, 1929);

Intracranial Tumours: Notes upon a Series of Two Thousand Verified Cases with Surgical-Mortality Percentages Pertaining Thereto (Springfield, Ill. & Baltimore: Thomas, 1932; London: Baillière, Tindall & Cox, 1932);

Papers Relating to the Pituitary Body, Hypothalamus and Parasympathetic Nervous System (Springfield, Ill. & Baltimore: Thomas, 1932; London: Baillière, Tindall & Cox, 1932);

From a Surgeon's Journal, 1915–1918 (Boston: Little, Brown, 1936; London: Constable, 1936);

Meningiomas: Their Classification, Regional Behaviour, Life History, and Surgical End Results (Springfield, Ill. & Baltimore: Thomas, 1938);

The Medical Career and Other Papers (Boston: Little, Brown, 1940);

A Bio-Bibliography of Andreas Vesalius (New York: Schuman, 1943);

A Visit to Le Puy-en-Velay: An Illustrated Diary (Cleveland: Rowfant Club, 1944);

Selected Papers on Neurosurgery, edited by Donald D. Matson, William J. German, and a Committee of the American Association of Neurological Surgeons (New Haven, Conn. & London: Yale University Press, 1969).

OTHER: Giovanni Battista Canani, *Musculorum Humani Corporis Picturata Dissectio,* facsimile edition, annotated by Cushing and Edward C. Streeter (Florence: Lier, 1925);

"The Doctor and His Books," in *Cleveland Medical Library Association: Addresses Delivered at the Dedication of the Dudley P. Allen Memorial Medical Library, November Thirteenth, 1926* (Cleveland, 1927), pp. 18–41.

SELECTED PERIODICAL PUBLICATIONS–
UNCOLLECTED: "The Holders of the Gold-Headed Cane as Book Collectors," *Johns Hopkins Hospital Bulletin,* 17 (May 1906): 166–169;

"The Value of Books to the Medical Profession," *Medical Journal Record,* 124 (1 December 1926): 712–713;

"Exercises in Celebration of the Bicentenary of the Birth of John Hunter," *New England Journal of Medicine,* 200 (18 April 1929): 810–823;

"The Binding Influence of a Library on a Subdividing Profession: An Address at the Dedication of the William H. Welch Medical Library of the Johns Hopkins University School of Medicine, October 17, 1929," *Science,* 70 (22 November 1929): 485–491;

"Remarks at the Presentation of the Henry Barton Jacobs Collection to the Welch Medical Library, January 14, 1932," *Johns Hopkins Hospital Bulletin,* 50 (May 1932): 307–309;

"A Bibliographical Study of the Galvani and the Aldini Writings on Animal Electricity," *Annals of Science,* 1 (July 1936): 239–268;

"Perry Williams Harvey, 1869–1932: Books and the Man," *Yale University Library Gazette,* 11 (January 1937): 43–52.

Harvey Cushing achieved an international reputation as a neurological surgeon, medical historian, and bibliophile. He received honorary degrees from nine American and thirteen European universities as well as the Distinguished Service Medal; was made a Companion of the Bath and an Officier de la Légion d'Honneur; and belonged to the Order of El Sol del Peru. He, Dr. Arnold Carl Klebs of Switzerland, and the Yale physiologist Dr. John Farquhar Fulton donated their personal collections of rare medical books to form the Historical Library as a wing of the new Yale University Medical Library in 1941.

The sixth son and the youngest of ten children, Harvey Williams Cushing was born in Cleveland, Ohio, on 9 April 1869 to Henry Kirke Cushing and Betsey Maria Williams Cushing. His father was professor of obstetrics and gynecology at Western Reserve University; his paternal grandfather and great-grandfather had also been physicians. Book collecting was an interest shared by Cushing and his father, who had a modest collection, and Cushing's initial book-collecting efforts were met with fatherly cooperation and, more important, financial assistance.

Cushing received his baccalaureate from Yale University in 1891 and entered Harvard Medical School. He graduated cum laude in 1895 with the A.M. and M.D. degrees and served his internship in surgery at Massachusetts General Hospital in Boston. In 1896 he joined the staff of the Johns Hopkins Hospital in Baltimore. There his association with the famous physicians William Osler, William Henry Welch, and William Stewart Halsted sparked his lifelong interest in medical history and bibliography. Osler, a serious book collector who had a library at Montreal's McGill University named after him, often left rare-book catalogues for Cushing to peruse.

In 1900–1901 Cushing visited the great medical libraries in London, Glasgow, Bern, and several cities in Italy. Returning to Baltimore, he began a general surgical practice but also specialized in surgery of the pituitary gland; he thus became the first American to devote his career to neurological surgery.

Having inherited a strict self-discipline from his Presbyterian father, Cushing would spend long days at the hospital attending to patients, then devote his evening hours to writing books and articles on medicine, medical history, and medical bibliography. On 10 June 1902 he married Katherine Stone Crowell of Cleveland; they had five children. Despite his growing family and small salary, Cushing began seriously collecting books at this time. Initially he collected histories, biographies, and volumes from the sixteenth century onward that could be had at a modest price. His first purchase of a work by the sixteenth-century anatomist Andreas Vesalius occurred in 1905, when he obtained the second edition of Vesalius's *Thesis* from Boas of Berlin. His interest in Vesalius would continue throughout his life.

Cushing's removal of a brain tumor from Gen. Leonard Wood—the Spanish-American War hero who had gone on to conquer yellow fever in Cuba—in 1910 and his appointment as surgeon-in-chief of the newly established Peter Bent Brigham Hospital in Boston and as professor of surgery at Harvard Medical School in 1912 firmly established his reputation. His *The Pituitary Body and Its Disorders: Clinical States Produced by Disorders of the Hypophysis Cerebri* (1912) enhanced that reputation and established neurological surgery as a new medical specialty.

During World War I Cushing took a volunteer medical group from Harvard to work at a military hospital in France. Returning to the United States, he organized Base Hospital No. 5, which would serve British and American units from May 1917 until the Armistice in November 1918. These experiences led to the publication of *The Story of U.S. Army Base Hospital No. 5, by a Member of the Unit* (1919). Cushing's war service, however, also resulted in polyneuritis, an inflammation of the spinal nerves marked by paralysis, pain, and wasting of muscles. Previously an active man who kept in shape by playing tennis, by the early 1930s he would be in almost constant ill health.

In 1925 Cushing published *The Life of Sir William Osler,* which won a Pulitzer Prize. The biography, which he had been asked by Lady Osler to write, was a labor of love and admiration for the man who had influenced his interests in medical history and bibliography. Republished in 1940, the work remains the definitive biography of one of the great physicians of early-twentieth-century America.

Cushing's Cameron Prize Lectures at the University of Edinburgh in October 1925 were published as *Studies in Intracranial Physiology and Surgery: The Third Circulation, the Hypophysics, the Gliomas* in 1926. That year also saw the publication of *A Classification of the Tumors of the Glioma Group on a Histogenetic Basis with a Correlated Study of Prognosis,* co-authored with Percival Bailey.

Cushing's bookplate, designed by Cushing and executed by Edwin Davis French

In "The Doctor and His Books," an address delivered at the dedication of the Dudley P. Allen Memorial Medical Library in Cleveland on 13 November 1926 and published in 1927, Cushing says that

a library must make unselfish use of its possessions even at the risk of an occasional loss. An open shelf, like an open shop, encourages the real worker who often chooses to browse for himself and should at least be put on probation. A library unexercised, and which takes no chances in life, is susceptible to the deterioration and scleroses certain to attend a poor circulation. To be sure, with some people there is no mine and thine in the matter of books; but one must take the chance and fill in the gaps when they occur, however painful, temporarily, the loss. It's far better than not to be used at all.

Published in 1928, *Tumors Arising from the Blood-Vessels of the Brain: Angiomatous Malformations and Hemangioblastomas,* by Cushing and Bailey, describes, with Cushing's usual exactness and attention to detail, twenty-nine cases of one of the rarest and most interesting groups of brain tumors. That year Cushing also published *Consecratio Medici, and Other Papers,* a collection of essays on medicine that displays the breadth of his interests and knowledge.

Cushing retired from Harvard Medical School and from active practice as a surgeon in 1932. That year was marked by the publication of two of his most original contributions to clinical medicine: *Intracranial Tumours: Notes upon a Series of Two Thousand Verified Cases with Surgical-Mortality Percentages Pertaining Thereto* again displays the meticulous attention to detail that was also evident in his book-collecting efforts; *Papers Relating to the Pituitary Body, Hypothalamus and Parasympathetic Nervous System* describes what is now known as Cushing's disease. In recognition of

Cushing just prior to his departure for France to work at a military hospital during World War I

his contributions, the Harvey Cushing Society was founded in 1932; today it is known as the American Association of Neurological Surgeons.

Cushing was appointed Sterling Professor of Neurology and Director of Studies in the History of Medicine at Yale University in 1933. Feeling that his duties were too minimal to warrant the salary Yale was paying him, he decided to recompense the university by leaving it his book collection. Additionally, he hoped that his books would be the first step in establishing a department of the history of medicine.

Cushing's book collecting was influenced by his friendship with Arnold Carl Klebs, a retired physician living in Nyon, Switzerland. When they first met in 1906 Klebs was working to bring together under one title all available information on medical and scientific incunabula; in 1938 he would publish *A Short-Title List of Incunabula Scientifica et Medica,* which would become a standard work in the field. Cushing knew little about incunabula at the time he

met Klebs, but his knowledge of the field grew under Klebs's mentorship. One of Cushing's first incunabulum purchases was a copy of Pietro d'Abano's *Conciliator* (Mantua, 1472), annotated by the Nuremberg physician Hartmann Schedel, which he bought in Zurich in 1929. The work would become one of the earliest of the medical incunabula in Yale's Historical Library.

Two more books by Cushing would appear before his death on 7 October 1939: *From a Surgeon's Journal, 1915–1918,* based on his experiences in World War I and illustrated with Cushing's own photographs and pencil sketches, published in 1936, and *Meningiomas: Their Classification, Regional Behaviour, Life History, and Surgical End Results,* an eight-hundred-page text with 685 illustrations, published in 1938. John Farquhar Fulton, a bibliophile who had been responsible for bringing Cushing to Yale in 1933, became his literary executor and published Cushing's final two books posthumously. *The Medical Career and Other Papers* appeared in 1940, while *A Bio-Bibliography of Andreas Vesalius,* which Cushing had completed during the summer of 1939, was published, as Cushing had wished, in 1943—the four hundredth anniversary of the publication of Vesalius's *De Humani corporis fabrica*. The Vesalius book was the result of nearly forty years of research and book collecting. Fulton also published a catalogue, *The Harvey Cushing Collection of Books and Manuscripts* (1943), and a biography of Cushing (1946).

Cushing, Klebs, and Fulton had agreed to donate their respective collections to the Yale Medical School, and on 15 June 1941 the school's Historical Library was dedicated. Cushing's and Fulton's books were in place in time for the dedication; World War II would prevent Klebs's collection from arriving from Switzerland until December 1946. The name Historical Library came about because a Yale advisory board decided that it would be unfair to name the facility after any one of the three major donors while to use all three names would be unwieldy. In addition, it was thought that a library named for a donor would be perceived as a static, little-used collection, when the opposite was intended. As Cushing had stipulated, the library is housed in a Y-shaped building with one section devoted to modern medical books and the other to rare books. Both sections are open to students and faculty.

The book collection Cushing donated to the Historical Library comprises some 15,000 items. It includes the 60 manuscripts on medical and scientific subjects that Cushing had begun collecting in the 1930s; the earliest is the thirteenth-century vellum codex of the *Compendium Medicienae* of Gilbert

Anglicus. There are 168 incunabula, the oldest dating from 1472. Orientalia are represented by 17 Arabic, Persian, and Sinhalese manuscripts from the thirteenth century and 17 printed books, the oldest of which is the *Handbook of Medicine* (1486) by Haly Abbas. General works number 7,498, dating from 1501 to the twentieth century. Authors in this part of the collection include Vesalius, Galen, Leonardo da Vinci, Ambroise Paré, Edward Jenner, Robert Boyle, and William Harvey.

The significance of Harvey Cushing as a physician lies in his work as a pioneer in the field of neurological surgery. As a medical historian his publication of *The Life of Sir William Osler* established his reputation. His extensive book-collecting activities in the field of medical bibliography, his establishment of the historical library at Yale University and his efforts to have the field of medical history recognized established Cushing as a bibliophile of international stature.

Letters:

The Making of a Library: Extracts from Letters, 1934–1941, of Harvey Cushing, Arnold C. Klebs and John F. Fulton, presented to John Fulton by His Friends on His Sixtieth Birthday, 1 November 1959 (New Haven, Conn.: Yale University Press, 1959).

Bibliography:

Harvey Cushing Society, *A Bibliography of the Writings of Harvey Cushing: Prepared on the Occasion of His Seventieth Birthday, 8 April 1939* (Springfield, Ill. & Baltimore: Thomas, 1939).

Biographies:

John Farquhar Fulton, *Harvey Cushing: A Biography* (Springfield, Ill. & Baltimore: Thomas, 1946);

Elizabeth H. Thomson, *Harvey Cushing: Surgeon, Author, Artist* (New York: Schuman, 1950).

References:

John Farquhar Fulton, *The Harvey Cushing Collection of Books and Manuscripts* (New York: Schuman, 1943);

E. P. Goldschmidt, "A Doctor and His Books: Harvey Cushing and His Library. Recollections of Harvey Cushing and His Book-Collecting," *Journal of the History of Medicine,* 19 (April 1946): 229–234;

Harvey Cushing Society, ed., *Harvey Cushing's Seventieth Birthday Party, 8 April 1939: Speeches, Letters and Tributes* (Springfield, Ill. & Baltimore: Thomas, 1939);

Geoffrey Jefferson, "Harvey Cushing and His Books," *Journal of the History of Medicine,* 19 (April 1946): 246–253;

David L. Reeves, "The Harvey Cushing Library," *Journal of Neurosurgery,* 20 (1963): 547–556;

Madeline E. Stanton, "Harvey Cushing: Book Collector," *Journal of the American Medical Association,* 192 (12 April 1965): 141–144;

Stanton, "The Medical Historical Library on the Hundredth Birthday of Harvey Cushing," *Yale University Library Gazette,* 44 (1969): 30–37;

Edward Towpik and Nicholas L. Tilney, "Harvey Cushing and His Books," *Surgery, Gynecology and Obstetrics,* 169 (October 1989): 366–370;

E. Weil, "The Formation of the Harvey Cushing Collection," *Journal of the History of Medicine,* 19 (April 1946): 234–246.

Papers:

Harvey Cushing's manuscripts and archives are housed in the Yale University Sterling Memorial Library. Diaries and correspondence are housed in the Harvey Cushing/John Hay Whitney Medical Library, Yale University.

Robert Dechert
(29 November 1895 – 8 November 1975)

John Pollack
University of Pennsylvania

WORK: "Las Casas in Italy," in *The Grolier Club: Iter Italicum,* edited by Gabriel Austin (New York: Grolier Club, 1963), pp. 167–169.

A lifelong Philadelphian, Robert Dechert achieved prominence both locally and nationally as a lawyer and a public servant. As a book collector, however, Dechert only began to gain recognition two decades after his death in 1975. He came to bibliophily relatively late in life and never devoted himself exclusively to the pursuit of rare books, yet what he lacked in time he made up in energy. Before he gave his collection of Americana to the University of Pennsylvania in 1962, it was one of the most important such collections in private hands. Begun by Dechert's mother-in-law, Helen Godey Wilson, the collection links two generations, forming a bridge between the world of nineteenth-century American book collecting and that of the late twentieth century.

Dechert was born in Philadelphia on 29 November 1895 to Henry Taylor Dechert and Virginia Louise Howard Dechert. The first American Dechert, Andrew Porter Dechert, had arrived in Philadelphia from Ireland in 1754 and had become an officer in the Continental Army. Robert Dechert's grandfather Henry Martyn Dechert and his great-uncle Robert Porter Dechert served as officers in the Civil War; his father was a colonel in the Spanish-American War. All three went on to careers as Philadelphia lawyers. Robert Dechert would continue the family traditions of military service and legal practice.

After attending the Phillips Brooks School in West Philadelphia and the Lawrenceville School in New Jersey, Dechert received his bachelor of arts degree from the University of Pennsylvania in 1916 and was commissioned a lieutenant in the Seventh Infantry, part of the Third Infantry Division. After training at Gettysburg, he was assigned to the Signal Corps and posted to Charlotte, North Carolina. In the spring of 1918 the Third Division received orders to leave for France, where it took up positions

Robert Dechert

near German lines along the Marne River. Fighting was intense between 23 and 25 July. According to the official report:

When the attacking battalion had been held up by machine-gun fire, Capt. Dechert (then first lieutenant), who was on duty as regimental signal officer, personally carried wire across an open field in full view of the enemy and established a telephone station within 200 yards of the front line. He then went forward under heavy shell fire to report to the battalion commander, and returning to the telephone kept it in operation for 24 hours under intense artillery and machine-gun fire.

For his heroism Dechert was awarded the Distinguished Service Cross.

After serving in the Argonne campaign and, after the Armistice, with occupation forces on the Rhine, Dechert was sent to St. John's College, Oxford, for five months in 1919 as a U.S. Army student. He admired the town's medieval atmosphere; several decades later he would seek to re-create it by acquiring carved wooden panels from a fifteenth-century house in Chester, England, and installing them in several rooms of his Revolutionary-era mansion, Ballygomingo, in Gulph Mills, near Philadelphia.

Dechert returned to Philadelphia at the end of 1919. He received his law degree, with honors, from the University of Pennsylvania Law School in 1921 and joined his father's old firm, Hepburn, Dechert and Norris. On 24 May 1922 he married Helen Hope Wilson; they had three children: Peter, Hope, and Marian. In 1923 he began to teach part-time at the law school of his alma mater; he would continue to do so for nineteen years. His course on taxation may have been the first ever taught at a major American law school. To institute the course he had to overcome objections that taxation was not an appropriate subject for legal study. In 1927 he left Hepburn, Dechert and Norris and founded the legal department of the Penn Mutual Life Insurance Company. In 1930 he established his own firm, Dechert and Bok, while continuing as head of the Penn Mutual legal department. He served in many insurance and bar association posts, as well as in civic and charitable groups.

Dechert's wife belonged to a Philadelphia family that was well known both in social and literary circles. One of her great-grandfathers was Louis A. Godey, the founder of *Godey's Lady's Book;* another was Morton McMichael, an editor of the *Saturday Evening Post* and the *Philadelphia North American.* Book collecting seems to have been an informal tradition in the Godey family. Helen Dechert's mother, Helen Godey Wilson, had inherited some rare American books, including Louis Godey's original set of *Godey's Lady's Book* in a red leather binding that, Dechert recalled in a 1957 interview, the eminent Philadelphia collector A. S. W. Rosenbach called "the finest early American binding he had ever seen." From this beginning Wilson gradually

acquired a small but rich collection of works relating to the French in North America and to the American West. Treasures from the era of New France included a 1558 first edition, second issue of André Thevet's *Les Singularitez de la France Antarctique* (Paris: Les heritiers de Maurice de la Porte, 1558); a first edition of Claude Charles LeRoy Bacqueville de la Potherie's *Histoire de l'Amérique Septentrionale* (Paris: Jean-Luc Nion and François Didot, 1722) in original calfskin, with plates in excellent condition; the exceedingly rare *Histoire du Canada,* by Gabriel Sagard-Théodat (Paris: Claude Sonnius, 1636), in original vellum; and the *Historiae Canadensis* of François du Creux (Paris: Sebastien Cramoisy and Sebastien Mabre-Cramoisy, 1664), with a perfectly preserved plate showing Jesuit martyrs. Wilson's western Americana treasures included several early editions of works by Meriwether Lewis and William Clark; a first edition of Alexander Mackenzie's *Voyages from Montreal* (London: R. Noble, 1801); George Catlin's *Illustrations of the Manners, Customs, and Condition of the North American Indians,* with rarely found colored etchings (London: Henry G. Bohn, 1866); and the extraordinary *Das illustrirte Mississippithal,* by Henry Lewis (Düsseldorf: Arnz, 1857), in original printed boards, with eighty plates depicting the Mississippi River. Wilson also cultivated a particular interest, uncommon for her time, in women's lives during the colonial era. She acquired the rare biographies of Marie de l'Incarnation, director of the Ursuline convent in Quebec, by Dom Claude Martin (Paris: P. de Bats, M. Jouvenel, and A. Vuarin, 1684) and Pierre François Xavier de Charlevoix (Paris: Ant. Claude Briasson, 1724), as well as several lives of Marguerite Bourgeoys, founder of the Community of Notre-Dame in Montreal.

Many of Wilson's books came from her longtime friend, the New York bookseller Lathrop C. Harper. In 1932 Wilson, after perusing the sale catalogue of the collection of the Marquise of Lothian, wrote to Harper what Dechert later characterized as "an amusing letter, pronouncing curses that she did not have sufficient funds to buy all the great books she coveted." Harper sent a tongue-in-cheek response:

> We had no intention of poisoning your life with the Lothian catalogue—we just thought we would provide you with a little light reading on the train which would later induce that holier-than-thou feeling that manuscripts and incunabula had no allure for you. But we might have known you would start coveting something—we have never known such an omnivorous person! You could do a neat little job of like-poisoning yourself if you ever broadcast a catalogue of your collection. You need never indulge in any self-deprecation or green-eyed

Title page for one of the books in Dechert's collection of works relating to the French in North America (courtesy of University of Pennsylvania Special Collections)

goddessing, for your library is a healthy infant and a credit to its mother; suffering from anything but rickets or anaemia and quite capable of standing on its own legs.

Wilson never did "broadcast a catalogue" of her collection. She did, however, pass on her appetite for collecting to her son-in-law, and, as Dechert recalled in the 1957 interview: "In 1936, after the death of her legal advisor, she came to me to have a new will drawn and said she wanted her books to go to me instead of to Hope, who was her only child. 'Hope and I have talked this over and decided that you are nuttier than she is, and are more apt to do something about them,' she said."

Dechert took an immediate interest in the collection that would have become his, and his enthusiasms blended seamlessly with Wilson's. In October 1936, using funds from a legacy he had received

from Wilson, Dechert acquired a copy of Samuel de Champlain's *Les Voyages du Sieur de Champlain* (Paris: Jean Berjon, 1613), with all maps and plates, in its original vellum with ties—a work that Wilson had been seeking in vain. Not long afterward Dechert purchased from E. D. Church a second edition of Thevet's *Les Singularitez de la France Antarctique* (Antwerp: C. Plantin, 1558), a fitting match for the Thevet that Wilson had obtained in 1929. Although he was never as active in the Philadelphia book-collecting community as Americana specialists such as William Elkins, who was then amassing his own splendid collection, Dechert was known to Rosenbach and his circle and was considered a "hard bargainer."

In 1939 Dechert, Rosenbach, and Elkins were among the many bibliophiles who attended the sale of the western Americana collection of Herschel V. Jones. One of Dechert's purchases was *Nehiro-irinui aiamihe massinahigan* (Uabistiguiatsh, [Quebec]: Massinahitsetuau, Broun gaie Girmor, 1767), a primer by Jean-Baptiste de La Brosse written in the Montagnais language of eastern Canada. This rare title was a find of great value for Dechert. In his notes on the book he wrote:

> This book is of particular interest to us because: (1) It is an early and interesting French-Indian contact; (2) The Montagnais Indians were those we knew at Mingan River and Village (north shore of St. Lawrence, about 30 miles east of St. John River) on our salmon fishing trips with Mr. and Mrs. Wilson; (3) It is from the great H.V. Jones collection.

Throughout his collecting career Dechert sought books with personal as well as scholarly significance.

In 1942 Dechert, Smith and Clark, as Dechert's law firm was then known, merged with the firm of Barnes, Myers and Price; Dechert, Price and Rhoads became one of the largest firms in the United States. By the end of the 1940s Dechert had become an expert on the legal aspects of the insurance industry, and he frequently traveled to give speeches to regional bar associations. His wife died in 1950; on 1 December 1951 he married Helen Branson.

Dechert acquired some of the most precious works in his collection during these busy years. He obtained Champlain's extraordinarily rare *Des Sauvages* (Paris: Claude de Monstr'oeil, 1603) in 1950 and the equally rare *Contrat d'association des jesuites au trafique de Canada* (Paris, 1613) in 1956.

In 1957 President Dwight D. Eisenhower named Dechert general counsel to the Department of Defense. The most difficult crisis Dechert faced during his time in office was a controversy over the classification of documents by the department. Despite congressional pressure, Dechert refused to relax the secrecy procedures.

In 1958 Dechert was invited to give the commencement speech at the University of Pennsylvania. Instead of focusing on the activities of the administration in Washington, Dechert chose to stress broader themes. "The export from one country to another of tangible goods—and even the activities of individual men on the stage of world history—seem to me to be of mere trifling insignificance as compared to the export of ideas," he told the graduates. He described the power of works by the missionary Bartolomé de Las Casas, the explorer Jedediah Smith, and the mapmaker David Thompson—all of which were in his collection. Finally he presented the university's president, Gaylord Harnwell, with a second edition of Dr. William Smith's *Discourses on Public Occasions in America* (London: A. Millar, 1762). Dechert could not resist telling the story behind his acquisition of the book, "in the interest of creating other book collectors among those here today": the day after the Japanese attack on Pearl Harbor, he had gone book hunting "as a relief from the tension" and had found the *Discourses* in the attic of a book dealer in Cynwyd, near Philadelphia.

In 1959 Dechert returned to private practice in Philadelphia. A trustee of the University of Pennsylvania from 1927 until his death, he became chairman of the university's Board of Libraries and played a major role in planning the Van Pelt Library. At the groundbreaking ceremony in 1960 Dechert announced that he had decided to donate his Americana collection to the new library. The first installment of the collection arrived with the opening of the building in 1962.

Dechert's collection of the French Jesuit *Relations* had been growing rapidly; by the mid 1960s he lacked only seven of the *Relations* listed by James Comly McCoy in his extensive bibliography *Jesuit Relations of Canada, 1632–1673* (1937). Perhaps the most extraordinary French Jesuit text he acquired was the *Copie de deux lettres envoiées de la Nouvelle France* (Paris: Sebastien Cramoisy and Gabriel Cramoisy, 1656), a work published when that year's *Relation* was lost. Dechert's is one of only five known copies.

On his many travels Dechert took the opportunity to forage in bookstalls whenever he could. In a 1964 interview he recalled: "Some of my happiest memories of this kind are among dusty shelves in Stockholm, Madrid, Mexico City, London and on the Left Bank of the Seine, to name only a few. Common interests in rare books seem to overcome possi-

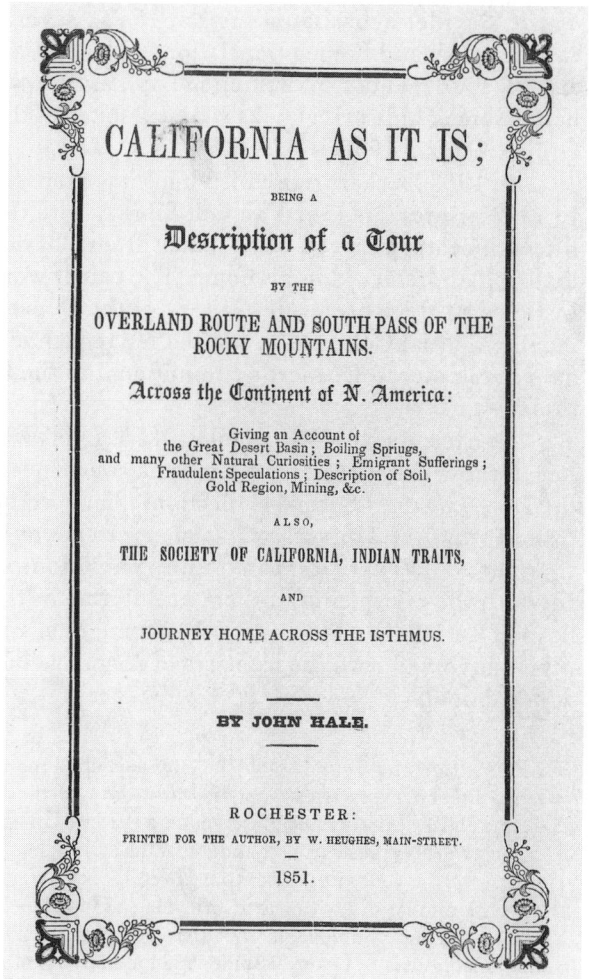

Title page for one of the travel narratives in Dechert's collection of Western Americana

ble language difficulties." Dechert continued the family tradition of traveling to the Saint Lawrence to fish for salmon. His trips gave him opportunities to buy books and, on one occasion, to meet Pierre-Georges Roy, archivist of the province of Quebec, with whom he consulted about the bibliographical rarities of New France.

Gradually Dechert's collection came to the attention of a wider public. In interviews he would tell his collecting stories and show the books he treasured most, including his Jesuit *Relations*, his Champlains, the first authorized edition of Lewis and Clark in original pasteboard covers (Philadelphia: Bradford and Inskeep, 1814), and Lansford Hastings's extremely rare *Emigrant's Guide to Oregon and California* (Cincinnati: George Conclin, 1843). Dechert became active in New York's Grolier Club, and in 1963 he gave a speech there, "Bartolomé de Las Casas: Bulwark or Bogeyman?," in which he discussed his fine printed copy of Las Casas's *Nine*

Tracts (Seville: Sebastian Trugillo, 1552), several early English and French translations of Las Casas, and his 1520 manuscript written in Las Casas's own hand. Some of his prize books were exhibited at the Grolier Club in 1966.

In 1968 Dechert retired from his law practice. In 1972 he presented the Van Pelt Library with the fifteenth-century carved wood panels from Chester that he had preserved in his home. The panels were installed in the Rosenwald Gallery of the Department of Special Collections, where they remain elegant testimony to Dechert's commitment to the library.

Dechert died on 8 November 1975. In his will he left the remainder of his Americana collection to the Department of Special Collections "in appreciation of what the University has meant to me over the years, and of what it can do for generations of the future by inspiring in them an interest in the days of Frenchmen, Indians and Mountain Men and others involved with the frontiers of America." He added a note:

> I hope that so far as practicable the emphasis upon the early French exploration and the early days of the Plains and Rockies will be preserved and that the University will also preserve a reminder that the early inspiration for the collection came from Helen Godey Wilson, the mother of my deceased wife, Helen Hope Dechert, and the granddaughter of the early American bookman, Louis A. Godey, founder and for many years editor of *Godey's Lady's Book*.

Dechert belongs to the generation of collectors who succeeded the great Americanists Jones, Elkins, James Ford Bell, and William Clements. Because he followed their lead and that of Wilson, Dechert staked out little new bibliographic territory for future collectors. But by focusing closely on two areas, the French in North America and western Americana, he built a collection that is remarkable for its thoroughness. It is a small collection of approximately 750 volumes, but for New France and for the American West it is of extraordinary quality. His Jesuit *Relations* and other early French publications rival the far-better-known collections at the University of Minnesota and the John Carter Brown Library, while his western Americana includes titles difficult or impossible to locate in other major libraries. The meticulous detail in which Dechert recorded the provenance of his acquisitions insures

that his collection will remain of value to future bibliophiles.

Dechert wanted his collection to have not only antiquarian but also intellectual value. Scholars have yet to explore many of the sources Dechert acquired; but as historians and literary critics come to recognize the importance of the texts, interest in the collection will grow. In the Dechert Collection at the Van Pelt Library a rare Lewis and Clark first edition sits near John Neihardt's *Black Elk Speaks* (New York: Morrow, 1932); Zebulon Pike's diaries rest next to equally rare but nearly unknown diaries of women on their journeys west, while Indian tribes are pictured and described by whites in extravagant folios and fragile pamphlets. Many new histories of New France and of the West remain to be written using the sources Dechert so painstakingly acquired. Reflecting on Helen Godey Wilson's faith that he was "nutty" enough to become a lover of book collecting, Dechert observed in 1957: "I think I have proved myself worthy of the word which she applied to me!"

Interviews:
"Bob Dechert's Collection of Rare Books," *Eastern Underwriter,* 13 December 1957, pp. 28, 40;
Samuel Stillman, "Soldier, Scholar, Lawyer, Teacher, Politician. . . . In a World of Specialists, Robert Dechert Is a General Practitioner of Living," *Sunday Bulletin Magazine,* 29 March 1964, pp. 6–7.

References:
Robert V. Massey Jr., *Dechert Price & Rhoads: A Law Firm Centennial, 1975* (Lancaster, Pa.: Intelligencer Printing Co., 1975);
Frank K. Walter and Virginia Doneghy, *Jesuit Relations and Other Americana in the Library of James F. Bell* (Minneapolis: University of Minnesota Press, 1950);
Edwin Wolf II and John F. Fleming, *Rosenbach: A Biography* (Cleveland: World, 1960), p. 477.

Papers:
Robert Dechert's letters and other papers are in the University of Pennsylvania archives. Dechert typed copious provenance notes for most of the books in his collection; these notes are housed with the Robert Dechert Collection of Americana in the Department of Special Collections of the Van Pelt Library at the University of Pennsylvania.

Everette Lee DeGolyer

(9 October 1886 – 14 December 1956)

Kevin J. Hayes
University of Central Oklahoma

BOOKS: *Geology of Salt Dome Oil Fields: A Symposium on the Origin, Structure, and General Geology of Salt Domes, with Special Reference to Oil Production and Treating Chiefly the Salt Domes of North America,* by DeGolyer and others (Chicago: American Association of Petroleum Geologists, 1926);

The Development of the Art of Prospecting, with Special Reference to the American Petroleum Industry: An Address Delivered before Princeton University on December 12, 1939, in the Cyrus Fogg Brackett Lectureship in Applied Engineering and Technology (Princeton, N.J.: Guild of Brackett Lecturers, 1940);

Bibliography on the Petroleum Industry, by DeGolyer and Harold Vance, Bulletin of the School of Engineering Station, Agricultural and Mechanical College of Texas, no. 83 (College Station, Tex., 1944);

The Antiquity of the Oil Industry, with Copious Notes and References by the Author (Dallas: Peripatetic Press, 1946; revised edition, Godley, Tex.: Peripatetic Press, 1947);

Science, a Method, Not a Field: Commencement Address Delivered at the University of Oklahoma, the Evening of May 31, 1948 (Norman: University of Oklahoma Press, 1948);

Landmarks in Science: An Exhibition from the Collection of Mr. E. DeGolyer to Illustrate the History of Science. Browsing Room, Fondren Library, Southern Methodist University, May 10–16, 1950, bibliographical and descriptive notes by DeGolyer (Dallas, 1950);

Spindletop 1901–1951 (Dallas: DeGolyer & MacNaughton, 1951).

OTHER: "Historical Notes on the Development of the Technique of Prospecting for Petroleum," in *The Science of Petroleum,* volume 1, edited by Ernest Dunston and Benjamin Brooks (New York: Oxford University Press, 1938), pp. 268–275;

Everette Lee DeGolyer (photograph by Lawrence Joseph)

Elements of the Petroleum Industry, edited by DeGolyer (New York: American Institute of Mining and Metallurgical Engineers, 1940);

Frank Hamilton Cushing, *My Adventures in Zuñi,* edited by DeGolyer (Santa Fe: Peripatetic Press, 1941);

David Ingram, *Across Aboriginal America: The Journey of Three Englishmen across Texas in 1568,* edited by DeGolyer (El Paso: Peripatetic Press, 1947);

"Seventy-Five Years of Progress in Petroleum," in *Seventy-Five Years of Progress in the Mineral Indus-*

61

try, edited by A. B. Parsons (New York: American Institute of Mining and Metallurgical Engineers, 1947), pp. 270–302;

"Some Aspects of Oil in the Middle East," in *The Near East and the Great Powers,* edited by Richard N. Frye (Cambridge: Harvard University Press, 1951), pp. 119–136;

Thomas J. Dimsdale, *The Vigilantes of Montana; or, Popular Justice in the Rocky Mountains: Being a Correct and Impartial Narrative of the Chase, Capture, Trial and Execution of Henry Plummer's Road Agent Band, Together with Accounts of the Lives and Crimes of Many of the Robbers and Desperadoes, the Whole Being Interspersed with Sketches of Life in the Mining Camps of the "Far West,"* introduction by DeGolyer (Norman: University of Oklahoma Press, 1953);

Katharine S. Lovell, *General Index to Petroleum Publications of the American Institute of Mining and Metallurgical Engineers, 1921–1952,* edited by De-Golyer (Dallas: Petroleum Branch, American Institute of Mining and Metallurgical Engineers, 1954);

David J. Cook, *Hands Up; or, Twenty Years of Detective Life in the Mountains and on the Plains: Reminiscences, a Condensed Criminal History of the Far West,* introduction by DeGolyer (Norman: University of Oklahoma Press, 1958).

SELECTED PERIODICAL PUBLICATIONS–
UNCOLLECTED: "Origin of North American Salt Domes," *American Association of Petroleum Geologists Bulletin,* 9 (1925): 831–874;

"New Mexicana," *Saturday Review of Literature,* 25, no. 32 (1942): 6;

"E. DeGolyer Picks Ten Unusual Books He Would Have Most Hated to Miss," *Dallas Times Herald,* 7 January 1945, I: 10;

"How Men Find Oil," *Fortune,* 40 (1949): 97–100, 103–104;

"Coronado's Northern Exploration," *Southwest Review,* 35, no. 2 (1950): 115–123.

Everette Lee DeGolyer's bookish interests led him in three different directions. He began by collecting literary first editions. Later, his upbringing in Oklahoma and early experiences as a petroleum geologist in Mexico sparked his enthusiasm for the history of Mexico and the American Southwest, which led him to assemble a fine collection of books on Spanish colonial history and the trans-Mississippi West. During the last decade of his life he gathered many books pertaining to the history of science with the idea of creating a permanent collection for students and researchers.

DeGolyer was born in Greensburg, Kansas, on 9 October 1886, the first child of John William De-Golyer and Narcissa Kagy Huddle DeGolyer. During his youth his father—a sometime farmer, cook, and zinc prospector—moved the family to southwestern Missouri and from there to central Oklahoma, finally settling in Norman.

DeGolyer began attending the University of Oklahoma preparatory school in 1904 and entered the university in 1906. An English course with Vernon Louis Parrington encouraged his love for books, but his science courses more profoundly influenced his career path. The University of Oklahoma was the first university in the United States to offer a degree in petroleum geology; DeGolyer enrolled in the new program and studied with Professors E. G. Woodruff and Charles N. Gould. Woodruff helped him get summer jobs with the United States Geological Survey (USGS) in 1906 and 1907, first as a cook and later as a field assistant for chief geologist C. Willard Hayes. During the summer and fall of 1908 DeGolyer worked on the Oklahoma Geological Survey. Through Hayes's influence he left college that winter to take a position with the USGS in Washington, D.C. Late in 1909, following Hayes, he left the USGS to join the staff of geologists at the British-owned, Mexico-based Mexican Eagle Oil Company and began fieldwork near Tampico.

DeGolyer briefly returned to Norman to marry Nell Virginia Goodrich, a dentist's daughter he had met at the University of Oklahoma five years before; they would have four children. The wedding took place on the morning of 10 June 1910; in the afternoon the couple boarded a train to Mexico. Later in 1910 DeGolyer discovered Potrero del Llano Number 4; the biggest oil well ever found, it established Mexico as an important oil-producing country and established DeGolyer's reputation as a petroleum geologist. Despite this important discovery and many others, in 1911 he interrupted his work to return to Norman and finish his bachelor's degree. Immediately afterward he went back to Mexico as chief geologist for Mexican Eagle. The following year he became chief of the company's land department.

During a visit to Mexican Eagle's headquarters in 1914 DeGolyer explored the London bookshops. It was then that he began his lifetime of book collecting. Sir Weetman Pearson (later Lord Cowdray), managing director of Mexican Eagle, gave him a first edition of Charles Dickens's *David Copperfield* (London: Bradbury and Evans, 1850) to commemorate his visit to England. The Dickens volume marked the beginning of what would become a fine collection of literary first editions.

Returning home, DeGolyer established a geological consulting firm in Norman; he and Mexican Eagle agreed that he would spend six months of each year working for the oil company and the other six months on his own business. In 1916 he moved his headquarters to New York City. Although he made the move for business reasons, it also presented him with book-buying opportunities unavailable in the middle of Oklahoma. He augmented his literary first editions by collecting works by Thomas Hardy, Rudyard Kipling, Herman Melville, and Robert Louis Stevenson.

In 1918 DeGolyer went to London to arrange to sell Mexican Eagle to Royal Dutch Shell. After the sale Lord Cowdray commissioned him to organize the Amerada Petroleum Corporation to operate in the United States and Canada and the Rycade Oil Company to concentrate exploration and drilling efforts in Mexican lands bordering the Gulf of Mexico. DeGolyer became vice president and general manager of Amerada in 1919.

In 1924 DeGolyer acquired copies of Melville's privately published volumes of poetry *John Marr and Other Sailors* (New York: De Vinne Press, 1888) and *Timoleon* (New York: Caxton Press, 1891). On 1 July 1924 he excitedly wrote a friend:

> I also picked up a book, two books in fact, that would interest you. They were Herman Melville's *John Marr* and *Timoleon*. They were published in '88 and '90 [*sic*] in editions of twenty-five copies each. I just missed getting these two books about two years ago when I saw them in a catalogue at $25.00 each. The result is that they cost me about four times that much now.

A few years later he acquired the copy of John Galsworthy's *A Man of Devon* (Edinburgh & London: Blackwood, 1901) that Galsworthy had presented to Joseph Conrad.

Encouraged by fellow geologist and bookman William E. Wrather, during the 1920s DeGolyer began collecting works about Mexico: its church history, biographies of its important leaders, travel narratives from the sixteenth through the nineteenth centuries, reminiscences of the Mexican War, and many others. He significantly augmented his burgeoning collection when he purchased the Mexican library of William Baker Stevens in 1924. He soon developed a modest reputation as an expert in Mexican history and biography and was asked to contribute the entry on the Mexican general and president Antonio López de Santa Anna for the 1930 edition of the *Encyclopaedia Britannica*.

DeGolyer's book stamp

DeGolyer's collection soon branched out from Mexicana to western Americana, and he became the best customer of the New York book dealer Edward Eberstadt. DeGolyer made his first purchase from Eberstadt in October 1928, and his frequent purchases during the Depression kept Eberstadt from financial ruin several times. After DeGolyer left New York, Eberstadt would continue to send him catalogues a month early, and DeGolyer would remain a good customer for many years.

DeGolyer became president and general manager of Amerada in 1926. He left the firm in 1932 and founded the Atlatl Oil Royalty Corporation; two years later he founded the Felmont Oil Corporation. Atlatl and Felmont were oil-finding companies, and DeGolyer served as president of each. In 1936 he moved to Dallas and joined Lewis MacNaughton in establishing DeGolyer and MacNaughton, which became the world's leading petroleum-engineering consulting firm. This innovative venture met the new need for independent appraisals of petroleum reserves for investors.

In Dallas, DeGolyer built his dream home: a one-story, 21,000-square-foot Spanish colonial on forty-four wooded acres; it was the first air-conditioned house in the city. A prominent part of the home was the library, located in the west wing. Shelves covered the walls except for the middle of the south one, which was dominated by a massive stone fireplace. Often shelved two rows deep, De-

*Title page for one of the books in DeGolyer's collection of early
scientific works, which includes many herbals, the first printed
attempts to formulate the science of botany*

Golyer's books were nevertheless easy to access because he kept them carefully arranged and catalogued. He took on many civic responsibilities in Dallas, including serving as a trustee of the public library.

DeGolyer's enthusiasm for books was part of his general enthusiasm for learning and discovery. The same impulse compelled him to publish his most important findings. His many discoveries and innovations made him one of the most important and influential oilmen of his day. As Daniel Yergin says in *The Prize: The Epic Quest for Oil, Money, and Power* (1991):

> No man more singularly embodied the American oil industry and its far-flung development in the first half of the twentieth century than DeGolyer. Geologist—the most eminent of his day—entrepreneur, innovator, scholar, he had touched almost every aspect of significance in the industry. . . . DeGolyer was more responsible than any other single person for the introduction of geophysics into oil exploration. He pioneered the development of the seismograph, one of the most important

innovations in the history of the oil industry, and he championed its use.

DeGolyer's prominence in the industry and his scholarly bent attracted the attention of the University of Texas, and in 1940 he was named Distinguished Professor of Geology. He was not inexperienced at the podium, having delivered the Aldred Lectures at the Massachusetts Institute of Technology in 1929 and the Brackett Lectures at Princeton University in 1939. In 1941 and 1942 he donated several important specialized works to the geology department's Petroleum Reference Library. Since he had started collecting books about Mexico and the American West he had gradually stopped collecting literary first editions. He lent much of that collection to the university library; later he made an outright gift of it. Altogether he gave the university more than twelve hundred volumes. In 1947 he became chairman of the newly formed Friends of the University of Texas Library.

DeGolyer enjoyed reading *The Saturday Review of Literature,* mainly for the columns of Christopher Morley. When Norman Cousins became its editor in 1940 the magazine had not turned a profit for some time. In 1942 Cousins contacted DeGolyer about a special issue he was planning on the Southwest. DeGolyer agreed to contribute an article, "New Mexicana"; more important was his agreement to provide sorely needed financial backing. He became the magazine's chief stockholder; with his money and Cousins's skillful editing and aggressive marketing, circulation greatly increased, and the magazine began to turn a profit. DeGolyer became chairman of the board of *The Saturday Review* in 1948.

DeGolyer had done some consulting work for the government before and during the early stages of World War II, but in 1943 he was given a special mission to appraise the oil potential of Saudi Arabia and the other countries of the Persian Gulf. DeGolyer became the first to recognize the profound importance of the Middle East for oil production. His findings were prophetic: "The center of gravity of world oil production is shifting from the Gulf-Caribbean area to the Middle East—to the Persian Gulf area . . . and is likely to continue to shift until it is firmly established in that area."

After the war DeGolyer carried on his consulting work with MacNaughton and continued to pursue a hobby he had taken up a few years earlier: small-press publishing. Sporadically he brought out works he had written or edited under the imprint of the Juan Pablos Press, named after the sixteenth-century Mexican printer, or the Peripatetic Press, so called because it moved from Santa Fe to El Paso to Dallas to Godley, a small town west of Dallas where DeGolyer owned a ranch. Several of the publications were printed by Carl Herzog, the "cowboy printer of El Paso." DeGolyer edited Frank Hamilton Cushing's *My Adventures in Zuñi* (1941), which included, in addition to the title piece, Sylvester Baxter's "An Aboriginal Pilgrimage"– both taken from the *Century Illustrated Monthly Magazine* (1882–1883)–and David Ingram's *Across Aboriginal America: The Journey of Three Englishmen across Texas in 1568* (1947), excerpted from Richard Hakluyt's *Principall Navigations, Voyages, and Discoveries of the English Nation* (1589).

James Bryant Conant's *On Understanding Science* (1947) convinced DeGolyer that to understand science one must understand its history, and he soon began collecting early editions of the fundamental scientific works, from incunabula describing animal husbandry to mimeographed reports on atomic energy. He collected some manuscript materials–lecture notes by Louis Agassiz, for example–but his emphasis was on printed works. He acquired the earliest edition of the *Elementorum Euclidis: In artem geometrie incipit qua foelicissime* (Venice: Echardus Ratdolt, 1482), the first substantial book to be printed with geometrical figures; John Dee's English translation of Euclid, *The Elements of Geometrie* (London: John Day, 1570), a bibliographic curiosity containing paste-ins that stood up to give a three-dimensional effect to the drawings; Andreas Vesalius's *De humani corporis fabrica* (Basel: Oporini, 1543), which undermined the classical authorities and prepared the way for empirical observation in anatomy and clinical medicine; the first edition of Nicolaus Copernicus's *De revolutionibus orbium coelestium* (Nuremberg: Johann Petreium, 1543) as well as a later edition, *Astronomia instaurata* (Amsterdam: Wilhelm Jansson, 1617); a copy of John Gerard's *The Herball or Generall Historie of Plantes* (London: John Norton, 1597) with an elaborately illustrated and colored title page; Galileo's *Siderius nuncius magna* (Venice: Thomas Baglionum, 1610), a presentation copy inscribed by Galileo to his friend, the poet Gabriello Chiabrera; Galileo's *Dialogo* (Florence: Giovanni Batista Landini, 1632) with marginal notes believed to be in Galileo's hand; John Napier's *Mirifici logarithmorum canonis descriptio* (Edinburgh: A. Hart, 1614), which explained the discovery of logarithms; Robert Hooke's *Micrographia* (London: J. Martyn and J. Allestry, 1665), one of the earliest-known works to describe the use of a microscope; Isaac Newton's *Principia* (London: Joseph Streater, 1687); Thomas Robert Malthus's *An Essay on the Principle of*

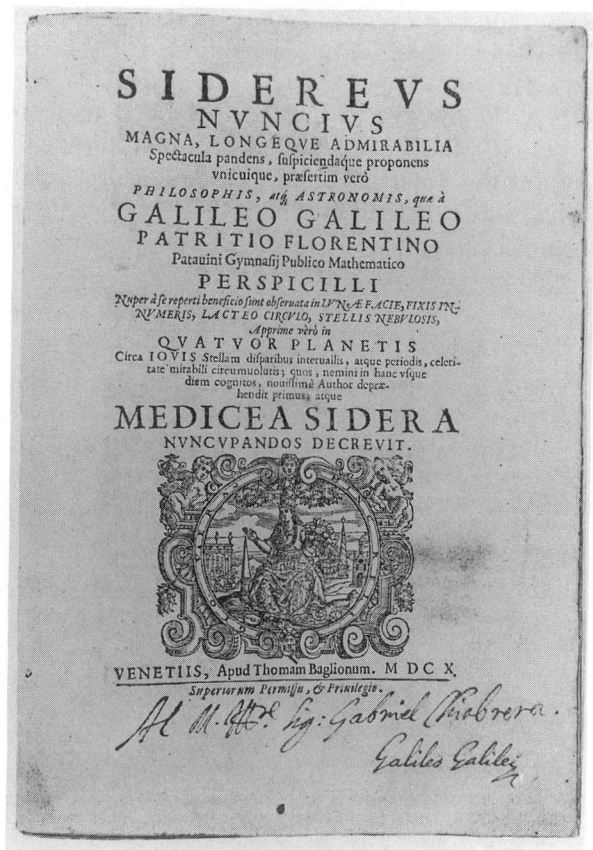

Title page for DeGolyer's copy of Galileo's first major astronomical work, inscribed by the author to poet Gabriello Chiabrera

Population (London: Printed for J. Johnson, 1798); and the copy of the corrected second edition of Charles Darwin's *Journal of Researches into the Natural History and Geology of the Countries Visited during the Voyage of H.M.S. Beagle round the World* (London: Ward, Lock, 1845) that Darwin presented to the veterinary writer William Youatt and inscribed: "With the author's compliments as a most trifling acknowledgement of the instruction derived from Mr. Youatt's work, and in admiration of his never-tiring zeal in the cause of humanity." In 1949 De-Golyer turned over six hundred rare volumes to the University of Oklahoma to form the basis of a new program in the history of science. He later added nearly two thousand more books and established a fund to further augment the collection. He also presented volumes on oil and gas law and on western and Mexican history to Southern Methodist University.

DeGolyer's health began to decline in 1949 when he lost the sight in his right eye due to a detached retina; he also suffered from aplastic anemia, which required him to take a series of blood transfusions, and had a series of minor strokes. In December 1956 he shot himself in his office at DeGolyer and MacNaughton. His will established the DeGolyer Foundation, which has helped to augment his library, funded publication of several works concerning the American Southwest, provided scholarships, and benefited DeGolyer's many civic interests in Dallas. In 1982 his home and property became the Dallas Arboretum.

Bibliography:

A. Rodger Denison, "Everette Lee DeGolyer: October 9, 1886–December 14, 1956," *National Academy of Sciences (U.S.) Biographical Memoirs*, 33 (1959): 65–86.

Biography:

Lon Tinkle, *Mr. De: A Biography of Everette Lee De-Golyer* (Boston: Little, Brown, 1970).

References:

Carl C. Branson, "E. L. DeGolyer, 1886–1956," *Oklahoma Geology Notes*, 17 (1957): 11–21;

"The Great DeGolyer Collection," *Fortune*, 63 (April 1961): 138–144;

John H. Murrell, *Science–Skill–Service: The Story of DeGolyer and MacNaughton* (New York: Newcomen Society, 1964);

"O.U.'s Prized Possession: The DeGolyer Collection," *Sooner Magazine*, 28 (February 1956): 14–19;

Duane H. D. Roller, "The Core of a Program," *Sooner Magazine*, 30 (October 1957): 12–14, 31;

Daniel Yergin, *The Prize: The Epic Quest for Oil, Money, and Power* (New York: Simon & Schuster, 1991), pp. 391–393.

Papers:

Everette Lee DeGolyer's papers are at Southern Methodist University.

Theodore Low De Vinne

(25 December 1828 – 16 February 1914)

Michael E. D. Koenig
Dominican University

BOOKS: *The Profits of Book Composition* (New York: Associated Employing Printers of New York, 1864);

The Printers' Price List: A Manual for the Use of Clerks and Book-keepers in Job Printing Offices (New York: Hart, 1869; enlarged, 1871);

The State of the Trade: Observations on Eight Hours and Higher Prices, Suggested by Recent Conferences between the New-York Typographical Union and the Employing Book and Job Printers of That City (New York: Hart, 1872);

The Invention of Printing: A Collection of Facts and Opinions Descriptive of Early Prints and Playing Cards, the Block-Books of the Fifteenth Century, the Legend of Lourens Janszoon Coster of Haarlem, and the Work of John Gutenberg and His Associates (New York: Hart, 1876; London: Trübner, 1877);

Historic Printing Types: A Lecture Read before the Grolier Club of New York, January 25, 1885, with Additions and New Illustrations (New York: Grolier Club, 1886);

Christopher Plantin, and the Plantin-Moretus Museum at Antwerp (New York: Printed for the Grolier Club, 1888);

The Roman and Italic Printing Types in the Printing House of Theodore L. De Vinne & Co. (New York: De Vinne Press, 1891);

The Practice of Typography: A Treatise on the Processes of Type-Making, the Point System, the Names, Sizes, Styles and Prices of Plain Printing Types (New York: Century, 1900);

The Practice of Typography: Correct Composition; a Treatise on Spelling, Abbreviations, the Compounding and Division of Words, the Proper Use of Figures and Numerals, Italic and Capital Letters, Notes, etc., with Observations on Punctuation and Proof-Reading (New York: Century, 1901);

Title-Pages as Seen by a Printer, with Numerous Illustrations in Facsimile and Some Observations on the Early and Recent Printing of Books (New York: Grolier Club, 1901); enlarged as *The Practice of Typography: A Treatise on Title-Pages, with*

Theodore Low De Vinne

Numerous Illustrations in Facsimile, and Some Observations on the Early and Recent Printing of Books (New York: Century, 1902);

The Practice of Typography: Modern Methods of Book Composition; a Treatise on Type-Setting by Hand and by Machine, and on the Proper Arrangement and Imposition of Pages (New York: Century, 1904);

Notable Printers of Italy during the Fifteenth Century, Illustrated with Facsimiles from Early Editions and with Remarks on Early and Recent Printing (New York: Grolier Club, 1910);

Printing in the Nineteenth Century (New York: Lead Mould Electrotype Foundry, 1924).

OTHER: *A Decree of Star Chamber Concerning Printing,* preface by De Vinne (New York: Grolier Club, 1884);

Joseph Moxon, *Moxon's Mechanick Exercises; or, The Doctrine of Handy-Works Applied to the Art of Printing,* 2 volumes, preface by De Vinne (New York: The Typothetae of the City of New York, 1896).

SELECTED PERIODICAL PUBLICATIONS–
UNCOLLECTED: "Medieval Printing," *Printer,* 5 (April 1864): 65–67;

"Giambatista Bodoni," *Printers' Circular,* 6 (1871): 8–9;

"William Caxton," *Printers' Circular,* 7 (1872): 241–243, 281–283, 321–323, 353–357;

"The Mazarin Bible," *Printers' Circular,* 8 (1873): 233–235;

"Old Specimen Books," *Printers' Circular,* 9 (1874): 45–47;

"John Gutenberg," *Scribner's Monthly,* 12 (May 1876): 73–85;

"The Growth of Woodcut Printing," *Scribner's Monthly,* 19 (April 1880): 860–874; 20 (May 1880): 34–45;

"The First Editor," *Scribner's Monthly,* 22 (October 1881): 889–898;

"The 'Century's Printer' on the 'Century's Type,'" *Century Magazine,* 29 (March 1896): 794–796;

"The Printing of William Morris," *Bookbuyer,* 13 (January 1897): 920–923;

"Fads in Typography," *Inland Printer,* 26 (January 1901): 601–604.

Theodore Low De Vinne was a printer and bibliophile of prodigious energy and scope. He was one of the great historians of printing; indeed, he was the one who ascertained that Johannes Gutenberg was the true inventor of printing in the Western sense. He built an impressive book collection on the history of printing, which, when it was sold in 1920, was described by Henrietta Bartlett, rare books librarian at Yale University, as "the finest library on the history of printing which has ever been offered for sale in this country." He was a type designer and trendsetter in book-composition styles, an enthusiastic adopter of new printing technology, and the originator of many innovations. He was an organizer of the printing trade, one of the seven founders of the Grolier Club, and a prolific author of both scholarly and popular works. All the while he was a successful businessman and a practicing

printer; in the latter capacity he was frequently called the greatest of his age.

The second of six sons in a family of eight children, Theodore Low (rhymes with *now*) De Vinne was born in Stamford, Connecticut, on Christmas Day 1828 to Daniel De Vinné and Joanna Augusta Low De Vinné. His father had emigrated from Ireland, to which his family, originally Van der Vinné, had fled during the sixteenth-century religious wars in Holland. Daniel De Vinné was a Methodist circuit rider, an ardent abolitionist who was a major factor in his church's gradual adoption of that cause, and the author of *The Methodist Episcopal Church and Slavery* (1857) and *The Irish Primitive Church* (1870).

Theodore De Vinne attended public schools in Catskill, Amenia, and White Plains, New York, and learned Latin from his father. At fourteen he was apprenticed to the printer of the *Newburgh* (New York) *Gazette.* In 1848, having fulfilled the obligations of his apprenticeship, he moved to New York City. After holding various jobs with several printing offices and a stereotype foundry he began work in 1850 as a journeyman compositor in the office of Francis Hart, a job printer in lower Manhattan. That same year he married Grace Brockbank. He quickly assumed operational responsibility for Hart's press, and in 1858, when he was considering the purchase of a printing establishment in Ogdensburg, New York, his employer countered with the offer of a partnership and one-third ownership in the Hart firm. De Vinne accepted, and the firm became Francis Hart and Company.

De Vinne soon became active in the organization of the printing trade. In 1859 he was one of a group of New York printers who began assembling at lunch to discuss business matters. On 21 March 1865 the group organized itself as the Typothetae of the City of New York, the first such organization in the country, with De Vinne, the youngest of the group, as secretary. When the United Typothetae of America was created in 1887, De Vinne was chosen as its first president. Another important contribution to the organization of the printing trade was De Vinne's *The Printers' Price List: A Manual for the Use of Clerks and Book-keepers in Job Printing Offices* (1869), a work that helped printers establish realistic prices.

In 1872 Francis Hart and Company secured the printing of Scribner and Company's *St. Nicholas,* the preeminent children's magazine of its time. The illustrations and artwork were particularly distinguished; the *Quarterly Illustrator* remarked in 1893 that "nearly every illustrator of talent and note has got his handiwork between the covers of *St. Nicholas.*" The quality of the printing of that artwork made De Vinne famous and led to the firm's being awarded the printing of *Scribner's Monthly* in 1876. *Scribner's Monthly,* which in 1881 became the *Century Magazine,* was for more than a quarter of a century the foremost example of American magazine publishing. It achieved a penetration (circulation relative to the population of the country) and an importance that has never been equaled by any other "quality" American magazine. The *Century* was particularly noted for its illustrations, featuring such engravers as Timothy Coles, William J. Linton, Francis C. Altwood, Frederick Juengling, and George Kruell and such artists and illustrators as Frederic Remington, Charles Dana Gibson, Maxfield Parrish, Howard Pyle, André Castaigne, E. W. Kemble, N. C. Wyeth, and Jules Guérin. Frank Luther Mott notes in his *History of American Magazines* (1938–1968) that "the *Century* gained the reputation of being the best-printed magazine in the world."

The quality of the magazines that he printed was the contribution in which De Vinne took the greatest pride. When he referred to himself, he almost invariably chose the phrase "the printer of the *Century.*" The firm, the balance of which De Vinne purchased over a six-year period after Hart's death in 1877 and renamed the De Vinne Press in 1883, also did a substantial amount of book printing and gained a reputation as the place to have fine quality printing done; forty-five of the first fifty-five publications of the Grolier Club, for example, were produced at the De Vinne Press. At its peak it employed more than three hundred persons and was housed in a handsome seven-story building specifically designed for it by George Fletcher Babb.

De Vinne was the force behind the designing and cutting of two fonts of type, the Century family and the Renner. The Century family of type, designed by De Vinne and Linn Boyd Benton in 1896, was, as the name suggests, created specifically for the *Century Magazine.* The basic font in the family was Century Expanded, designed for double-column magazine printing. Adaptations of Century Expanded included Century Broadface, used by the Century Company for book work; Century Schoolbook; and Century Catalog. The Century family has consistently rated high in studies of legibility, and a poll in the 1980s revealed it to be the third most popular type in the United States after Helvetica and Times Roman.

The Century types were important for another reason: they were the first to introduce the notion of a proportional family of types. That is, the larger type sizes were made proportionate to the size used in books and were designed to be used with it. This design allowed a unity of style that was particularly appropriate for advertising, where one would want to use several sizes together. This innovation was widely accepted, and today there are few general-purpose types that do not incorporate the feature of a family of sizes.

De Vinne and Henry Brehmer designed the Renner typeface in 1898. It was derived from a copy of Roberto Caracciolus's *Quadragesimale de Poenitentia,* printed by Franz Renner in Venice in 1472. The design was inspired by William Morris's work at the Kelmscott Press, but unlike virtually every other printer who was influenced by Morris at that time, De Vinne did not imitate him. Rather, De Vinne attempted to do the sort of printing that Morris had done but to do it better. The De Vinne Press printed *The Elizabethan Shakspere* (1903) in Renner type; in a 28 November 1902 letter the work's editor, Mark Harvey Liddell, told James Bothwell, De Vinne's foreman: "We have secured the prime beauty of early printing without having to resort to medieval man's revisions, and so far *we have beaten William Morris at his best*—no borders, no black illegible type, no crowding of matter, no sacrificing of sense to aesthetic demands—all clear straight legible printing—single, direct and forceful."

Though the typeface known as "De Vinne" is, of course, associated with him, De Vinne did not design it; the name is purely complimentary. In fact, De Vinne disliked the face, calling some of the capitals "grotesque," and debated with himself whether he should allow his name to be used with it, but he concluded that it would be rude to refuse the honor.

Though he was interested in style, legibility of type was always De Vinne's principal concern. He expressed his philosophy in the slogan "Legibility first, decoration last." De Vinne's tastes ran to the simple, the strong, and, above all, the legible. He disliked hyperrefined, overornamented, and overelaborate types with razor-edged hairlines and eye-irritating serifs.

From the beginning of his career De Vinne was interested in the technology of printing, and he rapidly adopted new technologies. The list of printing innovations in which he was either directly involved or of which he was one of the earliest adopters is impressive. For example, Francis Hart and Company is generally credited as the first to use dry paper for quality work, with De Vinne being the actual innovator. Similarly, the first use of a cylinder press, or any sort of nonplaten press, for quality work was accomplished, after much experimentation, at Francis Hart and Company under De Vinne's tutelage.

Perhaps De Vinne's most important contribution to printing technology occurred in 1875 when he conceived the idea of using coated paper for printing woodcuts. Charles M. Gage, a Springfield, Massachusetts, papermaker, produced the first "coated-one-side" paper for De Vinne, and it proved quite successful. In 1879, when Gage went to work for the S. D. Warren Paper Company, De Vinne transferred his business there. In 1881 S. D. Warren succeeded in producing paper coated on both sides, and De Vinne used it in printing the *Century;* that grade of paper was known for many years as "Century Enamel."

De Vinne's experimentation with coated paper was particularly timely: in 1882 wood engraving began to be supplanted by photoengraving, which allowed quicker and easier production, and coated paper proved to be essential for the halftone plates used in that process. The coating process buffered the acidic paper used in the late nineteenth century, and the paper has—in comparison with other papers of the time—excellent survival and preservation characteristics.

De Vinne also worked with the Hoe brothers in the design of printing presses. In 1886 the Hoes produced a new rotary-web perfecting press to De Vinne's specifications for the printing of the *Century.* It was, as Robert Hoe points out, "the first, and for three years the only, web press being used in this country for good book work." The success of this experiment led to the "rotary art" press for the printing of illustrations; in 1890 De Vinne became the first American printer to do quality work on such a press. And in 1891 the De Vinne Press became one of the first—if not *the* first—to use the Linotype machine, commercialized in 1890, for quality book work.

The technological preeminence of the De Vinne Press continued into the twentieth century. The firm was one of the first to experiment with the newly emerging methods of color reproduction, and in 1908 it was awarded the gold Special Medal of Award of the American Institute of Graphics Arts for the results it obtained with four-color process printing. It was, therefore, appropriate that when the *Scientific American* devoted a special issue in 1903 to printing technology it concluded the issue with an interview with De Vinne. "A Morning with Theodore L. De Vinne" is, in fact, a history of the development of printing technology in the nineteenth century and an assessment of the state of the art.

Although he took his greatest pride in being a printer, it may have been as a historian of printing that De Vinne made his most lasting contribution. His signal achievement in this regard was to resolve, decisively and permanently, the question of who invented printing in the sense in which the term is commonly used. In the mid nineteenth century the debate over the issue raged with considerable ferocity, the Germans determined to document that it was a German, the Dutch that it was Laurens Janszoon Coster, and the French that it was anyone but a German. De Vinne's approach to the issue was that one must define what is meant by "the invention of printing" before one can make an attribution. His thesis was that the invention of printing did not consist of printing from movable type because the Koreans and Chinese had done that for many centuries. Nor was it the invention of the press, nor was it printing from wooden blocks. Rather, De Vinne posited, the essence of the invention of printing in the sense commonly used was the invention of the type mold, which allowed the mass production of interchangeable pieces of type. Such type was uniform in height and depth but variable in width and could be laid on a composing stick to make a line of type, and line could be laid on line to make a page. This definition is now taken for granted, but at the time it was a penetrating insight that had escaped scores of scholars. De Vinne went on to document the evidence that linked Gutenberg to the invention of the type mold. It is probably true that no other historical dispute has occupied so many people for so long and has been as effectively laid to rest with one publication as was the "who invented printing?" dispute with De Vinne's *The Invention of Printing* in 1876.

De Vinne was also the author of other significant books on the history of printing. His *Historic Printing Types* (1886), originally a lecture before the Grolier Club, and *The Practice of Typography:* (1900) include much information on the history and evolution of printing types. Other important works were *Christopher Plantin, and the Plantin-Moretus Museum at Antwerp* (1888), a history of the famous Plantin family of printers and a description of the remarkable museum they left to their home city; *Title-Pages as Seen by a Printer* (1901), which was enlarged as *The Practice of Typography: A Treatise on Title-Pages* (1902); and *Notable Printers of Italy during the Fifteenth Century* (1910), on the printers whose choice of types and styles shaped the development of printing in the Western world. De Vinne was also a prolific contributor of articles on the history of printing to general-interest periodicals, particularly to *Scribner's Monthly* and the *Century,* for which he wrote such articles as "John Gutenburg" (1876), "The Growth of Woodcut Printing" (1880), and "The First Editor" (1881). And he was a frequent contributor of historical articles and prefaces to books and compilations. For example, he contributed the prefaces to the Grolier Club's first publication, a reprint of *A Decree of Star Chamber Concerning Printing* (1884), and to the

Typothetae's reprint of Joseph Moxon's text, *Moxon's Mechanick Exercises* (1896). He also sought to educate his fellow printers in the history of their craft. His inclusion of "Plain Printing Types: A Treatise on the Selection of Types and the Contexts in Which They Should Be Used" in his 1900 *Practice of Typography* is the most obvious example, but he also contributed articles on historical aspects of printing to various trade publications. Pieces such as "Medieval Printing" (1864), "Giambatista Bodoni" (1871), "William Caxton" (1872), "The Mazarin Bible" (1873), and "Old Specimen Books" (1874) helped to give printers a sense of identity and of the continuity of their craft.

In researching the invention of printing De Vinne had used the collections of David Wolfe Bruce, to whom he dedicated *The Invention of Printing,* and James Lenox, a founder of the New York Public Library, but he determined that he needed more material and that he would have to acquire it himself. His fame as a book collector rests largely on the resulting collection's strength in the history of printing, but he also indulged a strong interest in Americana. Notable items in the latter category included Claude Dablon's *Relation de se qui s'est passé de plus remarquable aux missions des peres de la Compagnie de Jesus en la Nouvvelle France* (Paris: Sebastien Marbre-Cramoisy, 1672). Also known as "The Jesuit Relations," this work was the first extensive and generally factual ethnographic study of indigenous North Americans. Also in De Vinne's library were William Hubbard's *A Narrative of the Troubles with the Indians in New England* (Boston: John Foster, 1677), the first printed account of King Philip's War; Isaac Backus's *An Address to the Inhabitants of New England Concerning the Present Bloody Controversy Therein* (Boston: S. Hill, 1787), dealing with Shays's Rebellion; and John Eliot's "Indian Tracts" of 1643 to 1652. Also included were autographs of nineteen Revolutionary War generals, predominately American but a few British; several Revolutionary War broadsides; and an original painting of the battle between the *Constitution* and the *Guerrière.* De Vinne also collected some literary items, for example, the manuscript for Bret Harte's "Mrs. Skaggs's Husbands" (London: Hotten, 1872).

Still, the collection's main value lay in its books about the history of printing and its exemplars of work of the great printers of the past. Eighty-seven incunabula are listed in the 1920 auction catalogue of De Vinne's library. His interest in early printers in Italy was particularly strong: he owned twenty-seven fifteenth-century items from seventeen Italian printers, including five by Erhardt Ratdolt, four by Renner, three by Nicolas Jenson,

and one by Andrea de Toresanis, Aldus Manutius's father-in-law. There were also twelve sixteenth-century Aldines, handsomely printed editions of Greek and Roman classics. While there were fourteen items from the Plantin press, eight from John Baskerville, six from Bodoni, five from the Riverside Press, and fourteen from the Ashendene Press, there were only two from the Kelmscott Press. This is perhaps an indication of De Vinne's lack of regard for the quality or importance of Morris's work.

The collection was strong in books about printing, from *Moxon's Mechanick Exercises* (London: Printed by Joseph Moxon, 1683), the first book in English extensively describing the printing process–about which the auction catalogue notes, "Much used and considerably repaired"–to Theodor Goebel's *Friedrich König und die Erfindung der Schellpresse* (Stuttgart: F. Kravis, 1906), the first account of the invention of the power press. De Vinne also secured bibliophilic items such as Joseph Ames's *Typographical Antiquities* (London: Printed for the Editor [William Herbert], 1785–1790), the first account of the history of printing in the British Isles, and Henry Lemoine's (London: S. Fisher, 1797) and Thomas Frognall Dibdin's (London: W. Miller, 1810–1819) extensions thereof; this trilogy served as the principal want list for more than a generation of book collectors seeking the landmarks of the history of printing and the most beautiful examples of the art.

The collection also contained items important to the history of printing as communication and to printing's role in society. Examples include *A Decree of the Starre-Chamber* of 1637, from which the Grolier Club's reprint of 1884 was made; the first edition of John Milton's *Aeropagitica* (London, 1644), his response to the *Decree of the Starre-Chamber* and to the 1643 licensing act imposed by Parliament; and *The Trial of John Peter Zenger, of New York, Printer: Who was charged with having printed and published a libel against the government; and acquitted. With a narrative of his case* (London: J. Almon, 1765), the first major freedom-of-the-press case in what is now the United States.

The reputation and the utility of De Vinne's collection are illustrated by the fact that Horace Hart of the Oxford University Press wrote in 1910 requesting information concerning an English manual of typography, John Smith's *The Printer's Grammar, Containing a Concise History of the Origin of Printing, also an Explanation of the Superfices, Graduation & Properties of the Different Sorts and Sizes of Metal Types* (London: T. Evans, 1787), which the Bodleian Library did not possess but of which De Vinne had two copies plus the original edition–without the history–of

1755 (London: Printed for the Editor). The collection inspired a poem by Carl Purington Rollins, printer to Yale University, "On Buying at Auction a Book Once in the Library of Theodore Low De Vinne," published in his *Off the Dead Bank* (1949). In 1941 Carl L. Cannon described De Vinne's books on printing as "the most distinguished collection on the subject ever dispersed in America."

At De Vinne's death on 16 February 1914 his collection was dispersed in three groups. The sizable typographical library he had maintained at the De Vinne Press was acquired in toto by Henry Lewis Bullen's Typographic and Graphic Arts Library in Jersey City, New Jersey; with that library's demise the De Vinne books were largely acquired by the Columbia University library. This material had been used primarily for reference in the operation of the press. The historical works, which had been kept at De Vinne's home, were divided into two parts: the Americana was sold at auction in 1919 by Scott and O'Shaughnessy of New York City, and the material on the history of printing was sold at auction in 1920 by the Anderson Galleries in New York City. The newly formed Wing Foundation of the Newberry Library of Chicago, whose curator was Pierce Butler, was the major purchaser at the latter auction, acquiring 250 of the 300 items for which it bid.

Theodore Low De Vinne achieved prominence in almost all major facets of printing that no one else has ever matched. He was the foremost historian of printing of his time, a book collector whose collection not only served to preserve and illuminate but also fostered scholarly contributions, a technologist who contributed to important advances in the art of printing, a type designer and a voice for more aesthetically pleasing book design, an organizer of the trade, and a successful entrepreneur. In 1911 he was recognized for his contributions with honorary degrees from both Columbia and Yale Universities. Perhaps the pithiest encapsulation of the man is a comment he made in addressing the Yale Club of New York shortly thereafter: "I have given the best part of my life to the making of books that have been sold and read and are not rated as bits of typographic bric-a-brac."

Interview:
"A Morning with Theodore L. De Vinne," *Scientific American,* no. 89 (14 November 1903): 339.

References:
Catalogue of Work of the De Vinne Press, Exhibited at the Grolier Club (New York: Grolier Club, 1929);

Frank Hopkins, *The De Vinne and Marion Presses* (Meriden, Conn.: Columbia Club, 1936);

Michael E. D. Koenig, "Theodore Low De Vinne: His Contributions to the Art of Printing," *Library Quarterly,* 41 (January 1971): 1–24;

The Library of the Late Theodore Low De Vinne . . . The Anderson Galleries . . . New York, sale no. 1455, 12–16 January 1920 (New York: D. Taylor, 1920);

Frank Luther Mott, *A History of American Magazines,* 5 volumes (Cambridge, Mass.: Harvard University Press, 1938–1968), III: 467;

Carl Purington Rollins, "Theodore Low De Vinne," *Signature,* new series 10 (1950): 3–21;

Rollins, *Theodore Low De Vinne* (New York: Typophiles, 1968);

Selections from the Fine Private Library of Mr. Theodore Low De Vinne (New York: Scott & O'Shaugnessy, 1919);

Virginia G. Smith, "Longevity and Legibility: Two Types from the De Vinne Press and How They Have Fared," *Printing History,* 8 (1986): 13–21;

Theodore Low De Vinne, Printer (New York: Privately printed at the De Vinne Press, 1915);

Irene Tichenor, "Theodore De Vinne: Unlikely Leader (Prominent Printer)," *Printing History,* 11 (1989): 17–26.

Papers:
Collections of Theodore Low De Vinne's papers are at the American Antiquarian Society, Worcester, Massachusetts; the Grolier Club Library, New York City; and in Special Collections, Columbia University Library.

Samuel Gardner Drake

(11 October 1798 – 14 June 1875)

Francis J. Bosha

Kawamura Gakuen Woman's University

BOOKS: *Indian Biography, Containing the Lives of More Than Two Hundred Tribal Chiefs: Also Such Others of That Race as Have Rendered Their Names Conspicuous in the History of North America* (Boston: J. Drake, 1832); revised and enlarged as *The Book of the Indians of North America: Comprising Details in the Lives of about Five Hundred Chiefs and Others* (Boston: J. Drake, 1833); revised and enlarged as *Biography and History of the Indians of North America; Comprising a General Account of Them, and Details in the Lives of All the Most Distinguished Chiefs, and Others Who Have Been Noted, among the Various Indian Nations* (Boston: Perkins / New York: Collins, Hannay, 1834; revised and enlarged edition, Boston: J. Drake, 1835; revised and enlarged edition, Boston: Antiquarian Institute, 1836; revised and enlarged, 1837); revised and enlarged as *The Book of the Indians; or, Biography and History of the Indians of North America, from Its First Discovery to the Year 1841* (Boston: Antiquarian Bookstore, 1841; revised and enlarged edition, Boston: Mussey, 1845); revised and enlarged as *Biography and History of the Indians of North America, from Its First Discovery* (Boston: Mussey, 1848; revised and enlarged, 1851); revised and enlarged as *The Aboriginal Races of North America: Comprising Biographical Sketches of Eminent Individuals, and an Historical Account of the Different Tribes, from the First Discovery of the Continent to the Present Period* (Philadelphia: Desilver, 1860);

Indian Captivities: Being a Collection of the Most Remarkable Narratives of Persons Taken Captive by the North American Indians to Which Are Added Notes, Historical, Biographical, &c. (Boston: Antiquarian Bookstore and Institute, 1839); republished as *Tragedies of the Wilderness; or, True and Authentic Narratives of Captives, Who Have Been Carried Away by the Indians from the Various Frontier Settlements of the United States, from the Earliest to the Present Time* (Boston: Antiquarian Bookstore and Institute, 1841); republished as *In-*

dian Captivities; or, Life in the Wigwam: Being True Narratives of Captives Who Have Been Carried Away by the Indians, from the Frontier Settlements of the U.S., from the Earliest Period to the Present Time (Auburn: Derby & Miller, 1850);

Catalogue of a Private Library, Chiefly Relating to the Antiquities, History, and Biography of America, and in an Especial Manner to the Indians . . . to Be Sold at Auction by Howe, Leonard & Co. . . . May 27th, 28th, 29th, & 30th (Boston: Coolidge, 1845); republished as *Catalogue of the Private Library of Samuel G. Drake, of Boston, Chiefly Relating to the Antiquities, History, and Biography of America, and* in an Especial Manner to the Indians, Collected and Used by Him in Preparing His Works upon the Aborigines of America (Boston: Published by Samuel G. Drake, printed by George Coolidge, 1845);

Genealogical and Biographical Account of the Family of Drake in America (Boston: Printed at the private press of G. Coolidge for S. G. Drake, 1845);

Genealogical and Biographical Account of the Descendants of Elder William Wentworth, One of the 1st Settlers of Dover, N.H. (Boston, 1850);

Recovery of Some Materials for the Early History of Dorchester, General and Particular, Prepared for the New England Historic-Genealogical Register (Boston: Office of the New England Historical and Genealogical Register, 1851);

History of the Buccaneers of America: Containing Detailed Accounts of Those Bold and Daring Freebooters; Chiefly along the Spanish Main, in the West Indies and in the Great South Sea, Succeeding the Civil War in England (Boston: Bazin, circa 1851);

Some Memoirs of the Life and Writings of the Rev. Thomas Prince, Together with the Pedigree of His Family (Boston: Office of the New England Historical and Genealogical Register, 1851);

A Memoir of the Rev. Cotton Mather, D.D., with a Genealogy of the Family of Mather (Boston: Printed by C. C. P. Moody, 1851);

The History and Antiquities of the City of Boston: The Capital of Massachusetts and Metropolis of New England. From Its Settlement in 1630 to the Year 1670, 16 parts (Boston: Stevens, 1854–1856); enlarged as The History and Antiquities of Boston, the Capital of Massachusetts and Metropolis of New England, from Its Settlement in 1630, to the Year 1770 (Boston: Stevens, 1856);

Bibliotheca Americana: Catalogue of an Extensive and Valuable Collection of Books Relating to America . . . from the Library of . . . Samuel G. Drake, Esq., of Boston (New York: Bouton, circa 1858);

Result of Some Researches among the British Archives for Information Relative to the Founders of New England: Made in the Years 1858, 1859, and 1860. Originally Collected for and Published in the New England Historical and Genealogical Register, and Now Corrected and Enlarged (Boston: Office of the New England Historical and Genealogical Register, 1860);

Memoir of Sir Walter Ralegh (Boston: Privately printed, 1862);

A Catalogue of Rare, Useful and Curious Books, and Tracts, Chiefly Historical, Offered for Sale, 17 volumes (Boston, 1864–1875);

Drake of Hampton, New Hampshire (Boston, 1867);

Annals of Witchcraft in New England, and Elsewhere in the United States, from Their First Settlement: Drawn up from Unpublished and Other Well Authenticated Records of the Alleged Operations of Witches and Their Instigator, the Devil, Woodward's Historical Series, no. 8 (Boston: Printed by J. Munsell for W. Elliot Woodward, 1869);

A Particular History of the Five Years French and Indian War in New England and Parts Adjacent, from Its Declaration by the King of France, March 15, 1744, to the Treaty with the Eastern Indians, Oct. 16, 1749, Sometimes Called Gov. Shirley's War: With a Memoir of Major-General Shirley, Accompanied by His Portrait and Other Engravings (Boston: S. G. Drake, 1870);

Early History of Georgia, Embracing the Embassy of Sir Alexander Cuming to the Country of the Cherokees, in the Year 1730 (Boston: Printed by D. Clapp & Son, 1872);

Narrative Remarks, Expository Notes, and Historical Criticisms, on the New England Historical and Genealogical Society, and Incidentally on the Massachusetts Historical Society, anonymous (Albany, N.Y.: Printed by J. Munsell, 1874).

OTHER: Benjamin Church, The History of King Philip's War; Also of Expeditions against the French and Indians in the Eastern Parts of New-England, in the Years 1689, 1690, 1692, 1696 and 1704. With Some Account of the Divine Providence towards Col. Benjamin Church. By His Son, Thomas Church, Esq., edited by Drake (Boston: Printed by Howe & Norton, 1825); republished as History of Philip's War, Commonly Called the Great Indian War, of 1675 and 1676 (Boston: Printed by J. H. A. Frost, 1827); revised as The History of the Great Indian War of 1675 and 1676, Commonly Called Philip's War (New York: H. Dayton, 1845);

The Present State of New-England with Respect to the Indian War: Wherein Is an Account of the True Reason Thereof, (as Far as Can Be Judged by Men.) Together with Most of the Remarkable Passages That Have Happened from the 20th of June, till the 10th of November, 1675 . . . Composed by a Merchant of Boston. . . . London, Printed for D. Newman, 1675, edited by Drake (Boston: J. Drake, 1833);

A Continuation of the State of New-England; Being a Farther Account of the Indian Warr . . . London: Printed by T. M. for D. Newman, 1676, edited by Drake (Boston: J. Drake, 1833);

The Old Indian Chronicle: Being a Collection of Exceeding Rare Tracts Written and Published in the Time of King Philip's War, by Persons Residing in the Country; to Which Are Now Added Marginal Notes and Chronicles of the Indians from the Discovery of America to the Present Time, edited by Drake (Boston:

Antiquarian Institute, 1836; enlarged, 1838; enlarged edition, Boston: Samuel A. Drake, 1867);

Thomas Prince, *A Chronological History of New-England, in the Form of Annals . . . from the Discovery of Capt. Gasnold in 1602 to the Arrival of Governor Belcher in 1730,* edited by Drake (Boston: Antiquarian Bookstore, 1852);

Increase Mather, *The History of King Philip's War,* edited by Drake (Boston: Printed for the editor, 1862);

Mather, *Early History of New England: Being a Relation of Hostile Passages between the Indians and European Voyagers and First Settlers,* edited by Drake (Boston: Printed for the editor, 1864);

William Hubbard, *The History of the Indian Wars in New England from the First Settlement to the Termination of the War with King Philip, in 1677. . . . Carefully Revised, and Accompanied with an Historical Preface, Life and Pedigree of the Author, and Extensive Notes,* 2 volumes, edited by Drake, Woodward's Historical Series, nos. 3, 4 (Roxbury, Mass.: Printed by J. Munsell for W. Elliot Woodward, 1865);

Samuel G. Bishop, *Eulogium on the Death of George Washington,* edited, with an introductory letter, by Drake (Roxbury, Mass.: Privately printed at the Bradstreet Press for W. Elliot Woodward, 1866);

Francis Baylies, *An Historical Memoir of the Colony of New Plymouth, from the Flight of the Pilgrims into Holland in the Year 1608, to the Union of that Colony with Massachusetts in 1692,* 2 volumes, edited by Drake (Boston: Wiggin & Lunt, 1866);

Cotton Mather and Robert Calef, *The Witchcraft Delusion in New England: Its Rise, Progress, and Termination, as Exhibited by Dr. Cotton Mather, in The Wonders of the Invisible World; and by Mr. Robert Calef, in His More Wonders of the Invisible World,* 3 volumes, edited by Drake, Woodward's Historical Series, nos. 5–7 (Roxbury, Mass.: Printed by J. Munsell for W. Elliot Woodward, 1866);

John Norton, *Narrative of the Capture and Burning of Fort Massachusetts by the French and Indians, in the Time of the War of 1744–1749 . . . Written at the Time by One of the Captives,* edited by Drake (Albany, N.Y.: Printed by J. Munsell for S. G. Drake, 1870).

SELECTED PERIODICAL PUBLICATIONS–
UNCOLLECTED: "Recollections in the History of Northwood, N.H.," as A–N. B–E, *Collections of the New-Hampshire Historical Society,* 3 (1832): 67–94;

Daniel Gookin, "An Historical Account of the Doings and Sufferings of the Christian Indians in New England," edited by Drake, *Archaeologia Americana,* 2 (1836): 423–534;

"Genealogical Memoir of the Farmer Family," *New England Historical and Genealogical Register,* 1 (1847): 21–34;

"Passengers of the Golden Hind," *New England Historical and Genealogical Register,* 1 (1847): 126–131;

"A List of Names Found among First Settlers of New England," *New England Historical and Genealogical Register,* 1 (1847): 137–139;

"The Parsons Family," *New England Historical and Genealogical Register,* 1 (1847): 263–275;

"Principal Events in the Life of the Indian Chief Brant," anonymous, *New England Historical and Genealogical Register,* 2 (1848): 345–348; 3 (1849): 59–64;

"Early Settlers of Essex and Old Norfolk," *New England Historical and Genealogical Register,* 6 (1852): 205–208, 243–254, 339–346; 7 (1853): 83–88, 357–360; 8 (1854): 49–54, 163–168;

"A Genealogical Memoir of the Doolittle Family," anonymous, *New England Historical and Genealogical Register,* 6 (1852): 293–296;

"New Publications: *The History of New England, from 1630 to 1649,* by John Winthrop, Esq. . . . [edited] by James Savage," anonymous, *New England Historical and Genealogical Register,* 7 (1853): 361–368; 8 (1854): 83–90;

"An Address Delivered at the Annual Meeting of the New England Historical and Genealogical Society, Held, by Adjournment, at Its Room, No. 5 Tremont Street, Boston, January 20th, 1858," *New England Historical and Genealogical Register,* 12 (1858): 97–105;

"Sir Humphrey Gilbert's Last Letters," *New England Historical and Genealogical Register,* 13 (1859): 197–199;

"The Savoy," *New England Historical and Genealogical Register,* 13 (1859): 205–206;

"Petition of Some 'Falsly Called Brownists' 1592," *New England Historical and Genealogical Register,* 13 (1859): 259–260;

"Pedigree of Joselyne," *New England Historical and Genealogical Register,* 14 (1860): 15–16;

"A Letter from the Rev. Cotton Mather, D.D., to George Vaughan, Esq.," *New England Historical and Genealogical Register,* 16 (1862): 348–351;

"Will of Herbert Pelham, 1672," *New England Historical and Genealogical Register,* 18 (1864): 172;

"Thomas Prince: A Reminiscence Extracted from My Private Diary," *New England Historical and Genealogical Register,* 19 (1865): 121;

"Books Published by Subscription," *American Historical Record*, 1 (January 1872): 19–22;

"Books Published by Subscription," *American Historical Record*, 1 (February 1872): 60–62;

"Books Published by Subscription," *American Historical Record*, 1 (March 1872): 116–117;

"Books Published by Subscription," *American Historical Record*, 1 (April 1872): 167–169;

"Books Published by Subscription," *American Historical Record*, 1 (August 1872): 356–357;

"A Rare Book," *American Historical Record*, 2 (August 1873): 359–360;

"The First Englishmen in North America," *American Historical Record*, 3 (August 1874): 344–353.

The Boston historian, bookseller, and printer Samuel Gardner Drake opened the first antiquarian bookstore in America in 1830. He collected a vast range of mostly American historical and literary texts, which he subsequently used to write his authoritative studies of American Indians as well as his New England histories and genealogies. He also reprinted many Colonial-era works and in the course of nearly five decades as a bookseller helped build the libraries of such collectors as Henry Stevens and George Brinley Jr.

Drake was born in Pittsfield, New Hampshire, on 11 October 1798, the third of five children of Simeon Drake, a farmer, and Love Muchmore Tucke Drake. The Drakes could trace their ancestry to Robert Drake, who immigrated to Exeter, New Hampshire, from Essex, England, around 1640; the family's history would become the subject of one of Samuel Gardner Drake's books, and genealogy in general would be one of his lifelong interests.

In 1805 Simeon Drake sold his farm and moved the family to the neighboring town of Northwood, where he opened a country store. In the autumn of 1816 Samuel Drake moved to Boston, where he joined his older brother, John Tucke Drake, as a clerk for their uncle, Samuel J. Tucke, an importer of paint and oils. Shortly thereafter Tucke relocated his business to Baltimore, and his nephews accompanied him. The move proved unsuccessful for Tucke, and within six months Samuel Drake returned home. During his stay in Baltimore, however, Drake was able to do more than develop his growing business acumen: he became acquainted with a French family, and according to John H. Sheppard, a contemporary of Drake's, he gained "a considerable knowledge of the French language."

On his return to Northwood, Drake studied for several months under John Kelly, an attorney. In 1818 he began teaching in Loudon, New Hampshire; he was paid eight dollars a month until the school ran out of money after a few months. He taught elsewhere for the next five years; in 1819–1820 he was employed at an academy in Columbia, near Morristown, New Jersey. He left New Jersey due to his poor health and returned home, where he studied medicine under Dr. Thomas Shannon of Pittsfield while continuing to teach in the local public schools until the spring of 1824.

For some time Drake—who has been described by his friend of more than forty years, William B. Trask, as having had even then "an antiquarian turn of mind"—had been considering entering the trade of bookselling. His conversations with the antiquarians Jacob B. Moore and John Farmer, two of the founders of the New Hampshire Historical Society in 1823, encouraged him to pursue this interest. On 12 April 1825 Drake married Louisa Elmes. They had six children; four survived to adulthood, including Francis Samuel Drake, born in 1828, and Samuel Adams Drake, born in 1833, who became historians.

In the summer of 1824 Drake had come upon a copy of the 1772 edition of Benjamin Church's *The Entertaining History of King Philip's War* (Newport, R.I.: Reprinted and sold by Solomon Southwick); he so enjoyed reading it that he decided to write a preface and appendix for it and republish it with the help of his younger brother, Josiah. To cover costs he obtained nearly one thousand subscriptions. In the summer of 1825 he published the duodecimo *The History of King Philip's War*, thereby beginning his career as a historian, publisher, and bookseller. Within three months the edition netted Drake a profit of between $400 and $500. Its success led him to search for other old books and manuscripts that he might be able to edit and reprint or use for his own historical research. This activity launched him on his career as a book collector.

Drake experienced a major setback nearly at the outset of his enterprise when a trunk of manuscript notes "relating particularly to the biography of the principal persons that figured in the Indian wars" was stolen during Boston's Court Street fire of 10 November 1825. Nevertheless, Drake continued to gather antiquarian material. In 1827 he enlarged and republished the Church volume under the slightly modified title *History of Philip's War*; it was one of the first books to be printed in Boston from stereotype plates. The second edition was less profitable than its predecessor. In 1828 he tried his hand at the book auction business; he failed after two years. In some measure his inexperience was to blame; John H. Sheppard, however, suggests that the failure was "more from the faithlessness of one who unfortunately was in the concern."

On 10 July 1830 Drake opened the first antiquarian bookstore in America at 63 Cornhill in Boston. The following year he moved the business across the street to 56 Cornhill.

Pursuing his interest in Indian history, Drake continued to seek primary-source material. In 1832 he published his major historical study, the duodecimo 348-page *Indian Biography, Containing the Lives of More Than Two Hundred Tribal Chiefs*. He expanded it the following year to discuss an additional three hundred chiefs, along with "the lives, customs and events" of the Indians, and retitled it *The Book of the Indians of North America*. As Drake would note in the preface to the eighth edition of the work (1841), the 1833 edition "contained three times as much as before, and yet my materials were scarcely half exhausted." In the preface to the eleventh edition (1851) he would write that, having added "a very particular Index, at a great expense of labor," he was submitting the study "as finished, though not as a *finished* performance." Thomas W. Field describes the eleventh edition as "the last and most complete edition of this very excellent and carefully compiled collection of the materials of Indian history. It is the result of a lifetime of labor, by one who spared no pains to be at the same time faithful to the completeness and truthfulness of history."

It is not surprising that Drake's activities would bring him into contact with the American Antiquarian Society, based in nearby Worcester, Massachusetts. While he was never a member, he helped the society secure books for its library and sold its publications at his bookstore. His relations with the society's librarian, Christopher Columbus Baldwin, were quite cordial, as is evident from their extant correspondence. When Baldwin died in 1835, Drake tried to secure the office of librarian. In a 16 September 1835 letter to the society he wrote that "some friends urged" him to apply for the position, which, he said, would be "the most congenial of all employments to me." In a 16 October letter to society member Samuel Jennison, Drake stressed that the office "would, of all others, be to me the most desirable." He added, "Small importance is attached to the salary." In a letter of the same date to another member, John Davis, he confided that it was at the urging of a "very much esteemed friend," George Bancroft, that he was applying. In the end, despite his and Bancroft's efforts, the post went to Maturin Fisher.

Drake edited *The Old Indian Chronicle* (1836) and wrote *Indian Captivities* (1839). For the latter work he drew on accounts of white settlers who had been taken captive by Indians; he republished the work two years later under the title *Tragedies of the Wilderness*. According to Justin Winsor, Drake "was for many years the most assiduous promoter of this class of books. This compiler's sympathetic sentiment clearly affected his rhetoric and sometimes the accuracy of his state-

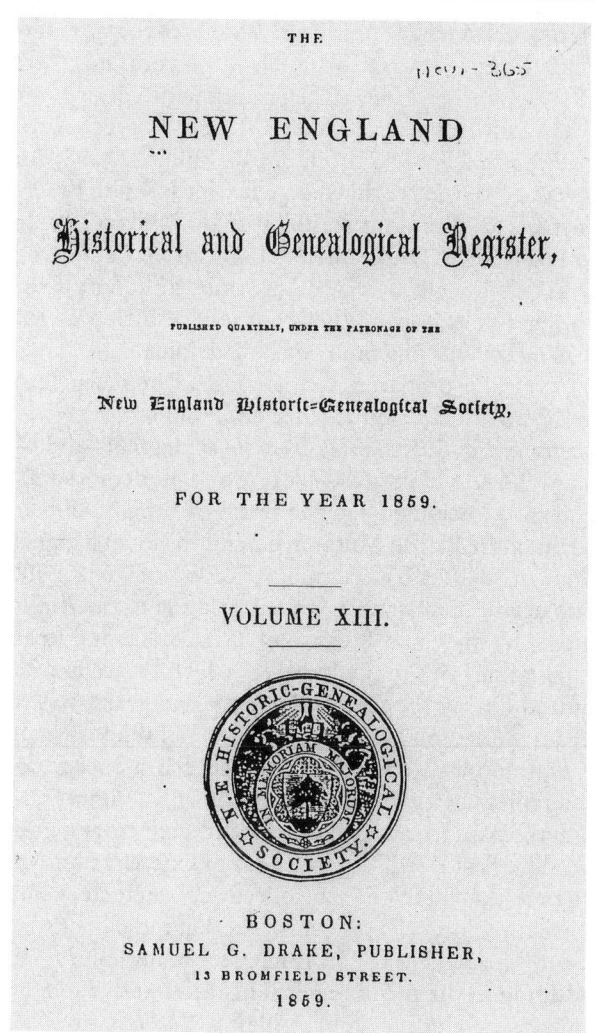

THE

NEW ENGLAND

Historical and Genealogical Register,

PUBLISHED QUARTERLY, UNDER THE PATRONAGE OF THE

New England Historic=Genealogical Society,

FOR THE YEAR 1859.

VOLUME XIII.

BOSTON:
SAMUEL G. DRAKE, PUBLISHER,
13 BROMFIELD STREET.
1859.

Title page for a volume of the periodical that Drake published from 1847 until 1861

ments." Nonetheless, in recognition of his work as a historian Drake was made a member of the Society of Northern Antiquaries of Copenhagen in 1840; in 1843 New York's Union College awarded him an honorary master of arts.

While continuing to work as a publisher and historian, Drake proceeded to sell many of the books and manuscripts he had reprinted or consulted. A collector with whom he dealt for more than three decades was the antiquarian Lyman C. Draper of Buffalo, who would serve as corresponding secretary of the State Historical Society of Wisconsin from 1854 to 1887. In a letter to Draper of 23 May 1843 Drake reported: "I have in my private library most of the works you desire but not many of them for sale." Among the volumes Drake did provide Draper at that time were William Johnson's two-volume *Sketches of the Life and Correspondence of Nathanael Greene* (Charleston, 1822) for $5.50 and James Hall's *Letters from the West* (London:

Henry Colburn, 1828) for $1.25. Over the next few years Draper secured from Drake several numbers of the *American Almanac,* beginning with volume one (1830), for fifty cents; Thomas Ashe's *Travels in America Performed in 1806* (London: R. Phillips, 1808) for seventy-five cents; and George Heriot's *Travels through the Canadas* (London: R. Phillips, 1807) for $5.00. In some instances Drake ordered books from London on Draper's behalf, and at other times he referred the younger collector to other booksellers, including the firm of Daniels and Smith of Philadelphia.

Drake prepared a collection of between four hundred and five hundred schoolbooks "which had been used in this country from its settlement" and offered them to Harvard College "for a moderate sum." Harvard "declined for the want of funds," but an agent of the British Museum bought the lot at a higher price in 1843. A collection of 1,517 lots of some 3,000 books and manuscripts "chiefly relating to the Antiquities, history, and Biography of America, and in an especial manner to the Indians," which Drake had acquired during the previous twenty-one years, was to be auctioned on 27 May 1845, but eight days before the announced date Drake concluded a special arrangement with Brinley of Hartford, Connecticut, whereby the twenty-eight-year-old collector—whom Drake considered "a gentleman of extensive knowledge in the value of such collections"—agreed to buy the entire library. Trask surmises that these books became "the nucleus of Mr. Brinley's famous library." In addition to the many regional histories and works on Indians, including James Adair's *The History of the American Indians* (London: Printed for Edward and Charles Dilly, 1775), Brinley acquired books dealing with the Age of Discovery, such as an excellent 1614 folio edition of Samuel Purchas's *Purchas His Pilgrimage. Or, Relations of the World and Religions Observed in All Ages and Places Discouered, from the Creation vnto This Present* (London: Printed by William Stansby for Henry Fetherstone) and the 1577 quarto of John Frampton's translation of Nicolas Monardes's *Ioyfull Newes out of the New Founde Worlde* (London: W. Norton). The sale also included several works by the Mathers, including Increase's *The Mystery of Christ Opened and Applyed* (Boston: Printed by Richard Pierce, 1686) and the 1702 London edition of Cotton's *Magnalia Christi Americana* (Printed for Thomas Parkhurst), along with dozens of New England tracts printed in the late 1690s. He also secured a Paris edition of *Jesuit Relations* by Paul Raguenau (1651), Joel Barlow's poem *The Columbiad* (Philadelphia: Printed by Fry and Krammer for C. and A. Conrad and for Conrad, Lucas and Company in Baltimore, 1807) in its original binding, and a copy of a Thomas Prince sermon that was printed in Boston

by James Franklin in 1718, the first year his brother Benjamin worked for him as an apprentice.

Closely allied to Drake's work as an antiquarian was his keen interest in genealogy. His history of his forbears, *Genealogical and Biographical Account of the Family of Drake in America,* was privately published in 1845. Also in 1845 Drake, along with the Boston bookseller Charles Ewer, John Wingate Thornton, Lemuel Shattuck, and William H. Montague, founded the New-England Historic Genealogical Society. Ewer, who had formulated the idea of creating such a society, became its first president; Drake served for twelve years as corresponding secretary.

When the society established its quarterly journal, the *New England Historical and Genealogical Register,* in 1847, Drake suggested that David Reed be its publisher. Ewer, however, persuaded Drake to take on the task. Drake, who by then had had his share of setbacks in the book trade, had doubts as to whether such a journal could succeed. The following year, however, it was Drake's business, not the journal, that failed. He sent out a printed announcement dated 2 June 1848 that said:

> The undersigned, owing to pecuniary embarrassments, finds it necessary to lay his circumstances before his creditors. He has, therefore, appointed Monday, June 5th, 1848, for a special meeting of said creditors; and you, being of the number, are respectfully requested to meet at the store of the subscriber, at half past three o'clock, on the day above mentioned.

Drake suspended his bookselling business and seemed ready to abandon the journal. He wrote to the Reverend Samuel H. Riddel of the New-England Historic Genealogical Society on 10 July:

> You have heard, I doubt not, of my, to me, very serious condition in the world.–I am entirely without property, & now, at the age of fifty, am to provide, somehow, for a family: & in poor health too.–I have had more upon my mind than a strong man ought to have, without the trouble I have had from the Periodical.

Drake, however, would continue to publish the *Register* until 1861, serving also as its editor for nine and one-half of those years. He had to cease his work, however, as an agent for the American Antiquarian Society's publication, *Archaeologica Americana,* and return the unsold copies he had in his store. According to the minutes of that society's meeting of 23 October 1848, Drake "has failed in business, and a small balance against him appears in the account he has rendered of debt and credit between himself and the Society."

Amid his financial and professional setbacks, Drake also faced the deterioration of his marriage, which ended in divorce in the early 1850s. In November 1855 Louisa married George Washington Tyler, an early editor of the *Boston Herald*. She would outlive both husbands and die in Buffalo, New York, in 1890.

Drake gradually rebuilt his bookselling business, and he ran on the inside back cover of the *Register* advertisements for books he hoped to sell. He also frequently contributed articles to the journal, many of them unsigned. In 1853 the building in which Drake's bookshop was located was demolished to make way for the construction of the Sears Block (the area is now occupied by Government Center), and Drake moved to 13 Brattle Street.

Drake's extant correspondence reveals that he continued to supply Brinley with books into the early 1870s. A letter to Brinley dated 29 December 1854 reveals Drake acting as an intermediary between the Hartford collector and other booksellers and conveys his frustration with setbacks and delays:

> I did not reply to yours of the 23d because I had not a copy of [Peter] Force's Tracts–I will willingly give you a copy as soon as I can get it from Washington–wh. you may *not* know is a ------ hard job. I am almost sure of them, but not quite–Peter is slow in such matters, but I can *conquer* him, as he must come to me for some things. The order for the Tracts is out.

In 1856 Drake relocated to 26 Bromfield Street. In 1858 he was elected to a one-year term as president of the New-England Historic Genealogical Society. That year he moved his business to 13 Bromfield Street. Also in 1858 he, Thomas Waterman, Frederick Kidder, Jeremiah Colburn, John Ward Dean, John Wells Parker, and William H. Whitmore founded The Prince Society for Mutual Publication; Drake would serve as its president until 1870. The object of the society, which was established on the centenary of the death of the New England annalist Thomas Prince, was to publish manuscripts and reprint scarce books "relating to the early history of this country." Each volume was to be issued in the form of an uncut, muslin-bound quarto and priced at no more than three dollars.

Drake held his first major book auction in 1858, offering his personal library for sale. The Vermont bookseller Stevens, who supplied such major collectors as John Carter Brown and James Lenox, purchased the library en bloc for $10,000. He later wrote that he did so "having in my eye . . . certain choice 'Historical Nuggets' for Mr. Lenox, who was ever ready to pay good prices for an early choice." In 1859 Stevens bought from Drake an 1827 duodecimo copy of Edgar Allan Poe's "unique pamphlet entitled 'Tamerlane,'" which he sold to the British Museum the following year; Stevens noted that it was finally "paid for in 1867 one shilling!"

Drake also played a role in Draper's work to expand the library of the State Historical Society of Wisconsin. After getting Draper elected a corresponding member of the New-England Historic Genealogical Society, Drake presented to the society Draper's proposal to begin an exchange of publications with the Wisconsin group. In addition to selling volumes to the Wisconsin society, Drake circulated among his friends and colleagues Draper's letters pleading for gifts of books and periodicals and allowed the donations to be dropped off at his store for shipment to Madison. He wrote Draper on 17 November 1854 that he had even asked the Adams family for volumes "out of Pres. John Adams works" that might be contributed to the Wisconsin library. Drake was forced to stop storing and shipping the donated books in 1865, explaining in a letter to Draper on 9 May that "I am up three flights of stairs, & do not employ even a boy at present, so that I am not able to do anything that way," but he resumed his efforts a few years later. The Wisconsin society's holdings grew from fifty volumes in 1854, when Draper began working in Madison, to fifty thousand volumes in 1873. In appreciation, in January 1875 the Wisconsin society named Drake an honorary vice president.

Meanwhile, Drake continued his historical projects, principally *The History and Antiquities of the City of Boston,* which he published in sixteen parts between 1 September 1854 and 2 April 1856. The work traced Boston's history from its settlement in 1630 to 1770. As Drake explained to the Reverend Henry M. Dexter in a letter dated 30 March 1868, the publisher of the series, Luther Stevens, "complained continually of the want of interest in the work . . . and that the patronage did not pay the expense of publication." As a result Drake added, "I received nothing for my labor, saving a few copies of each number of the work." Despite the fact that Drake felt "anxious to continue" the series to the present, the number of potential patrons "was too small to make the work remunerative." Ownership of the stereotype plates and the unsold volumes "passed into the hands of Messers. Piper & Co.," and the plates were melted. After Drake's death Samuel Adams Drake wrote that he thought that this work gave his father "greater pride" than "any other of his productions." He also maintained that "the book would have eventually proved a not unprofitable venture had not the stereotype plates been destroyed."

Drake went to England in November 1858 to locate materials for a history of New England that he hoped to write; he also traveled on the Continent. While abroad he purchased what his friend Sheppard

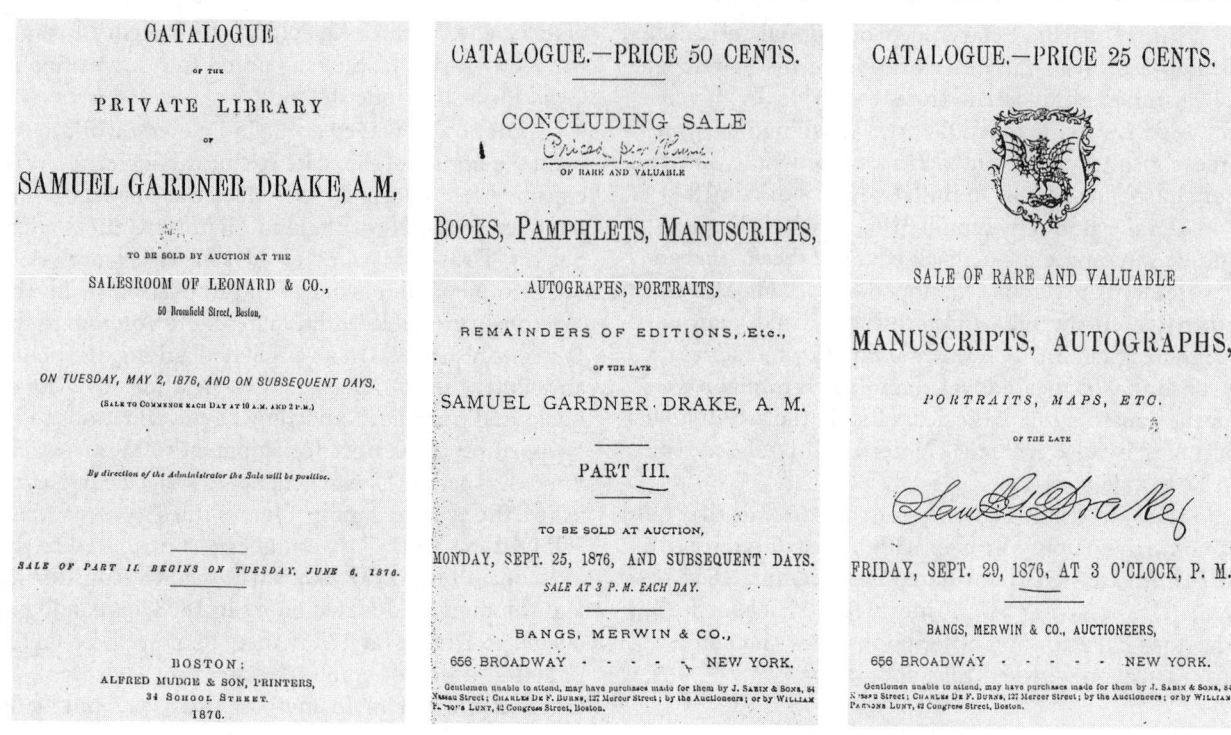

Catalogues for the sales of Drake's collection that were held after his death in June 1875

termed "many very rare" volumes; for these books and manuscripts Drake paid about £400, according to Samuel Adams Drake. He remained in England until May 1860. On his return to Boston he resumed his bookselling business. On 17 January 1861 Drake married a relative, Sarah Jane Drake. That year he moved his shop to 17 Tremont Street; in 1862 he returned to 13 Bromfield.

Drake's library continued to expand; according to Sheppard it contained "a very large collection of antique and selected works and literary relics." Sheppard further notes that "numerous visitors, some from distant parts of the country, often call either to consult him or make a purchase." According to Samuel Adams Drake, over the years these visitors included such notable scholars and collectors as Bancroft, William Hickling Prescott, George Hilliard, Samuel Prescott Hildreth, George Lunt, Orestes Augustus Brownson, Edward Everett, and Nathan Hale. Oliver Wendell Holmes, as a medical student, was also known to stop by when "searching for books on the healing art." Drake's Antiquarian Book-Store not only proved to be "the resort of men who made the literature of that day," as the younger Drake observed, but also was a training ground for future bookmen. A case in point is William Lee, whom Drake hired as an apprentice in 1837 when Lee was eleven. Lee worked for Drake from six in the morning until nine at night for a dollar a week for several years before leaving to clerk for Ol-

iver L. Perkins; soon afterward he became a book auctioneer. While at 56 Cornhill, according to John Tebbel, "Lee learned much besides the elements of bookselling from Drake." Years later Lee would become the senior partner in the publishing house of Lee and Shepard, which would number Samuel Adams Drake among the authors it published; he would spend some sixty years in the book trade.

In 1867 Drake's bookstore settled, finally, at 17 Bromfield Street. Drake devoted the last decade of his life to his histories; although he did not complete his project on New England, he wrote *Memoir of Sir Walter Ralegh* (1862) and *Annals of Witchcraft in New England, and Elsewhere in the United States, from Their First Settlement* (1869). He also reprinted Increase Mather's *A Relation of the Troubles Which Have Hapned in New-England* (1677) as *Early History of New England* (1864) and edited William Hubbard's *The History of the Indian Wars in New England* (1865) and Francis Baylies's *An Historical Memoir of the Colony of New Plymouth* (1866), adding a fifth part to the latter. During these years Drake's work continued to be based on the manuscripts and books he collected.

Drake also remained active as a book dealer. Between 1864 and June 1875—just a few days before his death—he issued seventeen detailed catalogues, totaling nearly one thousand pages, that included some of his British purchases. Drake's forty-three-page 1864 catalogue of "Rare, Useful and Curious BOOKS and

Tracts" includes a wide range of town histories and many inexpensive religious tracts and sermons; Bishop Ezra Ripley's 22 December 1819 sermon at the ordination of E. Q. Sewall at Barnstable (Cambridge, Massachusetts, 1820), which Drake priced at twenty-five cents, is typical of the latter. The 1864 catalogue also offers copies of sales catalogues of Boston private libraries, including those of Nathan Hale (1835) and Edward Augustus Crowninshied (1859), for fifty cents each. British volumes, some of them likely acquired on his trip to England, include the quarto *Tomus alter et idem or, The Historie of the Life and Reigne of That Famous Princesse, Elizabeth* (London: Printed by T. Harper, to be sold by W. Web in Oxford, 1629), Sir Thomas Browne's translation of the fourth part of William Camden's *Annales rerum Anglicarum et Hibernicarum, regnante Elizabetha, ad annum saltus M.D.LXXXIX* (1615, 1627), for three dollars; a folio original edition of Daniel Defoe's *Jure Divino: A Satyr in Twelve Books* (London, 1706) for five dollars; and Nicholas Rowe's "curious & rare book," as Drake describes the 1715 octavo edition of Rowe's translation of Claude Quillet's *Callipaedia,* for three dollars. Among the American nuggets is an unbound and uncut duodecimo edition of volume 1 of Prince's *A Chronological History of New-England in the Form of Annals* (Boston: Printed by Kneeland and Green for S. Gerrish, 1736) for five dollars.

Brinley made several purchases from Drake's catalogues. Among those in 1868 were Cotton Mather's sixteenmo blank-verse translation of the Psalms, *Psalterium Americanum* (Boston: Printed by S. Kneeland for B. Eliot, S. Gerrish, D. Henchman, and J. Edwards, 1718), for eight dollars, and Nathaniel Morton's unbound and "Somewhat imperfect" duodecimo second edition of *New-Englands Memoriall* (Boston: Printed by Nicholas Boone, 1721) for $1.25. The following year Brinley purchased Nathanael Low's *New-England Farmer's Almanack and Repository* (Boston) for 1777 to 1816 (lacking 1808 and 1815) for six dollars. The latest surviving record of a Drake-Brinley transaction is a memo on the back of Drake's letter of 19 December 1872 thanking Brinley for his "check for payment in full for Books," in which Brinley notes that the net cost was $110.00.

Drake was a member of the board of directors of the New-England Historic Genealogical Society for twenty-six years until his death, and he continued to publish in the *Register* into the 1870s. In 1874 he had his *Narrative Remarks, Expository Notes, and Historical Criticisms on the New England Historical and Genealogical Society, and Incidentally on the Massachusetts Historical Society* printed anonymously. This fifty-six-page pamphlet, as Winsor puts it, embodies "some personal grievances and notes of his career, not pleasantly expressed."

Sheppard's memoir of Drake portrays the elderly scholar in his library above the bookshop: visitors would find him seated at his desk in "a long attic chamber . . . a solitary man—arrayed in black— small in stature—but well proportioned . . . ready to lay down pen and receive the caller one or a dozen . . . answer his questions about the past—or sell him a long sought gem of antiquity." Drake made his last visit to his vast library on 8 June 1875; the seventy-six-year-old antiquarian appeared "much fatigued," according to his son Samuel Adams, who saw him "at about four o'clock in the afternoon." Earlier in the day Drake had attended the first day of the sale of Daniel Webster's library at Leonard and Company's auction in Boston, dutifully recording in what would be the last entry in a diary he had kept since 23 January 1816: "1875, June 8. At the sale of the Webster books." That night he contracted pneumonia, and on 14 June he died.

In the course of fifty years Samuel Gardner Drake distinguished himself as an antiquarian and a historian. As Drake observed of himself in 1841, in the preface to the eighth edition of *The Book of the Indians,* "The study of American History in general, and of Indian History in particular, has long been the favorite employment of many of my hours; I cannot say 'leisure hours,' for such are unknown to me; but time amidst a variety of cares and business, and before and after 'business hours.'" According to David L. Greene, "Few contemporaries below the level of a Prescott or a Parkman surpassed [Drake] in scholarly achievement." He collected and thereby preserved for posterity an important archive of American historical and genealogical material as well as magazines, almanacs, newspapers, scarce editions, maps, and manuscripts.

Less than a year after Drake's death his library, which included some 15,000 bound volumes and 30,000 pamphlets, was auctioned off. Leonard and Company held a two-part auction in Boston, each part lasting several days. The sale of part one (A through K), comprising 5,405 lots, began on 2 May 1876; part two (L through Z), comprising 5,012 lots, began on 6 June. According to the *Boston Daily Advertiser* of 3 May 1876, the books offered for sale "were mainly brought together during the last twenty years of Mr. Drake's life, and represent the breadth and scope of his personal interest in historical investigation." Three months later Bangs, Merwin and Company held two supplementary sales in New York, offering 2,533 lots of books, pamphlets, manuscripts, autographs, and portraits on 25 September and 1,014 lots of manuscripts, autographs, portraits, and maps on 29 September. This enormous collection contained some fifty-nine volumes of tracts on American history, scores of town histories, genealogies—including manuscripts by Drake—Indian studies, sermons, and works of literature. It encompassed engravings, manuscripts, autographs, and rare editions as well as many issues of newspapers and magazines from the Colonial and early Republic eras—not the least of which were the early volumes of the *American Magazine,* from its origin in Boston in 1743.

Quite a few of the works in Drake's library concerned the great voyages of discovery; among the rarest was the First Folio edition of Richard Hakluyt's *The Principall Navigations, Voiages and Discoveries of the English Nation* (London: Printed by George Bishop and Ralph Newberie, 1589), printed in black letter, and an extra-fine copy of the 1598–1600 edition (London: Printed by George Bishop, Ralph Newberie, and Robert Barker). Other nuggets were *Sir Francis Drake Revived,* edited by "R. D." (London: Nicholas Bourne, 1653 [i.e., 1652]), its flyleaves and margins filled with Drake's extensive notes—a practice that is evident in thousands of the volumes in his library; Lewes Roberts's folio *The Merchants Mappe of Commerce* (London: R. Mabb, 1638) with a map of New England; and Louis Hennepin's *A New Discovery of a Vast Country in America* (London: Printed for M. Bentley, Jacob Tonson, H. Bonwick, T. Goodwin, and S. Manship, 1698) with several maps—a book that includes the first written descriptions of Niagara Falls.

Other noteworthy volumes in Drake's library were several editions of Francis Bacon's essays; Nathan Bailey's *Dictionarium Britannicum* (London: Printed for T. Cox, 1730); scarce editions of essays by the philosopher George Berkeley; and some five hundred volumes of American poetry, including works by Edgar Allan Poe, Philip Freneau, Henry Wadsworth Longfellow, and William Cullen Bryant. Also auctioned in 1876 were a very rare edition of Patrick Campbell's *Travels in the Interior Inhabited Parts of North America in the Years 1791 and 1792* (Edinburgh: Printed for the author and sold by J. Guthrie, 1793) and a copy of "the first Western book of local history printed," Daniel Drake's *Natural and Statistical View, or Picture of Cincinnati and the Miami County* (Cincinnati: Printed by Looker and Wallace, 1815).

Bookman to the end, Drake had purchased several books at the Webster sale he had attended on what turned out to be his last active day as a collector. These volumes, too, were auctioned in 1876 and included Adam Anderson's *Historical and Chronological Deduction of the Origins of Commerce* (Dublin: Printed by P. B. Byrne, 1790) and Joseph Blunt's work on Indian tribes, *A Historical Sketch of the Formation of the Confederation* (New York: G. and C. Carvill, 1825). Among the many sermons and religious tracts in the collection,

works by Jonathan Edwards, John Cotton, and William Ellery Channing were well represented; also present were thirty-five lots of works by Cotton Mather and twenty-two lots of works by Increase Mather, including a sixty-page manuscript for Increase's *Cases of Conscience Concerning Evil Spirits Personating Men, Witchcraft, Infallible Proofs of Guilt in Such as Are Accused of That Crime* (Boston: Printed and sold by Benjamin Harris, 1692), twelve pages of which are in his hand. Another manuscript, also dealing with witchcraft, which Drake used in the preparation of his own publication on the topic, is the fifty-three-page "Examination of Hugh Parsons" (1650–1651), signed by William Pynchon, before whom Parsons appeared after being charged by his wife with witchcraft.

The vast collection of autographed letters and documents had as one of its rarest items a full-page letter from 1631 in the hand of William Bradford, governor of Plymouth Colony, which also bears the signatures of Myles Standish and John Alden. Documents signed by Massachusetts colonial governor John Endicott (1647) and William Penn (1681), as well as letters and official declarations signed by John Hancock, Samuel Adams, Royal Tyler, John Eliot, Thomas Jefferson, and John Quincy Adams, were also included.

Yet, Cannon observes, despite all this "rare game," sales totaled only $13,500. "This disappointing result was doubtless due to the crowding in of unimportant items until the prices of the better pieces were dragged down to their level." Thus, while several series of minor early American pamphlets, averaging two hundred items in each lot, went for as little as one, two and one-half, or three cents, an edition as valuable as Samuel Penhallow's *The History of the Wars of New-England with the Eastern Indians* (Boston: Printed by T. Fleet for S. Gerrish, 1726) brought only $8.25. Other unusually low prices fetched were $6.00 for a folio edition of Iodocus Hondy's *Historia Mundi: or Mercator's Atlas* (London: Printed by T. Cotes for Michael Sparke, 1635) in which Drake had inserted an impression of Capt. John Smith's map of 1614 and only $3.12 for one of the oldest volumes in the library, a Spanish-language quarto edition of Pedro Apiano's *Libro dela Casmographia* (Basilea: Gregorio Bonio, 1548). Among the highest book prices realized at the sale were $20.50 for Hubbard's *The Present State of New-England* (London: Printed for Thomas Parkhurst, 1677) with folding map and $41.00 and $41.75, respectively, for the two Hakluyts.

Late in his life Drake had often expressed his desire that his library not be dispersed—that it "should go to some institution, and be kept together," as he wrote in his catalogue of November 1870. He amplified this hope in a letter to Brinley, dated 19 December 1872: "Should you meet with any one who has a desire to erect an *everlasting* monument to his memory, by founding a library, please say to him mine is in the market." He pursued this theme in a letter to Draper, dated 9 May 1873:

> I doubt not there are many men who would seize upon the chance to secure the library, could they but know but half its value. I have proposed to give *two thousand* dollars from a fair valuation on the condition that it be kept together, &c.

While part of Drake's library was dispersed, his hope was realized to a degree by the California book collector Hubert Howe Bancroft. In his memoir, *Literary Industries* (1890), Bancroft numbers the auction of the library "of S. G. Drake of Boston in May and June, 1876" among the many sales "from each of which I secured something." Bancroft's Drake books were incorporated into what is now the Bancroft Library at the University of California, Berkeley.

In 1897 Samuel Adams Drake, using "a mass of materials in manuscript" that his father had gathered, along with other contemporary accounts, published *The Border Wars of New England*. The book had been, the younger Drake wrote, "a favorite project of my father" that he "did not live to see realized." On 7 May 1907, nearly a year and a half after the death of Samuel Adams Drake, a final auction was held in Boston by C. F. Libbie and Company to sell 2,096 lots of books, manuscripts, and broadsides that had belonged to him and his father, Samuel Gardner Drake.

References:

Hubert Howe Bancroft, *Literary Industries* (San Francisco: History, 1890);

Catalogue of the Private Library of Samuel Gardner Drake, A.M. (Boston: Mudge, 1876)—includes "Samuel Gardner Drake: His Life-Work and His Library," by Samuel Adams Drake, pp. iii–x;

Samuel Adams Drake, *The Border Wars of New England, Commonly Called King William's and Queen Anne's Wars* (New York: Scribners, 1897);

Luther Farnham, *A Glance at Private Libraries* (Boston: Press of Crocker & Brewster, 1855); republished, with an introduction and annotated index by Roger E. Stoddard (Weston, Mass.: M & S Press, 1991), pp. 52–53, 86;

Thomas W. Field, *An Essay towards an Indian Bibliography* (New York: Scribners, Armstrong, 1873), pp. 107–108;

David L. Greene, "Samuel G. Drake and the Early Years of The New England Historical and Genealogical Register, 1847–1861," *New England Historical and Genealogical Register,* 145 (1991): 203–233;

Waldo Lincoln, ed., *Proceedings of the American Antiquarian Society, 1812–1849* (Worcester, Mass.: Published by the Society, 1912), pp. 301, 550;

Joel Munsell, *Bibliotheca Munselliana: A Catalogue of the Books and Pamphlets Issued from the Press of Joel Munsell from the Year 1828 to 1870* (Albany, N.Y.: Privately printed, 1872; reprinted, New York: Burt Franklin, 1969);

Joseph Sabin, *A Dictionary of Books Relating to America,* volume 5 (Amsterdam: Israel, 1961), pp. xlix, 526–530;

John H. Sheppard, *Memoir of Samuel Gardner Drake, A.M.* (Albany: Printed by J. Munsell, 1863);

Henry Stevens, *Recollections of James Lenox and the Formation of His Library,* revised by Victor Hugo Paltsits (New York: New York Public Library, 1951), pp. 64, 88–89, 91;

John Tebbel, *A History of Book Publishing in the United States,* volume 1 (New York: R. R. Bowker, 1972), p. 419;

William B. Trask, "Samuel Gardner Drake, A.M.," *Potter's American Monthly,* 5 (October 1875): 729–732;

Alice Smith Thompson, *The Drake Family of New Hampshire* (Concord: New Hampshire Historical Society, 1962).

Papers:

The New-England Historic and Genealogical Society has the 1,087-page manuscript draft of Drake's *The Book of the Indians;* some proof sheets from the 1832, first edition of *Indian Biography;* and letters, including correspondence in the Henry Bond Papers. Other letters and papers are scattered among several collections, including the George Brinley Papers at the University of Michigan, Ann Arbor; the Lyman Copeland Draper Papers at the State Historical Society of Wisconsin; and the Edmund Bailey O'Callaghan Papers at the Library of Congress. Two folders of Drake papers, including his corrected handwritten draft of a book review, notes, letters, and a compilation of notes on Boston printers and publishers from 1640 to 1800, are at the American Antiquarian Society in Worcester, Massachusetts.

Nicholas Gouin Dufief

(1776 – 11 April 1834)

Madeleine B. Stern

Leona Rostenberg and Madeleine Stern—Rare Books

BOOKS: *Nature Displayed, In Her Mode of Teaching Language To Man; or, A New And Infallible Method of Acquiring a Language in the Shortest Time Possible, Deduced from the Analysis of the Human Mind, And, Consequently Suited To Every Capacity. Adapted To The French,* 2 volumes (volume 1, Philadelphia: Printed by Thomas L. Plowman for the author, 1804; volume 2, Philadelphia: Printed by Thomas S. Manning for the author, 1804; second edition, enlarged, Philadelphia: Printed at the Press of J. Watts for the author, 1806; London: Printed for the author, 1818);

The Logic of Facts; or, The Conduct of Wm. Rawle, Esq. Attorney at Law, Towards N. G. Dufief (Philadelphia: Printed by A. Dickinson for the author, 1806);

A New Universal and Pronouncing Dictionary of the French and English Languages, 3 volumes (Philadelphia: Printed by T. & G. Palmer, 1810); republished in 1 volume as *A Universal, Pronouncing and Critical French-English Dictionary* (London: Allard, 1833);

Nature Displayed in her mode of teaching language to man: or, a new and infallible method of acquiring a language . . . adapted to the Spanish, by Don Manuel de Torres and L. Hargous, 2 volumes (volume 1, Philadelphia: Printed by T. & G. Palmer, 1811; volume 2, Philadelphia: Printed by T. L. Plowman, 1811; London, 1817);

Universal Book-Store. No. 118, Chesnut-Street, Corner of Carpenter's Court, leading to the Bank of the United States; Philadelphia. N. G. Dufief's Catalogue For 1819, of a Very Extensive Collection of New and Second Hand, Scarce and Valuable Books, (Ancient and Modern Authors) in Arts, Sciences, and Literature. In About Thirty Different Languages (Philadelphia, 1819).

Nicholas Gouin Dufief, Franco-American bookseller in Philadelphia during the late eighteenth and early nineteenth centuries, helped increase Franco-American understanding during a critical

Nicholas Gouin Dufief (engraving by David Edwin, after a portrait by Peter J. Meance)

period of history by teaching French and by selling French books. As a bookseller he numbered among his customers one of the first American collectors of rare books, William Mackenzie, as well as Thomas Jefferson, for whom he supplied many desiderata and with whom he carried on an extensive bibliophilic correspondence. Great books and great libraries passed through his hands, including the remnants of Benjamin Franklin's library and of the Westover (Virginia) library of William Byrd I and William Byrd II. Dufief thus helped alert an American readership to the intellectual value of antiquarian books, especially those in the French language.

Dufief, son of royalists and counterrevolutionaries Nicolas-Henri Dufief and Victoire-Aimée-Libault-Gouin Dufief, was born sometime in 1776 in Nantes, France. He inherited his parents' monarchist leanings, and at age sixteen he volunteered for the Corps de la Marine Royale at Enghein under Jean Charles, Comte d'Hector. Dufief's background was less literary than military.

By 1793 the royalist cause was lost, and the Dufief family, suffering severe deprivations, was scattered. Dufief, age seventeen, sailed first to England and then to the West Indies. After the insurrection in Santo Domingo in 1793 he moved with other émigrés to Philadelphia, where his interest in bookish matters manifested itself.

Young Dufief promptly purchased books and arranged for lessons in English, but the yellow-fever epidemic thwarted his plans, and he moved to Princeton, New Jersey. Remaining there for eight months, he taught himself English and developed the innovative language techniques that he later described as the method of nature, a method that eschewed grammatical rules and advocated the study of phrases and sentences rather than of single words. Before becoming a full-scale bookseller, Dufief taught French and subsequently compiled language texts that he sold to his students. Thus his pioneer work in modern French instruction was a stepping-stone to his career in bookselling.

By 1795 Dufief was back in Philadelphia. At this time he supervised an English-language edition of the *General View or Abstract of the Arts and Sciences* by his compatriot the Philadelphia bookseller Merédic Louis Elie Moreau de Saint-Méry (Philadelphia, 1797). He also announced but never published a "French Grammatical Companion; or Concise and Easy Practical Grammar of the French Tongue." In the *Aurora General Advertiser* of 15 November 1798 Dufief advertised a "day and evening school" at 63 South Second Street, where private tuition in French and translations were available. His teaching was by the conversation method, upholding the genius rather than the grammar of the language. Teaching was soon combined with bookselling. On 8 April 1799 Dufief gave notice in the *Aurora* that he had for sale "an assortment of some of the best French writers and a variety of other books in his line." By then he was at a new location, on Fifth Street between Chesnut and Market, where he combined his dual professions of language instruction and bookselling. In June of the same year he successfully petitioned for naturalization as an American citizen.

From the time of his naturalization Dufief coupled teaching with bookselling. It was a natural step from giving instruction in French to selling books to his pupils, and as his reputation advanced he widened his market to include the general public. With the new century Dufief announced that he had begun compilation of a text embodying nature's method of teaching language, and by that time he

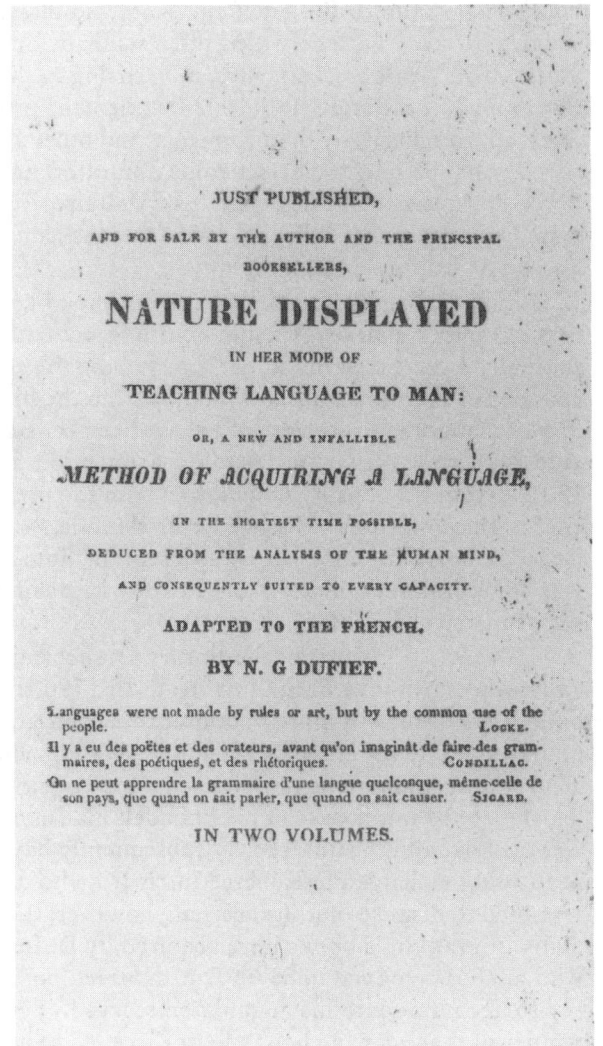

Title page for Dufief's first textbook, which sets forth his method of language instruction

had met Jefferson in Philadelphia. Jefferson, who was then vice president of the United States, was also a Francophile and a collector who soon became one of Dufief's most important customers. The stage was set for an influential career in bookselling.

Dufief's advertisements in the 1801 issues of the *Aurora* indicate that he already had a stock that could whet the appetites of book lovers, especially those with Gallic tastes. He offered "an assortment of the best French writers, and books for the use of the English and French schools" (2 April), "Books In Various Languages" (8 April), and "an Interesting and Valuable Collection of French Books" (14 May), including works by Honoré Riqueti, Marquis de Mirabeau; Jean François de La Croix; Jacques-Henri Bernardin de Saint-Pierre; and Bertrand de Moleville. In the aftermath of the French Revolution there was a strong American market for French books, especially in Philadelphia, where so many émigrés flocked. To satisfy their interests Dufief imported from dealers' catalogues, advertising in the *Aurora* on 25 June and 1 July 1802 that he had "just received from Paris, by the Tryphenia, and other arrivals, a handsome and select collection of French Books," among them the writings of Voltaire, Etienne Bonnot de Condillac, Comte Georges-Louis Leclerc de Buffon, and Montesquieu.

In 1801 Dufief—then operating his book business at Voltaire's Head, 68 South Fourth Street—substantially augmented his stock by acquiring the remainder of Franklin's library. Judging from the history of that library, it seems not to have been considered an extraordinarily desirable acquisition in 1801, except perhaps by Dufief, to whom the presence in the collection of French books doubtless appealed. Competition for what was left of the library was comparatively meager, and in 1801 it became the property of Dufief.

The early history of the library is uncertain and conjectural. On Franklin's death in 1790 the bulk of his library of more than four thousand volumes was left to his grandson Temple Franklin, who went to England and never returned. He may have left the books in the care of his Philadelphia friend George Fox, and the library may subsequently have been sold or pledged to Robert Morris Jr., who determined to dispose of it. It is certain, however, that many of Franklin's books were acquired by Dufief, who in 1801 removed to South Fourth Street, possibly to accommodate his augmented stock. In September of that year the bookseller proceeded to advertise the Franklin library both publicly and privately, and the *Aurora* of 14 September 1801 carried the following notice:

> G. Dufief, Bookseller Voltaire's Head, No. 68 South Fourth street Has the honor of informing the Lovers of Literature, that he has just added to his numerous collection of Books in various languages, a considerable part of the select and valuable Library of the celebrated Philosopher and statesman, the late Dr. B. Franklin.... He continues, as usual, to purchase, exchange, or sell on commission, libraries, or parcels of books.

The notice was repeated in October, and at the same time (22 October 1801) Dufief informed Thomas Jefferson of the acquisition: "I have recently added to my Collection the portion of B. Franklin's library left by him to his grandson Temple Franklin." The bookseller listed several available titles from which Jefferson selected a twenty-four-volume Parliamentary history priced at thirty dollars, which was shipped to him aboard the sloop *Highland*.

In September 1801 John Vaughan, as treasurer, authorized a purchase by the American Philosophical Society of a small collection of books from the Franklin library, including works by the Italian jurist Cesare Beccaria and the Puritan divine Cotton Mather as well as forty-six volumes of the *Philosophical Transactions* of the Royal Society (London, 1665–) and Thomas Birch's *History of the Royal Society* (London: Printed for Andrew Millar, 1756–1757). During the following months the American Philosophical Society added several other items to their purchases, among them the *Transactions of the American Philosophical Society* (Philadelphia, 1771–), in twelve volumes, and the *Oeuvres* (Paris: Ruault, 1777) of Bernard Palissy. In December 1801, through librarian Zachariah Poulson Jr., the Library Company of Philadelphia purchased from Dufief's Franklin stock fifty-one volumes of seventeenth- and early eighteenth-century tracts.

The unsold remnants from Franklin's library were perhaps more noteworthy than the items sold. Volumes of pre-Revolutionary tracts with notes in Franklin's hand remained undisturbed, and as late as 9 November 1802 Dufief informed Jefferson that William Duane, editor of the *Aurora,* had exhibited interest in an en bloc purchase of some two thousand volumes that "remain from Dr. Franklin's library . . . some containing marginal notes in the Dr.'s hand." That sale never materialized.

Next Dufief conceived a grandiose project to dispose of his Franklin collection, the sale of the whole to the Library of Congress. On 31 January 1803 he outlined his plan and purpose to President Thomas Jefferson, enlisting his support and intercession:

> I send you the catalogue of books remaining to me from the Library of Dr. Franklin. When you have looked it over, I beg you to deliver it to the Librarian of Congress to whom I propose, in the belief that he would be so authorized to make the purchase of the collection en bloc or in part....
>
> What worthier use for that money [allocated by Congress for the purchase of a library], Sir, than to use it to rescue the books of one of the founders of the American Republic and of a great man! It is not a spirit of speculation that makes me use this language for outside of the fact that these books belong in a national library, being in large part on the *politics,* the *legislation* and the affairs of *America,* I would dispose of them at a price so reasonable, that one could never accuse me of such a thing.

Jefferson acted with alacrity but without success. He selected a few books for his own library: the Venice 1556 edition of the *Dipnosophistarvm* . . . *Libri XV* of Athenaeus, published by A. Arrivabenus; Charles Blount's version of *The Two First Books of Philostratus* (London: Printed for Nathaniel Thompson, 1680), priced at one dollar; and William Derham's *Physico and Astro theology* (London: Printed at the Logographic Press, 1786). Those works were shipped by the bookseller aboard the sloop *Harmony* and bound for Jefferson by John March of Georgetown. In addition Jefferson informed the chairman of the congressional library committee of Dufief's proposal. The response was negative—the committee's funds were already exhausted.

Dufief was forced to turn reluctantly to his last alternative: disposal—and dispersal—of the collection of some two thousand volumes at auction. Accordingly, the *Aurora General Advertiser* of 23 February 1803 carried the following notice under the heading "Dr. Franklin's Library":

> Will be sold by public auction at Shannon & Poalk's auction store, on Saturday, the 12th. of March next, at 6 o'clock in the evening, unless previously disposed of by private sale, a great part of the library of the celebrated Dr. Benjamin Franklin.
>
> Persons desirous to purchase, or to become acquainted with such books as may be contained in so rare and valuable a collection as that of the abovementioned immortal statesman and philosopher, are invited to call on N. G. Dufief, No. 6, South Fourth-street—where also the amateurs of French literature may be gratuitously supplied with catalogues of a large and late importation of new French publications.

On 7 March the notice was enlarged to describe the collection more fully:

> This collection, besides a variety of excellent and scarce works in *English, French, Italian, German, Greek, Latin, &c.,* contains several manuscripts, all of which will be sold without reserve. It may with propriety be observed, that there never was yet sold at *public sale* the library of a man so illustrious, both in the annals of America and in those of the Arts and Sciences, which he so much aggrandized.... Every information concerning the ... library, will with pleasure be given by the proprietor at No. 6 south Fourth street—catalogues may be obtained the day before the sale, at the bookstores of Messrs. Carey, S. Bradford, Duane, P. Byrne, and Conrad.

On 12 March 1803 the remainder of Franklin's library was dispersed at public auction. Some of the items were sold to editor William Duane and to John Vaughan for the American Philosophical Society. Most of the lots were scattered and became untraceable. The catalogue of the library has never surfaced.

Dufief had been unable to sell Franklin's library on his own, but he had not overestimated its worth. Rather he had overestimated the contempo-

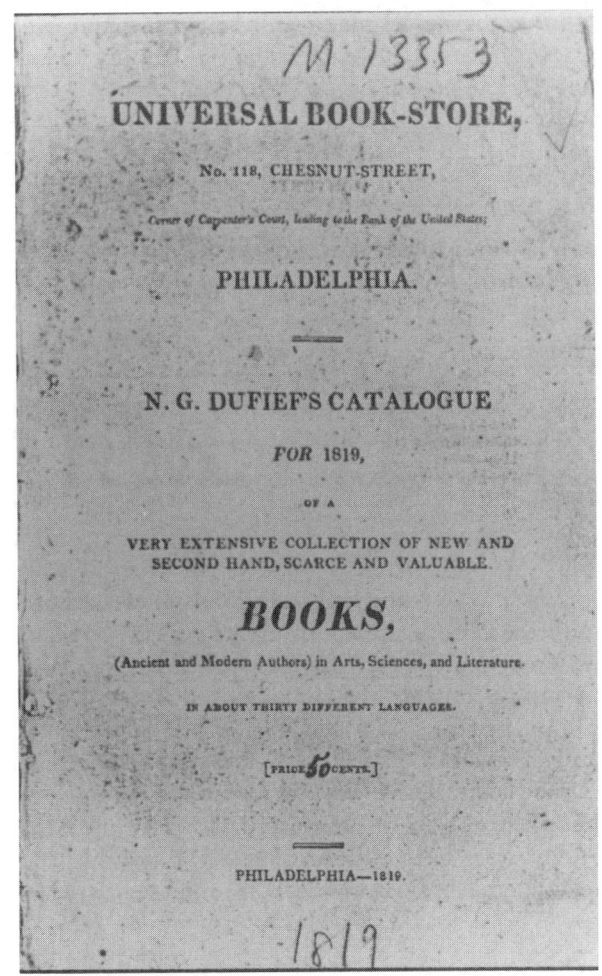

Title page for Dufief's most extensive catalogue of the books for sale in his Philadelphia bookstore

rary market. Not yet thirty, comparatively new to the bookselling trade, he had evinced the taste for and appreciation of books and their provenance essential in bibliophiles. These attributes served him well in his future bibliopolic enterprises.

In July 1803, shortly after the Franklin auction, Dufief visited New York City. His dual interest in language instruction and bookselling made him a welcome browser in the literary rooms of his New York colleague and compatriot Hocquet Caritat. There Dufief wrote the prospectus for his *Nature Displayed, In Her Mode of Teaching Language To Man; ... Adapted To The French,* which appeared in two volumes in 1804, a second enlarged edition following in 1806. Subscribers to the work included his Philadelphia colleague Mathew Carey as well as book collectors Mackenzie, Jefferson, and Vaughan. *Nature Displayed* also triggered a charge of plagiarism from a leading citizen of Philadelphia, William Rawle. Dufief replied with a defensive pamphlet, *The Logic of Facts* (1806).

At the same time that Dufief was seeking buyers for Franklin's library he was helping to sell books from another great collection. The Westover library, which Edwin Wolf II has called "a shining outpost of European culture on the American frontier," was begun by the merchant William Byrd I of Westover, Virginia (who died in 1704), was expanded by his son William Byrd II, and was catalogued and sold after the suicide of the third William Byrd in 1777. The manuscript "Catalogue of Books in the Library at Westover; Belonging to William Byrd, Esqr.," prepared by John Stretch, lists more than twenty-three hundred titles. Around 1778 Isaac Zane Jr., a Virginia land speculator and business associate of John Pemberton, bought the entire library for £2,000. Three years later the books were shipped to Philadelphia, and in 1781 and 1782 Robert Bell auctioned about half. The remainder was turned over to bookseller-stationer William Pritchard, who—over the next ten years or so—sold some of them from his shop. In 1791 Pemberton attempted, without much success, to dispose of the rest. Both Zane and Pemberton died in 1795, and five years later the Zane sisters gave away some of the remaining volumes and consigned the rest to booksellers.

In October 1801 Dufief paid $100 for the privilege of handling a large portion of the remainder of the Westover library. The Westover books apparently became part of Dufief's stock and were sold at intervals in the course of his career. For example, the American Philosophical Society bought nineteen volumes of the *Philosophical Transactions of the Royal Society of London* and the *Vocabolario degli Accademici della Crvsca,* a dictionary first published in Venice by G. Alberti in 1612. Mackenzie bought "The Catalogue of Books in the Library at Westover" and eventually bequeathed it to the Library Company of Philadelphia. A ten-volume Roman history by Livy (Utrecht, 1710) went to Thomas Jefferson in 1813.

The relationship between Dufief and Jefferson provides fascinating insight into bookselling operations during the early nineteenth century. Jefferson was Dufief's customer for twenty years, and their transactions are recorded in their correspondence. Dufief helped Jefferson build his second and greatest personal library (sold in 1815 to Congress) as well as the third collection Jefferson amassed in his later years. More than one hundred letters were exchanged between Dufief and Jefferson, Jefferson's in English, Dufief's—frequently signed "très-dévoué serviteur"—in French.

The sage of Monticello appreciated Dufief both as compiler of language texts and as bookseller, describing him as "the best person you can apply to for any French books you may want." Jefferson's requests were not confined to French books; his demands reflect the catholicity of his tastes and interests, as he sought "the favor of Mr. Dufief" in supplying a mathematical work by Thomas Simpson on fluxions or a Latin edition of Tacitus. A short desiderata list of 1813 included Arthur Young's experiments in agriculture, the memoirs of the English cleric and antiquarian Theophilus Lindsey, and Jeremiah Whitaker Newman's *The Lounger's Common-place Book* (first published, London: Printed for the author, 1792). Some of Jefferson's demands taxed the ingenuity of the bookseller. On 14 December 1816 he requested "an English bible, whose printed page shall be as nearly as you can find one of the size of the paper inclosed, and whose type shall be of such size as that the number of pages shall correspond with the numbers . . . on the same paper, as nearly as you can find one."

Dufief searched out Jefferson's desiderata from various sources: his own stock, other Philadelphia bookstores, catalogues from France. He sent the collector lists of his new acquisitions, and wherever possible he seems to have tried to cut prices. In addition he acted as literary adviser to Jefferson regarding forthcoming publications. Over the years Dufief served his Monticello correspondent not only as bookseller but also as local postal agent, fund distributor, or paymaster.

One of Dufief's services for Jefferson involved the bookseller in problems of censorship. Jefferson subscribed for Regnault de Bécourt's *La Création du Monde, ou Système d'Organisation Primitive* (Philadelphia: Printed by A. J. Blocquerst, 1813), and Dufief made payment from Jefferson's funds. When the author of that work was prosecuted for his religious and philosophical doctrine, Dufief found himself "innocently implicated" and asked that Jefferson clear up the matter. Jefferson's reply of 19 April 1814 was a ringing defense of freedom: "I am really mortified to be told that, *in the United States of America,* a fact like this can become a subject of enquiry, and of criminal enquiry too, as an offence against religion: that a question about the sale of a book can be carried before the civil magistrate. is this then our freedom of religion? and are we to have a Censor whose imprimatur shall say what books may be sold, and what we may buy?"

Jefferson encouraged Dufief as his bookselling expanded. On 9 August 1811 Dufief had informed Jefferson: "I propose, within a short time, . . . [to open] a French and English, Spanish, etc., book and stationery store. I flatter myself that through my connections in the United States and Europe I can assemble all the curious

Inscription in the copy of Nature Displayed *that Dufief presented to Charles X*
of France (Henry E. Huntington Library and Art Gallery)

and sought-for works in all subjects, and I dare to hope, Sir, that you will continue to honor me with your orders and that you will recommend me to those of your friends to whom I could be useful." In the *Aurora* of 26 February 1812 he announced "A New And Highly Useful Establishment" to be known as "The Repository, For the Sale and Purchase of Scarce and Valuable Books . . . in all languages." There he would "promote that laudable ambition in young persons for acquiring knowledge . . . by enabling them to obtain such Books as are necessary, at a price *considerably* below that of similar new productions; and those . . . desirous to instruct themselves, shall be directed in the selec-

tion of . . . works." "This establishment," he added, "holds out peculiar encouragement to the owners of Libraries or parcels of Books, (in good order) which may . . . be converted into cash, without resorting to the hopeless expedient of sacrificing them at auction."

The acquisition of books was not easy. In 1808 Napoleon's Bayonne Decree authorized seizure of American vessels in French ports. As late as 1811 the bookseller warned Jefferson of the difficulties involved. From the time of the Alien and Sedition Acts of 1798 until long after the War of 1812, however, Dufief's business survived, struggling during periods of conflict and hostility, profiting from improved Franco-American relations. In addition to his French speciality he sought books in other languages, supplying works for the private collectors Mackenzie, Duane, and David Bailie Warden, and for the librarians Zachariah Poulson Jr. of the Library Company and John Vaughan of the American Philosophical Society. In addition Dufief provided books for churches, public seminaries, public libraries, and private families.

Dufief's expanded interests are reflected in the renaming of his establishment. In 1818 he dubbed his shop at 118 Chesnut Street the Universal Book-Store. A "Universal Literary Repository," it was described by its proprietor in the *Aurora* of 15 September 1818 as "the largest and most extensive Repository of Books, in every department of Science, Literature, Arts, &c. in more than *twenty different languages,* than has before existed in the United States; and, for variety, is exceeded by very few in Europe.... In addition to their former stock, nearly 6000 volumes have been received by late arrivals, and 800 more are daily expected from Europe; ... Many of these are scarce works in Hebrew, Greek, Latin, Italian, Spanish, German, and French Literature and Theology ... many ... out of print."

By 1818 the Dufief firm had also begun the practice of inserting lists of selected stock in the pages of the *Aurora.* Those lists, reflecting the influx of books from abroad, include not only works by seventeenth- and eighteenth-century French authors–Jean Racine, Molière, Pierre Charron, Voltaire, Condillac, Crébillon–but also an assortment of early rare books such as a 1505 Saint Augustine and an *Imitation of Christ* by Thomas à Kempis bound in red morocco.

In 1819 such lists were climaxed by a monumental catalogue: *Universal Book-Store. No. 118, Chesnut-Street, Corner of Carpenter's Court, leading to the Bank of the United States; Philadelphia. N. G. Dufief's Catalogue For 1819, of a Very Extensive Collection of New and Second Hand, Scarce and Valuable Books, (Ancient and Modern Authors) in Arts, Sciences, and Literature. In About Thirty Different Languages.* "Most of the Books," he stated, "have been selected by himself, in Europe, with much care, at an auspicious period–auspicious, because of events, which may not again occur, that threw into circulation a multitude of works heretofore locked up in princely or public libraries, copies of which had long since ceased to be in the market." The catalogue reflects the bookseller's interest in rare and early printed books and their provenance–including, for example, a Greek Bible printed at the Cambridge University Press in 1665, formerly in the Colbertine Library, assembled by Jean-Baptiste Colbert, chief minister of Louis XIV

of France, and thrown into the market by "the vortex of the revolution." Books from the libraries of the celebrated French chemist Antoine-François de Fourcroy and the French peer Marie-Gabriel-Auguste Florent, Comte de Choiseul-Gouffier, were also listed. The proprietor boasted:

> This Catalogue contains, perhaps, the best selection of scarce and valuable works, in various languages, ever offered to the American Public.... Here may the Theologian, the Historian, the Politician, the Linguist, the man of Science or of Taste, embrace a wider range, at one view, than has ever before in this country been presented for sale.

In this ambitious 195-page catalogue the expanded range of Dufief's specialties is reflected. Eighteenth-century French works are still much in evidence (Jean-Jacques Rousseau, Mirabeau, Jacques-Pierre Brissot de Warville, Moreau de Saint-Méry), but rare books, some dating from the Renaissance, are also present, and Dufief's descriptions of them are quotable. A Greek Bible printed by Aldus Manutius at Venice is listed with Dufief's estimate of its publisher: "His reputation was such, that whatever was finely printed, was said, proverbially, to come from his press"; Dufief's catalogue also includes an Appianus printed in 1551 by Charles Estienne, who, according to Dufief, "died at Paris in 1564, leaving behind him a very learned daughter." A Greek and Latin lexicon prepared and published by Henri Estienne in Geneva in 1572 was purchased by Thomas Jefferson. Among early Italian literary works the bookseller offered a 1582 Petrarch described as "a very rare edition, and much sought after by the curious." Political pamphlets, Americana, and science were also well represented.

Dufief's comments on his books are often as interesting as the books themselves. Barthélemy d'Herbelot, whose *Bibliothèque Orientale* (first published, Paris: Compagnie des libraires, 1697) was listed, "was caressed by the literati of Europe, the ministers and princes of Italy and France." A Joseph Scaliger *Opera* was described as "Without title: very rare." From the viewpoint of twentieth-century bibliographical description, the entries are far from complete. Although place and date of publication are usually included, imprints are seldom cited fully. The titles are alphabetically arranged but unnumbered. Condition is frequently noted, but not a single price is indicated–a factor that evoked Jefferson's objection in an 11 April 1819 letter to John Laval: "It is a pity the prices of the books had not been printed. We are afraid to call for a book on seeing its title only, as books as well as other things have limits to their value beyond which we would not go."

By the time Dufief's 1819 catalogue appeared, he was in Europe, and his Universal Book Store was managed by his friend and associate John Laval. Dufief's 7 April 1817 passport application describes him: "height 5-7½, complexion light, with light brown hair and blue eyes, no scars or moles noted." In England and France, Dufief selected books for export to America, many of which were offered in his 1819 catalogue. As Laval wrote to Jefferson on 23 December 1818: "Mr. Dufief . . . has sent, from England & France, a large assortment of books in different languages & branches of literature, & amongst them, a considerable number of rare & Valuable Works, Some out of Print."

During Dufief's sojourn abroad, while he was buying on a grand scale and sending back an influx of stock, Laval conducted the business at home until his death in 1839. Laval also took Dufief's place as Jefferson's local book agent and correspondent, suggesting to the collector on 16 April 1823 that "any books that may be wanted for the Library of the University of Virginia, I will procure at the lowest commission & on the most moderate terms that can be obtained."

The last Philadelphia directory listing for Dufief appeared in 1828. Between that year and his death in 1834 he doubtless continued to ship books to his associate Laval for the shelves of the Universal Book Store. In addition, while abroad, Dufief presented an inscribed copy of a British edition of his *Nature Displayed in her mode of teaching language to man* (London: Printed for the author, 1828), elaborately bound by the great British bookbinder Charles Lewis, to Charles X of France. Another presentation copy—*A Universal, Pronouncing and Critical French-English Dictionary* (London: Allard, 1833)—went to Charles Lane, the connection between Dufief and Lane based on a shared interest in language pedagogy.

Dufief died on 11 April 1834 in Pentonville, near London, leaving his "literary property" to his executrix, Elizabeth Clarke of London, who had shown him kind attention during his last illness. His will was witnessed by Charles Lane.

A major bookseller, Dufief bought and sold notable books and libraries and served as book agent to a great American president. Through the works that passed through his hands, as well as through his innovations in language instruction, he increased Franco-American understanding. Moreover, during the late eighteenth and early nineteenth centuries he helped quicken an interest in antiquarian books in the United States and played a pivotal role in their distribution to collectors and libraries, including the Library of Congress.

Biography:

Madeleine B. Stern, *Nicholas Gouin Dufief of Philadelphia: Franco-American Bookseller, 1776–1834* (Philadelphia: Philobiblon Club, 1988).

References:

E. Millicent Sowerby, *Catalogue of the Library of Thomas Jefferson* (Washington, D.C.: Library of Congress, 1959);

Edwin Wolf II, "The Dispersal of the Library of William Byrd of Westover," *Proceedings of the American Antiquarian Society,* 68 (1958): 19–106;

Wolf, "The Reconstruction of Benjamin Franklin's Library: An Unorthodox Jigsaw Puzzle," *Papers of the Bibliographical Society of America,* 56 (1962): 1–16.

Papers:

The Dufief-Jefferson correspondence is preserved at the Library of Congress.

Charles Evans
(13 November 1850 – 8 February 1935)

Joseph Rosenblum

BOOK: *American Bibliography: A Chronological Diction-ary of All Books, Pamphlets, and Periodical Publica-tions Printed in the United States of America from the Genesis of Printing in 1639 Down to and Including the Year 1820, with Bibliographical and Biographi-cal Notes,* 12 volumes by Evans (Chicago: Pri-vately printed for the author, 1903–1934).

SELECTED PERIODICAL PUBLICATIONS-UNCOLLECTED: "The Sizes of Printed Books," *Library Journal,* 1 (1876): 58–61;
"Oaths of Allegiance in Colonial New England," *Proceedings of the American Antiquarian Society,* new series 31 (1921): 337–438.

Charles Evans contributed to American book culture in two ways. As librarian at the Indianapolis Public Library from 1872 to 1878 and from 1889 to 1892, assistant librarian at the Enoch Pratt Free Li-brary in Baltimore from 1884 to 1886, and librarian at the Chicago Historical Society from 1896 to 1901, he built, organized, and fostered the use of impor-tant collections. He was among the organizers of the American Library Association and served as its first treasurer. His bibliographic efforts were even more significant. From 1903 to 1934 he virtually single-handedly compiled, published, and even mailed the first twelve volumes of *American Bibliography,* a work that records the titles of all examples of printing in the United States from 1639 to 1820 and that Clar-ence Saunders Brigham of the American Antiquar-ian Society called "one of the greatest bibliographi-cal compilations of all time." Nearly a century after its inception, this work remains the fundamental list of early American imprints.

The second son of Charles Peter and Mary Ewing Evans, Charles Evans was born in Boston, Massachusetts, on 13 November 1850. In 1836 the Evanses had immigrated to the United States from Ireland, where they had married. After both of them died in 1859, on 13 July that year Charles was placed in the Boston Asylum and Farm School for Indigent Boys on Thompson's Island, where his

Charles Evans in 1875

older brother, Thomas John Evans, joined him the following year.

There Evans received a sound education. Classes were held from 8:30 A.M. until noon and 2:00 P.M. to 5:00 P.M. five days a week in summer and fall, with recitations in the evenings. Through the winter, classes lasted six hours during the day and another one and one-half to two hours after dark. Instruction included reading, spelling, writing, arithmetic, geography, and grammar. On Saturday evenings teachers read to the boys. Sundays included religious services and Sunday school; Sunday evenings were devoted to moral instruction. Evans learned his Bible well and used this knowledge in his study of early American title pages that included scriptural quotations.

Evans retained a lifelong fondness for and gratitude to the school. He sent an inscribed copy of each of the twelve volumes of his *American Bibliography* to the Farm School library, and he returned twice to address the students—in 1914 to celebrate the centennial celebration of the founding of the school, and in 1918 to speak at graduation exercises that year. In his 1914 speech he noted some of the qualities that he had acquired from his years at the Farm School and that he demonstrated in the decades that he spent compiling his magnum opus:

> The cardinal virtues taught at the School . . . are obedience, fidelity, individual character and industry. Possessed of these, there is nothing which may not be obtained in life. Genius is only the capacity for patient labor.

Among the managers of the Farm School was Samuel Eliot, a leading Boston educator, philanthropist, and historian as well as a trustee of the Boston Athenaeum, an association of literary men of the city. Eliot, who directed Evans's reading, encouraged diligence and high standards, and when Evans was sixteen years old, Eliot arranged for him to become assistant librarian at this institution. Evans assumed these duties on 12 June 1866.

According to Edward G. Holley, at the Athenaeum Evans met "some of the most prominent scholars, statesmen, and literary figures of the nineteenth century, including Charles Sumner, senior United States senator from Massachusetts, who became one of Evans's closest friends and for whom Evans named his third child." From Francis Parkman and John Lothrop Motley, Evans received further lessons in the patience and diligence necessary for historical research. From the librarian, William Frederick Poole, Evans learned to organize and direct a library. Poole, who was seeking to acquire Confederate imprints during Evans's tenure at the Athenaeum, also taught him the importance of building research collections and of gathering ephemera while they were still available.

William S. Fletcher, who worked under Poole at the Athenaeum at the same time as Evans and who also became a prominent librarian, said that his five years under Poole "were for me both an apprenticeship and a liberal education. Dr. Poole was everything that was kindly and stimulating, and I had no other ambition than to become like him, energetic and resourceful, able to mark out my own path guided by the light of common sense." Evans, who could have said the same, dedicated volume three of his *American Bibliography* to Poole, whom he addressed in the words that Dante speaks to his master, Virgil, in canto I of the fourteenth-century *Inferno*:

> Tu se' lo mio maestro e 'l mio autore,
>   tu se' solo colui da cu' io tolsi
>   lo bello stilo che m'ha fatto onore.
>
> (You are my teacher, and you are my author
>   You are the one alone from whom I took
>   The lovely style that has brought me honor.)

Evans called the Athenaeum "the alma mater of my bibliographical life." It served as his Yale College and his Harvard. Indeed, the Athenaeum provided Evans with a more useful education than he would have received at any college at the time, and he had access to a library better than most academic collections. In 1866 the Athenaeum owned about 100,000 volumes and 70,000 pamphlets. As Holley observes, "If Evans had purposely chosen a library in America in 1866 where he could develop strong bibliothecal tastes, he could not have chosen better than the Athenaeum."

In 1869 Poole left the Athenaeum for the Naval Academy at Annapolis and was succeeded by Charles A. Cutter. Evans and Cutter did not get along, and in 1872 Poole, who had become head of the Cincinnati Public Library and consultant to the board creating the Indianapolis Public Library, recommended Evans as head of the new institution. On 25 November 1872 Evans left the Athenaeum to assume his new post in Indiana.

Despite some local opposition to bringing in an outsider, the *Indianapolis Sentinel* for 6 February 1873 published a report that

> The library will open with over 12,000 books on the shelves, and a cursory examination of those already on hand will convince any one that the selections have been made by those who understand the needs of such an institution. Mr. Evans, the librarian, it is evident, thoroughly understands the requirements of his position, and the appearance of the library when opened to the public will testify to his ability.

John Hampden Holliday, owner of the *Indianapolis Evening News,* had opposed Evans's appointment, but on 28 March 1873 he praised Evans's arrangement of the library. Holliday became one of Evans's

The Indianapolis Public Library in 1873. Evans was the institution's first librarian.

closest friends and staunchest supporters, and his financial support helped make *American Bibliography* possible.

The library opened on 9 April 1873. It especially attracted young readers, and in recalling his youth George S. Cottman, a local Indianapolis historian, credits Evans with encouraging these patrons: "The courtesy he extended to a mere country boy, went far towards making me realize that all the wealth of the ages collected [in the library] was, in a sense, mine." By the end of the first year the library had operated, its circulation figures for patrons in Indianapolis, with a population of 65,000, ranked fifth among public libraries in the United States: 5,200 borrowers had made 101,821 withdrawals from the 14,000-volume collection. In 1876 the library ranked sixth in circulation figures among the public collections in the nation, and a writer in the *Indianapolis Sentinel* for 2 January 1876 credited the librarian for the success of the library and commented that Evans's

> courtesy, patience, and kindness in assisting teachers, authors, reporters and others seeking information is unlimited, [his] taste in selecting is discriminating and admirable, and [his] management of everything pertaining to the library is most excellent. To him and his courte-

ous assistants . . . the thanks of the public and of the writer are many times due.

By April 1876 the size of the collection at the Indianapolis Public Library had doubled, totaling 27,290 volumes and 2,241 pamphlets. Almost all of these were read; in 1877–1878 more than 25,000 titles circulated.

Evans defended the purchase of fiction to meet his patrons' needs, but he also sought to imitate the Boston Athenaeum in building a research collection. One of his early purchases was a rare pamphlet on the history of Vincennes, Indiana. He subscribed to all the local newspapers not only to provide current reading matter but also to build an archive for future research into local history. In his *First Annual Report of the Public Library of Indianapolis, 1873–74* (Indianapolis: Printing and Publishing House, 1874) Evans wrote:

> I would like to mention . . . the intention of the management to make the library the depository of everything in any way relating to the history of the city and the state, and would ask the cooperation of all friends of the library to assist them. No book or pamphlet, however trivial, can be of so little value as not to find a place in such a collection as it is our desire to make. At present there is no library in the State where the future historian can find his materials at hand.

Similarly, in his *Second Report of the Public Library of Indianapolis, 1874–1878* (Indianapolis: Issued by the Library, 1878) he defended his quest for government publications as a resource vital to future researchers:

> That the documentary literature of the country is now but seldom used, and by many considered of little value, does not, in the least, determine its worth in the future or furnish any criterion upon which to base an estimate of its importance to the student fifty or a hundred years hence. The degree of rarity to which this class of literature will attain in a few years, is a matter of astonishment to those who know how freely it has been distributed. . . . It, therefore, becomes a matter of great importance that this fleeting literature should be carefully collected and preserved while it can be had.

As he organized, catalogued, and built the public library's collection, Evans also helped create the Indianapolis Literary Club, patterned after similar groups Poole had founded in Cincinnati and Chicago. This organization was established in January 1877, with Evans as its first secretary. During its first two years of operation Evans gave papers on "Manners in Literature," "The Cincinnati Literary Club," and "An Evening with Dr. Johnson" (16 November 1878). According to Holley, this last paper, about the literary club created by Samuel Johnson, Sir Joshua Reynolds, and their circle, "recreated the eighteenth-century scene in vivid fashion and indicated considerable knowledge of the period."

Evans made an even greater contribution to American book culture in 1876 through his involvement with the Philadelphia meeting that created the American Library Association. To Melvil Dewey, the chief organizer of the gathering, Evans suggested the names of the committee on arrangements (Justin Winsor of the Boston Public Library; Poole, then at the Chicago Public Library; and Lloyd P. Smith of the Library Company of Philadelphia), and he addressed the gathering with "The Sizes of Printed Books." In this paper, published in the first volume of the American Library Association's *Library Journal,* he urges librarians to include the actual measurements of books in their catalogues instead of using the vague descriptions of folio, quarto, octavo, or duodecimo–designations that indicate how the sheets are folded rather than what their precise size may be. Cutter asked Evans to review three new library catalogues for the fledgling *Library Journal,* and all three of Evans's reviews concentrate on accuracy, full indexing, and usefulness to those seeking particular titles–the same concerns that were to inform his *American Bibliography.* In 1877 Evans became the American Library Association's

first treasurer, and in that year he traveled to England for an international conference to help the British organize a library association similar to that created in America.

Despite these successes that Evans enjoyed, his tenure at Indianapolis was about to end. In November 1874 the library committee had announced the purchase of the Sentinel Building from the Indianapolis Hall Company for $125,000 to house the public library, which had been maintained in the local high school. Evans and the local newspapers opposed the purchase, and they particularly attacked Austin H. Brown and other Democratic Party members of the board. Brown's anger festered, and in 1878 he was among the leaders of a movement to oust Evans from his post. On 31 August 1878 a local bookseller, Albert B. Yohn, took over Evans's position. Holley summarized Evans's achievements during his six years in Indianapolis by noting that "he had built good research collections for the student and the scholar. He had made these resources available to an ever increasing public. He had contributed much to the intellectual life of the city through the formation of a distinguished literary club."

Evans's activities for the next three years are unclear, but by summer 1881 he was working for the *Fort Worth* (Texas) *Democrat,* where he remained until the newspaper closed in June 1882. Evans was the business manager, but he probably also wrote for the paper. In 1883 he became bookkeeper for the firm of Max Elser, which sold pianos, organs, wallpaper, and books. In Fort Worth, Evans met Lena Young, daughter of Col. William Crawford Young, a rich rancher and businessman. Lena and Evans married early in 1884, and they eventually had four children: Gertrude, born in 1884; Eliot Howland, born in 1886; Charles Sumner, born in 1888 and later a renowned golfer; and Constance Evans, born in 1899.

On 16 December 1884 Evans was named assistant librarian of the newly organized Enoch Pratt Free Library of Baltimore, where he was to serve at a salary of $1,800 a year under Dr. Lewis H. Steiner, the head librarian. Pratt had given $833,333.33 to establish the institution, and the city had pledged at least $50,000 a year for operating expenses. When the library officially opened its doors to the public on 4 January 1886, the new central building housed 20,000 volumes, and the four branches held another 12,000. All were purchased and catalogued by Evans, who arranged the books according to Poole's system of fixed location, which did not necessarily group titles by subject.

In its first year the circulation figures at the main building of the library totaled 287,319–410,319,

Some of the 3" x 5" cards, cut in two, that Evans used in the preparation of his American Bibliography *(University of Illinois Library)*

including those from the branches. By the end of 1886 the collection had grown to a size of 45,109 volumes. Evans prepared a 153-page finding list that he periodically supplemented as new books arrived. Pratt was pleased with Evans's work, and he commented, "I don't think there is a more thoroughly organized library than mine & Mr. E. was very successful in it." Barely a month after the library opened, though, Evans and Steiner were quarreling, and later that year Steiner asked for and received Evans's resignation.

Evans's next job was at Omaha, Nebraska, where he was asked to catalogue the collection and prepare a finding list. Using Poole's system, Evans spent a year cataloguing 20,000 volumes and compiling a 252-page list of titles. Through the next year he was unemployed; then in March 1889 the Indianapolis Public Library rehired him at a salary of $2,000 a year. In his absence the library had deteriorated. No finding list had been issued since 1885; books had been lost, and damaged volumes had not been repaired. Evans set about restoring the library, and by April 1891 the collection held 50,000 volumes and was growing at a rate of about 5,000 books a year. Circulation figures for 1891 showed an impressive 269,542 charges.

Once again, however, Evans became enmeshed in controversy. The school board, which

oversaw the library, proposed a new building that would house 75,000 volumes; it would be overcrowded within a few years of opening, and Evans opposed the board's plans. Although the newspapers supported Evans as they had in 1878, he was dismissed in 1892.

Evans's mentor Poole, who in 1887 had become head of the Newberry Library in Chicago, hired him to replace Dr. William K. Williams as head of classification and reference. After Poole's death on 1 March 1894, Evans hoped to be named library director, but the trustees elected John Vance Cheney of the San Francisco Public Library. Cheney intended to reclassify the collection according to the Dewey decimal system, which groups books by subject. Evans argued to retain Poole's classification scheme, and in January 1895 Evans was fired.

His next job, which began in August 1895, was as librarian of the McCormick Theological Seminary in Chicago, where he undertook the reclassifying of the 20,000-volume collection. In April 1896 he also became a consultant to the Chicago Historical Society, and in July that year the society hired him as its librarian at a salary of $1,800 a year. Its collection included 20,000 books and 50,000 pamphlets. Evans not only organized the library in time for its opening on 15 December 1896 but also added to its collection through exchange programs with other historical societies and state libraries. He secured complete sets of reports of the Chicago Board of Trade (1871–1895) and the *School Reports and Proceedings* of the Chicago Board of Education (1854–1897). As secretary of the society Evans was responsible for arranging the publication of addresses presented at its meetings, and this experience proved valuable when he undertook the publication of his *American Bibliography*.

In 1901 Evans clashed with the executive committee over classification: a subcommittee recommended using Cutter's system—which, like Dewey's, organized materials by subject. Evans rejected this plan. The committee was also unhappy with Evans's *Charter, Constitution, By-laws, Roll of Membership, MDCCCLVI–MDCCCCI: List of Officers and Members, MDCCCCI* (Chicago: Printed for the Society, 1901), which contained various errors. Ordered by the committee to recall the flawed publication and to promise a corrected version, Evans did not comply, and in November he lost his library job. This was his last library position; he devoted the rest of his life to compiling *American Bibliography,* a work that became synonymous with his name.

While he had been looking for other jobs in August 1897, Evans had written to John Young in an attempt to secure the post of chief assistant librarian at the Library of Congress. In that letter he had declared:

> For the past ten years I have been engaged in the preparation of a Bibliography of all the publications issued in the United States for the first two hundred years; and this labor, happily approaching completion, has necessarily given a special knowledge of an important, but little known, period of American literature, not heretofore available to the Student and Collector.

In the printed circular announcing the imminent publication of the first volume of *American Bibliography* Evans dated the beginning of the project at about 1886 and claimed in January 1902 that he had begun work "more than sixteen years ago." Holley, the leading authority on Evans's career, believes that Evans probably had started working in earnest on his bibliography when he came to the Newberry Library. That library offered rich resources for such an undertaking, and Poole, who regarded bibliographical work as the foundation of librarianship, would have sympathized with Evans's ambition.

Evans's project coincided with a flurry of bibliographic work in both the United States and Great Britain. Thomas James Wise had published his first author bibliographies in 1897, and in 1885 Richard Rogers Bowker had published *The American Catalogue, 1886–1884,* followed in 1891 by *The American*

Catalogue, 1884–1890. Less-ambitious attempts to catalogue early American imprints had included Charles Benjamin Norton's *Literary Letter*. Norton had intended to print bibliographies of the imprints from each state, but he published only those for Maine, New Hampshire, and Vermont. Orville Augustus Roorbach's *Bibliotheca Americana* (1849) and four supplements had covered the period from 1820 through 1860. Much other work reflected the growing interest in the compiling of a national bibliography: Jeremiah Colburn's *Bibliography of the Local History of Massachusetts* (1871); Frederic Beecher Perkins's *Check List of American Local History* (1876); Joseph Sabin's *Bibliotheca Americana,* which had been begun in 1868; and Samuel Foster Haven's "Catalogue of Publications, in What Is Now the United States, Prior to the Revolution," which had been appended to the second edition of Isaiah Thomas's *History of Printing in America* (Albany: J. Munsell, 1874).

In January 1902 Evans issued an eight-page circular announcing the imminent publication of volume one of "A Chronological Dictionary of All Books, Pamphlets and Periodical Publications Printed in the United States of America from the Genesis of Printing in 1639 Down to and Including the Year 1820 with Bibliographical and Biographical Notes." This first volume was to cover the period from 1639 through 1740, and Evans was to publish the work himself. As soon as he received three hundred subscriptions for the first volume, which would cost fifteen dollars per copy, he would begin printing. Evans appealed not only to librarians but also to antiquarian booksellers, who, he said, would come to regard his bibliography as their bible.

When Evans had received 218 subscriptions—53 of them from foreign libraries—he began production. To underwrite the cost of this volume he borrowed money from the Union Trust Company of Indianapolis. This loan was guaranteed by Holliday, the president of the bank and Evans's old friend; Addison Clay Harris, an Indianapolis lawyer and politician; and George Towsey Porter, another Indianapolis lawyer. All had known Evans from his years as librarian in their city. Evans arranged for the Blakely Printing Company of Chicago to undertake the printing. He supplied the fine writing paper as well as the English red buckram used for binding, which was done by Brock and Rankin. Evans oversaw production, and when the books were finished, he packed and shipped them from his house, which he had purchased in 1899, at 1413 Pratt Avenue, Rogers Park, Chicago. In November 1903 he sent the first three copies to the men

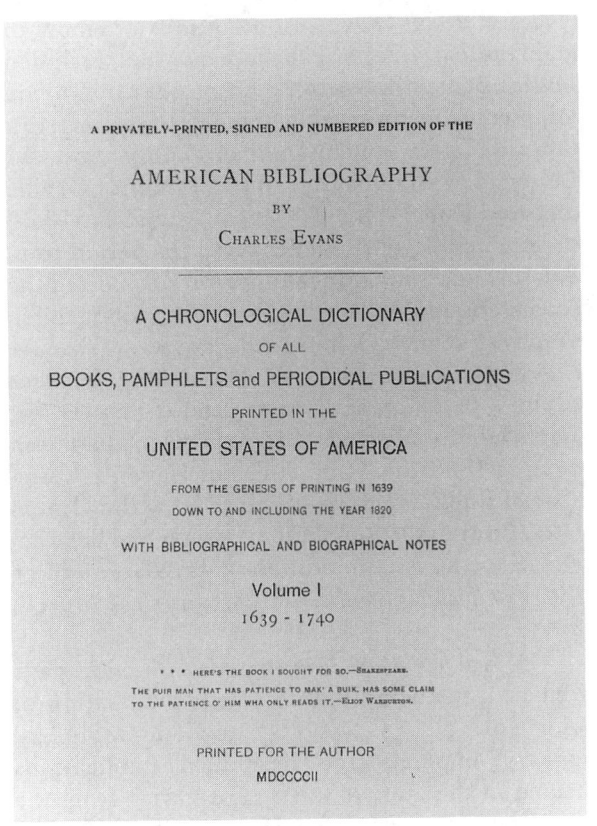

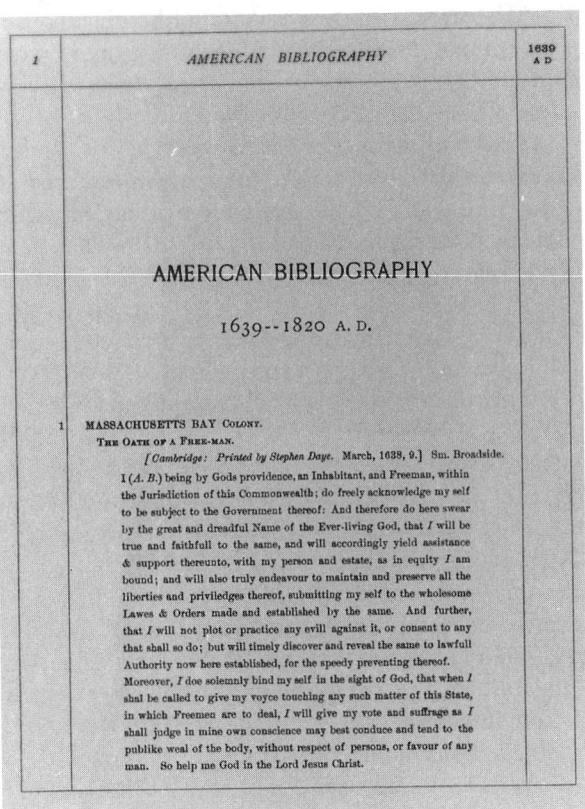

Title page and first page of the first volume of Evans's twelve-volume bibliography of American publications from 1639 to 1820

who had made possible the publication of this first volume by underwriting the loan, and he dedicated this volume to them.

Volume one covered the period 1639–1729 and contained 3,244 entries. As in all subsequent volumes, Evans left ample margins for librarians to add shelf marks and for bibliographers to add notes. He also provided his own annotations—nearly two pages on the first entry, "The Oath of a Free-man" (Cambridge, Mass.: Printed by Stephen Daye, March 1638–1639). Entries were arranged chronologically and under each year alphabetically by author (or by title, if the author was unknown). Evans defended his use of this chronological arrangement by arguing, "To the bibliographical student, and all book lovers are such, the date of publication is the most important fact in the identification of books and editions; it is the key to all investigation." He numbered each entry and listed auction values for works that sold for more than ten dollars. To assist researchers he listed libraries holding each item, and he included indexes of printers and publishers, subjects, and authors.

In the preface Evans discussed the history of the first century of printing in America and the na-

ture of the works produced there. He stressed the importance of this first volume of the bibliography, which he claimed provided

a record of first things in the literary history of the United States of America. It chronicles the birth of a National literature; the beginnings of National life in the Colonies and Provinces of Massachusetts, Pennsylvania, New York, New Jersey, Connecticut, Maryland and Rhode Island, in the chronological order in which printing was introduced in those States. It treats of much that has been forgotten; of a period all too little studied in the light of its printed records, and is an earnest endeavor to present in a fitting and enduring manner a faithful record of the literary activities of the true Founders of the American Republic.

The contents of the volume support Evans's claim to treat much that had been forgotten. Heretofore, Haven's list of colonial imprints, appended to Thomas's history of American printing in 1874, had been the most complete compilation of seventeenth-century American imprints. Haven's work had noted 648; Evans's listed 967.

Evans had hoped that Chicago industrialist Stanley McCormick would underwrite the cost of publication and provide the funds that Evans needed for travel to libraries with substantial holdings of early American imprints. When McCormick refused, Evans had already arranged the financing of the publication, but he could not afford to visit other libraries. So instead of making such visits he relied on local collections, especially those of the Newberry Library; Haven's list; the 1837 catalogue of the American Antiquarian Society; the ninety-five volumes of the British Museum's *Catalogue of Printed Books* (1881–1900); and Robert Watt's *Bibliotheca Britannica* (Edinburgh: Constable, 1824). Evans also drew on his own substantial bibliographical holdings, which included many auction catalogues; in 1934 he sent five barrels of such catalogues to the American Antiquarian Society. He also owned various library catalogues and the *Proceedings* of both the American Antiquarian Society and the Colonial Society of Massachusetts. Except for the bibliographies he acquired, Evans was not primarily a collector. He indefatigably pursued a needed volume, but once he had recorded it, the volume held no further fascination for him.

Forced to rely on records rather than personal inspection of volumes, Evans unwittingly included in his work some "ghosts," titles advertised or noted in bibliographies but never in fact published. On the other hand, his listing was not as complete as he claimed. When Roger B. Bristol published his *Supplement to Charles Evans' American Bibliography* (Charlottesville: University Press of Virginia, 1970), he added eleven thousand titles to Evans's listing of thirty-nine thousand. Evans's bibliography was especially weak on broadsides and Harvard dissertations. He refused to note line divisions on title pages, an important detail for distinguishing various states and editions of the same title, and he did not always give complete transcriptions of the title or of places of publication. His list of libraries holding particular titles was incomplete not only because he lacked complete information but also because he was willing to omit locations to save a line of type for an entry and thereby reduce production costs. He did not distinguish between books he had actually seen and those he had identified from newspapers or catalogues, and he did not cite sources for those that he included from citations in such newspapers and catalogues. He did not list many auction values, and those that he did are often misleading. For example, in one volume Evans records a value of $12 for item number 11,356–*A Brief of the Claim, on the Part of the Province of New Jersey* . . . (New York: James Parker, 1769)–but in 1880 the George Brinley Jr. copy had sold for $92.50. As another example of such misleading citations of values, Evans lists

a price of $100 for David Franks's New York directory (New York: Shepard Kollock, 1786); in 1911 the Robert Hoe III copy was sold for $2,275.

Reviewers of the first volume were not oblivious to its faults, but they recognized the importance of Evans's work. In January 1904 Varnum Lansing Collins of Princeton wrote in *Library Journal*, "This is one of *the* important bibliographies of Americana." An unsigned review in the February 1904 issue of the prestigious *Literary Collector* concluded that Evans's compilation would "undoubtedly prove of inestimable value to all workers in the field of colonial history, literature, and bibliography." In *A History of Printing in Colonial Maryland, 1686–1776* (Baltimore: Typothetae of Baltimore, 1922), Lawrence C. Wroth acknowledged his indebtedness to Evans:

> The compiler wishes to make an especial acknowledgement of the value to him of Charles Evans's *American Bibliography* in the preparation of the following list of Maryland imprints. Mr. Evans's contribution to American literary history has been of such character as to entitle him to the gratitude of all students in that and related subjects. His diligence and courage and single-minded devotion have cleared a high road through a wilderness in which, before his work was published, adventurers stumbled along uncertain trails.

Evans hoped to publish a volume a year, but before he could begin printing volume two he had to pay the $2,354.07 that volume one had cost to produce. By the end of March 1904 he had collected $3,432.35 from subscriptions; by March 1905, when he received volume two from the binder, he had secured $3,902.78 for the first volume. To reduce costs Evans printed only four hundred rather than five hundred copies of the second volume. This figure appeared to be more than sufficient since he had received only 312 subscriptions for the set, but in order to meet the demands of purchasers he later had to reprint volume two.

The second volume, dedicated to the Boston Athenaeum, contained 3,379 entries of works published between 1730 and 1750 and reflecting the progress of printing in British North America. Included were the first work of Benjamin Franklin and the first German Bible printed in the colonies, and Evans's preface remains a valuable survey of the printed production of the period. He noted that the number of works on religion remained dominant in the production of the presses, but religious debate was increasing. Volume two and all subsequent volumes are more accurate and complete than volume one because Evans was able to examine the holdings of various libraries on the East Coast before begin-

Evans at age sixty-eight

marized the history of printing in the colonies and noted landmark publications during these years. He again drew on bibliography to illuminate history: he observed, for example, that "the literary record of the Colonies is, in the main, a record of the influences exerted by the Colleges upon the spiritual and literary life of the people."

After shipping volume three to subscribers Evans again headed east to resume his work, which he began this time at the Library of Congress, where he had not previously examined materials. Edward G. Holley described his routine there: "I am usually the first reader to appear but leave about quarter of ten so the assistants can get away in time. I haven't found it necessary to take lunch but work steadily the twelve hours! . . . My breakfast is my one hearty, good meal every day." He followed this schedule for two months before heading north to Annapolis, Baltimore, and Philadelphia. In a letter to Lena on 1 September 1906 he wrote that he had completed a "successful summer, and for every dollar I have spent, the value of my work in extent and accuracy has increased twenty fold at least."

Volume four, dedicated to Samuel Eliot and covering the years from 1765 through 1773, was published in October 1907. It listed 3,201 entries, and in its sixteen-page introduction Evans traces the origins of the American Revolution, as these were reflected in the products of the colonial presses, and again surveyed noteworthy publications of the period.

In January 1908 Evans returned to the Library of Congress. After about three weeks in Washington, where he discovered at least eight hundred new titles, he traveled to Philadelphia, New York City, New Haven, Boston, and Salem. He had hoped to visit the Essex Institute before publishing volume four but had been unable to do so; this trip filled that gap. As the series continued to be published, its successive volumes were rendered more accurate than their predecessors both through Evans's personal visits to collections and through the help he began to receive from librarians and bibliographers such as William Beer of New Orleans (for early Louisiana imprints), Franklin B. Dexter of Yale, and George Parker Winship of the John Carter Brown Library. After 1907 Clarence Saunders Brigham of the American Antiquarian Society was one of Evans's chief supporters.

To print volume four Evans had bought the type from the Blakely Printing Company and hired his own compositors although he let the company do the actual press work. Production took longer than he had expected, and this left Evans with a debt of $600. Holliday, Harris, and Porter nonetheless

ning production. Using unpaid subscriptions as collateral in May 1904, he borrowed $300 and traveled to the Northern Indiana Historical Society, South Bend; Cleveland; the New York State Library; the American Antiquarian Society in Worcester, Massachusetts; Boston; Providence; Newport; Hartford; New Haven; and New York City. At the New York Public Library Wilberforce Eames was especially helpful in allowing Evans to work in the collection after it had closed and in pointing out titles that Evans might otherwise have overlooked.

Evans hoped to begin printing volume three in fall 1905, but he still owed $240 on volume two. He raised $140 from additional sales and borrowed the other $100, and in May 1906 volume three, dedicated to Poole, was sent to subscribers. By November enough copies of it had been sold to pay for its publication.

Volume three, with 3,267 entries, covers the years from 1751 through 1764. By this latter date all thirteen colonies had presses, Georgia being the last to get one in 1762 or 1763. In his preface Evans sum-

agreed to underwrite expenses for the fifth volume, which was printed at the Hollister Press of the Manz Engraving Company (Chicago), with Evans still managing the work.

In early May 1909 volume five appeared with 3,085 entries covering the years from 1774 through 1778. Evans dedicated it to the memory of six Americanists: Thomas Prince, Isaiah Thomas, Benjamin Franklin, John Carter Brown, George Brinley Jr., and James Lenox, whose collecting had done much to preserve American imprints from destruction. In his historical preface, the last that Evans provided for the volumes, he observes: "The literary record enters a period distinctively marked in character from what had been its prevailing characteristics up to this time," for politics supplanted religion as the primary concern of publications through these years. In this preface Evans traced the progress of the American Revolution through his record of works published during the period. He notes how even the press could become a casualty, as when on 27 November 1775 rebels destroyed James Rivington's printing office in New York City and melted down his type in order to make bullets. Publication of newspapers and other periodicals was also suspended because of the scarcity of paper, which forced printers to produce broadsides (a single leaf printed on one side) or broadsheets (a leaf printed on both sides) instead of pamphlets or books.

A deficit of $317.59 remained after volume five was sent to subscribers, but printing of volume six began in March 1910. Columbia Printing Company of Chicago became the printer, and it produced the next seven volumes. Volume six, which Evans dedicated to eight American bibliographers, was bound and ready for distribution in May 1910. Its 3,272 entries cover the period 1779–1785.

Before sending volume seven to the printer Evans once more traveled east, this time beginning in Savannah in order to survey southern collections. From there his itinerary included visits to collections in Charleston, Richmond, Washington, D.C., and New York City, where he checked imprints of the 1780s. In December 1912 volume seven, which included 2,849 entries covering the years from 1786 through 1789, was ready to go to subscribers. One measure of its success is in Evans's listing of fourteen previously unrecorded 1787 editions of the Constitution. Evans dedicated this volume to the American Antiquarian Society for all its help; in October he had sent the society a specially bound set of the first six volumes as another token of his gratitude.

He made another trip east before publishing volume eight, which was completed in April 1915 and included 2,777 entries covering the period 1790–1792. As World War I had broken out the previous August, Evans knew that he could not proceed with publication of his series: he relied too heavily on foreign orders that the war was interrupting, and the conflict raised his expenses. Nonetheless, he continued to prepare volume nine and also assisted Charles F. Heartman in compiling *The New England Primer Printed in America Prior to 1830: A Bibliographical Checklist* (New York: Heartman, 1915).

Not until 1925 was Evans able to resume publication of his bibliography. In a circular announcing an increase in price to twenty-five dollars a volume, Evans explained the significance of this ninth volume and its successors:

> From the year 1790 this work enters a period in the literary and political history of this country which has long lain fallow and almost untouched by the bibliographer. Its importance in the formation and growth of national and state governments nearly equals that of the better known and more stirring periods of our history, and the historian and research worker will find much to enlarge or modify, change or confirm opinions formed from an imperfect knowledge of existing sources of information, in this and succeeding volumes.

In January 1926 Evans sent the first copy of volume nine, with its 3,071 entries covering the years 1793–1794, to Clarence Saunders Brigham, the dedicatee. Although Evans had planned to extend the works included in his bibliographic series to 1820, the date at which Roorbach's *Bibliotheca Americana,* however inadequately, begins its coverage, by 1926 Evans decided that his series would conclude with the year 1800. He made another trip east in 1926 before publishing volume ten, dedicated to Lena, in February 1929. That volume covers 1795 and 1796 through the letter *M* and contains 2,687 entries.

As he neared completion of his great work Evans began to receive help from new sources. For the publication of volume eleven, published in February 1931 despite the onset of the Great Depression, he received a grant of $1,000 from the American Council of Learned Societies. This volume was dedicated to Josiah Quincy, a Massachusetts lawyer and the president of Harvard College from 1829 until 1845; Evans described Quincy in the dedication as a "Scholar Patriot Statesman—The Cato of New England." Volume eleven concluded the 1796 alphabet and covered the year 1797 in its 2,429 entries.

In the 1930s the Library of Congress, New York Public Library, New York Historical Society, and New Hampshire Historical Society supplied Evans with photocopies, making it unnecessary for him to travel to these institutions to examine primary works. For volume twelve, the last that he published, Evans received $3,000 from the American Council of Learned Societies, which passed a resolution thanking him "for his distinguished and self-sacrificing services to American scholarship." Published in February 1934, this volume covered works published in 1798 and 1799 to the letter *M,* contained 2,593 entries, and was dedicated to Calvin Coolidge for his service as president of the American Antiquarian Society from 1930 to 1933. When the volume was published, Wroth wrote to Evans on 27 February 1934, "All of us who are working in Americana have cause to thank you every day of our lives."

Recognition came late to Evans. In 1910 he had been elected to the American Antiquarian Society, but not until 1926 was he elected to the Colonial Society of Massachusetts, and the American Library Association, which he had helped create, did not make him an honorary member until 1933. The last and greatest of his honors came in June 1934, when Brown University awarded him an honorary doctor of letters degree. The citation, which summarized Evans's career, in part acknowledged him as a

> Distinguished figure in the field of the library and of bibliography, associated with public libraries in Boston, Indianapolis, Baltimore, Omaha, Chicago, several of which he, himself, organized . . . ; pioneer in the American Library Association . . . ; author of American Bibliography, herculean achievement; . . . unquestioned authority in that field; . . . long working in quiet willingness to serve the world of scholarship and to contribute to the understanding of American life and letters in the first two centuries of our national history.

Lena, who helped and encouraged Evans, had died on 5 October 1933, and Evans died following a stroke on 8 February 1935. He was cremated, and his ashes were buried in Memorial Park Cemetery, Evanston, Illinois, beside his wife and his daughter Constance, who had died in 1900. Memorializing his friend, Clarence Saunders Brigham wrote in the American Antiquarian Society *Proceedings* in April 1935, "For years to come, Charles Evans will be honored as the author of an invaluable historical reference work, but those who were privileged with his friendship will revere him most for his courage, his perseverance and his loyalty."

In *Early American Books and Printing* (Boston: Houghton Mifflin, 1935) John T. Winterich notes the significance of Evans's work: "The simplest way

in which to make a survey of the printing field in America in 1763 is to turn to the third volume of Evans's bibliography and take a quick census," which would show that nearly half the items listed concern religion, followed by political works and almanacs. Thus, as Winterich also observes, "A glance through Evans presents a lightning-flash survey of the cultural growth of America to the end of Washington's Presidency. . . . A good bibliography is itself a biography—not merely a birth-record of books, but a life-history of books that have put on immortality."

American Bibliography is important not only as a monumental achievement, an indispensable guide to all students of American literature, history, and culture, but also as an inspiration to bibliographers who succeeded Evans. In 1955 Clifford K. Shipton compiled a thirteenth volume that extended the coverage of *American Bibliography* to the year 1800; Evans's work on this final volume had left it about one-third finished. Four years later Roger Pattrell Bristol published a cumulative author-title index, followed in 1961 by an index of printers, publishers, and booksellers and in 1970 by a supplement to the entire thirteen volumes. Meanwhile, in 1958 Ralph R. Shaw and Richard H. Shoemaker began to fill the 1801–1819 gap between the bibliographies of Evans and Roorbach, a task they completed five years later. Sixty years after Evans published his first volume, the task that he had set for himself was thus accomplished.

Biography:

Edward G. Holley, *Charles Evans: American Bibliographer* (Urbana: University of Illinois Press, 1963).

References:

J. Christian Bay, "Charles Evans, 1850–1935," *American Library Association Bulletin,* 29 (1935): 163–164;

Clarence Saunders Brigham, "Charles Evans," *Proceedings of the American Antiquarian Society,* new series 35 (1935): 14–21;

Joel Silver, "Annals of Bibliography: Charles Evans and *The American Bibliography,*" *AB Bookman's Weekly,* 88 (1991): 1780–1784;

George Parker Winship, "Recent Bibliographical Work in America," *Library,* fourth series 9 (1928): 59–85.

Papers:

A large collection of Evans's letters, donated by his family, is housed at the University of Illinois at Urbana.

Charles E. Feinberg
(27 September 1899 – 1 March 1988)

Richard Raleigh
St. Thomas University

See also the tributes to Feinberg in *DLB Yearbook: 1988.*

BOOK: *An Exhibition of the Works of Walt Whitman* (Detroit: Detroit Public Library, 1955).

OTHER: "Notes on Whitman Collections and Collectors," *Walt Whitman: A Catalog Based Upon the Collections of The Library of Congress* (Washington, D.C.: The Library of Congress, 1955), pp. v–xviii;

"Introduction," *Whitman at Auction, 1899–1972,* compiled by Gloria A. Francis and Artem Lozynsky (Detroit: Gale, 1978), pp. xxi–xxx.

SELECTED PERIODICAL PUBLICATIONS—UNCOLLECTED: "The Importance of Children's Books," *Michigan Librarian* (October 1947);

"A Whitman Collector Destroys a Whitman Myth," *Papers of the Bibliographical Society of America,* 52 (1958): 73–92;

"Walt Whitman, Spokesman for Democracy," *Friends of Milner Library,* Illinois State Normal University, 11 (1961): 2–12;

"Adventures in Book Collecting," *Among Friends,* Detroit Public Library, 26 (1962): 1–6;

"Walt Whitman and His Doctors," *Archives of Internal Medicine,* 114 (1964): 834–842.

Charles E. Feinberg

Noting that Charles E. Feinberg's name will forever be associated with Walt Whitman, University of Paris–Sorbonne Professor Emeritus Roger Asselineau was once moved to remark that "for nearly half a century Feinberg was in a way Whitman's representative on earth." During the course of his life Feinberg became the foremost collector and one of the most knowledgeable scholars of Whitman's work, and he was known for his benefactions to libraries, research projects, and charitable organizations. Feinberg was fabled for his generosity with his collection, and virtually everyone who wrote seriously about Whitman since the 1950s consulted Feinberg and used his material.

The son of Russian immigrants, Charles Evan Feinberg was born in London, England, on 27 September 1899. Soon after, the family moved to Canada and settled in Toronto. Feinberg liked to tell the story of his first literary awakening—and brush with Walt Whitman—while in the sixth grade at Ogden School. On Friday afternoons the students were assigned readings from various books, and on one of those occasions Feinberg was asked to prepare a Henry Wadsworth Longfellow poem from a book titled *American Poems* (1872), edited by William Michael Rosetti. Feinberg was intrigued that the book had been dedicated to one of the poets in the collection, Walt Whitman. Later that year the family moved to Peterborough, Ontario, where Feinberg's formal education stopped at age eleven. Feinberg worked as a delivery boy for a wallpaper store and shined shoes in a tobacco shop ("five cents for black shoes, ten cents for brown").

Mr. Neil, a local teacher, took an interest in Feinberg and told him about the new library that had opened in town as a result of a $3,000 gift from Andrew Carnegie. Mr. Neil started Feinberg on biography, and he soon stumbled upon the Whitman biography by Dr. Richard Maurice Bucke, a friend of the poet. Feinberg also frequented a secondhand bookstore in Peterborough where he could usually buy a book for five cents and then sell it back to the owner for three cents; there, at age fifteen, he bought his first book including a Whitman poem, *American Poems,* the book he had read from in his last year of school in Toronto. The Whitman poem that seized him was "There Was a Child Went Forth." The family moved back to Toronto, and it was there, at Britnell's Book Store on Yonge Street, that Feinberg, at age seventeen, began his life as a Whitman collector.

His first purchase was a first edition of *Good-Bye My Fancy* bearing the signature of James Mavor, a professor of economics at the University of Toronto who had been a friend of Bucke. The second item was a Whitman letter to Thomas Nicholson, a member of the staff at Bucke's hospital in London, Ontario. In "Profile of a Book Collector: Charles E. Feinberg" in *Pages* (1976) Feinberg recalled the purchase as a turning point in his life:

> They brought out a letter, and I bought it. I just had my pay. I was making $22.50 at the time clerking, and they asked $7.50. What was important was not that it was a third of my pay. It was the emotional impact. There was nothing in my background that readied me to understand or to comprehend that this was the paper that Whitman had held in his hands, these were the words that he had written. . . . It hadn't occurred to me to visualize that a writer was a living human being who wrote the same as I did, who used a pen the same as I would.

Then came the task of explaining the purchase to his parents, to whom it was his habit to hand over his entire weekly earnings, from which they would then give him an allowance. According to Feinberg, his parents "accepted" what he had done, though his father could not resist the quip, "I could have written you a letter for half the price."

In 1923 Feinberg moved to Detroit and was employed by the Regal Shoe Store. Within two years he had become a manager and was opening up other stores in the Detroit area. Later he became a salesman for an oil burner company and then, along with attorney Alex Groesbeck, founded the Argo Oil Corporation, a business unique in that it provided delivery of fuel oil to private homes on evenings and weekends. All the while Feinberg was purchasing books, many by Whitman, mostly at the bookstore owned by B. C. Claes, a man he had befriended and helped financially, and at Sheehan's Book Shop. Feinberg developed an interest in the limited editions put out by Kelmscott and Nonesuch presses of England and admitted that he developed a bit of an "addiction" for fine editions which taught him "how to admire a good page."

When he began traveling on business he said that he could "always find the bookshops in all the towns." But not until the 1930s, when Philadelphia dealer Dick Sessler visited his home and remarked on his Whitman holdings, did Feinberg become conscious that he was a collector. "A collector to me had meant somebody possibly a little wealthier. I would have placed it more on a level with well-to-do people." When years later a dealer representing a large university came to Feinberg's home and offered him $1.5 million "for everything in the house," Feinberg's response was "What would I live with? Have you ever lived with money? I don't live that way." In later life Feinberg observed that "I never bought books from the standpoint of money; I had more confidence that I knew more about books than I did about money."

In 1927 Feinberg married Lenore Brown; they had three children (Bartley, Judith, and Suzanne) and seven grandchildren. Feinberg often stressed how important his understanding family was to him, acknowledging especially the patience of his wife with whom he shared his sometimes frenetic life as a collector for some sixty years. Of his early years as a collector, Feinberg admitted that he was "trying to prove something, that people with modest means could collect, and not wait until they were old and rich." Just as Samuel Johnson defined *lexicographer* as "a harmless drudge," so Feinberg could laugh about the often compulsive nature of collectors. Indeed, in his introduction to *Whitman at Auction* (1978) he quoted Whitman's remark to Horace Traubel: "The whole mania for collecting things strikes me as evidence of a disease—sometimes of a disease in an acute form."

In 1939, at age forty, Feinberg had the first in a series of heart attacks that he suffered through for the rest of his life. After the first attack, he pursued health as single-mindedly as he would a Whitman manuscript, consulting his doctors regularly, confining his eating largely to fresh fruits and vegetables, and exercising religiously—in his last years on sta-

Walt Whitman's working draft for "O Captain, My Captain" (Feinberg Collection, Library of Congress)

tionary bicycles that he kept at his Detroit and Miami residences.

In 1942 Feinberg cofounded the Friends of the Detroit Public Library and helped to arrange their first exhibition. They chose Mark Twain as the subject, largely because Twain's daughter was married to the conductor of the Detroit Symphony Orchestra, Ossip Gabrilovich, and she promised to make available some of her father's materials. At the exhibition the item that drew the most comment was the manuscript of Twain's *Adventures of Tom Sawyer*. The literary world invariably associates Feinberg with Whitman, but Feinberg, who began his reading life back in Canada with Frank Merriwell and Horatio Alger, collected many American writers besides Whitman, including Ralph Waldo Emerson, Henry David Thoreau, Karl Shapiro, Stephen Crane, Ernest Hemingway, and especially Robert Frost, with whom he shared a close friendship.

Realizing the advantages of having a generous Whitman collector on its Board of Directors, the Friends of the Detroit Public Library decided to mount a Whitman exhibition commemorating the ninetieth anniversary of the first printing of *Leaves of Grass* (Brooklyn, N.Y.: Rome Brothers, 1855). The exhibition, featuring some 322 items, with more than a third of them coming from Feinberg's collection, began in May 1945. Among Feinberg's contributions were several editions of *Leaves of Grass,* including a first, and many manuscripts and letters, but the item that Feinberg would later call "the star of the show" was one that the University of Michigan library owned and that he discovered there while searching for materials for the exhibition. It was a first edition of *Leaves* that had been rebound in full morocco, about which the library had little information except that it had been acquired sometime in the early 1900s. On the flyleaf was this inscription: "F. N. Sanborn, Nov. 9, 1855. This book Mr. Emerson received from the author and I from Mr. Emerson." Feinberg identified Sanborn as a young friend of Emerson and realized that the book had been rebound because it originally had a flimsy paper cover; it was one of only three or four copies of the first edition to have been bound in this manner. Feinberg delighted in the significance of the find, the book which "produced possibly the most famous letter in American literature of one great writer recognizing the future of a writer he had never heard of." Feinberg would one day own the letter.

Feinberg first met Annie Traubel, the wife of Whitman's friend and biographer Horace Traubel, the year before the Detroit Whitman exhibition. Considering the fruitful friendship that they would

eventually have, the first meeting was an inauspicious one. Traubel lived in Germantown, Pennsylvania, and Feinberg, in Philadelphia on business, made a quick decision to take a taxi to her home, arriving at her door unannounced. "Of course I should have called her first, but I didn't," he would say later. Feinberg introduced himself as a collector who was about to put on a Whitman exhibition in Detroit. Traubel responded to his greeting frigidly: "I didn't send for you," she said, and closed the door. Saddened but determined, Feinberg asked his friend Albert Boni, formerly of the publishing firm of Boni and Liveright, to intercede for him. Boni had known both Horace and Annie Traubel. Boni wrote Traubel assuring her that Feinberg was a serious Whitman collector she could trust. Later, Feinberg sent her a copy of the 1945 Detroit exhibition catalogue. A correspondence ensued, and soon she invited Feinberg to visit her home, which was a virtual storehouse of Whitman items.

Feinberg described the inside of the Traubel house as "unbelievable." The hallways were so littered with books, old copies of *The Conservator,* and stacks of letters and manuscripts that he had to walk sideways. Feinberg expressed concern about the safety of the materials, for among them was the still largely unpublished manuscript of her husband's *With Walt Whitman in Camden* (Boston: Small, Maynard, 1906–) and the famous letter from Emerson to Whitman on receiving *Leaves of Grass* on 21 July 1855 ("I greet you at the beginning of a great career. . . ."). Feinberg urged Traubel to publish a fourth volume of *With Walt Whitman in Camden* and contributed $2,000 to help defray expenses when the project was later undertaken by Sculley Bradley, Harold W. Blodgett, and the University of Pennsylvania Press.

As their friendship grew, Feinberg approached Traubel about purchasing the Emerson letter, but she indicated that she had promised to offer it first to Whitman collector Oscar Lion, whom she had known for many years. Feinberg suggested she write to Lion offering him the letter. Feinberg also said that he would pay her a thousand dollars more than Lion offered. Lion's response to Traubel's offer was curt, something to the effect that twenty years ago he had offered her $1,000 for the letter, and that he was prepared to give her the same today.

Feinberg suggested that she get the letter properly appraised, which she did, receiving an offer of $5,000 from Mabel Zahn of Sessler and Company and $6,000 from David Randall of Scribners. Feinberg responded by paying her $8,000 for the letter "to make sure she got enough." In the meantime

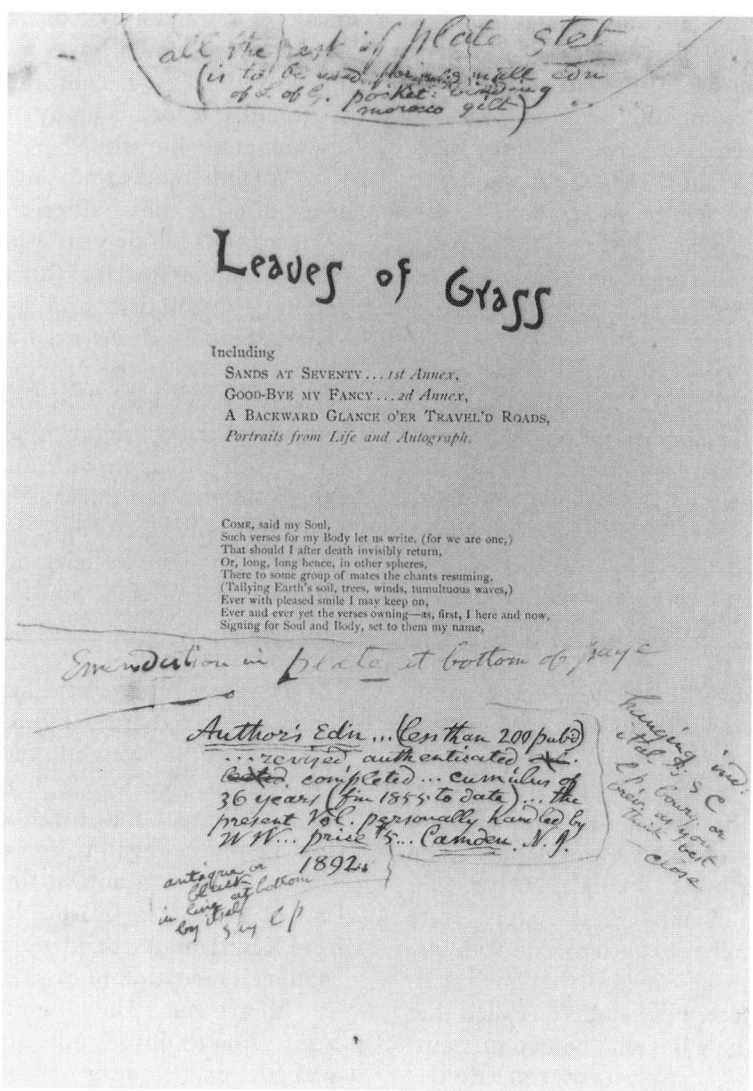

Trial title page, with Whitman's directions to the printer, for the so-called ninth edition of Whitman's best-known book, published by David McKay of Philadelphia in 1892

Feinberg had been helping Traubel financially, frequently paying her rent and even getting back for her the cemetery plot—which she had lost—next to her husband in Harleigh Cemetery in Camden, New Jersey, where Whitman is buried. When Traubel died, Feinberg gave the eulogy. There were only five or six mourners at Harleigh Cemetery that day, among them Oscar Lion.

In March of 1954 Feinberg traveled to Europe as a guest of the United States Information Agency (U.S.I.A.), and he spoke at the American Library in London where his Whitman items were being exhibited. The experience abroad encouraged him to carry the Whitman banner to foreign lands. Feinberg embarked on the project of preparing several sets of a traveling exhibit of laminated photographic reproductions from his collection of Whitman manuscripts. These were shown in the United States the next year (the centennial year of *Leaves*) and then throughout Europe and Latin America. The reproductions were viewed at more than 170 American colleges and universities before being sent off to Sweden, France, England, Romania, Israel, Ecuador, Venezuela, and Japan. In recognition of his efforts to promote better understanding of American culture abroad, the U.S.I.A. awarded Feinberg the Certificate of Merit. Later, he donated the laminated panel sets to several American institutions, with the promise that they would display the reproductions and lend them to deserving groups.

Also in 1954, one of Feinberg's dealers, David Kirschenbaum of Carnegie Bookshop in New York

City, alerted him to the upcoming auction of a manuscript page from the first edition of *Leaves of Grass*. Feinberg was surprised to hear of the existence of such a page, thinking that all of the pages of the manuscript had been destroyed. Whitman himself had told Horace Traubel that the manuscript had been destroyed by fire in an accident at the printer. And there were other questions: If one page survived, how many others might have? Were there more pages of the 1855 *Leaves* manuscript that would sell later for less?

On the day of the auction a collector from London was spreading the word that there were already a half dozen of the manuscript pages at Duke University. But Feinberg was confident that the London collector was wrong and equally confident that when he saw the page in question he would know if it was indeed a page from the 1855 manuscript. The other bidders were not so confident, apparently scared off by the uncertainty of the situation.

Bidding began at $500 and slowed at $1,300, going up in increments of fifty dollars. Feinberg got the page for $1,500 plus commission. After the sale David Anton Randall, manager of the rare-book department of Charles Scribners Sons, approached Feinberg and offered him $5,000 for the page. The incredulous Feinberg asked Randall, "Dave, you were there. Why didn't you bid on the page?" Randall replied: "The people who authorized me to pay the $5,000 said not to buy it until *you* bought it, which would authenticate it." Feinberg replied that the remark was flattering but that he had just purchased "the keystone" of his Whitman collection.

No doubt the reason that the manuscript page survived the fate of the rest of the pages was that Whitman wrote on the verso a list of ninety-one words in columns (initialed *g, f, c,* and *l*), apparently for use in some future poem. Feinberg's friend from the University of Detroit, C. Carroll Hollis, later to become Specialist in American Cultural History at the Library of Congress, solved the puzzle: the letters indicated Greek, French, Celtic, and Latin origin, and more than a third of the words were found in Whitman's poem "Song of the Broad-Axe," which first appeared in the 1856 edition of *Leaves.* No other page from the manuscript of the 1855 *Leaves of Grass* has been discovered.

The year 1954 had been busy and rewarding for Feinberg. The one-hundredth anniversary of the first publication of *Leaves of Grass,* 1955, would be a watershed. In that year Feinberg, whose formal education ended after the seventh grade, received his first honorary degree—from Southern Illinois University, Carbondale, where he had been invited to speak on Whitman by Robert Faner of the English Department. Feinberg was awarded a doctorate in humane letters for his contributions to the study of Whitman and for his many benefactions to American university libraries.

What happened next at Carbondale also happened at other universities, notably the University of Detroit that same year and St. Thomas University in Miami in the last years of Feinberg's life. The Feinberg magnetism and generosity took hold. When Feinberg discovered that Southern Illinois University was in the process of building a new library, he remarked, "No Friends of the Library? You must have a Friends to give the library a separate identity, to sponsor lectures and social events, and to help in the purchase of books and manuscripts the university might not otherwise be able to afford." University officials agreed and named Feinberg First Friend of the Southern Illinois University, Carbondale, Library. "No rare book room in the architectural plans for the new library?" he asked. "Every great university library has a treasure room," he told them. "If you create one I will help you fill it." Plans were altered; the rare-book room was built in what was later named the Delyte W. Morris Library; and in the next few months gifts from Feinberg began to arrive: first and early editions of Whitman books; fine printing and works from private presses; Bruce Rogers imprints; books from Kelmscott, Ashendene, and Doves presses. In 1956, at a reception following the dedication of the new library auditorium, Feinberg met local optometrist and James Joyce collector Harley Croessmann, who invited Feinberg to his home. Impressed by Croessmann's collection, Feinberg urged Ralph E. McCoy, director of libraries at Southern Illinois University, to stage a Joyce exhibition, and he did. Later, following Feinberg's advice, Southern Illinois University acquired Croessmann's Joyce collection, the beginning of what would become extensive holdings on the Irish Renaissance. Writing in the Morris Library publication *Southern Exposure* (May 1988), McCoy said that it was largely through Feinberg's efforts that Southern Illinois University published two volumes of Traubel's *Walt Whitman in Camden,* a work based on the Traubel diaries owned by Feinberg. Among the items Southern Illinois University later acquired from Feinberg were Thoreau's annotated copy of *The Dial* (the transcendental journal that appeared in the early 1840s), the manuscript of Thornton Wilder's *Bridge of San Luis Rey* (New York: Boni, 1927), the typescript of Hemingway's "The Short Happy Life of Francis Macomber," and some lecture notes of Dylan Thomas. In 1968 Feinberg contributed to the purchase of a first-edition *Leaves of Grass* as the one millionth book of the Morris Library.

Meanwhile, much the same thing had been happening at the University of Detroit. Feinberg's next-door neighbors on Boston Boulevard were Jesuit priests who administered and served on the faculty at the University of Detroit. In May of 1955 they invited him to give an address on Whitman at the university; Feinberg agreed and also promised to lend the university Whitman materials for an exhibition to complement the lecture. A friendship developed, and once again Feinberg preached the need for a Friends of the Library. His background with other Friends groups around the United States helped in setting up a constitution and bylaws for this Friends group. After functioning informally for two years, the Friends of the University of Detroit Library held a formal election in May 1957; they elected Feinberg vice president. Feinberg worked indefatigably for the Friends, contributing service, books, leadership, enthusiasm, and hospitality at his home and elsewhere to board members, who in May 1958 elected him president. Between 1955 and 1959 the University of Detroit Library staged seven exhibitions of materials lent by Feinberg, including an exhibit of rare Jewish ceremonial silver, and items associated with Whitman, Father Gabriel Richard (book collector, printer, and administrator at the University of Michigan), Benjamin Franklin, and William Shakespeare. Feinberg also spoke regularly to English classes at the university and donated items to the library, including more than one hundred volumes by and about Whitman, works of Saint Teresa, thirty-five volumes on Chaucer, letters of Rousseau, various items from the seventeenth century, and an illuminated Catholic missal from the fifteenth century.

The event of that centennial year of *Leaves of Grass* that got Feinberg the greatest national attention and, ironically, probably furthered the Whitman cause the most, was an act committed by a criminal. Writing in the *Walt Whitman Quarterly Review* (Summer 1988), Hollis recalled the 1955 Whitman exhibition at the Detroit Public Library, which was composed entirely of materials collected by Feinberg. One item of the hundreds on display at the exhibition was the *Day Book,* a large volume in Whitman's hand including addresses, notes, and records of purchases of *Leaves of Grass.* The day before the official opening of the exhibition Feinberg himself noted the book was missing. Police were called; articles appeared in the press; and there were suggestions to close the exhibition. "Close it? Not at all," Feinberg replied. "With all this publicity about the Whitman theft everybody will want to come and see what's left." A $5,000 reward was announced for the safe return of the Whitman diary, and, when crank callers seeking the reward became a problem, Feinberg asked Hollis, who was the only scholar to have examined the diary carefully at Feinberg's home before the exhibition, to screen the calls. The *Day Book* was finally recovered months later, mailed to Feinberg's home several days after Hollis made a special appeal on his weekly radio show. Wrapped in a brown paper grocery bag, the undamaged *Day Book* included a note: "The book wasn't stolen. I'm sorry I didn't return it earlier."

Theft or nontraditional loan, the ten-month disappearance and eventual safe return at Christmastime of the Whitman diary made a great story, the most memorable of several Feinberg-related stories that appeared in *The New York Times* that year. The year had begun with *The Times* coverage of a Feinberg lecture titled "Whitman Collections and Collectors" on 3 January at the Library of Congress in conjunction with the publication of the first complete catalogue (with a Feinberg introduction) of the 1,055 Whitman items in its various collections. Later in January *The Times* reported that the New York University Press planned the publication of the *Walt Whitman Newsletter* and the *Collected Writings of Walt Whitman* in twelve volumes, both publications to be edited by Gay Wilson Allen—the *Collected Writings* probably the most ambitious project on an American poet ever undertaken. Feinberg had strongly encouraged the two projects, and his collection made them possible.

In February *The Times* covered an exhibition of Feinberg Whitman items at Brooklyn College, including the Emerson letter, and on 4 March reported the theft of the Whitman diary in Detroit. Two days later *The Times* identified its owner as "Charles E. Feinberg, Detroit oil executive." They placed the value of the diary at $25,000 and indicated that the exhibition had been insured for $200,000. On 28 December the paper reported the safe return of the Whitman *Day Book.*

What Feinberg called his single most exciting acquisition as a collector was not a Whitman item and, as he would say with delight, enjoying the paradox, was "an item I would never own." Feinberg told *Pages* (1976) of his acquisition of a *Memorbuch* of the Jewish community of Frankfurt, buried by the last rabbi of that community during the Holocaust.

I knew when I bought it that I was buying a piece of history I would never own. It should never belong to an individual. Eventually it was given anonymously to the Hebrew University in the memory of three great pioneers who were instrumental in the rebuilding of Israel.

Feinberg's catalogue for the 1955 exhibit of manuscripts, books, and other items from his Whitman collection

It's exhibited in the rotunda of the Jewish National and University Library of Jerusalem. It's one of their historical treasures, as it should be. Originally started about 1626, all the entries were written by hand of all the communities that were destroyed, beginning with that period and with the death of some of the most prominent Jewish families of the German community of Frankfurt, right down to the last Baron Wilhelm von Rothschild.

Indeed, Feinberg's identity as a Jew was as strong as his passion for Whitman. As a child in Canada he was a member of the only Jewish family in Peterborough, Ontario. One of the reasons he maintained a lifelong devotion to the Boy Scouts was the sensitivity that group showed when, as a scout, he required special dietary considerations. Just as he collected Whitman, he collected Judaica and had an extensive collection of Jewish art treasures. In 1958 he founded the Lubavitch Foundation of Michigan, a humanitarian organization which later became part of the international Lubavitch Foundation. He was active in B'nai B'rith, the National Jewish Committee, the Jewish Historical Society, the National Commission on Jewish Americans, and a founder and member of the American Friends of Hebrew University, which awarded him a fellowship in 1969 and the S. Y. Agnon Gold Medal for intellectual achievement in 1988.

Feinberg also collected items related to Robert Frost and became friends with the poet in the early 1940s. They met frequently at the Bread Loaf conferences in Vermont where they both lectured. In 1960 Frost, as Feinberg's guest, visited Israel, where Feinberg surprised him with a special exhibition of his Frost collection at the library of Hebrew University, which eventually received the collection as a gift. In 1962 Frost, again as a Feinberg guest, made history when he read his poetry to an audience of more than eight thousand people at the University of Detroit. The aging Frost began his reading by acknowledging the hospitality of Feinberg but for several seconds seemed to have trouble remembering Feinberg's name. Later Frost would tell reporters, "I looked out into the audience and saw so many people that the only name I could think of was "Lindbergh." Until Feinberg's invitation to stay at his home, Frost had long avoided Detroit. Frost died shortly after the Detroit visit. Feinberg enjoyed inviting visitors to sit in Frost's favorite chair and told of the poet's long walks alone through the aging neighborhood while Feinberg, worried about the poet's safety, dispatched his brother Frank to follow in his car discreetly behind Frost.

In 1963 William White, having spent some eight years researching the Feinberg Collection, had some trouble estimating its size but not the generosity of the collector himself, for Feinberg had become known as the collector who was always willing to open his collection to scholars. In *The Long Islander* (30 May 1963) White observed that getting a true count of the items in the collection was difficult because so much of it was being lent to scholars at the time. White found more than twelve hundred unpublished Whitman manuscripts which he transcribed onto some two thousand filing cards and noted,

> But even this is not an accurate picture. For it does not include the poetry: these manuscripts, if they have anything to do with *Leaves of Grass* have been sent (in photostat) to Prof. Harold W. Blodgett (Union College) and Prof. Sculley Bradley (University of Pennsylvania). They are working on the variorum edition of the *Leaves* for the New York University Press *Collected Writings of Walt Whitman*.

> Material dealing with the early poems and the fiction was sent to Prof. Thomas L. Brasher (Southwest Texas State College), whose edition of this writing has just been published by the N.Y.U. Press.

> My list of 1,200 plus manuscripts does not include prose pieces having any connection with *Specimen Days*. For this was sent (on microfilm) to Prof. Floyd Stovall (University of Virginia), whose first volume of *Prose*

Works 1892 has also just been issued by N.Y.U. Press as another part of the collected Whitman.

Finally, it does not include letters and postcards, either to or from the poet. These were sent to Prof. Edwin H. Miller (New York University) for his edition of *The Correspondence of Walt Whitman.* Two volumes of these letters were published in 1961, and three more are in preparation of the collected edition.

White estimated that Whitman wrote approximately three thousand letters and cards. Of the 2,032 then believed extant, the Feinberg Collection included 1,028, more than all the other collections in the world combined. The collection also included about fifteen hundred letters sent to Whitman by such correspondents as John Greenleaf Whittier, Alfred Burroughs, and Tennyson, not to mention the prized Emerson letter and one from Oscar Wilde sent from Chicago on 1 March 1882 during Wilde's American tour. It concluded with the words "There is no one in this wide great world of America whom I love and honour so much."

By the late 1960s the Feinberg Collection included ten copies of the first edition of *Leaves of Grass.* Feinberg liked to recall how he bought his first copy of the first edition, how when he walked into Goodspeed's of Boston one day the owner greeted him with, "Well this must be your lucky day" and went on to tell him of the availability of a first edition of *Leaves* in the third binding. (Feinberg estimated that Whitman saved about thirty cents a copy on the second and third bindings of the first edition by eliminating the three rows of gilt on the front cover and the marbled paper linings.) Feinberg happily paid $100 for the book.

In 1969, the year the Library of Congress began acquiring the Feinberg Collection, the library prepared a major exhibit of more than two hundred items drawn entirely from the Feinberg Collection in the Great Hall of the library on the opening of the sesquicentennial exhibit commemorating Whitman's 150th birthday. Eight cases were devoted to Whitman's life and eight to his work. In the *Quarterly Journal of the Library of Congress* (April 1970), John C. Broderick, the assistant chief of the Manuscript Division, called the Feinberg Collection "unique in its size, its comprehensiveness, the surpassing quality of its choicest items, and the extraordinary range of interest which it encompasses." Noting the diversity of the collection, he went on to identify "curious relics and memorabilia" that Feinberg had acquired: a walking stick made from a calamus root—a gift to Whitman from naturalist John Burroughs, whose present echoed Whitman's series of poems titled "Calamus"; the battered haversack in which Whit-man carried presents for hospitalized victims of the Civil War; Whitman's pen and spectacles; and a collection of labels from a line of canned vegetables bearing Whitman's name.

The Feinberg Collection was transferred to the Library of Congress in ten installments, the last in 1979. But Feinberg never found it easy dealing with the library and blamed Congress for not providing the money to build collections and adequately house them. In his later years Feinberg was known to telephone scholar friends like Matthew J. Bruccoli to lament the way the library was "mistreating" his collection. Whatever the circumstances Feinberg realized his dream of seeing the great majority of the items he had collected for seven decades safely in the bosom of the American people, the works of the Poet of Democracy at last come home to rest. The Feinberg Collection at the library consists of approximately twenty-five thousand items in 209 large containers occupying 83 linear feet of shelf space. The collection was organized and arranged between 1980 and 1981 by Michael McElderry, who also compiled a register and prepared material that was microfilmed. An endowment that Feinberg arranged, the Feinberg Foundation, allows the library to buy other manuscripts or letters should they become available.

Over the years Feinberg contributed several articles in the service of Whitman scholarship, though he belittled his writing efforts with the remark, "I'm a fuel oil peddler, not a poet." In "The Importance of Children's Books" the *Michigan Librarian* (October 1947), Feinberg writes of the Nazi propaganda in children's books that had contributed to the climate of hate in Germany and how Abraham Lincoln, on reading Whitman's poem "I Hear America Singing" began to jot down the titles of all the songs he could remember. In "Notes on Whitman Collections and Collectors" in *Walt Whitman: A Catalog Based Upon the Collections of The Library of Congress* (1955), Feinberg writes that Whitman's "manuscripts, letters, postcards, and books continue to be game in a happy hunting ground for the collectors." In "Walt Whitman, Spokesman for Democracy" in *Friends of Milner Library* (May 1961), he writes about the joy of finding in manuscripts he has acquired "ideas which have never been published. This gives me the opportunity of doing what I call crawling into another man's creative brain box, because this is really the closest that I can ever come to this tremendous creativity." In "Adventures in Book Collecting" in *Among Friends* (Spring 1962), he recounts how, detective-like, he searched for more than twenty years for a man named Al to whom Whitman had written some letters, finally tracking the family down in Kansas and purchasing the Whitman letters after a tip from a faculty member at the University of Nebraska. In "Walt Whitman and his Doctors" in *Archives of Internal Medicine* (December 1964), Feinberg gives from Whitman's own case history and the notes of his doctors a compelling account of the poet's courage in his last days and hours. In "Civil War Friends of Walt Whitman" in *The Long Islander* (28 May 1970), Feinberg details his search for photographs of the boys and men Whitman nursed in the hospitals and with whom he later corresponded. And in the introduction to *Whitman at Auction* (1978) he writes about his disappointment when he was outbid for an 1855 *Leaves* inscribed by Whitman to the Irish patriot John Boyle O'Reilly and when he was outbid for a postcard by a man who later told him he just wanted to prove that "there were other dealers in the world" besides the one who always represented Feinberg.

In a telling paragraph in *Whitman at Auction* Feinberg captures a bit of the magic of collecting:

> In my acquisitions I have discovered and recovered, as is possible in no other way, a great many of Whitman's rejected thoughts, his discarded phrases, his canceled passages and stillborn paragraphs. Many of the manuscripts reveal Whitman's mind at work, correcting, rejecting, and substituting. All these furnish a clue to his taste and the process of his thought.

In 1981, learning that St. Thomas University in Miami was raising funds to build a new library, Feinberg phoned head librarian Margaret Elliston and invited her to his North Bay Village home. Ensuing events mirrored those at Southern Illinois and the University of Detroit in the 1950s. Soon Feinberg was meeting with Elliston and university president Father Patrick O'Neill to form a Friends of the St. Thomas University Library, which was subsequently founded on 24 May 1982. In his frequent visits to the campus Feinberg brought gifts for the library, among them three items chosen for an exhibit at the Historical Museum of Southern Florida in 1994 titled "Treasures of Florida Libraries": a Spanish *Patent of Nobility* (10 October 1737) consisting of thirty-nine manuscript pages on vellum; a signed Author's Edition of *Leaves of Grass* (1882); and a signed and dated proof page of the title page from *Good-bye My Fancy* with Whitman corrections prepared for the Death Bed Edition of *Leaves of Grass*.

Feinberg urged the Friends to acquire special items and helped in their purchase; the first was a facsimile edition of the Gutenberg Bible derived from the Insel Verlag edition and hardbound in goatskin by Thomas Thompson of Santa Barbara, California. As he had at the University of Detroit,

Feinberg spoke frequently to English classes at St. Thomas University, always beginning his talks with a tribute to librarians, who became his teachers when he left school back in Canada at age eleven. On one occasion the professor for whose class Feinberg was to speak was delayed in traffic. Arriving half an hour late, the professor was relieved to find that Feinberg, at age eighty-six, had already begun the freshman class on his own. An expert showman, he had broken the ice with the eighteen-year-olds by conducting a raffle of several copies of Gay Wilson Allen's *Walt Whitman* (1969) and was showing the students, who delighted in his childlike enthusiasm, some of his recent acquisitions. By 1987 Feinberg had donated about six hundred items—including first editions, proof sheets, manuscripts, and photographs—to the St. Thomas University Library. On 1 May 1987 the university awarded him the degree Doctor of Humane Letters, citing his "passion for the word" and quoting from Whitman's Preface to the 1855 *Leaves of Grass:* "You shall be marked for generosity and affection, without monopoly or secrecy, glad to pass any thing to any one. You shall not be careful of riches and privilege, you shall be riches and privilege."

In 1986 Sotheby's in New York City auctioned many of the printed materials and manuscripts relating to Whitman and Horace Traubel remaining in Feinberg's private collection. Traubel had spent his life advancing the cause of his friend Whitman. In addition to the multivolume *With Walt Whitman in Camden* his works included the *Conservator,* a monthly journal published until his death in 1919, the *Walt Whitman Fellowship Papers* (1894–1918), and his ten-volume edition of the *Complete Writings of Walt Whitman* (1902). In the 1980s Feinberg gave more than five thousand items from the archives of Horace Traubel to the Library of Congress. The Sotheby's catalogue for the auction, *Fine Books and Manuscripts Including Americana* (December 1986), included some 160 Feinberg items in fifty-eight lots, including correspondence between the Traubels and such figures as artists Marsden Hartley, Rockwell Kent, Maurice Prendergast, writer Christopher Morley, photographer Alfred Stieglitz, and architect Louis Sullivan; Whitman manuscripts, canceled checks, and corrected proof sheets; and Whitman's signed copy of William Rounseville Alger's *The Poetry of the East* (1856) with a Whitman note explaining that the stain on several pages of the book was from "breaking a bottle of Virginia wine in a trunk where it was stored down South in the war."

Feinberg won many accolades from scholars because, as he was fond of saying, he thought of himself as a "custodian, not a possessor." He felt

Feinberg and Robert Frost

that collecting was valuable because collections bring together items that scholars might otherwise have to travel half the world over to study and compare. Some called Feinberg "greedy" for attempting to buy up everything he could connected with Whitman, but in doing so he brought a new rationale to collecting and showed the interdependence between scholar and collector. As Feinberg would often say, he collected all he could of Whitman "to complete a picture" of the man, a picture that he knew he could not complete alone. To that end Feinberg collected items others might ignore, including empty envelopes as long as they had postmarks, because at least they proved that a letter had been written from a particular place at a certain time. Indeed, for four decades almost every serious Whitman scholar consulted him and made use of his collection.

Matthew J. Bruccoli is typical of the many scholars and collectors whose lives were changed by an encounter with Feinberg, whom Bruccoli calls "the most generous collector I have known." The two men first met in the late 1950s, when Bruccoli was a graduate student and Feinberg lectured on Whitman for the Bibliographical Society of the University of Virginia. Others had advised Bruccoli that he was not rich enough to become a serious collector, but Feinberg, the first prominent book collec-

tor to encourage him, told Bruccoli that he had started buying books with money he had earned by shining shoes. "The longer I knew Charlie," Bruccoli says, "the more I cherished him."

After Feinberg's death on 1 March 1988, tributes poured in from grateful scholars all over the world. The Summer 1988 issue of the *Walt Whitman Quarterly Review* devoted sixteen pages to scholars who wished to share their thoughts on their collector friend. Noting that Feinberg had assembled "the largest Whitman collection in the world," Ed Folsom spoke of Feinberg's ceaseless activity on behalf of Whitman studies that "wove a kind of magical field of good will and friendship" among Whitman scholars. Gay Wilson Allen recalled how generous Feinberg was in permitting scholars to use his unpublished manuscripts, even though it decreased their market value, and how Feinberg had invited him to stay at his home in Detroit to study more conveniently the manuscripts he needed for writing his Whitman biography *The Solitary Singer* (1967). Writing from Paris, Americanist Roger Asselineau said that Feinberg "did a scholar's job in particular by tirelessly hunting in all likely and unlikely places for new Whitman documents." Arthur Golden remembered Feinberg once saying to him that he was "a kind of amateur" at Whitman studies, a remark

Golden found amusing. Edwin Haviland Miller said that Feinberg was his "collaborator" in the editing of the five volumes of letters for *The Collected Writings of Walt Whitman* and spoke of Feinberg as a tireless correspondent—the two exchanging some two thousand letters which are now themselves part of the Feinberg Collection at the Library of Congress, silent record of the "trials, tribulations, and, above all, excitement of collector and editor." William White wrote that it if were not for Feinberg there would be no *Walt Whitman Quarterly Review,* no *Collected Writings,* and "the world would have been a lesser place." C. Carroll Hollis told the story of Whitman's watch, a revealing account which showed a different side to the confident, cheerful Feinberg. The watch was among the many items Feinberg had acquired from the Traubel collection. Since Whitman had willed the watch to Horace Traubel, Feinberg felt it was only fitting that it should go to Horace's grandson, who had run away from home. Feinberg hired a detective to track the grandson down and then mailed him the watch, with a note inviting him to reply about his Whitman interests and memories. Some days later the watch was returned, smashed almost beyond recognition, with no note. Hollis recalled the collector's genuine confusion and honest hurt at the grandson's response to his act of kindness. "What did I do wrong?" he asked Hollis, sadly holding the watch in his hand.

Still spirited and generous despite failing health, Feinberg consented to a videotaped interview, which took place two months before his death. Feinberg reminisced fondly about a life lived with books, about how fortunate he was to have had the friendships of librarians, book dealers and collectors, writers and scholars. At the conclusion of the interview, he shuffled to a living room wall and took down a photograph of the poet and scholar John Ciardi at Bread Loaf in 1955. Feinberg had recently framed this photograph, which Ciardi had inscribed to Feinberg and his wife. "John was quite a man," he said. "We had a lot of fun together. In those days I used to put out a bottle of Jack Daniel's. Between the two of us we'd finish it—but he drank most of it. 1955? Well, that's only thirty odd years ago."

Then pausing and thinking back on some seventy years of collecting, he smiled broadly at the camera and added, "Gosh, it's been a lot of fun."

References:

John C. Broderick, "The Greatest Whitman Collector and the Greatest Whitman Collection," *Quarterly Journal of the Library of Congress,* 27 (1970): 109–128;

Ed Folsom, Gay Wilson Allen, Roger Asselineau, Arthur Golden, Jerome Loving, Edwin Haviland Miller, William White, and C. Carroll Hollis, "Charles E. Feinberg: A Tribute," *Walt Whitman Quarterly Review,* 6 (1988): 39–54;

The Library of Charles E. Feinberg, three volumes (Detroit & New York: Parke-Bernet Galleries, 1968);

"Profile of a Book Collector: Charles E. Feinberg," *Pages,* edited by Matthew J. Bruccoli and C. E. Frazer Clark Jr. (Detroit: Gale, 1976), pp. 272–289.

Papers:

The Feinberg Collection in The Library of Congress includes extensive Feinberg correspondence.

Paul Louis Feiss

(3 June 1875 – 20 January 1952)

Jeanne Somers
Kent State University

BOOK: *The Sentiment of Book Collecting: Read at the Rowfant Club Saturday Evening, April the Eleventh, Nineteen Hundred and Eight, by Paul Louis Feiss,* Rowfantia, no. 6 (Cleveland: Rowfant Club, 1908).

OTHER: "Address of the President," *The Rowfant Club Yearbook, 1922* (Cleveland: Rowfant Club, 1922), pp. 13–32.

Sometime around 1895 a developing interest in Arthurian legend led Paul Louis Feiss to acquire a copy of Sir Thomas Malory's *Le Morte d'Arthur* (1485) at a secondhand book sale. There is no record of the edition or distinguishing features of this particular book; but around what was most likely a modest initial purchase, Feiss began to build a library of medieval romances and histories. His interest and acquisitions soon expanded to embrace British and European history, classics of French and English literature, and examples of fine printing. Through a deep love of books and commitment to scholarship, Feiss achieved encyclopedic knowledge in his areas of interest and until his death in 1952 enjoyed a reputation among Ohio book collectors as an expert in incunabula, the early history of printing, and rare editions of the sixteenth and seventeenth centuries, as well as pre-Victorian and nineteenth-century authors.

Feiss was born in Cleveland on 3 June 1875, the eldest son of Julius and Carrie Dryfoos Feiss. In early boyhood he was sent by his father to the family's native Bavaria for a year of schooling, and he recalled many years later that it was there he first read James Fenimore Cooper's Leather-Stocking Tales (*The Pioneers,* 1823; *The Last of the Mohicans,* 1826; *The Prairie,* 1827; *The Pathfinder,* 1840; *The Deerslayer,* 1841) in German. In 1899 he played in the first Cleveland scholastic football game, between University School and Central High School; one year later he graduated with the first class of University School. He eschewed college and instead

Paul Louis Feiss

entered the Joseph and Feiss Company, a family clothing manufacturing business established in 1846. Feiss worked his way up from the most menial tasks on the payroll to the presidency of the company, which by the late 1920s was distributing its "Clothescraft" apparel throughout the United States. Feiss married Edith Lehman in 1903; they had four children. As a businessman he cultivated a warm relationship with his employees, crediting his success in life to his many friends. He railed against mandatory retirements and once commented, "There is no other country in the world where there is so little respect for the valuable quality of stability." He himself never considered retirement, believing that "Spiritual relaxation is needful, but life is too interesting today for a man to want to retire from it."

Many activities besides his clothing business helped keep life interesting for Feiss. In 1915, as chairman of the Housing Committee of the Cleveland Chamber of Commerce, the young industrialist wrote the report of the first housing survey of the city and helped to write legislation seeking to control tenements. He served as the Chamber's president in 1917–1918. During World War I, Feiss was a member of the Emergency Housing Board and the Council of National Defense. He also served as the public member of the War Industries Board under Bernard Baruch. In 1918 Serbia decorated him with the Order of Saint Sava for war relief work. He was the founder of the New York–based National Information Bureau, which published a directory of national and international philanthropic campaigns, and he served as its president for more than thirty years. Feiss was the first president of Mount Sinai Hospital in Cleveland and served as one of the hospital trustees until his death. He worked for many years as chairman of the Cleveland chapter of the National Policy Association and was a member of the executive committee of the Cleveland Round Table of the National Conference of Christians and Jews. Feiss's involvements extended to the world of the arts: he was a founder and first trustee of the Cleveland Museum of Art; an adviser to the Board of the Cleveland Public Library; and, in 1919, he helped found the Cleveland Orchestra.

Feiss was a member of the Grolier and Aldine Clubs in New York. He was also an active participant in the regular meetings and frequent lectures which comprised the program of the Rowfant Club in Cleveland, a group named after the home of Frederick Locker-Lampson, British poet and bibliophile, whose collection of William Shakespeare quartos and other rare items was known as "the Rowfant Library." Since 1892 the club had been a prominent force in the lives of midwestern bookmen. As a member of the Rowfant Club's 1920 Publication Committee, Feiss supervised the production of *The Battle of Lake Erie,* a collection of historical documents edited by Charles Paullin and pertaining to Oliver Hazard Perry's 1813 defeat of the British fleet off Put-in-Bay, Ohio. The work was printed on Venetia handmade paper by the Arthur H. Clark Company in an edition of 150 copies. In that same year Feiss's annual committee report included the unhappy news that the cost of the club's publication program was outstripping its receipts; he proposed a new policy which imposed a rule of compulsory purchase on members. Despite his part in recommend-

ing such stern measures, Feiss was elected club president in 1922; he served subsequently on the Rowfant Board and was made a fellow.

In a memoir about his father, Feiss's eldest son, Julian, remarks that his father's library, though "not a Huntington or a Morgan, reflected the discernment of a fine mind, the inner sensibility of a scholar, and that of a devoted lover of books." Julian Feiss also describes the oak-paneled room which housed the collection in the Feiss family home: a wide bay window faced north, overlooking the terrace and lawn; the large stone fireplace invariably held a crackling fire; a solid old refectory table, oriental rugs, and deep lounge chairs invited repose. Most of the collection was organized by subject and accessible on open shelves. Fragile pieces and books bound in leather or vellum were shelved behind glass. These sumptuous surroundings, familiar to the many bibliophiles who visited there, seem to reflect the mood of Feiss's presidential address to the Rowfant Club on Candlemas in 1922, in which he urged his fellow Rowfanters to "gather the fruits of their book shelves about them and, with the world whirling madly by, sit down pleasantly to idle the hours away."

Julian Feiss recalls that his father "always knew what he wanted and . . . had the instincts of a book scholar," but regrettably he kept no systematic record of the sources of his acquisitions. A few partial listings, clippings from book catalogues, and an occasional pencil note in the books themselves indicate that Feiss actively sought and purchased desired pieces at auction or from American and European dealers, building the major portion of his collection from 1895 to 1915 through the exercise of the qualities he identified as essential to the true collector: "patient discrimination, deliberate selection, and courage."

Feiss's wide-ranging interests and good judgment were reflected in holdings that featured significant early printed books, including Hartmann Schedel's monumental *Liber Chronicarum* (Nuremberg, 1493), published by Anton Koberger. One of the most celebrated books of the fifteenth century, this history of the world is lavishly illustrated by Michel Wohlgemuth and Wilhelm Pleydenworff with views of all the major cities of the known world, as well as portraits of popes, saints, kings, emperors, and mythological figures. The work was published in a Latin edition of fifteen hundred copies in July 1493; one thousand copies of a German translation by Georg Alt were published in December the same year. Feiss's copy, one of eight hundred remaining of the Latin edition, was bound in stamped calf over boards and bore the bookplate of the bibliographer and bookman Percy Fitzgerald. The Feiss library also included a copy of an early printing of the *Decretales Cum Glossa* (Venice, 1491), Pope Gregory IX's contribution to canon law, collected by St. Raymond Penafort and printed by Johannes Hamman with a miniature in gold and colors on the first page and the text and commentary in black and red. Feiss's copy of the *Iliad* (Paris, 1554) was printed by Adrien Turnebe, the royal printer of Greek to Henry II. This edition, extra-illustrated and bound by Joseph William Zaehnsdorf, also included the *Batrachomyomachia* and the *Hymni,* works ascribed to Homer though not composed by him.

Holdings in British and European history featured Johannes Dun Scotus's *Scriptum Super Tertio Sententiorum* (Venice, 1481), in contemporary German stamped pigskin over oak boards, from the library of Theodore Low DeVinne and bearing his bookplate. Its colophon (Johannes Herburt for Johann von Köln, Nicholas Jenson and associates) was reproduced in DeVinne's *Notable Printers of Italy During the 15th Century* (New York: Grolier Club, 1910). Feiss also owned a fourth edition of *The Chronicle of Fabian* (London: J. Kyngston, 1559), a work used by both Shakespeare and Christopher Marlowe as a source for historical plays, and a second edition of Raphael Holinshed's *Chronicles of England, Scotland, and Ireland* (London: Printed at the expenses of J. Harison, G. Bishop, R. Newberie, H. Denham, and T. Woodcocke, 1587), enlarged and improved but without the illustrations found in the first edition—a book that also served as a resource for Shakespeare and his fellow Elizabethan dramatists.

Literary landmarks included Ludovico Ariosto's *Orlando Furioso* (Venice, 1550), published by Gabriele Giolito, an early and important promoter of Italian national literature; the first English edition of Cyrano de Bergerac's *Comical History of the States and Empires of the Worlds of the Moon and Sun* (London: Henry Rhodes, 1687); the edition of Edward Young's *The Complaint and the Consolation* (London, 1797) with forty-three engravings executed by William Blake; Henry Fielding's *Journal of a Voyage to Lisbon* (London, 1755), a first edition printed for A. Millar, which also included "A Fragment of a Comment on L. Bolinbroke's Essay"; and a first printing of the first book edition of Charles Dickens's *The Posthumous Papers of the Pickwick Club* (London, 1837), originally published by Chapman and Hall in twenty parts.

Examples of fine printing included books from the press of Jean Elzevir, the Ballantyne Press, and the DeVinne Press. Feiss's copy of the *Essays* of Ralph Waldo Emerson (Hammersmith, 1906), with a preface by Thomas Carlyle, was printed at the Doves Press in London and bound in vellum at the Doves Bindery. Among Feiss's several books from the

Feiss's bookplate

Kelmscott Press were *The Romance of Sir Degrevant* (Hammersmith, 1896), bound at the Rowfant Bindery in Cleveland and finished by L. Maillard and G. Pilon in crushed green morocco with blue, brown, yellow, and gray inlays, marbled endpapers, and dentelle borders; William Caxton's translation of *Reynard the Foxe* (1892), from the Dutch prose of Reinaert de Vos; Dante Gabriel Rossetti's *Sonnets and Lyrical Poems* (1894); and William Morris's *The Defence of Guenevere, and Other Poems* (1892).

Feiss's personal favorites included a seventh edition of Robert Burton's *Anatomy of Melancholy* (1660), which he found to be "overflowing with wisdom as to furnish an inexhaustible storehouse of contemplative suggestion." Another favorite, at the opposite end of the spectrum, was a second edition of John Swan's fantastic *Speculum Mundi* (1643), a book which discusses the dragon's appetite for elephant blood and enumerates the sovereign virtues of unicorn horn.

A 1936 appraisal of the contents of the Feiss residence listed more than 1,300 individual titles and 2,410 "miscellaneous books, partly old, partly of a later date" at a total value of approximately $39,000.

In the late 1940s John B. Nicholson, director of the Kent State University Library, approached Feiss to express his interest in making arrangements to purchase the greater part of the collection after Feiss's death. Kent, established as a normal school in 1915, had recently achieved the status of state university, and strengthening the holdings of its library was a high priority at the rapidly growing institution just fifty miles from Feiss's Cleveland home.

In his 1908 reflection, *The Sentiment of Book Collecting,* which appeared as number six in the Rowfantia series, Feiss spoke of his attachment to books as one of "pure friendship" and the act of reading as "a kind of conversation." This address reveals the intensely personal and active relationship he maintained with the "noble company" of his library. At the same time, however, he viewed himself as a "custodian" rather than an owner of books and found satisfaction in the thought that books "pass quietly and steadily, having their impress on countless minds, spreading knowledge and joy and forgetfulness of present ills and baleful memorials." This point of view, coupled with his reverence for scholarship, predisposed Feiss to embrace the idea of placing his books in a university setting. In a 1974 letter to his brother Julian, Carl Feiss also recalls that, in arriving at a decision to enter an agreement with Kent State, his father was "particularly touched by the thoughtfulness embodied in the provision that the University take entire charge of packing and transporting the books to their new home, which would considerably lighten the burden for the heirs."

Upon Feiss's death, therefore, the majority of his collection of more than five thousand volumes was transported to Kent State. Approximately forty-five hundred items were catalogued for the general collection, including large sets of Charles Reade, Théophile Gautier, Guy de Maupassant, Alexandre Dumas *père,* Oliver Goldsmith, Leo Tolstoy, Ivan Turgenev, and Prosper Mérimée. Another 450 volumes, which included incunabula, fine bindings, association copies, and first editions, were selected for the library's Department of Special Collections where they could be given appropriately detailed bibliographic description and housed under controlled conditions. Selections from the Feiss Collection were exhibited at Kent in 1974.

Feiss had made no arrangements for the disposition of his manuscripts, however. After his death his heirs donated a Book of Hours (Rouen, circa 1470) to the Cleveland Museum of Art in memory of their parents. Another late-fifteenth-century Book of Hours bearing Horace Walpole's bookplate was purchased by Wilmarth Sheldon Lewis, who was then reassembling Walpole's Strawberry Hill Library for Yale University. The Feiss family, acting on the recommendation of the executors of the estate, then made arrangements to sell the remaining manuscript collection at auction through the Parke-Bernet Galleries.

The Parke-Bernet exhibition and sale took place in December 1953. The more than thirty items listed from Feiss's collection included a thirteenth-century Sanskrit manuscript of the *Chandi,* an extract from the Hindu mythological text, the *Markandeyapurana,* with fine calligraphy on 161 leaves of bombazine paper, each edged by a filleted border of red, blue, and gold, and featuring twenty-one miniatures in colors and gold. Also sold were Feiss's *Opera* of Johannes Gerson (Nuremburg, 1489) printed by George Stuchs, two parts bound in one volume, with a full-page woodcut attributed to Albrecht Dürer; and *L'Office de L'Eglise* (French, late fifteenth century), a manuscript on vellum with six large-topped illuminated miniatures, bound in full seventeenth-century French calf. This last manuscript, written by more than one scribe, opens with the Vulgate text of Saint John "in principio erat verbum" and, facing the first page, features a miniature of the apostle on the Isle of Patmos, writing the Gospel. From the press of Erhard Ratdolt, Parke-Bernet auctioned Feiss's "exceedingly fine copy" of Jacobus Publicius's *Artes Orandi Epistolandi et Memorandi* (Venice, 1485), divided into two books instead of the usual three, with considerable changes in the text and added woodcut illustrations.

Feiss found many ways to contribute to his community in his lifetime. But perhaps the most enduring of his achievements is his acquisition and preservation of magnificent books. His son Julian recalls "the adventure of prowling through the shelves and the excitement of discovery as the world of literature, romance, philosophy, and history was unfolded during the forty years that the library was in our old home." Feiss's transfer of his rich collection to an institutional setting has guaranteed that same adventure to generations of students and researchers.

References:

Julian W. Feiss, "The Paul Feiss Library: A Memoir," *The Feiss Collection: An Exhibition of Books from the Library of Paul L. Feiss in the Kent State University Libraries,* edited by Dean H. Keller (Kent, Ohio: Kent State University Press, 1975), pp. xi, ix;

Parke-Bernet Galleries (New York), *Rare Books, Manuscripts, Broadsides . . . including property from the Estate of the Late Paul L. Feiss* (New York: Parke-Bernet, 1953).

Donald Gallup
(12 May 1913 –)

William Baker
Northern Illinois University

BOOKS: *A Catalogue of English and American First Editions of Writings by T. S. Eliot, Exhibited in the Yale University Library, 22 February to 20 March, 1937* (Portland, Maine: Southworth-Anthoensen Press, 1937);

A Catalogue of the Published and Unpublished Writings of Gertrude Stein, Exhibited in the Yale University Library, 22 February to 29 March 1941, by Gallup and Robert Bartlett Haas (New Haven: Yale University Library, 1941);

A Bibliographical Check-list of the Writings of T. S. Eliot; Including His Contributions to Periodicals and Translations of His Work into Foreign Languages (New Haven: Yale University Library, 1947);

T. S. Eliot: A Bibliography, Including Contributions to Periodicals and Foreign Translations (London: Faber & Faber, 1952; New York: Harcourt, Brace, 1953); revised again as *T. S. Eliot: A Bibliography* (London: Faber & Faber, 1969; New York: Harcourt, Brace & World, 1969);

80 Writers Whose Books and Letters Have Been Given over the Past Twenty Years to the Yale University Library by Carl Van Vechten, Compiled in Honor of His 80th Birthday, 17 June 1960 (New Haven: Yale University Library, 1960);

A Bibliography of Ezra Pound (London: Hart-Davis [Soho Bibliographies], 1963); revised as *Ezra Pound, A Bibliography* (Charlottesville, Va. & Godalming, U.K.: University Press of Virginia, St. Paul's Bibliographies, 1983);

On Contemporary Bibliography, with Particular Reference to Ezra Pound (Austin: Humanities Research Center, University of Texas, 1970);

T. S. Eliot & Ezra Pound: Collaborators in Letters (New Haven: H. W. Wenning / C. A. Stonehill, 1970);

A Curator's Responsibilities (New Brunswick, N.J.: Graduate School of Library Services, 1976);

Ezra Pound (1886–1972): The Catalogue of an Exhibition in the Beinecke Library 30 October–31 December 1975 Commemorating His Ninetieth Birthday (New Haven: Yale University Library, 1976);

Carl Van Vechten, 17 June 1880–17 June 1980: A Centenary Exhibition of Some of His Gifts to Yale . . .

Donald Gallup with Eleanor Anderson (widow of novelist Sherwood Anderson), Yvette Schumer, and Norman Holmes Pearson examining Anderson items in the Yale Collection of American Literature, January 1958 (Yale News Bureau). On the wall above them is Karl Anderson's portrait of Sherwood and their brothers.

(New Haven: Beinecke Rare Book and Manuscript Library, 1980);

Pigeons on the Granite: Memories of a Yale Librarian (New Haven: Beinecke Rare Book and Manuscript Library, 1988);

What Mad Pursuits!: More Memories of a Yale Librarian (New Haven: Beinecke Rare Book and Manuscript Library, 1998);

Eugene O'Neill and His Eleven-Play Cycle, "A Tale of Possessors Self-Dispossessed" (New Haven: Yale University Press, 1998).

OTHER: Gertrude Stein, *Unpublished Writings,* 8 volumes, edited by Gallup and Carl Van Vechten (New Haven: Yale University Press, 1951–1958);

"Picasso, Gris, and Gertrude Stein," in *Picasso, Gris, Miró: the Spanish Masters of Twentieth Century Painting* (San Francisco: San Francisco Museum of Art, 1948), pp. 15–23;

"Baretti's Reputation in England," in *The Age of Johnson: Essays Presented to Chauncey Brewster Tinker* (New Haven: Yale University Press, 1949), pp. 363–375;

The Flowers of Friendship: Letters Written to Gertrude Stein, edited by Gallup (New York: Knopf, 1953);

Eugene O'Neill, *Inscriptions to Carlotta Monterey O'Neill,* edited by Gallup (New Haven: Privately printed by the Yale University Library, 1960);

O'Neill, *More Stately Mansions,* edited by Gallup (New Haven & London: Yale University Press, 1964);

Stein, *Fernhurst, Q.E.D., and Other Early Writings,* edited anonymously by Gallup (New York: Liveright, 1971; London: Peter Owen, 1972);

"The Collection of American Literature," in *The Beinecke Rare Book and Manuscript Library: A Guide to Its Collections* (New Haven: Yale University Library, 1974), pp. 73–85;

Thornton Wilder, *The Alcestiad, or, A Life in the Sun* [with] *The Drunken Sisters,* edited anonymously by Gallup (Franklin Center, Pa.: Franklin Library / New York: Harper & Row, 1977);

O'Neill, *Poems, 1912–1942,* preliminary edition, edited by Gallup (New Haven: Yale University Library, 1979); final edition published as *Poems, 1912–1944* (New Haven: Ticknor & Fields, 1980; London: Cape, 1980);

Wilder, *American Characteristics and Other Essays,* edited by Gallup (New York & London: Harper & Row, 1979);

O'Neill, *The Calms of Capricorn,* preliminary edition, 2 volumes, edited by Gallup (New Haven: Yale University Library, 1981); final edition published as *The Calms of Capricorn: A Play, Developed from O'Neill's Scenario by Donald Gallup; with a Transcription of the Scenario* (New Haven & New York: Ticknor & Fields, 1982);

O'Neill, *Work Diary, 1924–1943,* preliminary edition, 2 volumes, transcribed by Gallup (New Haven: Yale University Library, 1981);

Kathryn Hulme, *Of Chickens and Plums: Selections from the "Kokee Cabin Log-Book" (1968–1979),* edited anonymously by Gallup (New Haven: Yale University Library, 1982);

Wilder, *The Journals of Thornton Wilder, 1939–1961: Selected and Edited by Donald Gallup, with Two Scenes of an Uncompleted Play, "The Emporium"* (New Haven & London: Yale University Press, 1985);

Ezra Pound, *At the Circulo de Recreo,* edited by Gallup (New Haven: Beinecke Rare Book and Manuscript Library, 1985);

Pound, *Plays Modelled on the Noh (1916) . . . ,* edited by Gallup (Toledo: Friends of the University of Toledo Libraries, 1987);

Wilder, *The Collected Short Plays of Thornton Wilder,* volume 1, edited by Gallup and A. Tappan Wilder (New York: Theatre Communications Group, 1997).

SELECTED PERIODICAL PUBLICATIONS– UNCOLLECTED: "On Hawthorne's Authorship of 'The Battle Omen,'" *New England Quarterly,* 9 (December 1936): 690–699;

"Exhibition of Writings by T. S. Eliot," *Yale University Library Gazette,* 11 (April 1937): 94–95;

"The Gertrude Stein Collection," *Yale University Library Gazette,* 22 (October 1947): 21–32;

"Aldis, Foley, and the Collection of American Literature at Yale," *Papers of the Bibliographical Society of America,* 42 (January/March 1948): 41–49;

"A Book Is a Book Is a Book," *New Colophon,* 1 (January 1948): 67–80;

"The Weaving of a Pattern: Marsden Hartley and Gertrude Stein," *Magazine of Art,* 41 (November 1948): 256–261;

"The Making of *The Making of Americans,*" *New Colophon,* 3 (1950): 54–74;

"Carl Van Vechten's Gertrude Stein," *Yale University Library Gazette,* 27 (October 1952): 77–86;

"The Value, Disadvantages, and Use of Letters," *Yale University Library Gazette,* 28 (October 1953): 56–70;

"Gertrude Stein and the *Atlantic,*" *Yale University Library Gazette,* 28 (January 1954): 109–128;

"Some Notes on Ezra Pound and Censorship," *Yale Literary Magazine,* 126 (December 1958): 37–41;

"Eugene O'Neill's 'The Ancient Mariner,'" *Yale University Library Gazette,* 35 (October 1960): 61–86;

"The Mabel Dodge Luhan Papers," *Yale University Library Gazette,* 37 (January 1963): 97–105;

"A Check-list of the Books in the [Frank] Altschul Collection [of the Arts of the French Book, 1838–1967]," *Yale University Library Gazette,* 44 (October 1969): 61–102;

Gallup, a local pastor, Gertrude Stein, Cpl. Clark Rowland, and Stein's poodle, Basket II, at Choisy-le-Roi, France, 4 March 1945

"Du côté de chez Stein," *Book Collector,* 19 (Summer 1970): 169–184;

"The Collection of American Literature," *Yale University Library Gazette,* 48 (April 1974): 241–252;

"The William Carlos Williams Collection at Yale," *William Carlos Williams Review,* 7 (Spring 1981): 1–8; reprinted in *Yale University Library Gazette,* 56 (October 1981): 50–59;

"The First Separately Published Atlas Entirely Devoted to the Americas: Wytfliet's *Descriptionis Ptolemaicae Augmentum," Papers of the Bibliographical Society of America,* 76 (January/March 1982): 63–73;

"The Carter and Pollard *Enquiry* Fifty Years After," *Papers of the Bibliographical Society of America,* 78 (October/December 1984): 447–460;

"Taste, Technique, and Utility in Book Collecting," *University of Rochester Library Bulletin,* 38 (1985): 60–72;

"The Eugene O'Neill Collection at Yale," *Eugene O'Neill Newsletter,* 9 (Summer/Fall 1985): 3–11;

"The Ezra Pound Archive at Yale," *Yale University Library Gazette,* 60 (April 1986): 161–177;

"The Pleasure of Their Company," *Review,* 9 (1987): 53–65;

"T. S. Eliot, Emily Hale, and the *Letters* of Baron Friedrich Von Hügel," *Book Collector,* 42 (Spring 1993): 126–129;

"Ezra Pound's Experiment for *Esquire," Yale University Library Gazette,* 67 (October 1992): 37–46; reprinted in *Paideuma,* 22 (Spring/Fall 1993): 181–190;

"Introductory Note [to "The Wreck on the Five-Twenty-Five," by Thornton Wilder]," *Yale Review,* 82 (October 1994): 17–22.

Donald Gallup's descriptive bibliographies of Gertrude Stein, T. S. Eliot, and Ezra Pound, based in part on his own collections, have been admired by scholars of twentieth-century literature. Gallup is also known for his work on editions of the writings of Stein, Thornton Wilder, and Eugene O'Neill. His literary friendships have been instrumental in the acquisition of material for his own collections and for those of Yale University Library.

Donald Clifford Gallup was born on 12 May 1913 in Sterling, Connecticut, the son of Carl Daniel Gallup, a lumberman, and Lottie Stanton Gallup. He attended Plainfield High School, gaining a Milner Scholarship to enter Yale University in the fall of 1930, where he received his A.B. in 1934. As a self-supporting honors student he developed his interests in book collecting, American and English literature, and the theater. Early influences were Chauncey Brewster Tinker, Sterling Professor of English and Keeper of Rare Books in the Yale University Library; Professor William Lyon Phelps; and William Clyde DeVane, who introduced Gallup to the writings of the great moderns, including William Butler Yeats, Pound, and Eliot. In February 1933 Eliot visited New Haven to speak on "The English Poets as Letter Writers," and Gallup heard him. Four years later, at the Gotham Book Mart in New York, Gallup purchased Eliot's manuscript of lines beginning "How unpleasant to meet Mr. Eliot," in imitation of Edward Lear, which had been written out during his New Haven visit.

Upon graduation Gallup entered the Yale Graduate School in the English department on a John Addison Porter Memorial Fellowship (1934–1937). He continued to work part time in the library, helping with the cataloguing of the Falconer Madan Collection of Oxford books, the Henry Fielding and *Robinson Crusoe* collections, and other holdings. Gallup's subsequent involvement with American literature and the discovery of unpublished materials was foreshadowed in his second year of graduate school in 1936 when he had an article accepted by the *New England Quarterly:* the subject was a piece that Nathaniel Hawthorne had published anonymously in the *Salem Gazette.*

A course with Yale librarian Andrew Keogh provided the opportunity to compile a bibliography of Eliot, whom Gallup was already collecting. Through a friend of his landlady who knew both Eliot and his wife, Gallup wrote to Eliot, receiving a letter from him on 21 February 1936. Gallup notes in his autobiography, *Pigeons on the Granite: Memories of a Yale Librarian* (1988), that "this was the beginning of a long correspondence which enormously improved the quality of my bibliographical research." In the fall of that same year Gallup met Eliot after a reading at Wellesley, asked him to inscribe the acting edition of *Murder in the Cathedral* (Canterbury: H. J. Goulden, 1935), and made contact with Eliot's brother Henry, from whom Gallup obtained help for both the Eliot bibliography and his extensive Eliot collection. Gallup exhibited this collection for the Yale Library Associates in 1937, and he prepared a catalogue of Eliot's writings.

Another of the social contacts made in those early years was with Ellen Strong Bartlett, historian of New Haven, who took Gallup to symphony concerts and to tea with prominent Yale hostesses. She helped finance Gallup's trip to France, Switzerland, Germany, and England in the summer of 1937. While in London he met Eliot and A. J. A. Symons of the First Editions Club, and in the London Guildhall Gallup discovered and transcribed the records of the murder trial of Giuseppe Baretti, the Italian writer and lexicographer who was the subject of his 1939 Yale Ph.D. dissertation. In September 1937 Gallup became an instructor in the English depart-

ment at Southern Methodist University in Dallas. He reviewed books for the *Dallas News.* Offered a position in the cataloguing department at Yale University Library for approximately the same money he was earning at Southern Methodist University but without "the chore of reading themes and tests from some 120 students," Gallup returned to Yale in February 1940.

Initially Gallup worked under Julia Pettee, retired librarian of the Union Theological Seminary, recataloguing theological books, a plan soon dropped. With Professor Norman Holmes Pearson and librarian James T. Babb he also became involved in developing library collections of American writers. In 1941 Gallup collaborated with Pearson in arranging an exhibition of the papers Stein had deposited at the Yale library in 1937, and he wrote the accompanying catalogue, incorporating a listing by Robert Bartlett Haas of all Stein's writings.

In 1941 Gallup was drafted into the U.S. Army. After graduating from Officer Candidate School he flew to London as a second lieutenant in 1942. While in England, Gallup bought books, which he posted back to Connecticut. His greatest bargain of the war years was a copy of the Kelmscott Press edition of *Poems Chosen Out of the Works of S. T. Coleridge* (1896), which he bought for 5s. 6d. While stationed in Paris, Gallup met Stein, her companion Alice B. Toklas, and the art dealer Daniel-Henry Kahnweiler and received the Croix de Guerre. He spent the last three months of his European service at Magdalen College, Oxford, under a special U.S. Army quota, returning to the United States on 13 December 1945 and receiving his discharge in 1946 as a lieutenant colonel.

During a preliminary year of preparation for teaching bibliography, Gallup studied with Lawrence C. Wroth, librarian of the John Carter Brown Library at Brown University, working on Corneille Wytfliet's *Descriptionis Ptolemaicae Augmentum* (Louvain: Bogardi, 1597). (The result of that research was eventually published in the *Papers of the Bibliographical Society of America* in 1982.) On 1 July 1947 Gallup returned to work at Yale as assistant professor of bibliography, curator of the Collection of American Literature, and editor of the *Yale University Library Gazette,* the organ of the Yale Library Associates.

Gallup's friendship with the novelist, critic, and photographer Carl Van Vechten was instrumental in bringing to Yale collections of inscribed first editions and correspondence of various writers, including the novelists James Branch Cabell, Theodore Dreiser, and Joseph Hergesheimer; the critic

T. S. ELIOT

A BIBLIOGRAPHY

INCLUDING CONTRIBUTIONS TO PERIODICALS
AND FOREIGN TRANSLATIONS

by

DONALD GALLUP

*Assistant Professor of Bibliography
and Fellow of Jonathan Edwards College
Yale University*

NEW YORK
HARCOURT, BRACE AND COMPANY

A. *Books and Pamphlets*

A1   PRUFROCK AND OTHER   1917
                  OBSERVATIONS

First edition:

PRUFROCK | AND | OTHER OBSERVATIONS | BY | T. S. ELIOT | THE EGOIST LTD | OAKLEY HOUSE, BLOOMSBURY STREET | LONDON | 1917

40 pp. 18 × 12 cm. 1s. Stiff buff paper wrappers lettered in black on front cover.

500 copies were published in June 1917. 'The Egoist Subscription Form', a slip measuring approximately 9 × 12½ cm., was loosely inserted in some copies. The price was raised gradually to 5s., at which price the remaining copies were sold in 1920–1. This book was not published in the United States, but its contents were reprinted in *Poems by T. S. Eliot* (New York, Knopf, 1920), pp. 37–63.

A copy in my possession, with dimensions 18½ × 12½ cm., carries the following autograph inscription on the half-title: '. . . . One of twenty-five numbered copies of which this is No. 3. Justification de tirage T. S. E.' Concerning this copy Mr. Eliot wrote me on September 8, 1938: 'I had completely forgotten that any numbered signed copies of *Prufrock and Other Observations* had been issued. . . . I am sorry that my memory is so defective that I cannot tell you whether there really were 24 other numbered copies, or whether that was just my fancy, but if, as you say, the copy in your possession differs slightly from the ordinary edition, I can only suppose there was such a set, though what became of the other copies I have not the remotest notion.'

CONTENTS: The Love Song of J. Alfred Prufrock—Portrait of a Lady—Preludes—Rhapsody on a Windy Night—Morning at the Window—The Boston Evening Transcript—Aunt Helen—Cousin Nancy—Mr. Apollinax—Hysteria—Conversation galante—La Figlia che Piange.

A2   EZRA POUND   1917
             HIS METRIC AND POETRY

First edition:

EZRA POUND | HIS METRIC AND POETRY | NEW YORK [*ornament*] ALFRED A. KNOPF [*ornament*] 1917

31 pp. front. (port.). 19½ × 13 cm. 35c. Red boards lettered in gold on front cover; end-papers. Plain buff dust-wrapper.

Issued anonymously on November 12, 1917, in connexion with the publication, also by Knopf, of Pound's *Lustra* (1917). Concerning this book, Eliot writes in *The Cantos of Ezra Pound: Some*

[3]

Title page and first entries from the American edition of Gallup's first descriptive bibliography

---

H. L. Mencken; and Stein. His correspondence with Toklas following Stein's death led to important Yale additions of books, letters, and art objects. Increasing contacts over library work between 1920 Yale alumnus Thornton Wilder and Gallup culminated in Gallup's appointment as Wilder's literary executor, responsible not only for the papers at Yale but also for the posthumous publication of hitherto unpublished manuscripts.

Gallup's involvement with the Ezra Pound archive came in part through his friendship with Pearson, adviser to the Yale collection, a bookman who, according to Gallup, "cultivated the friendship of contemporary American writers and demonstrated his faith in their importance by buying not just their current books . . . but also by acquiring first editions of earlier works, many of them long out of print." The complicated story of how Yale obtained Pound's pa-

pers and Gallup's role in the negotiations is told in his *Pigeons on the Granite.*

Less well known is Gallup's association with the distinguished artist Georgia O'Keeffe, wife of photographer Alfred Stieglitz, around whom New York artists and writers had gathered. O'Keeffe gave to Yale the Stieglitz/O'Keeffe Archive, a rich resource for the study of American modernism. The presence in the Yale Collection of American Literature of the Stein and Stieglitz papers became an invaluable aid in securing similar material from other sources, including the papers of the *Dial*. From January 1920 until it ceased in 1929 that magazine published work by a pantheon of writers, including Hart Crane, E. E. Cummings, H. D., Eliot, D. H. Lawrence, Thomas Mann, Marianne Moore, Wallace Stevens, Paul Valéry, William Carlos Williams, Edmund Wilson, and Yeats, as well as reproductions of artwork by Oskar Kokoschka, Henri Matisse, Edvard Munch, and Pablo Picasso. The *Dial* papers came to Yale in 1950 as a deposit; in 1987 they were about to be dispersed at auction when the Beinecke Foundation made possible their purchase by Yale.

Other important collections of papers that Gallup had a role in acquiring for Yale are those of Carlotta Monterey O'Neill (the widow of Eugene O'Neill); the art collector Katherine Dreier; the artists Marsden Hartley (with five paintings) and Pavel Tchelitchev (with most of his sketchbooks); the writers Stephen Vincent and William Rose Benét, Leonard Bacon, Arthur Davison Ficke, Mabel Dodge Luhan, Robert Penn Warren, and William Carlos Williams; and the critic Edmund Wilson. Archives of other periodicals that came to Yale while Gallup was curator are those of *Blues, Hound & Horn,* the *Southern Review,* and *View.* He helped administer the Bollingen Poetry Prize from its establishment at Yale until he retired in 1980. At the time of his retirement Gallup was elected an honorary trustee of the Yale Library Associates.

As curator of a great collection of American literature Gallup went beyond the conservation of books to the conservation of literature in the form of the definitive bibliographies of Eliot and Pound. His *T. S. Eliot: A Bibliography* (1952), revised from his 1947 checklist, established Eliot's canon. A further revised and extended edition appeared in 1969. Rupert Hart-Davis, who produced the influential Soho Bibliographies in London, published Gallup's *A Bibliography of Ezra Pound* in 1963. A revised edition published for the Bibliographical Society of the University of Virginia and St. Paul's Bibliographies by the University Press of Virginia appeared in 1983. In 1972 Gallup became involved with a literary journal, *Paideuma* (Orono, Maine), devoted to Pound studies.

In addition to his bibliographical scholarship, Gallup edited publications by Kathryn Hulme, O'Neill, Pound, Stein, and Wilder. His important editorial work on O'Neill includes *More Stately Mansions* (1964), *Work Diary 1924–1943* (1981), and the development of *The Calms of Capricorn* from a scenario. In 1994 the Eugene O'Neill Foundation honored him with its Tao House Award "for what he has given to the American Theater."

Gallup's talk "Taste, Technique and Utility in Book Collecting," made at a 12 November 1984 meeting of the Friends of the University of Rochester Libraries and published in the *University of Rochester Library Bulletin* (1985), presents his philosophy as a bookman. Gallup follows John Carter's *Taste and Technique in Book Collecting* (1948) in believing that a collector should "anticipate the scholar and the historian, to find some interest where none was recognized before, to rescue books from obscurity, to pioneer a subject or an author." Gallup's attention to Van Vechten, O'Keeffe, and the relationship between art and literature illustrates this belief in practice. To commemorate Van Vechten's eightieth birthday on 17 June 1960 Gallup prepared a listing of books and letters given by Van Vechten over the previous twenty years to the Yale University Library; it comprises a galaxy of writers, artists, and musicians, many of whom still need to be researched. More recently his publication in the October 1994 *Yale Review* of a manuscript play by Wilder, "The Wreck on the Five-Twenty-Five," exemplifies not only his concern with the bibliography and description of dramatic literature but also his advocacy of the role of the collector in resurrecting the lost, the forgotten, or the stolen.

In "Taste, Technique and Utility" Gallup also raises the issue of "*how* one collects." One way is through bibliographical compilation; his friendships with Stein, Van Vechten, and others illustrate another way of collecting. Gallup's belief in following "instinct" is fully described in *Pigeons on the Granite.* His instinct has helped to build the Yale library collections, because his own first editions and manuscript material by or related to Pound, as well as his extensive collections of Edward Lear, Lawrence Durrell, Graham Greene, John Osborne, and other British and American authors, have been given to the university.

References:

John Carter, *Taste and Technique in Book Collecting: A Study of Recent Developments in Great Britain and the United States* (New York: R. R. Bowker, 1948);

Anthony Rota, *Points at Issue: A Bookseller Looks at Bibliography; A Lecture Delivered at the Library of Congress on April 24, 1984* (Washington, D.C.: Library of Congress, 1984).

John Work Garrett
(19 May 1872 - 26 June 1942)

Timothy D. Pyatt
University of North Carolina at Chapel Hill

WRITINGS: "Seventeenth Century Books Relating to Maryland," *Maryland Historical Magazine,* 34 (1939): 1–39;

"A Library of Four Generations," in *John Work Garratt and His Library at Evergreen House* (Baltimore: Privately printed, 1944), pp. 45–74.

John Work Garrett was raised in the tradition of encouraging and supporting the creative arts. All of Garrett's family were collectors, but John Work Garrett brought book collecting to a new level. His library of thirty-five thousand volumes included rare Marylandia with a special emphasis on the seventeenth century, particularly early voyages and maps, as well as ornithology, William Shakespeare, and other early imprints. Garrett also acquired a complete set of autographs of the signers of the Declaration of Independence. As John Pierpont Morgan and his private library were to New York, so John Work Garrett and his Evergreen House Library became to Baltimore. Like the Morgan library, Garrett's has become a research facility open to the public.

John Work Garrett was born in Baltimore, Maryland, on 19 May 1872 to one of the richest and most important families in the state. As captains of finance and transportation, members of the Garrett family played leading roles in the business and arts communities. The patriarch of the family, Robert Garrett (1783–1857), was born in Ireland and immigrated with his family to Pennsylvania in 1790. In 1801 he moved to Baltimore, where he started a dry-goods and grocery business in 1819. By 1840 it had developed into Robert Garrett and Sons. The firm grew to become an investment-banking house with interests in western trade. To support this business Garrett fostered the fledgling Baltimore and Ohio Railroad. His son, the first John Work Garrett (1820–1884), became president of this railroad in 1858, having been nominated for the post by his friend and neighbor Johns Hopkins, for whom the well-known Baltimore university is named. During

John Work Garrett, 1932 (photograph by Eva Barrett; courtesy of Evergreen House Foundation, Johns Hopkins University)

the Civil War this John Work Garrett, grandfather of the book collector, was sympathetic to the Confederacy, but he placed his railroad at the disposal of the federal government. He engineered the first military rail transport in history, moving Union troops from the Potomac to Chattanooga in 1863. Garrett's railroad also took President Abraham Lincoln to Antietam to visit Union soldiers. Because Garrett allowed the Baltimore and Ohio Railroad to supply Union troops and provide scouting reports, Maryland Confederates blamed him for the failure of Southern troops to capture Washington, D.C.

John Work Garrett's son Thomas Harrison Garrett (1849–1888) twice tried to run away and

Garrett's library at Evergreen House, Baltimore

join the Confederate army. The father of the book collector, T. Harrison graduated from Princeton in 1868 and joined the family business, becoming head of the banking house of Robert Garrett and Sons and a director of the Baltimore and Ohio Railroad. In 1870 he married Alice Whitridge. The couple had three sons, among them John Work Garrett, who was only sixteen years old when his father died in a yachting accident on 7 June 1888.

Despite his early death T. Harrison Garrett's influence was powerful. As a child John Work Garrett was impressed with his father's knowledge of books, prints, coins, and art. After T. Harrison Garrett's death, Alice Garrett shut up Evergreen House, the family estate, and took her sons abroad. This period of travel to Europe and the Near East fostered John Work Garrett's natural ability with languages and gave him an appreciation for other cultures.

In his youth Garrett displayed a wide range of interests. In addition to a love of books he enjoyed music, art, languages, and athletics. His fondness for the outdoors manifested itself in his study of ornithology and other fields of natural history. These interests endured throughout his life and led to some of his most prized acquisitions for the Evergreen House Library. While at Princeton University he participated in sports and was active in musical organizations and social clubs. After his graduation with a B.S. in 1895, he joined the Princeton Geological Expedition to the Yellowstone Valley as the ornithologist for the group. After the expedition

did not report back for more than two weeks, it was thought that the party had been massacred by Bannock Indians. All the members of the party returned safely, however, and Garrett had fallen in love with the West. For the next few years he and some of his Princeton friends helped to manage a New Mexico cattle ranch.

In 1896 and 1898 Garrett served as a delegate to the Fifth and Seventh National Irrigation Congresses, an experience that helped shape his desire to serve in the diplomatic corps. In 1901 he became secretary to the American Legation at The Hague, remaining at that post until 1903. He then served as secretary in the Netherlands and Luxembourg until 1905, when he became second secretary of the American embassy at Berlin. In 1908 he was promoted to first secretary of the embassy at Rome, remaining there until sometime in 1910. Garrett next served as U.S. minister to Venezuela (December 1910–November 1911) and Argentina (1911–1914) before being sent to France at the outbreak of World War I. From 1914 to 1917 he was in charge of German and Austro-Hungarian civilian prisoners of war while serving as a special agent assisting the United States ambassador to France. In 1917 he was appointed minister to the Netherlands and Luxembourg, a post he held for two years. He later served as secretary general of the Conference on the Limitation of Armaments, held in Washington, D.C., in 1921–1922. In 1929 President Herbert Hoover named Garrett American ambassador to Italy. He

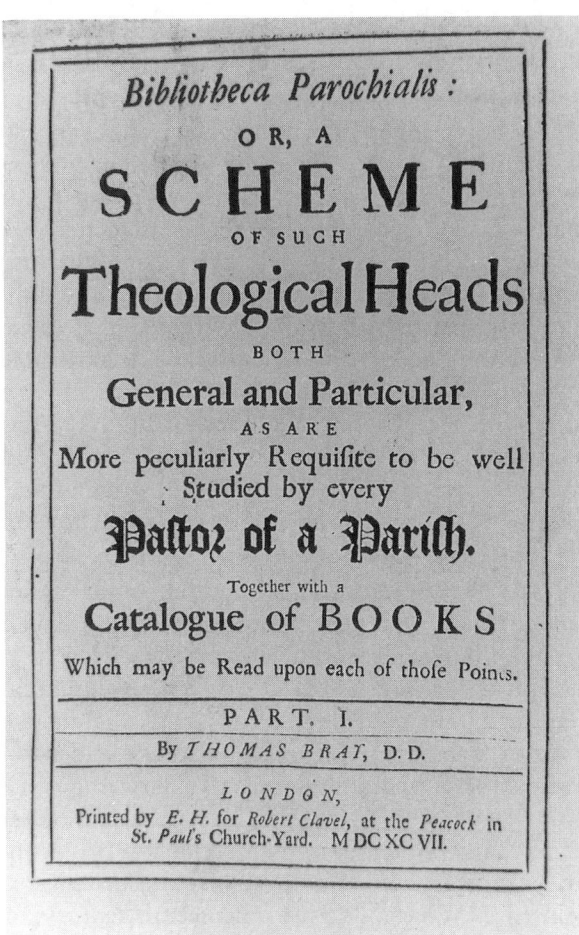

Title pages for two volumes in Garrett's collection of seventeenth-century books relating to Maryland: John Smith's account of his explorations in the New World, including the Chesapeake Bay, and a book by Reverend Thomas Bray, sent to Maryland to establish libraries for Anglican clergymen

retired from the diplomatic service in 1933 and devoted himself to the cultivation and refinement of his library.

Garrett's library was the product of four generations of collecting. While each Garrett played some role in its formation, the greater portion was built by John Work and his father. Few of Robert Garrett's books have survived, but much of the library of the first John Work Garrett was passed on to his namesake. Robert Garrett had insured his son's appreciation of literature and the arts by sending him to preparatory school to study French, Latin, and history. The elder John Work Garrett purchased paintings for the Maryland Institute of Art and donated casts of Greek and Roman statues to the Peabody Institute. He presented an entire library to a private school in his native city. Credited with suggesting the plan for Johns Hopkins University and hospital to his friend and neighbor, he served as one of the twelve original trustees for the university. Among the works that John Work Gar-

rett added to the family library was a first edition of Herman Melville's first book, *Typee* (New York: Wiley & Putnam, 1846).

In the next generation T. Harrison Garrett was a discriminating collector of books, prints, and coins. At Evergreen House, acquired by his father in 1878, he assembled the largest private library in Maryland and hired a personal librarian, John W. Lee. T. Harrison Garrett built a substantial collection of manuscripts, including autographs of most of the signers of the Declaration of Independence. He loved prints and gathered more than twenty-eight thousand, many at the important Claghorn sale in Philadelphia in 1885. He also collected southern Americana and Confederate imprints, and he secured an impressive group of Union and Confederate pamphlets relating to the Civil War, all of which he had attractively bound. He also started collections of pamphlets pertaining to the Revolutionary War, the War of 1812, and the Mexican-American War. Among his contributions to the Garrett Library is a bibliography of the Baltimore and Ohio Railroad, prepared by Lee and printed at T. Harrison's expense by the Chiswick Press in London.

The younger John Work Garrett began collecting books seriously while he was still in college. By 1928 the family library had grown to the point that he had a new library building constructed next to Evergreen House. Garrett was a discriminating collector, understanding the importance of condition and concentrating on the collecting areas of his grandfather and father. Bibliographer Lawrence Wroth, director of the John Carter Brown Library in Providence, Rhode Island, declared that Garrett with his financial resources could have collected vast numbers of books merely for the pride of possession but instead bought books slowly, showing great care and selectivity.

As Wroth said, Garrett built his library book by book, largely at auction or from one of the small group of booksellers with whom he dealt. His largest purchase consisted of fifteen seventeenth-century books relating to Maryland, which he acquired en bloc in 1937. These books had been owned by a former Baltimorean, Willard Augustine Baldwin of New York, whose estate held several items that were not part of any public or private library in Maryland. Books, maps, and broadsides printed in Maryland in the seventeenth century, or early items relating to Maryland but printed elsewhere, became Garrett's collecting focus after his retirement. His interest in this field stemmed from the seven early Maryland books already in the Evergreen House Library. During the final years of his life he expanded that small nucleus to ninety-two titles, the largest collection of its type. In 1939 Garrett wrote an article for the *Maryland Historical Magazine* about his efforts to identify seventeenth-century books relating to Maryland. It was his dream not only to document and collect in this field but also to make his volumes accessible to students and scholars. He acquired two of the three known copies of the 1632 Maryland charter, the earliest work to mention Maryland by name. One of the Garrett copies came to him as a gift from his friend Benjamin Howell Griswold Jr. Another choice piece of his Maryland collection is the unique copy of *An Almanac for the Provinces of Virginia and Maryland,* by John Seller (London: Printed for the author, 1685). The entire twenty-four-page work is engraved, not printed, and it includes two early maps of Virginia and Maryland. In 1949 Garrett's librarian, Elizabeth Baer, published *Seventeenth Century Maryland: A Bibliography,* outlining Garrett's research and collection. The work, underwritten by his widow, Alice

Warder Garrett, lists 209 titles and includes a survey of 250 institutions and private collectors.

The Americana in the Evergreen House Library was not limited to seventeenth-century Marylandia. The first book printed in Baltimore, *A Detection of the Conduct and Proceedings of Messrs. Annan and Henderson,* by John Redick (Baltimore: Printed by Nicolas Hasselbach, 1765), was placed in the library by Garrett's brother Robert (1875–1961), who had also inherited the family's collecting zeal. This book was the only known Baltimore imprint by Hasselbach until a second work, *Poor Robin's Almanac* (Baltimore: Printed by Nicolas Hasselbach, 1765), was discovered at the University of Maryland at College Park.

Garrett owned other early American imprints, including John Eliot's Indian Bible in Algonquian (Cambridge, Mass.: Printed by Samuel Green & Marmaduke Johnson, 1663), which was the first Bible of any sort published in British North America, and Increase Mather's *Kometographia. Or A Discourse on Comets* (Boston: Printed by Samuel Green for Samuel Sewall, 1683).

In part Garrett's library reflected his father's tastes. T. Harrison Garrett loved George Cruikshank, so the library includes many works illustrated by this nineteenth-century artist. John Work Garrett took it upon himself to complete the collection of manuscripts and autographs of the signers of the Declaration of Independence that his father had started, improving its significance—and value—by seeking manuscripts with Maryland associations or, at a minimum, substantive documents, because he disdained signatures cut from books. Garrett particularly sought letters written from Baltimore while the signers were attending the Continental Congress of December 1778 to February 1779. He succeeded in acquiring letters from John Hancock, William Whipple, Benjamin Harrison, Thomas Nelson, William Hooper, and Thomas McKean written from Baltimore (some directed to Robert Morris, another signer). This correspondence sheds light on the daily lives of the delegates, recording their complaints about living conditions and the weather. Harrison, for example, referred to eighteenth-century Baltimore as "the Damndest Hole in the World," where "in this infernal sink . . . there is not even a Tavern that we can ride to for Exercise and amusement." Garrett was also able to locate a deed signed by Button Gwinnett—Gwinnett is the most elusive of the signers—and one of two complete books that had survived from the library of Thomas Lynch Jr., signer from South Carolina.

Also interested in early printing, important typographers, and landmarks in the history of the book, Garrett acquired a thirteenth-century Chinese treatise on agriculture printed during the Sung Dynasty, two hundred years before the first book was printed from movable type in the West. He owned three Gutenberg imprints, including a fragment of his Donatus *Ars Minor* (Mainz, circa 1450), and a dictionary printed in Mexico City in 1571, nearly three-quarters of a century before printing came to British North America. Garrett also collected the work of William Caxton, the first to print a book in English. Garrett's prize Caxton was the *Chronicles of England* (Westminster, 1480). He also possessed the first medical treatise ever printed, *De Pollutione Nocturna* (Cologne: Printed by Ulrich Zel, circa 1470), by Joannes Gerson, chancellor of the University of Paris.

At the Jerome Kern sale, held at the Anderson Galleries in New York City in 1929, Garrett paid four thousand dollars for Kern's Fourth Folio of Shakespeare (London: Printed for H. Herringman and others, 1685), the last of the great folio editions of the seventeenth century. This book joined Garrett's many other editions of Shakespeare, including the Second (London: Printed by Thomas Coates for Robert Allot, 1632) and Third (London: Printed for T. C., 1663–1664) Folios bought by Garrett and a First Folio (London: Printed by Isaac Jaggard & Ed. Blount, 1623) that T. Harrison Garrett had purchased from William Pickering in 1865 when T. Harrison was just a sophomore at Princeton. Also in Garrett's collection of British literature was the first collected edition of the plays of Ben Jonson (London: Printed by W. Stansby, 1616) and of Francis Beaumont and John Fletcher's *Comedies and Tragedies* (London: Printed for Humphrey Robinson and Humphrey Moseley, 1647), and the first printings of Edmund Spenser's *The Faerie Queene* (London: Printed for William Ponsonbye, 1590), Samuel Johnson's *A Dictionary of the English Language* (London: Printed by W. Strahan for J. & P. Knapton and others, 1755), and James Boswell's *The Life of Samuel Johnson, LL.D.* (London: Printed by Henry Baldwin for Charles Dilly, 1791).

Garrett also added to his father's nice collection of natural history and art books, most notably by acquiring a complete set of the Audubon elephant folios of *The Birds of America* (London: Published for the author, 1827–1838). Garrett also secured two original Audubon drawings and *The Viviparous Quadrupeds of North America* (New York: J. J. Audubon, 1845–1848) by Audubon and John Bachman and rounded out his ornithological holdings with Alexander Wilson's *American Ornithology* (Philadelphia: Printed by Robert Carr for Bradford and Inskeep, 1808–1814) and thirty-five of John Gould's

folio volumes of three thousand color prints of birds throughout the world (1832–1888).

Garrett also sought travel and exploration literature. He secured Theodore De Bry's 1590 reprint of Thomas Hariot's *Virginia* (Frankfort: J. Wechel) with twenty-eight hand-colored engravings of John White's illustrations of North American natives. Another of such treasures was a copy of *De Insuli in Mari Indico* (Basel: Iohann Bergman de Olpe, 1494), in which Columbus recorded his discovery of the New World. Garrett did not limit his collecting to printed works. He owned several beautifully illuminated fourteenth- and fifteenth-century Books of Hours.

John Work Garrett's friends compared him to Jean Grolier, the Renaissance collector who had his book bindings stamped with the motto "IO. GROLIERII ET AMICORUM" (Jo. Grolier and Friends) to indicate his willingness to share his books with his friends. Garrett liked to share with his guests those books that he felt matched their tastes and personalities. For a corporate chairman, he might display Adam Smith's *Wealth of Nations* (London: W. Strahan and T. Cadell, 1776). Garrett's close friend and fellow collector Benjamin Howell Griswold Jr. remembered a meeting of the P. L. Club (Private Library Club) at Evergreen House. Garrett retrieved a rare and significant volume for each club member except Griswold, who was president of the club and was thus informed that he had the run of the entire library. To honor Griswold, however, Garrett displayed his favorite Audubon plate, an engraving of the canvasback duck with Baltimore in the background. For the visiting Samuel Johnson collector A. Edward Newton, whom Garrett called his greatest critic, Garrett displayed a copy of Newton's own *The Amenities of Book Collecting* (Boston: Atlantic Monthly Press, 1918). In 1937 Garrett agreed to serve as a member of the Johns Hopkins University board of trustees, and he willed his library, along with his art collection, house, and grounds, to the university, where his collection became the cornerstone of the rare-book collection. By this bequest Garrett ensured that future scholars would have access to his collections, just as they had during his life. Garrett stated in his will:

I make this gift of Evergreen House to the Johns Hopkins University as a memorial to my family. I should like it to be always hospitably open to lovers of music, art and beautiful things and to qualified and competent students and investigators, who could make use of its collections, and of additions that might be made to them from time to time.

Garrett understood the significance of his magnificent books as more than mere possessions. His contributions through his collections and bibliography of Marylandia ensure that his vision will continue.

References:

Elizabeth Baer, *Seventeenth Century Maryland: A Bibliography* (Baltimore: John Work Garrett Library, 1949);

John Work Garrett and His Library at Evergreen House (Baltimore: Privately printed, 1944);

Harold A. Williams, *Robert Garrett & Sons Incorporated: Origins and Development–1840–1965* (Baltimore: Schneidereth & Sons, 1965).

Papers:

The Garrett family papers are held at several repositories. The Manuscript Division of the Library of Congress holds business papers and personal correspondence dating from 1778 to 1925, with the greatest concentration in the 1830–1870 period. The Maryland Historical Society holds letters and related materials dating from 1884–1900. The majority of John Work Garrett's personal papers are at Evergreen House, Johns Hopkins University.

Belle da Costa Greene

(13 December 1883 – 10 May 1950)

Ruth Rosenberg
City University of New York

When J. Pierpont Morgan founded his library in 1905, he engaged twenty-one-year-old Belle da Costa Greene as his librarian. She continued to serve in that position to the end of Morgan's life in 1913 and remained as librarian under his son J. P. Morgan Jr. In 1924 Morgan gave over both ownership and administration of the library's collections and building to a board of trustees, and Greene was elected director of the library. She continued as such until her retirement in 1948, completing forty-three years of service and leadership to one of the great libraries of the world. The level of excellence attained by the Pierpont Morgan Library is due in no small measure to Belle Greene.

Belle da Costa Greene was born in Alexandria, Virginia, on 13 December 1883, the daughter of Richard Greene and Genevieve Van Vliet Greene. Her middle name came from her maternal grandmother, Genevieve da Costa Van Vliet. Belle's parents separated, and her mother, a native of Richmond and a woman of great pride and old-fashioned dignity, moved with her children to Princeton, New Jersey, where she gave music lessons to support them. Money was lacking for a college education, so Belle took employment at the Princeton University Library. There she learned the elements of cataloguing and the fine points of working with rare books. Ernest G. Richardson, a professor of bibliography and university librarian, was her first mentor. Her interest in early books attracted the attention of Junius Morgan, a Princeton man and nephew of the elder J. P. Morgan. Knowing that his uncle was seeking someone to manage his already considerable library of rare books and manuscripts, he recommended Greene. Her quick wit and receptive mind delighted J. P. Morgan, while she admired his decisiveness and the grand scale of his transactions. She carried out her duties with affection and loyalty. When Greene arrived in New York in 1905, the library building that Morgan had long planned was nearing completion on Thirty-sixth Street between Madison and Park Avenues. It was designed in graceful neo-Renaissance style with richly embel-

Belle da Costa Greene

lished interiors. Into this elegant atmosphere Greene entered with enthusiasm. Her first task was to sort, catalogue, shelve, and organize the diverse collections. She had the collaboration of a more experienced bibliographer, Ada Thurston, who was to be her associate for nearly thirty years, but the younger woman was the decisive personality on the staff.

When Morgan turned seventy he devoted himself with increasing intensity to his artistic interests, and Greene became his trusted and indispensable aide. By 1908 she was undertaking errands for him abroad. On these trips dealers opened to her their best treasures, and aristocratic houses welcomed her as a guest. Greene for her part did not hesitate to adopt the grand manner that she felt suited her role. For hotels she chose Claridge's in London and the Ritz in Paris; for clothes she visited the foremost couturiers. She sought out not only collectors who were wealthy but also scholars who were not. One of the latter was Sydney Cockerell, the director of the Fitzwilliam Museum in Cambridge, England, whom she met in 1908. He was to have a great influence on her development as a connoisseur of illuminated manuscripts. Cockerell devoted time to her, training her eye and her critical approach and furnishing introductions to the foremost scholars of Britain and the Continent. She developed her beautiful round handwriting in response to his criticism of her illegible scrawl. Thus the young woman who had no college degree became transformed into someone who, over the span of forty years, would be sought out by scholars, dealers, and the wealthy and powerful for her evaluation of rare treasures.

In rumor and gossip Greene was often linked romantically with Cockerell as she was years later with William Ivins Jr., the curator of prints at New York's Metropolitan Museum of Art. Unlike these or any other relationship, however, it was Greene's affair with Bernard Berenson, the world-renowned scholar of medieval and Renaissance Italian painting, that is supported by a mass of documentation. Late in 1908 Berenson and his wife, Mary, were invited by Morgan to visit his library. There they met Greene, "a svelte, dark-haired, strangely beautiful young woman, the dusky oval of her face suggesting an exotic origin–'Malay,'" Berenson later reflected. The attraction was mutual. For years Berenson and Greene wrote each other, sometimes daily, even when he was at his villa in Italy or elsewhere in Europe. Greene wrote to Berenson soon after their first meeting, "Dear Man of my Heart, I have been with you in thought every moment since you left me. I have wished for you at dinners, at the theater and opera; morning, afternoon and night, my thoughts have been wrapped around you, as I should wish to be." Berenson saved all six hundred of Greene's letters. Greene, however, destroyed all of Berenson's letters shortly before her death.

The marriage between Bernard and Mary Berenson was such that they shared information about their extramarital loves with each other. These attachments, they were convinced, did not detract from their own singular relationship and need for each other, since other deeply felt loves were necessary for spiritual growth and development. Upon Greene's arrival in London in 1910, Bernard dined with her, and they "chatted till midnight, so rapt in each other that for the life of me I could not recall who, or what, or why. I am all in a whirl," he told Mary, "for she is the most incredible combination of sheer childishness, hoydenishness, intermixed with sincerity, cynicism and sentiment." Mary's response was, "You are getting old. Make the most of it, if thee can without doing her harm." In a letter to Mary, Bernard wrote of Greene that "as yet she is much more cerebral than sensual. Of the erotic there is little in her and under the mask and manner and giggle there is something so genuine, so loyal, so vital, so full of heart that my impressions vary from minute to minute." He ended the letter, "Goodbye my darling. Even though polygamous I am not the less yours."

As time proceeded, however, Mary's acceptance of Greene as her husband's lover waned. In 1923 she wrote to Bernard's sister, "He is always in love and I put up with it all right, except when his mistress is an out-and-out vulgarian like Belle Greene." In 1926 she wrote of a "letter from Belle Greene which upset him a lot. It was evidently one of her sex-boasting letters, when she gets her silly head turned by people who make up to her thinking she is Morgan's mistress and can do great things for them. She has the worst taste in letter writing of any female I have ever known."

The affection that Greene and Berenson shared for each other never died. Though the fire that had ignited their passion in 1908 was banked by 1920, Berenson could still write to Greene in that year, "How simple it would be if I did not care so much for you." His letter elicited a lengthy homily: "I honestly cannot see that I am anything except an ineradicable memory." She reminded him that she had not made the slightest move to bring herself into his "active living–not even here in New York–as I so easily could, because I have a hunch that it is not *me* that you need but the rush and wear and tear. There is some antagonism on my side and a Christlike, all-enduring, all-suffering Patience and Forbearance on yours. I am trying to analyze my antagonism. I know that its roots lie in remembering the really innocent, utter and world-excluding worship I once gave you. It rarely occurs to me that you are someone with whom I have been in personal and acute touch. On the few times that I come closer to you, I cannot but sense an obscuring wall of Pretense and Effort. It is high time that we released each other." As soon as Berenson departed New York for Europe, however, Greene wrote, "Already it has begun, dear B. B. I *miss* you horribly, just horribly."

In 1908 Greene was crucial in arranging one of Morgan's great purchases. The family of Lord Amherst had in its possession fourteen books printed by William Caxton, England's first printer, in the fifteenth century. They had decided to put these volumes up for sale at public auction when Greene sought to convince them that their wiser choice would be to withhold them from auction and instead sell them to Morgan privately, through her. The night before the auction was to take place Greene attended a dinner in London with some book dealers, who wished to know if she might be bidding against them the next day. During the course of the dinner a telegram arrived for Greene. It was from the Amherst family, giving their approval to her proposal that they sell the Caxtons to Morgan. She was thus able to tell the book dealers, "You may now have your reply, gentlemen. I shall not bid against you tomorrow." Morgan paid $125,000 for the Caxtons.

When in one of his letters Bernard Berenson had written sarcastically of Morgan, Greene beseeched him not to "jeer at my dearly beloved Boss. In all the too few years I have known him in a unique way, he has been absolutely like a child in his confidences and the expression of his thoughts and feelings. I wonder how many other people know as I do the utter loneliness in his life. He gives all and gets what? Only a sickening realization of his money and the world power it brings him." Morgan's death in 1913 was a great shock to Greene. She wrote to a friend, "He was almost a father to me . . . his never-failing sympathy, his understanding and his great confidence and trust in me, bridged all the difference in age, wealth and position."

Greene and J. P. Morgan Jr. enjoyed an easy working relationship after he took over his father's responsibilities. In 1916 Greene was able, on her own initiative, to arrange the acquisition of the magnificent volume of "Old Testament Illustrations" that had been created in thirteenth-century France and presented to Shah Abbas the Great of Persia by the Primate of Poland in the seventeenth century. It had come into the possession of Sir Thomas Phillipps who, at his death in 1872, was reputed to have amassed the greatest collection of manuscript material that any private individual had ever gathered together. (His goal was said to be "to own one of everything.") Greene negotiated the sale of this volume from the Phillipps estate, and Morgan was impressed. The pattern that developed between them was that booksellers, or others with books, manuscripts, or prints to sell would write or call either Greene or Morgan. At times one or the other would go browsing or shopping. If one received an attractive offer or ran into an interesting item, the other would be promptly contacted. They would discuss

Greene early in her career

the item, possibly call in an outside expert, and then more often than not come to a joint decision about purchase or rejection.

A. S. W. Rosenbach, the great Philadelphia bibliophile and book dealer, was fascinated by Greene; he described her as "the dark, exotic, husky-voiced Belle, [who] had the knowledge, the appreciation, and the judgment to know when a great book was something she ought to go after" and, what was sometimes disconcerting to him, "when a great book was not so great or not so great that a better would not come along if she waited." Her judgment, he said, was "most sure and discriminating." Greene enjoyed the role in New York and international society that her position afforded her. She was known for the sweeping Renaissance gowns and matching jewelry that she wore. This style of dress slowly gave way to more businesslike attire after Morgan converted the library into an educational institution with Greene as its director. The imperiousness of Greene's manner remained, serving as protection against casual or incompetent visitors. True scholars were received warmly and aided in every conceivable way. She was generous with her counsel and practical help to other libraries and museums. (She was particularly helpful to the Walters Art Gallery in Baltimore.) For those who met

The J. Pierpont Morgan Library, where Greene served as librarian for forty-three years

her critical standards her capacity for friendship was astonishing; ever ready to make new friends, she kept older associations alive and glowing by a vigorous correspondence—little notes or voluminous letters, often written late at night after a long day at work and an equally long evening at play. Noted for her sharp tongue, she once called one of the scholars on the library's staff "a mule in sheep's clothing."

Though Greene had a reputation in society as a colorful and exciting personality, she preferred to keep much of her personal life private. Her friend Dorothy Miner said that "she refused to cooperate with any efforts to record her life, scorning such personal history as unimportant and of no concern to anyone."

Greene's friends were often introduced to her playful side. In 1928 she approached Rosenbach about buying the manuscript of Lewis Carroll's *Alice in Wonderland* (1865) as her personal gift to the library but then went on to say, "I do not doubt that it is rather silly of me to want to do this, but then as you know I am very silly." There was considerable sentiment in England that this manuscript had to remain within the country. Rosenbach purchased it at auction for £15,400, offering it to the British Museum if he were reimbursed this amount.

Greene was assiduous in guarding the library from acquiring items that were not quite what they were alleged to be. She had long been skeptical of the authenticity of a binding attributed to Benve-

nuto Cellini that had been purchased from the reputable Paris dealer Seligmann. Upon investigation her educated guess proved to be correct. The binding was, for the most part, of German provenance. Seligmann was mortified, and Morgan hastened to reassure him that he did not for a moment question his good faith.

Greene's eagerness, or lack thereof, for certain acquisitions did not always coincide with Morgan's. In 1922 she wrote to her employer: "In regard to Rosenbach's Thackeray items . . . I have made him an offer of ten thousand dollars. . . . My only enthusiasm in the matter is that it *finishes* the Thackeray question in the Library, for all time, and *in so far as I know,* would make your Thackeray collection the finest known." Greene received approval by cable to pay Rosenbach the $10,000. In a 1924 letter to Morgan, Greene underlines her opinion of some of his acquisitions: "In regard to the Tennyson items which, personally I loathe, it is a question of perfecting your already very large and fine collection of imbecilities." Morgan's reply was, "I reluctantly confirm that we ought to have the Tennyson idiocies."

Though Greene acceded to Morgan's desires, particularly in the case of purchases that would round out the library's holdings of an author's work, she had her limits. Thirteen years after the Alfred Tennyson episode, the library was offered the manuscript of Charles Dickens's *Life of Our Lord* (published 1934). Greene wrote, "This is an appalling product" and directed Morgan's secretary to reject it. She added: "Inasmuch as the lady [the seller] states that the Dickens manuscripts are all in museums or private collections, it might be another pleasant blow to let her know that we have complete original manuscripts of *Battle of Life, Christmas Carol, Cricket on the Hearth, Frozen Deep* (with Wilkie Collins), *Holiday Romance, Hunted Down, Sketches of Young Gentlemen,* and over 500 autograph letters."

Greene was interested in prints, and when several mezzotint portraits were coming up for sale at Sotheby's in November 1924 she wrote, "I rather fear that they may not interest you particularly," but then went on to invoke, as she almost never did, the memory of Morgan's father: "Mr. Morgan had such a splendid and representative collection of mezzotints and, this Library being what it is, I felt that you ought to cover the entire field of mezzotinting." Morgan authorized her to bid.

Over Greene's objections, the Morgan Library sometimes lent books and manuscripts to other libraries and museums for exhibitions. Her misgivings were justified in the fall of 1932, when the library lent the manuscript of Sir Walter Scott's *Guy Mannering* (1815) to Columbia University for an ex-

The East Room of the Morgan Library

hibition of Scott material. On 25 October it was discovered that the manuscript had disappeared. On 17 April 1933, however, President Nicholas Murray Butler of Columbia wrote to Morgan that the manuscript had mysteriously reappeared. It was never publicly explained, but Morgan learned from a friend who had been in contact with the underworld that the burglar who had stolen the manuscript had been unable to sell it and had since died. The criminal contact wished to know if Morgan would like to have the manuscript back, and it was subsequently returned wrapped in plain paper. Greene was able to arrange that no such loans would be made in the future, unless the borrowing institution's security measures could meet her exacting demands.

The last exchange of letters between Greene and Morgan occurred during the summer of 1939, when many people had come to New York for the World's Fair. Greene complained about the visitors to the library who had come to see the special exhibition of books and manuscripts assembled in conjunction with the fair: "The visitors, few or many,

are so damn respectful, never speaking above a whisper, that I occasionally think of importing a hoodlum (I should say another hoodlum) to keep myself company." Morgan replied, "I do not think I should feel as badly as you seem to about the respectfulness of the visitors. They ought to feel that way whether they show it or not, though of course I can quite understand your desire to have *some* hoodlumism around somewhere, for company's sake, now that I am abroad."

During the later 1920s and the 1930s Greene's duties included the promotion of publications and lectures by the library. Among public lectures during this period were "Aspects of Renaissance Book Illustration" (a series of ten presentations); "Arthurian Legends and Their Representation in Medieval Art"; "William Blake, Poet, Artist, and Seer"; and "The Early History of the Christmas Festival." Illustrated publications based on these lectures were published by the library. Graduate study courses, qualifying for credit at New York area universities, were also offered at the library during these years.

Among them were "Armenian Illuminated Manuscripts," "Manuscript Illustration of German Secular Literature from the Thirteenth to the Fifteenth Century," "French Illuminated Manuscripts from the Eleventh to the Thirteenth Century," and "Painting in Islam."

Besides her other activities Greene made time for scholarly work with her beloved illuminated manuscripts. It was Greene who bestowed upon the "Spanish Forger" his name, brought his work to greater professional attention, and compiled a basic list of his works. In 1939 her list included 39 items; now more than 150 items are attributed to him. Greene dubbed him the Spanish Forger because she discovered that he had created the panel portraying a *Betrothal of St. Ursula* that had been attributed to Maestro Jorge Ingles, an artist active in Spain about the middle of the fifteenth century. In actuality no one knows if the Forger was actually Spanish. He flourished in the 1890s and early 1900s and produced works attributed to many artists of various nationalities.

In the 1940s Belle Greene's world slowly began to disintegrate. Her mother, who had lived with her in New York since 1905, died. Then her nephew, whom she had put through college, was killed in World War II, and Morgan died in 1943. In 1948 she retired from the library. Among the many tributes she received at the time was one from paleographer E. A. Lowe: "What a reign you have to look back upon: What riches passed through your hands, what treasures your good taste acquired, what great men did you not meet . . . what fame you brought to the Library and what generosity and sympathy you have shown."

Belle da Costa Greene died in New York on 10 May 1950. Her reputation endures in the collections she oversaw and in the remembrance of those who worked with her among her rare and beautiful books. In 1953 Bernard Berenson dedicated the British edition of his book *Seeing and Knowing* "To the Memory of Belle Greene, Soul of the Morgan Library."

References:

The First Quarter Century of the Pierpont Morgan Library, a Retrospective Exhibition in Honor of Belle da Costa Greene (New York, 1949);

John Douglas Forbes, *J. P. Morgan, Jr. 1867–1943* (Charlottesville: University of Virginia Press, 1981);

Dorothy Miner, ed., *Studies in Art and Literature for Belle da Costa Greene* (Princeton: Princeton University Press, 1954);

Ernest Samuels, *Bernard Berenson: The Making of a Legend* (Cambridge, Mass.: Harvard University Press, 1987);

William Voelkle, *The Spanish Forger* (New York: Pierpont Morgan Library, 1978);

Edwin Wolf II and John J. Fleming, *Rosenbach: A Biography* (Cleveland: World, 1960).

William B. Greenlee

(25 April 1872 – 1 March 1953)

Robert Coale
The Newberry Library

BOOK: *The Voyage of Pedro Álvares Cabral to Brazil and India from Contemporary Documents and Narratives,* edited and translated by Greenlee (London: Printed for the Hakluyt Society, 1938); translated into Portuguese by António Alvaro Dória as *A Viagem de Pedro Álvares Cabral ao Brasil e à India, pelos documentos e relações Coevas: Introdução e notas de William Brooks Greenlee* (Oporto: Livraria Civilização, 1951).

SELECTED PERIODICAL PUBLICATIONS–
UNCOLLECTED: "A Descriptive Bibliography of the History of Portugal," *Hispanic American Historical Review,* 20 (August 1940): 491–516;
"The First Half Century of Brazilian History," *Mid-America,* 25 (April 1943): 91–120;
"The Captaincy of the Second Portuguese Voyage to Brazil, 1501–1502," *Americas,* 2 (July 1945): 3–12;
"The Background of Brazilian History," *Americas,* 2 (October 1945): 151–164.

William B. Greenlee

William Brooks Greenlee was a Chicago businessman who, as a young man, became interested in the Portuguese and their far-flung overseas empire. During a trip around the world after graduating from college he began his lifelong pursuit of books relating to Portugal. In 1937 he gave his collection to the Newberry Library in Chicago, and at his death he left funds that enable the library to continue adding to the collection. Today the William B. Greenlee Collection is probably the best in the United States on Portuguese history and literature before 1820, and some scholars consider it the best and most complete of its kind anywhere. No collector has done more to encourage the study of Portuguese history, especially Portuguese colonial history, than Greenlee; these contributions were recognized by the Portuguese government in 1950 when it conferred on him the rank of commander of the Order of Saint Iago, an order founded in the thirteenth century, together with a decoration for the highest merit and services in the fields of science,

arts, and literature. Four years earlier Dickinson College had awarded him an honorary LL.D. His achievements also earned him membership in the Sociedade de Geografia de Lisboa, the Royal Geographical Society of Great Britain, the American Geographical Society, the Instituto Historico e Geografico de São Paulo, the Royal Institute of Philosophy, and the Hakluyt Society.

Greenlee was born in Chicago on 25 April 1872 to Robert Lemuel and Emily Brooks Greenlee. After a preparatory education at Beloit College Academy he entered Cornell University. He majored in geology, a field that would be useful to him in the family's manufacturing business, which involved metallurgy. Among the other courses he took was modern European history, taught by Henry Morse Stephens, who had recently published *Portugal* (1891). Stephens stimulated Greenlee's interest in history, especially that of Portugal during the period when Portuguese sailors found their way around Africa to India and across the Atlantic to America and beyond. Greenlee was tempted to switch his major to history, but his sense of duty to his family business prevailed. After graduating from Cornell in 1895 he took a yearlong trip around the world during which he visited many areas where the Portuguese had left their mark.

Returning to Chicago in 1896, Greenlee became secretary of Greenlee Brothers and Company, manufacturers of copper, iron, and machinery. On 16 January 1902 he married Adeline Denham. The couple had three children: Richard Fargo; Martha, who died in infancy; and Isabel.

On his trip around the world Greenlee had collected books from Macao to Lisbon, and during his business years he slowly enlarged his collection. As early as 1903 he was buying from such noted London booksellers as Bernard Quaritch Ltd. and Maggs Brothers. There is no record of the purchase of large collections en bloc by Greenlee; he preferred to buy individual items that he knew and wanted.

Greenlee served as president of Greenlee Brothers from 1902 to 1916, becoming vice president and treasurer in the latter year. He also served as chairman of the board of the Greenlee foundry company, created by his father in 1886; under the younger Greenlee's direction it became one of the world's largest manufacturers of stoves and furnace parts. In 1926 Greenlee retired from active participation in the family businesses, though he continued to hold titular offices with Greenlee Brothers–vice president and treasurer until 1944 and chairman of the board from 1944 until his death. At last he had the time to pursue the life of scholarship that had tempted him at Cornell. He began spending more of his time at the Newberry Library, where the Ayer collection had already brought together much of the original source material for the study of the Spanish, Dutch, French, and English encounters in the New World but was lacking in Portuguese materials. In 1932 he was elected to the Newberry board of trustees. Five years later he gave his collection to the library, and he continued to add to it for the rest of his life.

While he was interested in Portuguese history and literature in general, Greenlee focused his atten-

tion on the Portuguese voyages of discovery and early colonial experiences. Believing that insufficient attention had been given to the voyage of Pedro Álvars Cabral in 1500–1501, which he considered the first truly commercial expedition to India via the Cape of Good Hope, Greenlee sought documentation of the journey in research libraries in England, France, and Italy.

Greenlee's research led to *The Voyage of Pedro Álvares Cabral to Brazil and India from Contemporary Documents and Narratives* (1938), only the third American work accepted for publication by the Hakluyt Society of London. It was the first book to bring together the primary documents relating to Cabral's voyage, which led to the discovery of Brazil. Greenlee translated the documents into English, edited them, and provided a lengthy introduction and annotations. With the publication of this book Greenlee became recognized as a leading scholar in the field and was named an honorary member of the Instituto Historico e Geografico de São Paulo. He was invited to be a member of the National Advisory Committee for the Commemoration of the Portuguese double centennial and asked to write "A Descriptive Bibliography of the History of Portugal," which appeared in the special number of the *Hispanic American Historical Review* (August 1940) published for the occasion. Like his study of Cabral, this piece remains an important contribution to Portuguese historiography.

According to Charles Ralph Boxer, a scholar of Portuguese history, "No man [did] more to foster the study of Portuguese history, and especially Portuguese colonial history, than William B. Greenlee did by founding the collection at the Newberry Library which bears his name." Greenlee worked closely with the staff of the Newberry so as not to duplicate books already in the library. In 1948 the Greenlee collection held about seventeen hundred volumes. In 1949 Greenlee accompanied Ruth Lapham Butler, curator of the Ayer collection, to Spain and Portugal to buy books for the library's Greenlee, Ayer, and general collections. By 1950 the Greenlee collection included more than four thousand volumes; in 1951 Boxer estimated that it contained "about ninety per cent of all the books which a discriminating student would wish to find"; and in 1953 Greenlee's *New York Times* obituary put the total at six thousand volumes. Greenlee's benefactions were not confined to the Newberry Library: in 1945 he gave money to Dickinson College in Carlisle, Pennsylvania, to fund a collection of books on paleography and library history. He also donated antiquarian books, including incunabula, to the Deering

Library of Northwestern University in Evanston, Illinois.

One of Greenlee's greatest satisfactions was a request by the Portuguese government for a translation of his Cabral book into Portuguese, the language of the nation he had so long and sincerely admired. The translation, by António Alvaro Dória, appeared in 1951.

Greenlee saw his collection primarily as a working scholar's library rather than an assemblage of rare or precious books. He believed that for most scholarly work the best available printed text is as useful as, or more useful than, an exceedingly rare first edition. Although the collection contains many rare and original imprints, it is surpassed in that regard by other collections, such as the Palha Library at Harvard.

As Boxer's assessment indicates, though, the collection includes most of the works that a scholar would wish to consult. It is rich in periodicals, gazetteers, bibliographies, and documents. The bibliographical section is especially complete: every bibliography, new or old, on Portugal and its colonies is in the collection, including those by the two leading Portuguese bibliographers, Diogo Barbosa Machado and Inocencio Francisco da Silva.

Many books of travel, social life, customs, and biography are present, such as the monumental thirteen-volume *Historia genealógico da Casa Real Portuguesa desde a sua origem até o presente* (Genealogical History of the Royal Portuguese Family from Its Beginnings to the Present [Coimbra: Atlântida, 1946–1954]), by António Caetano de Sousa. Almost all the standard Portuguese histories by all the leading Portuguese and foreign scholars in the field are also present. This section, which comprises about half the collection, includes the complete works of such authorities as Alesandre Herculano, Rebello da Silva, Visconde de Santarem, João Lucco de Azevedo, and Damião Peres.

The ecclesiastical subsection, containing most of the standard histories of the monastic orders, is by far the richest in antiquarian books. Particularly rare and significant are some forty Jesuit relations and letters dealing with missionary efforts in the Orient between 1559 and 1677, most of these in sixteenth- and seventeenth-century editions. Also in the collection is Antonio de Silva Rego's important multivolume history of Portuguese missionary efforts in the Orient, *Historia das missões do Padroado Portguês do Oriente* (History of the missions of Portuguese Ecclesiastical Patronage in the Orient [Lisbon: Agência Geral das Colónias, 1949–]), as well as Rego's editions of the primary sources on which he based his account.

Catalogue of the

GREENLEE COLLECTION

The Newberry Library

Chicago

Volume 1
A – Lim

G. K. HALL & CO., 70 LINCOLN STREET, BOSTON, MASSACHUSETTS
1970

Title page for the first volume of the catalogue of the collection of works relating to Portugal that Greenlee established in 1937

The collection is extraordinarily rich in works on the colonial expansion of Portugal, including the great bulk of the historical works published by the Agência Geral das Colónias in Lisbon. The French *Archives Marocaines* (Paris: E. Leroux, 1904–1934), François Valentijn's *Oud en Nieuw Oost-Indien* (Dordrecht: J. van Braam, 1724–1726), Charles Athanase Walckenaer's *Histoire générale des voyages* (Paris: Lefèvre, 1826–1831), and Camillo Beccari's *Rerum Aethiopicarum Scriptores* (Rome: C. de Luigi, 1903–1917)—the last work beautifully bound by the Lisbon bookbinders Santos and Alves and full of documents regarding mission history in Ethiopia—are illustrative of foreign works, new and old, in the Greenlee collection.

Greenlee formed a substantial library of works dealing with art and literature. All of the standard works dealing with Portuguese art are present, such as Luis Reis Santos's *Vasco Fernandes e os Pintores de Viseu do século XVI* (Vasco Fernandes and the Painters at Viseu in the Sixteenth Century [Lisbon: Published for the author, 1946]), Américo Cortez Pinto's *Da Famosa Arte da Imprimissão* (Of the Renowned Art of Printing [Lisbon: Editora "Ulisseia," 1948]), and the 1943–1947 three-volume reprint of Jose Duarte Ramalho Ortigão's *Arte Portuguesa* (Lisbon: Libraria Classica Editora). Major authors such as Luis de Camões and Padre António Vieira are well represented. Among notable older and rarer books in the Greenlee collection is the fifth edition of Camões's *Os Lusiadas* (Lisbon: M. de Lyra, 1597), the major Portuguese epic poem, which describes the glorious deeds of the Portuguese, their victories over the enemies of Christianity and the forces of nature, and their impressive geographical explorations and discoveries. The collection also includes, along with other later copies of *Os Lusiadas,* a facsimile of the extremely rare 1572 first edition.

Another example of the rare original editions that figure in the Greenlee collection is the *Cronica do muyto alto e muito poderoso rey destes reynos de Portugal dom João o III desta nome* (Chronicle of the Most Exalted and Most Powerful Kings of Portugal, John the Third of That Name [Lisbon: I. Rodriguez, 1613]), by Francisco de Andrade. The work is a detailed account of the sixteenth-century reign of João III, a time when Portugal was subject to a strong Spanish influence that led to many years of Spanish domination.

Shortly before his death on 1 March 1953 Greenlee oversaw the compilation of *A Catalog of the William B. Greenlee Collection of Portuguese History and Literature and the Portuguese Materials in the Newberry Library,* prepared by Doris Varner Welsh. Francis Millet Rogers, dean of the Graduate School of Arts and Science at Harvard University, calls this work "invaluable . . . for the mature scholar and graduate student" concerned with the subjects treated. The catalogue's 5,833 entries begin with general reference materials (223 titles). The next section deals with history (2,928 titles), followed by a section on individual colonies with 1,227 items about Brazil alone. In the *Hispanic American Historical Review* (May 1953) Alexander Marchant of the Institute for Brazilian Studies at Vanderbilt University praised Welsh and Greenlee for the catalogue and predicted that it would fulfill its announced purpose: "to encourage Portuguese studies in the United States."

Since Greenlee's death the Newberry Library has continued to build the collection, using funds established by the collector and supplemented by spe-

cial gifts from other members of the Greenlee family. Some of the more notable of these later acquisitions are a collection of several thousand Portuguese pamphlets printed from the sixteenth to the nineteenth centuries, added between 1954 and 1957; the *Regimentos & Ordenações da Fazenda* (Lisbon, 1516), given by Greenlee's widow in 1962; and the *Comentarios do Grande Afonso D'Albuquerque* (Lisbon, 1576), given by his daughter, Isabel Greenlee Farrar.

William B. Greenlee was that rara avis, a businessman and book collector who was also a scholar. In a 1951 letter to a granddaughter he reiterated his often-expressed belief that "the more interests you have the more lives you live." He urged everyone to "cultivate a hobby. . . . What it is does not much matter, though a hobby which engages the mind, such as book collecting, is more absorbing and is longer lived than a manual hobby, but whatever it is, choose and cultivate it." Greenlee's bibliophily, which grew into far more than a hobby, has advanced the study of Portuguese history. The Newberry Library and American book culture are the richer for his efforts.

References:

Catalog of the Greenlee Collection, The Newberry Library, Chicago, 2 volumes (Boston: G. K. Hall, 1970);

Alexander Marchant, Review of *A Catalog of the William B. Greenlee Collection of Portuguese History and Literature and the Portuguese Materials in the Newberry Library, Hispanic American Historical Review,* 33 (May 1953): 298–299;

Francis Millet Rogers, "William Brooks Greenlee, Scholar and Benefactor of Portuguese Studies," *Hispanic American Historical Review,* 33 (November 1953): 587–589;

Doris Varner Welsh, comp., *A Catalog of the William B. Greenlee Collection of Portuguese History and Literature and the Portuguese Materials in the Newberry Library* (Chicago: Newberry Library, 1953);

"The William B. Greenlee Collection," *Newberry Library Bulletin,* second series 6 (May 1951): 167–178.

Papers:

The Newberry Library in Chicago houses William B. Greenlee's papers.

Charles Frederick Heartman

(4 April 1883 – 8 May 1953)

Beth E. Clausen
University of Northern Iowa Library

BOOKS: *Phillis Wheatley (Phillis Peters): A Critical Attempt and a Bibliography of Her Writings* (New York: Printed for the author, 1915);

Checklist of Printers in the United States from Stephen Daye to the Close of the War of Independence, with a List of Places in Which Printing Was Done (New York, 1915);

The New England Primer Printed in America Prior to 1830: A Bibliographical Checklist (New York, 1915); expanded as *The New England Primer Printed in America Prior to 1830: A Bibliographical Checklist, Thirty-seven Additions and Corrections, Embellished with Cuts* (New York, 1917); revised as *The New England Primer Issued Prior to 1830: A Bibliographical Checklist for the More Easy Attaining the True Knowledge of This Book, Embellished with a Hundred Cuts* (New York, 1922);

Geschichte der kriege in und ausser Europa vom anfange des aufstandes der brittischen kolonien in Nordamerika an: Bibliographical Description of a Complete Set of This Rare Item, Relating to the American Revolution (New York, 1916);

Bibliographical, Historical and Commercial Notes for the Americana Collector (New York: Heartman, 1917);

Bibliography of the Writings of Hugh Henry Brackenridge Prior to 1825 (New York: Printed for the compiler, 1917);

The Liberty Loan: Why Americans of German and Austrian Origin Should Buy Bonds (New York: Heartman, 1918);

The Necessity of Prohibiting German Newspapers, from a Different Viewpoint (New York: Privately printed, 1918);

The Cradle of the United States, 1765–1789: Five Hundred Contemporary Broadsides, Pamphlets, and a Few Books Pertaining to the History of the Stamp Act, the Boston Massacre and Other Pre-Revolutionary Troubles. The War for Independence and the Adoption of the Federal Constitution, Alphabetically Arranged with Index to Items Issued Anonymously but Listed under Author's Name, Bibliographically, Historically and Sometimes Sentimentally

Charles Frederick Heartman

Described by the Owner, Charles F. Heartman (volume 1, Perth Amboy, N.J.: Heartman, 1922; volume 2, Metuchen, N.J.: Heartman, 1923);

The Untimeliness of the Walt Whitman Exhibition at the New York Public Library (New York, 1925);

Obstructions of the Hudson River during the Revolution (Metuchen, N.J., 1927);

Preliminary Checklist of Almanacs Printed in New Jersey Prior to 1850 (Metuchen, N.J.: Privately printed, 1929);

Americana, Printed and in Manuscript: Bibliographically, Historically, and Sometimes Sentimentally Described and Offered for Sale by the Owner (Metuchen, N.J.: Heartman, 1930);

A Census of First Editions and Source Materials by Edgar Allan Poe in American Collections, by Heartman and Kenneth Rede, 3 parts (Metuchen, N.J.: Heartman, 1932);

Charles F. Heartman Presents John Peter Zenger, and His Fight for the Freedom of the American Press, Together with a Genuine Specimen of the New York Weekly Journal Printed by John Peter Zenger (Highland Park, N.J.: Weiss, 1934);

American Primers, Indian Primers, Royal Primers, and Thirty-seven Other Types of Non-New-England Primers Issued prior to 1830: A Bibliographical Checklist Embellished with Twenty-six Cuts, compiled by Heartman (Highland Park, N.J.: Weiss, 1935);

Patrick Kevin Foley: An Appreciation and a Few Reminiscences, as C. F. H. (Hattiesburg, Miss.: Book Farm, 1937);

Twenty-five Years in the Auction Business and What Now? Reminiscences and Opinions (Hattiesburg, Miss.: Privately printed, 1938);

What Constitutes a Confederate Imprint? Preliminary Suggestions for Bibliographers and Catalogers (Hattiesburg, Miss.: Book Farm, 1939);

Bibliography of the Writings and Speeches of Gabriel Wells, L.H.D. (Hattiesburg, Miss.: Heartman, 1939);

Protesting against the Nomination for Librarian of Congress (Hattiesburg, Miss.: Book Farm, 1939?);

A Bibliography of First Printings of the Writings of Edgar Allan Poe, Together with a Record of First and Later Printings of His Contributions to Annuals, Anthologies, Periodicals and Newspapers Issued during His Lifetime; Also Some Spurious Poeiana and Fakes, by Heartman and James R. Canny (Hattiesburg, Miss.: Book Farm, 1940; revised, 1943);

Books and Pamphlets Relating to the Confederate States, Confederate Imprints, Confederate Sheet Music (Hattiesburg, Miss.: Book Farm, 1940);

Bibliographical Checklist of the Writings of the Poet Charles West Thomson (Hattiesburg, Miss.: Book Farm, 1941);

Aphrodisiac Culinary Manual: Being in Part, the Squire of Baudricourt's Cuisine de L'amour, in Use for Many Centuries, Especially Designed for Physical Regeneration, Vigor, and Health, Renewed through the Appropriate Use of Condiments and Aromatics in the Preparation of Dishes and Beverages; Containing a Modern Adaptation of Nearly Two Hundred Selected Historical Recipes Originating from Many Countries and Chosen from Famous Cooking Manuals and Herbal

Lore. Also Perfumes and Diversified Dainties (New Orleans: Gourmets' Company, 1942);

McMurtrie Imprints: A Bibliography of Separately Printed Writings by Douglas C. McMurtrie on Printing and Its History in the United States and Elsewhere, on Typography and Printing Practice, on Type Design and Typefounding, on Bibliography and Bibliographical Practice, and on a Variety of Historical Subjects, with an Appraisal of McMurtrie's Work (Hattiesburg, Miss.: Book Farm, 1942);

There Must Be No Germany after This War: Let Us Forget Most Peace Plans. Opinions of a German American (Hattiesburg, Miss.: Book Farm, 1942);

Thoughts upon Reading Thomas W. Streeter's Essay "North American Regional Bibliographies" (Hattiesburg, Miss.: Book Farm, 1943);

George D. Smith G.D.S. 1870–1920: A Memorial Tribute to the Greatest Bookseller the World Has Ever Known, Written by a Very Small One (Beauvoir Community, Miss.: Book Farm, 1945);

Americana, Printed and in Manuscript: A Most Interesting Collection. While There Is an Emphasis on the Subject of Negro and Slavery Most of Such Items Are of Interest Otherwise—The Offering Embracing the American Scene and Its Cultural Life—Offered for Sale at the Affixed Prices by the Owner (Biloxi, Miss., 1947?).

OTHER: Phillis Wheatley, *Poems and Letters: First Collected Edition,* edited by Heartman (New York: Heartman, 1915);

Samuel Bigelow, *A Poem Suitable for the Present Day, in Five Parts. Worcester, 1776,* preface by Heartman (New York: Heartman, 1915);

Jupiter Hammon, American Negro Poet: Selections from His Writings and a Bibliography, edited by Oscar Wegelin (New York: Heartman, 1915);

Bibliographica Americana: A Series of Monographs, edited by Heartman, 2 volumes (New York: Heartman, 1916);

Philip Freneau, *Unpublished Freneauana,* edited by Heartman (New York: Heartman, 1918);

William Nelson, *Notes toward a History of the American Newspaper,* edited by Heartman (New York: Heartman, 1918);

The Americana Collector: A Monthly Magazine for Americana-lore and Bibliography, edited by Heartman, volumes 1–2 (October 1925–June 1926); retitled *The American Collector,* edited by Heartman, volumes 2–6 (July 1926–September 1928);

The American Book Collector, edited by Heartman and Harry B. Weiss, volumes 1–6 (January 1932–June 1935);

The "Blue Book": A Bibliographical Attempt to Describe the Guide Books to the Houses of Ill Fame in New Or-

leans as They Were Published There, Together with Some Pertinent and Illuminating Remarks Pertaining to the Establishments and Courtesans as Well as to Harlotry in General in New Orleans, as Semper Idem (New Orleans: Privately printed, 1936);

An Immigrant of a Hundred Years Ago: A Story of Someone's Ancestor, Translated and Retold by an Old Hand, translated by Heartman (Hattiesburg, Miss.: Book Farm, 1941);

Traugott Bromme, *Mississippi: A Geographic, Statistic, Topographic Sketch for Immigrants and Friends of Geography and Ethnology,* translated by Heartman (Hattiesburg, Miss.: Book Farm, 1942);

Samuel B. Arnold, *Defence and Prison Experiences of a Lincoln Conspirator: Statements and Autobiographical Notes,* edited by Heartman (Hattiesburg, Miss.: Book Farm, 1943);

The Charles F. Heartman Collection of Material Relating to Negro Culture, Printed and in Manuscript, News Sheets 1–7 (Hattiesburg, Miss.: Heartman, 1945);

U.S.-iana, a New Bibliography: One Commercial Bibliographer to Another (New Orleans: Friends of Bibliography, 1952);

Johann Carl Buettner, *Narrative of Johann Carl Buettner in the American Revolution,* translated by Heartman, edited by William Hobart Royce (New York: Heartman, n.d.).

SELECTED PERIODICAL PUBLICATIONS–
UNCOLLECTED: "Famous American Book Sellers, Past and Present: Number One, Joseph F. Sabin," *Americana Collector,* 1 (1925): 17–21;

"Famous American Book Sellers, Past and Present: Number Three, Lathrop Colgate Harper," *Americana Collector,* 1 (1926): 139–143;

"The American Book Collector's Attitude toward First Editions: A Statement," *American Book Collector,* 1 (1932): 24–30;

"Incunabula in the United States: A Tribute to R. Otto H. F. Vollbehr," *American Book Collector,* 1 (1932): 88–90;

"Fakes, Forgeries and Frauds," *American Book Collector,* 2 (1932): 261–269;

"The Curse of Edgar Allan Poe," *American Book Collector,* 4 (1933): 45–49;

"The Yellow Parrot: The Story of an Association Book," *American Book Collector,* 5 (1935): 60–70.

Charles Frederick Heartman was one of the most important antiquarian booksellers and book collectors in the first half of the twentieth century. For most of his career he specialized in rare Americana in both his bookselling and auction stocks and was a noted, careful cataloguer and bibliographer

Heartman's leather bookplate

who established a reputation for discovering more unrecorded Americana materials than any of his predecessors or contemporaries. Heartman was also active in editing, publishing, and scholarly writing.

The personality of Heartman was perhaps atypical of an antiquarian bookman. He was outspoken, impatient, and energetic, and, as the varied and voluminous activities of his career attest, he was ambitious and hardworking. He was an intellectual who was especially passionate about his chosen specialization of Americana, a field in which he exhibited broad interests. Although a subject rarely held his attention long, some did not bore or disappoint him quickly, and he displayed deep interests in certain subjects, particularly Afro-Americana and Edgar Allan Poe. He often faced the dilemma of having to choose between pursuing bibliographic perfection and making a living, and he usually chose the former. Heartman moved often during his career, and he operated his bookselling and auction businesses and related concerns in various locations in the northeastern and southern regions of the United States.

He was born in Braunschweig, Germany, on 4 April 1883. His mother died when he was two years old, and he was raised by his grandmother and his father, a furniture dealer. Heartman was an ambitious youth, and after graduating from high school he became a journalist for a German newspaper and served briefly as a foreign correspondent in the Balkans. He edited a literary magazine, *Der Literate,* while still in his teens and later published and edited

Der Berliner Beobachter, a small newspaper. In 1907 Heartman left an increasingly unstable Germany and moved to London, where he met and married Martha Esche, a fellow German, who worked to support her husband's writing and to help him get started in the book business. They saved money for passage to the United States and emigrated in 1911; the two arrived in New York City with forty dollars between them. The couple became naturalized citizens in September 1916. The Heartmans had one daughter, Dolley Madison Heartman McKinney.

Following their arrival in the United States the Heartmans' forty dollars in savings did not last long. To support himself and his wife Heartman sought a job as a journalist for a German-language newspaper because he had experience, but the editor discovered that Heartman was married and therefore would not hire him. Heartman soon secured a low-paying job as janitor of an apartment building. Meanwhile, he frequented the bookshops of Fourth Avenue and met a bookseller named Deutschberger who, according to Harry B. Weiss, promised to introduce Heartman to the "mysteries of the books business" while he worked for the bookseller "for nothing during his spare time." Heartman stayed in this apprenticeship for two months and made rapid progress. During this period he bought mainly German books, including first editions of early authors. He paid pennies for these works, which no one else recognized on the outside book stands, and he sent some of his finds to Germany.

After being fired from his job as janitor, Heartman started a book business in what Weiss describes as the "worst [part] of the New York gashouse district." The prospects for Heartman's becoming a successful bookseller improved when, browsing on Houston Street, he found a cart of German pamphlets about socialism and anarchism. Among these pamphlets he discovered a report that no one believed to exist–a report of the first Social Democratic Convention held in Germany. Heartman bought the pamphlets for five dollars and sold them for two hundred dollars to Dr. Heinrich Eisemann of Baer and Company, Frankfurt, whom he met in 1911 at the Robert Hoe III sale in New York. These pamphlets became the first of many important discoveries and financial successes made by Heartman.

In 1912 he was able to open a shop on Twenty-second Street, and in that year he relocated his business to the more desirable address of 36 Lexington Avenue. At the beginning of his career Heartman bought books at auction on credit. This common practice was encouraged by auction houses be-cause the houses could settle the debts not by cash but by choosing prime titles from the stocks of those indebted clients. In *Twenty-five Years in the Auction Business and What Now? Reminiscences and Opinions* (1938) Heartman writes that because he "was ambitious and hardworking," he "constantly over-bought" himself and was "quite often in hot water and had to meet . . . obligations . . . through consignments." He did not like this bondage and thought that continuing in this manner would be "business suicide." Along with his indignation at the outrageous fees–sometimes as much as 60 percent–that consignors were charged, this fear of losing his business drove him to hold his own auction sales.

With R. E. Sherwood serving as auctioneer, Heartman's first sale was held on 9 and 10 June 1913 in rented space above his Lexington Avenue shop. He had been advised by collectors and others in the book trade to own at least half of the items offered, so he chose and catalogued particular items from his stock and solicited consignments for the balance of his auction. The sale drew a large audience and was successful even though, according to Heartman, consignors used the occasion as an opportunity to get rid of "plugs, or otherwise undesirable material."

After drawing up proofs for the sale catalogue, Heartman showed them to Herman Sauer, who was temporarily his mentor and who suggested that Heartman use a pseudonym on the catalogue. The catalogue for Heartman's first auction sale reads: "Heartman's Auctions, The First Part of the Library of G. H. Mayer, of Brooklyn, NY." This title became a source of embarrassment for Heartman, for several who attended the sale asked who G. H. Mayer was. Because of this experience Heartman never invented the name of another collector, and he was reluctant to use legitimate names on the catalogues even when such a name would have added prestige to, and interest in, the sale.

Heartman's decision to join the ranks of auctioneers had an immediate impact. He writes that his influence was one of "great stabilizing" in the auction business and that he brought about "the revolutionary change of a top charge of twenty-five percent" to the consignor for advertising, printing, and mailing costs in addition to the commission fee. The inflated auctioneer's charge–which had reached as much as 60 percent–was just the first of the ills in the book trade that Heartman tackled during the following decades.

Heartman was known for fairness in his business dealings, and he began his auction career with a philosophy that he claimed to maintain throughout his life. His motto, which first appeared as the conclusion of a message on a broadside sent with his first auction catalogue, stated: "I aim to protect the seller, because the buyer can protect himself." Some people interpreted this to mean that Heartman's offerings were protected by fixed prices below which an item would not be sold, and this motto was therefore taken as a statement defending the advantage of the seller. But Heartman writes that his motto meant that the owner was treated fairly, through proper cataloguing of items and reasonable charges for them and for services, and Heartman soon realized that the buyer also needed protecting, frequently from consignors or sellers. In "scrupulously guarding the interests of the buyer," as he writes, Heartman decided that there would be no protection of items at his sales, and he worked to earn the confidence of the mail-order buyer by supplying the name of the underbidder upon request.

His practice of not protecting materials began with his seventh auction sale, the materials for which are advertised in his catalogue *Rare Americana, Chiefly the Property of a Lawyer in Manhattan.* Heartman writes that this auction, which opened the New York book auction season in 1913, was the first sale that made him truly proud and opened his eyes "to the real possibilities of careful cataloguing of Americana." At this auction he offered rare items such as a collection of letters and documents related to the establishment of Robert Fulton's steamboats. Many rare almanacs were also sold—including a 1757 copy of Benjamin Franklin's *Poor Richard improved: Being an Almanac and Ephemeris* that was printed in Philadelphia and brought a price of $160 and the only extant copy of the first almanac that was printed in 1752 by Hugh Gaine in New York and that sold for $150. Gaine's almanac inspired Heartman to begin his lifelong publishing project, Heartman's Historical Series, after he realized the value of reprinting select specimens of rare Americana.

This series consists of bibliographies, original works by contemporary writers and scholars, and reprinted pieces of rare Americana, and some copies of the limited-edition volumes are often published on Japan vellum and handmade paper. Although publishing many of the volumes proved to be financially disastrous for Heartman, he took immense pride in this series and continued to publish it between 1913 and 1953, by which time he had completed a total of seventy-eight volumes.

The general purpose of the series was to preserve works for study by scholars and for reading by future generations. Heartman also contributed reference materials to the field of bibliography, and the variety of subjects covered in this series reflects his broad interests in Americana and his strong in-

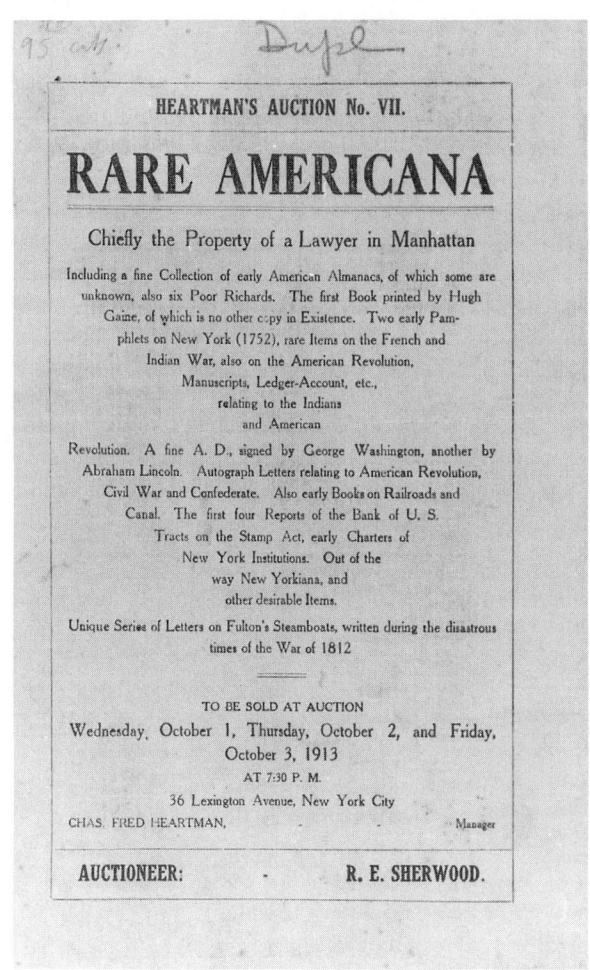

Catalogue for the book auction that showed Heartman "the real possibilities of careful cataloguing of Americana"

terest in Afro-Americana. In addition to the Hugh Gaine almanac his publications include *Bibliography of the Writings of Hugh Henry Brackenridge Prior to 1825* (1917), which Heartman compiled; *The "Blue Book": A Bibliographical Attempt to Describe the Guide Books to the Houses of Ill Fame in New Orleans as They Were Published There, Together with Some Pertinent and Illuminating Remarks Pertaining to the Establishments and Courtesans as Well as to Harlotry in General in New Orleans* (1936); *A Bibliography of First Printings of the Writings of Edgar Allan Poe, Together with a Record of First and Later Printings of His Contributions to Annuals, Anthologies, Periodicals and Newspapers Issued during His Lifetime; Also Some Spurious Poeiana and Fakes* (1940); and checklists of early American printers and New England primers. Publications on Afro-Americana topics include *Phillis Wheatley (Phillis Peters): A Critical Attempt and a Bibliography of Her Writings* (1915) and Wheatley's *Poems and Letters: First Collected Edition* (1915), the seventh and eighth works in the series, and *Jupiter Hammon, American Negro Poet: Selections from His Writ-*

THE CRADLE
OF THE UNITED STATES

1765-1789

A Collection of Contemporary Broadsides, Pamphlets
and a Few Books Pertaining to the History of
The Stamp Act, The Boston Massacre and
Other Pre-Revolutionary Troubles.
The War for Independence and
The Adoption of The
Federal Constitution

Alphabetically arranged with Index to Items issued anonymously
but listed under Author's Name

Bibliographically, Historically
and Sometimes Sentimentally Described by
CHARLES F. HEARTMAN

With Frontispiece

VOLUME TWO
(Number 501-1000)

ONE HUNDRED COPIES ISSUED BY THE COMPILER
Metuchen, New Jersey
NINETEEN HUNDRED AND TWENTY-THREE

*Title page for volume two of Heartman's bibliography of works relating to the early
history of the United States*

ings and a Bibliography (1915), edited by Oscar Wegelin, the antiquarian bookseller.

In 1916 Heartman published *Bibliographica
Americana: A Series of Monographs,* a short-lived series
of only two volumes including *A Bibliographical
Checklist of the Plays and Miscellaneous Writings of William Dunlap (1766–1839),* edited by Wegelin, and *A
Bibliographical Checklist of American Negro Poetry,* compiled by Arthur A. Schomburg. A sales pamphlet
found among Heartman's papers indicates that the
series fell short of his expectations as he had intended it to provide "the foundation of an organization for dealing with American subjects, a gathering
place for reference, a combination of energies now
scattered . . . something which should develop into
an institution."

Although successful in New York, Heartman
moved to Rutland, Vermont, in the fall of 1920 to
reduce his overhead. Gary A. Donaldson speculates
that Heartman, in deciding to move to Rutland,
may also have believed that the death of well-known
book dealer and bibliographer Henry Stevens had
"created a vacuum in that part of the world that he
could fill." Heartman failed in Rutland, however,
and soon moved to Perth Amboy, New Jersey, before he moved again, in 1922, to Metuchen, New
Jersey, where he stayed for thirteen years. In Metuchen his book business prospered, and he reported

that he "forever [surprised] collectors with hitherto undescribed material." According to Heartman, Metuchen "became a place for bookish people to gather" during his tenure there, and in this community he built his reputation through what the *American Book-Prices Current* in 1944 called "skillfully [combining] country dinners, pecans and books."

Heartman held his most famous auction sales in Metuchen. His mansion, decorated entirely in the Colonial style, provided the perfect backdrop for these affairs, which were distinguished by gracious hospitality and meals carefully prepared by Martha. Heartman writes, "I think Mrs. Heartman's cooking has become quite famous all over the United States and because of her unbounded hospitality, often visitors arrived already the day before the sale or stayed a day after."

Dealers, librarians, and collectors from New York and around the country attended the sales. One of the greater auction parties Heartman held in Metuchen was for the 19 December 1931 sale of the A. Edward Newton collection formed by George Henry Sargent. Barton Currie, the collector, and Newton himself acted as auctioneers, and Heartman spent almost $1,000 providing food and liquor for this affair.

Heartman often held sales on holidays, including the birthday of George Washington, and the 1927 Washington sale, another elaborate event, was Heartman's most famous auction. According to Clarence S. Brigham this sale brought bookmen such as bibliographer Wilberforce Eames, dealer Lathrop C. Harper, and collectors William L. Clements and Otis G. Hammond to Metuchen, where they "gathered in an upstairs room and discussed collectors and collections for most of the afternoon." This sale was also a surprise party for New York bookseller Gabriel Wells, who was presented with Temple Scott's booklet *Gabriel Wells, the Philosopher: An Essay* (Metuchen, N.J.: Heartman, 1927). Heartman provided a typical end to the day by returning his guests to New York City in a Pullman car he had hired.

This auction was reported in newspapers as being one of the more important single-session sales of the season, and the three hundred lots described in the auction catalogue, *Americana Printed and in Manuscript: Mainly Commemorative of George Washington and the American Revolution,* included items from Heartman's stock as well as consignments. The highest price paid was $1,960 for an orderly book kept at Washington's headquarters by Alexander Hamilton from 17 April 1779 to 8 August 1779. Another notable item offered, which sold for $1,550, was Washington's twenty-four-page, morocco-

bound memorandum cash account that included records from 10 September 1747 to 10 October 1749 as well as some later entries. Receipts from the auction totaled $30,134, an amount partly attributable to Heartman's cataloguing skills that were evident at this sale. Three items together were sold for more than $2,000; he had acquired these pieces months earlier at a sale for $400. According to Heartman, "so cleverly was the cataloging done" that the buyer, who had been an underbidder at that earlier sale, did not recognize these pieces.

The quality of Heartman's cataloguing and the detail presented in his catalogues helped distinguish him from his contemporaries. His auction and sales catalogues contain precise, detailed bibliographical notes and descriptions of his collections formed for sale. His extensive reference collection and knowledge of books added to the excellence of his catalogues. Between 1913 and 1953 Heartman issued 312 auction catalogues and 160 special-price catalogues and lists of Americana and materials on related subjects. Bibliographers, collectors, and scholars continue to appreciate the descriptions in his catalogues, which have been collected by such great research institutions as the Bibliothèque Nationale, the British Museum, the Library of Congress, the New York Public Library, and the American Antiquarian Society.

The quality of Heartman's catalogues is consistent. Weiss reports that Heartman received praise, although it was mixed with condescension, for his catalogues as early as 1916 when the overseas firm of Henry Stevens, Son and Stiles sent this message: "We think you are doing good work, and that your catalogues are prepared with a great deal of attention to bibliographical details, more so than any other we have seen, emanating from your side of the Atlantic." Weiss asserts that American book-auction catalogues benefited from Heartman's copious descriptions, which "pointed the way to more careful work" by other catalogue compilers.

Some of the sales catalogues issued by Heartman incorporated themes such as Lincolnia or the American Revolution, but many were simply titled *Americana, Printed and in Manuscript* or *Rare Americana.* This latter title was "fully justified," according to Brigham, who wrote that "No dealer in recent years has uncovered so many scarce and unusual items in this field as Mr. Heartman. Early Cambridge imprints, including two before 1660, a dozen undescribed Indian captivities, New England primers by the hundred, scarce Franklin and Washington titles, and literally thousands of unrecorded imprints are but samples of what were offered in his catalogues." Some of his remarkable success in discovering mate-

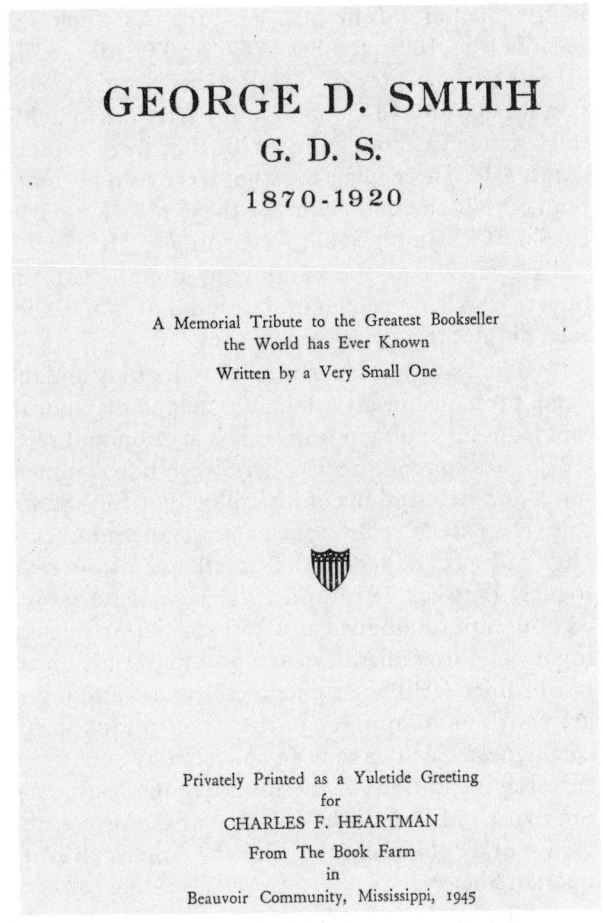

GEORGE D. SMITH

G. D. S.

1870-1920

A Memorial Tribute to the Greatest Bookseller
the World has Ever Known
Written by a Very Small One

Privately Printed as a Yuletide Greeting
for
CHARLES F. HEARTMAN
From The Book Farm
in
Beauvoir Community, Mississippi, 1945

*Heartman's tribute to the New York bookseller called by
playwright John Drinkwater "The Napoleon
of Bookdealers"*

rials such as these perhaps can be explained by the zeal and intelligence with which Heartman collected rare Americana, an activity that he viewed as a mission. In the introduction to the October 1925 *Americana Collector: A Monthly Magazine for Americana-lore and Bibliography* he writes of this view, "It is not a hobby, it is a creed. . . . [T]o me it seems that only the Americana collector has reached the heights of supreme contentment." He continues to explain why he is passionate about Americana: "Americana . . . represents not merely an accumulation of utilitarian and quaint objects . . . but with it goes the assimilation of a state of mind. . . . Every piece of Americana somewhat represents pioneer condition."

An important 119-page catalogue is *Six Hundred Pamphlets, Broadsides and a Few Books, Written in the English Language and Relating to America Issued Prior to Eighteen Hundred; Bibliographically, Historically, and Sometimes Sentimentally Described* (1919). Almost all the pieces listed in it were bought by bibliophile

Henry E. Huntington. Many items Heartman collected for sale were hitherto undiscovered and sometimes quite valuable. One catalogue, published in 1930 with the standard title *Americana Printed and in Manuscript,* describes some of the most famous as well as the most valuable and rare pieces sold by Heartman. This illustrated work, which Weiss calls "a model of careful cataloguing," contains a description of the only known copy of the book that includes John Filson's first map of Kentucky. A large folding color reproduction of this map appears in the catalogue. The original manuscript of the first eight stanzas of Edgar Allan Poe's "For Annie" is also listed—for $17,500. The most interesting and historically significant lot includes the Stuart-Bute Papers, which consist of letters sent by Lt. Gen. Sir Charles Stuart to his father, John Stuart, third Earl of Bute, from 1775 through 1779, and other manuscripts and documents related to the American Revolution. The whole collection, enclosed in 120 full morocco cases, sold for $27,300. Heartman's catalogues are notable for the reproductions they include, the remarkable items they list, the detailed descriptions they give for these items, and the often interesting and informative prefaces they provide. For example, the preface that appears in a 30 November 1929 catalogue is "virtually an essay on the collecting of first editions," according to Brigham.

Americana, Printed and in Manuscript: A Most Interesting Collection (1947?) lists and describes printed books and manuscripts with an emphasis on the subject of African Americans and slavery. The 2,282 items listed include the large gold medal presented to the first black voter in the United States. Ten Wheatley items, including two London first editions of her work, are listed and described, as are an American first edition (1744) and a London edition (1747) of Daniel Horsmanden's journal documenting the "Negro conspiracy" of the early 1740s in New York and an 1831 narrative of the slave rebellion led by Nat Turner of Virginia.

To the amusement of Heartman many of the bibliographically unusual materials that passed through his sales came from other auction sales because of their "at times abominable cataloging and bunching." Yet Heartman's seemingly unending supply of rare Americana that he offered at sale could not be guaranteed only by his superior cataloguing and intelligence: his reputation and carefully cultivated relationships were also necessary to ensure that he had a steady supply of unusual sales items. Librarians often reserved their unusual duplicates for him, and scouts and dealers also helped him maintain his supply.

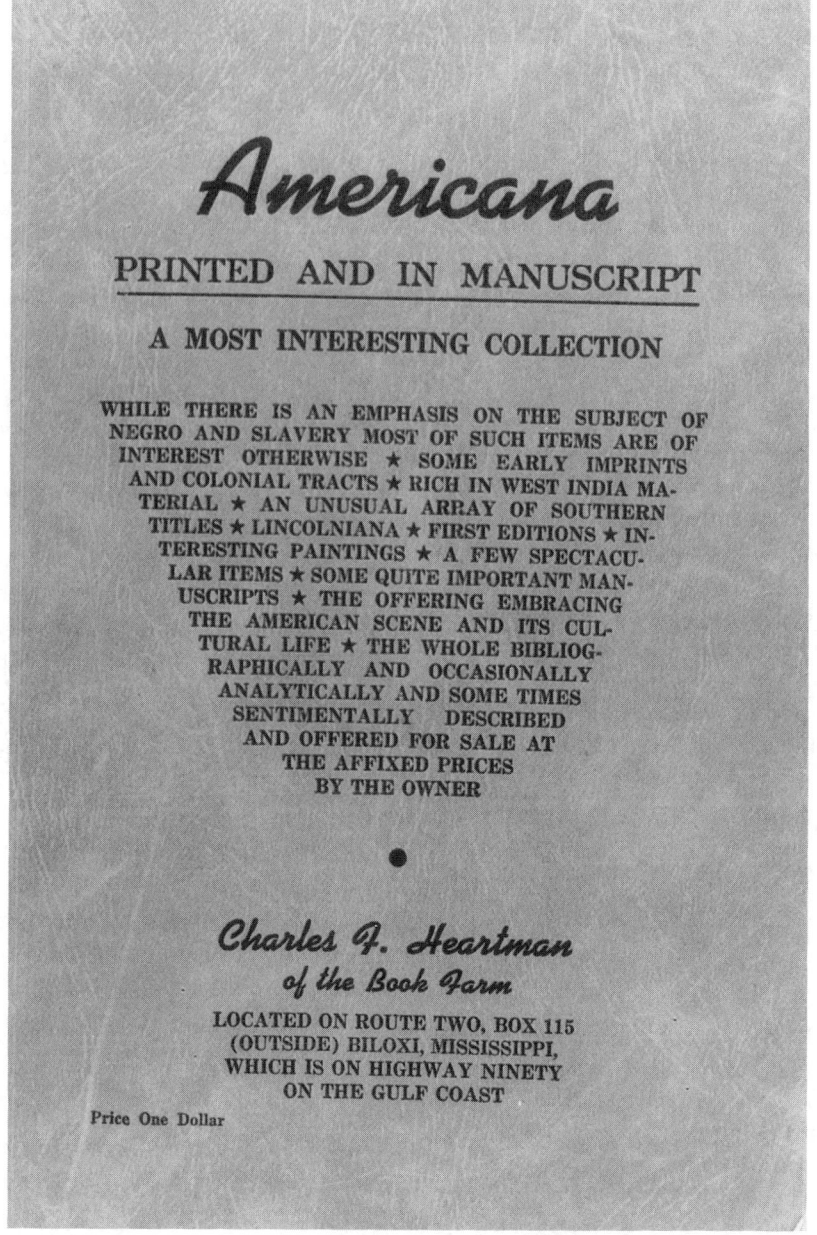

Cover of the last catalogue issued by Heartman in 1947 before he transferred to Texas

Like many other booksellers, Heartman encountered financial difficulties in the 1930s. He left Metuchen in 1935 and moved to New Orleans, where he hoped to reduce his overhead and live comfortably on little money. There he established the Pelican Galleries, and, with Charles R. Knight as his associate, he held book auctions and conducted a retail business in the French Quarter on Toulouse Street. After about one year he grew disenchanted with New Orleans and moved to another location about one hundred miles northeast of the city, near Hattiesburg, Mississippi. There he bought from the federal government a four-hundred-acre farm that he called The Book Farm and intended at first to establish as "a cooperative colony for intellectuals," according to James R. Canny.

Heartman advertised his vision of and desire for this Utopia, but no one joined him in making this vision a reality. He again turned his attention to bookselling and auctioneering, and by this time his mail-order business had become important. Wherever or however often he relocated his business, his reputation attracted buyers. Heartman found that in the South, a region that he described as being "hungry for books" and that he grew to love, conditions of book supply and demand differed from those he had encountered elsewhere in the United States. He notes that few book dealers in the South could "properly supply needs or create demand," and he writes that he "was shocked about the absence of research facilities in so many libraries in the deep South." He asserts that to be in the business of "book supply is not just [to be in the business of] offering merchandise for sale, but to develop an educational desire." He also felt that to be valuable in stimulating a book supply, a service would have to grow "from the soil of the religion, or must have such a cultural or historical background as to be identified with the particular needs of the territory." Heartman believed that what the South needed was "an intelligent force"—a bookseller such as he—who could help librarians and collectors by providing "a certain amount of unselfish advice," and he sought to stimulate the growth of the book supply and nurture the demand for books by focusing on the cultural heritage while living in that region.

Heartman edited two journals on book collecting during his career. From 1925 to 1927 he was also the publisher of the first of these, the *Americana Collector,* a journal that became the *American Collector* in its July 1926 issue. Many issues of this magazine feature biographical sketches of famous American collectors, printers, and booksellers. Heartman wrote some of these articles, such as the profiles of Joseph F. Sabin in the October 1925 issue and of Lathrop C. Harper in the January 1926 issue.

Between 1932 and 1935 Heartman coedited, with Weiss, a second journal, the *American Book Collector: A Monthly Magazine for Book Lovers.* This periodical proclaims itself to be slightly controversial, contains information on all details of book collecting, and is concerned with book-related subjects such as autographs, manuscripts, bibliographies, literary essays, and reviews of books and auctions. The editorials of this journal, as do those of the *Americana Collector,* present a record of how outspoken Heartman was in seeking "to introduce more ethical practices in the book business," and they were "always sought out by the subscribers as the first things to be read," according to Weiss. The editorial pages are especially interesting because Heartman wrote about what was on his mind, and, as Weiss reports, Heartman "never sugar-coated his bitter pills." Among the topics he frankly addressed in this forum are forgeries, fakes, and the selling of stolen materials. He also used the journals for "shouting time and time again that no second printing could be a first edition," as he insisted in "The American Book Collector's Attitude toward First Editions," a seven-page statement in the January 1932 issue of the *American Book Collector.*

Heartman had not limited his outspokenness to book collecting, and his speaking out had earned him some notoriety years earlier. In 1918 he had published *The Necessity of Prohibiting German Newspapers, from a Different Viewpoint,* a pamphlet that was reprinted in periodicals throughout the United States. This work conveyed Heartman's belief that newspapers printed in German impeded the "Americanization" of German immigrants, and Theodore Roosevelt wrote to Heartman to thank him "as an American" for this pamphlet. Heartman also wrote other essays that demonstrated his pro-American sentiments during the world wars.

After years of publishing, bookselling, and hosting weekend barbecues for friends and bibliophiles in Hattiesburg, Heartman moved to Biloxi, Mississippi, in 1943. He relocated to New Braunfels, Texas, in 1947, and in 1951 he returned to New Orleans, where he remained until he died of a heart attack in his home on 8 May 1953. The catalogue for what was his final sale had already been prepared, and at the urging of his wife the sale was held as planned on 24 May 1953. Martha Heartman, who had long assisted her husband in the business, continued selling books until 1963 when poor health forced her to quit.

Heartman was not only a bookseller and an exceptional cataloguer but also a serious bibliographer, scholar, and author. He produced important studies of Phillis Wheatley and completed exceptional bibliographic work on Edgar Allan Poe, and at the time of Heartman's death he was best known for this latter. His bibliographic work and publishing of bibliographic works by other scholars made materials accessible to researchers. His greatest contribution is that so much primary Americana now available to researchers in institutions would have been lost if Heartman had not undertaken his bibliographic and collecting work. Although his discoveries were not always commercially valuable, they often "supplied a definite link in the endless chain of bibliography," according to Weiss.

Many library collections have also been enhanced through his work. Two institutions especially benefited from his work in Afro-Americana heritage and culture. Heartman first became interested in Afro-Americana in the 1910s, a time when there was little interest in such material and prices for it were therefore low. His interest in this subject remained, and through the decades he built a significant collection of these materials before he disposed of them in the late 1940s.

In 1948 about eleven thousand pieces of this collection were bought by Texas Southern University, Houston, and these thousands of books, pamphlets, newspaper clippings, and oil paintings became one of the larger black history and culture collections in the United States. Xavier University in New Orleans also acquired much of Heartman's African-American history collection, which includes more than four thousand pieces covering the period from 1724 through 1897 and consists of materials in French, Spanish, and English languages. Most of these pieces are manuscript materials related to the economic, civil, and legal status of slaves and freedmen in Louisiana, especially in the area of New Orleans.

References:

Clarence S. Brigham, "History of Book Auctions in America," in *American Book Auction Catalogues, 1713–1934: A Union List,* edited by George L. McKay (New York: New York Public Library, 1937), pp. 1–37;

James R. Canny, "Charles F. Heartman, 1883–1953," *Antiquarian Bookman,* 7 (1954): 732–735;

Gary A. Donaldson, "The Career of Charles F. Heartman and the Tradition of Collecting Americana," *Papers of the Bibliographical Society of America,* 84 (1990): 377–396;

Sister Patricia Lynch, editor, *Guide to the Heartman Manuscripts of Slavery* (Boston: G. K. Hall, 1982);

Pamela Petro and Richard Newman, "'Remarks Called for and Otherwise': The Career of Charles F. Heartman, Bookseller," *American Book Collector,* 7 (1986): 9–15;

Madeleine B. Stern, "Charles F. Heartman," in her *Antiquarian Bookselling in the United States: A History from the Origins to the 1940s* (Westport, Conn.: Greenwood Press, 1985), pp. 203–209;

Harry B. Weiss, *The Bibliographical, Editorial, and Other Activities of Charles F. Heartman* (New Orleans: Privately printed, 1938).

Papers:

The McCain Library and Archives at the University of Southern Mississippi in Hattiesburg houses the Heartman Papers, a collection that includes catalogues, correspondence, business records, materials published by Heartman, and photographs.

Robert Hoe III

(10 March 1839 – 22 September 1909)

Joseph Rosenblum

BOOKS: *A Lecture on Bookbinding as a Fine Art, Delivered before the Grolier Club, February 26, 1885* (New York: Grolier Club, 1886);
A Short History of the Printing Press and of the Improvements in Printing Machinery from the Time of Gutenberg up to the Present (New York: R. Hoe, 1902);
Catalogue of Books (New York: Privately printed, 1903–1909).

OTHER: Joseph Maberley, *The Print Collector: An Introduction to the Knowledge Necessary for Forming a Collection of Ancient Prints,* edited by Hoe (New York: Dodd, Mead, 1880).

SELECTED PERIODICAL PUBLICATION—UNCOLLECTED: "Of Bibliophilism and the Preservation of Books," *Bibliographer,* 1 (1902): 304–308.

In the preface to the first volume of the Robert Hoe auction catalogues, Beverly Chew wrote of his late friend and fellow collector, "Possessed of ample means, with knowledge and the true bookman's taste, this library he has brought together is, beyond all question, the finest this country has ever contained, and its final dispersion by auction the greatest of book sales." In his fifty years of collecting Hoe created a library of some thirty thousand volumes that included the finest examples of illuminated manuscripts and printing, from a twelfth-century copy of the Venerable Bede's *Commentaries* and Johannes Gutenberg's Bible on vellum (Mainz, 1450–1454) to William Morris's 1896 Kelmscott Press *Chaucer,* the greatest production of one of the greatest private presses. Hoe also assembled the landmarks of literature, from the first printed edition of Homer (Florence: Nerlii, 1488) and Shakespeare's First Folio (London: Printed by Isaac Jaggard and Ed. Blount, 1623) to a play in manuscript by George Bernard Shaw. All were in exquisite bindings, one of Hoe's particular interests. The dispersal of this library in 1911–1912 proved Chew's prediction correct; it eclipsed all previous records and set its own

Robert Hoe III

that stood in America for over half a century until the Thomas Winthrop Streeter sales of 1966–1969 realized $3,104,982.50.

The son of Robert and Thirza Mead Hoe II, Robert Hoe III was born in New York City on 10 March 1839. His grandfather, the first Robert Hoe, had been born in Leicester, England, on 29 October 1784. Trained as a carpenter, he came to New York about 1802. Here he met Matthew Smith Jr. and Peter Smith, who were making wooden printing presses and type cases. In 1805 the three men formed Smith, Hoe and Company. Robert Hoe married Rachel Smith, daughter of Matthew and Rachel Mead Smith and the sister of his partners. Matthew Smith Jr. died in 1820, Peter in 1823, and Hoe continued the business under the name of R. Hoe and Company.

The firm succeeded through innovation and enterprise. In 1822 Peter Smith had devised a cast-iron press that was easier to operate than screw-driven models. When Samuel Rust of New York developed a metal press stronger than Smith's but lighter in weight (1827), R. Hoe and Company bought the patent. In 1832 Robert Hoe II sent Sereno Newton (who would later become a partner in the firm) to England to study the cylinder presses being manufactured there. Upon Newton's return R. Hoe and Company produced the first American cylinder press, superior to foreign models. After Isaac Adams of Boston patented steam power presses (1830, 1836), Hoe bought Adams's business. By the late 1800s this combination of technological expertise and entrepreneurship had made R. Hoe and Company the largest manufacturer of printing machinery in the world. The factory on Grand Street (New York City) covered twenty thousand square feet and employed twenty-five hundred workers. A second factory in London, opened in the late 1860s with six hundred workers, grew to employ eight hundred.

Heir to this printing giant, Robert Hoe III was educated at Quackenbush School in New York City and then by private tutors in Paris. His interest in French literature persisted throughout his life. By 1909 he owned some five thousand French books, the largest single section of his library. At age seventeen he entered the family business, learning all facets of the enterprise. His knowledge of the technical side of printing is demonstrated in his 1902 *A Short History of the Printing Press and of the Improvements in Printing Machinery from the Time of Gutenberg up to the Present*. While the work emphasizes the contributions of his family, it remains a valuable history. The continued prosperity of the firm under Hoe's leadership (1886 to 1909) testifies to his business acumen. As *The New York Times* for 23 September 1909 commented, "Since types were first made by Gutenberg and by Caxton, perhaps no man has developed the art of printing as Robert Hoe developed it." This obituary was printed on machinery developed by Hoe and manufactured by his company. Hoe married Olivia Phelps James, daughter of Daniel William James of New York City. The marriage took place at Watertree, England, on 12 August 1863. The couple had nine children, six of whom survived their father.

Catalogue for the sale of Hoe's vast book collection, which began on 24 April 1911

About the same time that Hoe began working for the family business, he started collecting books. Carl L. Cannon in *American Book Collectors* (New York: H. W. Wilson, 1941) recounts a conversation between Hoe and the bookseller-bibliographer James O. Wright, who helped catalogue Hoe's library. Wright had omitted some thirty or forty volumes from the catalogue because of their nugatory value. Hoe replied, "Keep them and put them in. They were the first books I bought, and I went without lunch money to buy them." The interest of Hoe's uncle Richard in books about typography—this collection was sold at auction in May 1887—and the concern of the firm with type led Hoe to the fine printing of the nineteenth-century British publisher William Pickering. From here he expanded to other examples of beautiful bookmaking: the works of Aldus Manutius of Venice; the Elzevirs, Dutch printers; other early printers; and illuminated manuscripts.

Although Hoe collected for most of his life, he enriched his library in the 1880s and 1890s through several important sales. Hoe and fellow collector

William Loring Andrews often bid jointly, dividing the spoils later. At the Syston Park sale (London) in 1884 they bought a fine Shakespeare First Folio for £590 ($2,950); the volume went to Hoe. That same year Hoe secured one of his four copies of the Christopher Columbus letter announcing the discovery of the New World. This edition, printed in Rome by Eucharius Silber (1493), came from the Henry Cruse Murphy sale in New York. The *Lettera di Amerigo Vespucci* (Florence, circa 1505), a sixteen-leaf quarto, came from the Court sale in Paris in 1884. Bernard Quaritch, noted London bookseller, bought this first collected edition of Vespucci's four voyages for 13,000 francs ($2,620) and sold it to New York collector Charles H. Kalbfleisch. Hoe later secured the work through Wright, who handled the sale of the Kalbfleisch library. Hoe's copy of the first edition of Robert Burns (Kilmarnock: Printed by John Wilson, 1786) also had belonged to Kalbfleisch and reportedly cost Hoe $500.

At the 1889 sale of Lord Ravelstone's library by Christie's of London, Quaritch paid $2,000 for *Helyas, Knight of the Swan* (London: Wynkyn de Worde, 1512). This is the only known copy of Wynkyn de Worde's printing of the English version of the Lohengrin story and one of only two known Wynkyn de Worde imprints on vellum. Quaritch, one of Hoe's major suppliers, sold the book to Hoe for $3,000.

The Brayton Ives sale in New York in 1891 yielded the fifteenth-century Pembroke Book of Hours. This manuscript of 231 vellum leaves includes 24 small circular miniatures, 29 full-page miniatures, and 267 other illustrations. The volume was created about 1440 for Sir William Herbert, Earl of Pembroke, who was beheaded by the Lancastians during the Wars of the Roses after the Battle of Hedgecote in 1469. Ives had secured the volume from the London bookseller Frederick S. Ellis for $10,000. Hoe paid $5,900 for it. Hoe's *Liber Sextus Decretalium* by Pope Boniface VIII, printed on vellum by Johann Fust and Peter Schoeffer (Mainz, 1465), also had belonged to Ives.

Hoe's two Gutenberg Bibles, one printed on vellum and the other on paper, came from the Ashburnham library sale of 1897. The copy on vellum, lacking only two leaves, had belonged to the English brewer Henry Perkins, who bought the two-volume work for £504 ($2,520). At the Perkins sale in London in 1873 Bertram, Fourth Earl of Ashburnham, bought the treasure for £3,400 ($17,000). In June 1897 Quaritch secured it for £4,000 ($20,000), a record auction price for a Gutenberg Bible, and sold it to Hoe for £5,000 ($25,000). The Gutenberg on paper had also belonged to Perkins and came to Hoe

through Quaritch for $17,500. Hoe's copy of William Caxton's first edition of *The Canterbury Tales* (Westminster, circa 1477), the first of Caxton's major publications on the first printing press in England, had also belonged to Ashburnham and cost Hoe $3,000. It lacked seventeen original leaves (supplied in facsimile) but was one of only eleven known copies. Of these only two were perfect; one belonged to the British Museum, the other to Merton College Library, Oxford.

Hoe bought much from the New York booksellers Frank Dodd and Luther Livingston. From them he secured Almon W. Griswold's copy of Ranulf Higen's *Polychronicon* (Westminster: William Caxton, 1482). Griswold paid £477 15s. for the work at the Lord Claremont sale at Sotheby's of London in August 1865. It lacked two leaves, folios 21 and 71, which Griswold supplied in facsimile. He also had the book rebound by Francis Bedford, one of the leading London craftsmen of the day. In 1888 Griswold sold the volume to Dodd, Mead and Company, who sold the work to Hoe for $6,750. Hoe's large-paper set of Ben Jonson's *Works* (London, 1616–1640) also had belonged to Griswold. The 1640 volume was the only large-paper copy known.

The most important contribution of Dodd, Mead and Company to the Hoe library was its handling of the sale of the Abbie Hanscom Pope collection after her death in 1895. Hoe bought many of her finest items. At the Osterly Park sale in London in 1885 she had outbid the British Museum for the only complete copy of the first printed edition of Thomas Malory's *Morte d'Arthur* (Westminster: William Caxton, 1485), paying £1,950. Also at the sale she paid £810 for one of the five known copies of Caxton's printing of the *Confessio Amantis* (circa 1483) by John Gower. Yet another important title in the Pope library was the "Charles VI Missal" presented by the French monarch to Henry V when the English monarch married Charles's daughter Catherine of Valois. The manuscript includes one hundred large and four hundred small miniatures. The volume later belonged to Henry VI, Henry VII, and Henry VIII of England. In the nineteenth century it became the property of Ambrose Firmin-Didot, a noted French collector. At the sale of his library in Paris in 1878 it brought 76,000 francs, the highest price of any of his books. Honoré de Balzac's daughter, the Comtesse Mniszeck, paid 100,000 francs ($20,000) for it, and after the comtesse's death in 1887 Abbie Pope secured it. Hoe acquired the two Caxtons, the missal, and Pope's fifteen Shakespeare quartos.

Hoe also frequented bookshops in New York, Paris, and London, making his own discov-

653. BYLAERT (HANS JACOB). [Dutch title.] Nouvelle maniere de Graver en Cuivre des estampes coloriées; de façon que, quoiqu'imprimées dans une Presse ordinaire, elles conservent l'air & le Caractère du Dessin. Traduit du Hollandais par L. G. F. Kerroux. *2 plates.* 8vo, half calf, uncut.　　　　　　　　　　　　　Leide, 1772

　　* The Dutch and the French texts are on opposite pages.

654. BYRON (GEORGE GORDON, LORD). English Bards and Scotch Reviewers. With the additional passages from the subsequent editions. 4to, dark blue straight-grain morocco, gilt edges (portion of back cover repaired).
　　　　　　　　　　　　　　　　　　　　[London] 1815

　　*Extra-illustrated copy from the Drury Collection, with special title-page and the original text inlaid to quarto, supplemented by manuscript readings of the variations in text of the 3rd, 4th and 5th editions. Twenty-six portraits are inserted, including a colored stipple of Madame Catalani, mezzotint by C. Turner of the Earl of Aberdeen, etc.

655. BYRON (GEORGE GORDON, LORD). The Works of Lord Byron; with his Letters and Journals, and his Life, by Thomas Moore. FIRST ISSUE. *Portrait, and 33 frontispieces and vignettes.* 17 vols. 12mo, cloth, uncut.
　　　　　　　　　　　　　　London: John Murray, 1832–33

BIBLES.

(SEE ALSO UNDER MANUSCRIPTS, NOS. 2425-2428.)

THE FAMOUS GUTENBERG (OR "42-LINE") BIBLE.

656. BIBLIA LATINA. *Gothic characters, double columns. 642 unnumbered leaves without signatures or catchwords, including last blank. Leaves 1–5 r. with 40 lines to the page, leaf 5 v. has 41 lines ; leaf 6 and the succeeding pages generally have 42 lines. Rubricated throughout and with numerous large and small ornamental initials painted in blue, red, etc , the titles of the books in red on the upper margins throughout. Fol. 1 r., col. 1:* Incipit epistola sancti iheronimi | ad paulinum presbiterum de omnibus | diuine historie libris. capitulū p'mū (*printed in red*). [F]Rater ambrosius | tua michi munus- | cula pferens. detulit | sil' et suauissimas | lrās. q a principio | amicicia 2l̃. fidē pba- | te iam fidei z̄ veteris amicicie noua: | . . . *Fol. 5 r., col. 1:* Incipit liber bresith quē nos genesim | dicim' (*printed in red*) | [I]N principio creauit deus celū | et terram. Terra autem erat inanis et | vacua: et tenebre erāt sup faciē abissi . . . *Fol. 324 v., col. 1. line 21 :* . . . laudet dūm. All'a. *Fol. 325 r., col. 1:* [I]ungat epistola quos iūgit sacerdoti- | um: immo carta non diuidat: quos | xpi nectit amor . . . *Fol. 641 v., col. 2, line 40 :* Venio

101

cito amen. Veni domine ihe- | su. Gratia dn̄i n̄ri ihesu cristi tū omni- | bȝ vobis amē. *Fol. 642 blank.* Bound in 2 vols. folio, red levant morocco, blind tooled panels, the titles of the work printed in gold letters around the inner panels of the front covers, doublures of light brown levant with gilt tooled borders, vellum fly-leaves, gilt edges, by MERCIER, in morocco cases.

　　[MOGUNTIÆ, JO. GUTENBERG et JO. FUST, 1450–55]

　　* EDITIO PRINCEPS OF THE BIBLE. Whereas all copies vary slightly, the above is one of the few with headings at the commencement of the Epistle of St. Jerome, the prologue to Genesis, and the first book of Genesis printed in red, it being presumed that on account of the difficulty encountered in printing in a second color, this undertaking was discontinued. In the British Museum copy these spaces were left blank. The other chapter headings throughout are written in red, thus preserving the symmetry of the pages. THE PRESENT COPY IS ABSOLUTELY PERFECT AND GENUINE THROUGHOUT, AND MEASURES 15 X 10¾ INCHES.

　　At the end of each volume there is a Latin inscription dated March 7, 1471, and authenticated by a notary, showing that this Bible belonged to a certain Jan Vlieghet, priest and beneficiary of the Cathedral of Utrecht, and that he left it to the monastery called *ad Castrum,* near Amersford. The Hoe catalogue states that this copy was formerly in the library of Lord Ashburnham, and that it was sold a year before his death. Hain, 3031; Pellechet, 2265; Hessels, p. 170, No. 6; Proctor, 56. Twenty-seven copies on paper (four containing Vol. I only, and one only Vol. II) are known to exist. By calculations based on the proportionate use made of two of the four kinds of paper used for the book, Dr. Schwenke suggests that the total number of paper copies printed may have been 180.

657. BIBLIA LATINA. *Gothic character. double columns; 481 unnumbered leaves without signatures and catchwords; 48 lines to the page; first page ornamented with a* SEMI-BORDER AND A LARGE INITIAL ILLUMINATED IN GOLD AND COLORS; *rubricated throughout and initials painted in red and blue.* Bound in 2 vols. Folio, old red morocco, gilt edges, probably by Padeloup (binding rubbed).　　　　　　Nurnberg: Antonius Koberger, 1475

　　* A magnificent copy of this very rare Bible, and one of the most noted books from the celebrated press of Coburger. From the libraries of Cardinal Lomenie de Brienne and Michael Wodhull. Hain, 3056; Proctor, 1970.

658. BIBLIA LATINA. *Gothic character, double columns, 470 unnumbered leaves [including 2 blank leaves]. with 52 lines to the page. 2 large* HISTORIATED INITIALS ILLUMINATED IN GOLD AND COLORS, *representing St. Jerome and a View of the Garden of Eden; a few other illuminated initials and the remainder painted in blue and red.* Folio,

102

Pages from the catalogue for the evening session, 24 April 1911, of the Hoe sale, with a description of the Gutenberg Bible. The Bible was bought by George D. Smith for Henry E. Huntington at $50,000, a record price for a single book at that time.

eries. London bookseller Walter T. Spencer recalled that Hoe's first purchase from him was a collection of works by Alexander Pope, and Hoe typically spent £200 to £250 with Spencer on each visit to London. Damascene Morgand of Paris was Hoe's favorite bookseller and supplied many works during the last decade of Hoe's life.

　　Hoe demonstrated and fostered bibliophily in ways other than collecting. In 1866 he encouraged David G. Francis of New York to publish a reprint of John Payne Collier's important *Bibliographical Account of the Rarest Books in the English Language* (1865), and in 1880 Hoe edited Joseph Maberley's *Print Collector: An Introduction to the Knowledge Necessary for Forming a Collection of Ancient Prints* (1844). In 1884 he was one of the nine

founders of the Grolier Club in New York, still the preeminent American association of book collectors. Hoe suggested the name, derived from the French Renaissance bibliophile Jean Grolier, noted for his generosity with his books. Grolier often had his books bound with the motto "GROLIERII (later IO. GROLIERII) ET AMICORUM"–belonging to Grolier and his friends–to indicate his willingness to share. Hoe served as the Grolier Club's first president from 1884 to 1888. An admirer of fine bindings, Hoe addressed the Grolier Club on the subject, and in 1895 he paid for the publication of *Historic and Artistic Book Bindings* in two oversize volumes, illustrating 176 examples from the fifteenth through nineteenth centuries. All were drawn from his collection. In that same year, together with other Grolier Club members, Hoe created the Club Bindery to foster fine craftsmanship in America. By 1900 the Club Bindery was unequaled in this country, and when Thomas James Coben-Sanderson, founder of the Doves Bindery in England, visited New York in 1902, he was amazed at the high quality of the work. Hoe provided much business for the bindery and directed its operations from 1906, but financial difficulties forced it to close in 1909.

Hoe also contributed to bibliophily through the sixteen catalogues of his collection prepared by Wright and Caroline Shipman Whipple, which remain important bibliographies. The *Catalogue of Books of Emblems* (New York, 1908), for example, describes 463 titles. The first of the series, *A Catalogue of Books by English Authors Who Lived Before the Year 1700* (New York, 1903), which appeared in five volumes, describes 2,875 titles. Excluding manuscripts, the series discusses 14,030 titles in 20,962 volumes. His eight volumes of auction catalogues, largely prepared by Arthur Swann and Giuseppe Martini, also constitute an important bibliographic resource for book lovers. A member of the English Bibliographical Society, Hoe also was a member of the Société des Amis des Livres, which promoted the production of fine modern French books.

Hoe died unexpectedly at his London apartment at 11 Whitehall Court on 22 September 1909. His will left most of his $8 million to his six children and one grandchild. His house at 11 East Thirty-sixth Street in New York City went to his wife. He also stipulated the sale by auction of his art collection and books. *The New York Times* for 9 February 1911 wrote of Hoe's art, "Mr. Hoe obviously never reached that stage at collecting in which he would consider only the best of a kind, and therefore the knowledge and taste of the connoisseur will be brought sharply into requisition at the forthcoming sale. But it will be a dull mind that cannot find stimulus in the hunt for certain treasure amid uncertainties. Hoe's interest in art was sincere, and he was a founder of the Metropolitan Museum of Art.

For a variety of reasons Hoe chose to disperse his collections rather than donate them to institutions. In the preface to the first of the Hoe auction catalogues Beverly Chew wrote that a visit to a major European library filled Hoe with

feelings of surprise and disgust at the utter lack of reverence and appreciation he found as shown in the want of care given to the great monuments of printing. The catalogue of this library was rich in the masterpieces of the early printers, and when he asked for them, volume after volume was brought to him covered with dust, with leaves stained and bindings broken and in every way proclaiming the effects of indifference and neglect. "This," he said, "confirms me in the conviction that those who love books should have them in their custody and will take the best care of them."

Hoe also recognized the need to restock the sources of book collecting. As he observed to Chew, "If the great collections of the past had not been sold, where would I have found my books?"

The art was auctioned first and proved a harbinger of events at the book sales to follow. At Mendelssohn Hall in New York on 17 February 1911 his "Young Girl Holding Out a Medal on a Chain" (1640–1643) by Rembrandt brought $70,500, an American record for a painting by that artist. His Rembrandt sketch "Christ Healing the Sick" brought $4,500, an American record. Rembrandt's sketch "An Arched Landscape with a Flock of Sheep" went for $2,800. On a smaller scale, Chew paid $180 for Sir Godfrey Kneller's portrait of John Dryden. Altogether, Hoe's art brought $608,816.

The books were auctioned in a series of four sales spread over a year and a half, beginning on 24 April 1911. *The New York Times* for 1 April 1911 correctly predicted that "the sale will bring the highest aggregate total of any collection ever sold at auction, not only in America, but in the world, and . . . at least one of its literary treasures will bring a higher price than has ever before been realized for a single work in the public market." Before the Hoe sale the record price for a printed book at auction was $24,750, set at the 1884 London sale of the library of Sir John Thorold (1734–1815). Bernard Quaritch, acting for J. P. Morgan, had paid this sum for the Mainz Psalter, printed by Fust and Schoeffer in 1457–the first printed book with a date and the first example of color printing. This price would be surpassed three times by printed books and twice more by manuscripts at the Hoe sales.

The Hoe sale opened at the new location of the Anderson Auction Gallery at Madison Avenue and Fortieth Street, formerly the residence of Clarence M. Hyde. The auction was a major social event with each of the four hundred reserved seats filled. Every major American bookseller and collector was present, as were many Europeans. Bookseller George D. Smith sat beside Henry E. Huntington; these two would dominate the buying. Other collectors present were Ives, who was assembling a second library to replace the one sold in 1891; Harry E. and Joseph E. Widener; Walter T. Wallace, a collector of English and American literature; Chew; Shakespeare collector Henry Clay Folger; and Belle da Costa Greene, formidable librarian of J. P. Morgan. Walter M. Hill of Chicago, Frank Dodd and Luther Livingston of New York, and A. S. W. Rosenbach of Philadelphia were among the American dealers vying with Quaritch and Ernest Maggs of London, Mme. Théophile Belin of Paris, and Ludwig Baer of Frankfurt.

George Parker Winship of the John Carter Brown Library had planned to attend but was uncertain of the opening date. He was aboard the *Segurania* outside the harbor of Havana when he learned that the auction had begun. So important was this sale that the captain skipped the usual stop at Nassau and steamed directly to New York, cutting two days off the trip and so allowing Winship to attend at least some of the sessions.

All were competing for volumes from one of the greatest of American libraries. As Carl L. Cannon wrote, it included "some of the world's finest copies of books and manuscripts in such widely differing fields that they appealed to all classes of collectors and excited competition from every civilized country." Here were more than 150 incunabula, with 16 examples on vellum; 2 Gutenberg Bibles; 75 printed Books of Hours; 465 emblem books; 250 illuminated manuscripts, including 80 Books of Hours; important Americana; manuscript letters and poems by Robert Burns, Edgar Allan Poe, Catherine de Médicis, and Cardinal Richelieu; and hundreds of fine bindings by the leading practitioners from the fifteenth through the nineteenth centuries, books from royal libraries and noted collectors. Hoe had spent $500,000 to $750,000 on his books and another $250,000 on bindings, although he was criticized for binding many of his books and so destroying their original covers. In his 1902 essay for *The Bibliographer,* "Of Bibliophilism and the Preservation of Books," Hoe defended his practice: "As all books must have bindings, it is surely better to have them well done and even elaborately decorated, no matter when their covers may be placed upon them. The better they are, the better the chance of the survival of the volumes, and the best will wear out soon enough."

Daniel P. Kennedy, the regular auctioneer for Anderson Auction Gallery, presided over the opening afternoon session that indicated the direction the Hoe sales would take. St. Augustine's *De Civitate Dei* (Venice: John and Wendelin Spira, 1470), the fourth book printed in Venice, richly illuminated in gold and one of eight copies printed on vellum, went for $2,700 to Smith for Huntington, who outbid Greene, who was representing Morgan.

For the evening session Anderson Auction Gallery imported Sidney Hodgson of London to

Page from the Catholicon, *printed by Gutenberg in 1460 (from* The Library of Robert Hoe, *part 2, no. 304)*

preside—to the chagrin of Kennedy. The highlight of this session, indeed of the entire sale, was the Gutenberg on vellum. Smith began the bidding by winking at Hodgson's request for $10,000. Rosenbach, Dodd, Quaritch, and Joseph Widener all competed initially. Brief applause interrupted the proceedings when the bidding at $21,000 surpassed the previous record for a Gutenberg at auction. At $30,000 Quaritch withdrew, leaving the field to Smith and Widener. Huntington was prepared to withdraw as well when the bids passed $40,000. "Too much money. Nothing doing," he whispered to Smith. "Leave me alone," Smith replied. "If you don't want it, I'll buy it myself." Widener offered $49,000. Smith winked once more, and at $50,000 the two volumes were his. Huntington immediately relented, and Hodgson announced that Huntington was the buyer. Huntington stood and bowed to an audience cheering the owner of the world's most expensive book. Also that evening, for $12,000 Hun-

Title page for one of the books at the Hoe Sale: a work by Saint Bernardine of Sienna, abridged by Thomas Varnet and Natalis Beda, translated by Thomas Watson, and printed in London by Wynkyn de Worde in 1511 (from The Library of Robert Hoe, part 3, no. 271)

tington acquired Dame Juliana Berners's *The Book of St. Albans* (St. Albans: St. Albans Printer, 1486), one of the two perfect copies known and the first example of English color printing. At the Ashburnham sale Hoe had paid £386 ($1,925) for it. By the end of the two sessions on the first day the Hoe library had realized $134,866, already more than the previous American record of $127,138 for an entire library set by the five George Brinley sales (1879–1893).

Subsequent sessions continued to yield high prices. William Blake's *Milton* (London: Author, 1804), the finest of the three known copies, was knocked down to Smith ($9,000), who again defeated Greene for the title. Greene secured Blake's *The Marriage of Heaven and Hell* (London: Author, 1790) for $3,500, but every other Blake item sold in that session went to Smith: for $725 a presentation copy of *Poetical Sketches* (London: Author, 1783), Blake's first book; for $725 *Songs of Innocence* (London: Author, 1789), Blake's first engraved volume; for $700 *Songs of Experience* (London: Author, 1794); for $210 *Illustrations for*

the *Book of Job* (London: Author, 1825); and for $180 a Blake letter dated 27 November 1805. Smith defeated Rosenbach at $3,800 for Samuel Daniel's *Delia* (London: Printed by John Charlwood for Simon Waterson, 1592), one of two known copies of the first edition, first issue of this important Elizabethan sonnet cycle. The other copy of this issue was at the Bodleian Library at Oxford. Smith paid $2,800 for ninety-three manuscript pages of Washington Irving's *Life of Washington* (New York: Putnam, 1855–1859) that included the description of the treason of Benedict Arnold, $540 for the twelfth-century manuscript of Bede's *Commentaries,* and $1,850 for a thirteenth-century Vulgate Bible on vellum executed at Cremona by a scribe named Viviano. This manuscript includes fifty-six large and another fifty-six small historiated and ornamented initials. A copy of Milton's *Poems* (London: Printed by Ruth Raworth for Humphrey Moseley, 1645), presented by the author to Peter Heimbach (counselor of state to the elector of Brandenburg and Milton correspondent), went to Smith for $1,520. The first New York Directory, compiled by David Franks and printed by Shepard Kollock in 1786, was knocked down to Smith for $2,275. On May 3 the Shakespeare First Folio from the Syston Park sale went to Smith for $13,000. Pliny's *Historia Naturalis* (Venice: Nicolas Jenson, 1472) on vellum became Smith's for $2,725. John Winthrop's *Declaration of Former Passages and Proceedings Betwixt the English and the Narrowgansets* (Cambridge, Mass.: Stephen Daye, 1645), one of the first books printed in British North America and one of only four known copies, was sold to Smith on 5 May 1911 for $10,000, a record for an American book. By the time the first sale ended on that day, the 3,538 lots, comprising about a quarter of Hoe's library, had realized $997,363—already more than the combined sales of the Sunderland library (1881–1883) at $237,905 and Ashburnham library (1891–1898) at $479,645—and these were two of the finest collections in England. Of the nearly $1 million, Smith, almost always acting for Huntington, had spent $523,700. Quaritch was a distant second at $90,000.

As Walter M. Hill observed in *The New York Times* on 28 April 1911, "In bidding against Mr. Smith the rest of us are practically attacking a brick wall." Hill had commissions from the Newberry Library, Chicago, for three hundred titles. He secured none. Hill joined the chorus of critics of the sale. On 28 April 1911, with the first sale not even half over, *The New York Times* quoted him as saying,

I think many of the books have brought absurdly high prices. Take for instance the *Adam Bede* sold last Monday. It is not worth more than $25, yet Smith paid $330. The rarities in the sale have not sold too high. The price paid for the Gutenberg Bible, for example, was perhaps not excessive, but the common run of books are going at ridiculously high prices.

Quaritch, too, said that "some of the prices seem absurdly high." Madame Belin remarked, "Your prices are as tall as your buildings." Belle da Costa Greene, accustomed to having her way in the auction room, claimed that "the prices that are being paid for rare books at the Hoe 'sale' are perfectly ridiculous. They are more than ridiculous—they are most harmful. They establish dangerous precedents" (*The New York Times*, 30 April 1911).

The New York Times disagreed, dismissing such complaints as resentment by unsuccessful bidders. In a letter to *The New York Times* published on 2 May 1911 Whipple, Hoe's librarian, defended the high prices:

> Robert Hoe was a great book-collector in the truest sense of the word—one of the greatest that the world has ever known, and the prices now being paid for his library are in a large measure a tribute to his perspicacity and his intelligent, long-standing, and unfailing interest in books. It is very evident to the spectator that buyers want not only a certain edition or issue of a book, but also the very copy once owned by this famous bibliophile. That fact accounts in part for the high prices now obtaining.

Despite the Smith-Huntington juggernaut and the complaints of high prices, the first sale included enough treasures to allow many to secure choice items.

The day after *The New York Times* published Greene's objections, she bought the Caxton *Morte d'Arthur* for $42,800, the second-highest price paid for an item at the Hoe sales; it was also beyond Morgan's previous record for the Mainz Psalter. This purchase apparently did not set a dangerous precedent. Greene had the satisfaction of defeating Smith for this item, though in this case Smith was not bidding for Huntington. Though Hill could not buy anything for the Newberry Library, for $21,000 he did secure *Helyas, Knight of the Swan* for Edith Rockefeller McCormick, daughter of John D. Rockfeller. He also bought the *editio princeps* of Homer for $3,800; for $3,400 Richard Hakluyt's *Principall Navigations, Voiages, and Discoveries of the English Nation* . . . (London: Imprinted by G. Bishop, R. Newberie and R. Barker, 1598–1600), an important account of sixteenth-century British exploration and colonization; and a letter of Edgar Allan Poe for $300.

Rosenbach did not get the 1786 Kilmarnock Burns with a letter from the author to Capt. John Hamilton of Dumfries; Smith bought it for $5,800. But for $3,000 Rosenbach did get a presentation copy of Burns's *Poems* (Edinburgh: T. Cadell, 1793) given by the author to Thomas White of Dumfries. This volume is now at Harvard. For $4,900 Belin secured a fine copy of Boethius's *De Consolatione Philosophiae* (Ghent: Arend de Keysene, 1485); at the 1891 Ives sale Hoe had paid $145 for this work. Walter T. Wallace, New York broker, paid $3,800 for the rare first printing of *The Embargo* (Boston: Printed for the purchasers, 1808) by the twelve-year-old William Cullen Bryant, and for $3,200 he obtained a Third Folio of Shakespeare (London: Printed for P. C., 1664). New York bookseller Ernest Dressel North paid $4,500 for the first edition of Thomas Gray's *Elegy Wrote in a Country Churchyard* (London: R. Dodsley, 1751); the previous record for this item at auction had been $740 in 1902.

For $33,000 Arthur Hoe apparently kept the *Pembroke Hours* in the family, though he may have been acting for Courtland Field Bishop, collector of French illustrated books in fine bindings. Hoe's granddaughter, Thirza Benson, paid $24,000 for the *Hours of Anne de Beaujeu*, made for the daughter of Louis XI of France. This fine Book of Hours includes 107 full-page miniatures. The missal given by Charles VI of France to his daughter went to Dodd and Livingston for $18,900. Among the items Quaritch secured was a fifteenth-century manuscript of Richard de Bury's *Philobilon* for $1,450, the first treatise on book collecting, originally composed in Durham, England, about 1345. The *Opera* of Lactantius (Subiaco: Konrad Sweynheym and Arnold Pannartz, 1465), the first printed book to use a complete Greek font, also went to Quaritch, for $1,700.

More serious than the complaints about prices were Ludwig Baer's claims that two expensive items in the first sale were forgeries. Baer denounced a sixteenth-century binding purportedly executed by Nicolas Eve for Henry III of France, for which Smith had paid $2,600, and the twenty-one miniatures in a fifteenth-century manuscript of Ovid that had belonged to Anne of Brittany, for which Smith had given $10,000. The latter had passed through the hands of the infamous nineteenth-century biblioklept Count Libri-Carrucci, who had restored medieval manuscripts, but Libri was not known to manufacture miniatures as Baer claimed the count had in this case. Smith, Chew, and other authorities rallied to defend the Hoe items, and when Baer returned to Germany, his accusations vanished with him.

Part 2 of the Hoe sale began on 8 January 1912 and ran for twenty sessions. Though the offerings were less spectacular than those of the first sale, by any other standards the 3,621 lots were impressive. They included ninety-eight illuminated manuscripts, sixty-nine incunabula—among these a Gu-

Hand-illuminated page from the Latin Lives, *by Cornelius Nepos, printed in Venice by Nicolas Jenson in 1471, that was in Hoe's collection in 1895 (from O. A. Bierstadt,* The Library of Robert Hoe, *1895)*

tenberg Bible on paper and another incunabulum Bible printed on vellum in Venice by Nicolas Jenson (1476), two Caxtons, Aldus Manutius's first Latin book (Pietro Bembo's, *De Aetna,* Venice, 1495), and two copies of the Columbus letter—important Americana, fine bindings, and rare literary first editions. Once more the auction attracted an international crowd, with Quaritch back from London, Paul Gottschalk coming from Berlin, and Heinrich Eisemann representing C. Lange of Rome. American dealers and collectors again helped fill the seats. Smith dominated this sale as he had the first, paying $5,000 for Caxton's *Canterbury Tales* and $8,000 for Caxton's *Polychronicon.* The first issue of the first edition of Milton's *Paradise Lost* (London: Peter Parker, 1667) went to Smith for $1,150. Of the $471,619.25 realized in this second sale, Smith spent $130,000.

Quaritch was a close second at $123,000. A substantial percentage of that sum was for the Gutenberg Bible on paper, which Quaritch secured for Joseph Widener, underbidder for the vellum copy. Quaritch had sold the paper copy to Hoe for $17,500 and repurchased it for Widener for $10,000

more. Quaritch also secured Hoe's copy of the *Catholicon,* also printed by Gutenberg (Mainz, 1460), for $1,625. This work lacked one leaf. *De Aetna* went to Quaritch for $255.

Hill fared better in the second sale than he had in the first, spending $30,000 and securing at least some of the titles sought by the Newberry Library. For that institution at $8,000 he bought the *Lettera di Amerigo Vespucci* (Florence, circa 1505), one of five known copies. *Mundis Novis* (Rome: Eucharius Silber, 1504), one of four known copies of the account of Vespucci's third voyage, went to Hill for $2,500. Two other early accounts of the voyages of Vespucci, Columbus, Vasco da Gama, and other explorers cost Hill an additional $5,800. For $2,500 Hill bought John Smith's *General Historie of Virginia, New England, and the Summer Islands* (London: Printed by I. D. and I. H. for Michael Sparkes, 1624), a large-paper copy with the arms of James I and the feathers of the Prince of Wales on the front cover, the arms of the Duchess of Richmond on the back.

Dodd and Livingston secured other important Americana, buying a 1493 Columbus letter for $1,650, twice what Hoe had paid for it at the Henry Cruse Murphy sale in 1884. The firm paid $875 for Theodore De Bry's French version of Thomas Hariot's *Virginia* (Frankfort: Joannes Wecheli, 1590), one of thirteen known copies, not all of them perfect. Another Dodd purchase was a first edition of Oliver Goldsmith's *The Vicar of Wakefield* (Salisbury: B. Collins, 1766) for $1,450.

Isaac Seligman—who lived near Washington Irving's house, Sunnyside, at Tarrytown, New York, and collected Irving material—secured three Irving manuscripts: his journal for 1 July 1804 to 23 January 1805 ($825), a notebook of the same period ($750), and four other notebooks ($160) with material for *A Tour on the Prairies* (Philadelphia: Carey, Lea & Blanchard, 1835). Wright paid $900 for a complete set in Latin of De Bry's *Grand Voyages* (Frankfort, 1590–1634). Rosenbach, who had spent $11,646 at the first sale, now secured a complete run of the 635 numbers of the *Spectator* (London, 1711–1714) with contracts between the authors, Joseph Addison and Richard Steele, and their publisher, Sam Buckley ($950). Goldsmith's *The Haunch of Venison* (London: J. Ridley, 1776) went to Rosenbach for $635, almost twice the $350 Hoe had paid for it. For $925 Rosenbach secured the two-volume first edition of Michel de Montaigne's *Essais* (Bordeaux: S. Millanges, 1580). He paid $140 for a George Bernard Shaw manuscript, $535 for a first edition presentation copy of Samuel Richardson's *Clarissa* (London: Printed for S. Richardson, 1748 with a sixteen-line note by the author), and $1,910 for Sir Walter Scott's manuscript *Life of Jonathan Swift* (Edinburgh: A. Constable, 1814) that belonged to the English collector Sir Thomas Phillipps and in 1893 had been sold for £230 ($1,150).

Part three included 3,412 lots. Among these were thirty-eight manuscripts, seventeen of them from the fifteenth century and nine from the sixteenth century; Grolier's copy of Baldassare Castiglione's *Il libro del cortegiano* (Venice: Aldus, 1528); Cicero's *Epistolae Familiares* (Venice: Aldus, 1522); choice incunabula; a Third Folio of Shakespeare; the first engraved view of New York; two more copies of the Columbus letter; and sixteen printed Books of Hours. The sale opened on 15 April 1912, the day after the sinking of the *Titanic*. Harry E. Widener had examined the books to be offered at this sale and had planned to bid on John Gower's *Confessio Amantis* (Westminster: Caxton, 1483), one of seven perfect copies known. Widener was among the fifteen hundred people lost when the *Titanic* sank.

On 18 April 1912, the night that the extent of the *Titanic* disaster became known, the Gower went to Smith for $10,500. Of the $200,159.50 this sale realized, Smith spent $115,000. Forty-four leaves of the *Legenda Aurea* printed by Caxton in 1484 went to Smith for $2,100. The complete *Legenda Aurea* printed by Caxton's successor, Wynkyn de Worde (London, 1527), cost Smith $3,100. John Dryden's first book, *A Poem on the Death of His Late Highness, Oliver, Lord Protector of England, Scotland, and Ireland* (London: William Wilson, 1659), was Smith's for $262.50. Smith paid $775 for the Kelmscott Chaucer and $1,400 for a second edition of the Columbus letter (Rome: Stephen Planck, 1493). Most of the sixteen printed Books of Hours offered on 19 April went to Smith, and on 22 April most of the seventeen manuscript Horae followed them. On 24 April, Smith bought for $500 the first collection of Mexican laws, compiled by Vasco de Puga (Mexico City: Pedro Ocharte, 1563) and printed seventy-five years before British North America had a press. The following day Smith bought for $450 a copy of the third edition of Philip Sidney's *Arcadia* (London: William Ponsonbie, 1593) with Queen Elizabeth's arms on the binding, for $1,160 a Shakespeare Third Folio (London: Printed for P. C., 1664), and for $220 Hartmann Schedel's *Nuremberg Chronicle* in German (rarer than the Latin version) printed in Nuremberg by Anton Koberger in 1493 with eighteen hundred woodcuts.

At this sale Rosenbach spent about $10,000. Among his purchases was the manuscript of Lope de Vega's *Carlos V en Francia,* signed and dated by the author at Toledo, Spain, 20 November 1604, for

$125. New York bookseller James F. Drake also spent about $10,000, about a quarter of that ($2,350) for the Grolier copy of Castiglione. He also bought for $1,500 *Le manière de traciter les playes* (Paris: Jean de Brie, 1551) by the sixteenth-century French physician Ambrose Paré. The work was printed on vellum, and the binding carries the arms of Henry II of France and Diane de Poitiers.

The last part of the Hoe sale was conducted between 11 and 22 November 1912, with two afternoon sessions on 25 and 26 November to dispose of bibliographical material. Part four was the largest of the sales, with 4,017 lots, and it realized $262,924.85, about half of that sum, $123,000, coming from Smith. The sale included eighteen manuscript Books of Hours: eleven of these went to Smith; Quaritch bought three; Ernest Dressel North, two; Rosenbach and Leo Berg, one each. Smith secured for $510 Hoe's copy of William Congreve's *Incognita* (London: Peter Buck, 1692), so rare that the British Museum lacked a copy. The first English translation of Thomas More's *Utopia* (London: Abraham Vele, 1555) went to Smith for $465, and for $200 he got *Salve Deus Rex Iudaeorum* (London: Printed by Valentine Simmes for Richard Bonian, 1611) by Aemilia Lanier, a candidate for the role of Shakespeare's Dark Lady of the sonnets. Yet another Shakespeare Third Folio went to Smith for $3,000, and the second issue of the first quarto edition of Shakespeare's *Troylus and Cresseida* (London: Imprinted by G. Eld for R. Bonian and H. Walley, 1609) went to Huntington through Smith for $7,300, about ten times what the Ives copy had realized in 1891 ($790).

Courtland Field Bishop secured through Drake the only known uncut copy of the *Ecole de Salerne, envers Burlesques* (Paris, Elzevir, 1651) in a nineteenth-century citron Levant morocco binding by George Trautz-Bauzonnet ($3,500) and *Homélies ou sermons* of Joannes Chrysostom (Paris, 1693) in a blue morocco binding by the skilled eighteenth-century French binder Anthony Michael Padeloup ($3,125). Altogether Drake spent $20,300 in this fourth sale. Through Hill, Cyrus H. McCormick of Chicago paid $4,600 for two early editions of Vespucci's voyages (Augsburg: Johann Otmar, 1504; Milan: Io. Iacobo & Fratelli de Lignano, 1508). Hill spent $14,400 in the November sessions. Belin took many French books back to Paris. Sebastian Brant's *Stultifera Navis* (Basel: J. Bergman de Olpe, 1497), which includes an early reference to the discovery of America on leaf 76, went to Lathrop C. Harper ($155). Quaritch, who spent $23,000 in part four, paid $1,200 for the beautifully illustrated Fermier Generaux edition of Jean de la Fontaine's *Contes et nouvelles en vers* (Paris, 1762) and $3,750 for a vellum manuscript of Petrarch's *Trionfi* copied at Florence in the late fifteenth century. Joseph Baer and Company of Frankfort was the fifth largest purchaser in part four, buying $10,200 worth of books.

The four sales together included 14,592 lots and realized $1,932,056.60, or $132.41 per lot. By comparison, the Syston Park sale of 1884 realized £14 ($70) a lot, which Quaritch had called a "singularly high average." The sale of Hoe's bibliographical works on 25 and 26 November added $1,927.10 to the total (468 lots).

The Hoe sales enriched private and public collections. They marked the emergence of Huntington as a force in the auction rooms, which he continued to dominate until 1924 when he withdrew from public purchases, and of the Anderson Auction Gallery, which thereafter used the slogan "Where the Hoe Library was sold." Even more significant, as Matthew J. Bruccoli writes in *The Fortunes of Mitchell Kennerley, Bookman* (San Diego: Harcourt Brace Jovanovich, 1986), "The Hoe sale made New York a serious contender for the position of rare book center of the world." Wesley Towner notes in *The Elegant Auctioneers,* "The English traders, stunned and openly resentful, said no good would come of this vulgar demonstration of American exuberance. Americans grinned, and French and German dealers hurried to New York to open branch establishments." Foreign dealers had scoffed at the idea of a major book sale in America, but those who came for bargains remained to pay record prices. The sale also showed that old books were increasingly moving beyond the purses of scholars and had become, like art, the province of the rich.

References:

Oscar Albert Bierstadt, *The Library of Robert Hoe, a Contribution to the History of Bibliophilism in America* (New York: Duprat, 1895);

Gelett Burgess, "The Battle of the Books," *Collier's,* 48 (10 February 1912): 17;

The Library of Robert Hoe of New York, 8 volumes (New York: D. Taylor, 1911–1912);

Frederick King, "The Complete Collector," *Bookman,* 36 (January 1913): 310–523;

William Roberts, "Recent Book Sales," *Nineteenth Century,* 72 (November 1912): 1030–1039;

Wesley Towner and Stephen Varble, *The Elegant Auctioneers* (New York: Hill & Wang, 1970), pp. 258–280.

Thomas James Holmes

(26 December 1874 – 7 February 1959)

Dean H. Keller
Kent State University

BOOKS: *Fine Bookbinding: A Paper Read Before the Rowfant Club at an Exhibition of Bindings Executed by the Rowfant Bindery, December Fourth, Nineteen Hundred and Nine* (Cleveland: Rowfant Club, 1912);

The Mather Literature (Cleveland: Privately printed for W. G. Mather, 1927);

Increase Mather, His Works: Being a Short-Title Catalogue of the Published Writings That Can Be Ascribed To Him (Cleveland: Printed for private distribution, 1930);

English Ballads and Songs in the John G. White Collection of Folk-Lore and Orientalia of the Cleveland Public Library, and in the Library of Western Reserve University; Being a List of the Collections of English, Scottish and Anglo-American Ballads, Traditional Songs, Rhymes, Carols, Political Ballads and Songs, and Critical Material Concerning Them, by Holmes and Gordon W. Thayer (Cleveland: Library Club, 1931);

Increase Mather: A Bibliography of His Works, 2 volumes (Cleveland: Printed at the Harvard University Press for W. G. Mather, 1931);

Cotton Mather: A Bibliography of His Works, 3 volumes (Cambridge, Mass.: Harvard University Press, 1940);

The Minor Mathers: A List of Their Works (Cambridge, Mass.: Harvard University Press, 1940);

The Education of a Bibliographer: An Autobiographical Essay (Cleveland: Western Reserve University Press, 1957);

On the Road with Holmes: Memoranda of a Trip to New York, Worcester, and Boston, February 7–14, 1928, edited, with a preface, by Robert A. Tibbetts (Akron: Northern Ohio Bibliophilic Society, 1989).

OTHER: "The Surreptitious Printing of One of Cotton Mather's Manuscripts," in *Bibliographical Essays: A Tribute to Wilberforce Eames,* edited by Lawrence C. Wroth, George P. Winship, and Randolph G. Adams (Cambridge, Mass.:

Printed at Harvard University Press for the Subscribers, 1924), pp. 149–160;

Cotton Mather, *Manuductio ad ministerium: Directions for a Candidate of the Ministry,* bibliographical note by Holmes and Kenneth B. Murdock (New York: Published for the Facsimile Text Society by Columbia University Press, 1938);

"A Letter on Books and Witches," in *Bookmen's Holiday: Notes and Studies Written and Gathered in Tribute to Harry Miller Lydenberg,* edited by Deoch Fulton (New York: New York Public Library, 1943), pp. 443–445;

"The Rowfant Bindery," in *The Rowfant Club Yearbook* (Cleveland: Rowfant Club, 1958): 71–86.

SELECTED PERIODICAL PUBLICATIONS– UNCOLLECTED: "Cotton Mather and His Writings on Witchcraft," *Papers of the Bibliographical Society of America,* 18 (1924): 31–59;

"Notes on Richard Mather's 'Church Government,' London, 1643," *Proceedings of the American Antiquarian Society,* new series 33 (1924): 291–296;

"Book Collecting and William G. Mather," *Cleveland Topics,* 72 (2 July 1927): 8–10;

"Samuel Mather of Witney, 1674–1733," *Publications of the Colonial Society of Massachusetts,* 26 (1928): 313–322;

"The Bookbindings of John Ratcliff and Edmund Ranger, Seventeenth Century Boston Bookbinders," *Proceedings of the American Antiquarian Society,* new series 38 (1929): 31–50;

"Additional Notes of Ratcliff and Ranger Bindings," *Proceedings of the American Antiquarian Society,* new series 39 (1930): 291–306;

"The Mather Bibliography," *Papers of the Bibliographical Society of America,* 31 (1937): 57–76.

Perhaps best known for his bibliographical work on the Mathers, an early American family of clergymen and writers, Thomas James Holmes enjoyed careers as a master bookbinder, librarian, bibliographer, scholar, and author. It is remarkable

Members of the Rowfant Club, 22 September 1928: Frank [?], H. D. Piercy, Thomas J. Holmes, Ernest Kirkwood, Ted Robinson, John R. Owens, Charles W. Chestnut, William Thompson, William O. Mathews, Charles A. Post, John MacGregor Jr., Louis Rorimer, George F. Strong, William T. Higbee, Cyrus W. Faxon, Benjamin P. Bourland, Clark D. Lamberton, Clarence Stratton, Horace Carr, William R. A. Hays, Frank H. Ginn, W. T. Holliday, Frank H. Baer, I. T. Frary, Dwight L. Smith, and Francis H. Herrick (photograph by William Higbee; courtesy of the Rowfant Club)

that such a range of accomplishments was achieved with a minimal amount of formal education.

Holmes was born on 26 December 1874 in Newcastle-Under-Lyme, Staffordshire, England, the son of Elisha and Maryjane Rhodes Holmes. He attended public school, and later, evening school, in his hometown. Once he began his education he never stopped, even though he did not attend a college or university. The description of his reading found in the early pages of *The Education of a Bibliographer: An Autobiographical Essay* (1957) reveals the substantial depth and breadth of his self-study program.

He was an avid reader of the Bible, notably in the King James version, and he read much in theology and church history, especially the writings of Martin Luther, John Calvin, and the English and Scottish nonconformists. These readings would prove to be especially useful to Holmes later in life when he began his bibliographical and scholarly work on the Mather family. Holmes also found useful his readings in the medical journal *Lancet,* which helped him understand Cotton Mather's interest in medicine.

He read through a set of Thomas Carlyle's works, except for the "ponderous" *History of Friedrich II. of Prussia, called Frederick the Great* (6 volumes,

1858–1865); and Carlyle's writings on the French Revolution led him to the Encyclopaedists and other French writers, including Blaise Pascal, whose *Pensées de M. Pascal sur la religion et sur quelques autre sujects* (1670) he read with "intense pleasure." Carlyle also was instrumental in awakening his interest in German history, literature, and philosophy. Holmes read many poets and was especially attracted to Dante, John Milton, and Alfred Tennyson.

When Holmes was thirteen years old he began a seven-year apprenticeship in a bookbindery which was connected to a printing office and bookshop in Newcastle-Under-Lyme. The proprietor was David Dilworth; later the shop was taken over by George Thomas Bagguley, who is credited with inventing a color tooling process on vellum. Holmes recalls that the workday was nine and one-half hours, for which he was paid two shillings and sixpence a week, equivalent to about sixty cents in American money; each year he received a raise of one shilling a week. From this salary he began to purchase books from Dilworth's and then Bagguley's stock.

Bagguley, besides running his business, was also visiting librarian for the duke of Sutherland, whose library was at Trentham Hall in Staffordshire about four miles from the bindery. Holmes spent three summers at the library, where his chief duty was the dressing of the leather bindings—a chore that also provided an opportunity to widen his acquaintance with classical and European literature, which was strongly represented in the duke's library. Holmes later worked for a few weeks in the library of the bishop of Lichfield, the earl of Exeter. Since Lichfield is the birthplace of Samuel Johnson, Holmes deepened his knowledge of Johnson and James Boswell, and he took an interest in Joseph Addison and Richard Steele as well.

It was also at about this time in his life that Holmes began to question the fundamentalist religion in which he had been raised. He was moved by the morning and evening services that the bishop of Lichfield conducted for his family and household staff in the chapel; later, in London, some Unitarian friends introduced Holmes to the writings of the Americans William Ellery Channing and Theodore Parker. His reading of them confirmed in him a sort of Christian humanism that he practiced for the rest of his life.

When Holmes was twenty-one, in 1895, he moved to London, where he joined the staff of the firm of Rivière and Son, staying until 1899 when he returned to Bagguley. His particular talents were forwarding—preparing a book for the finisher by performing assemblage tasks such as affixing the cover—and gilding, or overlaying surfaces with gold powder or leaf. He perfected these skills to such a degree that he was awarded a diploma and bronze medal for a binding exhibited at the Paris International Exposition of 1900. For a few months in 1902 he returned to London to work for the binder Joseph Zaehnsdorf.

While in London, Holmes discovered the writings of John Ruskin and became acquainted with the work of William Morris, T. J. Cobden-Sanderson, and others involved in the revival of the arts of printing and binding that was taking place in England at that time. He also attended lectures on art given by Lucking Tavener, a Ruskin admirer and critic for the *Westminster Gazette;* it was at these lectures that he met Alice Mary Browning, whom he married on 24 December 1901. Less than a year later Thomas and Mary Holmes left England for America, where they would eventually become naturalized citizens.

They arrived in New York on Saturday, 12 October 1902; on the following Monday Holmes began to work at the Club Bindery. This business was founded by several prominent book collectors, including William L. Andrews, Beverly Chew, Walter Gilliss, Robert Hoe III, Edwin B. Holden,

Marshall C. Lefferts, Junius S. Morgan, Arthur H. Scribner, and James O. Wright, and it was incorporated in 1895. Most of these men were members of the Grolier Club in New York, but the bindery had no official connection with that club. Besides Holmes, the Club Bindery employed several other skilled craftsmen, most notably the Frenchmen Henri Hardy, who served as foreman of the business; Léon Maillard, considered by some to be the best finisher in Paris; and his brother Paul, also a fine finisher. Women such as Anna Berger, Cornelia Hopkins, and Mary Neill also were valued members of the staff. Holmes worked mostly as a forwarder, almost exclusively on rare books. Unfortunately, by 1902 most of the work of the Club Bindery came only from the celebrated library of Hoe and patronage could not seem to be expanded, so the business consistently operated at a loss. Inevitably, the Club Bindery closed its doors in April 1909. Holmes's work at the Bindery ended in grand style, for the last book he forwarded was a copy of Francesco Colonna's *Hypnerotomachia Poliphili* printed in Venice in 1499 by Aldus Manutius and considered by some to be the most beautiful book ever printed.

While the Club Bindery was struggling toward closure, some members of the recently established and flourishing Rowfant Club in Cleveland, Ohio, were talking about establishing a fine bindery in the city to furnish their needs. Judge Willis Vickery, a club member, traveled to New York for discussions with Hardy, Maillard, and Holmes about coming to Cleveland. Within a month of the closing of the Club Bindery in New York, the Rowfant Bindery was established in Cleveland with Hardy as manager and Holmes as business manager. Between the time it opened on 24 May 1909 until it closed on 15 January 1913, the Rowfant Bindery finished 1,360 orders that totaled 4,051 volumes.

Shortly before the Rowfant Bindery closed, Holmes resigned to pursue other interests. He never lost interest in fine binding, however, and in 1912 he prepared for publication a paper called "Fine Bookbinding," which he had delivered at the opening of an exhibition of bindings executed by the Rowfant Bindery. One hundred copies of Holmes's first publication were printed by the Rowfant Club. He also spoke to the convention of the Master Bookbinders Association of America which met in Cleveland in 1918; that paper was published in the journal of the association under the title "Good Bookbinding." From 1908 to 1911 he conducted the bookbinding column for the *Progressive Printer* of Saint Louis, and at the May 1919 show he was

Title page for Holmes's descriptive bibliography of the prominent Boston clergyman who was the father of the Puritan divine Cotton Mather

awarded the Penton Medal for excellence by the Cleveland Museum of Art.

After leaving the Rowfant Bindery, Holmes began his career as a librarian. While he had no formal training in librarianship, his entire life had been devoted to books. He knew how books were printed and constructed from the handling of countless examples from all periods as well as the contents of many works through years of wide-ranging reading. His summer work in the duke of Sutherland's library, which was rich in ballad literature and similar material, had at least partly prepared Holmes for his first library position as part-time assistant to Gordon W. Thayer, head of the John G. White Collection of Folklore and Orientalia at the Cleveland Public Library. Holmes worked with Thayer for four years, and together they produced a catalogue of *English Ballads and Songs in the John G. White Collection of Folk-Lore and Orientalia of the Cleveland Public Library and the Library of Western Reserve University,* which was published by the Library Club of Cleveland in 1931. Holmes also devised an inexpensive method for preserving and restoring fragile material in the collection. In 1916, while working part-time

for the Cleveland Public Library, Holmes also began to work as librarian for the private collector William Gwinn Mather, and this relationship led to Holmes's greatest scholarly achievement: the publication of the bibliographies of Cotton and Increase Mather and the minor Mathers in six volumes from 1931 to 1940.

William Gwinn Mather, an eighth-generation descendant of Richard Mather, had begun to collect the works of his forebears almost as a whim in 1886 when he attended the fourth of five George Brinley sales and bought a few minor titles by Increase and Cotton Mather. His interest in collecting these works grew steadily, and with the assistance of book dealers such as Patrick K. Foley, Charles E. Goodspeed, Lathrop C. Harper, A. S. W. Rosenbach, George D. Smith, and Henry Stevens he was able to assemble 342 of the 621 works which were then identified as having been written by the Mathers. William Mather's collection soon equaled that of the American Antiquarian Society, making it one of the two largest in the country. A significant amount of collateral material was also made part of William Mather's collection, bringing the total number of volumes to approximately twenty-one hundred in 1933.

Holmes's relationship with William Mather began in July 1912 when Holmes was invited to Mather's library at Gwinn, the family's home in a suburb of Cleveland, for the purpose of making suggestions about arranging, cataloguing, and some rebinding of the collection. Mather evidently valued Holmes's advice, for he soon employed him as his librarian, a relationship that lasted through the sale of Mather's collection in 1935.

Holmes and Mather worked diligently to increase, improve, and describe the collection, and they formed the idea of publishing a series of bibliographies that would record the works of fourteen Mathers, from Richard (1596–1669) to Moses (1719–1806). Holmes made several trips on Mather's behalf to libraries and book dealers, mostly on the East Coast, doing research on the books and their backgrounds and making purchases for the collection at Gwinn. He recorded one such trip in diary form as "Memoranda: Trip to New York, Worcester and Boston, February 7 to 14, 1938." It was published in 1989 as *On the Road with Holmes,* and it is rich in references to bookseller Lathrop Harper, printer-typographer Bruce Rogers, librarians Wilberforce Eames and Clarence S. Brigham, historian Samuel Eliot Morison, and others as well as descriptions of visits to the Grolier Club, the Morgan Library, the New York Public Library, the American Antiquarian Society, and the

Boston Public Library. On 13 February, two hundred years after the burial of Cotton Mather in Copp's Hill Burying Ground in Boston, Holmes and Mather scholar Philip G. Nordell made a pilgrimage to the grave site, an event which Holmes recorded in some detail.

As plans began to develop for the Mather bibliographies, Holmes and William Mather consulted several eminent bibliographers, among them Brigham, Eames, George Parker Winship, and Lawrence C. Wroth; in "The Mather Bibliography" in *Papers of the Bibliographical Society of America* some years later Holmes looked back on their ambitious undertaking:

> The design was to compile a census, with location of every extant copy of these writings; to photograph and to reproduce in zinc etching every known Mather title-page, and other significant pages, such as those which contained colophons, etc.; and to examine, identify, and authenticate every known work; to give to it a full technical description by sheet signatures, by number of leaves, by pages, and by a description of its contents, according to the most approved modern practice.

The plan also called for the inclusion of imprint and textual variants, and summaries of the substance and backgrounds of the most notable works.

Holmes and Mather considered the works of Increase Mather to be the most important, so they determined that his works would be the subject of the first bibliography. In preparation they published a checklist in 1930, handsomely printed by Horace Carr in Cleveland and bound by R. R. Donnelly Company of Chicago; it was to be distributed, along with a paperbound copy, to libraries and collectors with the expectation that the paperbound copy would be corrected, amended, and returned so that information could be recorded in the bibliography. The Increase Mather bibliography, substantially funded by William Mather, appeared in two volumes in 1931 with an introduction by Winship, supplementary material by Kenneth B. Murdock and George F. Dow, and a binding executed by the R. R. Donnelly Company from designs by Holmes.

Shortly after the publication of the Increase Mather volumes William Mather decided to sell his collection and also to curtail his support of the planned bibliographies. Whether the Depression put too great a burden on his resources, whether he was ill, whether he simply lost interest, or whether, as Holmes suggests in "The Mather Bibliography," he was just "tired," is not clear; but in any case Holmes began a search for a new home for the collection. He had serious discussions with representatives of Yale University and then the University of Chicago but

to no avail. Finally Randolph G. Adams, librarian of the Clements Library at the University of Michigan, put him in touch with Tracy William McGregor of Detroit and Washington, D.C. McGregor was interested but not at the $200,000 Holmes and Mather hoped to realize from the sale. He offered $80,000 for the collection and Mather accepted. The sale took place in September 1935, but McGregor, who suffered from a heart ailment, died on 6 May 1936 before he could fully appreciate the great collection that he had bought. Happily, the collection ended up intact at the Alderman Library of the University of Virginia where it formed the basis of the McGregor Americana Collection.

Before he died McGregor allocated funds for the continuation of the work on the Mather bibliographies, to be administered by the American Antiquarian Society in Worcester, Massachusetts. After McGregor's death William Mather resumed his patronage of the project and supported it until its completion in 1940. Holmes moved to Worcester in 1936 to continue his work on the bibliographies. The three volumes of Cotton Mather's bibliography were published in 1940, and one volume comprising the minor Mathers appeared later in the same year.

The bibliographies were well received by scholars and librarians, and Holmes recorded comments from written notices by Morison, Wroth, Eames, Lyon N. Richardson, Ralph L. Rusk, R. W. G. Vail, Leonard L. Mackall, Jesse H. Shera, and others in *The Education of a Bibliographer*. In his historical and critical survey "The Descriptive Bibliography of American Authors" in *Studies in Bibliography* (1968), G. Thomas Tanselle called Holmes's six volumes one of the monuments of American bibliography and went on to say:

> At the time of its inception, this work represented the most serious bibliographical attention which had yet been paid to an American author (or group of authors) and the first extensive use of title-page reproductions in an American bibliography. It employed format terms accurately, reported gatherings in concise fashion, located copies, and noted later printings. One objection which may be raised is that its alphabetical arrangement of material is not as meaningful as a chronological one would have been; also, the generous inclusion of title-page facsimiles for all major titles does not obviate the bibliographer's responsibility for complete quasi-facsimile transcriptions. Even with its faults, the *Increase Mather* demonstrated more clearly than any previous American work that descriptive bibliography was a scholarly discipline, and I think it may fairly be said it is the earliest American author-bibliography which does not need to be done over.

To crown his achievement, in 1941 Holmes was awarded an honorary doctor of letters degree by Trinity College in Hartford, Connecticut, William Mather's alma mater.

In 1941 Holmes moved back to the Cleveland area, settling in rural Newbury, Ohio, on a twenty-acre farm a few miles east of the city. He continued to take a lively interest in matters relating to books, and on 1 January 1944 he was appointed as one of the honorary consultants to the Army Medical Library. Since Holmes was the only member among the eighty-nine consultants with both practical and managerial experience in the preservation and conservation of rare books, he was called upon to give advice to the Medical Library in this area. He prepared an illustrated lecture, "The Form of the Book and the Restoration Program of the Army Medical Library," which he delivered at the second general meeting of the consultants. The paper was printed in the *Report of the Proceedings of the Second General Meeting of the Honorary Consultants of the Army Medical Library,* and he delivered it again at the Rowfant Club in Cleveland on 23 November 1945.

Holmes was an active member of the Rowfant Club from the time he joined in 1924 until his death in 1959. On 8 March 1957 he spoke at the club about the history of the Rowfant Bindery; lengthy excerpts from that lecture were published in the 1958 *Rowfant Club Yearbook.* He addressed the club on at least four other occasions, with the lectures "Books from the Library of William Gwinn Mather," "Increase Mather and the New England Witchcraft Persecutions," "The Bibliography of Increase Mather," and "Exploding the Witchcraft Myth in 1692, and Its Bearing on Coexistence."

Late in 1951 Holmes was urged by his friend Lyon N. Richardson, a fellow Rowfant Club member and professor of English at Western Reserve University, to write a short account of his life. In 1952 several typewritten copies of what Holmes called "An Autobiographical Letter" were prepared for distribution to some of his friends. A few

years later he revised the "Letter" and added a bibliography of his writings; it was published in 1957 by the Western Reserve University Press as *The Education of a Bibliographer.*

Holmes's wife died in 1957; Holmes died on 7 February 1959. He was survived by his son, John, and daughter, Alice Rosa Hubbard. A third child, Thomas, had died earlier.

Holmes summed up his love of books and learning in *The Education of a Bibliographer:* "From childhood I was an insatiable reader, with a flair for dictionary study and a taste for writing. I learned early the helpfulness of correct punctuation and the importance of clarity. I acquired a shelf of books on writing, the favorite of which was Arthur Quiller-Couch's *On the Art of Writing,* which contains his amusing, devastating, and often reprinted chapter, 'Interlude on Jargon.' My small world seemed always one of books. I was hungry of learning." That hunger remained with him for a lifetime.

References:

Lyon N. Richardson, "Thomas James Holmes," *The Rowfant Club Yearbook* (Cleveland: Rowfant Club, 1960): 51–53;

G. Thomas Tanselle, "The Descriptive Bibliography of American Authors," *Studies in Bibliography,* 21 (1968): 1–24;

Elbert A. Thompson and Lawrence S. Thompson, *Fine Binding in America* (Urbana, Ill.: Beta Phi Mu, 1956);

Willis Vickery, *The Rowfant Bindery: Paper Read at an Exhibition of Rowfant and Other Bindings at 16924 Edgewater Drive, Lakewood* (Cleveland: Privately printed, 1928).

Papers:

Correspondence, manuscripts, and other material relating to Thomas James Holmes, especially concerning William Gwinn Mather's collection and the writing of the Mather bibliographies, are located in the Department of Rare Books and Special Collections in the library of Ohio State University in Columbus.

Donald Hyde
(17 April 1909 – 5 February 1966)

and

Mary Hyde
(8 July 1912 –   )

Judith A. Overmier
University of Oklahoma

BOOKS (by Mary Hyde): *Playwriting for Elizabethans, 1600–1605* (New York: Columbia University Press, 1949);

The Impossible Friendship: Boswell and Mrs. Thrale (Cambridge, Mass.: Harvard University Press, 1972; London: Chatto & Windus, 1973);

The Thrales of Streatham Park (Cambridge, Mass.: Harvard University Press, 1977).

OTHER: "Shakespeare, Jr.," by Mary Hyde, in *To Doctor R.: Essays Here Collected and Published in Honor of the Seventieth Birthday of Dr. A. S. W. Rosenbach, July 22, 1946,* edited by Percy E. Lawler, John Fleming, and Edwin Wolf II (Philadelphia, 1946), pp. 85–96;

Samuel Johnson, *Johnson's Diaries, Prayers and Annals,* edited by E. L. McAdam Jr. and Donald and Mary Hyde, The Yale Edition of the Works of Samuel Johnson, volume 1 (New Haven: Yale University Press / London: Oxford University Press, 1958);

"Dr. Johnson's Second Wife," by Donald and Mary Hyde, in *New Light on Dr. Johnson,* edited by Frederick W. Hilles (New Haven: Yale University Press, 1959), pp. 133–152;

"Randolph Greenfield Adams, 1892–1951," by Donald Hyde, in *Grolier 75: A Biographical Retrospective to Celebrate the Seventy-Fifth Anniversary of the Grolier Club in New York,* edited by R. W. G. Vail (New York: Grolier Club, 1959), pp. 237–240;

"Not in Chapman," by Mary Hyde, in *Johnson, Boswell and Their Circle: Essays Presented to Lawrence Fitzroy Powell in Honour of His Eighty-Fourth Birthday,* edited by Mary M. Lascelles and others (Oxford: Clarendon Press, 1965), pp. 286–319;

Donald Hyde

Bernard Shaw and Alfred Douglas, A Correspondence, edited by Mary Hyde (New Haven: Ticknor & Fields, 1982; London: John Murray, 1982).

SELECTED PERIODICAL PUBLICATIONS–

UNCOLLECTED: "Johnson and Journals," by Donald and Mary Hyde, *New Colophon,* 3 (1950): 165–197;

"The History of the Johnson Papers," by Mary Hyde, *Papers of the Bibliographical Society of America,* 45 (1951): 103–116;

Draft of Johnson's Latin letter to Dr. Huddesford, vice-chancellor of Oxford University when the degree of Master of Arts was conferred upon Dr. Johnson by the university in 1755 (Catalogue of the Johnsonian Collection of R. B. Adam, 1921)

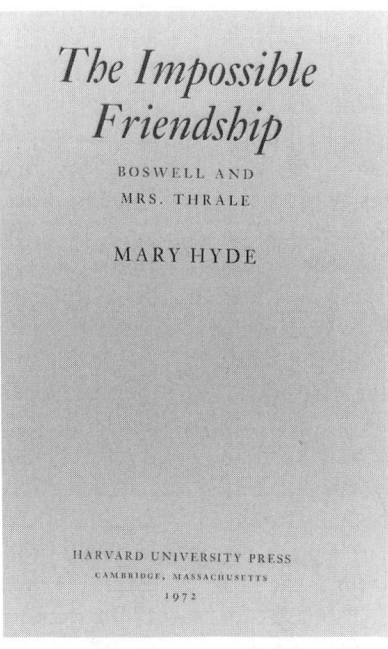

Title pages for books by Mary Hyde

"Contemporary Collectors VI: The Hyde Collection," by Donald and Mary Hyde, *Book Collector,* 4 (Autumn 1955): 208–216;

"Tetty and Johnson," by Mary Hyde, *Transactions 1957: Addresses and Transactions of the Johnson Society* (1957): 34–46;

"A Library of Dr. Samuel Johnson," by Mary Hyde, *Vassar Quarterly* (1966): 2–6.

The prescient and comprehensive collecting efforts of Donald and Mary Hyde have provided America's scholars with unequaled resources for the study of Samuel Johnson, James Boswell, and their circle. The Hyde collection also encompasses other authors in the eighteenth-century intellectual milieu, with in-depth holdings of Henry Fielding materials. Additional notable holdings include substantial collections dealing with Oscar Wilde and Bernard Shaw, a fine group of Elizabethan works, one of the best gatherings of Japanese manuscripts in the West, English bindings, and miscellaneous manuscripts of important literary and historical figures, among them Jane Austen, Desiderius Erasmus, and King Edward IV of England. As a husband-and-wife collecting team, the Hydes were exemplars of bibliophiles with an intense commitment to the scholarly use of their collection.

The son of Wilby Grimes Hyde, a lawyer, and Helen May Frizell Hyde, Donald Frizell Hyde was born in Chillicothe, Ohio, on 17 April 1909. The Hydes contributed to their son's love of books by reading aloud to the family the works of Sir Walter Scott, Charles Dickens, and Robert Burns. At Ohio State University, Professors Harlan Hatcher and William Graves imparted to Donald Hyde their love of eighteenth-century British literature. After graduating Phi Beta Kappa in 1929, Hyde went to Harvard Law School. He received his law degree in 1932 and worked briefly for the Goodyear Tire and Rubber Company before moving to Detroit to join the firm of Angell, Turner, Dyer, and Meek.

In Detroit, Hyde met Mary Morley Crapo, a scholar with an interest in the theater and the Elizabethan period. The daughter of Stanford Tappan and Emma Caroline Morley Crapo, she was born in Detroit on 8 July 1912 and received a B.A. from Vassar College in 1934 and an M.A. from Columbia University in 1936. She and Hyde were married on 16 September 1939. From their first Detroit home ("half a gardener's cottage," the Hydes recalled), with its floor-to-ceiling bookcases, books were an essential element of their life. During the first year of their marriage Mary Hyde bought first editions of Boswell's *The Life of Samuel Johnson, LL.D.* (London: Printed by Henry Baldwin for Charles Dilly, 1791) and Johnson's *A Dictionary of the English Language* (London: Printed by W. Strahan for J. and P. Knapton, T. and T. Longman, C.

Hitch and L. Hawes, A. Millar, and R. and J. Dodsley, 1755), thus laying the foundation for the Hydes' great Johnson collection.

In November 1940 the Hydes moved to New York City, where Donald joined the firm of Greene and Greene. They were quickly initiated into the New York book-collecting world. Their friend Randolph Greenfield Adams, a collector and director of the William L. Clements Library at the University of Michigan, visited the Hydes and orchestrated an extraordinary day during which they met the booksellers Gabriel Wells (who taught them about buying now and trading up later for better copies) and A. S. W. Rosenbach (who taught them about buying only the finest copies) and the experienced collector Arthur A. Houghton Jr.

Shortly after the Hydes' arrival in New York on 31 January 1941, the Darwin P. Kingsley sale was held at Parke-Bernet Galleries. Kingsley owned nine copies of the four folios of William Shakespeare's plays, including a First Folio (London: Printed for Isaac Jaggard and Edward Blount, 1623) that Wells bought for $5,200. Through their agent David Randall of Scribner's Book Store, to whom they had been introduced by Adams, the Hydes bought a copy of the first issue of the Third Folio (London: Printed by Philip Chetwinde, 1663) for $2,600.

The death of the famous collector A. Edward Newton in 1940 and the sales of his books at Parke-Bernet on 16 April, 14 May, and 29 October 1941 were major events in the book-collecting world. In the second of the three sales the Hydes bought Johnson manuscript materials, letters, and books, and Johnson's silver teapot. For $530 they secured thirty-two manuscripts and letters dealing with the case of the Reverend William Dodd, who had forged the signature of his pupil, Philip Stanhope, fifth Earl of Chesterfield, on a note for £4,200 and had been condemned to death; Johnson had interested himself in the case and had tried unsuccessfully to save Dodd, who was hanged in 1777. Among the manuscripts in Johnson's hand that the Hydes purchased were Dodd's petitions to the king, queen, lord chancellor, and the City of London. For $275 they bought "Considerations on the Case of Dr. Tripp's Sermons," a sixteen-hundred-word manuscript in Johnson's hand. Written in 1739 and first published in the *Gentleman's Magazine* in July 1787, after Johnson's death, it denies that Edward Cave's publication of an abridgment of Tripp's work was a violation of copyright.

At the third Newton sale the Hydes paid $650 for Hester Lynch Thrale Piozzi's commonplace book, kept between 1809 and 1820, which includes anecdotes about Johnson, and $275 for her forty-six-thousand-word manuscript "Lyfford Redivivus," a cu-

rious compilation of the etymology of names, written about 1815. At this sale they also bought a copy of the fourth quarto of Shakespeare's *Hamlet* (London: Printed by W. S. for John Smethwicke, [circa 1619]) for $900. In 1943 the Hydes acquired another Newton item when Eric Sexton sold them Hester Piozzi's journal of her 1774 tour through Wales with Johnson; her first husband, Henry Thrale; and the Thrales' oldest daughter.

The Hydes' collecting interests in the early 1940s took two main directions: Elizabethan theater books and manuscripts for her and eighteenth-century material for him. They patronized virtually every major dealer in the United States and Britain; among their principal suppliers were Rosenbach and Charles Sessler in Philadelphia; Charles Goodspeed in Boston; the Robinsons, Pickering and Chatto, Peter Murray Hill, Maggs Brothers, and Bernard Quaritch in London; and Blackwell's in Oxford. Rosenbach was a particularly productive source. Among the Elizabethan treasures the Hydes procured from him in the early 1940s were Robert Wilson's *The Three Ladies of London* (London: John Danter, 1592), Thomas Nashe's *Summer's Last Will and Testament* (London: S. Stafford for W. Burne, 1600), and Henry Petowe's *Eliza's Funerall* (London: Printed by E. Allde for M. Lawe, 1603). From William H. Robinson of London they bought the Leicester Harmsworth copy of Shakespeare's Fourth Folio (London: Printed for H. Herringman, E. Brewster, and R. Bentley, 1685). Among the rarities in early English drama in the Hyde collection were three quarto plays by Francis Beaumont and John Fletcher, together with the first collected edition of their works (London: Humphrey Robinson and Humphrey Moseley, 1647); four plays by George Chapman; two by Henry Chettle; three by Thomas Dekker; four by Thomas Heywood; the first collected edition of Ben Jonson's plays, in two volumes (London: Richard Meighen, 1616, 1640); three plays by Philip Massinger; nine Shakespeare quartos, together with the Second (1632), Third, and Fourth Folios; and four plays by James Shirley.

Among eighteenth-century items added by Hyde through Rosenbach in the early 1940s were Boswell's manuscript "Boswelliana," the manuscript for Johnson's dedication to John Hoole's translation of Torquato Tasso's *Jerusalem Delivered* (London: Printed for the author, 1763), and a letter from Johnson to Frederick North, eighth Baron North.

In 1943 Donald Hyde joined the Grolier Club; other collectors' groups with which he was affiliated during his life included the Philobiblon Society of Philadelphia and the Odd Volumes of Boston. Also in 1943 the Hydes purchased Oak Hill Farm near Somerville, New Jersey; it was renamed Four Oaks Farm,

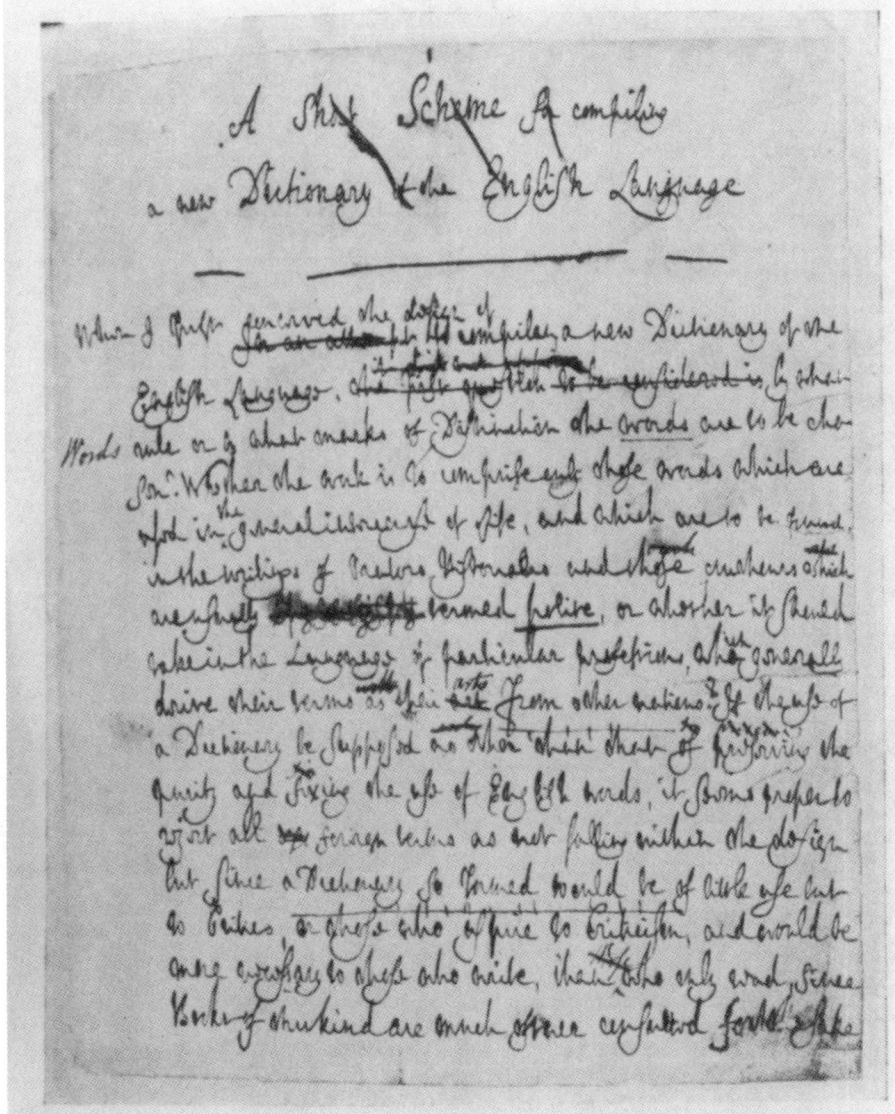

The first draft of Johnson's plan of a Dictionary of the English Language *(Catalogue of the Johnsonian Collection of R. B. Adam, 1921)*

after Donald Hyde's grandfather's farm in Ohio. That same year Donald Hyde entered military service as a lieutenant commander in the U.S. Naval Reserve. In 1946, toward the end of his term of service, he read *The History of Henry Fielding* (1918) by Wilbur L. Cross and was stimulated to collect Fielding material. The Hydes already had a few Fielding items, including the manuscript "Of Outlawry in Criminal Cases," and they continued to build that portion of their collection mainly by purchasing individual pieces. They did, however, secure several important items at the 1948 Parke-Bernet sale of the library of the New York philanthropist Herbert L. Carlebach. The Hydes' Fielding collection included two items that were so rare even Cross had not seen them: *The History of the Present Rebellion in Scotland* (London:

Printed for M. Cooper, 1745) and *Ovid's Art of Love Paraphras'd, and Adapted to the Present Time* (London: Printed for M. Cooper, A. Dodd, and G. Woodfall, 1747).

In the mid 1940s Rosenbach introduced Donald Hyde to Ralph Heyward Isham, the book collector noted for his efforts to recover, consolidate, and make available to scholars the papers of Boswell. Hyde became Isham's lawyer and lent him money interest free to complete the purchase of Boswell manuscripts found at Fettercairn House in Scotland. Though most of Isham's material was sold to Yale University in 1949, many important pieces went to Four Oaks; among them were 119 of Johnson's letters from the Fettercairn collection for which Hyde paid $14,000. From Isham the Hydes also secured the guest book

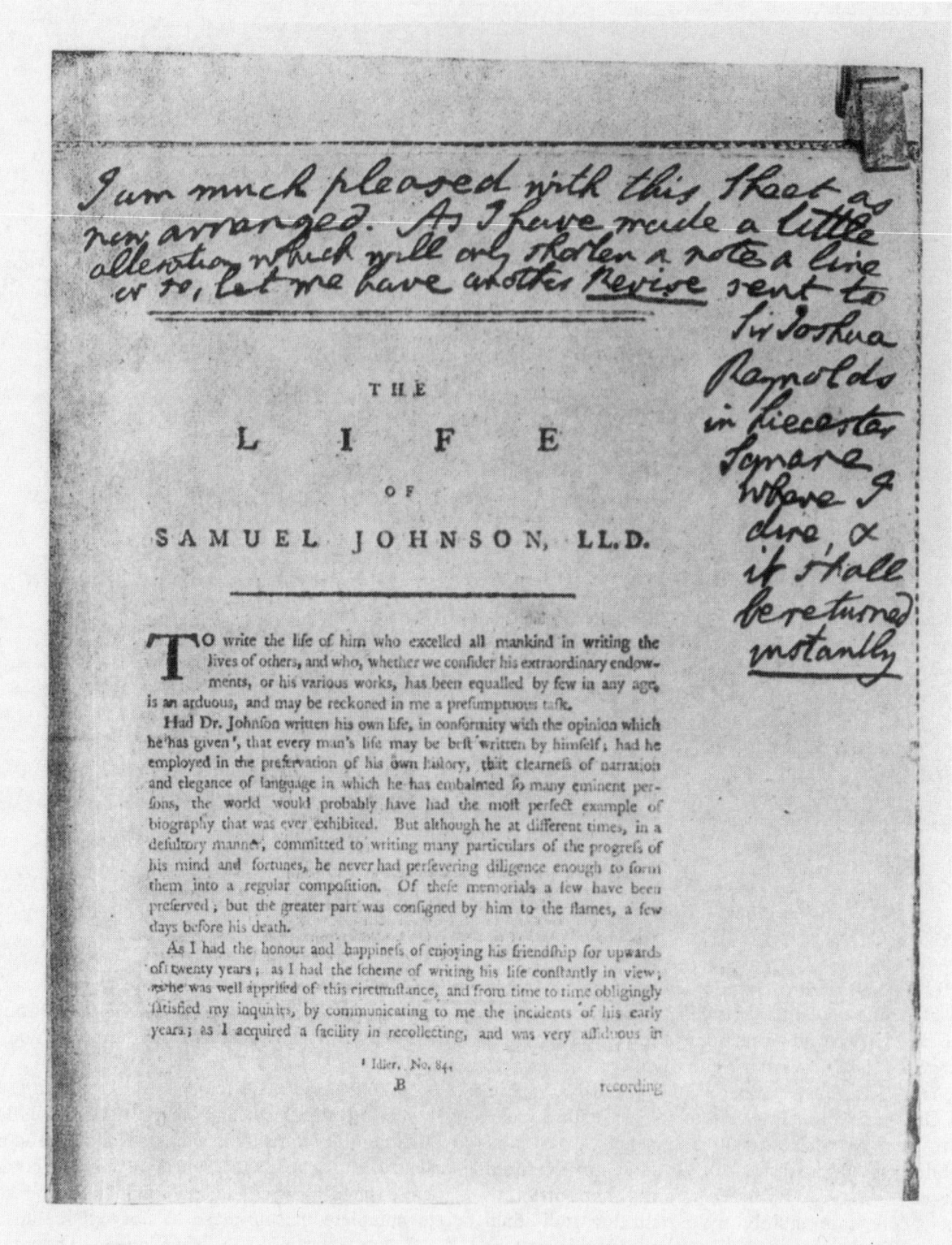

Page from James Boswell's original proof sheets (Catalogue of the Johnsonian Collection of R. B. Adam, 1921)

from Boswell's home at Auchinleck; the printer's copy and proof sheets of his controversial *A Letter to the People of Scotland* (London: Printed for Charles Dilly, 1785); some seventy letters by Boswell, including seven of his ten known letters to the Thrales; Johnson's drafts of *London* (London: Printed for R. Dodsley, 1738) and *The Vanity of Human Wishes* (London: Printed for R. Dodsley and sold by M. Cooper, 1749); Johnson's manuscript translation of Sallust's *Catiline;* transcripts of two Johnson diaries; and two fragmentary diaries, from 1729 and 1734, in Johnson's own hand.

A major purchase made by the Hydes in the late 1940s was the Robert Borthwick Adam collection. In 1936 Adam had deposited at the University of Rochester the collection that he and his uncle had assembled, thus making it available to scholars; after his death in 1940 his estate took considerable time to settle because his three heirs did not want to divide it. In 1948 they agreed to sell it in one piece, and the Hydes paid $75,000 for it. The Adam collection, joined with the Newton collection, Isham's Boswell papers, and individual items they had acquired from various sources, established the Hydes' Johnson collection as the preeminent one in the world.

The Adam purchase and subsequent acquisitions gave the Hydes the largest cache of Johnson manuscripts in existence. As Gabriel Austin noted in 1970, "Almost every significant contribution to Johnsonian studies [since 1948] has been indebted to the collection at Four Oaks Farm, and to the generosity and cooperation of its owners." In Austin's *Four Oaks Farm/Four Oaks Library* (1967) Robert F. Metzdorf describes the treasures the Hydes gathered:

> Johnson letters known at present to exist number more than 1000; of these more than half are at Four Oaks Farm. An analysis of the collection shows one letter to Boswell [of two letters and two fragments known]. There are in the collection 191 letter from Johnson to Mrs. Thrale. . . . Some of the other major series are 32 to [Johnson's stepdaughter] Lucy Porter, 32 to [his friend] Bennet Langton . . . and 18 to Sir Joshua Reynolds. In all there are Johnson letters to 108 identified correspondents.

The collection included Johnson's first known letter, written on 30 October 1731 to Gregory Hickman; his only known letter to his wife, Tetty, dated 31 January 1740; the two letters marking the end of his twenty-year friendship with Hester Lynch Thrale Piozzi; and a letter to James Macpherson of 20 January 1775 maintaining that the Ossian poems Macpherson had claimed to discover were forgeries: "I will not desist from detecting what I think a cheat, from any fear of the menaces of a Ruffian." The first and second drafts of *The Plan of a Dictionary of the English Language* (Lon-

don: Printed for J. and P. Knapton, T. Longman and T. Shewell, C. Hitch, A. Millar, and R. Dodsley, 1747), the proof sheets of the life of Alexander Pope for *Prefaces, Biographical and Critical, to the works of the English Poets* (London: Printed by J. Nichols for C. Bathurst and others, 1779–1781) that Johnson gave to Fanny Burney, and Lord Chesterfield's copy of Johnson's *Dictionary* were in the Hydes' collection. They also had seventeen books from Johnson's library, including two he had used in composing the *Dictionary*.

The acquisition of the Adam collection left the Four Oaks Library second only to Yale in its holdings of Boswell material, and the Piozzi portion of that collection gave the Hydes a group of her manuscripts, including more than three hundred of her letters, that is rivaled only by the John Rylands Library in Manchester, England, which houses the Thrale family papers. The Hydes also secured thirteen titles from her library, all with annotations in her hand. Among them was her copy of the 1807 edition of Boswell's *Life of Johnson* (London: T. Cadell and W. Davies), which had belonged to Isham and had been used by Edward G. Fletcher in preparing the 1938 Limited Editions Club edition.

In 1946 Mary Hyde joined other scholars and collectors in writing an essay for the volume *To Doctor R.,* in honor of Rosenbach's seventieth birthday. Her contribution, "Shakespeare, Jr.," deals with *Vortigern,* a forgery by William H. Ireland that purported to be a previously unknown play by Shakespeare, was accepted as such, and was produced at Drury Lane Theatre on 2 April 1796; Rosenbach owned the manuscript for the play. Hyde points out how the forgery deviates from sixteenth-century playwriting conventions in characterization, action, theme, and stage directions. She received her Ph.D. from Columbia University in 1948, and her dissertation was published the following year as *Playwriting for Elizabethans, 1600–1605.*

Her degree achieved and her book published, Mary joined Donald Hyde wholeheartedly in the pursuit of Dr. Johnson, Boswell, and Mrs. Thrale. To house the Adam collection the Hydes built a fireproof library that was opened in April 1949. Metzdorf describes the site: "These quiet, air-conditioned rooms, looking out on gardens, water, woods, and fields, have a vibrancy and vitality found in all too few libraries. It is a shrine of scholarship, but a workshop as well."

In 1950 the Hydes wrote an article for the *New Colophon* about Johnson's rules for keeping journals. In 1951 Mary Hyde wrote "The History of the Johnson Papers" for the *Papers of the Bibliographical Society of America*. During the 1950s she served on the editorial board of the *Shakespeare Quarterly*. The Hydes established the Four Oaks Foundation in 1953 to provide financial aid to students. In 1955 they wrote an article about their collecting adventures for the *Book Collector*. They served on the editorial board of the Yale Edition of the Works of Samuel Johnson and helped edit the first volume, *Johnson's Diaries, Prayers and Annals* (1958); of the manuscript materials published in the volume more than one-third was in their collection. Mary Hyde's presidential address to the Johnson Society in Lichfield, England, in 1957 was "Tetty and Johnson." In 1959 the Hydes contributed "Dr. Johnson's Second Wife" to *New Light on Dr. Johnson,* a volume commemorating Johnson's 250th birthday sponsored by The Johnsonians, a group the Hydes had organized in 1946. The Hydes' contribution speculates about women who might have become Johnson's second wife, had he remarried after Tetty's death.

In 1953 H. Montgomery Hyde (no relation), a longtime Wilde collector, had visited Four Oaks Farm to examine the Hydes' recently acquired letters from Wilde to Reginald Turner; he later wrote, "I have a feeling that our long talk . . . provided a great stimulus to [the Hydes'] interest in Wilde." In 1962 Donald and Mary Hyde acquired H. Montgomery Hyde's extensive collection through the bookseller Lew David Feldman; the purchase made Four Oaks Library second only to the William Andrews Clark Memorial Library at UCLA as a repository of Wilde material and the largest Wilde collection in private hands. Among the Wilde poems in manuscript at Four Oaks are *The Sphinx* (1894), "The Harlot's House," "Sonnet to Liberty," "Sonnet on the Sale of Keats' Love Letters," and "Roses and Rue," written to the actress Lily Langtry. The manuscript for "The Function of Criticism," first published in *The Nineteenth Century* in 1890, is in the Hyde collection, as are parts of the manuscripts for Wilde's verse plays *The Duchess of Padua* (1883) and *A Florentine Tragedy* (1908). The more than 150 autograph Wilde letters at Four Oaks range from his undergraduate letters to Reginald Harding through his correspondence with Louis Wilkinson after his release from prison. The collection is also rich in presentation and association copies of Wilde's books, including three copies of his *Poems* (London: D. Bogue, 1881) presented to his mother, his wife, and Robert Browning, and *The Importance of Being Earnest* (London: S. French, 1893), inscribed to the actor-manager Sir Charles Wyndham.

On a trip to Japan in 1960 the Hydes acquired *Daihannya Kyō* (730), *Hyakuman Tō Darani* (770), and an ornamented scroll with a fragment of a late-eleventh-century manuscript. By 1967 the Four Oaks collection of Japanese books and manuscripts had grown to 176 items, all of the greatest rarity and highest quality. These works illustrate the literary tradition of Japan, its printing history, and its art. Among the manuscripts is the oldest known complete *Genji monogatari* (The Tale of Genji), dating from the early twelfth century. The manuscript *Makura no sōshi* (Pillow Book), dated 1583, is one of only two known from before 1600. Printed works range from A.D. 770 to the modern period. Shigeo Sorimachi claimed that "the Hyde collection may be the best in the Western World, particularly in superior manuscripts earlier than the 17th century." The Japanese collection was sold in 1988 for the benefit of the Pierpont Morgan Library.

The expansion of the Hydes' Shaw collection was facilitated by Donald Hyde's affiliation in 1961 with the British publisher Constable and Company; from that firm's files that they acquired more than one thousand items of Shaw manuscript materials and correspondence. According to Dan H. Laurence these items "provide a unique record of the dramatist's publishing methods and negotiations from the early 1800's . . . until his death at the age of ninety-four." The archive includes hundreds of letters from Constable to and about Shaw.

During the 1960s Donald Hyde began collecting bindings. The largest group, comprising twelve items, is from eighteenth-century England; other English bindings include one from the sixteenth century and eight from the seventeenth. A visit to Italy led him to purchase examples from that country, including two from sixteenth-century Venice that enclose beautiful Renaissance manuscripts. The finest binding in the collection, for Lodovico Ricchieri's *Lectionum antiquarum* (Basel: Froben, 1517), was executed for John Grolier by Claude de Picques in the 1540s and later embellished with fanfare tooling. The volume has eight marginal notes in Grolier's hand. Hyde purchased the book from Warren Richardson Howell of San Francisco in 1960.

In 1965 Mary Hyde wrote "Not in Chapman" for *Johnson, Boswell and Their Circle,* a volume honoring their friend, the Boswell and Johnson scholar Lawrence Fitzroy Powell, on his eighty-fourth birthday. Her article updates the comprehensive edition of Johnson letters edited by R. W. Chapman in 1952. Hyde's contribution is a list of eighty-four Johnson letters identified since the publication of Chapman's edition; the article also provides the texts of thirty of these letters. The Hydes' collecting efforts made possible a more complete and accurate five-volume edition of Johnson's letters, edited by Bruce Redford for the Princeton University Press (1992–1994); Redford's acknowledgment thanks Mary Hyde for her assistance.

Both Hydes were active members of bibliophile and scholarly associations. Donald was chosen president of the Grolier Club in 1961; he reinvigorated the

Sir Joshua Reynolds's 1756 portrait of Dr. Johnson, engraved for the frontispiece of
Boswell's Life *(Catalogue of the Johnsonian Collection of*
R. B. Adam, 1921)

organization, its library, and its clubhouse and in 1962 organized a memorable Italian tour that his fellow members praised highly. The Hydes also were members of the Bibliographical Society of America (Donald served as president of the group in 1959); the Shakespeare Association of America; the Keats-Shelley Association of America; and the Johnson Society of Lichfield, England. Mary was president of the Shakespeare Association of America in 1956 and of the Johnson Society of Lichfield, England, in 1957. The Hydes served on the Harvard Libraries visiting committee and the council of the Friends of Princeton Libraries and as chairman of the council of fellows of the Pierpont Morgan Library, council member of Friends of Columbia University Libraries, trustee of the Yale Libraries Association, and member of the Council of Friends of the Folger Shakespeare Library. Their activities in connection with these libraries and others included lending materials for exhibits, giving talks, providing funding for acquisitions and activities, and contributing to publications. One notable example of their generosity occurred when they paid for the restoration of the historical ceiling of the Duke Humphrey Library of the Bodleian Library at Oxford University.

The Hydes had warm relationships with many librarians. One example is their long association with Randolph Greenfield Adams. Donald Hyde wrote the entry on Adams for *Grolier 75* (1959), which celebrated the seventy-fifth anniversary of the Grolier Club and included biographical sketches of eminent bookmen. When they purchased the Robert Borthwick Adam collection from the University of Rochester, the curator, Metzdorf, gave them his notes about the collection and suggested how to catalogue the books. William Jackson of the Houghton Library at Harvard University showed them the value of bibliographies and the importance of a book's condition; the Pierpont Morgan Library staff taught them how to clean their books; and the Princeton University Library staff allowed Mary Hyde to use their photocopying and microfilming facilities to reproduce material from the Hydes' collection for other scholars.

During the last year of his life Donald Hyde became a member of the oldest book collector's society, the Roxburghe Club of London; he was only the fourth American member. He died on 5 February 1966. His obituary in *The New York Times* identified him as "one of America's leading book and manuscript collectors" and noted that the Hydes owned more than half of the thirteen hundred Johnson letters extant and the only known manuscript page of Johnson's *Dictionary* and that the Hydes' collection of Wilde materials was the largest in private hands. Donald Hyde's Fielding collection was given to the Houghton Library, Harvard University.

In the summer of 1965 Donald Hyde had planned the two-volume *Four Oaks Farm/Four Oaks Library*. He selected subjects and authors for the essays. After his death, all the authors accepted, and the book, edited by Austin, was privately printed in 1967 as a tribute to Donald Hyde. In 1970 a memorial volume of eighteenth-century scholarly studies was published by the Grolier Club in honor of Donald Hyde. Among the articles in the Festschrift are G. J. Kolb's "Establishing the Text of Dr. Johnson's Plan of a Dictionary of the English Language," which draws on the manuscript and printed sources at Four Oaks Library, and Powell's "Tobias Smollett and William Huggins," in which the Smollett letters that the Hydes had purchased from Col. R. G. Parker in January 1952 are

published for the first time. In 1973 Princeton University presented Mary Hyde with the sixth Donald F. Hyde Award for Distinction in Book Collecting and Service to the Community of Scholars.

Mary Hyde's involvement in the Anglo-American world of scholarship has continued. Inspired by four letters from Boswell to the Thrales that were in the Robert Borthwick Adam collection, she wrote *The Impossible Friendship: Boswell and Mrs. Thrale* (1972). She has published two additional scholarly books, *The Thrales of Streatham Park* (1977) and *Bernard Shaw and Alfred Douglas, A Correspondence* (1982), both based on the rich resources of the Four Oaks Library. She had acquired the Shaw-Douglas correspondence in 1969; it represents one of the ways she has continued to develop the Four Oaks Library. She is a trustee of Dr. Johnson's House (London), a vice-president of the Johnson Society of London, president of the Boswell Society, council member and vice-president of the Grolier Club, and vice-president of the Association of International Bibliophiles. Redford accurately and succinctly summarizes her achievement: "As joint creator of the Hyde collection, [she] has formed an archive of incomparable rarity and coherence; as discerning scholar and benefactor, she has played a crucial role in the development of Johnsonian studies."

On 26 September 1984 Hyde married David McAdam Eccles, first Viscount Eccles. They have established the Eccles Centre for American Studies at the British Library.

References:

Gabriel Austin, "Donald F. Hyde: A Memoir," in *Eighteenth-Century Studies in Honor of Donald F. Hyde,* edited by W. H. Bond (New York: Grolier Club, 1970), pp. ix–xiii;

Austin, ed., *Four Oaks Farm/Four Oaks Library,* 2 volumes (Somerville, N.J.: Privately printed, 1967);

David Buchanan, *The Treasure of Auchinleck: The Story of the Boswell Papers* (New York: McGraw-Hill, 1974);

Robert F. Metzdorf and J. M. Edelstein, "Donald Frizell Hyde, 1909–1966," *Papers of the Bibliographical Society of America,* 60 (1966): 101;

Frederick A. Pottle, *Pride and Negligence: The History of the Boswell Papers* (New York: McGraw-Hill, 1982);

Lawrence S. Thompson, "American Bibliophiles XII: Donald F. Hyde," *American Book Collector,* 16 (March 1966): 10–11.

Irvin Kerlan
(18 September 1912 – 28 December 1963)

Karen Nelson Hoyle
University of Minnesota

BOOKS: *Newbery and Caldecott Awards: A Bibliography of First Editions* (Minneapolis: University of Minnesota Press, 1949);
A Helen Sewell Bibliographic Checklist (New York: American Artists, 1957);
A Roger Duvoisin Bibliography (Charlottesville: Bibliographical Society of the University of Virginia, 1958);
Caldecott Medalists 1938–1958, by Kerlan, Richard Hurley, and Colette M. Heck (Washington, D.C.: Catholic University of America Press).

OTHER: "Collecting Contemporary Books for Children," in *Bibliophile in the Nursery,* edited by William Targ (Cleveland: World, 1957), pp. 457–467.

SELECTED PERIODICAL PUBLICATIONS–
UNCOLLECTED: "Collecting Leads On," *Antiquarian Bookman,* 9 (5 January 1952): 24–25;
"On Collecting Contemporary Books for Children," *District of Columbia Libraries,* 25 (October 1954): 1–6;
"Panorama of Children's Books, 1950–1957," *Book Production,* 67 (May 1958): 53–54, 63;
"Sunday to Sunday: One Week of Children's Book Collecting," *American Book Collector,* 10 (December 1959): 23–26;
"Angelo to Zimnik," *Virginia Librarian,* 6 (April 1960): 39–42;
"The Bernard Meeks Collection: Three Hundred Years of Children's Books, 1657–1957," *American Book Collector,* 10 (April 1960): 6–11;
"Collecting Children's Books: A Rewarding Pastime," *Pediatrics,* 26 (October 1960): 684–688;
"Winnie Ille Pu and Dr. Alexander Leonard," *American Book Collector,* 12 (September 1961): 48–52;
"Collecting Children's Books," *Private Library,* 5 (January 1964): 1–4.

From the 1940s until his death at the age of fifty-one in 1963, Irvin Kerlan collected first editions of

Irvin Kerlan (courtesy of the Kerlan Collection, Children's Literature Research Collections, University of Minnesota)

American and British children's books, which he began to donate to the University of Minnesota in 1949. He also compiled an important bibliography of Newbery and Caldecott Award books and wrote essays explaining and sharing his enthusiasm. Acquainted with the work of Percy Muir, who collected classic British children's books, and A. S. W. Rosenbach, who collected early American children's books, Kerlan preferred contemporary works.

Page from the manuscript and the dust jacket for the book that won the Newbery Medal in 1936 (courtesy of the Kerlan Collection, the Children's Literature Research Collections, University of Minnesota)

In "Collecting Contemporary Books for Children" (1957) Kerlan acknowledged, "One sound approach to the collecting of children's books . . . is based on the principle that only works by authors and artists of the nineteenth and earlier centuries that have been acclaimed and stood the test of time are meaningful." Collecting such works, he said, marks no "departure from already established paths of collecting." Contemporary children's literature, however, presented challenges "since selections are predicated on what gives pleasure at the moment and is most likely to survive in the future. The collector must have courage and a strong conviction that what he chooses will maintain a place of distinction."

Born in Saint Cloud, Minnesota, to Isaac and Jennie Zack Kerlan, Irvin Kerlan completed eighth grade at McKinley School and entered Saint Cloud High School. Before graduating from high school he enrolled at the University of Minnesota to pursue a career in medicine, acquiring bachelor of science (1931), bachelor of medicine (1933), and doctor of medicine (1934) degrees and a certificate in public health (1939). He then moved to Washington, D.C., to work for the Food and Drug Administration, where he was medical officer (1939–1952), acting

medical director (1952–1954), and director of the Division of Research and Reference (1954–1962). On 28 December 1963 he was hit by a taxi and killed as he stepped off a curb in Washington.

Throughout his professional career Kerlan collected books. His first interest was rare books, but his salary as a civil servant precluded his building a large library. Around 1946 a Washington friend, Marcia Owen, gave him a copy of Margaret Friskey's new book, *Johnny Cottontail* (Philadelphia: McKay, 1946). As Granville Smith wrote in "Irvin Kerlan, M.D.: Founder of the Kerlan Collection," the gift changed Kerlan's life: "Something about it captured interest to an overwhelming degree," and Kerlan "was off at a gallop on a hobby that was to bring him enduring fame."

Kerlan first collected winners of the Newbery Award, established in 1922 to honor the best-written children's book of the year, and of the Caldecott Award, created in 1938 to recognize outstanding illustration of children's books. He then expanded his search to include winners of the Carnegie Award, created in Great Britain in 1937 as the British version of the Newbery, and of the Kate Greenaway Award, established in 1955 as the British equivalent of the Caldecott. He later pursued

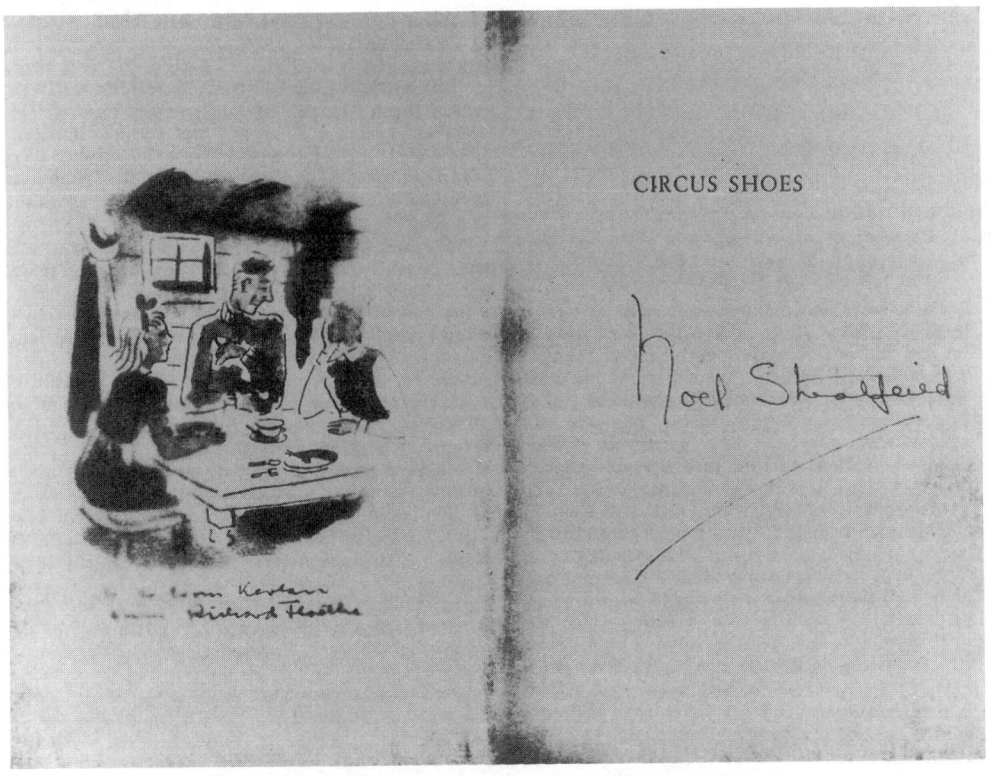

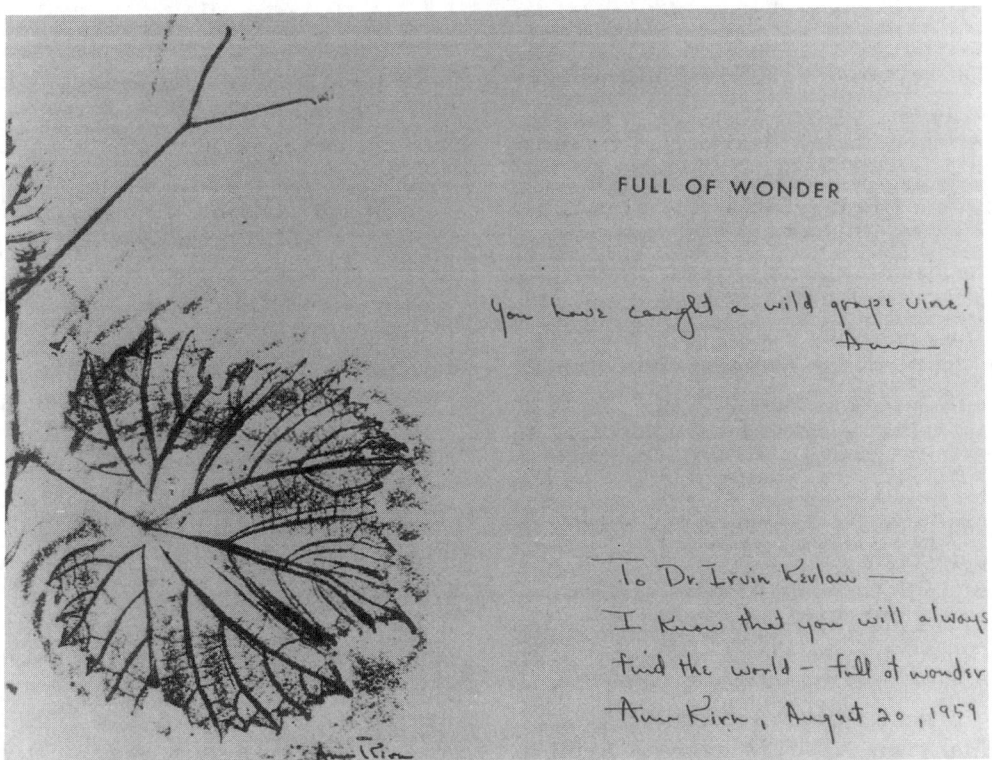

Inscriptions and original artworks in Kerlan's copies of Circus Shoes *(1939), by Noel Streatfeild with illustrations by Richard Floethe, and* Full of Wonder *(1959), written and illustrated by Ann Kirn (from Irvin Kerlan, "Sunday to Sunday,"* American Book Collector, *10 [December 1959])*

winners of the Hans Christian Andersen Award, created in 1956, and the Laura Ingalls Wilder Award, created in 1954. He sought not only first editions but also translations into other languages. As Kerlan noted, there were few guideposts for collectors of contemporary children's literature, but he was able to rely on Jacob Blanck's *Peter Parley to Penrod: A Bibliographical Description of the Best-Loved American Juvenile Books* (New York: Bowker, 1938; revised, 1956). Another valuable source of information was an American Institute of Graphic Arts exhibit of important children's books published between 1920 and 1952, which made Kerlan aware of gaps in his collection that he set about filling.

Broadening and deepening the scope of his collection, Kerlan added photographs of authors and illustrations, Caldecott and Newbery Award medals, and memorabilia relating to children's books as well as their authors and illustrators. Because he particularly wanted his collection to trace the evolution of a book from conception to publication, he also pursued manuscripts, original artwork, and book dummies.

Kerlan gathered much of his collection through conventional means—reading book catalogues and frequenting bookstores. One of his favorite haunts was Power's bookstore in Minneapolis, where he was served by Harold Kittleson, later of Random House, who played a major role in the growth of Kerlan's library. Many of Kerlan's treasures, however, reflect his friendships with authors and illustrators. His guest book of visitors to his brownstone on 1613 Riggs Street N.W. in Washington, D.C., reads like a "Who's Who in Contemporary Children's Literature." Among those who signed the book are Caldecott Award winners Marcia Brown and Leonard Weisgard and Newbery Award winners Jean Lee Latham and Virginia Sorensen as well as Clement Hurd, illustrator of Margaret Wise Brown's *Goodnight Moon* (New York: Harper, 1947).

Frequently these friends wrote inscriptions in Kerlan's copies of their books as well as giving him original manuscripts and illustrations. His copy of James Thurber's *Many Moons* (New York: Harcourt, Brace, 1943) includes a note from the author—"Jolly Times to Irvin Kerlan"—as well as illustrator Louis Slobodkin's drawings of twelve moon faces with the caption "Many many merry moons." Another friend was Jean Charlot, who visited with his family in 1957 and left gifts. Anita Brenner's *A Hero by Mistake* (New York: W. R. Scott, 1953), with illustrations by Charlot, had been selected by *The New York Times* as one of the best illustrated children's books of 1953, and Miriam Schlein's *When Will the World Be*

Mine? (New York: Scott, 1953), also illustrated by Charlot, had been named a Caldecott Honor Book. Charlot gave studies for illustrations in these books to Kerlan, along with his art for the Newbery Award–winning *Secret of the Andes* (New York: Viking, 1952) by Ann Nolan Clark and Newbery Honor Book *The Corn Grows Ripe* (New York: Viking, 1956) by Dorothy Rhoads.

When writers and artists could not visit, Kerlan mailed their books to them for inscription. He often sent them gifts on special occasions—a box of candy or a handkerchief to Katherine Milhous or Virginia Sorensen for Valentine's Day, for example—and they sometimes reciprocated with original manuscripts and artwork. In "Collecting Contemporary Books for Children" Kerlan wrote of receiving the manuscript and an inscribed copy of *Haunt Fox* (New York: Holiday House, 1954) from its author, James Kjelgaard, who dedicated the book to Kerlan. Later, Glen Rounds, who illustrated the book, and Lee Ames, who painted the book jacket, sent their original work too.

Among Kerlan's prized presentation copies was a first printing of *The Egg Tree* (New York: Scribners, 1950), which won the Caldecott Award for artist Katherine Milhous. Kerlan's copy includes a drawing and inscription by Milhous: "To Irvin Kerlan, his book and egg." Milhous gave him not only the art for the book but also eggs hand-painted in Pennsylvania Dutch designs on a white tree branch.

Kerlan's collection is further enriched by his preservation of every piece of correspondence related to children's books. He filed letters from editors and personal friends, including such important figures as illustrator Kurt Weise, poet Myra Cohn Livingston, and fiction writer Virginia Sorensen.

Kerlan was also an important bibliographer of children's books. For example, he identified the first edition of Carolyn Sherwin Bailey's *Miss Hickory* (New York: Viking, 1946), and he understood the importance of minor details in distinguishing printings and editions. Such sleuthing produced not only a fine collection but also important publications. Kerlan knew firsthand of the need for bibliographies to help those who shared his interests. His most important contribution in this area was his *Newbery and Caldecott Awards: A Bibliography of First Editions* (1949). This book was the first attempt to provide full bibliographic descriptions of the winners, and it is a landmark for collectors and bibliographers of children's literature. As L. S. Bechtel wrote in the *New York Herald Tribune Book Review* (5 February 1950), "This descriptive bibliography will be of importance to collectors, and may stimulate many, young and old, to a new interest in collecting in this field." Kerlan's later attempts to find a publisher for an updated edition of the book were unsuccessful. He also published bibliographies of author and illustrator Helen Sewell—who illustrated seventy-two children's books, most notably Laura Ingalls Wilder's Little House series (1932–1943)—and of his friend Roger Duvoisin, who illustrated more than 130 children's books. Kerlan also wrote articles describing his collection and sharing his enjoyment of children's books.

Kerlan shared his collection through exhibits. He selected, documented, packed, and shipped books and other materials for more than one hundred exhibitions at locations ranging from elementary schools to university libraries. Exhibit sites included art museums in Memphis, Minneapolis, and Washington, D.C.; public libraries in Atlanta, Baltimore, Chicago, Cleveland, and San Francisco; and the libraries of Northwestern and Howard Universities. During the month before he died Kerlan prepared and shipped books for eleven exhibits across the United States. Three international exhibits sponsored by the Department of State in 1953–1955 traveled to the Middle East, Far East, and Western Europe.

Because of his enthusiasm and expertise Kerlan was popular among children's book publishers and children's librarians, and he gave freely of his time. In 1951 he served on the committee to found the *Washington Post* Community Children's Book Fair, acting as chair of the event for its first seven years and later as adviser. In 1951 he also became honorary consultant on acquisition of children's books to the Library of Congress, serving until 1960. In 1955–1956 he was president of the Washington chapter of the American Institute of Graphic Arts and a member of the executive committee of the Children's Book Guild of Washington. In 1957 he was a juror for the Western Writers of America Juvenile Award, and the following year he served as vice chairman of the District of Columbia Citizens Committee for National Library Week. From 1958 to 1961 he acted as honorary consultant on children's literature for the Smithsonian Institution Traveling Exhibition Service. He also lectured at the library schools of George Washington University, the Catholic University of America, and the University of Maryland. In recognition of his work he received citations from the University of Minnesota (Regents' Citation of Honor, 1952; Outstanding Achievement Award, 1961); Catholic University of America; the Children's Book Guild of Washington, D.C.; and the District of Columbia Education Association. He participated in the White

Bookplate for the Kerlan Collection

House Conference on Children and Youth in 1960. When Kerlan died, memorial donations paid for a plaque with his name on a designated seat at the John F. Kennedy Center for the Performing Arts.

In 1949 Kerlan donated his collection to the University of Minnesota, remaining an active collector and continuing to contribute new items to the university. He was actively involved in administering his gift, and to encourage others to add to the holdings he urged the university to confer honorary degrees on authors and artists who gave their work to the institution. He also consistently expressed concern for the preservation of the art and manuscripts in the collection, and in an 8 July 1963 letter to the head of special collections he urged, "These materials should be carefully held in special slipcases with a touch of elegance." He lamented what he regarded as university officials' lack of enthusiasm for building the Kerlan Collection, and he explored the possibility of joining the library staff so that he could be with and help care for the collection.

By the time of his death Kerlan's donations and bequests totaled nine thousand volumes, and the collection has continued to grow. By 1995 the Kerlan Collection included some seventy-two thousand volumes, with manuscripts for twenty Newbery Award winners, from Elizabeth Coatsworth's *The Cat Who Went to Heaven* (New York: Macmillan, 1930) to Lois Lowry's *The Giver* (Boston: Houghton Mifflin, 1993); Marie Hall Ets's Caldecott Award medal for *Nine Days to Christmas* (New York: Viking, 1959); and Marguerite Henry's Newbery Award medal for *King of the Wind* (Chicago: Rand McNally, 1948). A Friends of the Kerlan Collection group began to meet informally in 1974, the twenty-fifth anniversary of the initial donation, and it was formalized with a constitution in 1987. This group encourages donations by giving the Kerlan Award "in recognition of singular attainments in the creation of children's literature and in appreciation for generous donation of unique resources to the Kerlan Collection for the study of children's literature." Recipients have included Ets, Duvoisin, Tomie de Paola, and Madeleine L'Engle.

The Kerlan Collection at the University of Minnesota has become a major center for research in a field that Kerlan pioneered, and it remains a living, growing testimony to Kerlan's belief that "collecting is demanding, yet thoroughly rewarding when the search yields the desired book."

References:

Karen Hoyle, "The Kerlan Collection," *Children's Literature Newsletter* (Spring–Summer 1978): 13;

Karen Nelson Hoyle and others, *The Kerlan Collection Manuscripts and Illustrations for Children's Books: A Checklist* (Minneapolis: Kerlan Collection, University of Minnesota Libraries, 1985);

Carolyn Clugston Michaels, *Children's Book Collecting* (Hamden, Conn.: Library Professional Publications, 1993);

Juanita Pacifico Opstein, "Man Behind the Irvin Kerlan Collection," *Gopher Grad,* 58 (February 1959): 4–7ff;

Glanville Smith, "Irvin Kerlan, M.D.: Founder of the Kerlan Collection," in *The Kerlan Collection* (Minneapolis: Kerlan Collection, University of Minnesota, 1974);

Peggy Sullivan, "A Tale of Washington's Irvin," *Horn Book,* 27 (June 1961): 288–289.

Papers:

The Kerlan Collection, University of Minnesota Libraries, holds books, articles, and interviews by and about Kerlan as well as memorabilia related to his life as a physician and collector of children's books. Also included in the collection is the correspondence of Kerlan and Linda Fishman, a Baltimore young-adult librarian and collector of children's books whom Kerlan served as mentor.

Jerome Kern

(27 January 1885 – 11 November 1945)

Theodore Spahn
Rosary College

Jerome David Kern, one of the leading American popular-song writers of the twentieth century, wrote more than 1,000 songs for 104 shows and movies. Most of these songs have been forgotten, but millions of people have heard and enjoyed such melodies as "Ol' Man River" (from *Show Boat*), "The Last Time I Saw Paris," "Smoke Gets in Your Eyes," and "They Didn't Believe Me." He was also a serious and knowledgeable collector of books and manuscripts, and the auctioning off of his collection was the most spectacular sale of books in this country before World War II.

Kern was born on 27 January 1885 in New York City. His father, Henry Kern, had been born in Germany in 1842. His mother, Fannie Kakeles Kern, had been born in New York in 1852. Both parents were from well-to-do Jewish families, but after their marriage in a synagogue they had nothing more to do with their religion. Altogether, the Kerns had seven sons, four of whom died in infancy or early childhood. Jerome was the sixth child.

Fannie Kern had some musical talent and was a competent piano player. She gave Jerome piano lessons, which both of them took seriously. He practiced faithfully, and she rapped his knuckles when he played a wrong note. Kern started writing songs while he was still young, and his music was first performed in a high school musical in 1902 when he was seventeen. His first published music, "At the Casino," appeared in 1902. (Of the many songs he had previously submitted to publishers, all had been rejected.) His father hoped to see him enter the family business, but he had no liking or talent for such a career. After he dropped out of high school, his parents permitted him to go to Europe to study music. He went to Germany—possibly Heidelberg, Germany—for several months, but the exact place and nature of his studies are unknown.

Returning to America, Kern found employment as a rehearsal pianist and as a song plugger for a music publisher. This latter job entailed play-

Jerome Kern

ing the firm's new songs for singers, dancers, and producers in the hope that they would be adopted for use in shows. He also continue to write his own songs, some of which were "interpolated" into musicals. The musicals of the day, many of which were imported from Britain, consisted for the most part of a succession of songs strung together by the flimsiest of plots. If a show had originally been staged in Britain or on the Continent, the producer would try to make it more appealing to a New York audience by replacing dull or "foreign" songs with newly commissioned ones. This is where the interpolating composers came in and how Kern first attracted attention, as some of his songs became hits. After the young composer's mother and father died, in 1907 and 1908, respectively, he spent most of his inheritance pursuing a showgirl who eventually jilted him.

During the first decade of the twentieth century Kern made several tips to London, where he collaborated with various lyricists in writing musicals. While in Britain he fell in love with Eva Leale, the teenage daughter of a hotel keeper. They were married in a Church of England ceremony in October 1910. The wedding seems to have been the last religious ceremony, either Jewish or Christian, in Kern's life. The young couple returned to the United States to live. Their friends regarded the marriage as a happy one, although Kern teased his wife constantly and was unfaithful to her. Elizabeth Jane (Betty), their only child, born in 1918, was adored by both parents.

In New York, Kern wrote scores of songs for Broadway shows. He became increasingly well known, and in 1914 he participated in the founding of the American Society of Composers, Authors, and Publishers (ASCAP). The motivation for founding this association was that composers were not receiving any royalties when their songs were played in public places such as restaurants.

In May 1915 the Kerns planned to sail for Liverpool and booked passage on the *Lusitania*. Through a fortunate mischance, Kern overslept on the day of sailing. He and Eva missed the boat, which was torpedoed some days later with the loss of more than a thousand lives, among them Elbert Hubbard, the founder of the Roycroft Press.

As a young man in London, Kern had started buying books. His means were still modest, and he could not afford the treasures he was later to acquire. The famous collection he was to build in later years was primarily of eighteenth- and nineteenth-century British authors. This focus may have been in part the result of his sojourns in London and visits to bookstores in Charing Cross Road. In New York City in the early days of his collecting, Kern haunted the secondhand bookshops on Fourth Avenue and Forty-second Street.

Kern said that his serious book collecting got its start at the suggestion of Harry B. Smith, a lyricist and librettist with whom he had collaborated and who took him to his first auction. As he came to enjoy a substantial income from composing, Kern was able to buy expensive and choice books, and he displayed good taste in doing so. Sometimes he bought at auctions, but usually he purchased from the stocks of expert dealers on whose advice and assistance he relied. Two such dealers were Charles Sessler and A. S. W. Rosenbach, both of Philadelphia. Sometimes Kern balked at the high prices of items offered to him; at other times he paid without demur, even when he knew that the price had been raised as soon as he was seen walking into the bookshop. Kern reflected: "In some cases . . . when I was carried away by personal enthusiasm, I paid more for volumes than they realized at the sale. This was the case with some of the Swinburne, Rossetti, Thackeray, and even Shakespeare volumes. Even dealers said that I had paid excessively high prices for some of my books, and I can recall times when ripples of laughter went around auction rooms at prices I paid that seemed too high."

He was sufficiently wealthy that even his passion for gambling, at which he sometimes lost thousands of dollars in an evening, did not prevent him from buying expensive books, many of which were association copies. He bought books—about half a million dollars' worth—because he liked them, not because he considered them an investment; he observed, "At the time that I bought my books, I had no idea of selling them," and he read the books he collected and took an interest in their paper, their bindings, and the methods used to print them. His books were never locked up: "They were like friends whom I wanted always about me," he explained in 1929. His collection was not utilitarian. Except for the autographs of classical composers, which he bought as a young man, the books and manuscripts in his collection had nothing to do with his vocation as a composer.

In late 1927 Kern disposed of several hundred books, many of them duplicates, at an auction. In 1928—partly because of his wife's reiterated complaints about the cost of housing and safeguarding the books, but largely because he had come to feel that the pursuit of books had become an obsession—he decided to dispose of his entire collection except for volumes he had received as gifts. Having made the decision, he quickly acted upon it. A contract was signed with Mitchell Kennerley, president of Anderson Galleries. Kern stipulated that dealers who had once given him credit should receive the same generous terms. An auction catalogue, *The Library of Jerome Kern, New York City . . . To Be Sold by His Order at Unreserved Public Sale,* was quickly printed, and its two volumes listed 1,488 items. The sale was well advertised by Kennerley and took place in ten sessions between 7 and 24 January 1929. Several dealers, of whom Rosenbach was the best known, were in the audience, sometimes buying for stock and sometimes bidding on behalf of wealthy collectors. Private collectors on whose behalf bids were entered included Richard Gimbel of the department-store family; Carl Pforzheimer, investment banker and collector of English literature; and Owen D. Young, chairman of General Electric, creator of the Radio Corporation of America, and a businessman who also entered some bids on his own behalf.

It was soon apparent that the proceeds of the sale would exceed the preliminary estimate of $1 million. Stock prices were rising, rich collectors were growing steadily richer, and the Depression was still in the future. A sort of euphoria filled the auction house, and when the sale was all over, the sum realized was $1,729,462.50. It was quite an event, and newspaper articles and editorials expressed wonder at the high prices paid.

First editions of Jane Austen's *Pride and Prejudice* (1813) and *Sense and Sensibility* (1811) sold for $4,800 and $3,600, respectively. A copy of Richard Doddridge Blackmore's *Lorna Doone* (1869), for which Kern had paid $45, brought $2,400. James Boswell's *The Life of Samuel Johnson* (1791), uncut, in a modern binding, with letters from Boswell and Johnson laid in, sold for $5,250.

A presentation copy of the first edition of Elizabeth Barrett Browning's first book, *The Battle of Marathon* (1820), printed in an edition of fifty copies by her father in her youth, went to Rosenbach for $17,500. Kern had bought it five years earlier for only $1,650. One of her manuscript notebooks sold for $2,200.

Of the thirty Robert Browning items, a first edition of *Pauline* (1833), his first book, in its original boards, went for $16,000. His own copy of the first edition of *Paracelsus* (1835), with his autograph corrections for a second edition, went for $2,900. Rosenbach bought a presentation copy of the Edinburgh edition of Browning's *Poems* (1844) for $23,500 but was never able to sell it.

The Kilmarnock edition of Robert Burns's *Poems, Chiefly in the Scottish Dialect* (1786) sold for $4,500. Various copies of this work had been sold on earlier occasions for $106 (in 1864), $155 (1876), $310 (1883), $2,700 (1898), $1,750 (1918), and $1,900 (1925). An inscribed second edition went for $23,500 in January 1929. During the Depression that followed this Kern sale prices fell to a range between $2,300 and $3,400.

The work of George Gordon, Lord Byron, was represented by fifty-seven items which brought in more than $96,000. Forty-nine pages of the manuscript for *Don Juan* (1821) went to Gabriel Wells for $20,000. The complete manuscript (142 pages) of *Marino Fallero* (1820), including letters, was purchased by Rosenbach for $20,000 on behalf of Carl Pforzheimer. Rosenbach also bought for $10,000, for stock, the "suppressed" first edition (1865) of Lewis Carroll's *Alice in Wonderland*. Various manuscripts and typescripts of Joseph Conrad included *Youth* (1902), which sold for $2,800, and *Under Western Eyes* (1911), which brought $7,250. A copy of Daniel Defoe's *Robinson Crusoe* (1719), bought by Kern in 1924 for $5,350, went for $11,500.

The most heavily represented author was Charles Dickens, with 113 items, including every first edition, three pages of the manuscript of *Oliver Twist* (1837), which sold for $8,500, and even the author's marriage license. Many of these items had been purchased from Rosenbach. A twenty-eight-page memorandum book in which Dickens had jotted down suggestions for names, plots, and dialogue from 1855 until his death sold for $15,000; Kern had paid $1,800. "The Perils of Certain English Prisoners," a manuscript with some leaves written by Dickens and others by Wilkie Collins, brought $15,000. *The Posthumous Papers of the Pickwick Club* (1836–1837), in parts, sold for a record $28,000; Kern had paid $3,500 (a copy of this edition sold at auction in 1991 for $3,400). One of a few genuine copies in existence of the first edition of *The Strange Gentleman* (1837), accompanied by a letter, sold for $10,500, and a presentation copy of *A Tale of Two Cities* (1859) sold for $10,250.

Kern had purchased for about $3,000 an uncut copy of Henry Fielding's *Tom Jones* (1749), the only copy known to exist in its original boards. At the sale it went to Rosenbach for $29,000. He sold it to Owen Young for that amount plus 10 percent. In 1931, two years after the sale, Young's librarian collated the six volumes of the work and found that eight leaves were missing. The work was returned temporarily to Rosenbach, but Young eventually took it back. In 1937 it was sold to Lord Rothschild. In 1940 John Hayward, a bibliographer working in Rothschild's library, found that five of the volumes had been repaired with leaves inserted from a later edition. This discovery led to much legal maneuvering, after which Lord Rothschild was reimbursed and the volumes returned to Rosenbach. (In December 1992 a copy with minor defects sold at Sotheby's for £3,800. In 1994 a dealer offered a similar copy for $3,750.)

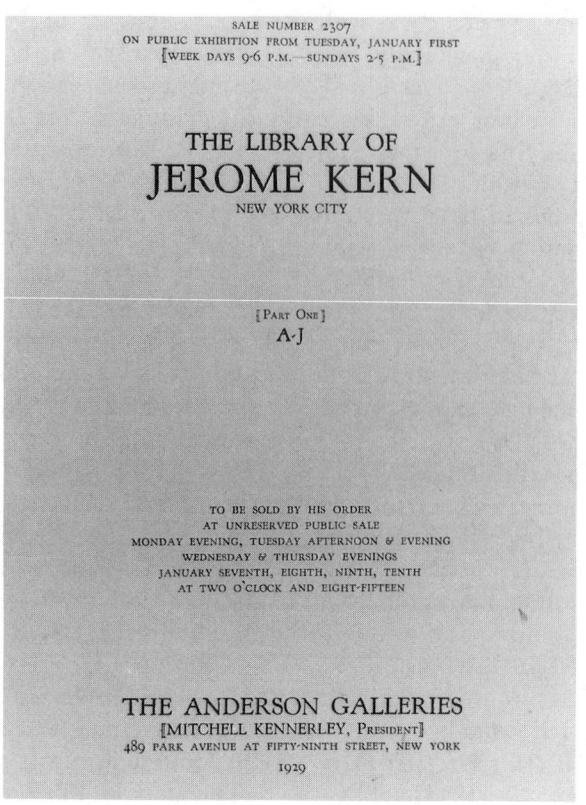

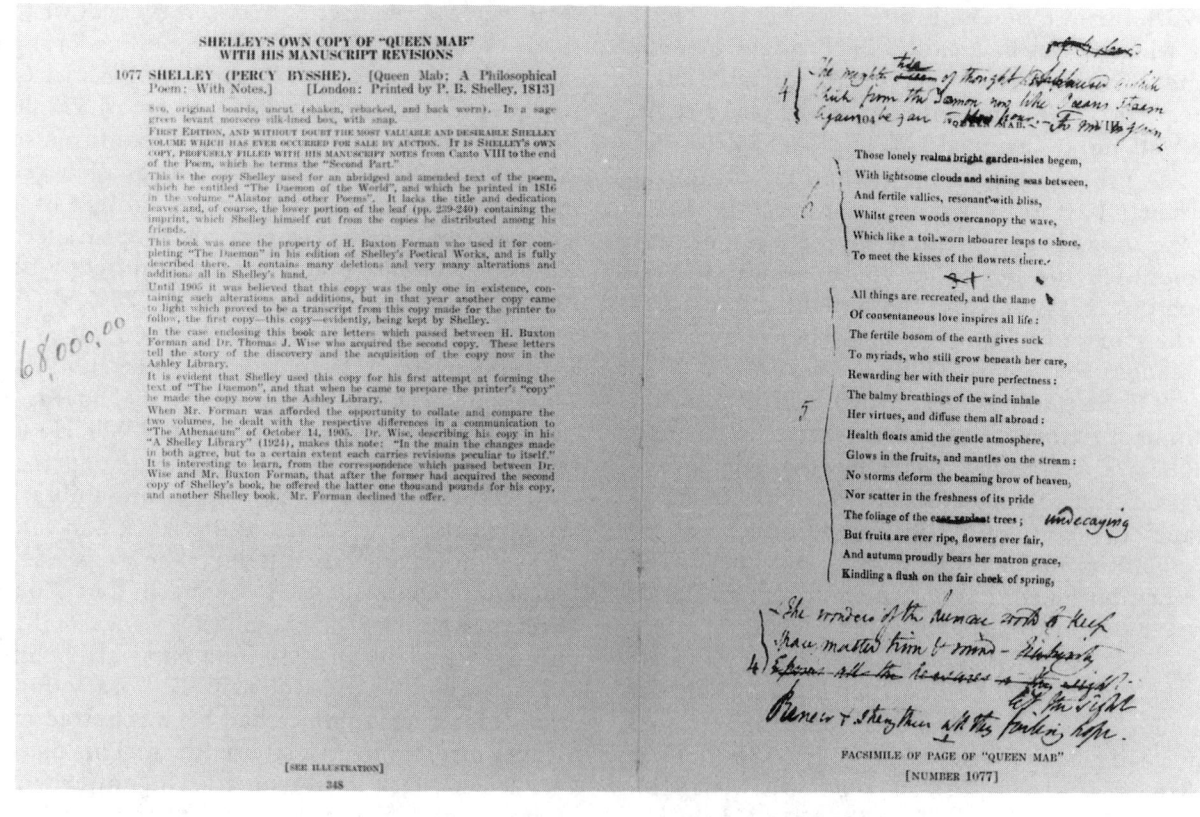

Title page for part one and pages from part two of the catalogue for the most glamorous literary sale held in the United States, marking the high point of the American book-collecting mania cut short by the stock market crash of October 1929. Gabriel Wells bought Shelley's copy of Queen Mab *for $68,000, the second highest price to that time for a book at an American auction.*

There were thirty-nine Oliver Goldsmith items. Young, bidding for himself, paid $27,000 for the thirty-four-page manuscript of Goldsmith's translation of Marcus Hieronymus Vida's *Scacchia, or Chess*—one example of a work that had failed to appreciate in value, for Kern had paid $33,000 for it only a year earlier. After Young bought it, the authorship of the work was disputed, and it was returned to the seller. Several years later Kern was still trying to have its authenticity established.

There were fifty-seven Thomas Hardy items in the sale. An inscribed copy of *Jude the Obscure* went for $4,100. Kern had purchased it in 1914 for only $47.50. An incomplete manuscript (160 pages) of *A Pair of Blue Eyes* (1873), for which Kern is said to have paid $10,000, sold for $34,000. This was a record for a manuscript of a contemporary author. *The New York Times* pointed out that "Within twenty-four hours of the first anniversary of the death of Thomas Hardy a record price was established here of a manuscript of one of his works." A presentation copy of *The Well-Beloved* (1897), with a few words written by Hardy on the flyleaf, sold for $1,200. As an illustration of the role played by a signature, another copy of the same edition with no inscription brought only $15. The manuscript of "Night in a Suburb" (five stanzas of seven lines each) sold for $2,600.

A single page of the manuscript of Samuel Johnson's *Dictionary* (1755) went for $11,000; Kern had paid $1,750. Another Johnson item was a copy of *The Lives of the English Poets* (1781) that had belonged to Hester Lynch Thrale, a close friend of Johnson. Johnson's own copy of *Rasselas, Prince of Abyssinia* (1759) with seven corrections in his own hand, presented by him to Samuel Richardson and inscribed "From the Author," brought $5,800. A letter about Thomas Gray's *Elegy Written in a Country Church-Yard* (1751) sold for $5,500.

John Keats's *Poetical Works* (1854), with the twenty-two-line manuscript of "I Stood Tiptoe upon a Little Hill," sold for $7,000, although it had cost Kern only $400. *Schoolboy Lyrics* (1881) was Rudyard Kipling's first book. A copy of the first edition, presented by his mother to a friend, sold for $4,000. A presentation copy of the first edition of Kipling's *Life's Handicap* (1891), with two verses of *Barrack-Room Ballads* (1892) written by Kipling on the verso of the title page, sold for $6,250; Kern had bought it for $50 in 1925. The first edition, first issue of *Under the Deodars* (1888) with a long inscription went for $5,000; Kern had paid $750.

There were thirty Charles Lamb items. Charles and Mary Lamb's *Poetry for Children,* one of the few copies then known, went to Rosenbach for $8,750, but he could never find a buyer for it. The forty-eight-page manuscript of Lamb's contributions to William Hone's *Table-Book* (1827–1828) sold for $48,000; it had sold for $2,250 in 1919, and Kern had paid $3,000 for it. The first edition of *Tales from Shakespear* (1807), uncut, with a letter from Lamb, sold for $5,700. The first edition, first issue of *The King and Queen of Hearts* (1805), catalogued as the only known copy in its original wrapper, sold for $4,500, considerably less than Kern had paid for it ($7,500). A presentation copy of the first edition of *Album Verses* (1830) went for $5,900.

A four-page letter by Edgar Allan Poe, quoting Elizabeth Barrett Browning's praise for *The Raven* (1845), sold for $19,500; Kern had paid only $1,250 for it. There were thirty items by Alexander Pope; forty pages of the manuscript of *An Essay on Man* (1733–1734) in a quarto notebook, for which Kern had paid $6,000, sold for $29,000. The manuscript of Sir Walter Scott's *Tales of a Grandfather,* first series (1827), on 156 folio pages, sold for $6,000.

There were only eight William Shakespeare items. A copy of the Second Folio, for which Kern had paid $7,500, fetched only $5,750. A copy of the Third Folio, first issue, fetched $8,000, and one of the second issue sold for $15,500.

An uncut copy of the first edition of Mary Shelley's *Frankenstein* (1818), with a letter from Percy Bysshe Shelley concerning the book, brought $4,600. There were forty-one items by Percy Bysshe Shelley, among them the author's copy of *Queen Mab* (1813) with his revisions. It had been published privately, and in 1929 only two copies were known. Gabriel Wells paid $68,000, up until that time the second-highest price ever paid for a book at an American auction; Wells was never able to find a buyer for it, and after his death his executors sold it at auction in 1951 to Carl Pforzheimer for $8,000. As an example of the rise of prices before the Crash, this copy had sold in 1896 for £6 ($30); in 1920 (to Rosenbach) for $6,000; and in 1927 (to Kern) for $9,500. Kern, who knew what Rosenbach had paid for the book a few years before, called him a robber for raising the price. Maurice Baring's copy of Percy Bysshe Shelley's *Adonais, An Elegy on the Death of John Keats* (1821), with the original wrappers bound in and containing two sonnets written and signed by Baring, sold for $6,000. The manuscript of six stanzas of "Laon and Cythna" sold for $4,700, and the

Jerome Kern (Gale International Portrait Gallery)

first issue of the printed poem, with a letter by the poet, went for $5,500.

The first issue, first edition of Tobias Smollett's *The Expedition of Humphrey Clinker* (1771) went for $6,200. An uncut set of the first edition of Laurence Sterne's *Tristram Shandy* (1760–1767) sold for $12,500. (In 1992 copies were sold at auction in New York for $3,400 and in London for £4,500.) One of the forty-two Robert Louis Stevenson items was the dedication copy of his *A Child's Garden of Verses* (1885) with his letter explaining why he dedicated the book to his nurse, Cummy. It sold for $8,500. (Kern had bought it five years before for $2,000.) A copy of the first edition of Jonathan Swift's *Gulliver's Travels* (1726) was sold for $17,000.

There were seventy A. C. Swinburne items. An early notebook brought $1,100, and the 114-page manuscript of *Chastelard: A Tragedy* (1865), with an inserted letter by George Meredith eulogizing Swinburne, brought $2,400. A twenty-three-page early manuscript draft of Alfred Tennyson's "The Coming of Arthur," for which Kern had paid $2,600, brought $8,000, and sixteen pages of the manuscript of *Maud* (1855) sold for $9,500. One of six copies of a privately printed trial edition of *The Lover's Tale* (1868) brought $4,500.

There were seventy-seven items by William Makepeace Thackeray. A copy of the first edition of *Vanity Fair* (1847–1848), presented by the author to Charlotte Brontë after she had dedicated *Jane Eyre* (1847) to him, sold for $3,600; Kern had paid $1,850. Eight original drawings by Thackeray for *The Book of Snobs* (1848) brought $2,800. A presentation copy of *Rebecca and Rowena* (1850), with the inscription incorporated in a drawing, went for $4,100; Kern had paid $875. In the early 1850s Thackeray had delivered a series of lectures called "The Four Georges"; a 155-page manuscript—some in his handwriting and some in the handwriting of others—his lectures on the British kings sold for $8,500.

A first edition of Walt Whitman's *Leaves of Grass* (1855), for which Kern had paid only $268, brought $3,400. (In the early 1990s copies brought $28,000 and $2,000.) Six stanzas of the manuscript of Oscar Wilde's *The Ballad of Reading Gaol* (1898) brought $1,600, and the 123-page manuscript of *A Woman of No Importance* (1893) sold for $550.

A few days after the auction ended Kern was interviewed by a writer for *The New York Times.* The headline read, "KERN SEES PRICES OF BOOKS MOUNTING: Composer Says Sums Paid at Sale of His Library Won't Seem High in a Few Years; Gathered It in 20 Years." Kern took most of his proceeds from the sale and invested them in the stock market. Unfortunately for him and many others, the market crashed later in that year. Fortunes were wiped out, and book prices collapsed. Kern had sold at the right time, when prices were high and buyers had money, but he invested the proceeds in an unsound market. Those who had bought Kern's books also suffered financially. In their biography of A. S. W. Rosenbach (who had spent $410,000 at the sale), Edwin Wolf II and John F. Fleming wrote, "The Kern sale was history, but the effects of the orgy were lasting. Kern bills and Kern books plagued dealers and collectors for two decades." A contemporary article in *The New York Times,* written after the first half of the auction was over, complained that the rare-book world was "sadly bewildered and disorganized" and that Kern and Kennerley had brought about a "tremendous upheaval" and evoked "cataclysms." The article concluded that "Undoubtedly the new prices must reduce the number of collectors for this class of books."

No sooner had Kern disposed of his book collection—and made a lot of money and attracted a lot of attention in doing so—than he started buying books again, but not on the same scale as before. Kern seems to have been an inveterate collector. At various times he collected the signatures (cut from letters) of classical composers, paintings, furniture, vases, lamps, and coins. His coin collection began at the suggestion of a masseur who was treating him after an illness. The masseur, who was an officer in the American Numismatic Society, brought some rare coins to show him. Kern was fascinated. He immediately bought several reference books on numismatics, familiarized himself with the terms and technicalities of the subject, and started building a valuable collection.

Kern was gregarious, enjoyed staying up late drinking and conversing with friends, loved practical jokes, and had an explosive temper. When his favorite piano was damaged through some workmen's carelessness, he was so enraged that he suffered a serious heart attack. He recovered, but in 1945 he collapsed on the street in New York City and died several days later, on 11 November, without having regained consciousness. His death was widely noted and regretted. His songs had brought pleasure to many listeners, but among bibliophiles he was remembered for his book collection, and the "Kern Sale" was referred to for years afterward as a high-water mark in the antiquarian trade.

Biographies:

David Ewen, *The World of Jerome Kern: A Biography* (New York: Holt, 1960);

Michael Freedland, *Jerome Kern* (London: Robson Books, 1978);

Gerald Bordman, *Jerome Kern: His Life and Music* (New York: Oxford University Press, 1980);

Andrew Lamb, *Jerome Kern in Edwardian London* (Brooklyn: Institute for Studies in American Music, Conservatory of Music, Brooklyn College of the City University of New York, 1985).

References:

Matthew J. Bruccoli, "The Kern Sale," *American Book Collector,* 7 (1986): 11–17;

John Carter, "Looking Backward," *Publishers' Weekly,* 119 (1931): 330–332;

The Library of Jerome Kern, 2 volumes (New York: Anderson Galleries, 1929);

Colton Storm and Howard Peckham, *Invitation to Book Collecting, Its Pleasures and Practices, with Kindred Discussions of Manuscripts, Maps, and Prints* (New York: R. R. Bowker, 1947);

Robert A. Wilson, *Modern Book Collecting* (New York: Knopf, 1980);

Edwin Wolf II and John F. Fleming, *Rosenbach: A Biography* (Cleveland: World, 1960).

John S. Van E. Kohn
(6 October 1906 – 18 December 1976)

and

Michael Papantonio
(25 February 1907 – 20 August 1978)

Marcus A. McCorison

WRITINGS (by Kohn): "Some Undergraduate Printings of Edna St. Vincent Millay," *Publishers' Weekly,* 138, no. 22 (1940): 2026–2029;

"Mark Twain's 1601," *Princeton University Library Chronicle*, 18 (Winter 1957): 49–54;

"Stephen Herrick Wakeman," in *Grolier 75,* edited by R. W. G. Vail (New York: Grolier Club, 1959), pp. 95–98.

WRITINGS (by Papantonio): "William Augustus White," in *Grolier 75* (New York: Grolier Club, 1959), pp. 35–37;

"John S. Van E. Kohn Memorial Tributes," by Papantonio, Clifton Waller Barrett, Robert H. Taylor, Walter Goldwater, George Goodspeed, Louis Cohen, and others, *AB Bookman's Weekly,* 59 (28 February 1977): 1203–1215.

In late January 1946 book collectors and librarians received a notice that a bookshop was about to open at 3 West Forty-sixth Street in New York City. The announcement was signed by John S. Van E. Kohn and Michael Papantonio, each of whom had had a New York bookshop of his own before entering military service in World War II. Rather than attaching their own names to the business, they preferred something with an "American" flavor. Both men having interests in American literature, they hit upon Seven Gables, from the Nathaniel Hawthorne novel, as the name of their new enterprise. Pooling their remaining stocks they opened Seven Gables Bookshop in February in a building that had no gables–nor, for that matter, much to indicate that a bookshop existed there. Their first catalogue appeared in April, launching what was to become one of the greatest American bookshops of its time.

John S. Van E. Kohn

John Sicher Van Eisen Kohn was born in New York City on 6 October 1906 to a well-established Manhattan family. He graduated from Williams College in 1928, having been elected to Phi Beta Kappa. In 1930 he received his M.A. from Harvard University. Already a collector of modern American literature, Kohn the next year applied for a job at the Argosy Book Store in New York City. When the proprietor, Louis Cohen, told him that money was unavailable for wages, Kohn offered to work for nothing. Ultimately he became a salaried staff member in charge of Argosy's First Editions Depart-

Michael Papantonio

ment. He remained with Argosy until he began his own business.

Kohn opened his new establishment, Collectors' Bookshop, in mid-November 1935 at 37 West Forty-seventh Street, stating his intention to deal in first editions of American literature published during the past seventy-five years. His stock was based on his own thousand-volume collection of modern American poetry and on books he had scouted during the previous six months in the Northeast and in Europe. He augmented this material by buying the collection of the late Edward E. Fuller of Connecticut, who for fifty years had purchased American literary works on publication and wrapped them, unread, in newspapers. R. F. "Doc" Roberts was Kohn's assistant at the time the store opened; a short time later Alexandra "Alex" Dobbs Schultze was hired as secretary. She would remain with Kohn, and then with Papantonio, for the next forty years.

Kohn's first catalogue came out in mid-March 1936. It listed Edwin Arlington Robinson's *The Children of the Night* (Boston: Badger, 1897) at $60. A fine copy of Herman Melville's *Moby-Dick* (New York: Harper, 1851) was marked "SOLD," while Mark Twain's *A Connecticut Yankee in King Arthur's Court*

(New York: Webster, 1889), with the half title, was available at $100 (the Twain book would appear in several more catalogues before it was sold). Catalogue 3 (October 1936), titled *First Books,* was the first of Kohn's famous series of catalogues that identified the initial publications of American authors, well known or not. The series included catalogue 10, *More First Books* (January 1937), and catalogue 11, *Fifty-Seven Fledglings* (May 1940). Catalogue 13, *First Books by Foley Authors* (February 1942), was the last catalogue issued by the Collectors' Bookshop. These catalogues, which were the fruit of Kohn's intense interest in and encyclopedic knowledge of American literature, as well as his sense of humor, would be resumed under the banner of Seven Gables Bookshop. They included items priced as low as $2.50. Kohn put them together because he loved the chase of obscure information and of the odd book.

Catalogue 5, *Modern American Poetry* (April 1937), included a selection of Robert Frost's books as well as Robinson's privately printed first book, *The Torrent*, which was priced at $300. Both authors—especially Frost—were favorites of Kohn's, and he formed outstanding collections of their works and another of those of Edna St. Vincent Mil-

AMERICAN

FIRST

EDITIONS

FIRST CATALOGUE OF
COLLECTORS' BOOKSHOP
37 WEST 47 STREET · NEW YORK

Kohn's first catalogue, March 1936

lay. Catalogue 12, *American Women Writers,* reached customers in May 1941. Kohn also issued brief, mimeographed specialized lists on such subjects as sports, Virginia fiction, the frontier, the American Revolution and the War of 1812, and belles lettres in the South. A final list, dated October 1942, was issued by Roberts and Schultze, who attempted to keep the business open after Kohn was drafted into the army infantry in April 1942. An announcement dated 15 January 1943 informed customers that Collectors' Bookshop had closed. Staff Sergeant Kohn was discharged in November 1945, having been awarded a bronze star for meritorious service.

Papantonio, the other member of the Seven Gables partnership, was born in Union City, New Jersey, on 25 February 1907, the son of Italian immigrants. He received his elementary education in Myerstown, Pennsylvania, and graduated from a New York City high school. He began his career in rare books in 1924 as an apprentice at the Brick Row Bookshop of E. Byrne Hackett at 19 East Forty-seventh Street. He remained there for a dozen years, receiving a thorough training in bookselling. In

1934 he married Eleanor Clermont; they had two sons, Jeremy and André.

Papantonio established his own business early in 1936 at 509 Madison Avenue, at Fifty-third Street. His first catalogue, issued that April, was *A Catalogue of First Editions and Rare Books.* It included a catechism of the Dutch Reformed Church, printed in New York by Hugh Gaine in 1763; the American Antiquarian Society in Worcester, Massachusetts, bought it for $12.50. Catalogue 7 (October 1940) included Papantonio's statement of purpose for his shop and his life: he said that after his twelve-year apprenticeship,

> I have a clear idea of what I am trying to do; and what is encouraging, is that the generous support I have received leads me to believe that booklovers and collectors understand me too.

> . . . I am a young man and would especially like to serve a group of young men who will appreciate and profit from what I can do for them. First, I want to give my assurance that whether you are an occasional or constant buyer, the volume of your business small or large, you shall always have the very best I can do for you. Naturally, you want every dollar that you spend to give you the best possible return: I shall labor unceasingly to bring to you what you want at the best possible price, and to furnish any information that you may ask for at any time. . . . I specialize in rare, choice and standard books of a diversified character. . . . American and English first editions, limited editions, special press books, important new books, autographs, magazine subscriptions, etc.

Papantonio never varied from this credo of service, and until the end of his days he continued to treat young and old, rich and poor alike, giving to each his best effort.

During their early years in business Papantonio and Kohn became good friends; like Kohn, Papantonio issued lists in addition to his catalogues, and a copy of one of them (now at the American Antiquarian Society), *Early American Fiction,* sent out in January 1941, bears the inscription "JS VanE Kohn from Michael Papantonio." Beginning in September 1941 his lists were headed "Papantonio Bookshop." His final catalogue, number 8, was issued in October 1942, shortly before he became an army medical corpsman. Like Kohn, he was discharged in November 1945.

Papantonio and Kohn had corresponded during the war, and a month or so after their return to civilian life they decided to go into business together as the Seven Gables Bookshop. The shop was located on the top floor of a nondescript four-story building at 3 West Forty-sixth Street, just off Fifth

Avenue. The ground floor was occupied by a marine-supply house, whose stock boy operated the primitive elevator in which Seven Gables customers ascended to the shop. The second floor housed the bookshop's excess stock, while the third floor held the marine-supply business's anchors, sails, and rope. Entering the bookstore, customers first encountered Schultze behind her typewriter, a smoldering cigarette in the ashtray. Beyond her was the main room, whose walls were lined with floor-to-ceiling bookshelves; in the middle of the room a long table was covered with books. The cases on the west wall held the shop's impressive collection of general reference books. Assistants working in the room at different times included William Kable, Bailey Bishop, Bart Auerbach, Jane O'Connor Callahan, and Andrea Tucher. Tony LaSalle, who wrapped books so thoroughly that his packages all but defied opening, worked in a cubicle off the room.

Papantonio's office was another large room at the front of the building. Illuminated by sunlight from a large, grimy window, it housed his stock, his reference books, and a large safe. The slightly built, dark-complexioned Papantonio could usually be found pacing about the office, tense and chain smoking. His interests and stock, which included English literature and Americana, were somewhat broader than those of Kohn, who concentrated on American literature. In his office at the rear of the main room Kohn typically sat at his cluttered desk, cataloguing stock. In the center of the rear wall of his crowded room stood two massive safes into which customers eagerly delved—as they also did into Papantonio's—hoping that the desired book would be there; often it was. Volumes of American literature filled Kohn's shelves and a table. His battered, annotated reference books—Lyle Wright's *American Fiction* and Merle Johnson's *American First Editions* chief among them—were constantly at his side, both at the office and at home.

Before the war Kohn had issued thirteen catalogues and Papantonio had put out eight; thus, the first catalogue issued by Seven Gables Bookshop was number 22. It appeared in April 1946 and included American literature and Americana. The next catalogue, for May 1947, offered Kohn's collection of Emily Dickinson materials en bloc at $1,250. Most of the catalogues were prepared by Kohn; Papantonio was more apt to quote books directly to favored customers. But both booksellers tended to place their best material directly with collectors or institutions, so their catalogues usually did not include major items. Kohn continued to issue lists of specific classes of mate-

Papantonio's first catalogue, April 1936

rials. List 1, April 1946, was the first of many offering American fiction, or American literature, or works of individual authors. In his March 1948 list, *Drama & Theatre,* he asked for his customers' help in sorting out the complex bibliographical history of American editions of plays in publishers' series. In addition to his printed lists, from time to time he mailed carbon copies of typed author lists to selected customers. Catalogue 25 (February 1953) had a photograph of Wright on its cover, a tribute from Kohn to the bibliographer of American fiction. Catalogue 26, *English Drama* (May 1953), was prepared by Papantonio. Catalogue 27, *Fifty Books & Manuscripts* (May 1954), featured outstanding material gathered from both their specialties. Catalogue 30, *First Books by American Authors, 1765–1964* (February 1965), continued the series begun by Kohn in his Collectors' Bookshop days. Introduced with a short essay by Roger Butterfield, a writer for Time-Life who had opened a

Papantonio, Kohn, secretary Alexandra Schultze, and the collector Robert H. Taylor

bookstore, it included, as usual, the odd book; for example, lot 167, Coates Kinney's *Keeuka and Other Poems* (Columbus, Ohio: Privately printed, 1855), went to the American Antiquarian Society for $35.

Seven Gables has been described as a "rialto" and a "club." Kohn and Papantonio presided over a congregation of characters, for once admitted—as most freely were—they tended to stay. Booksellers, great collectors, and students searched the shelves and gossiped with their hosts and with one another. What drew this disparate crowd to 3 West Forty-sixth Street was the intelligence, knowledge, integrity, generosity, and good humor of the proprietors. As an absolute beginner, Clifton Waller Barrett had called on Kohn at the Collectors' Bookshop and learned of the importance of condition; he never left. In time he established a well-appointed "office," with draper-

ies, in the back room of Seven Gables, where he and Kohn developed the great collection of American literature that is now at the University of Virginia. Later, Barrett's office became Kohn's office. Robert H. Taylor also had begun collecting before the war, but with Papantonio; he, too, never left. Taylor's outstanding collection of English literature, his gift to Princeton University, was formed with the help of Papantonio, who not only sent exceptional materials to Taylor but also handled auction bids for him in New York and London. Often a crowd would troop off to lunch as guests of one of the proprietors. H. Bradley Martin was frequently present. Papantonio would shepherd his disciples to the Miramar Restaurant on East Forty-sixth. Robert H. Taylor, also, was often in the shop, sometimes exercising an operatic voice in the rear room. Kohn tended to take his guests to a Horne & Hardardt Automat.

Kohn and Papantonio had an uncanny ability to keep their competing book collectors happy. Kohn kept extensive records in his head and on paper of who owned what book, who was looking for what book, and which collector should get the book. Kohn's field, American literature, was inhabited by many hopefuls, but he had a strict code of values by which he judged the quality and intentions of each collector—personal or institutional. Papantonio's clientele for early English literature was somewhat smaller, and he tended to concentrate on helping certain individuals—Taylor, Gordon Ray, Mary Massey, and Bradley Martin among them—build superlative collections. Above all, however, Papantonio was a businessman, and he would assist emerging collectors when the occasion arose: Jean and Donald Stralem's collection of American literature and Gerald E. Slater's of English and American literature were built with his help.

Kohn, who was quieter and more introspective than Papantonio, possessed a subtle mind: he suggested that the staff blow dust—which was abundant at Seven Gables—*onto* the tops of books so that customers would think the volumes had been in stock for years and the prices were, therefore, a bargain. Occasionally he would move ordinary books that had been in stock for long periods of time into the safe in his office; finding them there, customers would quickly snatch them up as treasures. He also had an impish sense of humor: he might pose conundrums to unwary visitors, ask them for definitions of impossible words, or request them to pick a number from one to ten—all for no reason except to confound the innocent victim. Pauses in conversation as he searched for the precise word he wanted could be unnerving. On one occasion, when he seemed to fail to respond to a question put to him, his wife, Frances "Frankie" Rosenbaum Kohn, admonished him, "Speak, John, speak!" (The Kohns were married after the death of Frankie's first husband, who was John's brother; she had two sons by her first marriage, and she and John had a daughter, Penny.) Papantonio's humor was a bit more acerbic; he was known to say that he could keep the business going forever just by selling copies of the first edition of *Gulliver's Travels* (London: Printed for Benjamin Motte, 1726).

Each summer John and Frankie Kohn would travel throughout New England in an informal Progress with another couple, such as Walter Goldwater of the University Place Bookshop and his wife, Eleanor Lowenstein of The Corner Bookshop, to visit country booksellers who had laid aside a year's supply of American literature to await their coming.

Seven Gables catalogue that continued the series begun by Kohn in his Collectors' Bookshop days

Kohn would search card catalogues for lacunae in library collections, marking his Wright and Johnson lists and then fill the holes by selling wants to the institution. William A. Jackson, the acquisitor for Harvard University's Houghton Library, who normally trusted no one but himself, put complete confidence in Kohn's judgment in matters of American literature as did many other private and institutional collectors. Papantonio traveled regularly to England, often accompanied by Taylor, Alexander Wainwright, and Robert Metzdorf, to look for rarities, to attend auctions, and to visit his many friends in the British book community. Papantonio's reputation as an outstanding bookman was possibly stronger among his English colleagues than among those in America; his dealings with Dudley Massey of Pickering and Chatto, Ted Dring of Quaritch's, and Brian Maggs of Maggs Brothers were extensive and profitable to all concerned—booksellers and book collectors alike.

Although very different in personality and temperament, Kohn and Papantonio got on famously with one another. They were social individuals, Papantonio being somewhat more so. Both were members of the Old Book Table, a group of

Thitieth

Anniversary

Catalogue

Seven Gables Bookshop, Inc.

3 West 46th Street   New York, N.Y. 10036

1976

The last catalogue to appear before Kohn's death

or bequeathed most of it to the American Antiquarian Society. His collection of ephemera pertaining to British circulating libraries, which is now in the hands of Henry Morris, proprietor of the Bird & Bull Press, is the subject of a 1992 book by Charlotte A. Stewart-Murphy. Kohn also collected the works of Robert Frost, with whom he had been friends since 1938, and of Edna St. Vincent Millay; he said that neither collection was truly great because he could not take the best material out of the shop's stock. Nonetheless, both holdings were exceptionally rich.

John R. B. Brett-Smith was especially important to the shop's running in its latter days. A collector of English Restoration drama, he arrived at Seven Gables from Oxford University Press around 1971. Eleanor Papantonio was a dynamic, lively person who set off Michael's more quiet manner. Eleanor and Mike had two sons, Jeremy and André. Her death in February 1972 was devastating to Mike, who moved from the Yonkers house to an apartment on East Forty-eighth Street in Manhattan, where he entertained friends and lived in increasingly ill health until his death on 20 August 1978. Kohn's last "first books" catalogue, the shop's thirty-fourth (February–March 1972), was *More First Books by American Authors, 1727–1977 [sic]*. Catalogue 37, Seven Gables' *Thirtieth Anniversary Catalogue,* was designed to celebrate the firm and Kohn's inestimable contribution to it. John Kohn died on 18 December 1976 after a period of ill health. His death created a chasm in the lives of those living not only at home in White Plains but also in the city. Catalogue 39, *Reference Books, Bibliography, and Auction Catalogues* (May 1978), was the last catalogue issued by Seven Gables. Papantonio died on 20 August of that year, and the Seven Gables Bookshop died with him. The closing of the shop was handled by Brett-Smith, Stephen Weissman of Ximenes: Rare Books, and Robert J. Barry Jr. of C. A. Stonehill, Inc. Kohn's Frost collection was sold in 1980 to the University of Tulsa; the Millay material went to a relative of Kohn's and in the summer of 1997 was being offered for sale by a bookseller. Now all that remains are memories, lost or fading, of gladsome gatherings of eager book people at Longworth's Shakespeare Gallery, Dodd & Mead, George D. Smith's, or Eberstadt's in New York; McClurg's or Nebenzahl's in Chicago; the Howell shop on Post Street in San Francisco; Jake Zeitlin's red barn on Figuero Street in Los Angeles; or Goodspeed's on Beacon Hill in Boston. Still, the great, learned collections that live on in the libraries of New Haven, Charlottesville, Princeton, New York, San Marino, Chicago, Worcester, Austin, Cambridge, Washing-

booksellers that met monthly for dinner. Richard Wormser and Howard Mott were also members, and George Goodspeed regularly came down from Boston. Guests from other parts of the book world were occasionally invited to meetings, and it was an invitation that one did not refuse. Dick Wormser, also a bookseller, and his wife, Carola Paine Wormser, were hosts of an annual New Year's party, originally held in New York City and later at their home in Bethel, Connecticut. Close friends gathered there for very lively times. In 1949 Papantonio was one of the founders of the Antiquarian Bookseller Association of America; he served as its president from 1958 to 1960.

Eleanor Clermont Papantonio and Frances Rosenbaum Kohn provided safe havens and more for their bookseller husbands. The Papantonios lived in Yonkers and the Kohns in White Plains in neat, well-appointed homes that were a contrast to the clutter of the shop. Their homes were filled with books—stock on which they were working in private and their personal collections. Papantonio built an outstanding library of American bindings; he gave

ton, and elsewhere stand as the monuments to those men and women in the antiquarian book world who built them.

References:

Clifton Waller Barrett, "John Sicher Van Eisen Hohn," *Proceedings of the American Antiquarian Society,* 87 (April 1977): 18–20;

Matthew J. Bruccoli, "Debts," *Private Library,* fourth series 4 (Winter 1991): 132–145;

Early American Bookbindings from the Collection of Michael Papantonio. Second Edition, Enlarged with a List of the Papantonio Collection Now at the American Antiquarian Society (Worcester: The Society, 1985);

Hannah Dustin French, "Early American Bookbindings from the Collection of Michael Papantonio," *Magazine Antiques* (June 1973): 1172–1177;

Walter Goldwater, "Michael Papantonio," *AB Bookman's Weekly,* 62 (4 September 1978): 1262;

William Spawn, "Michael Papantonio," *Proceedings of the American Antiquarian Society,* 88 (October 1978): 181–184;

Charlotte A. Stewart-Murphy, *A History of British Circulating Libraries: The Book Labels and Ephemera of the Papantonio Collection* (Newtown, Pa.: Bird & Bull Press, 1992).

Papers:
Letters of John S. Van E. Kohn from 1924 to 1973 are in the Williams College archives, the gift of Frances Kohn. Collectors' Bookshop financial records from 1935 to 1943 are at the Fred Lewis Pattee Library of Pennsylvania State University. The Seven Gables Bookshop's records from 1946 to 1978 are in the Rare Book and Manuscript Division of Butler Library at Columbia University.

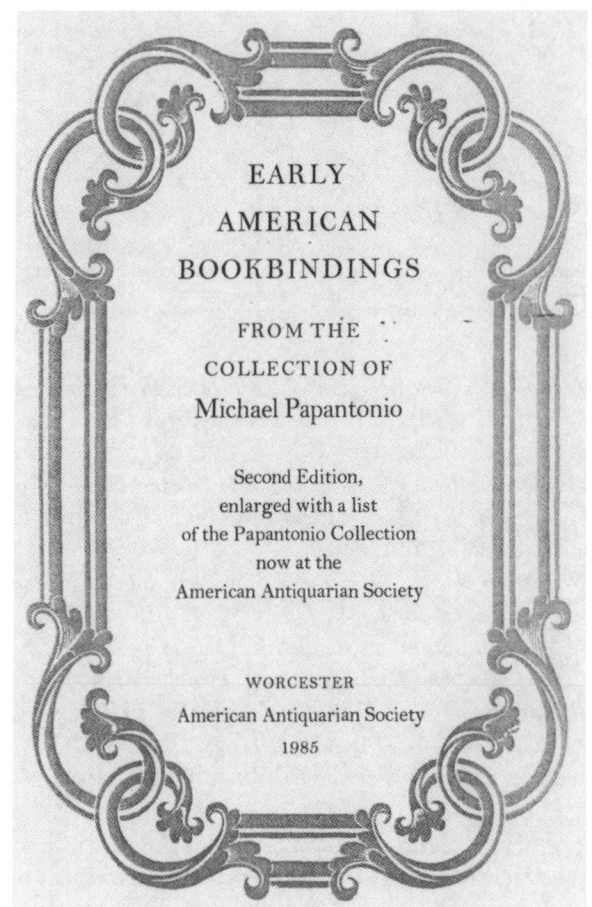

EARLY
AMERICAN
BOOKBINDINGS

FROM THE
COLLECTION OF
Michael Papantonio

Second Edition,
enlarged with a list
of the Papantonio Collection
now at the
American Antiquarian Society

WORCESTER
American Antiquarian Society
1985

Second edition of a catalogue of Papantonio's binding collection. The first edition was published in 1972 to accompany exhibitions of the collection at Cornell University Library, the University of Virginia Library, the J. Pierpont Morgan Library, the American Antiquarian Society, and Princeton University Library.

Hans Peter Kraus

(12 October 1907 – 1 November 1988)

Thomas M. Verich
University of Mississippi

BOOKS: *Inter-American and World Book Trade; Problems of Organization* (New York: Privately printed, 1944);

On Book Collecting; The Story of My Drake Library (Minneapolis: Associates of the James Ford Bell Library, 1969);

Sir Francis Drake, A Pictorial Biography with an Historical Introduction by David W. Walters & Richard Boulind and a Detailed Catalogue of the Author's Collection (Amsterdam: N. Israel, 1970);

A Rare Book Saga: The Autobiography of H. P. Kraus (New York: Putnam, 1978);

Gedichte (Mount Vernon, N.Y.: A. Colish, 1983).

Hans Peter Kraus was one of the preeminent twentieth-century dealers in rare manuscripts and early printed books. Once, when a journalist told him he was the greatest bookseller in the United States, Kraus retorted "in the world." His boast was not without foundation. In fact, the Western world was very much Kraus's province, the great auction houses his preferred stages. During an antiquarian book career that spanned nearly sixty years and two continents, Kraus bought, sold, or discovered many of the most celebrated illuminated manuscripts and early printed books handled by any dealer in the post–World War II period. He was a passionate collector in his chosen areas as well as a farseeing entrepreneur who established highly successful and important periodical and reprint enterprises. His competitive spirit and financial resources were forces to be reckoned with in the antiquarian book trade. In the introduction to Kraus's autobiography, *A Rare Book Saga* (1978), Herbert W. Liebert describes Kraus's career as "a history of the success of hard work, knowledge, skill, cunning, patience, and a great deal of good luck in dealing with some of the most valuable, most beautiful, and most significant objects created by man."

Born in Vienna, Austria, on 12 October 1907, Kraus was the only child of Emil and Hilda Kraus. His parents both came from families with medical backgrounds. Emil Kraus was a physician whose collecting interests, rather than his profession, influenced his son. Uninterested in his father's stamp collection, Kraus began his own specialized coin collection. Then in 1919 a chance find introduced Kraus to the world of rare books. An old atlas given to him because its owner thought the volume had no value as a geography text turned out to be a first edition Mercator Atlas of 1595 with engraved maps designed by the Flemish cartographer Gerard Mercator. Later Kraus sold the atlas to an antiquarian dealer to raise money for a trip to Italy to celebrate his graduation from The Viennese Academy of Commerce in 1925. At age seventeen Kraus had completed all the formal education he would ever receive.

Kraus entered an Austrian guild to apprentice himself as a bookseller. He learned an important lesson from his undemanding and ill-rewarded apprentice days: "Never leave employees alone and presume they're working." For a few years following his apprenticeship Kraus worked as a sales representative, calling on clients in Romania and Poland for a German publisher of architectural books.

In 1932 Kraus returned to Vienna from Berlin to start his own book business. Even though he lacked extensive technical knowledge of rare books, Kraus intended from the first to stock antiquarian books. Initially he made most of his profit not from rare-book sales but from reselling scholarly periodical runs purchased at distress-sale prices. More opportunist than specialist, Kraus even in his early selling days handled first editions of printed scores by Wolfgang Amadeus Mozart, a first edition of Jakob and Wilhelm Grimm's *Tales* (Berlin: Real Schulbuch Handlung, 1812–1815), and a first edition of William Harvey's *De Motu Cordis* (Frankfurt: G. Fetzer, 1628). Yet, he admitted, "I have never become specialized to the degree of some of my colleagues. I handle good books in all fields, so long as they show the chance

H. P. and Hanni Kraus at work in their New York bookstore

for profit. When I smell a profit I take a chance. Over the years my sense of smell has improved considerably." One such opportunity was the purchase of a volume of sixteenth-century maps lacking a title page, which he bought for approximately twenty-eight dollars. Kraus found the maps cited in a cartographic reference that confirmed them to be the earliest edition of a series of maps by Antoine Lafreri, a French engraver and publisher who did much of his work in Rome; only later editions of the maps included a printed title page. Kraus's investigation and careful collation led to his sale of the volume a year later for more than $3,000. The small-volume, first-edition Harvey was acquired from a monastery library in Wilhering, Austria. (Monastic libraries figured frequently in Kraus's book career.) Kraus sold this book quickly for a large profit: as he noted in his autobiography, "Small books had come into demand among collectors, as they could be transported more easily if one had to take sudden flight from the Nazis."

Kraus did not follow the example of those Austrian Jews who had elected to take flight. In 1938 he was arrested by the Nazi SS and dispatched first to Dachau and then transferred to Buchenwald. For reasons never fully explained in his memoir he was released and permitted to rejoin his mother in Vienna, becoming one of an extremely small number of survivors who spent time in both Dachau and Buchenwald. Formally deported from Austria, Kraus stayed briefly in Sweden and then sailed for New York, arriving on Co-

lumbus Day 1939. Fittingly, Kraus had brought with him to the New World a rare edition of a Columbus letter describing the discovery of America (Basle: Printed by Bergmann de Olpe, 1494). He also managed to have this possession—one of his few—publicized in a New York newspaper by a shipping-news reporter covering arriving passengers.

Kraus had landed in New York lacking both financial resources and any real fluency in the language of his new country. Indeed, throughout his life in the United States, Kraus spoke English with a distinctive and pronounced Middle-European accent. Shortly after arriving in New York, Kraus met a fellow Viennese émigré, Hanni Zucker, who became his wife in 1940. She was a member of an affluent family who had escaped the Nazis. The Zuckers' financial support was critical in Kraus's eventual success as a bookseller of the first rank. His intensely close relationship with his wife was of the upmost importance to Kraus: "We became not just husband and wife, and parents of five children, but business partners. . . . Sharing in the dramas of the auction room, celebrating together after an important purchase, preparing catalogues, tracking down rare books, negotiating purchases and sales, entertaining clients."

The war years were not a prosperous period in the antiquarian book trade. Despite a general paucity of sales Kraus did succeed in coming to the attention of a prominent American collector—Lessing J. Rosenwald. Rosenwald was the

Page from the Gutenberg Bible that Kraus bought in April 1970 and sold eight years later to the Gutenberg Museum in Mainz, Germany

first in a succession of leading American collectors—including William H. Scheide, Alastair Bradley Martin, James F. Bell, Edwin J. Beinecke, and Arthur A. Houghton Jr.—who became Kraus's clients. In 1940 Kraus's first sale to Rosenwald, $4,500 worth of books, encouraged the bookseller's father-in-law to lend him $10,000 as working capital. With this money Kraus bought valuable volumes available because of the war, particularly Spanish antiphonals and Russian books, the remainder of the czarist libraries at Tsarskoye Selo, the Winter Palace.

At the end of the war Kraus purchased a property located at 16 East Forty-sixth Street, transforming it into what he called "one of the handsomest bookshops in New York" and the only one "to occupy an entire building." During the third quarter of the twentieth century, from its location between Fifth and Madison Avenues, the firm of H. P. Kraus, in the words of its owner, "served as home for more great book rarities than any other dealer's address in the world."

As a bookseller in Europe, Kraus had discovered that there was more money to be made selling periodicals than rare books. Acting on this experience after the war, he established another branch of his business—Kraus Periodicals. In a short time the new firm became established as the leading dealer in back issues of scholarly journals.

While Kraus was hardly reluctant to sing his own praises in his autobiography, he does recount some failures and missed opportunities. Perhaps the most noteworthy was his rejection of several blackened and battered scrolls he was offered in 1949. These ancient manuscripts turned out to be the famous Dead Sea Scrolls.

One opportunity Kraus did not miss was the acquisition of more than twenty thousand volumes representing the rump of Prince Liechtenstein's private library. Cataloguing this library rich in sixteenth-century books, maps, and manuscripts cost Kraus nearly as much as the original purchase price for the entire library.

Over time Kraus's acquisitive appetite and financial resources permitted him to indulge his taste for illuminated manuscripts. Nevertheless, his bookman's grasp was sufficiently wide to embrace early Marxist tracts, including a first edition of Karl Marx's *The Communist Manifesto* (London: J. F. Burghard, 1848) and autograph letters to Lenin as well as a specialized collection on the Haymarket Riot in Chicago (4 May 1886), one example of Kraus's interest in important Americana.

In concert with another dealer Kraus handled a major Americana collection, the Washington-Rochambeau Papers, which included, among other important documents, Revolutionary War letters written by George Washington, Marquis de Lafayette, and Jean-Baptiste-Donatien de Vimeur, Comte de Vimeur Rochambeau.

Kraus published what he considered to be his first major catalogue in 1954, *The Cradle of Printing*, number 69 in a numerical sequence stretching back to catalogue 1, published in Vienna. Among the highlights of catalogue 69, which listed only fifteenth-century materials, was a William Caxton first edition of *The Canterbury Tales*, printed circa 1478; a leaf printed by Albrecht Pfister of Bamberg (circa 1463); and a leaf from the Fust and Schoeffer Psalter of 1457, the first book that included the printer's name and the date and place of publication.

In 1957 Kraus bought the *Hours of Catherine of Cleves* and two other manuscripts illuminated with beautiful miniatures from Eric-Engelbert, Duke of Arenberg, who was selling his library, which Kraus described as "one of western Europe's oldest, most coveted private collections." Almost reluctantly, Kraus sold the *Hours of Catherine of Cleves* to the American collector Alastair Bradley Martin. Years later Kraus purchased back the manuscript from Martin and sold it to the Morgan Library, New York, which owned the complementary half of the manuscript, which had been first divided by the Paris dealer J. J. Techener in the 1850s. Several years after his first visit Kraus revisited the duke of Arenberg to purchase some paintings and was given boxes of papers from the duke's garage. The duke dismissed them as "worthless old paper," but Kraus knew better. The boxes contained the fifteenth-to-seventeenth-century archives of Nord-kirchen, a German castle belonging to the Arenberg family. Kraus sold the lot to the University Library of Münster.

Another noteworthy manuscript purchase was the twelfth-century *Sigenulfus Codex*, once the property of the library of the monastery of Monte Cassino in Italy. In 1962 Kraus bought this masterwork of medieval illumination, which features many large initials embellished with animal figures. The owner had initially asked $60,000, which Kraus regarded as a fair price. Yet he finally paid only $30,000 and quickly sold it to Dr. Peter Ludwig of Aachen. Kraus, who bargained hard in this as in most of his purchases, once offered this piece of buying advice: "The chief rule in buying is not to show emotion, no matter how beautiful the books, no matter how badly you want them. Be unimpressed, even if all of western civilization's treasures should be spread before you." Selling, for Kraus, was distinctly another matter. In his autobiography he complains of one of his clients, "He was my kind of customer except in one regard. He never was moved to spend beyond his limit."

A turning point in Kraus's emergence as a dominant buyer of illuminated manuscripts was his active participation in three auction sales of the manuscript collection formed by the British collector C. W. Dyson Perrins, whose family's fortune derived from the sale of Lea & Perrins Worcestershire Sauce. Over the years 1958–1961, Kraus spent in total more than £360,000 at the London Sotheby sales. In 1959, for the *St. Albans Apocalypse*, an English illuminated manuscript dating from about 1250, he paid £65,000, the highest price ever paid for a book to that time. Back in New York, Kraus appeared on the television program *I've Got a Secret*. His "secret"–"I have a book backstage worth $182,000."

Clearly, Kraus preferred illuminated manuscripts to more prosaic books, and he certainly enjoyed buying and selling incunabula. He boasted that at one time his stock included a Gutenberg Bible and the Psalters of 1457 and 1459. Kraus also acquired the second known copy of the *Constance Missal*, or *Missale Speciale*. For a time this missal was thought to be contemporaneous with or even perhaps to predate the Gutenberg Bible. Only later was it demonstrated that the missal was printed years after the Gutenberg Bible, the first and most famous early printed book.

Kraus bought his Gutenberg Bible from Arthur A. Houghton Jr. for a seven-figure price in April 1970. An adherent of the buy low, sell high school of economics, Kraus quickly priced his prize at $2.5 million. Shortly after his purchase he

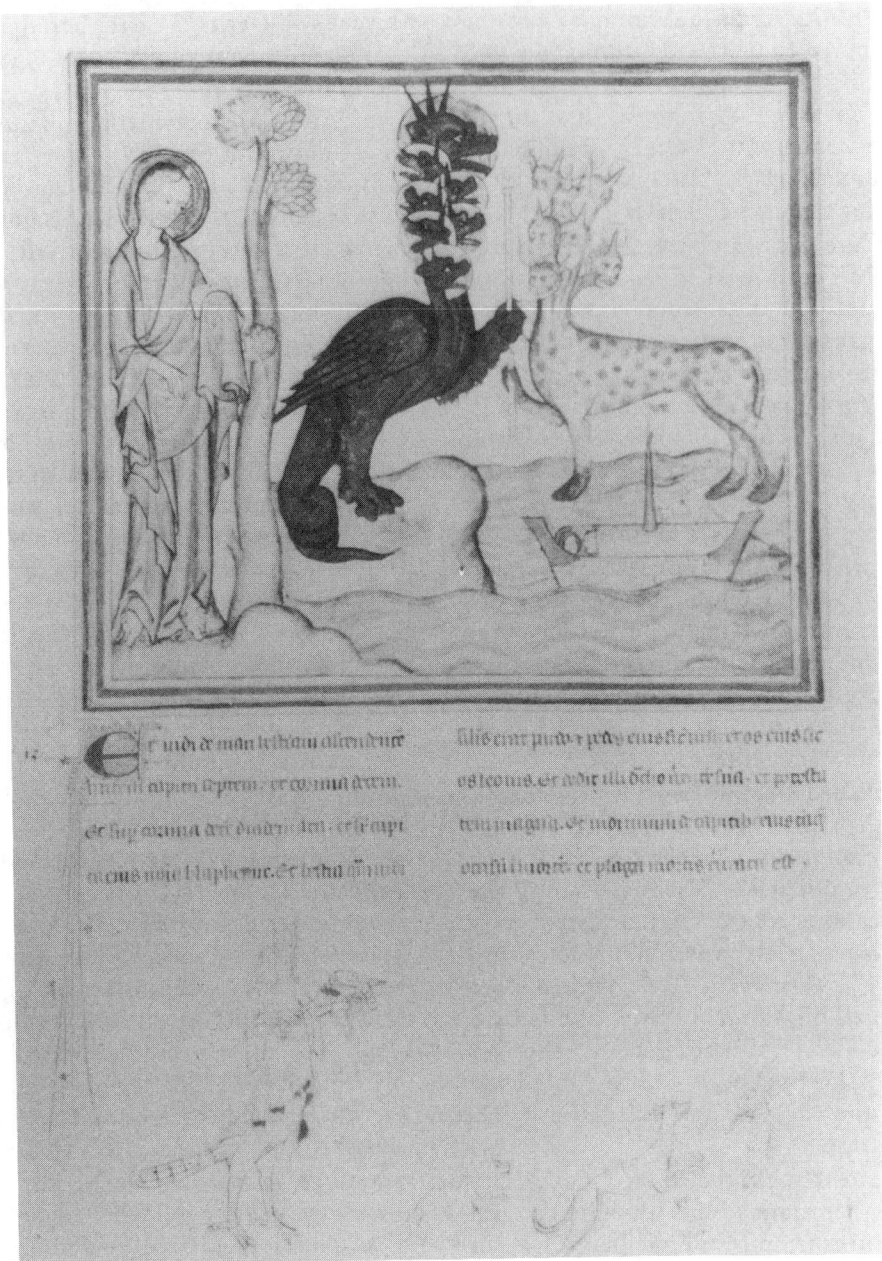

Page from the thirteenth-century Apocalypse manuscript that Kraus bought from a Rothschild family collection in 1968 and sold to the Metropolitan Museum of Art, New York, a few months later

was disturbed to learn of a putative second Gutenberg Bible entering the marketplace. According to an Eton College exhibition catalogue, a "newly discovered 'Gutenberg Bible' resided in the library at 'Blandings Castle.'"

Kraus, whose sense of humor was underdeveloped, looked for this castle on the map. Failing to find it, he sought the help of the British Information Service and the keeper of the Eton College library, who informed him that Blandings Castle was the fictional creation of P. G. Wodehouse,

who had furnished it with its own Gutenberg. Still not laughing, Kraus later wrote in his autobiography: "So that was the end of the Blandings Castle ghost, I had one less worry—one less possible competitor." Kraus's Gutenberg remained unsold until 1978, when it was bought by the Gutenberg Museum in Mainz, thus returning the book to the city where it had been printed 523 years earlier.

Caxtons were another of Kraus's special favorites. For the five hundredth anniversary of the first Caxton (1476), the first book printed in the

The first-floor showroom at H. P. Kraus, Rare Books, in New York City

English language, Kraus published a commemorative catalogue listing the largest number of Caxtons available for sale anywhere in the world—a grand total of six books. One Caxton he listed in his 1976 catalogue, *The Historye of Reynart the Foxe* (Westminster, 1481), remained in stock and was reoffered as recently as 1990 in H. P. Kraus catalogue number 182. Kraus had acquired *The Historye of Reynart the Foxe* as part of a remarkable transaction with the great Swiss collector Dr. Martin Bodmer. Kraus had been authorized by University of Texas interests to offer Bodmer $60 million for his entire library. Bodmer turned down this offer but agreed to sell Kraus several rarities, including such major works of English literature as the first editions of William Shakespeare's *King Lear* (London: Printed for Nathaniel Butter, 1608) and *Lucrece* (London: Printed by Richard Field for John Harrison, 1594) and the first edition of John Bunyan's *Pilgrim's Progress* (London: Printed for N. Porder, 1678).

The crowning glory of Kraus's purchase from Bodmer was a group of manuscripts, including the *Arenberg Missal,* and the *Juengere Titurel* of Albrecht von Scharfenberg. The *Arenberg Missal* is beautifully bound in silver and enamel and includes seven full-page paintings from the eleventh century. The *Juengere Titurel,* which includes eighty-five lovely miniatures, was produced in southern Germany in the early 1400s and is important as literature of the German High Middle Ages. Kraus, who had sold the *Juengere Titurel* to Bodmer shortly after World War II, repurchased it for ten times his selling price and resold it to the Bayerische Staatsbibliothek in Munich. In all, Kraus spent several million dollars on the deal, which caused Bodmer to say, "You have succeeded in denuding me." Kraus replied, "You have succeeded in making me broke."

Perhaps more than any other antiquarian book dealer of his time, Kraus had the financial resources not only to acquire expensive properties but also to retain them unsold for a considerable period of time. In 1968 Kraus paid more than a million dollars for nine illuminated manuscripts from the collection of a member of the Rothschild family, including a thirteenth-century manuscript of the Apocalypse that included seventy-two large paintings. This manuscript, which Kraus bought at auction in Paris for the equivalent of $221,000, did not remain in Kraus's stock for long. Both the Metropolitan Museum of Art in New York and the German collector Dr. Paul Ludwig offered to buy the manuscript from Kraus at more than triple the price he had paid, and it went to the Metropolitan for $750,000. This profitable turn of events elicited an enigmatic response from Kraus: "Such is the luck, the unpredictability, and the drama of the rare-book business."

One of Kraus's especially valued clients was Edwin J. Beinecke, the great benefactor of the Yale University libraries. In the 1960s, for slightly more than $1.1 million Kraus sold Beinecke for Yale a first edition of Saint Augustine's *De Civitate Dei* (Subiaco: Printed by Konrad Sweynheym & Arnold Pannartz, 1467); *The Bedford Book of Hours,* a fifteenth-century illuminated missal in French and Latin; an illustrated and signed manuscript of Dante's *Divina Commedia* from the late fourteenth century; *The Savoy Hours,* a gem of fourteenth-century illumination; an illuminated manuscript that includes the canticles of the Virgin (circa 1325); *The Capitularies,* or edicts of Charlemagne, his son Louis the Pious, and his grandson Charles the Bold, written in northern France in the ninth century and including eleven fine colored initials; and a fifteenth-century Bible written on vellum. Produced in northern Italy, it has 682 decorated leaves and hundreds of miniatures. Kraus described it as "one of the finest of all Italian late Gothic illuminated manuscripts."

Yet another record-breaking auction victory for Kraus occurred in July 1970 when he purchased for $750,000 a hitherto unknown Flemish Book of Hours with miniatures accomplished by the three leading masters of the Flemish arts: Sanders Bening, his son Simon, and Gerard Horenbout. Sotheby's of London had estimated the selling price as $180,000–$270,000. Again, Kraus had achieved a world record for the highest price ever paid for a manuscript in the salesroom. According to Kraus, its armorial bindings indicated that it had belonged to the Spinola family of Genoa, the same family that had owned the famous fifteenth-century *Très Riches Heures* of the Duc de Berry. Kraus sold the manuscript to Dr. Peter Ludwig.

The major auction houses were not the only places Kraus acquired new material. Frequently he was able to buy back books he had sold to collectors and to purchase deaccessions from institutions. On occasion he even traded items with such institutional owners as the Morgan Library and the Bibliothèque Nationale. In a 1969 exchange with the Bibliothèque Nationale, Kraus was able to acquire the Mainz Psalters of 1457 and 1459, important examples of early printing. In 1980 he acquired from an American university early Coptic texts written on papyrus—*The Crosby Codex.*

His purchase of objects seemingly almost without regard to future sale was an attribute that distinguished Kraus from most other dealers: "At heart I am a collector, I sell only because as a businessman, it would be impossible to do otherwise." Indeed, throughout his life Kraus continued to put together his own collections. He owned an important assemblage of maps, atlases, globes, and por-

tolans, navigational charts used in the fifteenth and sixteenth centuries. His cartographic interest—along with the chance mention by the American collector James Ford Bell that Sir Francis Drake had made a profit of 5,000 percent on his circumnavigation of the globe—inspired Kraus to build a Drake collection consisting entirely of original materials from Drake's own age. This collection of books, manuscripts, letters, maps, portraits, and medals documents Drake in the eyes of his own contemporaries and was the basis for a book on Kraus's collection published in 1970. In 1967 Kraus started a collection in an area completely new to him—Persian illuminated manuscripts.

While hardly dismissing the profit motive, Kraus could also be generous. In 1961 he gave Yale University, which he came to regard as his honorary alma mater, an important equestrian collection, the Robert Sterling Clark Collection of Books on Horses and Military History. In 1970, as a form of thanks to his adopted country, Kraus gave the Library of Congress a stunning collection of Americana highlighted by the *Amoretti Codex,* a contemporary copy of a seventeen-page letter written by Amerigo Vespucci, and an eight-page Bartolomé de Las Casas holograph from the sixteenth century concerning the plight of Indians in Peru. In October 1980 Kraus also gave his celebrated Sir Francis Drake collection to the Library of Congress. According to *The New York Times* of 12 October 1980 Kraus placed the value of his Drake collection at "exactly $950,000." "But," he said, "that is not much—it is very little. Just last month I bought a Boccaccio manuscript at an auction for $1,250,000."

One of the final chapters of Kraus's autobiography is titled "Why I Will Be Remembered." In this chapter Kraus mentions especially his firm's remarkable production of catalogues, which by that time numbered 150. Kraus did not usually take an active role in writing these catalogues. He relied on his house experts, Dr. Hans Nachod and Dr. Hellmut Lehmann-Haupt, for authoritative expertise. Many of the catalogues produced for the firm of H. P. Kraus are considered standard reference tools; nevertheless, Kraus was fond of saying about his catalogues: "Everybody admires them, nobody reads them." Kraus himself was a serious student of all he bought, sold, and collected. He maintained a personal reference library of more than fifteen thousand volumes, duplicates from the far larger reference collection housed at H. P. Kraus on East Forty-sixth Street.

In his autobiography Kraus paid scant attention to one of his most lucrative and far-reaching ventures—the reprint publishing business. While he may have been more proud of his Rare Books Monographs Series, Kraus's reprint firm, founded in 1957 and expanded to incorporate a European division headquartered in Liechtenstein, was an enormous success with a permanent impact on institutional collections. In 1965 Kraus merged his reprint business with holdings owned by Roy H. Thomson—Lord Thomson of Fleet, the Canadian-born English communications baron.

One of Kraus's final triumphs was the purchase of, in partnership with the London firm of Bernard Quaritch, the twelfth-century *Gospels of Henry the Second*—probably the finest medieval manuscript sold in the twentieth century. Acting on behalf of German institutions, Kraus won the manuscript at a London Sotheby-Parke-Bernet auction in 1983 for yet another world record price—an astonishing $11,720,000, the highest price ever paid for a book.

After a long illness Hans Peter Kraus died on 1 November 1988 at his home in Ridgefield, Connecticut. Through intense effort this driven and sometimes difficult man made an indelible mark on many of the great private and public collections in the United States and in Western Europe. He will be remembered as one of the supreme antiquarian bookmen of the twentieth century.

References:

In Memoriam Hans Peter Kraus 1907–1988 (Mount Vernon, N.Y.: A. Colish, 1989);

Hellmut Lehmann-Haupt, ed., *Homage to a Bookseller; Essays on Manuscripts, Books and Printing Written for Hans P. Kraus on his 60th Birthday. Oct. 12, 1967* (Berlin: Mann, 1967).

Paul Lemperly

(1858 – 4 May 1939)

Dean H. Keller
Kent State University

BOOKS: *Francis Adon Hilliard, 1850–1923* (Cleveland: Rowfant Club, 1924);

Among My Books (Cleveland: Rowfant Club, 1929);

Books and I (Cleveland: Rowfant Club, 1938).

OTHER: *The Courting of Dinah Shadd: A Contribution to a Bibliography of Rudyard Kipling,* edited by Lemperly (Jamaica, N.Y.: Marion Press, 1898);

A List of Book-plates Engraved on Copper by Mr. Edwin Davis French, compiled by Lemperly (Cleveland: Printed for subscribers, 1899);

Andrew Lang, *Bibliomania,* edited by Lemperly (Lakewood, Ohio: Privately printed, 1914);

Thomas Hardy, *Jude the Obscure: A Letter and a Foreword,* edited by Lemperly (Lakewood, Ohio: Privately printed, 1917);

"The History of The Rowfant Name," in *The Rowfant Manuscripts,* by H. Jack Lang (Cleveland: Rowfant Club, 1978), pp. 51–55.

An early and innovative collector of association books, Paul Lemperly was born in Cleveland, Ohio, in 1858. He grew up on the west side of the city, near the banks of the Cuyahoga River; attended public schools; and graduated from West High School. He was married on 19 April 1881; he and his wife, Emma, had two children: Lucia and Charles. Lemperly's long career in business was spent with the wholesale drug firms Benton Myres Company and Hall-Van Gorder Company.

Lemperly's home on Clifton Boulevard in the Cleveland suburb of Lakewood became a favorite gathering place for local book collectors and such out-of-town visitors as Eugene Field, DeWitt Miller, William Allen White, and Francis Wilson. On 19 February 1892 postcards signed by Lemperly, Francis Adon Hilliard, W. H. Gaylord, Clifford J. King, Charles Orr (the manager of the Austin-Taylor Bookstore in Cleveland), Charles A. Post, and Thomas Walton were sent to fifty Clevelanders known to be interested in books, inviting them to a meeting at the Hollenden Hotel on 23 February to consider the organization of a club for book collectors. Eighteen men attended the meeting and appointed a committee, which included Lemperly, to draw up a constitution and bylaws for the club. The committee sent out a draft constitution and bylaws on 25 February; they were ratified at a meeting on 29 February. Lemperly is credited with giving the organization its name, the Rowfant Club, after the Rowfant Library put together in England by Frederick Locker-Lampson; he wrote his account of the naming of the club in 1925 on the flyleaves of a copy of Arthur H. Clark's *A Bibliography of the Publications of The Rowfant Club* (1925). This bit of club history was published as an appendix to H. Jack Lang's *The Rowfant Manuscripts* (1978).

Lemperly was elected president of the club for the 1923–1924 term; he was a fellow of the club for several terms, served on its Publication and Library Committees, and in 1938 was made an honorary member. He addressed the club on several occasions, giving such talks as "Of the Intimate Satisfaction of the Pursuit and Capture of Books," "On Certain Matters Rowfantian," and "Some Association Books," which was published by the club in 1929 as *Among My Books*. The club also published Lemperly's presidential address—*Francis Adon Hilliard, 1850–1923* (1924)—and his *Books and I* (1938). Leland Schubert credits Lemperly with obtaining the typescript for H. M. Tomlinson's *War Books* for publication by the club in 1930. The typescript would be listed as lot 962 in the sale of Lemperly's library by Parke-Bernet New York Galleries in New York City in 1940; an additional thirty-nine Tomlinson items would also be included in this sale.

In his foreword to the catalogue for the sale of Lemperly's books Noel Lawson Lewis, a fellow Clevelander and member of the Rowfant Club, noted that

Paul Lemperly's especial interest as a collector began and continued to the end of his long life, with the most human of all bookish attributes, Association. He loved his books for their contents, for their binding, their type,

Paul Lemperly

their illustrations and for their features but, above all, he loved them for their association—in countless cases, personal association of the closest kind—with their authors.

Contemporary literature, both English and American, was dominant in Lemperly's library, and many of the associations were between himself and the authors of these books. His usual method of establishing such associations was to purchase a copy of the book he wanted, usually on publication; to write to its author for permission to send the book for inscription; and, if permission was granted, to send the book off to the author with sufficient postage for its return. Lemperly's courtesy of sending return postage was appreciated by at least one author; A. E. Housman wrote on 11 December 1899: "I think yours is the only letter containing no nonsense that I have ever received from a stranger, and certainly it is the only letter containing an English stamp that I have ever received from an American. Your countrymen generally enclose the stamps of your great and free republic."

A variation on this method of collecting association books involved the use of bookplates. A friend of the artist and bookplate designer Edwin Davis French, and also of the collector of and writer about bookplates Charles Dexter Allen, Lemperly was an avid collector and user of bookplates. In 1917 he and his wife gave their bookplate collection to Flora Stone Mather College of Western Reserve University in Cleveland in memory of their daughter, who had died in 1915 and who had attended the university. Of the several bookplates used by Lemperly, at least two were designed by French, and one of these was created especially to enhance Lemper-

ly's collection of association books. The plate, dated 1900, is rather large, measuring four and one-half by two and five-eighths inches. It consists of a panel surrounded by scrollwork, with a space in the center for the author's name, and the words "this volume, / for insertion in which the author / has been pleased to write his name, / is the property of / Paul Lemperly." Instead of sending books to authors for their inscriptions, a costly and sometimes hazardous practice, Lemperly could simply send copies of his bookplate. He used the plates liberally, and his success in having them signed and returned may be seen in references in the catalogue of the sale of his library where books are frequently described as "With [the author's name]'s signature on Mr. Lemperly's bookplate."

Never rich, Lemperly rarely bought books from antiquarian dealers. Most of the items he did acquire secondhand came from Dodd, Mead in New York. He was especially fond of Percy Lawler of that firm, but when Lawler joined the Rosenbach Company in 1916 Lemperly wrote that Lawler would not be getting any more of his business because Rosenbach's prices were too high.

Lemperly described many of the favorite books in his library in *Among My Books* and *Books and I,* but a broader look at his success as a collector may be gleaned from the catalogue of the sale of his library after his death on 4 May 1939. The sale took place in four sessions at the Parke-Bernet Galleries in New York City on Thursday and Friday, 4 and 5 January 1940. The 1,060 lots in the sale represented some 5,000 volumes; the sale realized approximately $21,000.

Two of Lemperly's bookplates

The catalogue shows that Lemperly collected the works of some of his favorite authors in considerable depth. Among these authors was Joseph Conrad, whose thirty lots included *Almayer's Folly* (London: Unwin, 1895), his first book, and the first edition, first issue of *Chance* (London: Methuen, 1913). Among seventeen Robert Frost lots were *A Boy's Will* (London: David Nutt, 1913) and *North of Boston* (New York: Holt, 1914), both inscribed by Frost to Lemperly. One of Lemperly's largest collections was of works by Thomas Hardy. Besides letters, including fifty from Florence Hardy to Lemperly, and manuscripts, the fifty-six lots included Hardy's first and second books, *Desperate Remedies* (London: Tinsley, 1871) and *Under the Greenwood Tree* (London: Tinsley, 1872), as well as a set of the first edition of *The Dynasts* (London and New York: Macmillan, 1903–1908).

There were thirty-seven Rudyard Kipling lots, including a copy of *Departmental Ditties and Other Verses* (Lahore: Privately printed, 1886) inscribed by the author and with three letters from Kipling to Lemperly laid in it. Andrew Lang had twenty-nine lots, including twenty-six first editions of his *Fairy Books* and *Story Books,* and John Masefield was represented by thirteen lots, among them a first edition of his first book, *Salt-Water Ballads* (London: Richards, 1902), inscribed. There were large holdings of George Meredith's and Robert Louis Stevenson's works—twenty-three and twenty-five lots, respectively; William But-

ler Yeats also had twenty-five lots, including the first edition of his rare first book, *Mosada* (Dublin: Printed by Sealy, Bryers and Walker, 1886).

Among individual titles in the sale of Lemperly's library was James M. Barrie's first book, *Better Dead* (London: Swan Sonnenschein, Lowrie, 1888), in its original paper wrappers; described by the cataloguer as "excessively rare," it sold for $265. A copy of Robert Bridges's first book, *Poems* (London: Pickering, 1873), was also in the collection, inscribed for Lemperly and containing a letter from Bridges to Lemperly regarding the suppression of the book and the reprinting of it for copyright. An inscribed copy of Stephen Crane's pseudonymous and first book, *Maggie: A Girl of the Streets* (New York: Privately printed, 1893) was present as was Ralph Waldo Emerson's own copy, with his corrections, of his *Poems* (Boston: Munroe, 1847).

An inscribed copy of the first separate edition of Edward Everett Hale's *The Man without a Country* (Boston: Ticknor & Fields, 1865) sold for $220, and A. E. Housman's *A Shropshire Lad* (London: Kegan Paul, Trench, Trübner, 1896), with the letter from Housman to Lemperly, brought $125. Henry James's own copy of his dramatization (London: Heinemann, 1891) of his novel *The Americans* (1877) was also in the library.

The sale included a presentation copy to Richard Henry Stoddard of Edwin Arlington Robinson's privately printed first book, *The Torrent and the Night Before* (Gardiner, Maine, 1896), with two letters from Robinson to Lemperly that apparently came from Lemperly's friend Miller. Lemperly's copy of Walt Whitman's *Leaves of Grass* (Brooklyn, 1855) was the second issue of the first edition and contained an autograph note by the author.

Lemperly was especially proud of two inscribed copies of books by Charles Dickens: volumes one and two of *Master Humphrey's Clock* (London: Chapman and Hall, 1840) and the first separate edition of *Barnaby Rudge* (London: Chapman and Hall, 1841). Both books were inscribed for Frederick Salmon, the surgeon who operated on Dickens in 1841, and *Master Humphrey's Clock* contained a letter from Dickens to Salmon. The books brought $160 and $270 respectively at the Lemperly sale.

Not all of the books in Lemperly's library were association copies. For instance, he had eight books printed at William Morris's Kelmscott Press, four of which were titles by Morris. He also had several fine Ohio items, including *An Act to Incorporate the City of Cleveland* (Cleveland: Rice and Pennington, 1836), the first Cleveland directory (Cleveland: Sanford and Lott, 1837), three tracts on the organization of the Ohio Company, and a lot containing five early Ohio imprints dating from 1815 to 1833.

To sum up the collecting career of this most extraordinary bibliophile, one could do no better than to quote from Lewis's foreword to the sale catalogue:

Quietly and modestly proud of his success, as he had every right to be, Paul Lemperly was a most shy and retiring collector withal, and forever credited to "bullheaded luck" (his favorite remark) what was in reality the result of his inborn book-collecting genius through many fruitful years of faithful, intensive, inspired and extraordinarily successful work and study. Surely the chronicle of book-collecting in America cannot properly be written without the personal history of his superlative achievements in that happiest of hunting grounds.

References:

Russell H. Anderson, *The Rowfant Club: A History* (Cleveland, 1955), p. 82;

Arthur Henry Clark, *A Bibliography of the Publications of the Rowfant Club* (Cleveland, 1925), pp. 12, 35, 66, 78, 123;

Donald C. Dickinson, "Lemperly, Paul," in his *Dictionary of American Book Collectors* (New York: Greenwood Press, 1986), pp. 201–202;

Sue Hanson, "The Lemperly Collection at Case Western Reserve University Libraries," *Book-*

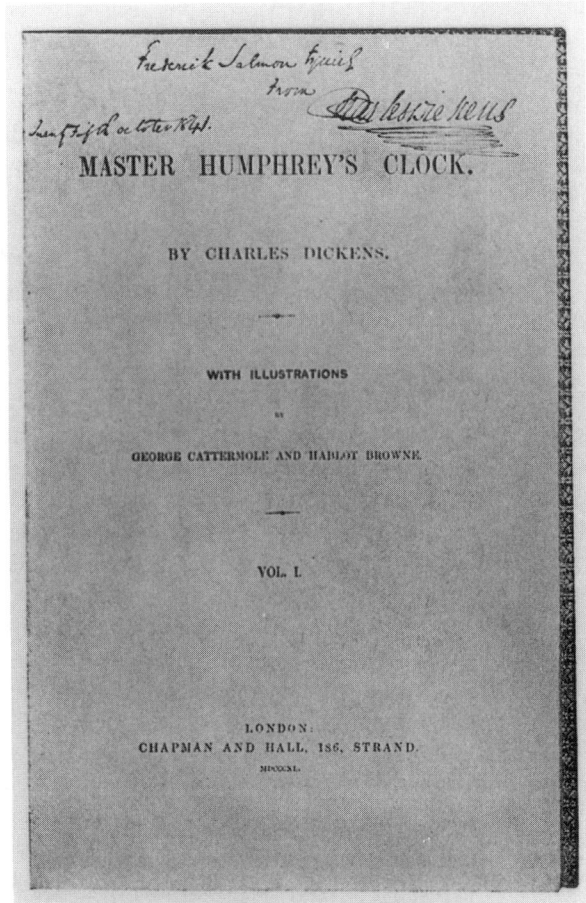

Title page for one of Lemperly's two inscribed works by Dickens. This book, which also included a holograph Dickens letter, was purchased for $160 at the January 1940 sale of Lemperly's library (from Lemperly's Books and I, *1938).*

plates in the News, no. 59 (January 1985): 539–542;

Dean H. Keller, "Paul Lemperly and His Bookplates," *Bookplates in the News,* no. 59 (January 1985): 535–537;

Library of the Late Paul Lemperly, Lakewood, Ohio: Sold by Order of Charles M. Lemperly, Executor of the Estate of Paul Lemperly, Deceased, sale no. 157 (New York: Parke-Bernet Galleries, 1940);

Leland Schubert, *A Bibliography of the Publications of The Rowfant Club: Part Two, 1925–1961* (Cleveland, 1962), pp. 18–19, 38–40, 53.

Papers:

Paul Lemperly's papers relating to the Rowfant Club are in the club's archives at the Western Reserve Historical Society, Cleveland.

William Mackenzie

(30 July 1758 – 23 July 1828)

Karen Nipps
Library Company of Philadelphia

William Mackenzie collected books for the sake of their rarity, age, or beauty. By the time he died in 1828, he had assembled one of the largest private libraries in the United States. It was the most valuable collection of antiquarian books gathered by an American to that point. His assortment of historical material, unprecedented in this country for its depth and breadth, sets Mackenzie apart as the first American rare-book collector. Bequeathed in part in Mackenzie's will to the Library Company of Philadelphia, which then purchased the rest, his library has remained intact for posterity, the legacy of an extraordinary collector.

Mackenzie was born in Philadelphia on 30 July 1758 to Kenneth and Mary Mackenzie. Kenneth Mackenzie had come to Philadelphia by way of Charleston, South Carolina, where his father, also named William, had helped to found a benevolent society for Scottish immigrants in 1730, suggesting that the first William may have been of Scottish birth. Mary was the daughter of Edward Thomas of Barbados, and ties with that country remained strong throughout her son's life. Kenneth and Mary Mackenzie had been married at Christ Church, the most prestigious Episcopal church in Philadelphia, on 12 December 1754. The records of Christ Church list a daughter, Temperance, born to a Kennath and Mary Mackinsey in 1755; it is likely that she was a sibling of William Mackenzie, but there are no other records extant relating to her.

In 1766 an eight-year-old William Mackenzie was admitted as a student to the Academy of Philadelphia. Philadelphia was the richest and most cosmopolitan city of the early republic, a setting ripe for the cultivation of a life of sophistication and erudition. The academy, which was the preparatory school for the College of Philadelphia, had been established in 1749 by Benjamin Franklin and offered one of the few structured curriculums in the city for the education of its young men, with such standard courses as Latin, Greek, history, English language, logic, and rhetoric. Mackenzie was not enrolled by

William Mackenzie; portrait by John Neagle (courtesy of the Library Company of Philadelphia)

his father, who had likely died before then, but by Capt. William Morrell, a Philadelphia merchant who had dealings in Barbados and also had two sons Mackenzie's age who attended the academy. Mackenzie spent four years at the academy and then entered the counting house of John Ross, one of the most prominent shipping merchants in Philadelphia and muster master of the Pennsylvania navy. There he prospered, gaining an extensive knowledge of accounting and mercantile affairs.

Mackenzie, who never married, resided his entire life on Union Street in the fashionable area of town known as Society Hill, not far from the bustling New Market. He must have been close to his

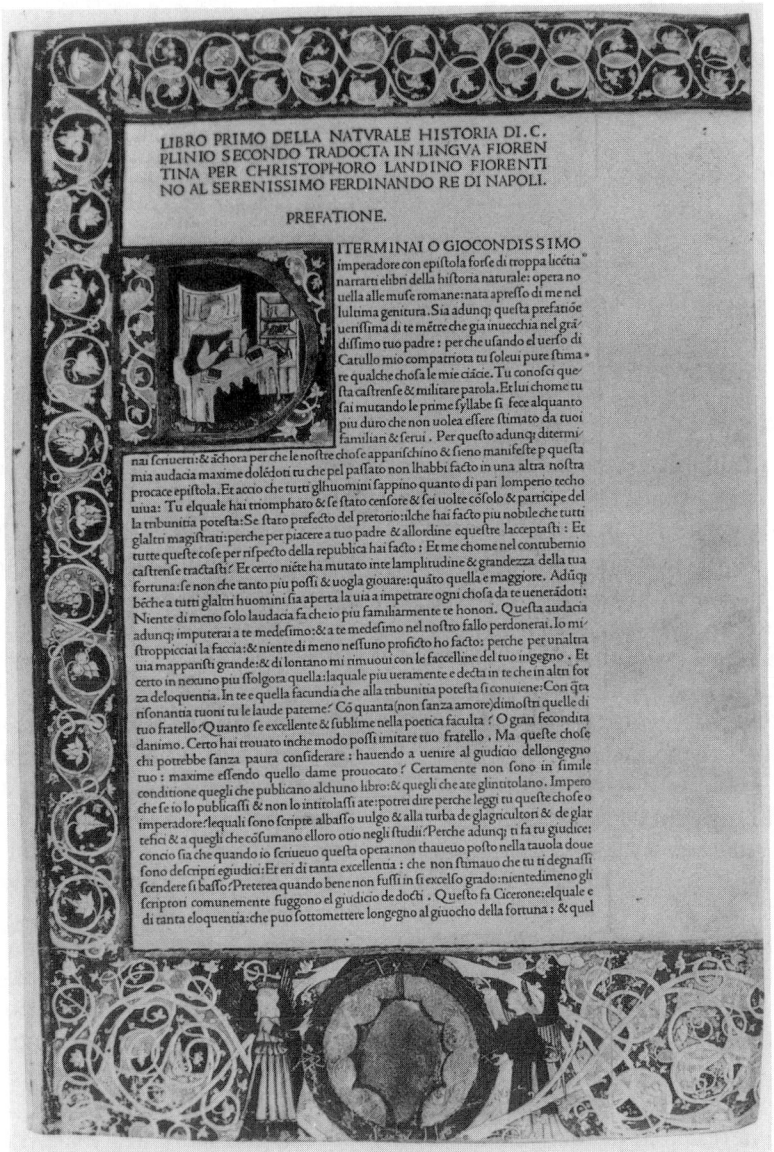

Page from Mackenzie's copy of the 1476 Italian edition of Pliny's Historia
naturale; *one of two copies printed for Ferdinand, king of Sicily (Library
Company of Philadelphia)*

mother, who always lived nearby and did not die until 1825, three years before Mackenzie's death. His closest known friendship was with James Abercrombie, an academy classmate and associate minister of Christ Church from 1794 to 1833. Mackenzie was an active member of Christ Church and its sister church, Saint Peter's, throughout his life. In 1786 he joined the Library Company of Philadelphia, the oldest cultural institution in the country and the dominant library in the city, where he could make use of the collections and interact socially with fellow book lovers. In 1791 he paid $300 for a share in the New Theatre on Chestnut Street, becoming one of the first contributors to that endeavor. He took a philanthropic interest in cer-

tain civic affairs; in 1789 he joined Benjamin Rush, Thomas Dobson, Joseph Claypoole, and almost one hundred other prominent citizens in petitioning the Pennsylvania Executive Council for the release and pardon of James Lange from the Pennsylvania Jail on the grounds that he was wrongly imprisoned. Mackenzie was a member of such charitable organizations as the Female Bible Society; the Society for the Relief of Poor, Aged and Infirm Masters of Ships; and in keeping with family tradition, the St. Andrew's Society, a charitable organization for Scottish immigrants.

Mackenzie retired at a relatively young age to pursue a life of scholarship and book collecting, though where he acquired sufficient income to support such a leisurely life is unclear. Certainly as a merchant he would have had ample opportunity to profit from the economic conditions during the Revolution. There is rumor of an inheritance, and his mother gave him power of attorney over her United States Treasury Bonds in 1796, though the worth of those bonds is not known. Except for his will, Mackenzie left behind no written records such as letters, diaries, or business papers; only his book collection remains as evidence of his unique character, revealing a gentleman of leisure, scholarship, and refinement who chose to apply himself to bibliophily in a distinctive way.

Much of Mackenzie's library consisted of contemporary imprints, common to lettered men of his day, including a wide variety of belles lettres, philosophy, and history as well as such popular periodicals as the *Port Folio,* the *American Museum,* and the *Gentleman's Magazine.* The many Episcopalian and Unitarian works, pamphlets on prison reform, Scottish-related material, works concerning the moral and social obligations of the gentility, early books on travel and the description of the Caribbean, and scholarly editions of the Greek and Roman classics found in his collection reveal his personal interests. He also possessed an excellent reference library of biographies, histories, dictionaries and encyclopedias. Copies of Guillaume François de Bure's *Bibliographie instructive* (Paris: De Bure le jeune, 1763–1768) and Joseph Ames's *Typographical Antiquities* (London: Printed by W. Faden and sold by J. Robinson, 1749) were purchased to support his extraordinary interests in the history of books; it is doubtful that there were any other Americans of Mackenzie's day so interested in printing history as to pursue these two early and rare bibliographical imprints. In addition he bought more contemporary works of bibliography, such as the second edition of Jacques-Charles Brunet's still useful *Manuel du libraire et de l'amateur de livres* (4 volumes, Paris: Brunet, 1814) and many of the works by Thomas Frognall Dibdin, now known to be filled with inaccuracies but which at the time were held in the highest respect.

What most distinguishes Mackenzie and his library, however, are those older and rarer items collected for their bibliographic qualities. Earlier American book collectors such as James Logan, William Byrd, Isaac Norris, and Cotton Mather had more utilitarian reasons for creating their libraries: books to them were to be read, studied, and used for practical as well as intellectual purposes. Mackenzie, while collecting on this level, also followed the lead of a growing number of European book collectors who were creating libraries based on aesthetic sensibilities and bibliophilic discernment. Such men as John Ker, third Duke of Roxburghe; the Count MacCarthy-Reagh of Toulouse; George John, second Earl Spencer; and George Spenser, Marquis of Blanford, broke new ground in their approach to book collecting at the end of the eighteenth and beginning of the nineteenth centuries and were no doubt models for Mackenzie's approach to books. For them, books were often to be admired and treasured for their antiquity and artifactual qualities alone.

A great majority of the volumes that these men sought had not even been available for purchase before Mackenzie's generation. The dispersal of hundreds of monastic and aristocratic libraries during the French Revolution and the Napoleonic Wars created an unprecedented opportunity for collectors such as Mackenzie, who were able to acquire a far greater amount of older and rarer material on the open market than had previous generations. Many of Mackenzie's volumes bear an early Continental provenance suggesting that they were among the spoils of this turbulent period. For instance, Mackenzie owned a copy of Konrad Sweynheym and Arnold Pannartz's 1471 Bible (Rome) that bears the early signature of eminent Italian antiquarian Onuphrio de Urbe and a seventeenth-century inscription from the Convent of St. Roche at Toulouse. His copy of Nicolas Jenson's Venetian printing of Eusebius's *De evangelica praeparatione* (1470), a hallmark in printing history as the first appearance of Jenson's influential roman type, was given by Giustiniano de Luzago to the Convent of San Domenico at Brescia in 1483.

Other volumes that Mackenzie owned bear only markings of late-eighteenth-century Continental and British ownership, implying that they were circulating during this period—many for the first time in centuries. For example, editions of two early illustrated French chivalric romances, *Meliadus de Leonnoys* (Paris: D. Janst, 1532) and *La treselegāte . . . hystoire du . . . Roy Perceforest* (6 volumes, Paris: E. Gormontius, 1531–1532), bear no previous provenance except that of the eighteenth-century English collector John Louis Goldsmid, whose library was sold in 1815; they probably had not been circulating much between their initial printing and Goldsmid's acquisition of them.

The greatest strength of Mackenzie's library is the wide array of fine incunabula and early-sixteenth-century books it included. Many of them are the only copies known in this country, among them a Dutch Book of Hours filled with woodcuts and printed by Adriaen van Liesvelt in 1494; the anony-

Three illustrations from Robert Gobin's Les loupes rauissans *(circa 1505), one of several books in Mackenzie's collection printed by Antoine Verard (Library Company of Philadelphia)*

mous *Legende des Flamens artisiens et haynuyers* printed by François Regnault in Paris in 1522, also copiously illustrated; and a folio edition of Boethius's *De consolatione philosophiae* printed by Jean Parix in Toulouse in 1480. At the time of his death Mackenzie had the largest collection of incunabula in the country–a total of three dozen titles. Perhaps the most outstanding among them is a copy of the first Italian edition of Pliny's *Historia naturale,* celebrated as the first important printed book of science, printed by Jenson in Venice in 1476. It is one of two copies known to have been specially printed on vellum and richly illuminated with gold and colors for the translator's noble patron, Ferdinand, king of Sicily, and presented to Ferdinand's nephew, Prince Lodovico of Aragon, by his tutor. Another incunabulum owned by Mackenzie was an English edition of Jacobus de Voragine's *Legenda aurea,* produced by the first printer in England, William Caxton, at Westminster around 1483. Mackenzie's copy is particularly renowned as being the first Caxton to reach America.

Mackenzie had an affinity for French imprints and French popular literary traditions; the French works he collected are diverse, ranging from fifteenth-century books to contemporary imprints. One of his earliest imprints was what was thought of at the time as the first New Testament in French, printed by the celebrated Lyonese printer Guillaume Le Roy around 1478 (it is now known to be the second, after another Le Roy edition). Among the many works by and about women authors that he acquired was the ten-volume roman à clef, *Artamène, ou le Grand Cyrus* (Paris: Augustin Coubré, 1649–1653), by Madeleine de Scudéry (but published as by her brother George). Scudéry, celebrated as an early female intellectual, presided over one of the most popular French salons in her day. Jean Benjamin de Laborde's five-volume quarto *Essai sur la musique ancienne et moderne* (Paris: Printed by P.-D. Pierres, sold by E. Onfroy, 1780) also would have been especially attractive to Mackenzie for its groundbreaking history of the art of the troubadour.

Mackenzie combined his Francophilic interests with his fondness for illustrated works, collecting some of the most striking examples of fifteenth- and sixteenth-century illustrated books. He owned many books printed by the Parisian Antoine Verard, the acknowledged master of the French illustrated book; among them is Robert Gobin's *Les loupes rauissans,* printed around 1505 and including several noteworthy illustrations depicting the villainous wolf Archilupus and his wicked cubs attempting to overcome the shepherdess Saincte Doc-

trine and her innocent sheep. Its vigorous cuts are complemented by a haunting Dance of Death series. Another unusual item is *Les illustrations de Gaule et singularitez de Troy* (Paris: De Marnes and Viart, 1521), by Jean Lemaire de Belges, historiographer to the queen of Brittany, with woodcuts by Le Roy. The first edition of the collected works of chief French patroness of letters Marguerite d'Angloulême, titled *Marguerites de la marguerite des princesses* and printed in 1547 by leading Lyonese printer Jean de Tournes, includes a series of delicate wood engravings; in addition, while Mackenzie did not collect ornate bindings routinely, this book is bound in a contemporary Lyonese binding with strapwork design, colored enamel ornament, and stippled ground.

Mackenzie took his interest in illustration beyond France, acquiring such highlights of printing history as the famous edition of Dante's *Divina Commedia* with woodcuts after Sandro Botticelli drawings (Venice, 1491); the first edition of Henricus Cornelius Agrippa of Nettesheim's *De occulta philosophia libri tres* (Cologne, 1533), filled with unusual characters and signs of the occult; and the first English edition of Rembert Dodoens's classic herbal (London, 1578), translated from French by H. Lyte with more than seven hundred botanical woodcuts. In chivalric literature Mackenzie acquired the 1596 edition of Edmund Spenser's *Faerie Queene* (London: W. Ponsonby) and the rare London edition of R. Le Vayer de Boutigni's *The Famous Romance of Tarsis and Zelie* (1685). He clearly relished original English editions. All early editions of George Herbert's *The Temple* are rare; Mackenzie owned a 1634 third edition, striking for its unusual *carmen figuratum,* or shaped poems, "Easter Wings" and "The Altar." Other early English works Mackenzie brought together included the principal authority for English canon law, William Lyndewode's *Constitutiones,* printed by one of the first printers in England, Richard Pynson (1505?); Andrew Marvell's *The Rehearsal Transpros'd: The Second Part* (London: N. Ponder, 1673); and many of the propaganda pamphlets written by John Milton while he was secretary for Oliver Cromwell.

Mackenzie was a connoisseur of the printing arts, filling his shelves with outstanding volumes by the fifteenth- and sixteenth-century fine printers Anton Koberger, Jean de Marnes, Johann Froben, Aldus Manutius, and the Estiennes, but he also sought out the handsomest books printed in the eighteenth and early nineteenth centuries. John Baskerville of Birmingham, who revolutionized book design with his sharply defined type, spare laying of type on the page, restraint in decoration, dis-

Page from William Byrd II's manuscript catalogue of his collection, one of the items purchased from his library by Mackenzie (Library Company of Philadelphia)

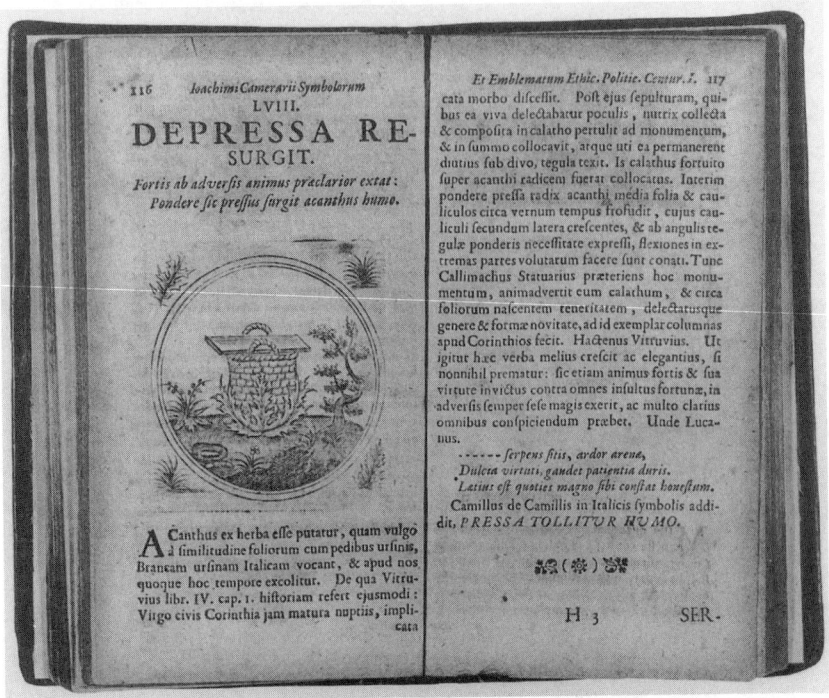

Benjamin Franklin's copy of the emblem book by Joachim Camerarius that inspired designs for
American currency and was purchased by Mackenzie (Library Company of Philadelphia)

tinct black ink, and unique practice of passing sheets through a hot press after printing, is represented with his first book, Virgil's *Bucolica, Georgica, et Aeneis* (1757). Mackenzie acquired one of the greatest bibliographic achievements of the rococo period, the four-volume folio edition of Jean de La Fontaine's *Fables choisies* (Paris: Printed by C.-A. Jombert for DeSaint & Suillant, 1755–1759) with copious illustrations by the celebrated artist Jean-Baptiste Oudry; this set is specially bound in a choice calf binding stained appropriately with a paw-print design. As both a scholar and a bibliophile Mackenzie collected several titles from the distinguished Glasgow press of Robert and Andrew Foulis.

In addition Mackenzie took a keen interest in the more common printing activities of his time, collecting scores of Revolutionary War pamphlets and related Americana. He acquired the rare early work of American political economy, Francis Rawle's *Ways and Means for the Inhabitants of Delaware to Become Rich* (Philadelphia: S. Keimer, 1725). The second known Antigua imprint, Samuel Martin's *An Essay Upon Plantership* (S. Jones, 1750), would have been attractive to both the merchant and the bibliographer in Mackenzie and may well have had practical uses. Mackenzie also collected Benjamin Franklin imprints, among them Franklin's handsomest piece

of printing, Cicero's *Cato Major* (1744). Many books in his collection, such as the first editions of Jean-Jacques Rousseau's *La Nouvelle Heloïse* (Amsterdam: Marc-Michel Rey, 1761); Thomas Paine's *Common Sense* (Philadelphia: R. Bell, 1776); and George Gordon, Lord Byron's *Childe Harold's Pilgrimage,* Cantos III and IV (London: John Murray, 1816, 1818), show Mackenzie to have been a discriminating buyer of the books of his own age.

Mackenzie sought books both abroad and locally. Many of his books bear eighteenth-century British and Continental provenances; while it is likely that he had a European agent looking out for his interests abroad, it is equally probable that he himself traveled to Europe to do at least some of his own buying. Mackenzie accumulated auction catalogues of French and English libraries being sold at the end of the eighteenth and early nineteenth centuries, and while most of these are not annotated (Mackenzie rarely put a mark in his books), it is possible that he was buying from some of these sales. Mackenzie owned the 1798 auction catalogue of the library of the Englishman Richard Farmer, which includes a description of Spenser's *Faerie Queene* as in two volumes with the first volume lacking its title page; this description corresponds exactly with Mackenzie's copy. Other items in the catalogue bear a striking resemblance to Mackenzie's copies of those titles as well.

Another auction catalogue that Mackenzie owned was that of the 1815 sale of the library of the renowned French collector Count MacCarthy-Reagh of Toulouse. Three entries in particular sound much like Mackenzie's copies. In 1814 Dibdin said he knew of no copies of the 1471 Sweynheym and Pannartz Bible except Earl Spencer's and the count's; the MacCarthy-Reagh copy lacked volume two, as does Mackenzie's. Only two copies of Jenson's printing of Pliny's *Historia naturale* are known to have been made on vellum for Ferdinand, king of Sicily; MacCarthy-Reagh owned a vellum copy, so it is quite likely that his and Mackenzie's copies are the same. The count also owned a copy of Jenson's first edition of Eusebius's *De evangelica praeparatione,* one of the highlights of Mackenzie's collection.

There is evidence that Mackenzie purchased books at the establishments of the local booksellers John Sparhawk, John Phillips, and Robert Bell. He most likely frequented the shop of the most literate Philadelphia bookseller of the time, Thomas Dobson. Many of his volumes bear local contemporary provenance, which suggests that he was buying at library sales occurring at the time. For example, Mackenzie possessed several volumes once owned by Joseph Priestley and by Robert Morris, a signer of the Declaration of Independence; the libraries of both of these men were dispersed locally while Mackenzie was actively collecting.

One of Mackenzie's most important local sources was the Franco-American author, professor, and bookseller Nicholas Gouin Dufief. Mackenzie bought from him and subscribed to his books. In addition, when Dufief orchestrated the piecemeal dispersal of the libraries of William Byrd II and Franklin, two of the most significant private American libraries assembled prior to Mackenzie's day, Mackenzie bought heavily at those sales. Among the twenty-nine Byrd books known to have been purchased by Mackenzie is Byrd's own manuscript library catalogue (circa 1751), richly bound in gilt-tooled red morocco, probably by its compiler, the Williamsburg binder John Stretch. It is fortunate that this item caught the collector's eye, as it is only from this catalogue that historians could know what a magnificent library Byrd constructed. Mackenzie acquired at least eighty-four books from Franklin's library; among them is Franklin's copy of *Symbolorum ac emblematum ethico-politicorum centuriae quator* (Mainz; Ludovico Bourgeat), a 1702 emblem book by Joachim Camerarius used by Franklin and the Continental Congress in designing the first American paper money.

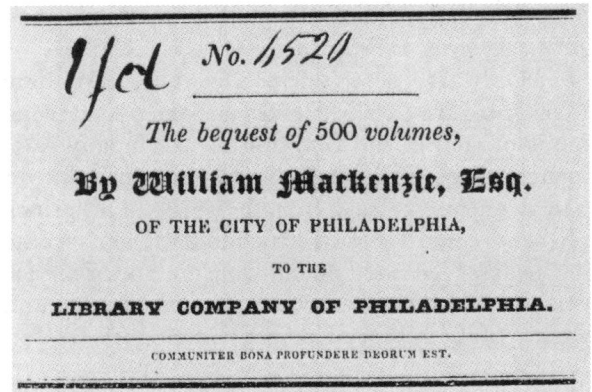

Bookplate for the volumes that Mackenzie bequeathed to the Library Company of Philadelphia

Mackenzie died on 23 July 1828. In his will he bequeathed almost $25,000 in cash to various friends and relatives, many of whom had connections with Barbados. He left $1,000 each to the St. Andrew's Society and to the Society for the Relief of Poor, Aged and Infirm Masters of Ships. When it was inventoried, his estate was valued at almost $50,000, a remarkable sum for the time. The library that he spent a lifetime accumulating, which comprised 7,051 volumes when he died, was estimated to be worth almost $3,400. (This amount would equal about $50,000 today, though of course the actual value of his collection far exceeds that amount now.)

Mackenzie bequeathed much of his collection to the Library Company of Philadelphia and its associated Loganian Library. No private library of the time is known to have been larger, and contemporary newspapers remarked on the unusual size and worth of such a bequest. As he itemized in his will:

> I give and bequeath to the Library Company of Philadelphia their successors and assigns forever five hundred volumes to be chosen by the Directors thereof from my English Books printed since the beginning of the eighteenth Century and I give and bequeath to the Library Company of Philadelphia aforesaid their successors and assigns forever in trust for the increase of the Loganian Library and subject to the direction of the trustees thereof all my books printed before the beginning of the eighteenth Century and eight hundred volumes more to be chosen by the said Trustees from my French Books and Latin Books printed since the beginning of the eighteenth century.

The remaining volumes were purchased under favorable terms by the directors for the two libraries. In 1829 two catalogues were printed for the library of the entire bequest, the *Eighth Supplement to Volume II.-Part I of the Catalogue of Books, Belonging to the Li-*

brary Company of Philadelphia and the *Catalogue of the Books, Belonging to the Loganian Library, Vol. II.*

Only two personal recollections of William Mackenzie are extant. His friend James Abercrombie is quoted in the 1829 Library Company catalogues as saying that he believed Mackenzie "never had an enemy, at least, from the purity of his principles and correctness of his conduct, I am sure he never deserved one." Judah Dobson, one of the executors of Mackenzie's estate and compiler and printer of the Library Company catalogues, wrote:

> His constitution, though vigorous, was not robust, his manners plain and conciliatory, his hand and his purse were ever open and ready to relieve individual and domestic distress, and contribute to public requisitions; in short, in every relation which he bore to society, he exhibited a truly estimable and exemplary character; as a son, dutiful, affectionate and attentive; as a man, benevolent, liberal, and honest; as a citizen, patriotic, generous, and amiable; as a friend, firm, sincere, and candid; as a companion, intelligent, entertaining, and courteous. He was an accomplished Belles Lettres and classical scholar, and the tenor of his life was an uniform illustration of his principles and the benevolence of his heart.

An oil painting presented to the Library Company by Abercrombie at the time of Mackenzie's death also suggests a man of gentility and learning.

Although Americans of the next generation avidly collected Americana, it was not until after the Civil War that collectors followed Mackenzie's lead and became keenly interested in early examples of European printing. Mackenzie presaged a revolutionary development in American book collecting by taking an interest in books for their artifactual value. As Edwin Wolf II, former librarian of the Library Company, wrote in his summary of Mackenzie's achievements in the *Gazette of the Grolier Club:* "the books themselves remain the monument of the man."

References:

Judah Dobson, comp., *Catalogue of the Books, Belonging to the Loganian Library, Vol. II* (Philadelphia: Dobson, 1829);

Dobson, comp., *Eighth Supplement to Volume II.–Part I. of the Catalogue of Books, Belonging to the Library Company of Philadelphia. (Including the Books of the Late William Mackenzie, Esq.)* (Philadelphia: Dobson, 1829);

Marie Korey, "Three Early Philadelphia Book Collectors," *American Book Collector,* 2 (November/December 1981): 2–13;

Edwin Wolf II, "Great American Book Collectors to 1800," *Gazette of the Grolier Club,* no. 16 (June 1971): 3–70;

Wolf and Korey, eds., *Quarter of a Millennium: The Library Company of Philadelphia 1731–1981* (Philadelphia: Library Company of Philadelphia, 1981).

Papers:

The only papers relating to William Mackenzie known to exist are his will and the inventory of his estate, both held by the Archives of the City of Philadelphia; records of his admission to the Academy of Philadelphia, held by the Archives of the University of Pennsylvania; a record of his birth, at Christ Church; and the document giving him power of attorney over his mother's U.S. Treasury Bonds and the James Lange petition with his name on it, both held by the Historical Society of Pennsylvania.

David Magee

(18 June 1905 – 17 July 1977)

Harlan Kessel
The Book Club of California

BOOKS: *Bibliography of the Grabhorn Press, 1915–1940,* by Magee and Elinor Raas Heller (San Francisco: Magee, 1940);

Jam Tomorrow: A Novel (Boston: Houghton Mifflin, 1941);

My Ascent of Grizzly Peak: The Adventures of a Middle-aged Gentleman, as David Catt (San Francisco: Privately printed, 1950);

The Duke and the Printer: An Improbable Conversation between John Ker, Third Duke of Roxburghe, and Don Augustín Vicente Zamorano (San Francisco: Printed at the Grabhorn Press for the Roxburghe Club, 1953);

Bibliography of the Grabhorn Press, 1940–1956, by Magee and Dorothy Magee (San Francisco: Magee, 1957);

The Hundredth Book: A Bibliography of the Publications of The Book Club of California and a History of The Club (San Francisco: Printed at the Grabhorn Press for the Book Club of California, 1958);

A Course in Correct Cataloguing; or, Notes to the Neophyte (San Francisco: Magee, 1958; revised edition, New York: International League of Antiquarian Booksellers, 1959);

Fine Printing and Bookbinding from San Francisco and Its Environs: A Representative Exhibition for the Grolier Club (San Francisco, 1961);

Two Gentlemen from Indiana Now Resident in California (San Francisco: Printed by the Grabhorn Press for the Grolier Club, 1961);

Shakespeare in Bohemia: Three Plays, by Magee, Loyall McLaren, and David Dodge (San Francisco: Grabhorn Press, 1961);

Lawton Kennedy, Printer (San Francisco: Book Club of California, 1962);

The Second Course in Correct Cataloguing; or, Further Notes to the Neophyte (San Francisco: Privately printed, 1962);

The Buccaneers, music by Leon C. Radsliff (San Francisco: Grabhorn Press, 1964);

The Book Club of California: A Catalogue of the Publications, Keepsakes and Ephemera Offered for Sale by

David Magee, 1969 (photograph by Ruth Teiser)

David Magee (San Francisco: Antiquarian Books, 1965);

Victoria R. I.: A Collection of Books, Manuscripts, Autograph Letters, Original Drawings, etc., by the Lady Herself and Her Loyal Subjects, Produced during Her Long and Illustrious Reign, 3 volumes (San Francisco: Grabhorn-Hoyem, 1969–1970);

The Bonny Cravat, music by George Shearing (San Francisco: Grabhorn-Hoyem, 1970);

The Golden Cave, music by Shearing (San Francisco, 1973);

Infinite Riches: The Adventures of a Rare Book Dealer (New York: Eriksson, 1973).

PLAY PRODUCTIONS: *The Buccaneers,* music by Leon C. Radsliff, San Francisco, Bohemian Grove, 31 July 1964;

The Bonny Cravat, music by George Shearing, San Francisco, Bohemian Grove, 31 July 1970;

The Golden Cave, music by Shearing, San Francisco, Bohemian Grove, 27 July 1973.

OTHER: *Eliza Farnham's Bride-Ship,* edited by Magee, Book Club of California Keepsake Series (San Francisco: Book Club of California, 1952);

Gambling in the Mines, edited by Magee (San Francisco: Book Club of California, 1953);

"Death of a Dentist," in *The Graveside Companion: An Anthology of California Murders,* edited by J. Francis McComas (New York: Obolensky, 1962);

"Afternoon of a Poet," in *Second Reading,* edited by Oscar Lewis (San Francisco: Book Club of California, 1965).

SELECTED PERIODICAL PUBLICATIONS–UNCOLLECTED: "The Fourth of July, 1862," *Battledore* (1946);

"They Come in Threes," *Atlantic Monthly,* 191 (March 1953): 90–91;

"Two Gentlemen from Indiana," *California Librarian,* 20 (October 1959): 238–243;

"A Course in Correct Cataloguing; or, Notes to the Neophyte," *Antiquarian Bookman,* 25 (25 January 1960): 251–252;

"Afternoon of a Poet," *Quarterly News-Letter, Book Club of California,* 27, no. 1 (1961);

"Pseudonymity, or The Art of Hiding One's Light," as Pseudonymous Bosch, *Quarterly News-Letter, Book Club of California,* 28 (Fall 1963);

"On Collecting P. G. Wodehouse," *Quarterly News-Letter, Book Club of California,* 29 (Spring 1964).

In the annals of antiquarian bookselling, bibliography, and cataloguing the name David Magee looms large indeed. During his half-century as an antiquarian bookseller in San Francisco he averaged slightly more than one subject catalogue of offerings annually; many of these catalogues are used as references and as models by book dealers, collectors, and librarians. As an antiquarian bookseller Magee specialized in early printing, modern presses, first editions, Western Americana, and Victorian literature. He was also a successful novelist, editor, book scout, and publisher. His autobiography, *Infinite*

Riches: The Adventures of a Rare Book Dealer (1973) is a standard work in antiquarian literature.

Born in Yorkshire, England, on 18 June 1905, David Bickersteth Magee was the fifth child of a vicar, Arthur Victor Magee, who later brought his family to his large parish, St. Marks, in St. John's Wood in northwest London. Magee's grandfather William Connor Magee, archbishop of York, is described by Magee in *Infinite Riches* as "perhaps the greatest orator in the House of Lords since the elder Pitt." William Connor Magee's father was the archbishop of Dublin from 1822 to 1831. All three paternal forebears were prolific authors of religious sermons and tracts, but they had no interest in antiquarian books. On his mother's side, however, Magee had a great-great-aunt, Frances Mary Richardson Currer, whom he calls "England's greatest woman book collector"; at the time of her death in 1861 she had assembled some twenty thousand volumes, including near-perfect copies of the first complete English version of Miles Coverdale's Bible (1535) and the succeeding five editions; superb collections of early English chronicles; a fourteenth-century manuscript for *The Travels of Sir John Mandeville;* and many other items that would be virtually priceless in the modern antiquarian market. Most of her collection was auctioned at Sotheby's a year after her death.

Magee's father died when Magee was in his teens; the family was soon reduced to penurious circumstances. Magee graduated from Lancing College, a private school, but a university education was out of the question. Unable to support even himself on his shipping clerk's salary, Magee came to believe that he was a burden to his mother and his two sisters who remained at home. America beckoned–particularly California, where he believed a fortune could be quickly gained in farming: "You just lie under a tree and hold out your hat to catch the dollars," Magee says in *Infinite Riches.* He successfully appealed to a wealthy uncle, Sir Mathew Wilson, for a loan to pay his sea and overland passage. With no more in the way of references than advice from Madame de Souza-Dantas–wife of the Brazilian ambassador to France, a Californian by birth and friend of Magee's aunt–to "look up a Johnny Stern in San Francisco," Magee sailed from England in January 1925. He crossed the United States in one of the coldest of American winters–an experience that no doubt enhanced his instant and lifelong love of San Francisco.

Stern introduced Magee to Albert M. Bender, a wealthy insurance executive, philanthropist, patron of the arts, and one of California's most notable collectors of antiquarian books; Bender in turn arranged an interview for Magee with the antiquarian book dealer John Howell, proprietor of John Howell: Books, at 434 Post Street. Magee thus became one of the first in a long line of distinguished book dealers who were trained in the Howell establishment before venturing out on their own. His salary was seventy-five dollars a month, plus ten dollars worth of books. He learned the art of cataloguing at John Howell: Books; the first full catalogue he compiled for Howell was Catalogue No. 5, *Catalogue of Elizabethan Literature, Including the Works of Shakespeare and His Contemporaries, with a Preface by David Magee* (1928).

Magee developed a strong clientele that included some of the great collectors and bibliographers of California—Robert E. Cowan, Henry E. Huntington, Henry R. Wagner, George D. Lyman, Lawrence Clark Powell, and Sanford Berger. But he wanted to deal in modern first editions, fine presses, and Victorian literature, fields in which the Howell offerings were not strong. Therefore, in 1928, with a $5,000 loan from friends, he sublet an eight-by-fifteen-foot room—"a miniature shooting gallery," as he described it in *Infinite Riches*—at 480 Post Street in the most fashionable shopping section of San Francisco; went on a buying trip to England; and opened his own shop. Although he had gone into competition with Howell, Magee and his former employer would remain friends until Howell's death in 1956.

Magee's first catalogue, *A Catalogue of Modern First Editions, Californiana, and Miscellaneous Literature,* issued in November 1928, included 261 offerings that ranged in price from $1 to $325. The catalogue was an instant success, enabling Magee to begin repaying his loans, to invest in new inventory (usually supplied by his London agents, B. F. Stevens and Brown—a relationship that would last for almost fifty years), and to visit international auctions and the libraries of collector-tycoons (as well as musty, spider-laden basements) in search of rare items for his growing clientele.

An early customer at Magee's shop was Edwin Grabhorn, founder of San Francisco's Grabhorn Press, one of the finest design and printing firms in America. In 1930 Magee tried to commission Grabhorn to print the first book under the David Magee imprint: a 240-copy edition of William Shakespeare's *King Lear,* with an introduction by G. K. Chesterton. Grabhorn refused without explanation; Magee surmises in *Infinite Riches* that a noted San Francisco collector, H. Flodden

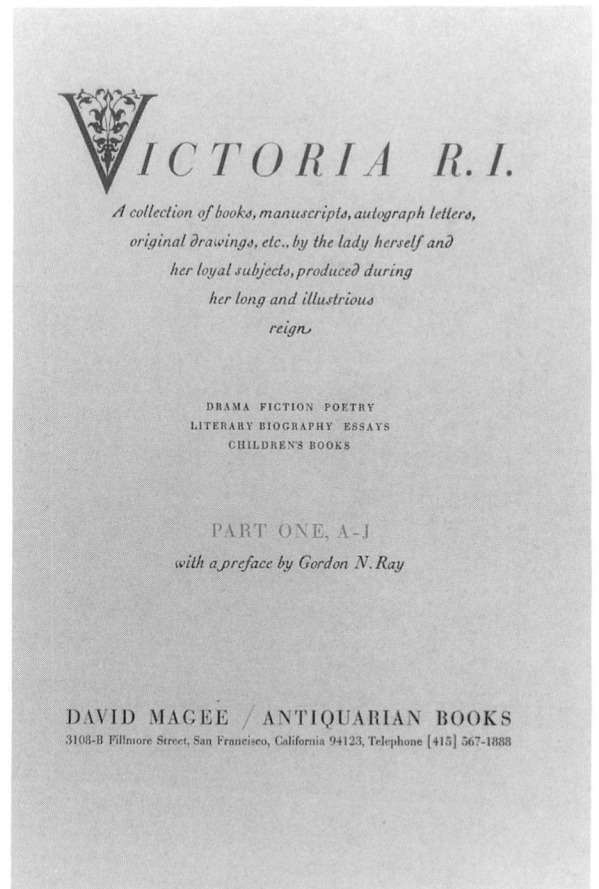

Title page for Magee's three-volume catalogue of what is considered the largest Victorian literature collection assembled by a bookseller. Brigham Young University bought the entire collection before the catalogue was published.

Heron, had told Grabhorn that Magee was short of funds so Grabhorn feared that he would never be paid. Magee commissioned a distinguished British firm, the Curwen Press, to design and print the edition on expensive handmade paper. The volume is a rare and expensive item today and is especially desirable to Chesterton collectors.

The second book published under the David Magee imprint, *Original Leaves from the First Four Folios* (1935), was designed and printed by the Grabhorn Press; Magee surmises in *Infinite Riches* that his credit rating with the Grabhorns had improved by that time. Perhaps the finest of all the leaf books published under the Magee imprint, each copy includes four leaves. The number of copies resulted from Magee's obtaining an incomplete First Folio (1623) with seventy-three leaves. He had planned to publish leaf books with one leaf each but then acquired some broken later Folios—a Second Folio (1632), a Third Folio (1663/1664), and a Fourth Folio (1685). He de-

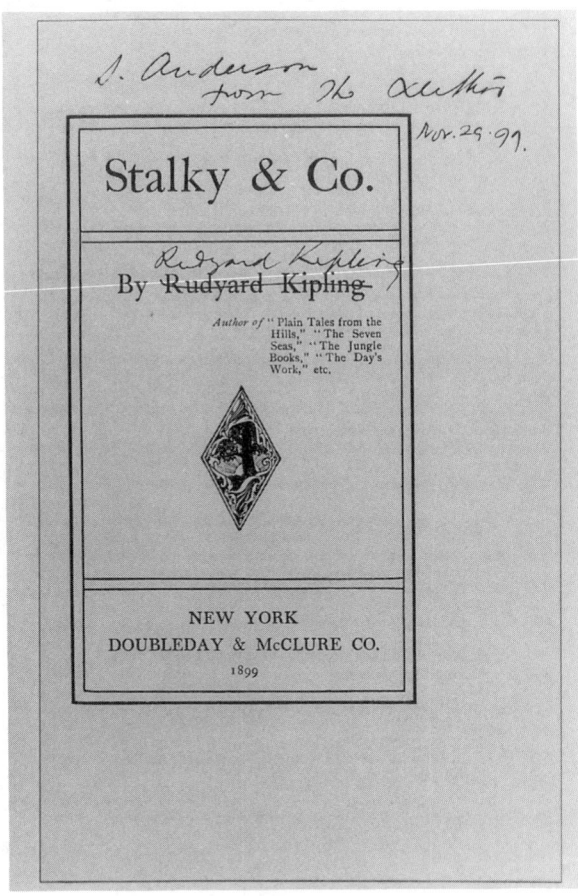

Inscribed title page for one of the books in the Victorian collection that Magee sold to Brigham Young University in 1959

cided instead to use one leaf from each of the four Folios to create seventy-three books, each with four leaves and an essay by Edwin E. Willoughby of the Folger Shakespeare Library in Washington, D.C. It quickly sold out. Subsequently Magee published a leaf book of the first English edition of Sebastian Brant's *The Ship of Fools* (1509), by the important London printer Richard Pynson; the original volume was one of the earliest examples in an English-language book of the roman typeface, the most commonly used typeface today. In addition to his own distinguished list of leaf books, Magee was an important influence on the Book Club of California's long tradition of leaf book publications.

Magee's greatest achievement as a bibliographer was the two-volume *Bibliography of the Grabhorn Press* (1940, 1957). The project represents a stupendous piece of investigative work: the firm kept poor records (some materials were stored in a bathtub, for example), and the Grabhorn staff's recollections of the firm's early efforts in Indiana, of its year in Seattle, and even of recent projects were quirky and

flawed. Occasionally, after experiencing vociferous denials, Magee had to produce a specific book in question to convince them that it was, indeed, a Grabhorn Press production. Fortunately for Magee, in 1933 he had purchased the personal library of the Grabhorn Press artist and designer Valenti Angelo, which contained many of the extremely rare early items from the firm's Indiana period. The 1940 bibliography, covering the years 1915 to 1940, comprises 358 entries and was compiled with the cooperation of the Grabhorn brothers, Edwin and Robert; Sherwood Grover, the chief pressman; and Jane Bissell Grabhorn, Robert's wife and a fine printer and writer in her own right. Carl Purington Rollins wrote in the *Saturday Review* that the volume "will take its place with the half dozen notable books printed in America in the past half century." The entries in the 1957 bibliography, dealing with the press's productions from 1940 through 1956, lack the spicy humor and playful anecdotes of the 1940 volume, but the bibliographic commentary is equally valuable. The Magee-Grabhorn relationship lasted for some thirty years, as Magee commissioned the Grabhorn Press for virtually all of his book publications and major catalogues.

In 1941 the venerable Boston firm Houghton Mifflin published *Jam Tomorrow: A Novel,* which Magee in *Infinite Riches* calls a novel written "in my unregenerate youth." *Jam Tomorrow* is a delightful comedy in which inside jokes and playful names—Lady Millicent Vanely (a scramble of Edna St. Vincent Millay, whom Magee knew), Lord Ravensbill, Tubby Oldersnaithe, Monstreley Castle—abound. The reader may recognize the influence of P. G. Wodehouse, whose work Magee collected. The plot revolves around a unique Victoria Jubilee stamp from a mythical British colony, Putumayo, that is shamelessly inflated in value to be sold to an American plumbing magnate and philatelist. The book was widely and favorably reviewed and went through two printings.

The Hundredth Book: A Bibliography of the Publications of The Book Club of California and a History of The Club (1958) was Magee's third major bibliographic endeavor in book form. When he began working on the project Magee discovered that the Book Club of California's records, which had been assembled for the most part by volunteers, were extensive but in utter disarray; thus, what had seemed to be a simple writing and editing assignment had become a major task of research and organization. The bibliography was designed and printed by the Grabhorn Press in an edition of

David and Dorothy Magee in his San Francisco bookshop, 1973 (photograph by Proctor Jones)

four hundred copies in an elegant fourteen-by-ten-and-a-quarter-inch trim size. It would serve as the model for the Book Club of California's *The Two Hundredth Book* in 1993.

Magee's *A Course in Correct Cataloguing; or, Notes to the Neophyte,* was published as a booklet in 1958 and revised in booklet form in 1959 and as an article in the *Antiquarian Bookman* in 1960. The pieces are minor classics in the lampooning of book dealers' cataloguing misdeeds and outright bloopers.

As a cataloguer Magee produced his magnum opus in *Victoria R. I.: A Collection of Books, Manuscripts, Autograph Letters, Original Drawings, etc., by the Lady Herself and Her Loyal Subjects, Produced during Her Long and Illustrious Reign* (1969–1970). The catalogue, in three volumes of 120 pages each, comprises 2,049 items and includes color frontispieces and many illustrations. Gordon W. Ray provided the preface, and 625 copies were printed at the Press of Robert Grabhorn and Andrew Hoyem. This massive catalogue, with its splendid and learned annotations, depicts what is considered the most extensive and important collection of Victorian literature ever assembled by a bookseller. At the end of the work Magee informed recipients that the entire collection had already been purchased by the Brigham Young University library: "We hope you will enjoy the perusal of these volumes even if denied the opportunity of purchase."

The title of Magee's 1973 autobiography is taken from a line in Christopher Marlowe's *The Jew of Malta* (produced circa 1590, published 1633): "As their wealth increaseth, so enclose / Infinite riches in a little room." The book displays Magee's characteristic zest, good taste, and grand style. Magee emerges in its pages as a book dealer who actually read what he sold. He relates inside stories of his dealings with Huntington, Chesterton, Wagner, Lyman, Bender, Sanford and Helen Berger, Bertram and Anthony Rota, J. K. Lilly Jr., and James Stephens. Among his anecdotes is an account of Doubleday's establishment of a San Francisco editorial office headed by the legendary Howard Cady, who later became editor in chief at Putnam and William Morrow in New York. Magee gave Cady the manuscript that would become the new office's first book: *920 O'Farrell Street* (1947), tales of Jewish-American life in San Francisco by Harriet Levy, the aunt of Magee's friend Ruth Elkins. Magee suggested that Levy also write about her experiences in Paris in the bohemian circle of Gertrude Stein, Alice B. Toklas, Pablo Picasso, and Henri Matisse in the 1920s; she did so, but her account was considered too libelous to publish. At Magee's urging, the manuscript was deposited in the Bancroft Library with instructions that it be sealed for twenty years.

Magee also tells the story of "the William Morris lot": while visiting Anthony Rota's London bookshop Magee learned of the existence of an enormous archive of the Morris, Marshall, Faulkner Company, founded by William Morris—the firm that made the Morris chair, the Morris wallpapers, and the tapestries, stained-glass windows, and countless other objects that decorated British homes during the latter half of the nineteenth century. The archive included "portfolios bulging with framed watercolors, tiles, pots, and a heap of books." Magee bought the entire lot and sold it to his friend Sanford Berger, a Berkeley architect and noted Morris collector. Today the Sanford and Helen Berger Collection is considered the finest Morris collection in the world.

Magee served as editor in chief of the Book Club of California's *Quarterly News-Letter* in 1950 and again from 1959 until 1971. He also served as president of the club and of the Antiquarian Booksellers Association of America, and as Master of the Press for the Roxburghe Club of San Francisco. He died of cancer on 17 July 1977; his wife, Dorothy Wilder Magee, had died two months earlier. At the time of his death Magee was working on a leaf book of the sixteenth-century Douay Bible—the first Catholic translation of the Bible into English—and had stored the leaves at the offices of the Book Club of California. The leaves were later rediscovered, and the book was published by the club in 1990 as *The Rhemes New Testament: Being a Full and Particular Account of the Origins of Printing, and Subsequent Influences of the First Roman Catholic New Testament in English with the Divers Controversies Diligently Expounded for the Edification of the Reader by Decherd Turner.*

David Magee is a major figure in twentieth-century bibliography and antiquarian bookselling. His catalogues are superb examples of critical evaluation, scholarship, and California fine-press printing. Those who visited his shop recall the Grabhorn-printed announcement he placed on the front door on suitable occasions:

> Notice to Patrons
>
> I have been obliged through sheer weight of fatigue and hunger to quit my post and repair to the nearest house of public refreshment until I have recovered my usual composure. This will probably transpire by a quarter past one o'clock post-meridian, at which time I shall reappear.
> DM.

Interview:

Ruth Teiser, *Bookselling and Creating Books: David Bickersteth Magee* (Berkeley: The Bancroft Library, University of California, Berkeley, Regional Oral History Office, 1969).

Papers:

The Department of Special Collections, Gleeson Library, University of San Francisco, has a small collection of David Magee printed and association ephemera, assembled by D. Steven Corey. More association items and ephemera are in the Book Club of California library, San Francisco. The David and Dorothy Magee papers, dating from 1947 to 1977 and comprising some 150 boxes, are in The Bancroft Library, University of California, Berkeley, a gift from the Magees' daughter, Jane Lundin. Access to all the Magee collections is restricted; prior arrangement is required.

Linton R. Massey

(27 January 1900 – 9 November 1974)

Edmund Berkeley Jr.
University of Virginia Library

BOOK: *William Faulkner: "Man Working," 1919–1962. A Catalogue of the William Faulkner Collections at the University of Virginia* (Charlottesville: Bibliographical Society of the University of Virginia, 1968).

SELECTED PERIODICAL PUBLICATIONS–
UNCOLLECTED: "The Voice of Urraca," *Smart Set,* 73 (1924): 55–58;
"Bibliographia Virginiana or Ledgerdemania," *Virginia Librarian,* 2 (1956): 41–42;
"Notes on the Unrevised Galleys of Faulkner's *Sanctuary,*" *Studies in Bibliography: Papers of the Bibliographical Society of the University of Virginia,* 8 (1956): 195–208.

Linton R. Massey is identified with the William Faulkner collections at the University of Virginia–those that he assembled and donated and those that came to the university largely through his friendship with Faulkner. But he should also be remembered as the pillar under the Bibliographical Society of the University of Virginia, which he served anonymously as a financial supporter and as president in 1948–1949 and from 1951 until his death in 1974.

Linton Reynolds Massey was born in Marietta, Georgia, on 27 January 1900 to John and Elma Massey. He lived in Washington, D.C., prior to World War I and trained as a naval aviation cadet, but the war ended before he saw active service. He then entered the University of Pennsylvania, from which he graduated in 1922. While in college he had begun submitting short stories to magazines, and in 1924 his story "The Voice of Urraca" was published in the *Smart Set,* edited by H. L. Mencken and George Jean Nathan.

Returning to Washington, Massey took a position with the Ford Motor Company. On 28 September 1926 he married Mary Ord Preston of Washington. After Massey retired from business the couple moved to their estate, "Kinloch," in Keswick, near

Linton R. Massey

Charlottesville, Virginia. There Massey supervised the extensive farming operation, renovated the estate's eleven gardens, and wrote unsigned book reviews for the *Virginia Quarterly Review.*

The Masseys shared a love of book collecting, with Mary concentrating on botanical books; her collection was ultimately donated to the Folger Library in Washington, D.C. Linton built broad collections of works by fiction writers, including Ernest Hemingway, James Joyce, Sinclair Lewis, Sherwood Anderson, Evelyn Waugh, Aldous Huxley, Eudora Welty, and Peter Taylor as well as many lesser-known Southern novelists and short-story writers.

His interest in Faulkner began when he read *As I Lay Dying* (1930); among the treasures he ac-

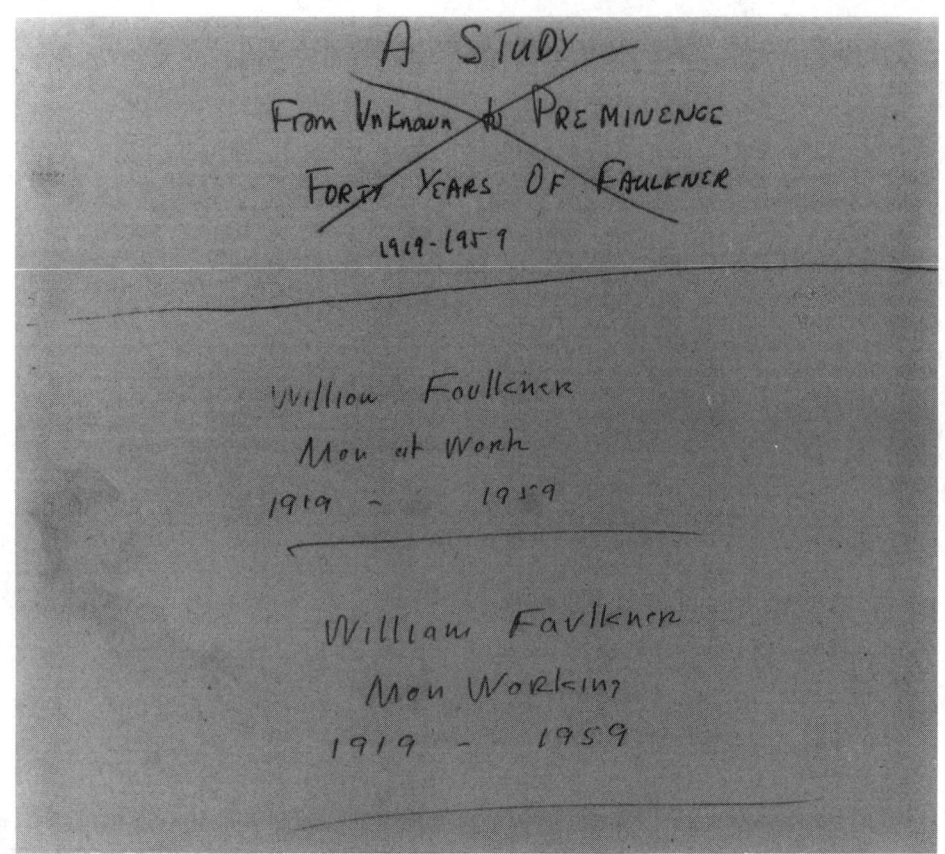

William Faulkner's suggested titles for the exhibition from the Massey Collection at the University of Virginia in 1959. The one at the bottom was selected (from Linton R. Massey, William Faulkner: "Man Working," 1919–1962, *1968).*

quired at a time when few others were interested in Faulkner was a copy of *The Marble Faun* (Boston: Four Seas, 1924) for $12.50.

The Bibliographical Society of the University of Virginia was founded in 1947. Its early years were a period of constant financial struggle, and the Masseys' generosity was largely responsible for the organization's survival. But Linton Massey's involvement was far more than monetary. After Fredson Bowers, editor of *Studies in Bibliography: Papers of the Bibliographical Society of the University of Virginia,* thanked him for a donation, Massey replied on 18 April 1949 that Bowers's letter "lets me share some of your enthusiasm for the Society, and at the same time gives me this chance to put into writing some of the plans I have advanced orally to John [John Cook Wyllie, then curator of rare books and later university librarian at the University of Virginia]. I am anxious to have it understood clearly that my motives in presenting these ideas spring solely from my interest in the Society itself, just as I have for similar reasons requested anonymity for my recent action." He went on to suggest several remedies for

the society's financial problems. He believed that the organization should not depend on private donors but should lay "plans for permanent financing . . . at once." While "our *Papers* should be as scholarly, erudite and technical as you can conjure them into being, our talks before the Society could be leavened with less heady stuff. . . . Let us have also, as a means of attracting a somewhat wider audience even unto the more literate students, extemporaneous talks." He listed a wide variety of possible topics for the talks, which he believed could be offered "without any lessening our dignity or permitting any indecent lifting of our academic gowns." Massey would put these ideas into practice during his twenty-five-year tenure as president of the society, but the organization would continue to struggle—especially for funds to publish the annual *Studies in Bibliography* volumes. Massey particularly advocated involving students in the society's activities: he strongly supported the annual awards given to student book collectors, a society tradition that continues today, and the presentation of talks by graduate students at society meetings. He also promoted joint meetings with such groups as the Bibliographical Society of America and the Grolier Club.

Wyllie often called on Massey for advice about acquisitions for the rare-book collection in areas in which Massey was knowledgeable. Gothic novels were one of his interests, and he demonstrated his bibliographic knowledge in responding on 30 December 1954 to a query from Wyllie about adding some material to the noted library's Sadlier-Black Gothic Novel Collection:

> The 19th century comic books dignified as GOTHIC NOVELETTES in the memorandum which you sent me . . . are obviously chap-books of the period. Louise Savage and I have previously discussed the propriety of acquiring such ephemera for the Black collection; and while we agreed that a few might properly grace the collection there was at the same time no compulsion about the matter. They were as you know cheap and usually abridged versions of previously published novels. Not all chapbooks were gothic, as you also are aware . . . if you do not subscribe to our opinion, then by all means sign up for the Mathews list so that we may later confer and make such selections as your judgment and my purse may allow.

Wyllie acknowledged Massey's first gift of a Faulkner item to the University of Virginia Library on 26 February 1951: "This is to acknowledge with very cordial thanks your gift to the Rare Book Room of the limited, signed edition of Faulkner's *Notes on a Horse Thief,* 1950 [Greenville, Mississippi: Levee Press, 1951]. I have discovered to my real chagrin that the only other Faulkner now in the rare book collections is *This Earth* [New York: Equinox, 1932]." Massey delivered a paper on the unrevised galleys of Faulkner's *Sanctuary* (1931) before the Bibliographical Society on 23 March 1955; Bowers persuaded him to turn the talk into a paper, and it was published in *Studies in Bibliography* the following year. It was his only contribution to the journal.

In January 1956 Massey donated his collection of books by and about James Branch Cabell–described by Wyllie as "notable for their fine condition, many with the original dust jackets and many with laid in clippings of contemporary reviews"–to the University of Virginia Library.

Massey purchased items for his Faulkner collection from many dealers, and friends contributed as well. On 20 April 1957 Massey thanked Wyllie for "the paperback editions of the Faulkner novels, particularly the first editions of the separately printed THE WILD PALMS [New York: Penguin, 1948] and THE OLD MAN [New York: Signet, 1948]. . . . I had scorned all the paper-backs as being editions later than the first until I realized my mis-

take. Most of the resulting gaps have now been closed, with your much appreciated help." A month later he thanked Wyllie for another gift: "I am deeply grateful for your kindness in presenting to me . . . the early [*sic*] nineteenth century edition of Col. W. C. Falkner's novel, WHITE ROSE OF MEMPHIS [1881], which will go on my shelves together with your interesting letter referring to your own grandfather, John Henry Cook." (Col. William Clark Falkner was Faulkner's great-grandfather; Faulkner added the *u* to his last name in 1918.) Massey's knowledge of Faulkneriana was vast, as is illustrated in a letter to Wyllie of 24 November 1957:

> Under the Smith & Haas imprint of Faulkner's SANCTUARY there were six editions from the same plates; when Random House took over the property they issued a second impression of the sixth edition using the same binding, and then later still, using the same plates, Random House issued their Modern Library Edition. I have been able to acquire for my collection the first, second, fifth, and Modern Library editions; and no doubt the missing third, fourth, and two impressions of the sixth will reach my hands in the course of time.

On 15 February 1957 Faulkner arrived at the University of Virginia, where he had been named writer in residence. A friendship quickly grew among William and Estelle Faulkner; their daughter and son-in-law, Jill and Paul Summers; and Linton and Mary Massey. The Faulkners often made use of the guest cottage at Kinloch, and they enjoyed holiday dinners with the Masseys. The close relationship between Massey and Faulkner led to important developments for the University of Virginia Library, the first of which was a major exhibition of Faulkner materials at the library in 1959. Many items from Massey's collection were included in the exhibition, and Faulkner cleared out the attic at his home in Oxford, Mississippi, for it. Massey suggested six titles for the exhibition; Faulkner considered them and then wrote his own: "William Faulkner: Man Working, 1919–1959."

The success of the exhibition and a lack of shelf space at Kinloch led Massey to decide to donate his Faulkner Collection to the university. On 6 April 1960 he wrote Wyllie:

> I want to confirm our understanding that I am presenting to the Alderman Library my entire collection of the first editions, manuscripts, letters, memorabilia, and ephemera of William Faulkner. . . . This constitutes my entire collection, except for a few association items that will come to the Library in the course of time . . . after the collection has been inventoried, appraised and cataloged it may be made available to qualified applicants. . . . I am particularly anxious to have my gift

"Man Working," 1919–1962

WILLIAM FAULKNER

*A Catalogue of the William Faulkner Collections
at the University of Virginia*

Compiled by Linton R. Massey

With an Introduction by John Cook Wyllie

Published by the Bibliographical Society of the University of Virginia
Distributed by the University Press of Virginia, Charlottesville

*Title page for Massey's catalogue of the Faulkner collections at the
University of Virginia, compiled with the aid of graduate students*

called the Faulkner Collection; and I hope you will help
me in concealing the identity of the donor.

The appraisal of the collection revealed that it
included more than 280 editions, variant issues, and
proof copies of books by Faulkner. Many of the first
editions had inscriptions—including a copy of *This
Earth* with a Faulkner signature, below which Faulkner had added in 1954 "This is a forgery" and his actual signature. Also included were about 180 magazine articles by and about Faulkner, 65 anthologies
with similar articles, 37 handwritten and typed
Faulkner letters, several short manuscripts for stories by Faulkner, paper and microfilm copies of theses about Faulkner, photographs, and other material. Although Massey had wished his identity kept
secret, soon a modest bookplate was designed for
the "Massey-Faulkner Collection."

Massey's gifts to the collection continued after
his original donation; he wrote Wyllie on 5 February 1962: "This Collection will continue to grow, I
am convinced, until it establishes itself as the largest
and most comprehensive devoted to a single, contemporary author." Massey worked diligently toward this goal, seeking and buying items and coop-

erating with library staff to ensure that microfilm
copies of dissertations about Faulkner were acquired for the collection.

In December 1960 Faulkner established the
William Faulkner Foundation; its articles of incor-
poration stated that its purpose was "to promote, encourage and advance knowledge, understanding
and appreciation of American literature, and, in particular, the works of American novelists." Other
goals were to assist in the education of "worthy negro students from the State of Mississippi" and "to
acquire source materials and to make such materials
available for study and examination." Before his
death in 1962 Faulkner gave the foundation some
funds as well as some of the manuscripts he had deposited in the University of Virginia Library; in his
will he bequeathed the remainder of the manuscripts to the foundation. Massey was president of
the foundation for most of the ten years of its existence. Its two most ambitious undertakings were the
establishment of the William Faulkner Prize for the
best first novel by an American and an award for the
best novels from various Latin American countries.
The first American award, for 1961, was to John
Knowles for *A Separate Peace*. The foundation's
funds were always extremely limited, and by 1970 it
was moribund. The directors dissolved it, transfer-
ring its assets to the University of Virginia. Thus,
joined permanently to the Massey-Faulkner Collection in the University of Virginia Library were the
manuscripts Faulkner had lent the library for the
1959 exhibition.

Massey had given the library a splendid collection of Southern cookbooks in 1964; there were also
many smaller donations of books as well as gifts of
cash and stock, always with strictures against publicity. Since 1960 he had been working on a catalogue of
the Faulkner collections at the university; it was a massive undertaking, and he drew others, including
graduate students at the university such as William S.
Kable, Jeffrey T. Gross, and Matthew J. Bruccoli into
the effort. Each entry was verified by four experts.
*William Faulkner: "Man Working," 1919–1962. A Cata-
logue of the William Faulkner Collections at the University of
Virginia* was published in 1968 with the imprint of the
Bibliographical Society of the University of Virginia,
of which Massey was then president. In the preface he
wrote, "This book makes no pretensions toward descriptive bibliography; it is not a check list, nor does it
advance any claims to completeness. . . . Despite these
and other omissions, a great quantity of source materials is readily at hand for research scholars, with
pointed emphasis on printed articles appearing in
Faulkner's own lifetime." Massey thanked Wyllie,
who had "advised, consoled, and, above all, encour-

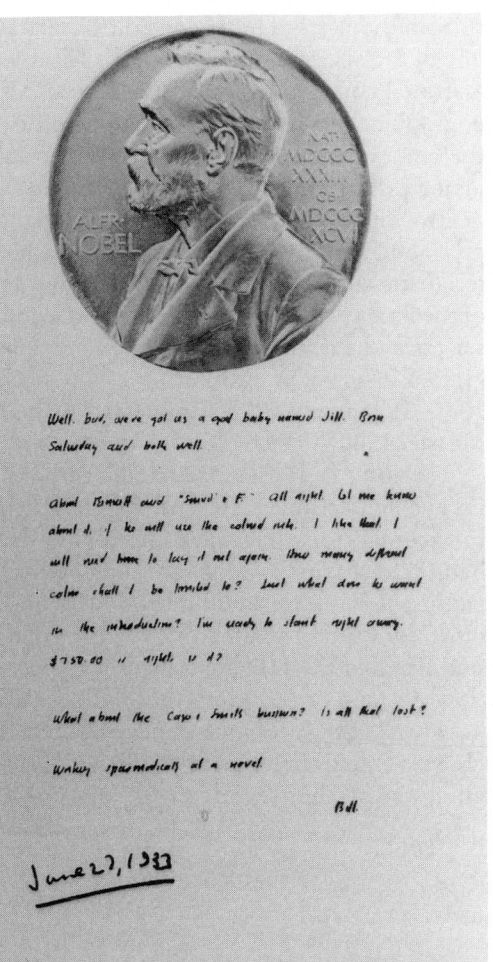

Pamphlet that was inserted in copies of Massey's Faulkner catalogue distributed at the lecture he presented at the University of San Francisco, 21 January 1968

aged during those forbidding moments when enthusiasm for the job in hand dwindled to the point where it became indistinguishable from apathy."

The Bibliographical Society continued to need his attention. As Kendon Stubbs, associate university librarian and assistant secretary-treasurer of the society, was to write in a letter of 27 November 1974, after Massey's death:

Linton's great gift was to be a gadfly to all of us, making sure that [Secretary-Treasurer] Pat Shutts' accounts were up-to-date or that I wrote to prospective authors, helping [University Press of Virginia director] Walker [Cowen] determine the retail price of a [society] publication, worrying with Fred [Bowers] about the costs of composition for studies. Even in a coldly objective analysis of administrative practices, it is hard to conceive that the Society would have survived without his kind of constant and courteous attention to every detail.

Massey's stature as a collector and bibliophile was widely recognized. He was a member of the Grolier Club, the Association of International Bibliophiles, and the Roxburghe Club of San Francisco; a fellow of the Morgan, Folger, and Newberry Libraries; and an associate of the libraries of Harvard, Yale, Princeton, and Brown Universities, the Gleason Library of the University of San Francisco, and the University of Virginia Library. In addition to being a member of the Bibliographical Society of the University of Virginia, he was a member of the bibliographical societies of America, London, Oxford, Cambridge, and Edinburgh.

Massey died on 9 November 1974. In his will he left $25,000 in trust to the University of Virginia, the income to be used for maintaining or adding to the Massey-Faulkner Collection.

The University of Virginia honored Massey's memory in several ways. With its own funds and contributions from his friends the library purchased one of the six copies of Faulkner's hand-lettered, illustrated copies of his play *The Marionettes;* the Bibliographical Society published a facsimile edition in the summer of 1975. The library also mounted a major exhibition that opened a year after Massey's death. The exhibition's title was derived from that given by Faulkner to the 1959 exhibit of his own material and subsequently used for Massey's catalogue of the Faulkner collections: "Man Collecting: Manuscripts and Printed Works in the University of Virginia Library On Exhibition . . . 16 November 1975–31 January 1976: Honoring Linton Reynolds Massey 1900–1974."

Linton R. Massey was a collector of cool, critical eye, impeccable taste, and the voracious appetite for acquisitions that mark all great collectors. He had the discerning judgment to recognize early the genius of William Faulkner and the means to acquire everything related to the writer that he could find. He had the rare good fortune to become an intimate friend of the subject of his collecting, whom he was able to influence to benefit the collections. He was a great benefactor to the University of Virginia and its library, donating not only his great Faulkner collection but also many other collections and gifts. His contributions to the Bibliographical Society of the University of Virginia ensured the organization's survival. A modest man, he avoided taking credit for many of his benefactions to the university and the society. His name will always be honored at the University of Virginia.

References:

Fredson Bowers, "Linton Reynolds Massey," *Chapter and Verse: A Report to the Associates of the University of Virginia Library,* 3 (1975): 5–8;

Joan St. C. Crane, "A Memorial to Linton Massey: William Faulkner's 'Marionettes,'" *Chapter and Verse: A Report to the Associates of the University of Virginia Library,* 3 (1975): 9–10.

Papers:

The University Archives, Special Collections Department, University of Virginia Library, holds records of the Bibliographical Society of the University of Virginia, certain of Linton R. Massey's personal papers, and his correspondence with John Cook Wyllie.

John Quinn
(14 April 1870 – 28 July 1924)

Joseph Rosenblum

BOOKS: *A Plea for Untaxed Contemporary Art: Memorandum in Regard to the Art Provisions of the Pending Tariff Bill* (New York: Association of the American Painters & Sculptors, 1913);

The Irish Home-Rule Convention, by Quinn, George William Russell, and Sir Horace Plunkett (New York: Macmillan, 1917);

The Library of John Quinn, by Quinn and Vincent O'Sullivan (5 parts, New York: Anderson Galleries, 1923–1924); republished, with a list of sale prices, as *Complete Catalogue of the Library of John Quinn* (2 volumes, New York: Anderson Galleries, 1924).

SELECTED PERIODICAL PUBLICATIONS– UNCOLLECTED: "Modern Art from a Layman's Point of View," *Arts and Decoration,* 3 (March 1913): 155–158, 176;

"Roger Casement, Martyr: Some Notes for a Chapter of History by a Friend Whose Guest He Was When the War Broke Out," *New York Times Magazine,* 13 August 1916, pp. 1–4;

"James Joyce, A New Irish Novelist," *Vanity Fair,* 8 (May 1917): 49, 128;

"Jacob Epstein, Sculptor," *Vanity Fair,* 9 (October 1917): 76, 114;

"Why Art Should Not Be Taxed," *Bulletin of the Metropolitan Museum of Art, New York,* 13 (September 1918): 198–199.

John Quinn

In the 1925 *Year Book* of the Association of the Bar of the City of New York, Richard Campbell wrote of John Quinn, "Whatever he did in life, he did with passionate intensity. If it was worth doing at all he considered it to be worth all of the exact thought, the penetrating precision that long training and experience could command." The echo of William Butler Yeats's poem "Second Coming" (1921) in Campbell's first sentence is apt because Quinn assembled a virtually complete collection of Yeats's manuscripts and first editions to 1923. An avid book lover throughout his life, Quinn built a library filled with the most important manuscripts of the early twentieth century, most notably T. S. Eliot's *The Waste Land* and James Joyce's *Ulysses* (both published in 1922) and most of Joseph Conrad's pre–World War I fiction. Not just a collector, Quinn acted as patron, literary agent, and—when necessary—attorney for Irish and English authors whose genius he recognized before most of his contemporaries. Quinn played a similar role in the modern-art movement. His judgments proved prescient and his support useful in securing the recognition of Georges Seurat, Gwen John, Jacob Epstein, and the Vorticists. In 1966 Alfred H. Barr of the Museum of Modern Art called Quinn the greatest American collector of early-twentieth-century art.

John Quinn was born at Tiffin, Ohio, on 14 April 1870; he was the oldest of the eight children of James William and Mary Quinlan Quinn. Both of his parents were emigrants from Ireland, his father from County Limerick and his mother from County Cork. Throughout his life Quinn admired Irish literature, and his earliest artistic passion was for Irish paintings. Shortly after John Quinn's birth the family moved to Fostoria, Ohio, where the elder Quinn became a successful baker. John attended the local public schools, graduating from Fostoria High School in 1888. Already he had shown himself a book lover. As Quinn wrote of the sale of his library in a 21 January 1924 letter to James Joyce,

> This collection of books goes back to 1887, when I bought $237 worth of books with money that my mother gave me, among them Walter Pater's first editions and a first edition of [Thomas] Hardy. She came into the room while I was on my hands and knees gloating over the treasures, and I can see her smile yet as she said: "Well, how long will they last you?"

Quinn offered similar recollections to Charles Culp Burlingham in August 1918: "I became a collector of books almost as soon as I ceased to be collector of marbles, and gave my marbles and bicycle away." Dr. U. H. Squires, principal of Fostoria High School, encouraged Quinn's bibliophily, and, as Quinn's letter to Joyce suggests, Quinn bought the works of Walter Pater, Thomas Hardy, William Morris, and George Meredith as their books were published.

In the fall of 1888 Quinn matriculated at the University of Michigan but remained only a year because he was chosen as private secretary to former Ohio governor Charles Foster, whom Quinn had nominated to run for Congress before Quinn himself could vote. President Benjamin Harrison had chosen Foster as secretary of the treasury, and Foster took his young protégé with him to Washington, D.C. Despite this early association with a Republican administration and a long friendship with Theodore Roosevelt, Quinn became active in the Democratic Party, serving as a delegate to the national conventions of 1908 and 1912.

In Washington Quinn continued his studies, attending the Georgetown University law school in the evenings and taking his law degree in 1893. He then went to Harvard University to take a second law degree, with a concentration in international law. While at Harvard he also studied philosophy under William James and aesthetics under George Santayana. After graduating from Harvard in 1895, Quinn began clerking for Gen. Benjamin F. Tracy of New York at ten dollars a week. Quinn spent his spare time at the Lenox Library at Seventieth Street and Fifth Avenue, where he read philosophy, theology, and literature. Quinn became one of the leading corporate lawyers of his day, and his colleagues attested to his legal knowledge. His passions, however, were literature and art; law provided the means for him to enjoy what he really loved. He wrote to George William Russell (better known by his pseudonym Æ) on 8 June 1915,

> If I had the time I should like to take up painting, and if I had more time I should like to take up writing. And if I had the money I should quit practicing law and would like to edit a paper and to gather some live young men around me.

When the bookseller Laurence J. Gomme offered Quinn a deluxe edition of William Blackstone's *Commentaries on the Laws of England* (first published 1765–1769), the lawyer replied on 7 December 1914, "I take great pride that I have not a single law book in my library of twelve or fifteen thousand volumes."

In 1900 Quinn became a junior partner in the law firm of Alexander and Colby. While there he gained recognition in the financial community as legal adviser to Thomas Fortune Ryan in the reorganization of the Equitable Life Assurance Company. In 1906 Quinn established his own practice at 31 Nassau Street, near Wall Street, in the National Bank of Commerce, which he served as legal counsel. He remained at that address for the rest of his career, which proved successful. In 1922 he paid income taxes of $25,424, indicating an income of somewhat more than $90,000. At the time of his death his estate was valued at $500,000, not including his extensive art collection.

Quinn regarded the Equitable Life Assurance Company reorganization as a turning point in his professional life, but an equally important milestone in his life was his first trip to Great Britain in the summer of 1902. In London he bought ten paintings from artist Jack Yeats and commissioned portraits of John O'Leary, Douglas Hyde, and George William Russell, his heroes of contemporary Irish politics and culture. In Ireland Quinn met Jack Yeats's brother, poet William Butler Yeats, whom Quinn had already read and admired, as well as George

Moore and Douglas Hyde. Quinn introduced Yeats to the works of Friedrich Nietzsche.

Back in the United States by October, Quinn helped organize a New York branch of the Irish Literary Society, which held its first meeting at Sherry's restaurant on 1 May 1903. Quinn hoped to raise money for Yeats, who was not well known in America, by arranging for the production of three of his plays as the society's first event. On 3 and 4 June 1903 at Carnegie Lyceum at Fifty-seventh Street and Seventh Avenue the society sponsored performances of *The Land of Heart's Desire* (first produced in London in 1894), *The Pot of Broth* (first produced in Dublin in April 1902), and *Cathleen-ni-Houlihan* (which opened in Dublin in April 1902). The plays just met expenses, but Quinn wrote optimistically to Yeats on 26 June 1903, "You are known now to a great many who before the Irish Literary Society of New York was started and the plays given did not know what you stood for."

When he returned to Ireland in 1903, Quinn became a patron of the Dun Emer crafts, predecessor of the Cuala Press, organized by Yeats's sisters, Lily and Elizabeth (Lollie). Quinn subscribed for multiple copies of their handprinted books, bought clothes and fabrics they were making, and promoted the sale of their products in America. Having urged Yeats to undertake a lecture tour of America to raise money, Quinn handled the arrangements and helped promote the tour, which took place in late 1903 and early 1904, earning the poet more than three thousand dollars. When James Gibbons Huneker was preparing an article on Yeats for the *New York Sun*, Quinn sent him a copy of Yeats's *In The Seven Woods* (New York & London: Macmillan 1903) and an astute commentary showing that Quinn read and understood the books he collected:

> Every year Yeats has grown more and more critical, more and more careful, more and more self-critical. . . . The loosening of the verse structure, instead of being a sign of decadence, is with Yeats the result of deliberate artifice and intention, and in this he is but following the best tradition of the last two hundred years.

Before returning to Ireland Yeats gave Quinn the page proofs of Lady Isabella Augusta Gregory's *Gods and Fighting Men* (London: J. Murray, 1904), and from Ireland Yeats wrote Quinn in March 1904, "I am facing the world with great hopes and strength and I owe it all to you and I thank you and shall always be grateful."

Yeats had much for which to thank Quinn. According to Allan Himber, editor of Quinn's letters to Yeats, Quinn regularly helped Yeats with securing

Quinn's bookplate, based on a drawing made by Jack B. Yeats in 1903

American copyrights for his works, acted as his New York agent, gave him legal advice and financial assistance, and worked at publicizing Yeats and the Irish literary movement of which he was part. In 1908 a group of actors, unhappy with the Abbey Theatre of Yeats and Lady Gregory in Dublin, came to America claiming to represent the Irish National Theatre. Quinn ensured that Yeats and Lady Gregory received royalties for the American performances of their plays. In that same year Quinn paid for the publication of fifty copies of Yeats's *The Golden Helmet* (New York: Quinn, 1908) to secure American copyright for the work. For the Yeats bibliography in volume eight of Yeats's *Collected Works* (Stratford-upon-Avon: Shakespeare Head Press, 1908) Quinn prepared the list of American editions. (Quinn had the only complete set of these works.)

The friendship between Yeats and Quinn was interrupted in 1909, when Quinn thought that the

First page of the manuscript for Joseph Conrad's first book, which Quinn bought from the novelist in 1912 (from Complete Catalogue of the Library of John Quinn, *1924). It was acquired by Dr. A. S. W. Rosenbach in November 1923 for $5,300.*

poet had been indiscreet in discussing Quinn's relationship with Dorothy Coates, the lawyer's mistress. For five years Quinn and Yeats did not correspond, but when Yeats came to America for his third lecture tour in 1914 the two met and resumed their ties. On 3 June 1914 Quinn wrote to Yeats,

> I think you know that I collect manuscripts, but only the manuscripts of men whose work I like. . . . So I should like to make arrangement with you, if you care to do it, to have you assemble your manuscripts, and pay you so much a year for them, depending on the quantity and the different things, taking articles as they are or poems as they are. . . . I would pay you a reasonable price for them, more perhaps than you would get of any dealer . . . . I would either make an arrangement for an annual amount with you, or for each article or essay or group of poems, after you have had them typewritten from your manuscript, depending on their length and their importance.

Quinn thus secured virtually all of Yeats's manuscripts to 1923, though he had to wait until after World War I to begin receiving them because German submarines rendered shipping uncertain for the duration of the hostilities.

On 16 May 1917 Yeats offered Quinn the manuscripts of *The Wild Swans at Coole* (published in 1917), "The Alphabet" (published as *Per Amica Silentia Lunæ,* in 1918), *At the Hawk's Well* (published in *Four Plays for Dancers,* 1921), *The Player Queen* (1922), and the essays "Witches and Wizards and Irish Folklore" and "Swedenborg, Mediums, and the Desolate Places" (both written in 1914 and published in 1920 in Lady Gregory's *Visions and Beliefs in the West of Ireland*). Quinn bought them all. His correspondence with Yeats also yielded Quinn 116 letters, eleven telegraphs, and one postcard from Yeats. Yeats dedicated the second volume of his autobiography, *The Trembling of the Veil* (London: Privately printed by T. W. Laurie, 1922), "To John Quinn my friend and helper and friend and helper of certain people mentioned in this book."

Quinn was equally supportive of the Irish playwright John Millington Synge, paying for American publication of his *In the Shadow of the Glen* (1904), *The Well of the Saints* (1905), and *The Playboy of the Western World* (1907). To help the ailing Synge, Quinn bought the manuscript of *The Playboy of the Western World* in 1908, and he offered to buy the manuscript for *Deirdre of the Sorrows* as soon as it was finished. Synge died before sending the manuscript, but Quinn still offered £30 for it and received it. To help the Synge estate Quinn also paid for publication of fifty copies of Synge's *Poems and Translations* (1909) and fifty copies of *Deirdre of the Sorrows*

(1910), thus securing the U.S. copyrights. His edition of the play cost him $250, and he spent $123 on a second printing to correct the errors in the first.

Quinn's manuscript holdings of works by Joseph Conrad were as impressive as his Yeats collection. In 1909 Quinn returned to Europe for the first time in five years. In London he met the author Arthur William Symons and Symons's companion, Agnes Tobin, who introduced Quinn to Conrad's works. In 1911 Quinn began buying Conrad manuscripts, paying between £40 and £150 each. In August 1911 Conrad sent Quinn manuscripts of *An Outcast of the Islands* (published in 1896), "Freya of the Seven Isles" (1912), and the preface to *Nigger of the Narcissus* (1897). In March 1912 Conrad sent Quinn manuscripts of *The Secret Agent* (1906), *Almayer's Folly* (1895), and the stories "Karain" (1897) and "The Brute" (1906). To replace the manuscript for "Karain," which sank with the *Titanic,* Conrad sent the manuscript for "The Informer" (1906). Conrad also gave Quinn the manuscript of Stephen Crane's "The Five White Mice" (1898), which he had been given by Crane.

The stream of Conrad manuscripts in 1912 continued with *Falk* (1903), and fragments of *Lord Jim* (1900), *Romance* (1903), by Conrad and Ford Madox Hueffer (later Ford Madox Ford), *Nostromo* (1904), and *The Nigger of the Narcissus* (1897). Conrad, who had found these manuscripts in the bottom of an old sea chest, wrote to Quinn on 12 May 1912, "How all this wreckage got preserved all these years is what astonishes me most." (Jessie Conrad, the author's wife, deserves the credit for their preservation.)

In May 1912 Conrad sent the roughly twelve hundred pages of the recently completed manuscript for *Chance* (1912). He also sent the manuscripts for "Typhoon" (1902), "Amy Foster" (1901), and "Tomorrow" (1902). Quinn paid £70 for these three manuscripts, and for another five Conrad added about three hundred pages of *Nostromo, Heart of Darkness* (1899), and *Lord Jim.* Conrad thought that by then he had sent Quinn every manuscript in his possession, but he soon found the holograph of his only play, *Tomorrow,* which Quinn bought for £40, a full manuscript of *The Nigger of the Narcissus* with Edward Garnett's editorial notes (£80), and 113 pages of "The Return." With these in hand Quinn had, as Conrad wrote, "a corner in" the author, being "in possession of *every scrap* of Conrad's MSS up to date, with the knowledge besides that you have befriended him in a time of difficulty." On 19 February 1913 Conrad again expressed his gratitude for a recent check: "The hundred pounds will pay last year's doctor bill and

Preface from the manuscript for William Butler Yeats's Reveries Over Childhood and Youth, *which Quinn bought from the poet in 1915 (from* Complete Catalogue of the Library of John Quinn, *1924)*

cover my overdraft at my bank. They save me from the necessity of putting aside the work I am busy with to write a couple of silly stories for the magazines." As long as Quinn kept his collection intact, Conrad promised not to sell or give away to others any of his manuscripts.

For a time Conrad kept that promise. In July 1914 Quinn paid Conrad £60 for the recently completed manuscript of *Victory* (1915) together with the first typed copy. In 1916 Quinn bought Conrad's manuscript description of his wartime trip to Poland, paying $320 that went to the relief of the Belgians. In February of that year Quinn paid Conrad £60 for the final typescript of *Victory,* the manuscript of *The Shadow-Line* (1917), and the promise of "The Humane Tomassov." But in 1919 Quinn learned from the British journalist Clement Shorter that

Conrad had sold the typed first draft of *The Arrow of Gold* (1919) and the incomplete manuscript of "Rescue" to British book collector and bibliographer Thomas James Wise. Conrad subsequently sent Quinn a few manuscripts, but Quinn did not buy any of the post–World War I works. When Conrad came to New York in 1923 he avoided Quinn despite the lawyer's efforts to meet with him. In *It Was the Nightingale* (1933) Ford Madox Ford described an interview with Conrad that explains Conrad's decision to sell to Wise. Noting Conrad's acknowledgment "that Quinn had been a real benefactor to him" and that Quinn was justly angry about not getting *The Arrow of Gold,* Ford continued:

But the war had been on. Conrad had been afraid of what the German submarines might do. He did not dare to send the MSS. to Quinn in New York and he had been dreadfully pressed for money. . . . And Mr. [Wise] had pressed and pressed, offering very large sums. . . . He had his family to think of.

Conrad had asked Ford to explain and apologize to Quinn, but Ford never did.

Another writer whom Quinn assisted and collected was Ezra Pound. In February 1910 Quinn wrote to the wife of his friend James F. Byrne, "I have done very little reading this winter," a statement belied by the long list of titles that follows in the letter. Among the works is *The Spirit of Romance* (London: Dent, 1910) by Pound, whom Quinn met that year. A close relationship did not begin until 1915, when Pound wrote in the 21 January 1915 *New Age* of "American collectors buying autograph MSS of William Morris, faked Rembrandts and faked Van Dykes." Quinn took the allusion personally, though the description hardly fit, and wrote to Pound on 25 February 1915 to defend himself. Pound wrote back, "My whole drive is that if a patron buys from an artist who needs money (needs money to buy tools, time and food), the patron then makes himself equal to the artist: he is building art into the world; he creates." This role was precisely the one Quinn had conceived for himself in relation to Yeats, Synge, and Conrad, and he went on to act similarly for Pound and his friends. Quinn served as Pound's literary agent in New York and urged Alfred A. Knopf to publish Pound's works. To encourage Knopf, Quinn agreed to buy forty copies of *'Noh' or Accomplishment* (New York: Knopf, 1917), by Pound and Ernest Fenollosa, and fifty copies of *Lustra* (New York: Knopf, 1917). Quinn read proofs of *Lustra* from the manuscript that Pound had sent him for his collection. Pound also gave him one of six proof sets printed by Elkin Mathews for the 1916 London edition of *Lustra*. Quinn bought not the promised fifty copies of the American edition but one hundred, which he had specially bound with a frontispiece portrait of the author. To enhance Pound's reputation in America Quinn paid $80 of the $100 cost of publishing T. S. Eliot's *Ezra Pound: His Metric and Poetry* (New York: Knopf, 1917), with Knopf absorbing the other $20. On 17 April 1917 Pound wrote to Quinn, "I can only say that I appreciate the cash and energy you are putting into booming my stuff. I will try to give you a run for your money." Soon thereafter Quinn also helped Pound to promote his friends' writings by subsidizing the British little magazine *The Egoist* and the New York–based *Little Review,* giving Pound, who had editorial positions with both magazines, considerable leverage in determining what they published.

Pound dedicated *Pavannes and Divisions* (New York: Knopf, 1918) to Quinn, who advanced $150 for the American publication (the money to be repaid in copies of the book), and again read proofs for Pound. Pound's *Instigations* (New York: Boni & Liveright, 1920) was also published through Quinn's efforts, and Quinn bought twenty-five copies. If not for Quinn, Pound claimed, his books would never have been published in America. Quinn had fulfilled Pound's—and his own—ideals of the true patron.

Pound introduced Quinn to T. S. Eliot and James Joyce, from whom Quinn would obtain two of the most important manuscripts in his collection. Early in 1918 Quinn, who was recovering from surgery for colon cancer, heard that the firm of Boni & Liveright was planning to publish an unauthorized edition of Eliot's poetry. Quinn investigated and discovered that the rumor was false. Eliot wrote to thank the lawyer for his efforts: "I appreciated it the more because I knew you had recently undergone a serious operation; I do not think that there are many people who, under such conditions, would bestir themselves so actively even for personal friends, still less for a man who was personally unknown to them."

Quinn secured American publication of Eliot's *Poems* (New York: Knopf, 1920), which was published a few days earlier by Ovid Press in London as *Ara Vos Prec.* Four copies of the London edition were printed on Japan vellum and bound in morocco. Eliot presented number one of these to Quinn. Quinn bought thirty-five copies of the American edition, characteristically distributing them to friends in his effort to familiarize readers with Eliot's poetry. Quinn negotiated the contract for the American edition of Eliot's *The Waste Land* (New York: Boni & Liveright, 1922). On 25 June 1922 Eliot wrote to Quinn, "I am sending you as quickly as possible a copy of the poem merely for your own interest, and I shall send you later the complete typescript with the notes in the form to be handed to the publisher." Quinn's biographer, Benjamin Lawrence Reid, suggests this first copy sent to Quinn is not the famous typescript with Pound's annotations, which Eliot also sent to Quinn and which Quinn's niece and goddaughter Mary Anderson Conroy sold to the New York Public Library in 1958 for $18,000. Eliot insisted on giving Quinn this second typescript, but Quinn wanted to compensate the poet and therefore asked to buy Eliot's other extant manuscripts. In January 1923 Quinn received the fifty-four leaves of the Pound-edited typescript of *The Waste Land* and a fifty-four-page notebook with six inserted pages of holograph poems. These po-

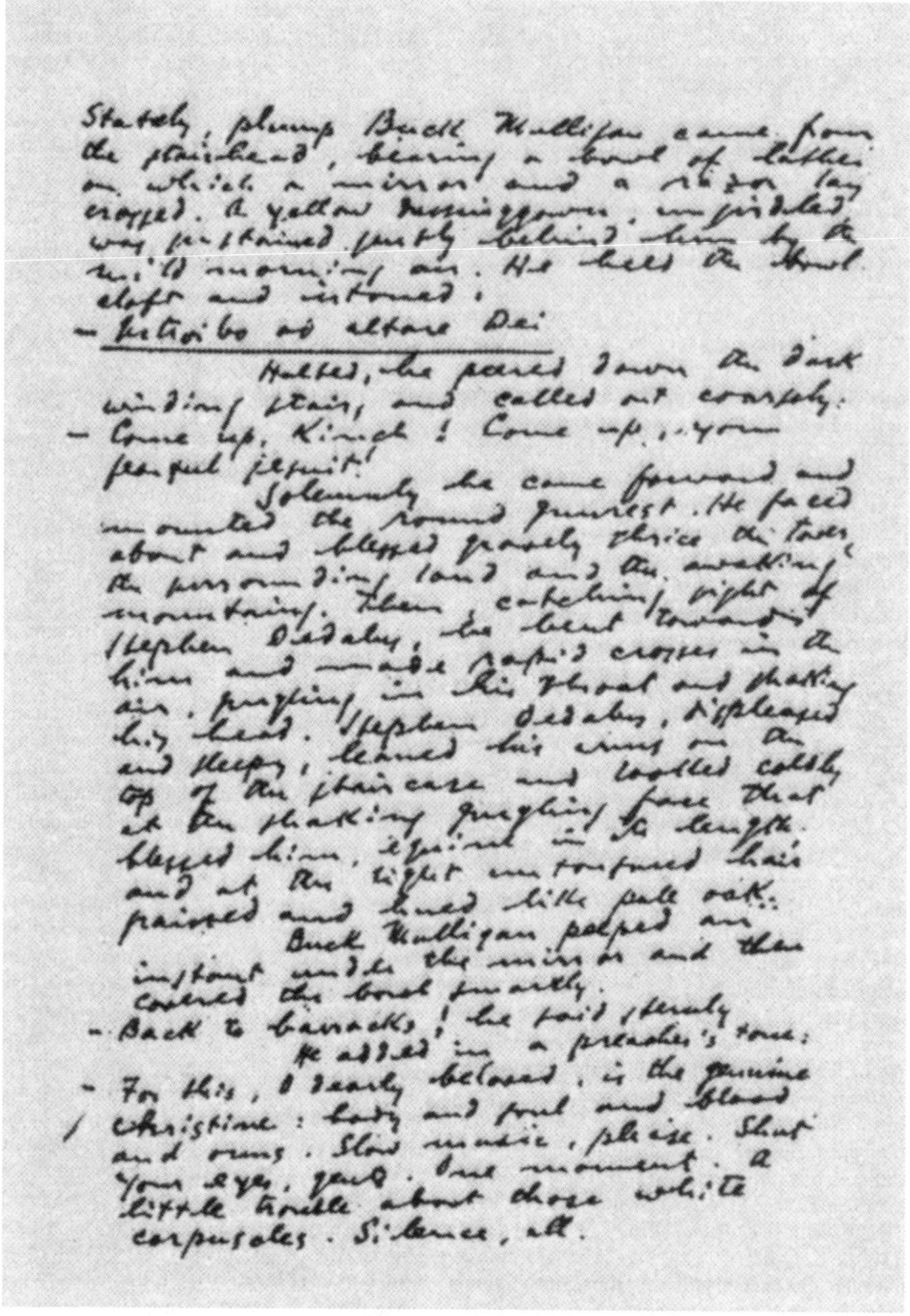

First page from the manuscript for James Joyce's Ulysses, *which Quinn bought from the novelist in installments, beginning in 1920 (from* Complete Catalogue of the Library of John Quinn, *1924). It was purchased by Dr. A. S. W. Rosenbach in January 1924 for $1,975.*

James Joyce, Ezra Pound, John Quinn, and Ford Madox Ford in Paris, 1923

ems, published as *Inventions of the March Hare* (New York: Harcourt Brace, 1997), offer valuable insights into the mind and craft of the young T. S. Eliot. Quinn took the notebook to the New York City bookseller James F. Drake, who appraised the manuscripts at two dollars a page, or $120 for the material excluding *The Waste Land*. Quinn sent Eliot a check for $140. Eliot wrote back on 12 March 1923, "I consider your payment for the manuscript very generous indeed, and feel that you have thwarted me in my attempt to repay you in some way for all that you have done." On 26 April 1923 Eliot again thanked Quinn, adding, "Perhaps I can only say that it is the greatest stimulus to me to commence the work I have in mind, which is more ambitious than anything I have ever done yet. And a stimulus to do my part to bring about the conditions which will make this work possible." Quinn was again acting as Pound's ideal patron, participating in the creation of literature. In addition to the Eliot manuscripts Quinn was also able to add to his collection twenty-two letters and six cables from Eliot, which are now in the Manuscript Division at the New York Public Library, having been donated by Mrs. Conroy.

In 1922, the year *The Waste Land* appeared, James Joyce's novel *Ulysses* was published in Paris by Sylvia Beach's Shakespeare and Company. Thus, two of the most important literary works of the twentieth century appeared almost simultaneously, and Quinn can claim some credit for the publication of both. Quinn's relationship with Joyce began in 1916 when, at Pound's urging, Quinn sent £10 to the Irish expatriate, who was then living in Zurich, Switzerland, and moved to Paris in 1920. Pound sent Quinn the manuscript of *A Portrait of the Artist As a Young Man,* which had been serialized in *The Egoist* (2 February 1914–1 September 1915) in the hope that Quinn could find an American publisher. Quinn was successful, and B. W. Huebsch of New York published the novel in 1916, providing 750 copies to *The Egoist* for publication in Great Britain. In 1917, to help Joyce further, Quinn offered $100 for the manuscript of *A Portrait of the Artist As a Young Man,* which was already in New York. For that sum Quinn also received seven pages of corrections for the novel and a single page of manuscript corrections for *Dubliners* (published in 1914). Quinn bought about thirty copies of the first edition of *A Portrait of the Artist As a Young Man,* as usual distributing copies to friends, including James Gibbons Huneker of the *New York Sun,* who praised the book in his article "Who Is James Joyce?" Quinn also promoted the book by writing an article for the May

*Catalogue for the first of five parts of the Quinn sale, considered
the greatest auction of modern books and manuscripts*

1917 issue of *Vanity Fair*. Quinn paid Joyce $125 for
the manuscript of his play *Exiles* (1918) and tried unsuccessfully to find an American producer for it. In
1920 Quinn began paying Joyce for portions of the
manuscript of *Ulysses*, eventually spending $1,200.
At the same time that he was buying the manuscript
in parts he was urging Margaret Anderson and Jane
Heap, editors of the *Little Review*, not to serialize the
novel because they risked prosecution for violating
the obscenity laws. Quinn feared, correctly, that if
the serialization were banned, no American publisher would bring out the work in book form, thus
depriving Joyce of substantial royalties (which
Quinn estimated at $1,500–$2,000). Quinn's fears
were justified. In September 1920 John Sumner of
the New York Society for the Prevention of Vice
swore out a warrant against the owners of the Washington Square Bookshop for selling the July–August
1920 issue of the *Little Review*, which carried the
"Nausikaa" episode of *Ulysses*. Quinn worked hard
to get the charges dismissed, and after that effort

failed, he defended the work unsuccessfully in
court. Further serialization was prohibited, and the
novel was not published in America until Random
House brought out its edition in 1934. Though
Quinn argued against banning the "Nausikaa" episode because it was too incomprehensible to be a
threat to public morality, he showed his appreciation of the work in a 21 June 1922 letter to Shane
Leslie, who criticized the work as "the suicide of the
whole Irish literary movement." Quinn was more
perceptive than Leslie, writing of *Ulysses*, "It is a
great tour de force, a very great work, indeed. . . .
Joyce is a great story-teller. He has done new things
with the English language. . . . Joyce has a great
sense of reality, a magical gift in the telling of a
story, and a style that is utterly his own." From Sylvia Beach, Quinn ordered five of the one hundred
copies of *Ulysses* printed on Dutch handmade paper
(350 francs each), three of the 150 copies on paper
D'Arches (250 francs each), and six of the 750 copies on less expensive handmade paper (150 francs
each). Altogether he spent $291.04 on copies of the
first edition. To avoid confiscation—the book was
banned in the United States, and customs officials
burned the copies they seized—Quinn had the volumes sent packed with works of art to prevent the
discovery of the books.

When Quinn sold his library in 1923–1924, he
placed a $2,000 reserve on the twelve-hundred-page
manuscript of *Ulysses*, intending to split the profits
with Joyce. Philadelphia bookseller A. S. W. Rosenbach secured the manuscript for $1,975. After pay-
ing the 15 percent seller's premium, Quinn realized
a profit of $478.75 and promised Joyce a check for
$239.37 as soon as Rosenbach paid him. Joyce re-
fused the sum as too small; he was especially angry
that Quinn had refused to sell two George Meredith
manuscripts for less than $1,400 but was letting
Ulysses go for only slightly more. Joyce hoped that
Rosenbach might sell the manuscript back, but after
briefly putting a $3,000 price on the work Rosen-
bach added it to his private collection.

Quinn's decision to sell his library was
prompted by several factors. He was becoming increasingly interested in French art and had resolved
to devote all his resources to the purchase of paintings. As early as 1909 he had written to Townsend
Walsh,

I am going to stop putting hundreds and in fact some
thousands a year into books. In fact I have got my collection about complete and I am not going into new
lines of book collecting. I am going in for some good art,
however. After all a picture is a more living thing than a
book. It represents life or a moment of life and the older

we get the more interest we ought to show in life and the less in a printed transcript of it.

Quinn did not stop buying books and manuscripts, adding between eight hundred and one thousand volumes a year to his collection for the rest of his life. He did, however, sell part of his collection in 1912. Before going to Europe in August 1911 Quinn had deposited his manuscripts in the Equitable Building for safekeeping. He retrieved them shortly before a fire struck the building. Recognizing the vulnerability of his collection and feeling the need for additional space—even though he had just moved from 79 Central Park West to a larger apartment on the ninth floor of 58 Central Park West at Sixty-sixth Street, where he would live for the rest of his life—Quinn decided to sell some of his manuscripts to Henry E. Huntington in spring 1912. Most of these were of works by dead authors: George Meredith, William Morris, George Gissing, Algernon Charles Swinburne. William Ernest Henley, Dante Gabriel Rossetti, and Thomas Hardy. Altogether Quinn sold Huntington 121 manuscripts, including twelve poems by Gissing, the final draft for Morris's *The Story of the Glittering Plain* (1890), and four essays by George Bernard Shaw. Having charged Huntington only what he himself had paid for the manuscripts plus whatever interest that sum would have earned, Quinn used the money to buy two oil paintings by the nineteenth-century French artist Pierre Puvis de Chavannes, *La Rivière* and *Le Vendage* (both executed in 1866); these two works cost him $28,000. In 1923 Quinn not only wanted more money to put into art, he also wanted more space in which to display it, and reducing his 18,000-volume library by two-thirds would help. Yet another reason for Quinn's decision to dispose of the bulk of his library was the sale of his apartment house in 1923. Quinn thought that he would be obliged to vacate his longtime residence, though at the last moment he was given a one-year extension on his lease.

Quinn and Vincent O'Sullivan prepared the catalogue, which listed 12,096 items. This catalogue is an important contribution to bibliography. As Carl L. Cannon wrote in *American Book Collectors and Collecting from Colonial Times to the Present* (1941),

Not only was [Quinn's] collection of "firsts" of many authors complete enough to constitute virtually a check list, but the biographical sketches that precede each author's works, the many portraits and facsimiles and full quotations from numerous manuscripts owned by Quinn, give it a literary flavor that well rewards casual reading.

The richness of Quinn's library in Irish and English literature makes the 1,205-page catalogue a comprehensive bio-bibliography of the major authors of the late nineteenth and early twentieth centuries. Author and bibliophile Christopher Morley praised Quinn's catalogue in the *New York Evening Post,* and the *Times Literary Supplement* for 22 November 1923 said that Quinn's "catalogue will always be useful as a book of reference" and mentioned the "brief and unconventional" biographical details that could not be found elsewhere because they are based on Quinn's personal knowledge of any correspondence with the writers.

On the back covers of each of the five parts of the catalogue Quinn had printed a quotation from the French author Edmond de Goncourt:

My wish is that my Drawings, my Prints, my Curiosities, my Books—in a word, these things of art which have been the joy of my life—shall not be consigned to the cold tomb of a museum, and subjected to the stupid glance of the careless passer-by; but I require that they shall all be dispersed under the hammer of the auctioneer, so that the pleasure which the acquiring of each one of them has given me shall be given again, in each case, to some inheritor of my own tastes.

To the first part of the catalogue Quinn added an introductory note explaining his reasons for the sale and describing his feelings for the books and manuscripts that had been an important part of his life, in some cases for decades. He concluded,

I cannot go through or attempt to write about or to tell what these books and manuscripts which contain a world of beauty and romance or enshrine the records of friendships and of interests and enthusiasms have meant or mean to me, for they seem to me to be a part of myself, even though I may smile a little at my own feeling.

The sale, described by Matthew J. Bruccoli as still "the greatest auction of modern literature," began at Mitchell Kennerley's Anderson Galleries, at 489 Park Avenue in New York City on 12 November 1923. The A–C catalogue covering this portion of the sale lists 2,272 items in its 236 pages; 230 of the lots were Conrad books and manuscripts. Quinn had paid about $10,000 for his Conrad collection; these items, lots 1780–2010, offered on the second evening of the auction, sold for about $111,000. New York dealer Gabriel Wells bought the manuscript of *Under Western Eyes* for $6,900. Composer and collector Jerome Kern bought the manuscript of "Youth" (1898) for $2,300. James F. Drake secured the 224 quarto pages of the manuscript for *Freya of the Seven Isles* for $3,500 and the

4929 ORIGINAL AUTOGRAPH MANUSCRIPT of "Exiles," written on 164 pages, quarto, together with title-pages and page of characters, 169 pages in all. In a crushed blue levant morocco solander case.
THE COMPLETE MANUSCRIPT, beautifully written in the author's unusually legible hand. Each of the title-pages is inscribed: "*Exiles: a play in three acts. By James Joyce*," and at the foot of each of these title-pages Joyce has written: "*Present address: Seefeldstrasse F 3ᵐ, Zurich: Switzerland.*"
Laid in with this Manuscript is an A.L.s. from Ezra Pound to Mr. Quinn, written on a wrapper for the Manuscript: "*Dear Mr. Quinn. Here at last are the two remaining acts of Joyce's Play.*" The mailing wrappers to Mr. Quinn in Ezra Pound's hand are also laid in.   *195.*

4930 EXILES. A Play in Three Acts. 12mo, boards, cloth back.   London, 1918   *4⁵⁰*
First Edition.

4931 EXILES. A Play in Three Acts. 12mo, boards, cloth back.
First American Edition.   New York, 1918   *.50*

4932 CHAMBER MUSIC. 16mo, cloth, uncut.   London, n.d. [1918]   *9⁵⁰*
First Edition.

4933 CHAMBER MUSIC. 12mo, boards, uncut.   New York, 1918   *1.*
First Authorized American Edition.

4934 EXILES. A Play in Three Acts. 12mo, cloth.   London, [1921]   *.25*
Second Edition.

4935 DUBLINERS. 12mo, cloth.   London, [1922]   *1⁵⁰*
Second Edition.

4936 ORIGINAL AUTOGRAPH MANUSCRIPT of "ULYSSES," written on over 1200 pages. In four blue morocco slip cases.
THE COMPLETE MANUSCRIPT of this remarkable work, one of the most extraordinary produced in modern times and hailed by critics as epoch-making in modern literature.   *1975.*
The first slip case contains: Part I: Telemachus, Proteus, Nestor. Part II: Calypso, Lotus Eaters, Hades, Eolus, Lestrygonians, Scylla and Charybdis.
The second slip case contains Part II continued, made up of the following: Wandering Rocks, Sirens, Cyclops, Nausikaa, Oxen of the Sun.
The third slip case continues Part II and contains: Penelope, Ithaca, and Part III down to page 618 of the book.
The fourth slip case contains from page 618 to the end of the work.
In a recent review of Ulysses by Mr. T. S. Eliot he refers to Mr. Aldington's attack upon Mr. Joyce as "a libel on humanity" and quotes Thackeray's shameful attack upon Swift, Thackeray having damned Swift for the conclusion of the Voyage to the Houyhnhnms, which Mr. Eliot writes "seems to me one of the greatest triumphs that the human soul has ever achieved." Referring to the form as well as the content of Ulysses, Mr. Eliot writes: "Psychology (such as it is, and whether our reaction to it be comic or serious), ethnology, and The Golden Bough

487

Priced page from the catalogue for the Quinn sale, held at the Anderson Galleries, New York, on 14–16 January 1924

235 pages of *The Shadow-Line* for $2,700. A. S. W. Rosenbach, who spent $72,000 overall at the Quinn sales, got the rest of the Conrad manuscripts, paying $6,000 for *Chance,* $5,300 for *Almayer's Folly,* $5,100 for "Typhoon," $4,700 for *Nostromo,* $4,500 for *The Nigger of the Narcissus,* $4,100 for *An Outcast of the Islands,* $3,900 for *Lord Jim,* the same price for *The Secret Agent,* $3,100 for *Falk,* $2,400 for "The Secret Sharer" (1910), $2,300 for "A Smile of Fortune" (1911), and $8,100 for the 1,139 pages of *Victory,* a record for a manuscript by a living author. Contrary to his usual practice, Rosenbach bought these items for his stock rather than for a collector who had commissioned him to secure them. He offered them to Henry E. Huntington, but the California collector thought the prices too high. Most of the Conrad manuscripts remained unsold at the time of Rosenbach's death in 1952.

Subsequent sessions of the Quinn sale were less successful. The second part of the sale, held on 10–12 December 1923, included books and manuscripts of Lady Gregory (75 items), the poet John Davidson (46 items), Thomas Hardy (69 items), John Galsworthy (80 items), and Lafcadio Hearn (71 items). The December sessions earned only $16,181.10 for 2,237 lots, and the highest price paid was $250 for the forty-seven-page manuscript of Hearn's "The Story of Mimi-Nashi-Hoïchi" (1903).

The third part of the sale—held on 14–16 January 1924 and covering the letters I–M) included extensive runs of Henry James (169 items), Rudyard Kipling (149 items), Andrew Lang (218 items), John Masefield (117 items), George Moore (142 items), and most notably, the manuscript of *Ulysses*. Prices were higher than in December—the rare first edition of Kipling's *Echoes* (Lahore, India: Civil and Military Gazette Press, 1884) went for $1,170, for example—but were still disappointing. The *Ulysses* manuscript failed to reach Quinn's reserve; the manuscript of Joyce's *Exiles* with a letter from Ezra Pound sold for $195, less than Quinn's $200 reserve. The 334-page manuscript of George Moore's *Esther Waters* (1894) brought only $600. Two manuscripts of George Meredith poems, "Alsace Lorraine: An Ode" and "Napoleon: An Ode," also failed to reach Quinn's reserve and were not sold. This part of the sale earned $31,705.85.

Part four of the Quinn sale, held on 11–13 February 1924 and covering letters M–S, offered Quinn's extensive holdings of materials by William Morris, one of Quinn's earliest enthusiasms (242 items). The 270-page manuscript of *The House of the Wolfings* (1889) brought $475. The first edition of Ezra Pound's *A Lume Spento* (Venice: A. Antonini, 1908), his first book, sold for a mere $52.50. Pound's second book, *A Quinzaine for the Yule* (London: Pollock, 1908), brought $3.25. Bruccoli notes that in 1984 a second printing of this rare book sold for $11,500. This portion of the sale also included sixty-two Dante Gabriel Rossetti items and ninety-eight by George Bernard Shaw. Like Morris, these two writers had interested Quinn from his youth. Altogether this part of the sale yielded about half the $32,000 Quinn had paid for the items, $16,967.70 for 2,201 lots. On 23 February 1924 Quinn wrote to the artist and critic Walter Pach, "I am getting sick and tired of all the blabber about the 'great' sale of my books. It was not a sale. It was a slaughter, the slaughter of each part being worse than the preceding part."

The final portion of the sale, which took place on 17–20 March 1924, was the largest, with 90 Robert Louis Stevenson items, 372 by Algernon Charles Swinburne, 277 by Arthur Symons, 54 by John Millington Synge, 117 by H. G. Wells, 149 by Walt Whitman, 180 by Oscar Wilde, and 273 by William Butler Yeats. Prices remained low. The twelve-page manuscript of Swinburne's "Athens" brought $35. Synge's typescript of *The Playboy of the Western World* (Synge composed on the typewriter) brought $750; *Deirdre of the Sorrows* sold for $410. The first edition of Whitman's *Leaves of Grass* (Brooklyn, N.Y., 1855) went for $160. Oscar Wilde's *The Happy Prince* (London: D. Nutt, 1888), inscribed by the author to his wife, went for $375. The manuscript of Yeats's "The

Wild Swans at Coole" brought $250. *Nine Poems Chosen from the Works of Williams Butler Yeats,* which Quinn had privately printed by Mitchell Kennerley in 1914, went for $12, about one-hundreth of its 1994 value. The total for part five was a disappointing $23,736.20 for 3,059 lots. Altogether the sale of the library realized $226,358.85. The average of $18.69 per lot is absurdly low. Without the Conrad items the average plunges to $9.71 per lot for a library filled with the gems of modern literature. Quinn estimated that after paying the 15 percent commission to the auction house and deducting the cost of books bought in for him because they failed to reach their reserve prices, he earned about $170,000 for material that had cost him about $250,000. Still, the sales gave Quinn money to buy paintings and some space in which to display them.

Quinn did not live long enough to increase or enjoy his art collection, but on 15 February 1924 he acquired Henri Rousseau's *La Bohémienne Endormie* (The Sleeping Gypsy) for 175,000 francs, or about $15,000. Of this painting, which is now in the Museum of Modern Art in New York City, Quinn wrote to the French art dealer Henri-Pierre Roche on 14 March 1924:

> It is indeed one of the most beautiful paintings that I have ever seen. . . . Rousseau was perhaps at the height of his power when that picture was painted in 1897. . . . This painting has a wonderful depth of color that even the later ones lack. . . . It is, as you say, "the gem of my collection."

This last statement is truly high praise because Quinn owned not only the best private collection of late-nineteenth- and early-twentieth-century British literature but also the finest private collection of modern art, on which he spent some half a million dollars over two and one-half decades and which sold, mostly after his death, for about $750,000. Among his acquisitions were more than sixty works by Pablo Picasso, fifty by Camille Pissarro, nineteen by Henri Matisse, eleven by Georges Seurat, and twenty-seven sculptures by Constantin Brancusi. Quinn had the most extensive private holdings of Matisse, Picasso, Rousseau, and Seurat. At the time of his death from liver cancer on 28 July 1924, Quinn owned about 600 oil paintings and 1,900 other works of art, including drawings, sculptures, and Oriental artifacts.

For his support of modern art the Association of American Painters and Sculptors made him an honorary member in 1913. In 1915 he was elected an honorary fellow of the Metropolitan Museum for life, and in 1919 he was named to the French Legion of Honor.

On the day following Quinn's death the *New York Sun* carried an obituary, probably written by Quinn's longtime friend Frederick James Gregg, which read in part:

> John Quinn . . . was probably the most courageous patron of the arts of his time. . . . He bought the pictures, sculptures and manuscripts of men whose names, when he made the venture, were known to but few but whose eminence is now undisputed.

This statement is even truer at the end of the twentieth century than it was in 1924. Aline B. Saarinen best summarized Quinn's achievement in 1958, when she wrote: "By the time he died . . . , John Quinn had become the twentieth century's most important patron of living literature and art." His library and art collection reflect a keen understanding, a love of beauty, and a desire to participate in the creation of that beauty by supporting writers, painters, and sculptors. What Percy Bysshe Shelley wrote of John Keats in "Adonais" (1821) applies to Quinn as well. Through his collecting Quinn became "a portion of the loveliness / Which once he made more lovely."

Letters:

The Letters of John Quinn to William Butler Yeats, edited by Alan Himber with the assistance of George Mills Harper (Ann Arbor, Mich.: UMI Research Press, 1983);

On Poetry, Painting, and Politics: The Letters of May Morris and John Quinn, edited by Janis Londraville (Selinsgrove, Pa.: Susquehanna University Press, 1997).

Biography:

B. L. Reid, *The Man from New York: John Quinn and His Friends* (New York: Oxford University Press, 1968).

References:

Matthew J. Bruccoli, *The Fortunes of Mitchell Kennerley, Bookman* (San Diego: Harcourt Brace Jovanovich, 1986);

Walter Pach, *Memorial Exhibition of Representative Works Selected from the John Quinn Collection* (New York: Art Center, 1926);

Aline B. Saarinen, "John Quinn," in her *The Proud Possessors: The Lives, Times and Tastes of Some Adventurous American Art Collectors* (New York: Random House, 1958), pp. 206–237;

Harvey Simmons, "John Quinn: An Exhibition to Mark the Gift of the John Quinn Memorial Collection," *Bulletin of the New York Public Library,* 72 (November 1968): 569–586;

James L. Walsh, "John Quinn: Lawyer, Book Lover, Art Amateur," *Catholic World,* 120 (November 1924): 176–184.

Papers:

The New York Public Library has a large collection of Quinn's correspondence.

Harry Ransom

(22 November 1908 – 19 April 1976)

Richard W. Oram
University of Texas at Austin

BOOKS: *The First Copyright Statute: An Essay on an Act for the Encouragement of Learning, 1710* (Austin: University of Texas Press, 1956);

The Collection of Knowledge in Texas (El Paso: Carl Hertzog, 1957?);

The Conscience of the University, edited by Hazel H. Ransom (Austin: University of Texas Press, 1982); republished and enlarged as *Chronicles of Opinion on Higher Education, 1955–1975,* edited by Hazel H. Ransom (Austin: University of Texas Press, 1990);

The Other Texas Frontier, edited by Hazel H. Ransom (Austin: University of Texas Press, 1984);

Snow in Austin: A Collection of Photographs from 1895 to 1985, by Ransom and Hazel H. Ransom (Austin: Clearstream Press, 1986);

The Song of Things Begun: A Selection of Verse, compiled by Hazel H. Ransom (Austin: University of Texas Press, 1988).

OTHER: *Coyote Wisdom,* edited by Ransom, J. Frank Dobie, and Mody C. Boatright (Austin: Texas Folk-lore Society, 1938);

In the Shadow of History, edited by Ransom, Dobie, and Boatright (Austin: Texas Folk-lore Society, 1939);

Mustangs and Cow Horses, edited by Ransom, Dobie, Boatright, and others (Austin: Texas Folk-lore Society, 1940);

Texian Stomping Grounds, edited by Ransom, Dobie, and Boatright (Austin: Texas Folk-lore Society, 1941).

Harry Ransom

Harry Ransom, educator, academic administrator, scholar, and bookman, was associated with the University of Texas at Austin for most of his career. He is best known as the founder of the Humanities Research Center, of which he served as the guiding spirit from 1957 until the early 1970s; it was renamed the Harry Ransom Humanities Research Center in 1982. During this time he was in charge of a massive library-development effort, one of the largest and most costly of the century, which re-sulted in the spectacular growth of Texas's rare-book, manuscript, and other special collections. Ransom was the first institutional collector of twentieth-century literary materials on a large scale, and his acquisitions revolutionized the market for modern manuscripts.

Harry Huntt Ransom was born in Galveston, Texas, on 22 November 1908 to Harry Huntt Ransom, a high-school Latin teacher, and Marion Goodwin Ransom. After his father's death his mother

Page proof for James Joyce's Ulysses, *with the author's corrections, acquired by the Humanities Research Center at the sale of the T. Edward Hanley library in 1958*

moved the family to Sewanee, Tennessee, where they lived in the hospital in which she worked. Ransom enrolled at a private academy associated with the University of the South, and in 1924 he matriculated at the university. While in college he worked as a stringer for a Nashville newspaper and for the Associated Press; his most important assignment required him to cover the Scopes "Monkey Trial" in nearby Dayton, Tennessee. In 1928 he graduated valedictorian, with honors in Greek, Latin, French, and speech, and entered the master's program in English at Yale University. He received the degree in 1930. While studying for his Ph.D. in English from Yale he taught English and journalism at State Teachers College in Valley City, North Dakota, from 1930 to 1934 and taught English and history at Colorado State College in 1934–1935.

Ransom's forty-one-year association with the University of Texas at Austin began with his ap-

pointment as a part-time instructor in English in 1935. After completing his doctorate in 1938, Ransom was promoted to assistant professor. His academic career was interrupted by service as an intelligence officer in the Army Air Corps from 1942 until his return to Austin in 1946. In 1947 he became a full professor and assumed his first administrative position, assistant dean of the graduate school. The list of Ransom's scholarly writings, which mostly deal with the history of copyright and with Texas folklore, is relatively modest in consequence of his early choice of a career in administration.

Ransom's creation of the Humanities Research Center at the University of Texas must be regarded as his single greatest accomplishment. In the course of roughly fifteen years he would build one of the world's outstanding literary research collections. Since becoming an instructor at Texas he had concerned himself with library issues, particularly library development and special collections, and to avoid any appearance of a conflict of interest he had ceased collecting books other than those he needed for research. The university possessed several significant book collections—notably the J. H. Wrenn library of English literature and the George Aitken collection of eighteenth-century British literature as well as important nineteenth-century manuscripts acquired with the Miriam Lutcher Stark Library—but no truly outstanding research collection had arrived in almost thirty years. Ransom recognized that Texas had to add to its holdings or lose its place of distinction in the field. What he would frequently refer to as "the plan for the library" began to take shape in 1948 when he served on a three-person committee that recommended greatly increased purchases of rare books and manuscripts and a commensurate increase in the budget, which then was less than $1,000, for such acquisitions.

In 1951 Ransom married Hazel Louise Harrod, one of his former students; they had no children. He became associate dean of the graduate school in 1953 and dean of the College of Arts and Sciences in 1954. That year he made contacts with a handful of booksellers, such as the New York City dealers Margie Cohn of The House of Books and James Drake, asking them to keep an eye out for important collections that would be suitable for the University of Texas. Most of the earliest purchases were in the area of modern literature: in 1955 and 1956 respectively, Ransom bought collections of first editions of works by T. S. Eliot and William Butler Yeats from Cohn and a theater arts collection from Drake. He soon encountered difficulties in financing these purchases; to his great embarrassment, Cohn had to beg the university repeatedly for payment for the Eliot collection. Ransom realized that he would need a relatively unrestricted source of funds if he were to attempt collection-building on a grand scale.

Ransom's December 1956 address to the Philosophical Society of Texas, meeting in Galveston, publicly unveiled his vision of Texas's library development. Published as *The Collection of Knowledge in Texas* (1957?), the speech begins with the proposal that "there be established somewhere in Texas—let's say in the capital city—a center of cultural compass, a research center to be the Bibliothèque Nationale of the only state that started out as an independent nation." After citing the examples of Henry Huntington and Henry Clay Folger, builders of great private libraries, Ransom goes on to identify two competing strains in Texas's history: a promise of future greatness on the one hand and a tendency toward antiintellectualism that stands in the way of that progress

on the other hand. One of the principal motivations for Ransom's library-development effort was the need to bring the state and its flagship public university to intellectual maturity.

Ransom's grandiose proposals began to be realized almost immediately. In 1957 the university regents approved the creation of the Humanities Research Center. They also formally recognized Ransom's leadership of the rare-books program by retiring the venerable Fannie Ratchford as head of Rare Books and Special Collections and appointing Ransom as her successor. Just as crucial was Ransom's promotion that year from dean of arts and sciences to vice president and provost of the university. As a top administrator he was in a position to lobby the regents directly for funding. He asked for and received a commitment of more than $1 million for research collections for the academic year 1958–1959.

The plan Ransom set before the regents in 1957 had four principal elements. First, he saw that an attempt to build a great library one book at a time was pointless; the university would have to buy entire collections. Second, since Texas could not challenge the great eastern libraries in the traditional rare-book-collecting areas such as early printed books, it would plunge into the collecting of modern English and American literature, territory in which relatively few institutions had set foot and prices were relatively reasonable. "Somebody should be paying more serious attention to the period since 1870: that will be our undertaking," he wrote Cohn on 10 May 1958. Third, works by both major and minor literary figures would be collected. Finally, Ransom stressed the acquisition of manuscripts as much as, or more than, that of rare books.

Although other institutions, such as the Lockwood Library at the University of Buffalo, had begun to collect modern manuscripts in the 1940s and 1950s, there was little widespread interest in the field. As a result, prices for manuscripts even of major twentieth-century writers were quite modest, and papers of minor authors were available at what now seem (even allowing for inflation) shockingly low prices. The market of the late 1950s presented an ideal opportunity for Texas. Moreover, as a literary scholar with a historical bent, Ransom recognized the importance of documenting the entire creative process, from the author's earliest notes through the progression of manuscript, proofs, and first and subsequent editions. The author's correspondence, royalty statements, and other personal papers might also shed light on the process of composition; such materials were already being used by scholars of nineteenth-century literature. Thus, Ransom saw the importance of acquiring intact the

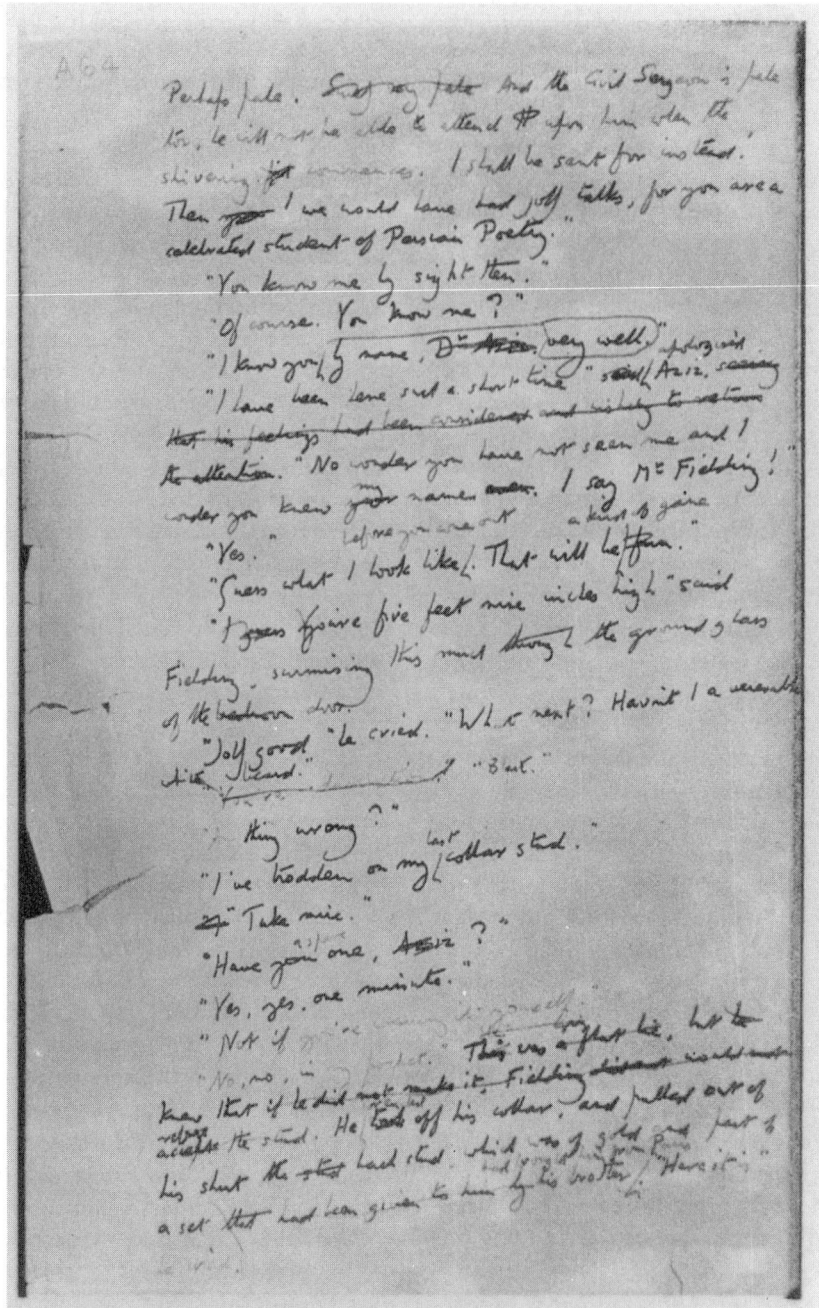

Page from the manuscript for E. M. Forster's A Passage to India, *purchased for the Humanities Research Center in 1960 by Lew David Feldman for £6,500*

entire corpus of a writer's papers. In large part because of his efforts the literary archive, rather than the single showpiece manuscript, became the focus of institutional collecting.

In 1958 the university's rare-book and manuscript holdings increased at a geometric rate. Two major acquisitions were the library of the Alexander Pope bibliographer and Texas professor R. H. Griffith and forty thousand volumes, including a Wil-

liam Shakespeare First Folio (London: Printed by Isaac Jaggard and Edward Blount, 1623) from the New Orleans collector Edward Alexander Parsons. The Parsons library, worth as much as $5 million, was known for its early Louisiana imprints and manuscripts, but it also contained fine holdings in English literature and the book arts. Ransom had had his eye on the Parsons library since 1954 and was able to acquire it with the help of private donations. It was also in 1958 that the Humanities Research Center acquired the core of its theater arts collections with financial assistance from the Texas theater owner Karl Hoblitzelle.

By far the most important event of the year, if not of Ransom's career, was the purchase of the bulk of the T. Edward Hanley library. Hanley, a wealthy industrialist, and his wife, Tullah, a former exotic dancer, had amassed an astonishing collection of modern art and literature that overflowed their home in Bradford, Pennsylvania, and spilled into the barn. Their insurance company refused to renew their homeowners policy unless they divested themselves of some of these holdings. Ransom, who had been aware of the Hanley library since 1954, saw an opportunity to steal a march on the major American collectors who had shown signs of interest in it. By the summer of 1958 Ransom had secured the necessary $1,075,000 from the university to buy the portion of the collection that was for sale. The Texas representatives had only a vague idea of what Hanley had sold them until they opened the boxes in Austin, at which point they were overwhelmed by the richness of the collection. Hanley held the largest private collections of George Bernard Shaw and D. H. Lawrence manuscripts, and his collections of Dylan Thomas, Samuel Beckett, Walt Whitman, and James Joyce (including the final page proofs for the first edition of *Ulysses* [Paris: Shakespeare and Co., 1922]) were nearly as spectacular. On 10 September 1958 Ransom wrote to William J. Burke, executive director of the State Board of Control, that "this action now puts the modern collections at Texas in the forefront of international libraries. We talk a good deal about 'first class.' In this regard we have now achieved the title." Over the next few years further acquisitions of Hanley material added luster to the collection.

The purchase of the Hanley Library put the name of the University of Texas—and that of Ransom himself—on the lips of every bibliophile in England and America. Drake, the New York dealer, reported back to Ransom rumors that the university had $7 million in hand to spend on rare items and that Ransom had empowered an agent to buy any available library. The English literary press viewed with alarm the rapid growth of American special collections and the gradual withdrawal of British writers' manuscripts from their homeland. This complaint was to become a frequent theme in foreign journalism over the next decade or so.

In 1960–1961 Ransom served as president of the Austin campus before being elevated to the chancellorship, the highest position in the University of Texas system. His years in that office saw

major building projects on the Austin campus—notably the Academic Center, known informally as "Harry's Place." Ransom also encouraged the hiring of promising younger faculty, expanded student counseling services, initiated the process of racial integration, and made many improvements in undergraduate education.

As Thomas F. Staley has pointed out, had it not been for the "fragile and yet crucial relationship . . . between the book trade and libraries," Ransom's plan for library development would not have become a reality. Being an administrator rather than a librarian or professional bookman, he relied heavily on the advice and market expertise of a handful of booksellers, most of whom specialized in modern literature. One of these was Margie Cohn, proprietor of the House of Books in New York and a dealer well known for her generosity and encouragement of young book collectors. During the late 1950s and early 1960s Cohn provided hundreds of titles to fill gaps in the university's modern-literature collection; the Lawrence, Thomas, Ernest Hemingway, and Ezra Pound materials are particularly noteworthy. Cohn, who knew Eliot's wife, Valerie, was also responsible for putting Ransom in contact with the poet and making possible Eliot's successful visit to Austin in 1958.

Another important bookseller associated with Ransom during the Humanities Research Center's formative years was James H. Drake, co-owner of the James F. Drake Company of New York. In 1958 Ransom bought a large group of John Steinbeck first editions from the Drake firm. He purchased the archive of popular American novelist Joseph Hergesheimer the next year and the papers and enormous performing-arts library of John Gassner in 1963. In addition, Drake put Ransom in contact with several important donors. One was Halsted VanderPoel, who in 1963 removed his comprehensive collection of Charles Dickens materials from Rutgers University, where it was deposited, and donated it to Texas. Drake's greatest coup was to act as matchmaker between Ransom and Alfred A. Knopf, publisher of some of the twentieth century's most notable literature. As a result of a meeting with Ransom in the summer of 1959 Knopf and his wife, Blanche, donated their personal library to Austin. A decade later the Knopf company's rich archive of correspondence with scores of major authors began to arrive. Drake died in 1965, and when the firm was dissolved, Texas acquired its entire stock of thirty thousand items and its business records, as well.

Ransom also developed close relationships with Jacob (Jake) Schwartz and Bertram Rota. Schwartz, an eccentric Los Angeles dealer who had

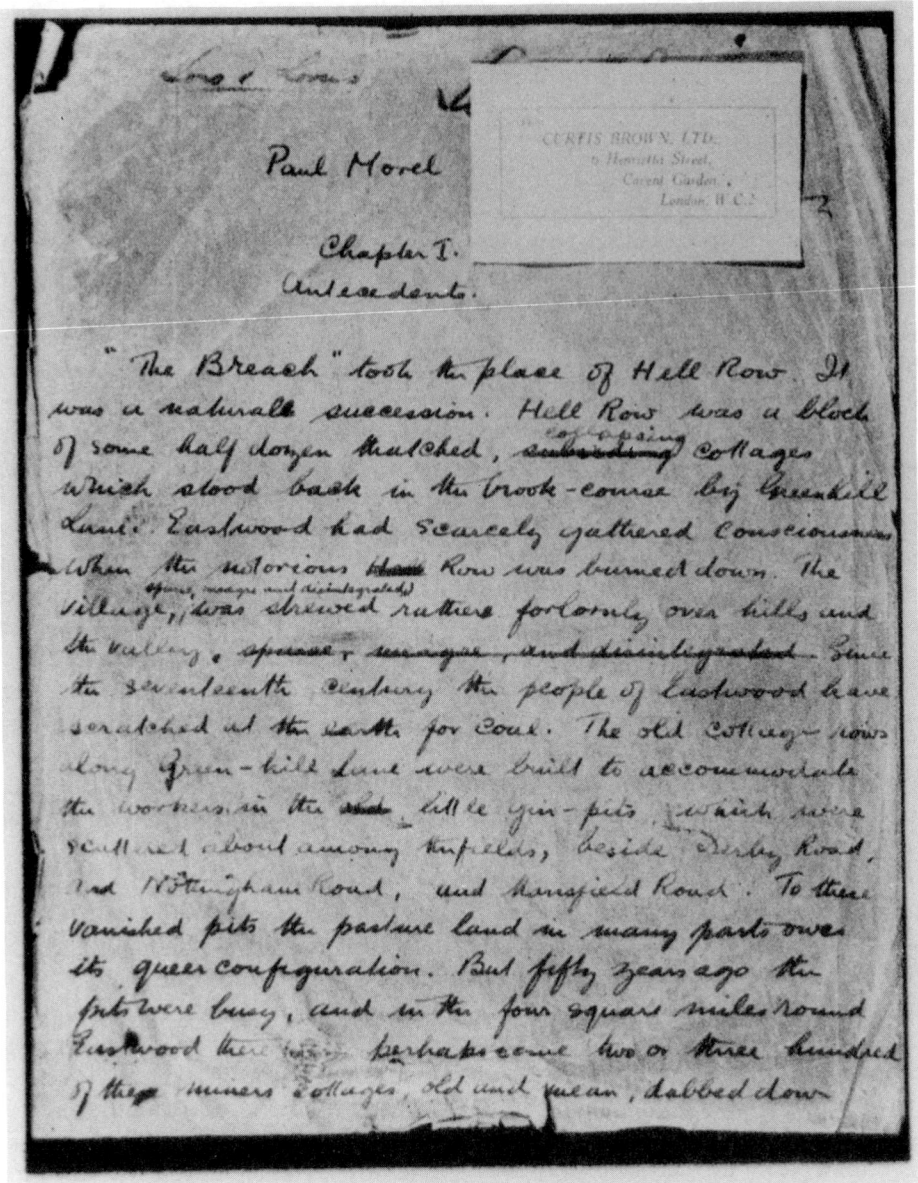

First page of the manuscript for D. H. Lawrence's "Paul Morel," the novel that was published as
Sons and Lovers (Harry Ransom Humanities Research Center, University of
Texas at Austin)

sold the bulk of the Hanley collection to its original owners and thus was indirectly responsible for shaping the Texas collections, brought the archive of the English short-story writer A. E. Coppard to Austin. Rota frequently served as Ransom's agent at London auctions and was the most important English dealer specializing in the moderns. In recognition of his services he was appointed an official adviser to the University of Texas in 1959. After his death in 1966 his son Anthony continued the close relationship. The firm sold the archives of Edith Sitwell, John Lehmann, and several members of the Powys family to Texas.

Ransom's closest adviser and confidant in the book trade was Lew David Feldman, president of the New York–based House of El Dieff (a pun on Feldman's initials). Feldman corresponded regularly, and at crucial points even daily, with Ransom and later with his associate F. Warren Roberts, who was appointed director of the Humanities Research Center in 1961. In early 1957 Ransom had confided the outlines of his plan to Feldman, who had aggressively begun to seek collections for sale. A year later Feldman negotiated the sale of the Ellery Queen collection of classic detective fiction, a forward-looking purchase since institutional genre collecting was still unusual.

Between 1958 and 1960 he also sold collections of Frank Harris and Mark Twain manuscripts, one of the most complete collections of dime novels, and papers of the Herschels, the English scientific family. Feldman was an especially valuable ally in the auction room. Armed with instructions from Ransom, he was in a position to terrorize other bidders for modern literature. At Christie's sale on behalf of the London Library on 22 June 1960 Feldman plucked about half of the lots for sale, including the autograph of E. M. Forster's *A Passage to India* (1924) for £6,500—by far the highest price paid for a modern English manuscript until that time—and a fair copy in the author's hand of Eliot's *The Waste Land* (1922) for £2,800.

The story was the same at the London Sotheby's sale of 8 November 1960, when Feldman bought the manuscript for Lawrence's *Etruscan Places* (1932) for £2,000, as well as letters by authors such as Robert Southey and Oscar Wilde. In May 1961 Feldman once again triumphed with the purchase of Pre-Raphaelite letters, architectural drawings by Thomas Hardy, and other manuscripts totaling more than £27,000, or 58 percent of the total proceeds of the sale. If they had not already done so, dealers and librarians began to take notice of Feldman's domination of the modern-literature market. In "Moderns in the Auction Room" English bibliographer John Carter observed that the phenomenal appetite of American libraries had had an astonishing effect on the prices paid for modern manuscripts and the archives of living writers.

Feldman's brashness, his successes in the auction rooms, and most of all the lucrative commissions he earned for his work on Texas's behalf earned him the enmity of many booksellers. He was, however, impervious to criticism of his "winner-take-all" style, believing, as he wrote Ransom on 16 November 1961, "that we must consistently sweep the field in all matters that apply to your interests" and that "we must continue to brook criticism, antagonism, and downright ill-will as long as we are convinced of the basic soundness of our acquisition policy." Until his death in 1975 Feldman continued to make important purchases at auction for the Humanities Research Center, notably manuscripts of Sitwell and many paintings and other artworks for the center's iconography collections. He was the intermediary for the acquisition of the papers of Louis Zukofsky, J. B. Priestley, and Elmer Rice; for the Artine Artinian collection of French literature; for the papers and libraries of Evelyn Waugh and Sir Compton Mackenzie; and for the superb Gernsheim collection of the history of photography. As a bonus, Feldman assisted Ransom by encouraging important writers such as Tennessee Williams and Arthur Miller to give their papers to Texas. Feldman regarded the Miller gift of 1962 as his greatest contribution to the Ransom effort.

Ransom himself was responsible for convincing many donors to give papers to Texas. In 1959 he was introduced to the prolific mystery writer Erle Stanley Gardner by the chairman of the university's board of regents. The two became friends, and Gardner began shipping his papers to Austin in 1961. The friendship culminated in the late 1960s with the arrival of the entire contents of Gardner's study, which was carefully re-created at the Academic Center. This gift was but one illustration of Ransom's singular powers of persuasion. Stocky and unassuming in appearance, serious and low key in demeanor, but nevertheless indefinably charismatic, Ransom was adept at charming money out of the university regents and collections out of donors. Those who fell under his spell often remarked afterward that they had been "Ransomized." Carlton Lake, who owned the premiere private collection of late-nineteenth- and twentieth-century French literary manuscripts and books, came to Austin in 1969 to discuss the disposition of his library. He left feeling that his magnificent collection must go to Texas, and it did go there in a gift-purchase arrangement. Ransom seemed "to have an infinite capacity to assume that the most impossible sort of thing is going to happen—and then proceeds to make it happen—not worrying about the minutiae that trouble the 27½ cent minds," a colleague once remarked.

The Humanities Research Center's remarkable progress in library development was marked by several milestones. The first was the 1964 exhibition "A Creative Century" and the accompanying catalogue, which put on public view such treasures as the typescript for Sinclair Lewis's *Main Street* (1920), the first draft of Lawrence's *Sons and Lovers* (1913), and Shaw's shorthand draft of *Pygmalion* (1913). The exhibit was held in the recently opened Academic Center, which housed both the undergraduate library and the modern special collections; the dual use of the building was in keeping with Ransom's belief that original materials could be an invaluable part of the teaching process. The next milestone was the appearance of Anthony Hobson's *Great Libraries* (1970), which surprised many by its inclusion of Texas as one of the five American institutions treated. Hobson regarded Ransom as the figure largely responsible for its success. The 1971 exhibit, titled "One Hundred Modern Books" and based on Mary Hirth's catalogue, *Cyril Connolly's One Hundred Modern Books* (1971), celebrated cornerstones of modernism (many of which were obtained

The Harry Ransom Humanities Research Center

by Feldman for the occasion), as well as Texas's widely recognized preeminence in this field. That same year a new building for the rare-book and literary collections was completed, and a professional association of rare-book librarians met in Austin with Ransom as the keynote speaker. He modestly but proudly looked back on the development of research collections since the 1950s.

Ransom had made another major contribution to Texas letters as founder and editor in chief of the *Texas Quarterly*, which had begun publication in 1958. The journal was partly inspired by the *Sewanee Review*, on which Ransom had served as a staffer. The *Texas Quarterly*, with its special issues devoted to the cultural life of individual counties, was highly respected but would outlive its founder by only a couple of years.

Increasingly criticized for what some regarded as his free-spending ways, Ransom resigned as chancellor in 1971 and became chancellor emeritus. He continued his association with special collections and occupied an office in the Humanities Research Center's new building. In retrospect it might be said that 1971 marked the end of "the Ransom era." The early 1970s was a time of relative austerity in the economy, and funds available for the purchase of rare books and manuscripts, which had been in the $2 million-per-annum range between 1967 and 1972, began to diminish. In the last few years of Ransom's career, the funding of the Humanities Research Center came under fire, as did what was per-

ceived as Ransom's favoritism toward special collections at the expense of general collections. In 1974 university president Stephen Spurr, who was attempting to bring library expenditures under tighter control, removed Ransom from all collection-development responsibilities and assigned him to work on a history of the university. Ransom died suddenly of a heart attack on 19 April 1976 at his in-laws' home near Austin.

At the time of Ransom's death commentators agreed that his most lasting accomplishment was the creation and development of the Humanities Research Center, which effectively "put Texas on the cultural map," as Knopf observed. Today the Harry Ransom Humanities Research Center holds some one million rare books, thirty-six million manuscripts, six million photographs, and thousands of artworks. Ransom's published and unpublished writings show that he intended the center to be much more than a storehouse for rare materials: its holdings were meant to promote research, discussion, and understanding of the humanities, broadly defined. This concept grew out of Ransom's humanistic education, and it was never fully realized. Ransom was at heart a nineteenth-century man, a bookman in the old-fashioned sense, though his reputation paradoxically rests on his visionary insight into the research value of manuscript materials relating to the modern movement in British and American literature.

Inevitably, the "grand acquisitor's" campaign to bring Texas into the forefront of modern libraries in the space of a decade and a half invited controversy and criticism. Estimates of Ransom's total acquisitions expenditures from state funds from 1958 to 1974 range between $11 million—Ransom's own figure—and $55 million, with the actual amount most likely in the neighborhood of $20 million. Some critics maintained that anybody with access to such vast sums could have assembled a great research library. These voices do not recognize that a less inspirational leader could scarcely have marshaled financial support on this scale, nor do they take account of the $30 million in gifts brought in by Ransom's tireless development efforts. Others accused him of buying indiscriminately and without regard to duplication. It is certainly the case that some lesser or peripheral collections were purchased during these years; Ransom acknowledged as much when he allowed that "as to mistakes, every research library makes them." He was not blind to the need for access to the books and manuscripts he acquired, but it is also true that he did not concern himself unduly with management and cataloguing issues, which he felt were best left to "library scientists." Withal, Ransom must be counted among the most important library collection builders of the postwar era. The proof may be seen today on any stack level of the institution he founded.

References:

John Carter, "Moderns in the Auction Room," *Times Literary Supplement,* no. 3093 (9 June 1961): 401;

Alan Gribben, *Harry Ransom* (Austin: University of Texas Press, forthcoming 1998);

Mary Hirth, *Cyril Connolly's One Hundred Modern Books from England, France, and America, 1880–1950* (Austin: Humanities Research Center, 1971);

Anthony Hobson, *Great Libraries* (New York: Putnam, 1970; London: Weidenfeld & Nicolson, 1970), pp. 307–310;

Alfred A. Knopf, "Harry Huntt Ransom," *Library Chronicle of the University of Texas at Austin,* new series 10 (1978): 11–12;

Gene Lyons, "The Last of the Big-Time Spenders," *Texas Monthly* (January 1978): 66–73, 142–148;

Bob Sherrill, "Ransom: Room at the Top," *Texas Observer,* 23 December 1960, pp. 1–2;

Thomas F. Staley, "Literary Canons, Literary Studies, and Library Collections: A Retrospective on Collecting Twentieth-Century Writers," *Rare Books and Manuscripts Librarianship,* 5 (1990): 9–21.

Papers:

Harry Ransom's official papers are held by the Center for American History of the University of Texas at Austin.

Lessing J. Rosenwald

(10 February 1891 – 24 June 1979)

Peter M. Van Wingen
Rare Book and Special Collections Division,
Library of Congress

BOOKS: *The 19th Book: Tesoro de Poveri* (Washington: Published for the Library of Congress, 1961);
Recollections of a Collector (Jenkintown, Pa., 1976).

OTHER: "The Story of an Unusual Purchase at Sotheby's," in *To Doctor R: Essays Here Collected and Published in Honor of the Seventieth Birthday of Dr. A. S. W. Rosenbach,* compiled by Percy E. Lawler (Philadelphia, 1946);
The Florentine Fior di Virtu of 1491, translated by Nicholas Fersen, introduction by Rosenwald (Philadelphia: E. Stern, 1953);
Three Erfurt Tales, 1497–1498, introduction by Rosenwald (North Hills, Pa.: Bird and Bull Press, 1962).

SELECTED PERIODICAL PUBLICATIONS—UNCOLLECTED: "The Formation of the Rosenwald Collection," *Library of Congress Quarterly Journal of Current Acquisitions,* 3, no. 1 (October 1945): 53–62;
"Rosenwald's Medal Acceptance Speech," *Art Alliance Bulletin,* 41, no.8 (May 1963): 16–17;
"The Mirror of the Collector," *Quarterly Journal of the Library of Congress,* 22, no. 1 (July 1965): 160–170;
"Experiences in Collecting," *The Record* (Gleeson Library Associates, University of San Francisco), no. 9 (June 1972): 14.

On 18 March 1943 both the *Washington Post* and *The New York Times* carried small pieces, overshadowed by the many articles of war news, reporting that the nation had received a most generous gift. Lessing Julius Rosenwald, a Philadelphia businessman and philanthropist, had donated his collections of prints and drawings to the National Gallery of Art and his collection of illustrated books to the Library of Congress. This was the beginning of a long relationship between Rosenwald and two national cultural institutions.

Rosenwald was born in Chicago on 10 February 1891. He was the son of Julius and Augusta Nusbaum Rosenwald. In 1895 Julius Rosenwald had purchased an interest in Sears, Roebuck and Company and was a main force in developing the company into one of the country's leading mail-order businesses. His son Lessing attended Cornell University (1909–1911). He then began work in the Sears stockroom and gradually made his way through the business at various levels. In 1920 Julius Rosenwald sent his son Lessing to Philadelphia to establish an East Coast merchandising center. He remained in Philadelphia for the rest of his life. In 1932 Rosenwald succeeded his father as chairman of the board of Sears. He held this position until his retirement in 1939.

In 1913 Rosenwald married Edith Goodkind. The couple enjoyed sixty-seven years of marriage and had five children. Rosenwald often remarked about the strong bond of this marriage and the great influence his wife had on his pursuits. In his own collection of essays, *Recollections of a Collector* (1976), he wrote, "By far the most important person in my life is my Edith. . . . Whatever I may have accomplished is due to her strong impetus, her understanding, and loving guidance."

Rosenwald began his collecting pursuits with a focus on prints. He bought his first significant prints in 1926. He started buying rare books in 1928. His early serious purchases were from the extraordinary Philadelphia book dealer A. S. W. Rosenbach. Rosenwald began by buying prints from Rosenbach, but before long the dealer was able to convince the new collector that his collection should be comprehensive, including woodcut prints and books with woodcut illustrations. Rosenwald's collections and his relationship with Rosenbach both grew quickly. In their biography *Rosenbach* (1960) Edwin Wolf and John Fleming record that in 1922 Rosenwald had purchased two Stephen Crane first editions for six dollars. In October 1928 Rosenwald again bought books from Rosenbach, but of a much different

Lessing J. Rosenwald

type. This purchase included German illustrated in-cunabula with a strong emphasis on the fifteenth-century woodcut, including *Die Cronica vander hilliger stat van Coellen* or the *Cologne Chronicle* (Cologne: Johann Koelhoff the Younger, 1499), Anton Koberger's illustrated edition of Jacobus de Voragine's *Legenda aurea* (Nuremberg, 1488), and the *Nuremberg Chronicle* (Nuremberg: Koberger, 1493). Rosenwald was back at Rosenbach's on an enormous buying spree on 5 March 1929. For the sum of $404,700 he purchased four block books and acquired the best of the William Blake material that had come from the estate of Brooklyn collector William A. White. These purchases included seven of Blake's illuminated books, among them the finest known copy of *The Book of Urizen* (Lambeth: William Blake, 1794 [i.e, 1815?]) and the only known copy of *The Book of Ahania* (Lambeth: William Blake, 1795). Rosenwald thus laid the foundation for what would become the best Blake collection in the country. In the short time between October 1928 and March 1929 Rosenwald had defined two of the major components of his collection of rare books: early illustrated books and the books of Blake. By 1930 both his print collection and his book collection were well established and moving toward gaining international prominence.

William Matheson, former chief of the Rare Book Division of the Library of Congress, has pointed out in his article on Rosenwald, "Lessing J. Rosenwald: 'A Splendidly Generous Man,'" in the Library's *Quarterly Journal* (Winter 1980), that as soon as the collections began to take form Rosen-wald initiated his policy of permitting the materials, both books and prints, to go on display. Exhibit loans were a constant feature of the Rosenwald Collection and followed his notion of a collector's responsibilities, which he firmly stated as "to care for the material he or she has assembled and to make it available for use." This generous attitude has led to the wonderful story, perhaps apocryphal, reported in the *Washington Post* (23 January 1972) that when a print was returned from an exhibit loan with visible insect damage, Rosenwald remarked, "Better to be seen and eaten, than not seen at all."

Rosenwald had the misfortune of starting his collection just before the stock market crashed in 1929 and while the economy was especially weak. From the early 1930s until 1935 there are virtually no records of his making any purchases. But Americans continued to patronize Sears in spite of the Great Depression, and so by 1935 Rosenwald was able to pay off his debt to Rosenbach and begin to collect again in a favorable market for book buyers. By this time the collection had taken its shape, focusing on the illustrated book. The major parts of the collection were illustrated books through 1520, William Blake, William Morris, and French books of the eighteenth and twentieth centuries.

From the mid-1930s Rosenwald made acquisitions in earnest. In 1935 he met with Rosenbach and came away with a *Danse macabre* (Paris: Printed by Guy Marchand for Geoffrey de Marnef, 1490), an early German edition of *Barlaam et Josaphat* (Augsburg: Gunther Zainer, 1476), and a 1493 Paris edition of Boccaccio's *De claris mulieribus* printed by An-

Page from a 1490 edition of Danse macabre *that Rosenwald bought from Dr. A. S. W. Rosenbach in 1935 (Rosenwald Collection, no. 406, Library of Congress)*

toine Vérard. Several book auctions in the late 1930s gave him more opportunities to add to his collection. In 1937 the William E. Moss Collection and the Clumber Library of the Dukes of Newcastle were sold. Rosenwald's collection of Blake materials was especially enhanced by purchases at the Moss sale. The Clumber Library sale was the first auction that Rosenwald attended, and he came away with five of the thirty-four items offered. These included a copy of William Caxton's edition of *Legenda aurea* (Westminster, 1483) and Boccaccio's *De casibus virorum illustrium* (Paris: Antoine Vérard, 1494), one of two known copies (the other is in the Bibliothèque Nationale), printed on vellum with miniatures painted over the woodcuts.

A year later the great auctions of the libraries of Mortimer L. Schiff and Cortlandt F. Bishop were held. From the Schiff sale Rosenwald acquired many fine bindings, French illustrated books, and Francesco Colonna's *Hypnerotomachia Poliphili* (Venice: Aldus Manutius, 1499), often regarded as the most beautiful book ever printed because of the fine correspondence between print and woodcut illustrations. At the Bishop sale he came away with a copy of the 1462 Mainz Bible printed by Johann Fust and Peter Schoeffer (the first printed Bible to bear a date) and two illuminated manuscripts. Especially noteworthy was a magnificent French Book of Hours dated 1524. This work of 113 leaves has an outstanding pedigree, having belonged to the eighteenth-century bibliophile William Beckford and later to Robert Hoe III before passing to Bishop. The vellum leaves include sixteen large and twenty-six small miniatures. The script and illumination were once attributed to Geoffrey Tory, but more recent scholarship has linked this Book of Hours to an anonymous workshop patronized by Louise de Savoy, mother of Francis I. *Rosenwald and Rosenbach: Two Philadelphia Bookmen, Organized by Kathleen Hunt Mang* (1983) describes the manuscript as embodying "all the stylistic elements of the High Renaissance. The brilliant color of the rich palette, which ranges from deep shadows to glittering highlights, shimmers on the fine vellum leaves. Each of the sixteen large miniature paintings is framed within a monumental Renaissance arch."

The Rosenbach-Rosenwald connection became even stronger with time. Rosenwald wrote in the *Library of Congress Quarterly Journal* (October 1945) that "the collection has been gathered from many places and from many people. In spite of this it should be said that its godfather is Doctor A. S. W. Rosenbach. That monarch of the auction room and eminent private collector has acted as a mentor, a tempter, and a super-salesman. To 'Doc' goes the major credit for the high quality of many of the rarest books in the collection; he has often refused to sell one which, in his estimation, did not meet the rigid specifications he had set for this library." This lesson on condition was practiced thoroughly by the collector. When addressing the Gleeson Library Associates he said, "Collect the best quality of anything which you can obtain." He developed a comprehensive collecting code. Matheson summarizes the code in his 1980 article for the *Quarterly Journal of the Library of Congress:*

1. Get to know as much about what you collect as possible.
2. Have an overall theme and stick to it.
3. Find a dealer you feel comfortable with and trust.
4. Be ahead of your time in your collecting interests.
5. Seize unusual opportunities when they present themselves.
6. Continuously refine your taste.

In 1939 Rosenwald initiated two major changes in his business involvements and collecting interests: he resigned his position as chairman of the board of directors of Sears, Roebuck and Company, and he moved with his family to Alverthorpe, an estate of 150 acres in Jenkintown just outside Philadelphia. This new home included storage cabinets for prints, shelving units for rare books, and exhibition space. The gallery allowed scholars a place for study and meetings with the collector. Furthermore, the space fulfilled Rosenwald's dream of making his collections available to his visitors, who ranged from academics to schoolchildren. He took the greatest joy in having students around his great mulga wood book table looking in amazement at the treasures laid out for them.

Rosenwald's plans to spend full time with his book and print collections in his new gallery were interrupted by World War II. During the war Rosenwald contributed his extensive business experience by serving as director of the Bureau of Industrial Conservation in the War Production Board. During this time spent in Washington he came to the decision to conjoin his collection of prints with those at the National Gallery of Art and his books with the collections at the Library of Congress.

In 1943 Rosenwald announced his decision to donate his collections to the nation, dividing them appropriately between the two national institutions. He established two stipulations in the deed of gift: he could retain the collections at the Alverthorpe Gallery during his lifetime, and he could add to the collections—that is, make further gifts—at any time. He immediately received praise for the gifts. In a letter dated 18 March 1943 Rosenbach wrote to Rosenwald: "Coming in on the train this morning I read of your gift. . . . I would like you to know what a thrill it gave me. It will not come as a surprise though, to people who know you because it is so consistent with your always generous, wise, and patriotic performances." The indenture, dated 30 January 1943, lists approximately 400 books, exclusive of the reference books. Among the rare books were 193 fifteenth-century books. Nearly 10 percent (37) of these items were otherwise not represented in any American library. The gift also included 66 volumes from William Morris's Kelmscott Press.

The decision for the placement of the collections gave Rosenwald an even greater impetus to collect. He was especially active in collecting during the period from 1945 to 1947. Although he remained focused on collecting books with illustrations, Rosenwald branched out to acquire those items that were monuments of early printing and those that were the foundation materials for the illustrated book. During this period he acquired such books as the Fust and Schoeffer printing of Guillaume Durand's *Rationale divinorum officiorum* (Mainz, 1459), the earliest complete printed book in the Rosenwald Collection, and Giovanni Balbi's *Catholicon* (Mainz, 1460), possibly printed by Gutenberg. By the end of 1947 the Library of Congress listed 250 newly acquired books as gifts from Rosenwald.

In 1947 the Library of Congress displayed seventy-nine of these recent acquisitions. Rosenbach's foreword to the exhibition catalogue noted the importance of these books:

The books described herein presented to the Library of Congress represent a great achievement in the field of collecting. In one year have been gathered together some of the most important volumes ever issued by the presses of Europe and America, from the days of Gutenberg to the end of the eighteenth century. Every one is significant in the history of culture. . . . The Rosenwald gift has given added prestige to the Library of Congress among scholars throughout the world. Through this great contribution to our national library these precious mementoes of the past have been made accessible to the public for all time.

Rosenwald's books remained at Alverthorpe Gallery, but special arrangements were made for materials to be sent to Washington so that readers could use them in the Rare Book Division Reading Room of the Library of Congress. The exhibit loan program also continued, with the Library of Congress becoming an especially frequent borrower. Another feature of Rosenwald's idea of using the collection for public education was his willingness to ship batches of the books to the Library of Congress cataloguing department for full cataloguing. These records then appeared in the public catalogues of the Library of Congress and were available through the card division to libraries around the country and the world. The Library of Congress has published two printed catalogues of the Rosenwald Collection based on these records.

Rosenwald was a collector who studied and knew his prints and books. In 1929 he purchased from Rosenbach the reference library put together by Howard C. Levis. The collection was the foundation of Levis's work titled *A Descriptive Bibliography of the Most Important Books in the English Language Relating to the Art and History of Engraving and the Collecting of Prints* (London: Ellis, 1912). The collection consisted of more than twenty-three hundred items and gave Rosenwald immediate background information on his collecting interests. The Levis books and several thousand other reference books were eventually divided between the National Gallery and the Library of Congress.

By good fortune Rosenwald found at the Library of Congress Frederick R. Goff (a curator and later chief of the Rare Book Division associated with the division from 1940 to 1972) who was a devoted scholar of fifteenth-century printing. The collector and the curator developed a close association and frequently communicated between Alverthorpe and Washington regarding acquisitions, exhibit loans, and scholarly inquiries. In his *Recollections* Rosenwald notes that Goff "has been a splendid advisor and has aided me in my collecting and in bibliographical knowledge. I have seldom gone wrong following his careful advice. . . . It is safe to say that

Fred Goff shares with Dr. A. S. W. Rosenbach the major credit for bringing to me the great pleasure and satisfaction of collecting books and learning about them."

Rosenwald's collecting passion remained intense. Although for the most part he acquired his books one at a time, there were two major exceptions: the 35 books (28 incunabula) purchased from the prince of Liechtenstein's library shortly after World War II and the 167 books from the dukes of Arenberg in 1956. The Arenberg books added considerable strength to his holdings of fifteenth- and sixteenth-century Dutch and Flemish books. This purchase had international significance because under Rosenwald's custody, books which were known in only one copy and had been inaccessible through the Arenberg family now became available to all. Rosenwald's book buying took on a steadiness that indicates the conviction of the collector with a cause. The gift indentures show his progress: in 1950 he purchased 175 books; in 1951, 85 books; in 1953, 100 books; in 1954, 85 books; in 1964, 700 books; in 1968, 10 books; in 1975, 10 books; and in 1978, 180 books. The year 1952, not in this list, was the year of two of his greatest individual gifts, the *Biblia Latina* or Giant Bible of Mainz (Mainz, 4 April 1452–9 July 1453) and Pierre Joseph Bernard's *Poëmes de P .J. Bernard* (Paris: P. Didot, 1796).

The Giant Bible of Mainz is often considered the most important book in the Rosenwald Collection. He acquired the Bible from New York rare-book dealer H. P. Kraus. Rosenwald and Kraus had met a decade earlier when Kraus was a struggling refugee bookseller. Rosenwald's 1941 purchase of books worth $4,500 served, Kraus said, as the dealer's "passport into the upper strata of rare book dealing." Though Rosenbach was Rosenwald's closest friend and chief supplier of books, Kraus continued to sell to Rosenwald, especially after Rosenbach's death. Kraus regarded Rosenwald not just as a customer but also as a "valued friend." Kraus knew that Rosenwald should buy the Giant Bible of Mainz and that it should go to the Library of Congress where it would join the extraordinary vellum copy of the Gutenberg Bible. The Giant Bible lives up to its name. The pages of this magnificent two-volume manuscript are about as large as the John James Audubon's elephantine folio *Birds of America* (1840–1844), and each volume is much thicker than the Audubon. Rosenwald paid $35,000 for the work, and on 4 April 1952 the manuscript went on display. This date marked the five-hundredth anniversary of the date that the scribe wrote on his first page. One volume of the Giant Bible and one volume of the Gutenberg Bible

Page from Rosenwald's copy of De proprietatibus rerum *(1486) by*
Bartholomaeus Angelicus, with an illustration of "The Ages
of Man" (Rosenwald Collection, no. 394,
Library of Congress)

have remained on permanent display at the Library of Congress ever since. Both Bibles were produced in the same city (Mainz) at the same time (early 1450s). They bear a remarkable resemblance. Nowhere else can one see this earliest transition from the manuscript books to the printed book.

Also in 1952 Rosenwald gave his copy of Bernard's *Poëmes* to the Library of Congress. This volume has illustrations by Pierre Paul Prud'hon. The

Rosenwald copy is Didot's own into which three pen-and-ink drawings on vellum are bound along with a fourth illustration, which is an engraving and etching. The drawings on vellum have a depth and intensity that are missing in the illustrations engraved after Prud'hon's drawings. Agnes Mongan, in writing about this book in *Vision of a Collector* (1991) says: "It is a brilliant example of the difference between the touch of a master and that of his

*Aeneas meeting Venus, an illustration in Rosenwald's copy of John Dryden's
1697 translation of Virgil's* Aeneid *(Rosenwald Collection, no. 1548,
Library of Congress)*

imitators, no matter how serious and dedicated they may be."

Rosenwald was especially pleased at the expanded educational role his collection took at the Library of Congress. Exhibitions flourished and facsimile reprints were initiated. The Library of Congress had never had such treasures at close hand before. The library did not have any strength in the category of illustrated books before it received Rosenwald's gift, but with the acquisition of its greatest collection of rare books came the opportunity for the Rare Book Division to attain a level of interna-

tional prominence. Though the division had strong holdings in incunabula with the Vollbehr Collection and the Thacher Collection, it took the draw of the Rosenwald books to bring researchers to the Library of Congress to find a full range of complementary materials.

Further educational possibilities developed with a series of Blake facsimiles. As a member of the Blake Trust and with the cooperation of the Library of Congress, Rosenwald permitted eight of his copies of Blake's illuminated books to be reproduced in a series of facsimiles printed by Arnold Fawcus at the Trianon Press in Bossia, Clairvaux. Rosenwald and countless Blake students have been grateful for the high quality of these facsimiles.

By the 1960s Rosenwald's collecting began to drop off. He was clearly thinking in long-range terms about his wife, children, and grandchildren. But he was also extremely busy with philanthropic and community efforts. At his memorial service, many of these activities were enumerated: board member of the Institute for Advanced Study; board member of Thomas Jefferson University (forty years); founding role in the establishment of *Scientific American* magazine; member of the American Philosophical Society; president of the Federation of Jewish Agencies of Philadelphia; chairman of the Julius Rosenwald Fund; trustee of the Abington Memorial Hospital; member of the board of directors of the Philadelphia Museum of Art, the Free Library of Philadelphia, and the Philadelphia Orchestra Association; president of the Philip H. & A. S. W. Rosenbach Foundation; founder and president of the Print Council of America (1956–1972); founder, president (1943–1955), and chairman (1956–1966) of the American Council for Judaism; a member of the American Council of Learned Societies; president of the Philobiblon Club; president of the Friends of the University of Pennsylvania Libraries; member and then Honorary Member of the Grolier Club; member of the Association Internationale de Bibliophiles; and member of the Royal Society of Arts. He received the Philadelphia Award in 1967.

Rosenwald died in Jenkintown on 24 June 1979 at age eighty-eight. Following his death the plan for the gift of his collection was put into action. During the end of 1979 and the beginning of 1980 the books and prints began to arrive at the National Gallery and the Library of Congress in huge wooden crates. A special space was created in the Rare Book Division vault for the books, which were arranged by their Rosenwald catalogue number. The number of rare books in the collection had reached just over 2,600 items, and it included another 5,000 reference books. (Approximately 22,000 prints went to the National Gallery of Art.) Within months the full collection of books was ready for immediate availability to Library readers. Another group of choice books—about 180—that had never been officially given before were transferred at this time. But the generosity of the Rosenwald donation had one further, final moment. In 1951 Rosenwald had given his wife Edith on her birthday a miniature Book of Hours produced in Paris in the 1370s. Thirty years later Edith Rosenwald presented this book to the Library of Congress during an occasion at the library honoring her husband.

In 1991 the Rare Book and Special Collections Division dedicated a room to Rosenwald. In it, furniture and fixtures from the book room at Alverthorpe are used to convey something of the atmosphere of the gallery. The great book table and the Carl Milles sculpture *Head of Orpheus* are especially noteworthy for setting the scene. The room is used as Rosenwald would have wanted—for seminars with book "show-and-tell" experiences for local college and university classes, for conversations with researchers, and for programs on the history and illustration of books.

References:

"Catalog of Fine Books and Manuscripts Selected for Exhibition at the Library of Congress from the Lessing J. Rosenwald Collection October 1945," *Library of Congress Quarterly Journal of Current Acquisitions,* 3, no. 1 (October 1945): 7–51;

A Catalog of Important Recent Additions to the Lessing J. Rosenwald Collection Selected for Exhibition at the Library of Congress, June 1947 (Washington, D.C.: U.S. Government Printing Office, 1947);

A Descriptive Hand-List of a Loan Exhibition of Books and Works of Art by William Blake, 1757–1827, Chiefly from the Collection of Mr. Lessing J. Rosenwald (California, 1936);

Early Printed Books of the Low Countries from the Lessing J. Rosenwald Collection, an Exhibition in the Library of Congress 2 April 1958 to 31 August 1958, Organized by Frederick R. Goff (Washington, D.C.: Library of Congress, 1958);

Ruth E. Fine, *Lessing J. Rosenwald: Tribute to a Collector* (Washington, D.C.: National Gallery of Art, 1982);

Frederick Richmond Goff, "A Catalog of Important Recent Additions to the Lessing J. Rosenwald Collection," *Library of Congress Quarterly Journal of Current Acquisitions,* 5, no. 3 (May 1948): 3–51;

Goff, "Contemporary Collectors VIII: The Rosenwald Library," *The Book Collector,* 5 (Spring 1956): 28–37;

Goff, *Early Belgian Books in the Rosenwald Collection of the Library of Congress* (N.p., 1947?);

Goff, "The Gift of the Lessing J. Rosenwald Collection to the Library of Congress: A Bibliographer's Survey of the Collection, from the 15th through the 18th Century," *Quarterly Journal of the Library of Congress,* 22, no. 3 (July 1965): 170–193;

Sandra Hindman, ed., *The Early Illustrated Book: Essays in Honor of Lessing J. Rosenwald* (Washington, D.C.: Library of Congress, 1982);

Hans Peter Kraus, *A Rare Book Saga: The Autobiography of H. P. Kraus* (New York: Putnam, 1978), pp. 117–126;

Lessing J. Rosenwald Collection: A Catalog of the Gifts of Lessing J. Rosenwald to the Library of Congress, 1943 to 1975 (Washington, D.C.: Library of Congress, 1977);

Livres anciens des Pays-Bas; la Collection Lessing J. Rosenwald (Brussels: Bibliothèque Royale de Belgique, 1960);

William Matheson, "Lessing J. Rosenwald: 'A Splendidly Generous Man,'" *Quarterly Journal of the Library of Congress*, 37, no. 1 (Winter 1980): 2–24;

Dorothy Miner, *The Giant Bible of Mainz 500th Anniversary; April 4, 1452–April 4, 1952* (Washington, D.C.: Library of Congress, 1952);

Paul Needham, *The Printer & the Pardoner: An Unrecorded Indulgence Printed by William Caxton for the Hospital of St. Mary Rounceval, Charing Cross* (Washington, D.C.: Library of Congress, 1986);

Oude drukken vit de Nederlanden: Boeken uit de Collectie Arenberg thans in de Verzameling Lessing J. Rosenwald. Tentoonstelling, De Haag, Museum Meermanno-Westreenianum, 29 Augustus tot 9 Oktober 1960 (The Hague: Nijhoff, 1960);

The Philadelphia Connection: An Exhibition in Honor of the 40th Anniversary of Lessing J. Rosenwald's First Gift to the Library of Congress Organized by Kathleen Hunt Mang (Washington, D.C.: Library of Congress, Rare Book and Special Collections Division, 1983);

Paul Richard, "Not a Giant, But a Gem," *Washington Post*, 23 January 1972, Section G: 2;

Rosenwald and Rosenbach: Two Philadelphia Bookmen, Organized by Kathleen Hunt Mang (Philadelphia: Rosenbach Museum & Library, 1983);

The Rosenwald Collection: A Catalogue of Illustrated Books and Manuscripts, of Books from Celebrated Presses, and of Bindings and Maps, 1150–1950 (Washington, D.C.: Library of Congress, 1954);

Merle Secrest, "Lessing J. Rosenwald, Collector of Great Prints, Rare Books," *Smithsonian*, 2, no. 12 (March 1972): 50–57;

A Selection of Printed Books, Manuscripts, Miniatures, Prints and Drawings in the Lessing J. Rosenwald Collection . . . Exhibited on the Occasion of the Visit of the Association Internationale de Bibliophiles, 3 October 1971 (Jenkintown, Pa., 1971);

Treasures from the Lessing J. Rosenwald Collection: An Exhibit Honoring Mr. Rosenwald's Eighty-second Birthday, Organized by William Matheson (Washington, D.C.: Library of Congress, 1973);

Vision of a Collector: The Lessing J. Rosenwald Collection in the Library of Congress, Organized by Peter Van Wingen 14 September 1991–23 February 1992 (Washington, D.C.: Library of Congress, Rare Book and Special Collections Division, 1991);

Edwin Wolf II and John Fleming, *Rosenbach: A Biography* (Cleveland & New York: World, 1960);

Carl Zigrosser, "So Wide a Net: A Curator's View of the Lessing J. Rosenwald Collection, 17th to the 20th Century," *Quarterly Journal of the Library of Congress*, 22, no. 3 (July 1965): 194–205.

Papers:

Lessing J. Rosenwald's papers (28,000 items in 81 containers) are housed in the Library of Congress. The papers date from 1819 to 1980, the bulk from 1932 to 1979.

Joseph Sabin

(6? December 1821 – 5 June 1881)

Joseph Rosenblum

BOOKS: *The Thirty-nine Articles of the Church of England, with Scriptural Proofs and References,* anonymous (Oxford: Printed by the author, 1844);

A Dictionary of Books Relating to America, from Its Discovery to the Present Time, volumes 1–14 (New York: Sabin, 1867–1884); volume 19 completed by Wilberforce Eames;

Better Advertising: A Refutation of Several False Standards, and a Statement of Some Principles and Rules of Economical and Effective Newspaper Advertising (New York: Sabin, 1870);

A Bibliography of Bibliography; or, A Handy Book about Books Which Relate to Books: Being an Alphabetical Catalogue of the Most Important Works Descriptive of the Literature of Great Britain and America, and More Than a Few Relative to France and Germany (New York: Sabin, 1877).

Joseph Sabin

In the 1943 Goodspeed (Boston) reprint of the first volume of Charles Evans's *American Bibliography* Lawrence C. Wroth writes that "One notable difference between our day in the book world and the old days of the nineteenth and early twentieth centuries is that now we have gigantic bibliographical projects while in the old days we had bibliographical giants." Joseph Sabin was such an oversized figure, a colossus of nineteenth-century American bibliographers and bibliophiles.

As an antiquarian bookseller he supplied many of the leading bibliophiles of the day and encouraged them to collect Americana when the field was still relatively new. As an auctioneer he presided over the major book sales of his day, and for many of these sales he prepared the catalogues. His publishing program made rare seventeenth- and eighteenth-century Americana more accessible, and his bibliographic works remain useful guides for scholars and collectors.

Born in Braunstron, Northamptonshire, England, in December 1821 (sources give the dates of 6 or 9 December), Joseph Sabin was educated in the Braunstron schools and later those of Oxford, to

which his family apparently moved in Sabin's youth. At the age of fourteen he was apprenticed to learn bookbinding from Charles Richards, an Oxford bookseller. Richards quickly recognized Sabin's skills as a bibliopole; after only a few months Sabin was transferred from the bindery to the salesroom, where, despite his youth, he was consulted by collectors. At the age of seventeen he became general manager of Richards's shop, a position in which he bought as well as sold books and prepared auction catalogues. When Sabin's apprenticeship ended in 1842 he established his own auction house in Oxford, where he joined with a Mr. Winterborn, son of a local architect and builder. In 1844 Sabin's firm published the young man's first book, *The Thirty-nine Articles of the Church of England,* with *Scriptural Proofs and References,* and in this year he married the sister of his partner.

Four years later Sabin, his wife, and their two sons (Joseph Jr. and Frank) left England aboard the *West Point* for New York City, where they arrived on 3 July 1848. William Reese notes that in 1848 the North Texas Colonization Company had circulated throughout London copies of *Texas: Its Resources, Climate, and Advantages for Colonization,* a brochure soliciting immigrants, and Sabin came to the United States to claim land that he purchased in that state. As Sabin's obituary in *The New York Times* reports, however, he soon learned "that [his land] was in much the same condition as Martin Chuzzlewit's Eden investment, and he never went near it."

Although Sabin may have been prompted by unscrupulous realtors to emigrate, he may also have regarded the United States as a better market for books than his native England, where the bibliomania of the Napoleonic era was followed by bibliophobia. In *Bibliophobia* (London: Bohn, 1832) and in *Reminiscences of a Literary Life* (London: Major, 1836) Thomas Frognall Dibdin acknowledges the depressed state of the book trade, and in the earlier work Dibdin remarks that "FEAR is the order of the day. To those very natural and long-established fears of bailiffs and tax-gatherers, must now be added the fear of *Reform,* of *Cholera,* and of BOOKS." Dibdin records London bookseller Henry Foss as saying, "Whenever we see cases of old books arrive from Milan, or from Paris, we absolutely lack the courage to open them," and, he adds, "Men wished to get for *five,* what they knew they would not formerly obtain for *fifteen,* shillings." In 1848 Edward Moxon sent sixty works from the library of his father-in-law, Charles Lamb, to New York to be sold there rather than offered in London.

Sabin did not find work in New York City and moved on to Philadelphia, where he went to work as assistant and salesman for George S. Appleton at 148 Chestnut Street. According to William Brotherhead, a Philadelphia bookseller, Sabin must have acquired some skill as a binder during his apprenticeship because at Appleton's shop he introduced Americans to half-binding in calf or morocco—that is, binding that covers the spine and corners with leather and the rest of the boards with paper or cloth. Soon after coming to Philadelphia, Sabin bought a farm at Chestnut Hill, where his family lived until 1861, even when Sabin had returned to New York City to work. In 1847 Appleton had published *Appleton's Library Manual . . . Upwards of 12,000 of the Most Important Works in Every Department of Knowledge,* and this bibliography, compiled to promote sales, may have given Sabin the idea of preparing a similar work when he opened his own business.

In 1850 Sabin moved to the store that Appleton operated in New York City, and in May, Sabin joined the auction firm of James Cooley and John Keese, 191 Broadway, at the corner of Broadway and Dey Street. In this position Sabin demonstrated his bibliographic skills in preparing auction catalogues such as that for Ithiel Town, a New York architect whose library was rich in foreign titles.

In 1851 the business of Cooley and Keese was sold to Lyman and Rawdon, and Sabin became a cataloguer for this latter firm. The first major collection that he catalogued for Lyman and Rawdon was that of the Reverend Samuel Farmer Jarvis. The task required much overtime, and when Sabin presented his bill, Lyman and Rawdon refused to pay. Sabin responded by refusing to surrender the manuscript of the catalogue, and his action delayed the sale. His employers were compelled to yield, but they proposed cutting his salary effective 1 January 1852, and Sabin at once took a new position with Bangs, Brother and Company, a rival firm of auctioneers at 13 Park Row.

With this new employer Sabin was exposed to much Americana, such as the stock of booksellers John Russell Bartlett and Charles Welford, a firm begun by Welford in 1840 at Astor Place. Bartlett and Welford were the first American dealers to carry a large antiquarian stock, including Americana, and their customers included ethnographer Henry R. Schoolcraft and Henry Cruse Murphy. In 1850 Bartlett was appointed a U.S. Boundary Commissioner to settle the southwest border with Mexico, and the firm was dissolved. In 1852 George Brinley Jr. sold his duplicates through Bangs, and Sabin may have catalogued this collection. One of the last catalogues that Sabin prepared for Bangs was that of the library of Edward Brush Corwin (New York: Baker & Godwin, 1856). Including fifty-three hundred lots, this was the largest collection of Americana to be sold at auction to that date, and the catalogue that Sabin compiled for it gave him the idea of preparing a comprehensive bibliography of books relating to the history of America.

Late in 1856 Sabin left Bangs's firm to open his own shop at the corner of Broadway and Canal Street. This shop, which dealt in "antique and miscellaneous fine books," was not successful, and in 1857 Sabin returned to Philadelphia, where his family was still living. Opening a store at 27 South Sixth Street, he prospered largely through the sale of books by catalogue to collectors in the South. Brotherhead claims that Sabin had the finest stock of antiquarian books in the city.

In May 1859 Sabin published in *Historical Magazine* a "Prospectus for an American Bibliographer's Manual" combining a sale catalogue such as Appleton's with a comprehensive listing of Americana, but increasing tension between the North and the South forced Sabin to delay his plans as orders from the South diminished and then ceased. Henry Stevens, a London dealer who sold to the leading American collectors of the day, notes the effect of the Civil War on the book trade: "On the first gun of Ft. Sumter [customers] shut up like clam shells, and began to practice those beautiful virtues of prudence and economy which protected themselves and at the same time ruined me." Brotherhead agrees:

> In 1861 the war was fairly commenced, business was fairly paralyzed, war, war was the cry everywhere, all business except that of war was thrown aside, old book collectors locked up their libraries, their engravings and autographs were thrown aside. . . . No one had any time to read except war-news, and amid all this excitement for one year books were forgotten.

Sabin returned to New York, bought a house at 3 Weinland Avenue, Brooklyn, and established an auction house with H. A. Jennings on Fourth Street. The first and last sale of J. Sabin and Company was that of the dramatic library of actor William E. Burton. The sale of these books brought little money; Jennings left the business; and the Burton estate sued. Sabin was forced to become an employee of Sheldon and Company, where he remained until 1863.

In that year Sabin contracted to catalogue the library of John Allan, a deceased New York collector whose holdings included more than fifty-two hundred lots and were expected to be sold for about $12,000. In fact, they brought $27,058.96, and his other collections added another $10,000. Sabin encouraged buyers to pay record prices, and he became an independent cataloguer, agent, and auctioneer. Brotherhead claims that "if an important sale of books in New York took place, Sabin was the man that was engaged to compile the catalogue and manage the sale." In 1863 he also prepared the library catalogue of actor Edwin Forrest, and the following year he compiled *A Catalogue of the Entire Library of Andrew Wight, of Philadelphia* (New York: Cooley, 1864), which Sabin describes as "the largest collection relating to the Unites States that has ever been offered for sale at auction on this continent." During his lifetime Sabin catalogued more than 150 libraries, including the William Shakespeare collection of Richard Grant White. Working with these libraries introduced Sabin to a wealth of Americana

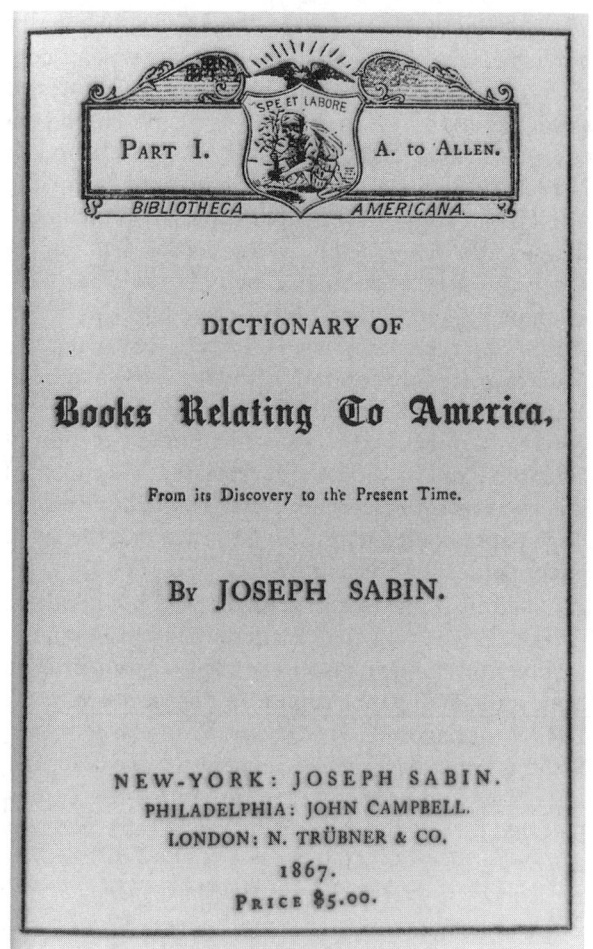

Title page for the first part of Sabin's major achievement, a bibliography of Americana for which he catalogued some 150 private libraries

that he later recorded in *A Dictionary of Books Relating to America, from Its Discovery to the Present Time,* his monumental bibliography.

In 1863 or 1864 Sabin paid $9,000 for the bookstore of Michael Noonan (or Nunan) at 84 Nassau Street in the heart of the rare book district, where he opened his own shop. Charles L. Woodward, who specialized in Americana, was at 78 Nassau Street; William Gowans, with the largest stock of books in the United States, was at 115 Nassau Street. Gowans was a rival to Sabin but also a friend, and Sabin wrote Gowans's obituary in the *American Bibliopolist* in March 1872. Gowans regularly published catalogues in which Americana predominated, and he kept in his office a list of works by American authors, a list that Sabin consulted in compiling his *Dictionary of Books*.

In addition to bookselling, cataloguing, and auctioneering, Sabin entered the publishing business in 1865 with his series of reprints. In his octavo series were six eighteenth-century titles, including

The Journal of Major George Washington, originally published in 1754. Each of the fifty large paper copies was offered at $3; for one of the two hundred small paper copies, the price was $1.50. Hugh Jones's *The Present State of Virginia,* first published in 1724, cost $8 for a large paper copy and $4 for the small paper copy. Large paper copies of William Stith's *The History of the First Discovery and Settlement of Virginia,* initially published in 1747, sold for $15, small paper copies for $7.50. The manuscript of *The Narrative of Colonel David Fanning,* covering the American Revolution in North Carolina, had been edited by Thomas Hicks Wynne of Richmond, Virginia, and published in 1861 in a limited edition of 50 copies, and in 1865 Sabin reprinted 250 copies of this work as the sole volume in his second series, the large paper copies selling for $10 each and the small paper copies for $5 each.

Sabin's quarto series of reprints included ten works drawn from the seventeenth rather than the eighteenth century and were also offered in both large and small paper copies. In this series were the 1643 *New England's First Fruits* ($3 for large paper, $1.50 for small); Thomas Shephard's *The Clear Sunshine of the Gospel* (1648) at $5 for large paper copies, half that for small; Henry Whitfield's 1651 *The Light Appearing More and More towards the Perfect Day; or, A Farther Discovery of the Present State of the Indians in New England* (large paper, $5; small paper, $2.50); and Nathaniel Byfield's 1689 *An Account of the Late Revolution in New England* ($4 for large paper, $2 for small).

Sabin also became involved in some bad feelings over his publication of Henry Harrisse's *Bibliotheca Americana vetustissima: A Description of Works Relating to America, Published between the Years 1492 and 1557* (New York: Philes, 1866). Harrisse and his patron, Samuel Latham Mitchell Barlow, had engaged George P. Philes, an impecunious bookseller, to act as publisher and to collect subscriptions for their edition. Yet before Harrisse's bibliography was published, Philes sold much of the edition at a discount to Sabin, who was able to offer the work at twenty-five percent less than its subscription price. Harrisse was thus cheated of much of his profit, and as late as 1897, more than fifteen years after Sabin's death, Harrisse remained furious. "I can only say that I have a very poor opinion of Sabin's first 12 or 13 vols.," he wrote, "and of Mr. Sabin himself."

Harrisse's view was not shared by collectors, who bought more than $1 million worth of books from Sabin between 1864 and 1874. His shop became a favorite haunt for rich bibliophiles. As the New York *Tribune* noted on 19 December 1874, "Every New Yorker who is thoroughly conversant with books knows the emporium of Sabins. . . .

[T]hey have books of all sorts, modern as well as ancient." Brayton Ives, president of the New York Stock Exchange, writes in the introduction to his 1891 sale catalogue that

> For many years I found rest after a hard day's work on Wall Street, by spending an hour or two on my way home in one or more places where I could look over recently purchased books. In those days Mr. Sabin's shop in Nassau Street was the favorite resort of book-collectors, and one could meet several of them there nearly every afternoon. The arrival of a box from London, containing new importations of books, was always an occasion of interest and usually gave rise to keen competition for the privilege of making first selections. Mr. Sabin was an enthusiastic student of Americana, and I was soon instilled with the same feeling.

By 5 December 1866 Sabin felt prosperous enough to circulate another prospectus for his bibliography in which he promised to provide a list "of all the books published in this country, or abroad, which relate to its History—using the word in its widest meaning." In this prospectus Sabin wrote:

> Had the magnitude and extreme difficulty of the undertaking been presented to my mind in full proportions at the outset, I should never have attempted it; and, indeed, I may remark, that I have more than once almost determined upon its abandonment; but a deep sense of its importance, however imperfectly it may be executed, and a strong partiality for bibliographical pursuits, have stimulated me to continue my labor, until the work has attained such a degree of completeness as to justify its publication, and render its conclusion a task of comparative ease.

The first number was published in January 1867, and through the first year Sabin published four parts—each of which cost five dollars, a substantial sum—and six each subsequent year until his death. These parts—each published in a run of 635 copies, with 110 on large paper and the rest on regular quarto size—were collected into volumes beginning in 1868. Sabin acted as publisher, and the printing was done by the Bradstreet Press of New York, a firm admired by bibliographers and collectors of the period.

Sabin arranged his bibliography by author, with anonymous works listed under subject or title. For each entry he included author, title (sometimes, however, citing the half-title rather than the actual title), place of publication, date of publication, size (in the traditional designations of folio, quarto, octavo, and duodecimo), and sometimes details of pagination and location. For some items he included annotations, and although these may be brief, they are useful. For example, he discusses the content and publication history of Pieter van der Aa's *Naau-keurige versameling der gedenk-waardigste zee en land-reysen naar Oost en West-Indiën* (Leyden: Printed by the author, 1707), and under the entry for Edward Strutt Abdy's *Journal of a Residence and Tour in the United States of America* (London: John Murray, 1835) Sabin writes: "The republication of this work was commenced in New York, but suspended on account of its remarks on slavery. The author accompanied Mr. [William] Crawford, who was sent by the English Government to inspect the prisons in the U.S. He gives much information on Public Institutions."

Sabin's was not the first attempt to compile a bibliography of books dealing with American history. As early as 1629 Antonio Rodriguez de León Pinelo had produced his *Epítome de la bibliotheca oriental i occidental* (Madrid: Gonzales, 1629). Bishop White Kennet's *Bibliothecae Americanae Primordia* (London: Churchill, 1713), a catalogue of Kennet's library of Americana donated to the Society for the Propagation of the Gospel in Foreign Parts, is another important early compilation. Leman Thomas Rede used Kennet's catalogue in compiling his *Bibliotheca Americana* (London, 1789). Early in the nineteenth century Obadiah Rich and Henry Stevens, two booksellers, had undertaken bibliographies with bibliographic interests and business motives similar to those of Sabin.

Rich's three-volume *Bibliotheca Americana nova* (London: Rich, 1835–1846) dealt with Americana of the eighteenth and nineteenth centuries. Stevens proposed to cover Americana before 1700, and in 1848 he published a proposal for a "Bibliographia Americana" but found no financial supporters. In 1854 he began his *American Bibliographer* (Chiswick: Whittingham, 1854) but got no farther than the letter *C*. Sabin drew on these bibliographies as well as institutional catalogues such as that of the Library of Congress, state bibliographies such as John Russell Bartlett's *Bibliography of Rhode Island* (Providence: Anthony, 1864), auction catalogues (including many that Sabin had prepared himself), and lists from booksellers. Sabin recognized that even the best bibliographies may err, and whenever possible he relied on personal examination. Repeatedly in his dedications he thanks individuals for allowing him access to their libraries. Yet he understood that an absolute commitment to perfection leads to paralysis. As he observed, "Should I wait to make this bibliography as full and exact on all points as I trust it will generally be found, I should never complete it."

Sabin's bibliography has its faults. Entries lack standardized forms, and he has no set guidelines to determine what to include or exclude. He includes some government documents and omits others; he also includes some, but hardly all, promotional fliers. Sometimes he relies on inaccurate sources, as when he draws on Quaker George Keith's *Journal of Travels from New Hampshire to Caratuck* (London: Printed by J. Downing for B. Aylmer, 1706) for a list of Keith's works. The bibliography that Keith includes in his *Journal* is based on a faulty memory and so leads Sabin into error.

Nonetheless, Sabin's work earned—and deserves—high praise. At the 1878 Paris Exhibition his *Dictionary of Books* was awarded a bronze medal in the category of "Printing, Books, Lithography, black or coloured, Special Collections, Periodicals, etc." A year earlier Justin Winsor, Librarian of Harvard College, wrote to Sabin on 4 December 1877:

> I am well acquainted with your Dictionary, and know well the competent labor that is put upon it. Its imperfections are inseparable from such a work. Its merits are positive, and no one can deal with titles of Americana, as I have to a considerable degree for years, without knowing the help it can afford, which is always opportune and often great. Its progress has been slow; but I have borne with it gratefully in the belief that when done, it was worth waiting for; and haste would imperil its character.

Adolph Growell, in *Book-Trade Bibliography in the United States in the XIXth Century* (1898), recognizes Sabin's omissions and occasional inaccuracies but remarks, "Inasmuch as a mass of material on a given subject is brought together in the 'Bibliotheca Americana' . . . it cannot fail, in however slight degree, to assist the collector and bookseller in their researches." More than sixty years later bibliographer Frederick Goff confirms Growell's estimate of the value of Sabin's work: "Scarcely a day passes when I am at my office that I do not have occasion to consult Joseph Sabin's *Dictionary of Books Relating to America.* . . . This is the most important single bibliography relating to America that has ever been compiled." Reese, a bookseller and historian of the book, agrees, writing in 1984 that "It is useless to complain about the shortcomings of the *Dictionary*. For all its faults, it is an amazing and endlessly useful work."

In addition to compiling his bibliography, between 1869 and 1877 Sabin published the monthly *American Bibliopolist,* which contained notices of auctions and other events of interest to bibliophiles and included articles on collectors, libraries, and other literary matters. Many of these pieces he wrote himself, and parts of his *Dictionary of Books* and his *A Bibliography of Bibliography; or, A Handy Book about Books*

Which Relate to Books: Being an Alphabetical Catalogue of the Most Important Works Descriptive of the Literature of Great Britain and America, and More Than a Few Relative to France and Germany (1877) were first published in this journal. He used the magazine to advertise his stock, and other dealers also promoted their businesses in its pages. The *American Bibliopolist* suggests that scope of Sabin's bookselling. For example, he advertised a stock of two hundred thousand engraved portraits and the largest American collection of materials relating to George Cruikshank, the nineteenth-century British illustrator.

While pursuing these bibliographic activities Sabin continued to dominate bookselling in the United States and to play an important role in Europe. He made twenty trips to Europe, most of them after the Civil War, to buy books. In 1869 he went to Leipzig to execute bids for American clients, including John Carter Brown, at the sale of the books that had belonged to Emperor Maximilian of Mexico. Sabin was also in Germany in 1873 for the sale of the library of Serge Sobolewski, and he bought about a quarter of the collection. In 1871 his son, Frank, opened a bookshop in London, and this gave Sabin even greater access to English and Continental rarities. Although Sabin promoted Americana, he dealt with all sorts of antiquarian books.

Yet in the United States his presence was most evident. At the 1868 James Bruce sale in New York, Sabin defeated Gowans in acquiring the John Eliot Bible (Cambridge, Mass.: Printed by Samuel Green and Marmaduke Johnson, 1663), the first Bible printed in the American colonies and hence much sought after, despite being written in Algonquian. Acting for John A. Rice of Chicago, Sabin bid $1,130, at that time a record price for a book sold at auction in America. Two years later Sabin bought the book again when Rice sold his library, and the volume became part of the library of the Americanist George Brinley Jr. Other leading Americanists of the day also patronized Sabin's shop and relied on him at auction. His customers included Almon W. Griswold and William Menzies of New York, and Henry Cruse Murphy and Thomas W. Field of Brooklyn. To New York collector Charles H. Kalbfleisch, Sabin sold Theodore De Bry's edition of Thomas Harriot's *A briefe and true report of the new found land of Virginia* (Frankfort, 1590) for $1,250 and encouraged Kalbfleisch to pursue the collecting of Americana.

Sabin sold heavily to Chicagoans after the Civil War. Volume five of his *Dictionary of Books* is dedicated to Edward G. Asay,

who placed for my use, as well as his own convenience, his entire library in my possession during his visit to Europe [in 1870–1871] and thus aided my researches, and saved his books from the flames which destroyed Chicago, and perhaps would have destroyed his library.

Volume six was dedicated to Ezra B. McCagg, who was not so fortunate as Asay; McCagg's collection of local history was destroyed in the Chicago Fire. Volume twelve was dedicated to Levi Z. Leiter–Asay's fellow Chicagoan, a partner of Marshall Field, and one of Sabin's better clients after 1870.

Sabin's best customer between 1866 and 1870 was John A. Rice of Chicago, part owner of the Sherman House Hotel. Rice attempted to corner the grain market, failed, and in 1870 was forced to sell his library. Sabin, who had sold Rice most of his books, prepared the catalogue and served as auctioneer for Bangs, Merwin. Sabin's skills as an auctioneer were evident, as the amount of the sale of this collection set a record for an American book auction: $42,263. J. Woods Poiner, a collector from Newark, New Jersey, wrote in his copy of the auction catalogue: "I think [Sabin] to be the very best book auctioneer 'extant.' Mr. Rice's library would have brought much less money if it had been sold by any other man than Sabin." Sabin was the largest buyer in this sale and bought the most expensive item, an extra-illustrated edition of Thomas Frognall Dibdin's *A Bibliographical, Antiquarian and Picturesque Tour in France and Germany* (London: Author, 1821) in three volumes extended to six with 242 plates and 130 original drawings. At the 1868 Windus sale by Sotheby's of London the set had brought $240; in 1870 Sabin paid $1,920. In 1896 the set again appeared at auction held in New York by Bangs and Company; it sold for $630 and was then broken up.

In May 1875 Sabin sold the library of Thomas W. Field, whose collection was rich in materials dealing with Native Americans. In 1873 Field had published the first major bibliography dealing with this subject, and the Panic of that year destroyed his fortune. The sale, which realized only $13,500, was not a success.

Much more profitable was the sale of the William Menzies library the next year. Sabin had compiled a catalogue of the library–a catalogue that is an important contribution to American bibliography–and Menzies then decided to sell his collection. With Sabin as auctioneer the proceeds from this sale set another record: $48,105.70. In an article perhaps written about the sale by Sabin himself on 21 November 1876 in *The New York Times,* the reporter closed with praise for the auctioneer: "Mr. Sabin's reputation as a bibliographer is unequalled, and no one can spend an hour in the auction room without noticing that the auctioneer was a man of rare wit, and had a profound knowledge of books. He kept the audience in a roar of laughter." In the December 1876 issue of the *American Bibliopolist* Sabin used this triumph to promote bibliophily and the sale of his bibliography:

> The result of the [Menzies] sale coincided with views we have often expressed—that good works are a mere investment; they pay good interest in the entertainment and information they afford the buyer, and when sold repay most of their original cost. In this particular library they have done much more. The entire collection cost Mr. Menzies in round figures $41,000, and has sold for $51,000 [*sic*]. The difference more than pays the cost of selling the books, so that the fortunate possessor of a library of rare and fine books may congratulate himself that his books may be a source of revenue as well as of comfort. The sale was not devoid of interest in other respects; it exhibited on the part of buyers a healthy desire to possess themselves of books relative to the fine arts, which all sold well. Books on Bibliography also sold well, the philosophy of which is that the American book buyers are in earnest search of information concerning literature and the fine arts.

Sabin retired in April 1879 to devote himself to his bibliography. The name of his firm was changed to J. Sabin's Sons, and the firm was moved to 64 Nassau Street. Yet he continued to serve as an auctioneer, and on 10 March 1879 he presided over the first of the George Brinley Jr. sales held by George Leavitt Company at Clinton Hall in New York City. In a week the proceeds from Sabin's performance set another auction sales record of $48,831, and in March 1880 Sabin sold the second part of the Brinley collection for an additional $32,690. The third part of the sale was to be held in March 1881, but Sabin was too ill to preside, and the auction was delayed a month. In Sabin's last sale he sold the first Gutenberg Bible offered at auction in the United States: in a duel between Ives and Hamilton Cole, a New York lawyer, the latter triumphed with a bid of $8,000, an amount that was yet another American auction record achieved by Sabin.

On 5 June 1881 Sabin died of chronic glomerulonephritis at his Brooklyn home, and he was buried on 7 June at Cypress Hills Cemetery. The writer for *The New York Times* concluded its obituary by observing, "Mr. Sabin, during his business career in Nassaustreet, became known not only throughout this country, but through Europe, as a bibliophile of great acquirements, and as an expert whose judgment in all matters relating to books could be implicitly relied on." William Loring Andrews, a prominent New York collector, commented that "Sabin was a genuine lover of books and a patient, painstaking student of bibliography. He was a better bibliophile than he was a merchant, and his customers would often find him more eager to discuss the bibliographical points of his literary wares than to effect a sale of them."

Sabin was certainly a lover of bibliography: he died poor, having expended the profits from his sales on his *Dictionary of Books*. By the time of his death the list of items covered in the *Dictionary of Books* had reached entry 58,796 (Nederland), and Sabin had completed entries 58,797–60,332. In 1884 Wilberforce Eames assumed responsibility for the work and prepared entries 60,333–82,714 (parts 83–116). In 1892 Eames's duties at the Lennox Library forced him to abandon the project, and work on it was not resumed until 1927, when Eames again continued work on it through part 121 (entry 84,556), which was published in 1929.

Robert William Glenroie Vail then became editor, and with a staff of assistants he completed the work with part 172 in 1936. The final entry is number 106,413, but many entries include more than one edition, so Sabin's completed *Bibliotheca Americana: A Dictionary of Books* actually includes more than 250,000 works. This bibliography remains a fitting monument to the man who devoted so much of his time and money to it, and it confirms what John Pyne said of Sabin: "His love for rare books passed into knowledge which he used for the benefit of all who had the pleasure and profit of knowing him."

References:

William Loring Andrews, *The Old Booksellers of New York and Other Papers* (New York: Printed by the author, 1895);

William Brotherhead, *Forty Years among the Old Booksellers of Philadelphia* (Philadelphia: Brotherhead, 1891);

Frederick R. Goff, *Joseph Sabin, Bibliographer (1821–1881)* (Amsterdam, N.Y.: Israel, 1963);

Adolph Growell, *Book-Trade Bibliography in the United States in the XIXth Century* (New York: Dibdin Club, 1898);

Edwin D. Hoffman, "The Bookshops of New York City, 1743–1948," *New York History,* 30 (1949): 53–65;

William S. Reese, "Joseph Sabin," *American Book Collector,* new series 5 (January–February 1984): 3–24;

Robert William Glenroie Vail, "Sabin's 'Dictionary,'" *Papers of the Bibliographical Society of America,* 31 (1937): 1–9.

Charles Sessler
(5 November 1854 – 4 September 1935)

David Klappholz
Stevens Institute of Technology

Charles Sessler sold important books and manuscripts to many of the great collectors of the twentieth century, including Henry E. Huntington, Henry Clay Folger, A. Edward Newton, Jerome Kern, Barton Currie, and Lessing J. Rosenwald. Sessler's greatest interest was in Charles Dickens; he was a friend of the Dickens family and bought many rarities from them. He aided John C. Eckel in writing his Dickens bibliography, still a standard in the field, and he helped create important Dickens collections. Sessler's activities were not confined to Dickens; he also did some work as a publisher, but primarily he bought and sold significant books and manuscripts of the fifteenth through the twentieth centuries. With his assistant Mabel Zahn, who was to take over the book business of the Sessler firm after its founder's death, Sessler helped usher in an era of book collecting in which those with smaller purses than Huntington, Folger, and Newton were able to build collections on previously ignored subjects.

Sessler was born Carl Sessler in Vienna, Austria, on 5 November 1854. Family legend has it that he attended the University of Vienna and that he traveled to Cairo for the premiere of Giuseppi Verdi's *Aïda* (1871). In 1880 he came to America, arriving with little money but with fluency in six languages. This skill would serve him well in the book business.

Sessler's first job in New York was selling Catholic Bibles for the George Kelley publishing company of 13 Barclay Street. Toward the end of 1881 or the beginning of 1882–having visited the city on business and found it to his liking–he moved to an upstairs room at 1018 Chestnut Street in downtown Philadelphia. His capital consisted of forty dollars. In 1883 Sessler married Caroline Abendroth; the couple had four children: Raphael Montgomery, Charlotte, Marguerite, and Joseph Leonard.

In an 1884 Philadelphia directory Sessler is listed as a clerk at 1007 Brown Street, and the following year he appears at the same address as a pub-

Charles Sessler, 1877

lisher. Entries in his account book for 1884–1887 indicate that a large portion of his business came from the sale of family Bibles and albums, with only the occasional set of Charles Lamb, Robert Burns, or Sir Walter Scott. Judging from the names of the majority of Sessler's customers, such as Funk, Schmidt, Kolberg, and Haberle, Sessler's Austrian background helped him attract business from the large German-speaking immigrant population.

The 1887 Philadelphia directory places Sessler at 1018 Chestnut Street, still as a publisher. He continued to be listed as a publisher through his 1903 move to 1003 Chestnut Street and a 1904 relocation

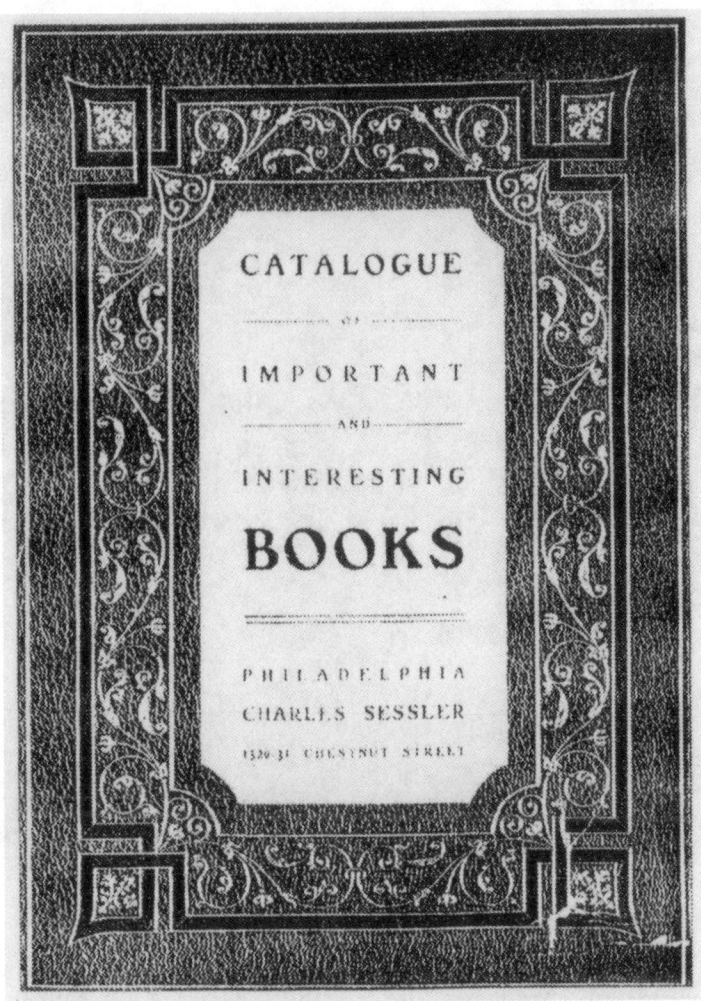

The only catalogue of books from Sessler's shop, prepared by John Eckel in
1904 (Free Library of Philadelphia)

to 1529–1531 Chestnut. Sessler probably did not publish many works himself but rather sold subscription sets for others. A collection of Sessler's receipts from the early 1900s shows that he sold the Daniel Boone edition of Theodore Roosevelt's *The Winning of the West* (New York and London: Putnam, 1900), limited to two hundred copies, for as much as $60 for the four octavo volumes bound in three-quarters levant morocco, crushed and polished, with gilt tops and deckle edges, or bound in full levant for $100. By this time Sessler's customer list was no longer limited to recent German and Austrian immigrants but also included at least one Biddle, scion of a prominent old Philadelphia family.

In 1904 Sessler published his only book catalogue. Prepared by Eckel, then managing editor of the *North American,* a local newspaper, the *Catalogue of Important and Interesting Books* included such collectibles as a copy of the Geneva Bible (London: Imprinted by the Deputies of Christopher Barker,

1592) for $100 and a two-volume set of Robert Burns that had belonged to the British poet and publisher William Morris, with Morris's signature on each title page. Also listed was an 1869 letter written and signed by Dickens and another Dickens item described as:

A $6000 set of Dickens for $1200, being #5 of the Edition Definitive, New York, 1902, publisher's price $6000. 60 vols. royal 8vo magnificently bound in full crimson crushed and polished levant with inlaid floral centerpiece of light blue levant, richly tooled on back and corners; doublure with light green levant within gold borders; ornamented with colored inlays in scroll and floral design, leather joints, silk end papers, solid gold edges.

Such luxurious shelf furniture dominated the catalogue; the most elaborate item was a magnificently illustrated edition of James Granger's *Biographical History of England from Egbert the Great to the Revolution*

273

Sessler's shop at 1314 Walnut Street in Philadelphia, circa 1915

(London, 1806–1824), "every leaf beautifully inlaid to royal folio size and extended to 18 volumes," for $5,000.

In 1906 Sessler, having moved yet again, to 1314 Walnut Street, was listed at last as a bookseller. This section of Walnut Street was becoming quite a bookseller's row, with the Rosenbach Company just a few doors away at 1320. A newspaper account of Sessler's latest move described his stock as consisting of "handsomely bound books, paintings and other works of art."

The factor that transformed Sessler from a purveyor of beautiful books into a leader in the rare-book trade was probably his interest in Dickens. According to a 1929 *Publishers' Weekly* article by Ruth Brown Park, Sessler claimed that Dickens's *The Life and Times of Nicholas Nickleby* (1838–1839) was the first book he had read in English before coming to America. Later he cited a different Dickens title and said that he had read it on the voyage across the Atlantic. Whatever the case, Dickens was Sessler's lifelong passion. In 1906, having learned of the existence of the Dickens Fellowship established in 1902 in London, Sessler placed the following notice in his shop window: "All interested in Charles

Dickens are invited to attend a meeting to be held in the St. James Hotel, 13th and Walnut Sts., object being to form in Philadelphia a Dickens Fellowship."

On 23 January 1907 sixty-six Dickensians met at the Saint James Hotel, and on 7 February 1907, Dickens's birthday, the Philadelphia branch of the Dickens Fellowship was founded with Eckel as its first president. Sessler did not run for office, but when one of those elected to the executive council declined to serve, Sessler accepted his office. Sessler remained a member of the executive council until 1915, serving as chairman from 1909. When he left the executive council, he was elected honorary president and served in that capacity until his death.

Between the founding of the Philadelphia branch of the Dickens Fellowship and the 1930s, Sessler transformed his store. He filled the large glass front window with beautiful books. Inside the door to the right of the window, shelves contained new books. Tables down the center held best-sellers. There was also a section of sporting prints on the first floor. On the left side, toward the front of the store, was a staircase which led to the second-floor art gallery. At the rear of the first floor, behind black wrought-iron Spanish-style grillwork, sat Sessler and Zahn among the rare books. There were no inexpensive secondhand books in the store, only new and rare books.

Local members of the carriage trade began to frequent his establishment, such as the owners of Strawbridge and Clothiers and of Lit Brothers, major Philadelphia department stores. Other customers included John B. Stetson and Harry Elkins Widener of Elkins Park, just north of Philadelphia; John Thomson, librarian of the Free Library of Philadelphia; Hampton L. Carson and John F. Lewis, whose collections would go to the Free Library; and William Langfeld and William J. Campbell, later to become bibliographers of Washington Irving and Benjamin Franklin, respectively. About 1907 A. Edward Newton discovered Sessler as a source of rare books and began buying Dickens association items from him. From farther away came such buyers as Ruth Grannis, librarian of the Grolier Club of New York, an association of book collectors; lyricist Harry Bache Smith, also of New York; wealthy businessman and collector John R. Clawson of Buffalo; John Howell, later to become dean of the San Francisco book trade; and others from Pittsburgh, the District of Columbia, Memphis, and Duluth.

Sessler's greatest American customer of the prewar era was Huntington. According to Ruth Brown Park,

> One snowy afternoon in the winter of 1907, Henry E. Huntington sat at a table in an upper Fifth Avenue club playing solitaire. It is said he looked up with little interest when Charles Sessler first spoke to him about the acquiring of certain rare books. Frankly, he was not interested. He had never been a rare book collector. However, it took just what Mr. Sessler has, a kind of passionate belief in collecting, to fire an imagination like Huntington's. To-day $27,000,000 worth of books rest in a beautiful Greek Temple Library. . . . However, as Mr. Sessler points out, he himself did not sell all the $27,000,000 library to Mr. Huntington.

Romantic as this story is, Sessler did not initiate Huntington into the field of rare books. Credit for that probably goes to Isaac Mendoza of the Ann Street Book Store in New York. It is not unlikely, though, that Sessler introduced Huntington to the pleasures of collecting association copies and manuscript material, for both of which Sessler had developed a strong appreciation.

Whatever Sessler's role in Huntington's becoming a book collector, Huntington enjoyed his relationship with Sessler. In response to Sessler's request Huntington wrote a letter of reference that, enlarged, graces the entrance of the Huntington Library:

> I am glad to say that my dealings with you in books have been very satisfactory to me, and I imagine equally so to yourself. The books I purchased from you were what I wanted and while, of course, I paid you too much for some, I got a good many at figures quite acceptable to me. When I paid you tall prices, I felt at the time I owed it to you as a tribute to your linguistic ability and your transcendent qualities as a salesman of literary commodities, both of which excited my sincere admiration. If I never run across a worse man than yourself to deal with, I certainly deserve congratulation, and if you always find as good a customer as myself, you will never want for the necessities of life.

Though Huntington bought most of his library through George D. Smith and A. S. W. Rosenbach, he continued to purchase important items from Sessler until he stopped collecting. For example, from the William Hermann sale by the Anderson Auction Company in New York in 1909, Sessler purchased a set of Dickens first editions in their original covers; he sold this set to Huntington. On a visit to Austria, Sessler found a copy of the *Catholicon* printed at Mainz and dated 1466. The item was reported to be in better condition than the copies of this work owned by American bibliophile Robert Hoe III or British collector Henry Huth. Sessler sold it to Huntington for $11,250.

The color-plate books in the collection of Samuel H. Austin came almost exclusively from Sessler, and Sessler probably deserves at least partial credit for creating Judge John M. Patterson's Dickens collection of some 250 first editions and rare Dickensiana. Col. Richard Gimbel would come to Sessler for aid in starting the Dickens collection now at Yale. Rosenwald, who would create one of the finest libraries of illustrated books, noted that the first print he purchased, an etching by D. Y. Cameron, had come from Sessler.

While expanding his interests, Sessler retained his passion for Dickens. In July 1909 a London newspaper reported, "Charles Sessler, of Philadelphia, has come to London expressly to bid on the favorite chair of Charles Dickens from the Gad's Hill residence, which figures in many of his portraits. . . . It is to be sold at Sotheby's July 14 and Mr. Sessler expects to take it to America with him. He it was who last year bought the last pen used by Dickens in writing *Edwin Drood*," Dickens's last (and unfinished) work. Sessler bought the chair for a client, but the ensuing furor convinced Sessler to allow it to remain in England. On 29 August 1910 the *Philadelphia Morning Ledger* reported that Sessler had bought six Dickens presentation volumes: three signed to Lord Francis Jeffrey, two to Thomas Beard (who recommended Dickens for a post on the *Morning*

Entrance to the Rare Book Room of Sessler's Walnut Street shop

Chronicle), and one to the artist Daniel Maclise (who painted a portrait of Dickens). About the same time Sessler initiated various schemes to raise money for three of Dickens's granddaughters who had fallen into relative indigence. In 1911 Sessler purchased a Dickens letter to Leigh Hunt, the only Dickens letter then known to include a word that Victorians would have regarded as improper: *damned*.

On his frequent and lengthy trips to Europe, Sessler visited Walter Spencer's shop at 27 New Oxford Street West, London. Spencer was a major source of literary relics of nineteenth-century British authors. He had a special affection for Dickens and bought extensively from such Dickens family members as Kate Perugini, the author's daughter, and Georgina Hogarth, his wife's sister. Sessler himself also bought from these women. A Dickens relic that Sessler never sold was given to him by Perugini as an expression of thanks for his many kindnesses to the Dickens family. The relic, suitably framed, was the tombstone of a Dickens family pet canary, bearing the inscription "This is the grave of Dick, the best of birds born at Broadstairs Mids. 1851, died at Gadshill Place 14th of October 1866."

The war years were relatively quiet for the rare-book trade. Once World War I ended, however, the race was on to secure British literary trea-

sures and to deposit them in American libraries. In early June 1920, having spent nine weeks searching for books on his second postwar trip to Europe, Sessler arrived in New York. *The New York Times* reported that he had returned with $325,000 worth of original manuscripts; the *Philadelphia Public Ledger* put the figure at $365,000. Included in this cache were letters from Charles Lamb to Samuel Taylor Coleridge; these went to Huntington.

On 20 May 1921 in London, Sessler bought at auction a defective Second Folio of Shakespeare with a six-line manuscript signed "Wm. Shakspeare." Lacking the portrait of Shakespeare, the verses by Ben Jonson, and pages 397–419 (though supplied in manuscript), the book sold for only £45 ($220). Sessler offered the book and manuscript to the preeminent Shakespeare collector Folger, who did not believe the manuscript to be in Shakespeare's hand. Nonetheless, Folger paid Sessler $1,500, writing on 25 October 1921,

You present the history of your folio in a most romantic way, and you certainly, in addition to being very fortunate, have been very clever in what you have gotten together. Of course, granting the writing is forged, it has some Shakespeare interest.... It is a satisfaction to meet anyone as enthusiastic as you are, and a great pleasure for me when that enthusiasm is centered on Shakespeare.

Sessler continued to sell to Folger. All the other items were of the highest quality, such as a fine Fourth Folio that Folger acquired on 10 November 1921 for $1,000.

The 1921 trip also yielded, for £910, a prime copy of *The Posthumous Papers of the Pickwick Club* (London: Chapman and Hall, 1836–1837) in parts. The copy had belonged to the English collector Henry William Bruton, whose library was sold in 1897. Judge Patterson, president of the Dickens Fellowship of Philadelphia, was the next owner, and Newton secured it from Sessler.

In 1922 the highlight of Sessler's European trip was the sale of the library of Baroness Burdett-Coutts, rich in Dickens material, by Sotheby's in London. Much of the bidding was dominated by two Philadelphians, Philip Rosenbach and Sessler. Though Rosenbach bought more, Sessler secured six Dickens first editions inscribed to the baroness.

After the Burdett-Coutts sale Sessler, nearing seventy, avoided British auctions, preferring private sales. On 11 May 1926 *The New York Times* reported that Sessler was about to leave Southampton with $400,000 of illuminated manuscripts and a silver map of the world that had belonged to

Sir Francis Drake. On 24 March 1927 *The New York Times* reported Sessler's purchase in London of Dickens's manuscript of "The Mud Fog Papers" for about $16,000 and a Burns manuscript for $20,000. Sessler also secured letters and autographs of James I; Mary, Queen of Scots; and Catherine de Médicis. The total value of his purchases on this trip to England was some $700,000.

At the 1929 Kern sale Sessler was among the top buyers, spending $150,000. Among his purchases were a single manuscript page of Samuel Johnson's *Dictionary of the English Language* (1755) for Colonel Gimbel at $11,000 and Lamb's eighty-page manuscript of his contributions to William Hone's *Every-Day Book and Table Book* for Currie at $48,000. The *Table Book* was originally published in fifty-five weekly numbers by Hunt and Clark (London) between January 1827 and January 1828.

Sessler was also involved in two controversies that emerged from the Kern sale. From Walter Spencer, Sessler had bought what he believed was the only copy of the first edition of Henry Fielding's *Tom Jones* (6 volumes, London: A. Millar, 1749) in original boards. Sessler sold the set to Kern for $3,000, and at the Kern sale Rosenbach bought it for $29,000. The volumes eventually became the property of Lord Vincent Rothschild, and in 1940 John Hayward, a bibliographer working in the Rothschild library, discovered that some of the leaves were not those of the first edition. Lord Rothschild sued, and Sessler's firm was among those that had to pay damages; the Sessler share amounted to $4,500.

The other questionable item in the Kern sale was a holograph translation, attributed to Oliver Goldsmith, of "Vida's Scacchis, or Chess." Sessler had bought it for Kern at Sotheby's in 1928 for $28,000 plus commission. Owen Young bought it at the Kern sale for $27,000 with Sessler as underbidder. After the sale Young showed it to A. S. W. Rosenbach, who expressed doubts about it, as did the Goldsmith scholar Katherine C. Balderston, who had originally authenticated the item. Young returned the manuscript to Kern, and Kern sued Sessler.

As Sessler approached the age of seventy-five, his son Joseph Leonard (known as Dick) was taking over increased responsibility for the print business. In November 1929 Sessler put out a catalogue of etchings, only the second catalogue in the company's history. At the same time the knowledgeable Zahn, who had gone to work for Sessler in 1905 when she was sixteen, was taking over much of the book business.

Sessler nonetheless remained active. In 1931 he spent £1 million buying books in England. The

Sessler in his seventies

following year he and Newton were both in London buying books, and in September, Sessler was soliciting material from the Dickens family. He was especially eager to secure the manuscript of the then-unpublished *A Child's Life of Christ*, owned by Henry Fielding Dickens, the author's son, who was not willing to part with it at that time. In April 1935 Sessler scored his last coup in the world of rare books when he located and bought the manuscript score, thought to have been destroyed, of Richard Wagner's first opera, *Die Hochzeit*.

Sessler died on 4 September 1935 at his home in Merion, a Philadelphia suburb. Sessler's firm continued to function under his son's leadership, with Zahn running the rare-book business. After the death of J. Leonard Sessler, Zahn continued the business until her death in 1975; the Sessler family sold the business to W. Graham Arader II in 1979.

Sessler was one of the major figures in the rare-book trade during the golden age of book collecting in America. If George D. Smith or Rosenbach bought and sold larger quantities of prime literary property, Sessler sold material equally desirable and important. Sessler had a deep appreciation for the content of what he sold, especially in the field of nineteenth-century English literature. An accomplished linguist and Dickensian, Sessler was also a supreme salesman; Newton once commented, "Sessler studies his customers' weaknesses—that's where his strength lies." He understood the nature of the collecting impulse and knew how to use it to his advantage.

References:

George Allen, "Old Booksellers of Philadelphia," in his *Four Talks for Bibliophiles* (Philadelphia: Free Library, 1958), pp. 33–34;

John C. Eckel, *Catalogue of Important and Interesting Books* (Philadelphia: Sessler, 1904);

Etching Since Nineteen Hundred as Viewed by D. O. C. (an Amateur) and Published (as an Advertisement) by Charles Sessler (Philadelphia: Sessler, 1930);

A. Edward Newton, *The Amenities of Book-Collecting and Kindred Affections* (Boston: Atlantic Monthly, 1918), p. 46;

Ruth Brown Park, "A Great Romantic," *Publishers' Weekly* (16 November 1929): 2399–2403;

Prints of Distinction, 1929 (Philadelphia: Sessler, 1929);

Edwin Wolf II and John F. Fleming, *Rosenbach: A Biography* (Cleveland: World, 1960).

Papers:

There is a set of three Sessler family scrapbooks at the Free Library of Philadelphia. The Free Library also holds Sessler family relics, including Dick the canary's tombstone, an account book from the 1880s, and volumes inscribed to Sessler by their authors. The Historical Society of Pennsylvania holds the business archives of the Sessler firm, though almost nothing remains from the period of Charles Sessler's lifetime except trays of customer cards. The archive of the Philadelphia branch of the Dickens Fellowship is currently in the possession of David Klappholz; it will be donated by the current officers of the Philadelphia branch to a suitable library in the near future. The major located collections of Sessler's correspondence are at the Folger Shakespeare Library in Washington, D.C., and the Huntington Library in San Marino, California. There are a few Sessler letters at Yale. A. Edward Newton's letters to Charles Sessler and Mabel Zahn are in Klappholz's collection.

Harry B. Smith

(28 December 1860 – 1 January 1936)

Judith A. Overmier
University of Oklahoma

BOOKS: *A Pleasaunt Comedie of the Life of Will Shakspeare, Player. . . .* (Chicago: Dial, 1893);

Lyrics and Sonnets (Chicago: Dial, 1894);

Stage Lyrics (New York: R. H. Russell, 1900);

A Sentimental Library, Comprising Books Formerly Owned by Famous Writers, Presentation Copies, Manuscripts and Drawings, Collected and Described by Harry B. Smith (New York: Privately printed, 1914);

A Catalogue of One Hundred Rare Books and Autographs (New York: Harry B. Smith, 1921);

Richard Wagner: His Life and Adventures Related in His Own Words with Music and Scenes from His Music Dramas (New York: Chauncey Holt, 1921);

First Nights and First Editions (Boston: Little, Brown, 1931);

First Editions, Association Books, Autograph Letters and Manuscripts by the Brownings, Dickens, Byron, Thackeray, Swinburne, Lamb and Other Esteemed Nineteenth Century English and French Authors, and An Important Collection of Books, Autographs, Relics, Prints, and Other Material by or Relating to Napoleon I, Collected and Catalogued by the Late Harry B. Smith (New York: American Art Association and Anderson Galleries, 1936).

OTHER: *The Begum: A Hindoo Comic Opera in Two Acts,* libretto by Smith (Chicago: Blakely, 1887);

Robin Hood: A Comic Opera in Three Acts, libretto by Smith (Chicago: Thompson, 1890);

The Fencing Master: A Comic Opera in Three Acts, libretto by Smith (Buffalo, N.Y.: Baker, Jones, 1892);

The Wizard of the Nile: Comic Opera in Three Acts, libretto by Smith (New York: Schuberth, 1895);

The Fortune Teller: Comic Opera in Three Acts, book by Smith (London: Ascherberg / New York: Witmark, 1899);

The Earliest Letters of Charles Dickens, edited by Smith (Cambridge, Mass.: University Press, 1910);

Gypsy Love: A Romantic Opera in Three Acts, book by Smith, lyrics by Smith and Robert B. Smith (New York: Chappell, 1911);

Harry B. Smith (photograph by Dudley Hoyt, New York)

Sweethearts: A Comic Opera in Two Acts, book by Smith and Fred De Gresac (New York: Schirmer, 1913).

SELECTED PERIODICAL PUBLICATIONS–
UNCOLLECTED: "Presentation Copies and Association Books," *Publishers' Weekly,* 102 (1922): 1544–1546;

"How Charles Dickens Wrote His Books," *Harper's Magazine,* 150 (December 1924): 50–60;

"Sherlock Holmes Solves the Mystery of Edwin
Drood," *Munsey's Magazine,* 83 (December
1924): 385–400;

"Gentlemen of the Old School," *Colophon,* 1, part 3
(1930): 1–8;

"Me and Napoleon," *Colophon,* 3, part 11 (1932):
1–16.

Librettist and lyricist Harry Bache Smith was
the earliest extensive collector of association copies:
books that can be linked to their authors or other
notable people through inscriptions, annotations,
bookplates, or other identifying marks. His passionate and articulate advocacy of that interest had established association copies as a legitimate and desirable collecting field by the turn of the century,
and his catalogue, *A Sentimental Library* (1914),
strongly influenced an entire generation of book collectors.

Smith was born in Buffalo, New York, but
grew up and established his first ties with the
book-collecting community in Chicago, where his
parents, Josiah Bailey Smith and Elizabeth Bach
Smith, had moved in 1864. He was called Harry (or
sometimes Hank), and although his name generally
appears as Harry B. Smith on title pages and as
Harry Bache Smith in reference books, he writes in
his autobiography, *First Nights and First Editions*
(1931), that his name was really Henry Bach Smith.
The name Henry derived from an uncle, Henry Tis-
dale Smith, and there was no *e* at the end of Bach,
which was his mother's maiden name. Smith added
the *e* himself, he says, because his childhood friends
always mispronounced his middle name. Also, there
is no evidence for conjectures that his musical talent
was inherited because he was related to Johann Sebastian Bach, but "wouldn't it be fun if he were [con-
nected]," Smith writes.

However, in his 1922 article "Presentation
Copies and Association Books," Smith asserts that
his bibliomania *is* inherited—and incurable, as well.
In various places in his articles and books he mentions early family influences on his collecting. He reports that as a child he received an unspecified edition of William Hazlitt's *Life of Napoleon Buonaparte*
(first published in four volumes, 1828–1830) from
his grandfather. He also tells of his admiration of an
1870 present from his grandmother to his parents of
William Henry Ireland's *Life of Napoleon Bonaparte*
(London, 1823–1828), a four-volume work with
prints by George Cruikshank. Smith reports that
these books burned in the Chicago Fire of 9 October
1871. Given his later notable collections of Napoleon and Cruikshank materials, it seems likely that

his assessment of the strength of early family influences on his book collecting is accurate.

According to Smith, the Chicago Fire curtailed
plans for his newly begun college preparatory education, presumably because of family finances. Instead he attended public school and then worked for
several years in a variety of occupations, some unsuccessfully, such as acting. He was successful as a
newspaper reporter and columnist for several different newspapers, including the *Chicago Daily News*
and the *Chicago Tribune,* writing drama, literature,
and music criticism. It was during this period of his
life, while he was working for the *Chicago Daily News,*
that he met the poet Eugene Field, who was the
newspaper's literary editor. Field introduced him to
the people who populated the "Saints and Sinners
Corner" of McClurg's Bookshop. That group of collectors influenced Smith in many ways. He was a so-
ciable person, and his connection with this lively
group ensured from the beginning that he became a
gregarious book collector, interacting with other
bibliophiles and writing about these interests.

Throughout his book-collecting career Smith
continued his writing about books, theater, and music; he also published fiction and poetry in newspapers; in major magazines such as *Scribner's, Harper's,
Atlantic Monthly,* and the *American Mercury;* and in
book form. His best-known writing took the form of
librettos and lyrics. He and the musician Reginald
De Koven began collaborating and wrote *The Begum: A Hindoo Comic Opera in Two Acts* (1887), the first
successful American operetta (in the style of Gilbert
and Sullivan's 1885 hit *The Mikado*). Smith and De
Koven's first smash hit was *Robin Hood: A Comic Opera in Three Acts* (1890). Smith wrote the librettos for
more than three hundred musicals and the lyrics for
more than six thousand songs from 1887 to 1932.
During this long and successful musical career he
collaborated with Victor Herbert, Jerome Kern,
Irving Berlin, John Philip Sousa, Franz Lehar, and
Sigmund Romberg. He wrote Florenz Ziegfeld's Fol-
lies from their inception in 1907 through 1912.
Smith's better-known lyrics include "Gypsy Love
Song" (1898), "The Sheik of Araby" (with Francis
Wheeler, 1921), and "Play, Gypsies, Dance, Gyp-
sies" (1926).

It was these musical successes that provided
him with the funds to support himself and his family
and to collect books. It seems probable that his first
marriage, to Lena Reed on 12 October 1887, was
based on the strength of the reception of *The Begum.*
His collecting efforts increased then, too, again often under the influence of the Saints and Sinners.
George Millard, for example, gave him a replacement set of Ireland's *Life of Napoleon* and thus en-

Page from the manuscript for a story written by Napoleon at eighteen and acquired by Smith for his Napoleon collection (from Smith's First Nights and First Editions, *1931)*

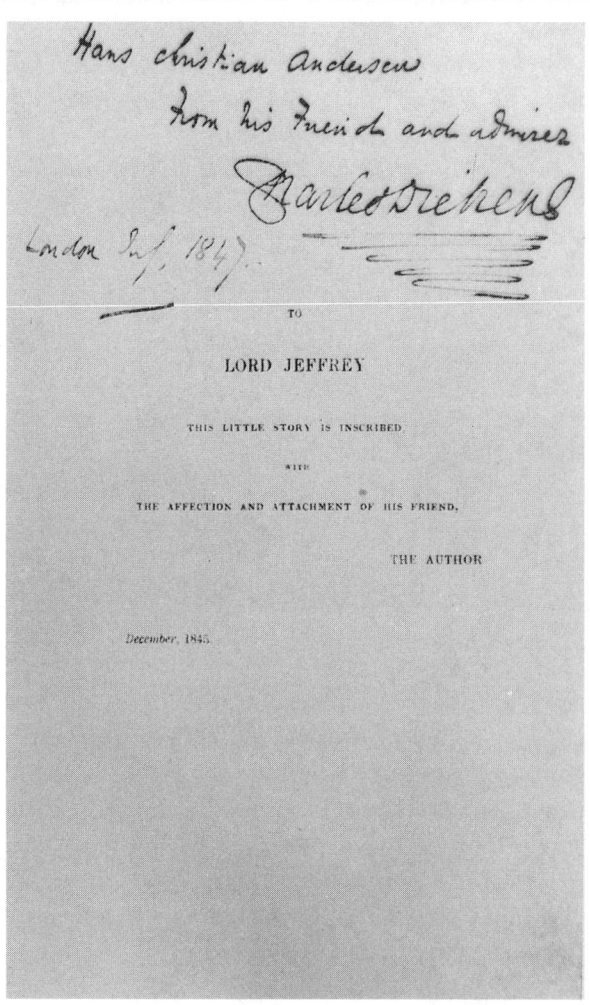

Inscription from Charles Dickens to Hans Christian Andersen on the dedication page in Smith's copy of The Cricket on the Hearth *(from Smith's* First Nights and First Editions, *1931)*

couraged the establishing of Smith's Napoleon collection and his affinity for books illustrated by Cruikshank. It was also his sixty-dollar acquisition from Millard in 1891 of an inscribed first edition of *The Pickwick Papers* (first published in twenty parts, London: Chapman and Hall, 1836–1837) that initiated his collecting of presentation copies. That particular volume was a copy that Charles Dickens had bound in green morocco for presentation to a friend, J. P. Harley. Eventually Smith owned three presentation copies of *The Pickwick Papers*. The second was also a specially bound copy and had been presented by Dickens to his friend the actor William C. Macready. Smith's third copy of *The Pickwick Papers* was in parts, with paper covers and advertisements, and had been presented by Dickens to Mary Hogarth, his wife's sister. Three presentation copies seemed excessive to Smith, so he sold the Harley

copy in 1905 for $130. Smith wrote later that he thought the "awkward and ambiguous term 'association copies' had not been coined" at the time of his acquisition of the Dickens.

A Shakespeare satire with no book-collecting connection was Smith's first publication, but his book-collecting passions show up in much of the rest of his writing. For example, his book *Lyrics and Sonnets* (1894) has an entire section titled "Bookish Ballads" that consists of ten poems. The poems include "A Ballade of Books Well Bound," in which he defends his taste for good bindings—"I like to see my friends well drest"—and "A Book-Lover's Vision," about a marvelous heavenly library where "Each book will be a treasure rare, / A perfect copy, tall and fair." "Editio Princeps" derides those who buy a first edition just because it is a first edition, and in "Extra Illustrating" a book speaks to the poet of its humiliation when someone has "despoiled" it by removing from it materials such as engraved portraits, prints, autograph letters, documents, or drawings that are then added to another book. The latter poem is ironic, given Smith's later efforts at extra-illustrating a life of Napoleon.

At the death of the collector Charles W. Frederickson in 1897 Smith's interest in association copies gained impetus with the $615 acquisition of Frederickson's copy of Percy Bysshe Shelley's poem *Queen Mab* (London: Printed by P. B. Shelley, 1813), which was inscribed by Shelley to Mary Wollstonecraft Godwin with the note "You see, Mary, I have not forgotten you." Her annotations, written in the book in 1814 shortly before they eloped, are more extensive. This book became the most written about and famous association copy known to the general public, and Smith reports in his 1922 article that its last known selling price was $9,000. It was Frederickson's collecting that Smith described in his 1930 article "Gentlemen of the Old School." Frederickson had turned away from the traditional interest in Americana and collected early-nineteenth-century literature, especially poets; he liked books that had been owned by their authors, particularly Charles Lamb. When Frederickson died in 1897, his books were sold at auction by Bangs and Company. Smith was a major buyer at that sale, and he lauded Frederickson as an early, perhaps the first, "sentimental" association copy collector. In his writings Smith frequently disparages the fact that everyone collected Americana, so his appreciation of Frederickson encompasses several shared collecting interests.

During the next two decades his success as a librettist and lyricist continued; a book of his lyrics, considered the first publication of collected musical song lyrics, was published with success in 1900. After Lena Reed's death, Smith remarried in November 1906; his new wife, Irene Bentley, was a successful musical comedy actress. His writing also continued, and his next book, *The Earliest Letters of Charles Dickens* (1910), highlighted the scholarly uses of association materials collected by Smith.

As World War I approached, Smith began to withdraw from collecting association copies, which were no longer comfortably within his financial reach. This retreat has been attributed to the increased interest shown in this field by extremely wealthy collectors, such as Henry E. Huntington and John Pierpont Morgan, and to the increase in the monetary value of association copies. Both factors could be considered, in part at least, due to the success of Smith's general championship of the genre. A specific individual whom Smith is often credited with addicting to collecting association copies was Jerome Kern. The composer reportedly accompanied Smith to a book auction and purchased a copy of John Keats's *Endymion* (1818), which he and Smith joyfully discovered bore a previously unknown Keats signature.

During this period Smith began to prepare his most influential work, *A Sentimental Library*. Smith's papers include his notes for the book and drafts of the manuscript. A 17 September 1913 letter from Luther S. Livingston, author of the "Appreciation," or introduction, to the volume, accompanied his return of the catalogue manuscript to Smith. Livingston writes that he is glad Smith was "pleased with the Introduction," and he tells Smith of his plans to write two or three articles of a column each in the *New York Evening Post* and in the *Boston Evening Transcript* about Smith's books, in conjunction with the publication of the catalogue. It was a volume well worth notice in the press. In the preface, which Smith titles "Apology," he makes his now famous confession: "It is not the yielding to temptation that oppresses me; but oh, the remorse for the times I yielded not!" He yielded often enough; *A Sentimental Library,* which does not even include his entire collection (not the Napoleon material, for instance), has 851 entries, 667 of which are nineteenth-century English authors. The Mary Hogarth *Pickwick* is part of the notable association collection. Smith had purchased this copy in 1899 at the William Wright sale for 100 guineas; he points out that when he sold his library in 1914 this item was valued at $6,000 and that the dealer then sold it in 1921 for $15,000. Smith had managed to purchase presentation copies of all but one of Dickens's books, and all are described in this catalogue. Robert Browning's presentation copy of *The Ring and the Book* (four volumes, 1868–1869) to Alfred Tennyson is nicely balanced

by Tennyson's presentation copy of *Enoch Arden* (1864) to Browning. Evidence of the connections between many nineteenth-century authors is found in the entries of *A Sentimental Library*.

While most of the entries are for printed books, manuscript materials are also present, ranging from single letters to the youthful correspondence of W. H. Kolle and Dickens that Smith published in 1910. Authors' manuscripts, such as a sixteen-page story by Charlotte Brontë, are also included, as are documents, such as George Gordon, Lord Byron's will and marriage license. Even a few artifacts, such as a brass candlestick used by Dickens, found their way into the catalogue.

Smith also included sections in *A Sentimental Library* for "Seventeenth and Eighteenth Century Authors," "French Authors," "German Authors," "American Authors," "Historical Celebrities," "The Drama," and "Bindings and Extra-Illustrated Books." These sections include such items as William Hogarth's copy of Henry Fielding's *Joseph Andrews* (two volumes, 1742); Smith's own copy of *Love-Songs of Childhood* (1894), presented to him by his friend Field, the author and Madame Pompadour's copy of the edition of Giovanni Boccaccio's *Il Decameron* printed by Daniel Elzevir in 1665.

It has been suggested by Edwin Wolf II that it was the en bloc purchase by A. S. W. Rosenbach in 1914 of the association copies comprising Smith's "Sentimental Library" that stimulated the career of the noted and colorful Rosenbach as a book dealer. Rosenbach reportedly paid $79,000 for the collection and then sold some of the items to such noted purchasers as A. Conger Goodyear, John L. Clawson, Henry Clay Folger, William K. Bixby, and A. Edward Newton. Rosenbach sold those titles remaining from the Sentimental Library through his catalogues, beginning in 1916 with Catalogue 18.

Smith kept on collecting, of course, and writing about his interests. One area which Smith continued to build after the 1914 sale of his Sentimental Library to Rosenbach was his Napoleon collection, but he also continued to acquire items connected to Shelley, Lamb, and Dickens. Vincent Starrett wrote to Smith on 23 November 1928 thanking him for his Edwin Drood paper, which Starrett says he will add to his own "(I think) rather notable collection of Drood-ana." Smith's article explaining how Sherlock Holmes solved the mystery of Drood had first appeared in *Munsey's Magazine* in December 1924, and it would certainly have appealed to the noted mystery collector. A 19 December 1931 postcard from bibliophile, editor, and book collector John T. Winterich includes the inquiry, "would you do another Colophon piece soon?" Presumably Smith's

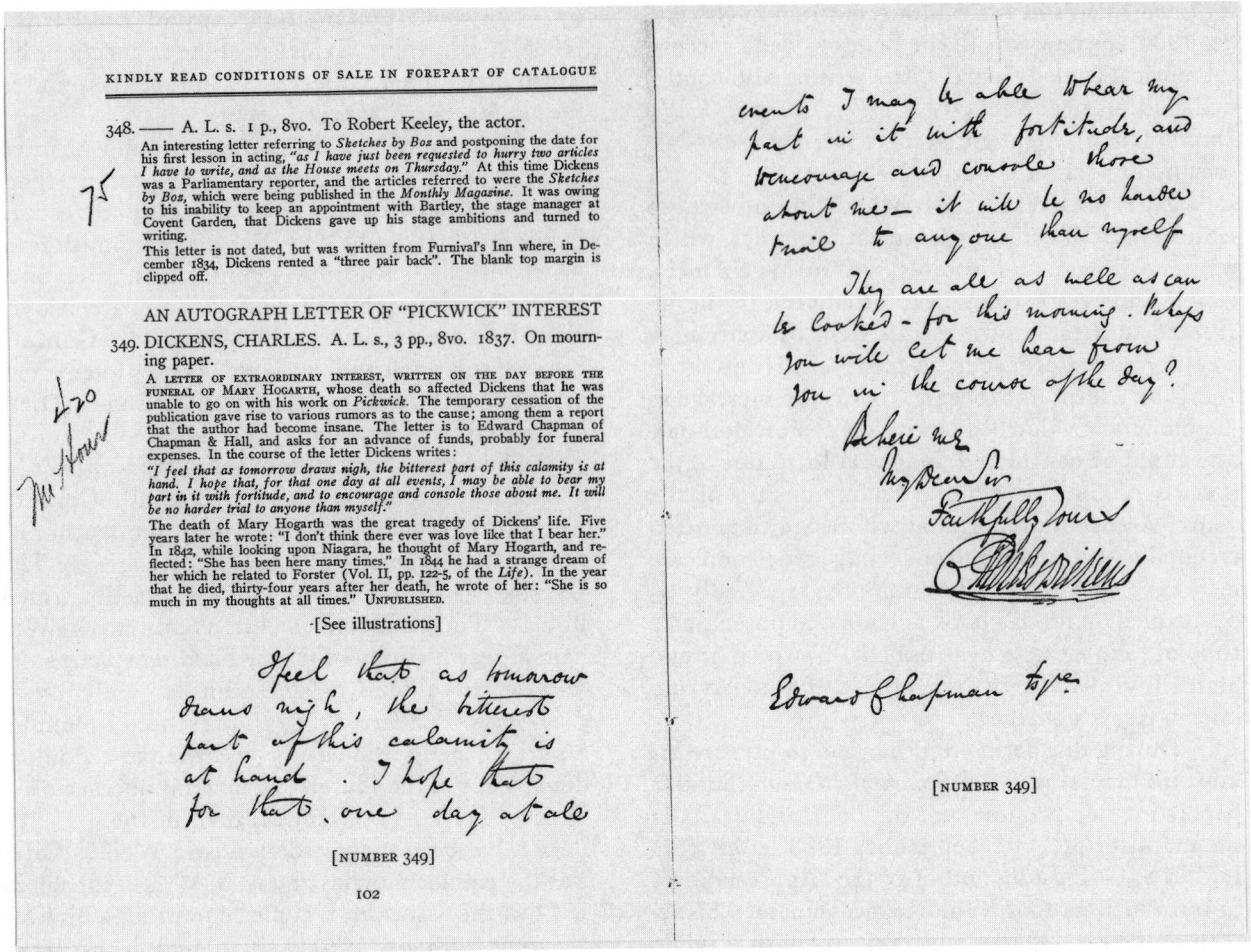

KINDLY READ CONDITIONS OF SALE IN FOREPART OF CATALOGUE

348. —— A. L. s. 1 p., 8vo. To Robert Keeley, the actor.

An interesting letter referring to *Sketches by Boz* and postponing the date for his first lesson in acting, "*as I have just been requested to hurry two articles I have to write, and as the House meets on Thursday.*" At this time Dickens was a Parliamentary reporter, and the articles referred to were the *Sketches by Boz*, which were being published in the *Monthly Magazine*. It was owing to his inability to keep an appointment with Bartley, the stage manager at Covent Garden, that Dickens gave up his stage ambitions and turned to writing.

This letter is not dated, but was written from Furnival's Inn where, in December 1834, Dickens rented a "three pair back". The blank top margin is clipped off.

AN AUTOGRAPH LETTER OF "PICKWICK" INTEREST

349. DICKENS, CHARLES. A. L. s., 3 pp., 8vo. 1837. On mourning paper.

A LETTER OF EXTRAORDINARY INTEREST, WRITTEN ON THE DAY BEFORE THE FUNERAL OF MARY HOGARTH, whose death so affected Dickens that he was unable to go on with his work on *Pickwick*. The temporary cessation of the publication gave rise to various rumors as to the cause; among them a report that the author had become insane. The letter is to Edward Chapman of Chapman & Hall, and asks for an advance of funds, probably for funeral expenses. In the course of the letter Dickens writes:

"*I feel that as tomorrow draws nigh, the bitterest part of this calamity is at hand. I hope that, for that one day at all events, I may be able to bear my part in it with fortitude, and to encourage and console those about me. It will be no harder trial to anyone than myself.*"

The death of Mary Hogarth was the great tragedy of Dickens' life. Five years later he wrote: "I don't think there ever was love like that I bear her." In 1842, while looking upon Niagara, he thought of Mary Hogarth, and reflected: "She has been here many times." In 1844 he had a strange dream of her which he related to Forster (Vol. II, pp. 122-5, of the *Life*). In the year that he died, thirty-four years after her death, he wrote of her: "She is so much in my thoughts at all times." UNPUBLISHED.

-[See illustrations]

[NUMBER 349]

102

[NUMBER 349]

Pages from a priced catalogue for the April 1936 sale of Smith's collection. Item 349 was bought by W. T. Howe.

1932 *Colophon* article, "Me and Napoleon," was the response. In it Smith describes the development of his interest in the collecting of Napoleon material, including the extra-illustrating of a *Life,* during which he accumulated so much material that he had to have it bound in Paris in seven large folio volumes with a special Empire cabinet built to contain them. The contents of this extra-illustrated life of Napoleon are chronological and comprise autographs, letters to and from relatives and friends, and nonpersonal letters from all over Europe, in many languages. Even battle plans are included in the collection; letters and documents of persons around Napoleon were also collected together with prints and portraits of these people and of Napoleon himself. It would be readily apparent from Smith's description of it that the collection got out of hand, even had he not so informed his readers.

Smith was often amusing about his affection for his books, as when he writes that they are loved and will be "until they go to the auction when each will be changed; yea, in the twinkling of an eye, from a sacred relic to a Lot." His love of books ex-

tended to a desire to run a bookstore. Smith's 1922 article on presentation copies is prefaced by an editorial comment that the "entrance of Harry B. Smith into the field of rare book selling was one of the interesting trade events of last year!" and that his collecting specialty of association books "has been continued in his bookshop" at 319 West 107th Street in New York. Smith published his first sale catalogue in 1921 with an introduction announcing to "bibliophiles, bibliopoles, bibliotaphs, and readers that he has engaged in the old book business. . . ." The catalogue includes notable association items, such as another copy of Browning's *The Ring and the Book,* this one with Browning's presentation inscription to Dante Gabriel Rossetti; a copy of the first edition of *Alice's Adventures Under Ground, Being a Facsimile of the Original MS. Book Afterwards Developed into "Alice's Adventures in Wonderland"* (1886), with Lewis Carroll's inscription to novelist Charlotte Yonge; and Charles Dickens's *The Cricket on the Hearth* (1845), with a presentation inscription to Hans Christian Andersen. Smith's catalogue descriptions are detailed and scholarly. His description of *The Cricket,* for example, notes that the influence of Andersen's works on Dickens led the latter to write *A Christmas Carol* (1843) and *The Cricket* in a new style, and that Andersen was a guest in Dickens's home when Andersen visited England. No wonder Smith wrote "Trade was brisk," and no wonder the reviews praised the catalogue so highly that Smith was as proud of his work "as a comedian praised for playing Hamlet."

Smith's intelligent and witty autobiography, *First Nights and First Editions,* successfully intertwined his professional careers and his primary avocation. Like much of his other writing it is light and amusing, full of plays on words, such as when he writes of the sixty-dollar purchase of the Harley *Pickwick Papers* during the early, less-solvent stage of his career that "the means did not justify the spend." It is clear from his reminiscences that his theater and book-collecting worlds overlapped often. For example, Kern and comedian Francis Wilson, both of whom were Smith's collaborators, were also book collectors. Smith recalls his first trip to London and his visits to bookshops in Charing Cross Road with Augustin Daly, New York theater owner, playwright, and book collector. His enormous zest and energy are evident throughout his entire life, never more so than when in his early sixties he wrote with pride about his bookshop and his first sales catalogue. He had started a second catalogue when he was called upon to write another comic opera, but he reports he fully intended to return to the bookselling business eventually. He was seventy years old when he wrote his lively, bookish autobiography.

When Smith died in Atlantic City, New Jersey, in 1936, he still had a substantial library; nearly a thousand volumes were sold in four sessions on the afternoons and evenings of 8 and 9 April, four months after his death, at Anderson Galleries. The University of California, Berkeley's copy of the sale catalogue has the prices neatly written in and records a total sale figure of $29,243.50. That final auction catalogue, its contents "collected and catalogued by the Late Harry B. Smith," includes sentimental associations of Smith himself. The auction catalogue lists two copies of Ireland's *Life of Napoleon,* that earliest influence on Smith, and items 579–671 are "Napoleonic Books, Autographs, Prints, and Relics." Dickens's presentation copy to Andersen of his *The Cricket,* which apparently had not sold from Smith's own cherished first catalogue, where it was listed for $1,400, brought $1,450 at the auction. One of the volumes sold, Field's *Love-Songs of Childhood* inscribed to Mr. and Mrs. Harry B. Smith, had been originally in Smith's Sentimental Library; Smith must have repurchased it at some point, no doubt for sentimental reasons.

Harry B. Smith was an eclectic collector "intrigued," he said, by everything "excepting Americana, incunabula, and telephone directories." His overarching interest in association copies was both sentimental and intellectual. He was sensitive to the emotional connotations of owning a volume held, inscribed, annotated, interleaved, or presented by its author; his collecting was informed by the knowledge that association copies comprised material that contributed to many fields of scholarship.

References:

Gerald Bordman, *Jerome Kern: His Life and Music* (New York: Oxford University Press, 1980);

Edwin Wolf II, "The 'Sentimental Library' and the War Years," in *Rosenbach: A Biography*, by Wolf and John F. Fleming (Cleveland: World, 1960), pp. 89–99.

Papers:

Smith's papers are in the Harry Ransom Humanities Research Center at the University of Texas at Austin.

Vincent Starrett
(26 October 1886 – 5 January 1974)

Alison M. Scott
Bowling Green State University

BOOKS: *Arthur Machen: A Novelist of Ecstasy and Sin* (Chicago: Walter M. Hill, 1918);

Estrays, by Starrett, Thomas Kennedy, George Seymour, and Basil Thompson (Chicago: Camelot Press, 1918);

The Escape of Alice: A Christmas Fantasy (Cedar Rapids, Iowa: Privately printed for the friends of Luther Albertus & Elinore Taylor Brewer, 1919);

Ambrose Bierce (Chicago: Walter M. Hill, 1920);

The Unique Hamlet: A Hitherto Unchronicled Adventure of Mr. Sherlock Holmes (Chicago: Privately printed for the friends of Vincent Starrett, 1920);

Rhymes for Collectors (Cedar Rapids, Iowa: Privately printed for the friends of Walter M. Hill, 1921);

A Student of Catalogues (Cedar Rapids, Iowa: Privately printed for the friends of Luther Albertus and Elinore Taylor Brewer, 1921);

Ebony Flame (Chicago: Covici-McGee, 1922);

Banners in the Dawn: Sixty-four Sonnets (Chicago: Walter M. Hill, 1923);

Buried Caesars: Essays in Literary Appreciation (Chicago: Covici-McGee, 1923);

Persons from Porlock (Chicago: Bookfellows, 1923); enlarged as *Persons from Porlock, and Other Interruptions* (Chicago: Normandie House, 1938);

Stephen Crane: A Bibliography (Philadelphia: Centaur Book Shop, 1923); revised by Starrett and Ames W. Williams (Glendale, Cal.: Valentine, 1948);

Coffins for Two (Chicago: Covici-McGee, 1924);

Flame and Dust (Chicago: Covici, 1924);

In Defense: Alfred A. Knopf—Arthur Machen vs. Covici-McGee Co.—Vincent Starrett. An Answer to an Open Letter to the Trade Issued by Alfred A. Knopf under Date of April 22, 1924 (Chicago: Covici-McGee, 1924?)

Ballad of Brobdingnag (Ysleta, Tex.: Edwin B. Hill, 1925);

Fifteen More Poems (Ysleta, Tex.: Edwin B. Hill, 1927);

Vincent Starrett, Robert Cromie, and Frederic Babcock at the Chicago Tribune

Seaports in the Moon: A Fantasia on Romantic Themes (Garden City, N.Y.: Doubleday, Doran, 1928);

Ambrose Bierce: A Bibliography (Philadelphia: Centaur Book Shop, 1929);

Murder on "B" Deck (Garden City, N.Y.: Published for the Crime Club by Doubleday, Doran, 1929; London: World's Work, 1936);

Penny Wise and Book Foolish (New York: Covici Friede, 1929);

All about Mother Goose (Glen Rock, Pa.: Apellicon, 1930);

The Blue Door: Murder—Mystery—Detection, in Ten Thrill-Packed Novelettes (Garden City, N.Y.: Published for the Crime Club by Doubleday, Doran, 1930);

Dead Man Inside (Garden City, N.Y.: Published for the Crime Club by Doubleday, Doran, 1931; London: World's Work, 1935);

The End of Mr. Garment (Garden City, N.Y.: Published for the Crime Club by Doubleday, Doran, 1932);

The Private Life of Sherlock Holmes (New York: Macmillan, 1933; London: Nicholson & Watson, 1934; revised edition, Chicago: University of Chicago Press, 1960; London: Allen & Unwin, 1961);

The Great Hotel Murder (Garden City, N.Y.: Published for the Crime Club by Doubleday, Doran, 1935; London: Nicholson & Watson, 1935);

Snow for Christmas (Glencoe, Ill.: Eileen Baskerville, 1935);

Midnight and Percy Jones (New York: Covici Friede, 1936; London: Nicholson & Watson, 1938);

Books and Bipeds (New York: Argus, 1937);

The Laughing Buddha (Mount Morris, Ill.: Magna, 1937); republished as *Murder in Peking* (New York: Lantern Press, 1946; London: Edwards, 1947);

Oriental Encounters: Two Essays in Bad Taste (Chicago: Normandie House, 1938);

An Essay on Limited Editions (Chicago: Black Cat Press, 1939);

Books Alive: A Profane Chronicle of Literary Endeavor and Literary Misdemeanor, with an Informal Index by Christopher Morley (New York: Random House, 1940);

First Editions: A Note for Beginners on the Proud and Profitable Hobby of Book Collection (Ottoman, Iowa: Privately printed by the Mercer Co. for Lawrence & Dorothy Cheever, 1940);

Bookman's Holiday: The Private Satisfactions of an Incurable Collector (New York: Random House, 1942);

Autolycus in Limbo (New York: Dutton, 1943);

A Catalogue of Original Manuscripts, and First and Other Important Editions of the Tales of Sherlock Holmes, as Written by Sir Arthur Conan Doyle; Together with Important Biographies, Pastiches, Articles, Etc., and a Few Extraordinary Association and Unique Items (New York: Scribners Rare Book Department, 1943);

The Case Book of Jimmie Lavender (New York: Gold Label Books, 1944);

Books and Bipeds (New York: Argus, 1947);

Stephen Crane: A Bibliography, by Starrett and Ames W. Williams (Glendale, Cal.: Valentine, 1948);

Brillig . . . Sonnets and Other Verse (Chicago: Dierkes Press, 1949);

Best Loved Books of the Twentieth Century (New York: Bantam, 1955);

Book Column (Chicago: Caxton Club, 1958);

The Quick and the Dead (Sauk City, Wis.: Arkham House, 1965);

Born in a Bookshop: Chapters from the Chicago Renascence (Norman: University of Oklahoma Press, 1965);

Late, Later and Possibly Last: Essays (Saint Louis: Autolycus Press, 1973).

OTHER: *In Praise of Stevenson: An Anthology,* edited by Starrett (Chicago: Bookfellows, 1919);

Stephen Crane, *Men, Women and Boats,* edited by Starrett (New York: Boni & Liveright, 1921);

The Wave, 8 issues, edited by Starrett, 1 (January 1922–October 1924);

Arthur Machen, *The Shining Pyramid,* edited by Starrett (Chicago: Covici-McGee, 1923);

Machen, *The Glorious Mystery,* edited by Starrett (Chicago: Covici-McGee, 1924);

Et Cetera: A Collector's Scrap-Book, edited by Starrett (Chicago: Covici, 1924);

George Gissing, *Sins of the Fathers and Other Tales,* edited by Starrett (Chicago: Covici, 1924);

Fourteen Great Detective Stories, edited by Starrett (New York: Modern Library, 1928; revised, edited by Howard Haycraft, 1949);

Lionel Johnson, *Three Poems,* edited by Starrett (Ysleta, Tex.: Edwin B. Hill, 1928);

Johnson, *Two Poems,* edited by Starrett (Ysleta, Tex.: Edwin B. Hill, 1929);

Gissing, *Brownie: Now First Reprinted from the Chicago Tribune Together with Six Other Stories Attributed to Him,* edited by Starrett, George Everett Hastings, and Thomas Ollive Mabbott (New York: Columbia University Press, 1931);

Crane, *Maggie: A Girl of the Streets, and Other Stories,* edited by Starrett (New York: Modern Library, 1933);

William Gillette, *Sherlock Holmes: A Play, Wherein Is Set Forth the Strange Case of Miss Alice Faulkner,* introduction by Starrett (Garden City, N.Y.: Doubleday, Doran, 1935);

A Modern Book of Wonders: Amazing Facts in a Remarkable World, edited by Starrett (Chicago: University of Knowledge, 1938);

221B: Studies in Sherlock Holmes, by Various Hands, edited by Starrett (New York: Macmillan, 1940);

Charles Dickens, *The Mystery of Edwin Drood,* introduction by Starrett (New York: Heritage Press, 1941);

Three Great Documents on Human Liberties: Magna Charta, Declaration of Independence, Constitution of the United States, edited by Starrett (Chicago: Normandie House, 1942);

World's Great Spy Stories, edited by Starrett (Cleveland & New York: World, 1944);

Two of Starrett's bookplates. The one on the right was designed by Gordon Browne.

John T. McCutcheon, *John McCutcheon's Book,* introduction by Starrett (Chicago: Caxton Club, 1948);

Arthur Conan Doyle, *The Adventures of Sherlock Holmes: A Definitive Text,* edited by Edgar W. Smith, introduction by Starrett (New York: Limited Editions Club, 1950);

Wilkie Collins, *The Moonstone,* introduction by Starrett (New York: Limited Editions Club, 1959).

Vincent Starrett was a journalist, essayist, poet, novelist, literary critic, and biographer of Sherlock Holmes. He earned the admiration of bibliophiles throughout the world and the honorary title "Number One American Bookman" through his many writings about the pleasures of books and his activities as a book collector and bibliographer.

Charles Vincent Emerson Starrett was born in Toronto on 26 October 1886. He was the first of four sons of Robert Polk Starrett, an accountant, and Margaret Deniston Young Starrett, a well-educated and deeply religious woman who was the daughter of the Toronto publisher and bookseller John Young; she would spend her last years as a missionary among the Native Americans of western Canada. The doctor, thinking that Starrett had been born dead, wrapped him in a newspaper and placed him under the bed

while attending to the mother; the baby's cries soon revealed the mistake. Starrett would later comment that "none of my writing colleagues can boast of an earlier appearance in print."

In 1890 the family moved to Chicago when Robert Starrett took a position as accountant for the Carson, Pirie, Scott and Company department store; he would remain with the firm until his death on 24 November 1918. Charlie, as Vincent Starrett was then known, made frequent visits to Toronto; some of his earliest and fondest memories were of his grandfather's bookstore and its treasures. He would title his autobiography *Born in a Bookshop: Chapters from the Chicago Renascence* (1965) in commemoration of the time he spent there. As a boy Starrett was devoted to the great nineteenth-century adventure writers G. A. Henty, Edward S. Ellis, James Otis, and Kirk Monroe. At ten he acquired his lifelong interest in the writings of Sir Arthur Conan Doyle when he read the Sherlock Holmes story "The Adventure of the Speckled Band."

Starrett dropped out of high school in 1904. He worked in the Chicago subscription office of Houghton Mifflin and in other temporary jobs before Harry Daniel, editor of the *Chicago Inter-Ocean,* hired him in 1905 to "chase pictures" for the illustrated newspaper for twelve dollars a week. Starrett's colleagues there included Ring Lardner and the cartoonist H. T. Webster.

After a year at the *Inter-Ocean,* where he signed his work C. V. E. Starrett or Charles Vincent E. Starrett, he went to work for the *Chicago Daily News.* In 1909, after his promotion to feature writer, he married Lillian Hartsig.

In 1916, after selling his first short story to *Collier's Weekly* for seventy-five dollars, Starrett left the *Daily News* to devote himself to creative writing. He sold material wherever he could, from the pulps to *The Pictorial Review,* from Sunday-school journals to *The Smart Set.* In 1918 he published his first book, *Arthur Machen: A Novelist of Ecstasy and Sin,* a revision of an earlier magazine essay. That same year Arthur Machen authorized Starrett to act as his literary agent. Starrett edited two volumes of Machen's early tales and essays, *The Shining Pyramid* (1923) and *The Glorious Mystery* (1924), which were published by Covici-McGee in Chicago. In the meantime the firm of Alfred A. Knopf had become Machen's authorized publisher in America. Machen failed to inform Knopf of his arrangement with Starrett, and the two volumes Starrett had edited led to accusations of literary piracy and threats of lawsuits from Knopf's lawyers. Starrett had letters from Machen granting him permission to publish Machen's works, and the lawsuits were dropped. Starrett and Machen resolved their differences on a trip to Europe in 1924.

Literary subjects and fiction were the mainstays of Starrett's writing, but bibliographical matters were among his favorite topics for essays. His first such article, "Have You a 'Tamerlane' in Your Attic?," appeared in *The Saturday Evening Post* on 27 June 1925 and was republished in his *Penny Wise and Book Foolish* in 1929. Dismissing Edgar Allan Poe's first published poem as "a stupid tale of a stupid monarch," Starrett discusses the astonishing monetary value of this near-mythical volume: only four copies were known to exist in 1925, and Starrett predicts that the price for the next discovery will begin at $10,000. Ordinary people, even the most bibliographically ignorant, were discussing the book: "Bridge parties disintegrate before the magic of that name and the resounding sum for which it stands." This essay set the tone of most of Starrett's bibliographical writing for popular and middlebrow audiences: he stressed the value of books as collectibles and recounted the lives and idiosyncrasies of authors, printers, publishers, and collectors.

Starrett demonstrated his skill as a technical bibliographer in the catalogues he compiled for dealers across the country, including the Centaur Book Shop of Philadelphia, and his bibliographical studies in American literature. He prepared the first comprehensive bibliography of the works of Ambrose Bierce in 1920 and performed a similar service for those of Stephen Crane in 1948.

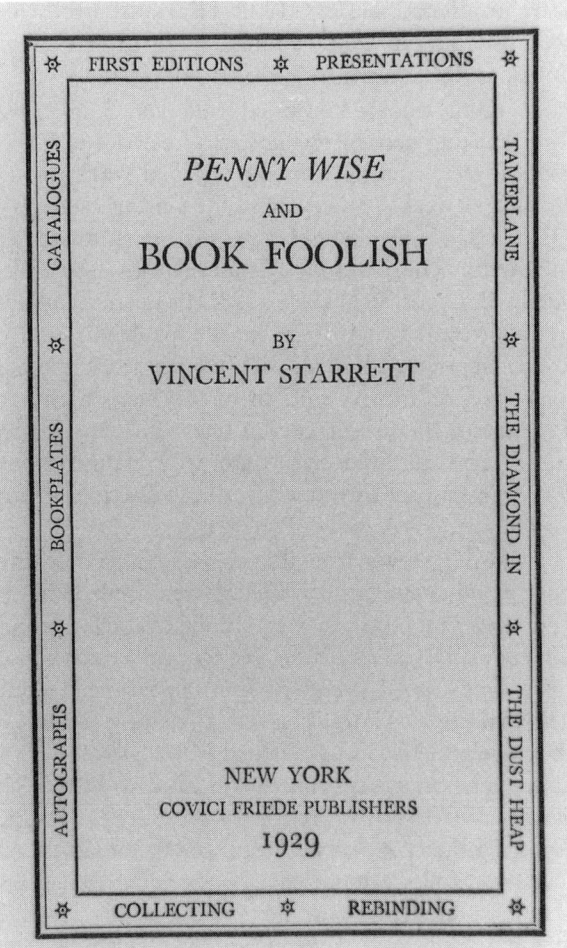

Title page for a collection of Starrett's essays on book collecting

Starrett's enthusiasm for Sherlock Holmes resulted in several books about the fictional consulting detective. His pastiche *The Unique Hamlet: A Hitherto Unchronicled Adventure of Mr. Sherlock Holmes* (1920) may be the finest of the many attempts to imitate Doyle's remarkable character: it details Holmes's search for the ultimate bibliographical rarity—a copy of an inscribed first edition of William Shakespeare's most famous play—while satirizing the foibles of book collectors and Shakespearean scholars.

As Starrett was making a reputation for himself as a writer of fiction, essays, and poetry in the years before World War I, Chicago was rising to national prominence as the home of an important literary movement: as Starrett writes in his autobiography, he had "a box seat for the famed Chicago renascence." His main contribution to the Chicago Literary Renaissance was the editing of a magazine, *The Wave,* which he produced at the urging and with the assistance of Steen Hinrichsen, a Danish immigrant printer. Starrett described the publication as "modest": after eight issues were published in 1921–1922, Hinrichsen returned to Copenhagen to escape the enterprise's rising debts, and the journal's life abruptly ended.

Though some magazines paid well, Starrett was forced to augment his income as a freelance writer by writing copy and performing editorial work for *The Austinite,* a weekly published in the Chicago suburb of Oak Park. He also taught classes in the short story at the Medill School of Journalism at Northwestern University in Evanston in 1922–1923. His financial difficulties contributed to growing marital problems, and he and Lillian were divorced in 1924. Starrett had to sell his collection of first editions of Machen's books for $2,000 to fulfill his obligations to his former wife (the couple had no children). Financial pressures would force him to part with several other collections during his lifetime.

Moving away from the relatively ill-paid fields of poetry and avant-garde fiction, Starrett drew on his experiences as a reporter to create the character Jimmie Lavender. Detective fiction was Starrett's main source of income from Lavender's first appearance in pulp magazines in 1925 until his last adventure in 1964 in the novelette "A Corpse Named Miles"; twelve of the Lavender stories were collected in *The Case Book of Jimmie Lavender* (1944). Starrett also wrote a series of stories featuring the crime-solving team of Walter Ghost and Dunstan Mollock, modeled after Sherlock Holmes and Dr. Watson, who made their debut in his first full-length detective novel, *Murder on "B" Deck* (1929). Starrett was a longtime member of the Mystery Writers of America, which has as its slogan "Crime does not pay—enough!" In 1958 Starrett received the organization's first Edgar award, designating him a Grand Master of mystery fiction. In 1961 he was elected president of the group.

Starrett had a long friendship with Christopher Morley, author of such works as *Parnassus on Wheels* (1917) and *The Haunted Bookshop* (1919). Morley prepared the index (which proved to be "so amusing it had to be moved from the back of the book to the front," as Starrett put it in *Born in a Bookshop* [1965]) to Starrett's collection of essays *Books Alive: A Profane Chronicle of Literary Endeavor and Literary Misdemeanor, with an Informal Index by Christopher Morley* (1940) and published many of Starrett's poems in his column, "The Bowling Green," in *The Saturday Review of Literature.* Like Starrett, Morley was an enthusiast for Sherlock Holmes, and the two were among the founding members of the premier society for Sherlockian admirers, the Baker Street Irregulars. The first formal meeting of the Baker Street Irregulars was held on 5 June 1934 when the charter members gathered in New York City. Starrett attended the society's "first state dinner" in December of that year; he brought as his guests Alexander Woollcott,

drama critic and host of the radio program "Town Crier," and William Gillette, whose portrayal of the great detective set the standard by which all subsequent actors have been judged. (The following year Starrett worked with Gillette on a definitive edition of Gillette's play *Sherlock Holmes.*) Starrett's "biography" of the fictional detective, *The Private Life of Sherlock Holmes* (1933), and the collection *221B: Studies in Sherlock Holmes, by Various Hands* (1940), which he edited, are regarded as groundbreaking works in the tongue-in-cheek field of Sherlockian scholarship. (In *The Private Life of Sherlock Holmes,* for example, Starrett speculates that Rex Stout's detective, Nero Wolfe, was the illegitimate son of Holmes and Irene Adler, a character in the story "A Scandal in Bohemia.")

One of Starrett's greatest commercial successes was *The Great Hotel Murder,* published in 1935 by Doubleday, Doran for the Crime Club; this novel, which marked the first appearance of Starrett's third series character, Riley Blackwood, was made into a movie by the Fox Film Corporation, starring Edmund Lowe, the same year. Throughout his life Starrett believed that many of his best-selling books were hackwork, while his better efforts failed to achieve more than moderate sales. Critics of mystery fiction regard him as a master of plotting but comparatively weak in characterization.

With the proceeds from *The Great Hotel Murder* Starrett embarked on a trip around the world in September 1935. He intended to be away from Chicago for three months; instead, the trip lasted for nearly three years. It was on this excursion that he met and married Rachel Latimer.

After his return to the United States in 1937, Starrett began to write extensively about the history of books for popular audiences. He collected these essays, written for *Coronet* and other mass-market magazines, in *Books Alive* and *Bookman's Holiday: The Private Satisfactions of an Incurable Collector* (1942). Racy and vivid, these pieces are anecdotal introductions to a wide range of bibliographic and bibliophilic topics, including the history of detective fiction, literary forgeries and frauds, and the intricacies of "high spot" collecting. Above all else, these articles convey the joy that Starrett found in books.

In the late 1930s Starrett was again under financial pressure, and he was forced to sell his collection of Sherlockiana at auction. The catalogue of the 1939 sale, which was published in 1943, has itself become a collector's item: it not only describes Starrett's own copies of Doyle's books and related titles but also includes extensive and witty accounts of such apocryphal titles as Sherlock Holmes's *Practical Handbook of Bee Culture, with Some Observations upon the Segregation of the Queen* and Col. Sebastian Moran's *Heavy Game of the Western Himalayas* (Moran, an outwardly respectable big-game hunter and

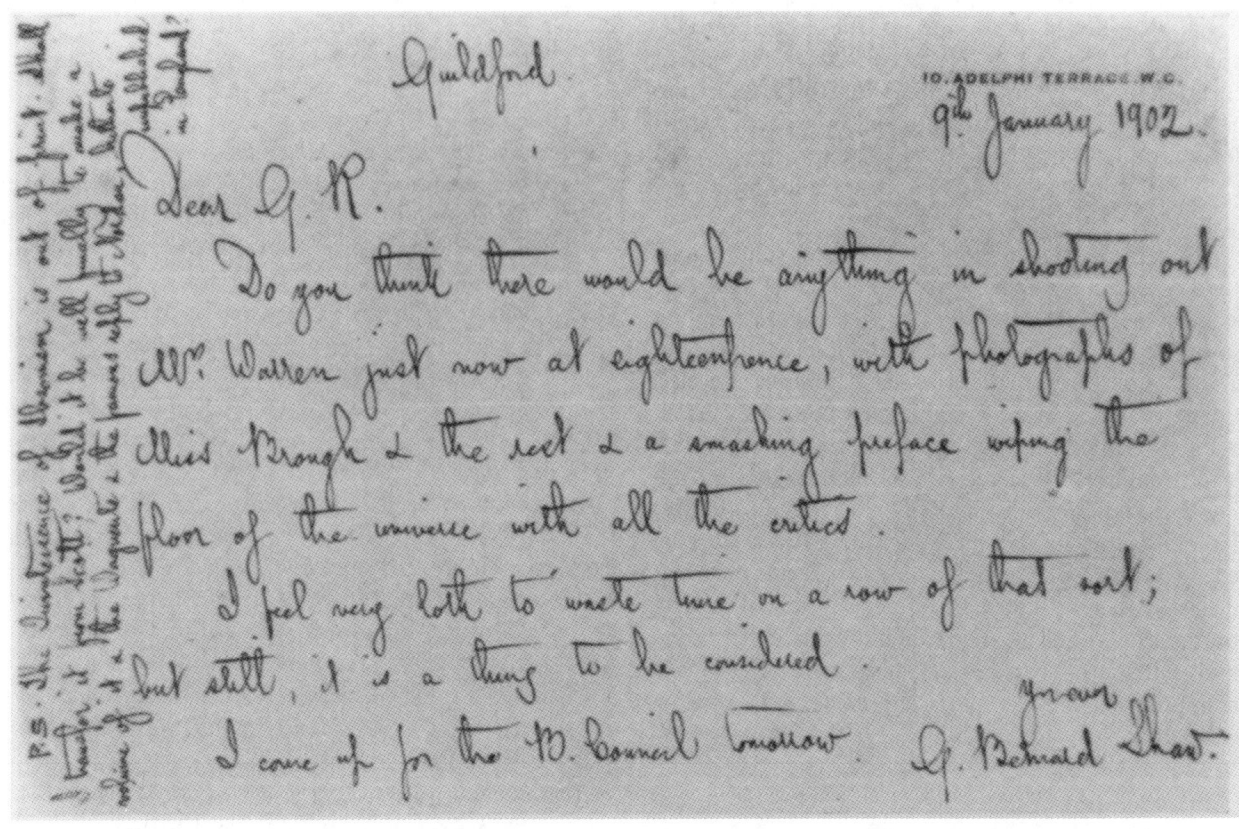

A postal card from George Bernard Shaw to his publisher, Grant Richards, that was in Starrett's collection (from Starrett's Penny Wise and Book Foolish, *1929)*

former soldier, is the confederate of Holmes's arch-enemy, Professor James Moriarty, who tries to assassinate Holmes in "The Adventure of the Empty House").

Starrett received commissions from the Limited Editions Club, the Heritage Press, and the Caxton Club to write introductions to limited editions of classic works, including Charles Dickens's *The Mystery of Edwin Drood* (1941), Doyle's *The Adventures of Sherlock Holmes* (1950), and Wilkie Collins's *The Moonstone* (1959). The introductions are informed by Starrett's deep knowledge of the publishing histories of the works and his fund of anecdotes about the authors. In 1942 Starrett began writing for the Sunday edition of the *Chicago Tribune* a column on books and book collecting that took its title from his 1940 collection *Books Alive*. He continued the column until shortly before his death. The column was popular and led to the publication of Starrett's *Best Loved Books of the Twentieth Century* (1955), a compilation of fifty-two essays he had written for the *Tribune* in 1954 on "the outstanding books of the century." On the strength of this volume, which became a best-seller, the influential biographer, literary critic, and anthologist Edward Wagenknecht characterized Starrett as the "Number One American Bookman."

Starrett proudly admitted that he was what Eugene Field, another Chicago bibliophile, had called a "DOFAB–a damned old fool about books." Throughout his life he spent as much time as he could in bookstores, and he gathered and dispersed several notable collections over the course of his eighty-seven years. As a young man he had frequented Powner's Bookstore in Chicago; the store's owner, Charles T. Powner, collected editions of Mark Twain's works. The Chicago bookseller Walter M. Hill was Starrett's first publisher, bringing out Starrett's book on Machen in 1918 and for many years distributing privately printed limited-edition pamphlets of Starrett's work as Christmas mementos. In the 1910s and 1920s Starrett patronized the Covici-McGee Bookshop, owned by Pascal Covici and William F. McGee. Covici-McGee also acted as a publisher; the firm brought out several of Starrett's books, including *Ebony Flame* (1922), *Buried Caesars: Essays in Literary Appreciation* (1923), and *Coffins for Two* (1924), as well as his editions of Machen's books. Kroch's bookshop (which later became Kroch's and Brentano's) and the book section of the Marshall Field's department store, under the direction of Marcella Bruns Hahner, were also among his favorites. On his many trips abroad he sought out books and booksellers wherever he could; he became one of the first English-speaking experts on Chinese detective stories through his forays into Beijing bookstores in the late 1930s, and his expeditions to English, French, and Italian bookstalls yielded not only additions to his collection but also a fund of anecdotes for his books and columns.

Starrett's taste in books was eclectic, but he pursued three main collecting areas. First, he was an avid and devoted collector of literary first editions, paying special attention to English and American writers of the 1880s and 1890s such as Machen, Bierce, Stephen Crane, Haldane Macfall, and Robert Louis Stevenson. Second, he collected works on certain subjects. His leading interest in this regard was Sherlockiana, including first and later editions of Doyle's Holmes books, Holmes stories in periodicals, secondary works on the character, and ephemera, but he also collected detective fiction in general. Third, he formed substantial and important collections of editions of individual titles. In the mid 1930s, after he had pruned his private library to accommodate a smaller apartment, he wrote to a fellow collector:

> I am tired of being a *general* collector. . . . My three most important collections are still intact. I hope they always may be. They are, as you know, *Sherlock Holmes, Edwin Drood,* and *Aucassin & Nicolette*. . . . From now on I shall be a specialist; but I hope I shall never fail to acquire anything genuinely fine and rare that is within my reach, since one of my specialties will be the real and outstanding books of earth, in the finest editions possible—*firsts,* if it may be; but where that is not possible, the next best thing whatever it may be.

In all his bibliophilic activities, whether buying books or writing about them, he emphasized the informed exercise of taste, but above all he emphasized the enjoyment of the pursuit. As he told the readers of his essay "The Rationale of Book Collecting" in *Penny Wise and Book Foolish:* "when we are collecting books, we are collecting happiness; and if that be not the absolute quested by us all, I do not know what is." Starrett died on 5 January 1974 and was buried in Chicago's Graceland Cemetery.

Letters:

Sincerely, Tony; Faithfully, Vincent: The Correspondence of Anthony Boucher and Vincent Starrett, edited by Robert W. Hahn (Chicago: Catullus Press, 1975);

"Dear Starrett—" "Dear Briggs—": A Compendium of Correspondence between Vincent Starrett and Gray Chandler Briggs (1930–1934), Together with Various Appendices, Notes, and Embellishments, edited by John Nieminski and Jon L. Lellenberg (New York:

Baker Street Irregulars; distributed by Fordham University Press, 1989).

References:

An Exhibit from the Vincent Starrett Library: Books, Periodicals, Manuscripts, Letters, Photographs, Memorabilia: September 1–October 13, 1989 (Minneapolis: Special Collections, Wilson Library, University of Minnesota, 1989);

First Editions of Esteemed Modern Authors Mainly in Original Bindings; Authors' Inscribed Copies, Autograph Manuscripts and Letters . . . Including Selections from the Libraries of Vincent Starrett of Chicago, Illinois, and Waldo R. Browne, of Wyoming, New York . . . to Be Sold on the Evening of Wednesday, November 18, and the Afternoon and Evening of Thursday, November 19, 1925 (N.p., 1925);

Charles Honce, *A Vincent Starrett Library: The Astonishing Results of Twenty-three Years of Literary Activity* (Mount Vernon, N.Y.: Golden Eagle Press, 1941);

Michael Murphy, ed., *Starrett vs. Machen: A Record of Discovery and Correspondence* (Saint Louis: Autolycus Press, 1979);

Murphy and others, *Vincent Starrett: In Memoriam* (Culver City, Cal.: Pontine Press, 1974);

Peter A. Ruber, *The Last Bookman: A Journey into the Life and Times of Vincent Starrett, Author, Journalist, Bibliophile,* introduction by Christopher Morley (New York: Candlelight Press, 1968);

Selections from the Literary Estate of the Late Henry Blake Fuller of Chicago; to Which Have Been Added Selections from the Library of Vincent Starrett of Chicago: To Be Sold at Unrestricted Public Auction, Tuesday Evening, November 22, 8 P.M. (Chicago: Book & Art Auctions, 1932);

Shaking Hands with Immortality: Encomiums for Vincent Starrett, 1886–1974 (Kirkwood, Mo.: Printery, 1975).

Papers:

Significant collections of Vincent Starrett's correspondence and manuscripts, as well as copies of his many privately printed and distributed works, are in the Beinecke Rare Book and Manuscript Library, Yale University; the Henry E. Huntington Library, San Marino, California; the Berg Collection, Research Library, New York Public Library; the Rare Book and Manuscript Library, Columbia University; the University of Iowa Libraries; the Popular Culture Library, Bowling Green State University; the Lilly Library, Indiana University; the Newberry Library, Chicago; the Harry Ransom Humanities Research Center, University of Texas at Austin; the Manuscript Division, Library of Congress; and the State Historical Society of Wisconsin, Madison.

Frances Steloff
(31 December 1887 – 15 April 1989)

Robert Hauptman
St. Cloud State University

and

Joseph Rosenblum

WRITINGS: "In Touch with Genius," *Journal of Modern Literature,* 4 (April 1975): 749–882;
"One for the Books," by Steloff, as told to Bobbie Stein, *People's Weekly* (26 January 1987): 87–88, 90.

Frances Steloff, founder of the Gotham Book Mart in New York City and friend and benefactor to some of the great twentieth-century writers, supported literature and authors both spiritually and physically by purchasing, selling, and defending their works despite legal and financial problems. She was instrumental in founding the James Joyce Society, which continues to meet at the Gotham Book Mart. Even at the age of 101 she was an indefatigable worker, coming down to the store each day to help. Steloff made the Gotham Book Mart one of the most influential bookshops in the United States, but the Gotham Book Mart is more than a mere purveyor of books: it is a force that helped shape modern literature.

Ida Frances Steloff was born on 31 December 1887 in Saratoga Springs, New York, a city that in summer bustled with the wealthy who came for the horse racing but which became a virtual ghost town during the dreary winter months. Her father, Gustav Stolov (later Simon Steloff) had emigrated from Russia in 1886 and earned a meager living as a peddler. He was not a good provider, but he doted on his daughter. Steloff's mother, Tobe Metzner Steloff, died in 1890, and three months later her father married a harsh and demanding woman fifteen years his junior. She did not allow Steloff to continue her schooling after the third grade. Instead, Steloff was forced to cook, clean, feed the animals, and care for her nine young siblings. The family remained extremely poor; to earn a little money Steloff sold flowers to the racing aficionados, showing

Frances Steloff

the entrepreneurial spirit that led to her success as a bookseller. Her siblings, grateful for the shoes and dresses her earnings bought them, dubbed her "Mrs. Vanderbilt."

Steloff owned few books as a child. Her first was a copy of Frances Hodgson Burnett's *Editha's Burglar* (1888). Its heroine, according to Burnett, "had always been very fond of books, and had learned to read when she was such a tiny child that I should almost be afraid to say how tiny she was when she read her first volume through." This volume may have contributed to Steloff's bibliophily, as did her father's reverence for the sacred volumes he cherished and devoured. As she remarked, "When my Dad dropped a book, one of those books he treasured, and then picked it up, he kissed it. That's my way, too. . . . I can hear books cry and groan when they are maltreated!"

One day while selling flowers Steloff attracted the attention of a rich Roxbury, Massachusetts, couple, who asked her parents whether she could come live with them. Everyone decided that this move would be in Steloff's best interest, and so at twelve and a half she went to live with these unusual people. Her adoptive father treated her kindly, and she was enrolled in the fifth grade at Phillips Brook school. She skipped sixth grade, but her adoptive mother made increasing demands on Steloff's time, so the girl once again had to give up her education. At the age of fifteen, tired of being treated as a servant, she ran away to New York. She soon returned to Roxbury, where she tended a one-year-old baby and clerked in a store, earning $3.50 a week. She attended Roxbury Evening High School, completing courses in elementary English and commercial arithmetic.

In 1907 Steloff moved permanently to New York City, where her first job was at Frederick Loeser's department store on Fulton Street. The store had a rare-book department run by George Mischke, whom she later described as "like a father. He was so good! He could almost be my own father." Mischke initiated Steloff into the mysteries of first editions and prints; he also gave her books to read and to own. Mischke's gifts constituted an important part of Steloff's small stock when she started her own bookshop in 1920. At Loeser's, Mischke arranged for Steloff to move from selling corsets to selling books and magazines. When her boss refused to give her a raise, she went to work for Charles P. Everitt at Schulte's at Twenty-third Street and Lexington Avenue (June 1909–January 1910). Impressed with Steloff's ability to locate out-of-print material, Mrs. Ralph Wilson of McDevitt-Wilson soon hired Steloff away from Schulte's. Steloff subsequently worked for Brentano's at Twenty-seventh Street and Fifth Avenue, where she met David Moss, her future husband; for S. Kahn and Son in Washington, D.C.; for Mischke's short-lived shop on Lexington Avenue near Twenty-third Street; and for Richard Davis on Vesey Street.

Late in 1919 Steloff saw a vacancy sign on Forty-fifth Street, and on 1 January 1920 she opened her own shop, Gotham Book and Art, at 128 West Forty-fifth Street in Manhattan. The rent was seventy-five dollars per month, and her entire stock consisted of 175 volumes. When she asked Mischke what books to carry, he replied, "Your customers will educate you." She soon began taking books and small artworks on consignment. Her first sales were to actors and other people who passed the store on their way to the many theaters in the district. Matinee idol Glenn Hunter was her first customer. Dancer-choreographer Martha Graham, actress Ina Claire, and playwright-director R. H. Burnside were other early patrons. Her clientele dictated her stock.

This same desire to please her customers led to her carrying books on the occult. She was at first hesitant because as a clerk she had noted that the customers seeking such works were not well regarded by her coworkers. She recognized, though, that "it wasn't good business or good service to turn away sales," and she came to believe that books on philosophy and religion comprised "the most important part of the shop, certainly the most rewarding." One of her earliest purchases was a portfolio of Japanese prints. She had bid on a series of hunting prints, but the auctioneer switched lots. Resignedly she took what she was given and priced the pictures, which she did not like, at one dollar apiece. A collector who bought several told her that she had underpriced them. "From five to ten dollars would be a fair value." He also invited her to view his collection. In this way she learned more about the subject and began stocking Oriental prints. As Mischke had predicted, her customers were educating her. Because she was an apt pupil; because she regularly spent eight, twelve, and even fifteen hours in the store every day; and because she had an unswerving service ethic the store prospered.

On 17 June 1923 Steloff married David Moss, who had been assisting her at the Gotham. She married primarily to please her father, who wanted to see his daughter married before he died. The couple celebrated their wedding by visiting London, Leipzig, Vienna, and Paris to purchase books.

After returning from her European honeymoon, Steloff moved to larger quarters at 51 West Forty-seventh Street, changed the name of the store to the Gotham Book Mart, and began publishing catalogues. At this new location she installed the famous sign proclaiming "Wise Men Fish Here," designed by John Held Jr. with the inscription supplied by Steloff. In her new location Steloff was among friends. Her neighbors included Brentano's (Fifth Avenue and Forty-seventh Street), J. Ray Peck at 34

WE MODERNS

GOTHAM BOOK MART
1920 - 1940

The Life of the Party at FINNEGANS WAKE in our Garden
on Publication Day
Painting by Ruth Bower   *Photograph by Carl Van Vechten*

*Catalogue of modern first editions published in 1940 to mark the
twentieth anniversary of the Gotham Book Mart*

West Forty-seventh Street, Mischke with yet another shop at 45 West Forty-seventh Street, and Charles P. Everitt next door to Mischke. The Beacon Book Shop and the Chaucer Head Book Shop were also nearby.

In 1925 Steloff and Moss went to Italy, where they bought Bleau atlases, which were in demand for their hand-colored, copper-engraved maps. In Milan they found books on modern art, in Florence works on sculpture, and in Venice fine leather bindings. The Gotham Book Mart also stocked expensive limited, signed editions from new publishers springing up in the prosperous 1920s.

While business was good, Steloff's personal life was not. By 1928 she was ill and depressed because her marriage was not working, and in 1930 she divorced Moss. At first she had planned to let Moss have the store, but friends and relatives convinced her that she should retain ownership. In October 1930 she paid Moss for his share and became sole owner of the Gotham Book Mart. Moss first

joined Martin Kamin to form the bookselling establishment of Moss and Kamin, and shortly before his death in 1936 he struck off on his own to start the Nonesuch Bookshop.

Despite being somewhat prudish, Steloff stocked, sold, and fought for books accused of being obscene. As early as June 1928 John S. Sumner, who represented the New York Society for the Prevention of Vice, seized almost five hundred of Moss's books, including editions of Giovanni Boccaccio's *Decameron,* James Joyce's *Ulysses,* Frank Harris's *My Life and Loves,* and Pierre Louys's *Aphrodite.* Moss had to pay a $250 fine. In 1932 Sumner discovered a Gotham Book Mart catalogue that listed illustrated copies of the Chinese classic *Chin P'ing Mei: The Adventures of Hai Men Shing and His Sixteen Wives* and *From a Turkish Bath.* Steloff became embroiled with lawyers, courts, and judges, wasting time and about a thousand dollars, only to have the case dismissed. She retaliated by preparing a list of and offering for sale those books that Sumner had failed to get the

John Malcolm Brinnin, Dylan Thomas, and Steloff at the Gotham Book Mart in 1952 (photograph © G. D. Hackett, New York)

courts to condemn as obscene. Three years later Sumner had Steloff arrested for selling André Gide's autobiography, *If It Die* (New York: Random House, 1935), published in a limited edition of fifteen hundred copies and priced at five dollars. Early in 1936 she was once again acquitted. In 1946 Sumner complained about a window display that André Breton and Marcel Duchamp had created to advertise Breton's *MIArcane 17* (New York: Brentano's, 1944). Steloff covered the offending bared breasts with Sumner's card, on which she wrote "Censored." Many years later she still became incensed when she thought about these occurrences: "To think that they banned *Ulysses* and D. H. Lawrence and Henry Miller in the United States is still outrageous to me."

Steloff also championed the little magazine. Her first success at Loeser's had been with magazines, and she preferred them to books. As she observed, "Books are wonderful. But they're not magazines. There's nothing like magazines. You remember them. They stick with you." She prominently displayed these inexpensive periodicals at the front of her shop. She sold *Yale Review, Partisan Review, Poetry, Transatlantic Review, Broom* (which carried examples of the work of Pablo Picasso, Juan Gris, Henri Matisse, and other important modern artists), *The Little Review* (whose contributors included T. S. Eliot, Wyndham Lewis, James Joyce, André Gide, William Carlos Williams, and Edgar Lee Masters), *transition* (which published Joyce's "Work in Progress," later called *Finnegans Wake*; Gertrude Stein; Kay Boyle; Hart Crane; Gide; and Archibald MacLeish), and Ezra Pound's *Exile*. Steloff acted as agent for many of these publications.

For example, she had a standing order for five hundred copies of *transition,* an eighth of the usual print run. She took one thousand copies of each issue of Cyril Connolly's *Horizon,* and she assisted Charles Henri Ford's *View,* a leading voice of French and English-language Surrealism, by accepting enough copies COD to pay the printer. She further supported these avant-garde magazines by purchasing advertisements in them and recommending them in her catalogues and conversations. In 1962 Louise Bogan called the Gotham Book Mart "one of the premier bookshops in America" for its support of fledgling authors.

Steloff used the shop and her own resources to assist ailing, penurious, even lazy authors, whom she generally venerated not necessarily because of their particularly incisive or successful works, but merely because of their choice of calling. On the bulletin board she posted Henry Miller's pleas from California for a cart, an ax, and thermos bottles or money. Later she posted Miller's request for funds that would allow him to go to Mexico for a year to finish *The Air-Conditioned Nightmare* (New York: New Directions, 1945). Someone who saw this notice sent Miller a check for $250 and a promise to repeat this gift every month for a year. Steloff sent Theodore Dreiser $200 and also aided Gertrude Stein and Ezra Pound. William Carlos Williams asked for her help in finding a publisher for a volume of his poetry. She interceded for writers, set up displays of their works, read manuscripts, gave parties and advice, and hired writers to work in her shop (employees included Tennessee Williams, Allen Ginsberg, and LeRoi Jones). She lent money to Anaïs Nin so she could buy a press on which to print editions of *Winter of Artifice* (New York: Gemor Press, 1944) and *Under a Glass Bell* (New York: Gemor Press, 1944), put copies of both works on display at the Gotham Book Mart, and sent a copy of *Under a Glass Bell* to Edmund Wilson. Wilson's review did much to establish Nin's American reputation. Steloff established a relief fund for distressed poets and protected authors' rights. When someone pirated J. D. Salinger's stories, she refused to sell the volume and notified Salinger of the violation of copyright. When Marianne Moore's *Selected Poems* (New York: Macmillan, 1935) was remaindered, Steloff bought all available copies.

Authors returned Steloff's admiration, making the Gotham a Mecca for literary figures. Christopher Morley, Theodore Dreiser, Eugene O'Neill, Edmund Wilson, Edith Sitwell, Marianne Moore, Padraic Colum, Dylan Thomas, W. H. Auden, Stephen Spender, Mary McCarthy, Eudora Welty, Arthur Miller, Jorge Luis Borges, Susan Sontag, William Heyen, W. S. Merwin, and Galway Kinnell have visited and bought books from Steloff. H. L. Mencken first came to buy up copies of his *Ventures into Verse* (New York: Marshall, Beek and Gordon, 1903) so he could destroy them despite their fifty-to-sixty-dollar price tag. Steloff hid one copy from Mencken because it was filled with his annotations. After he heard about it, he offered her the five-hundred-dollar asking price and two thousand dollars in free advertising in the *American Mercury,* but she protected the volume until she could sell it to a collector. James Laughlin dedicated *Spearhead: 10 Years' Experimental Writing in America* (New York: New Directions, 1947) to Steloff "because no one has done more than she to further the cause of good books by non-dead writers for whom writing is a thing to live for."

Over the years Steloff's best-selling authors were D. H. Lawrence, James Joyce, and Dylan Thomas. Steloff suggested that Thomas tour America, and on the first of his four American visits his first stop on landing in New York in the spring of 1950 was the Gotham Book Mart.

In the early 1920s Steloff bought up for $200 all remaining copies of Eugene O'Neill's *Thirst and Other One-Act Plays* (Boston: Gorham Press, 1914). By 1945 copies were selling for $150 each. She paid about fifty cents each for five hundred copies of the Harvard *Wake* issue dedicated to E. E. Cummings (Spring 1946), stored them in her basement, and later sold them for five dollars a copy. Seymour Lawrence, who edited the magazine and later directed Atlantic Monthly Press, said that Steloff had helped *Wake* more than any "other American bookshop ever did." At the same time Steloff was helping the Gotham Book Mart.

Steloff's interest in twentieth-century writers led her into publishing. Among her titles are the first *James Joyce Miscellany* (New York: James Joyce Society, 1957), edited by Marvin Magalaner; Leon Edel's *James Joyce: The Last Journey* (New York: Gotham Book Mart, 1947); Lucie Noël's *James Joyce and Paul L. Leon* (New York: Gotham Book Mart, 1950); Samuel Putnam's translation of André Gide's *Persephone* (New York: Gotham Book Mart, 1949); and poems by Gertrude Stein and Wallace Stevens. Some of her catalogues, *GBM Currents,* have become collectors' items, including the 1938 catalogue of books about movies, photography, and radio. The ninety-page *We Moderns,* which appeared in 1940 to mark the twentieth anniversary of the Gotham Book Mart, was another landmark catalogue, with introductory essays by avant-garde writers assessing their colleagues. John Dos Passos wrote about E. E. Cummings; Edmund Wilson dealt with John

Peale Bishop; E. E. Cummings discussed Ezra Pound; Carl Van Vechten assessed Gertrude Stein. *We Moderns* not only advertised modern first editions but also became a modern first edition in its own right.

Another manifestation of Steloff's devotion to modern letters was her sponsoring of lectures and parties. In the 1930s, shortly after launching his *New Review,* Samuel Putnam asked to give a lecture in the backyard of the Gotham Book Mart to promote contemporary French writers. The success of this talk led to others, as many as forty a year, such as the one described by A. J. Liebling in the *New York World-Telegram* as "The Return of the Natives," at which about one hundred former expatriates gathered to discuss Malcolm Cowley's *Exile's Return* (New York: Norton, 1934). From these gatherings arose an Artists and Writers Dinner Club, admission twenty-five cents. The publication of *Finnegans Wake* (London: Faber and Faber, 1939; New York: Viking, 1939) was celebrated at 51 West Forty-seventh Street with an Irish wake, with the proofs of the novel lying in a casketlike jewel case and Steloff assuming the role of widow. In February 1941 Steloff hosted a memorial for Joyce, who had died a month earlier.

In 1945 Steloff lost her lease. Publisher Mitchell Kennerley told her that Columbia University wanted to sell a nearby building at 41 West Forty-seventh Street. In 1946 the Gotham moved to this brownstone, which Steloff purchased for $65,000. Here the James Joyce Society was founded in 1947.

According to Philipp Lyman, secretary of the Joyce Society, William York Tindall, a Columbia University English professor, offered the first course on Joyce in the United States. When his students had questions about Joyce, they visited the Gotham Book Mart. Steloff could not always answer their questions. To assist them, as she always sought to aid her customers, she helped organize the James Joyce Society to "introduce Joyce students to scholars, maintain a Joyce library, further the publication and distribution of his works, . . . and issue occasional bulletins." According to William Garland Rogers's *Wise Men Fish Here* (1965), the society "has been the dominant influence in propagating the Joyce cult" in America. Steloff served as the first treasurer of the society, which publishes the *James Joyce Journal,* continues to flourish, and holds its quarterly meetings at the Gotham Book Mart.

Steloff's complete devotion to literature, books, and friends made her a demanding and difficult employer. She insisted on the same commitment from her workers that she herself made. The store was her life, and she could not comprehend that young

Steloff at the Gotham Book Mart

clerks might have other interests or needs. She was equally incredulous to discover that some employees stole books from her or forged Gotham Book Mart checks.

In 1967 she sold the store to Andreas Brown, but until her death at the age of 101 she continued to live in her upstairs apartment and came down every day to work in the shop as a consultant.

In 1987, to mark her centennial, she received tributes from around the world. Heads of state, including President Ronald Reagan, also conveyed their best wishes, and four hundred people came to the Gotham Book Mart to mark the occasion. Steloff died of pneumonia on 15 April 1989 at Mount Sinai Medical Center in New York City. She was buried in the family plot in the Jewish cemetery at Saratoga Springs.

To author and journalist Franklin Pierce Adams (F.P.A.) Steloff was "my favorite vendor of books." British writer Cyril Connolly claimed, "I've never seen so many books I'd like under one roof as in the Gotham Book Mart." Alastair Reid called the shop "one of the best places in the world." Book collector Charles E. Feinberg declared, "This is where collectors begin." Perhaps the best description of Steloff's achievement in fostering American book culture appeared in Samuel Putnam's general introduction to *We Moderns:*

> Dropped down in the heart of New York's "roaring Forties" . . . is a spacious and yet somehow curiously intimate ground floor shop the walls of which are lined with books, while the numerous close-crowded tables groan with all that is latest and best in the literature of America and a good part of the world.
>
> If its success has been somewhat phenomenal . . . this has been due to the fact that Frances Steloff, the Gotham's Founder, was at once so finely attuned to the literary age in which she lived, so catholic in her range

of sympathies, . . . and so courageous from both a financial and aesthetic point of view.

Biography:

William Garland Rogers, *Wise Men Fish Here: The Story of Frances Steloff and the Gotham Book Mart* (New York: Harcourt, Brace & World, 1965).

References:

Frances Steloff: Memoirs of a Bookseller, 16mm or video, 28 minutes, Winterlude Films (Direct Cinema Limited), 1987;

J. G., "Gotham's Grande Dame Turns Ninety," *Publishers' Weekly* (16 January 1978): 74;

Valerie Harms, *Maria Montessori, Anaïs Nin, Frances Steloff: Stars in My Sky* (N.p.: Magic Circle Press, 1976);

The Ineffable Frances Steloff: A Photographic Visit by Herta Hilscher-Wittgenstein (Chicago: Swallow Press, 1976);

Journal of Modern Literature, special Gotham Book Mart issue, 4 (April 1975);

Herbert Mitgang, "Doyenne of Booksellers is 100," *New York Times,* 30 December 1987, C9;

"Notes and Comment," *New Yorker* (25 January 1988): 25–26.

Papers:

Steloff's papers, correspondence, and books can be found in the Berg Collection of the New York Public Library and at Skidmore College.

John Boyd Thacher

(11 September 1847 – 25 February 1909)

Carol Armbruster
Library of Congress

and

Larry E. Sullivan
City University of New York

BOOKS: *Address of John Boyd Thacher to the American Exhibition of the World's Columbian Exposition, Delivered at Music Hall, Jackson Park, August 12, 1893* (Chicago?, 1893?);

Charlecote; or, The Trial of William Shakespeare (New York: Dodd, Mead, 1895);

The Continent of America: Its Discovery and Its Baptism (New York: Benjamin, 1896);

Little Speeches by John Boyd Thacher: Being a Collection of a Dozen Short Addresses on Various Topics (Albany, N.Y.: Fort Orange, 1896);

"Some-one, Some-one in the World Apart" and Other Poems (N.p.: Brandow, 1897?);

Awards at the World's Columbian Exposition (Albany, N.Y., 1898);

Christopher Columbus: His Life, His Work, His Remains, as Revealed by Original Printed and Manuscript Records, Together with an Essay on Peter Martyr of Anghera and Bartolomé de las Casas, the First Historians of America, 3 volumes (New York & London: Putnam, 1903–1904);

A Short History of the French Revolution Told in Autographs, Exhibited at the Rooms of the Albany Historical Society, March 19, 1904 (Albany, N.Y.?, 1904);

Outlines of the French Revolution Told in Autographs, Exhibited at the Lenox Branch of the New York Public Library, March 20, 1905 (Albany, N.Y.: Weed-Parsons, 1905).

SELECTED PERIODICAL PUBLICATION–
UNCOLLECTED: "The Cabotian Discovery," *Transactions of the Royal Society of Canada,* second series 3, section 2 (1897–1898): 279–307;

"A Bibliographical Romance," *The Bibliographer,* 1 (1902): 269–284.

John Boyd Thacher

John Boyd Thacher was a wealthy nineteenth-century American industrialist who had the money, time, and interest to indulge in both politics and the collecting of books, manuscripts, and autographs. His social and political positions helped place him in roles that reflected and encouraged his collecting interests. He lived in an era when extensive and quality collecting of early European and American rare books and manuscripts was popular and possible. He collected not only as an avocation but also, in part, in order to write histories of major world events such as the European discovery of the Americas and the French Revolution. His extensive collections included many rarities of research and were of great monetary value. After his death the fate of several of his collections, as determined by his wife, Emma Treadwell Thacher, continued Thacher's legacy in a manner that was consistent with Thacher's public-service career. To the acquisition of several of Thacher's collections the Library of Congress attributes a turning point in the history of its Rare Book and Special Collections Division as well as in the tradition of patriotic giving to establish a national collection of rare and special materials.

John Boyd Thacher, the oldest son of George H. and Ursula Jane Boyd Thacher, was born at Ballston Spa, New York, on 11 September 1847. His father's paternal forebears included distinguished Puritans such as the Reverend Thomas Thacher, who had arrived in New England in 1635. His father's maternal ancestry was equally distinguished; he was descended from Judge George Hornells, founder of the city of Hornell, New York. George Thacher was politically active, serving as mayor of Albany four times between 1860 and 1874.

John Boyd Thacher attended Williams College, where he graduated cum laude in 1869. In 1872 he married Emma Treadwell of Albany, whose great-grandfather had been the last of the Puritan governors of Connecticut and also a member of the Continental Congress. She shared many of her husband's interests and became his constant traveling partner and intellectual companion. They had no children.

In addition to serving as mayor of Albany, Thacher's father was a wealthy manufacturer of car wheels for railroads. John entered the family business after graduation and assumed ownership of the firm with his brother, George Hornell Thacher, following his father's death in 1887. His wealth allowed him to enter politics as well as become an avid collector of books and manuscripts.

Thacher is best known in New York history for his political career. He helped organize the Albany Board of Health, and he was twice elected to terms in the state senate (1883–1886). As a Democrat he campaigned for Grover Cleveland, and, as

his father had done, he served terms as mayor of Albany (1886–1887 and 1896–1897). He helped abolish contract labor in prisons and aggressively pursued a politically unpopular resolution to provide Ulysses S. Grant a pension while the former president lay dying in 1885.

During his first term as mayor in 1886 Thacher followed the practice of presenting a report to the Albany Common Council, and his first report concerned the bicentennial celebrating the granting of the charter to the city by Thomas Dongan, Second Earl of Limerick, the colonial governor of New York. He subsequently delivered three other addresses or lectures on this event, and these were collected and published with other speeches as *Little Speeches by John Boyd Thacher: Being a Collection of a Dozen Short Addresses on Various Topics* (1896). President Benjamin Harrison appointed him to be the New York state representative to the World's Columbian Exposition of 1893. He was made chairman of the awards committee for the exposition, and one of his areas of research interest and collecting developed from this experience. In 1896 the Democratic Party of New York proposed to nominate Thacher for the governorship, but he, advocating a gold standard, declined to run on the free-silver platform of presidential candidate William Jennings Bryan in that election.

In 1887 Thacher became nonresident member forty-one of the premier book-collecting society in the United States, the Grolier Club, based in New York City. Though his motives for collecting remain obscure, it seems likely that his interests in American history, as evidenced by his addresses, led him to that subject. The late nineteenth century was a great age for Americana collectors such as James Lenox, John Carter Brown, and Samuel Latham Mitchell Barlow, and their interests may also have prompted Thacher's. His collecting interests included Americana beginning with Columbiana, or that fifteenth-century period that also interested others such as bibliographer Henry Harrisse; American autographs; European autographs; the French Revolution; and incunabula.

To the collector and researcher the lasting legacy of Thacher's activities are the incunabula holdings. Thacher's method of collecting incunabula dates from the publication of Georg Wolfgang Panzer's eleven-volume *Annales typographici ab artis inventae origine ad annum MD. (ad annum MDXXXVI. continuati)* (1793–1803). Panzer was the first to arrange incunabula in chronological order within the geographical limits of country and place of

John Boyd Thacher

EX LIBRIS

Thacher's bookplate

printing rather than in an alphabetical arrangement by subject matter. His greatest contribution to the study of incunabula was his view that one must consider the typographical origin of early printing from a geographical point of view. Later incunabulists, such as Ludwig Friedrich Theodor Hain and Walter Arthur Copinger, arranged material alphabetically by authors, and because Copinger's work was widely used by scholars, the geographical method was not firmly established until Robert Proctor began his work on his six-volume *An Index to the Early Printed Books in the British Museum from the Invention of Printing to the Year MD, with Notes of Those in the Bodleian Library* (1898–1903), which arranged the books according to their places of printing. Proctor also attempted the technical identification of early printing, a method valuable in untangling the printing history of undated books. Proctor's index shows that by 1501 approximately 1,080 presses existed at more than 238 places of printing, and his bibliography was fashionable among incunabula collectors, including Thacher, in the late nineteenth and early twentieth centuries.

Gen. Rush Hawkins, whose collection went to the library named after his wife, Annemary Brown, at Brown University, was the leading American exponent of collecting according to the Proctor model, and his example probably influenced Thacher's collecting of incunabula. Hawkins had been a friend both of Proctor and of Henry Bradshaw, who devised the method of classifying incunabula according to type forms, and enticed Alfred W. Pollard to compile a catalogue of Pollards holdings. Thacher thus had a good model on which to pursue his collecting, although he apparently had little contact with the work of scholarly bibliographers other than through his membership in the Grolier Club. Beginning in approximately 1889 Thacher bought incunabula with great enthusiasm, and a decade later he wrote:

I bought at Libbie & Co.'s sale, Boston, and paid for it June 3, 1899, a Benedicti Regula printed by Geoffrey Marnef, Paris, September 7, 1500. This book completed my 500 presses of the fifteenth century. I take it as a good augury that the first book of my incunabula and the one to round out my five hundredth press should have been found in America. It is seldom my collection finds specimens of incunabula already brought to America.

Ten years ago it did not seem possible that I should get from one to ten examples of 500 presses of the fifteenth century. No other private collection has so great a number of separate presses.

Thacher gathered 840 incunabula as well as sixty-four duplicates, a total of 904 works arranged by countries, places, and printers. His collection began with imprints from Mainz, Germany, the earliest being a vellum copy of Johann Fust and Peter Schöffer's printing of Bishop Gulielmus Duranti's *Rationale divinorum officiorum* (1459). Ownership records of this copy begin with Anthony Askew's sale of 1775, through Augustus Frederick, Duke of Sussex, to the sale of the collection of Bertram, fifth Lord Ashburnham, in 1897 when the book was bought by Bernard Quaritch, who apparently sold it to Thacher. Another early book Thacher collected was the second edition of Cicero's *De Officiis* (1466), a copy that had belonged to Michael Woodhull, the first translator of the works of Euripides into English verse. Entries in the collection include six other Mainz imprints (among a total of eight), and then record items published by the presses of Strassburg, works beginning with Johann Mentelin's edition of Vincent of Beauvais's *Speculum historiale* (1473).

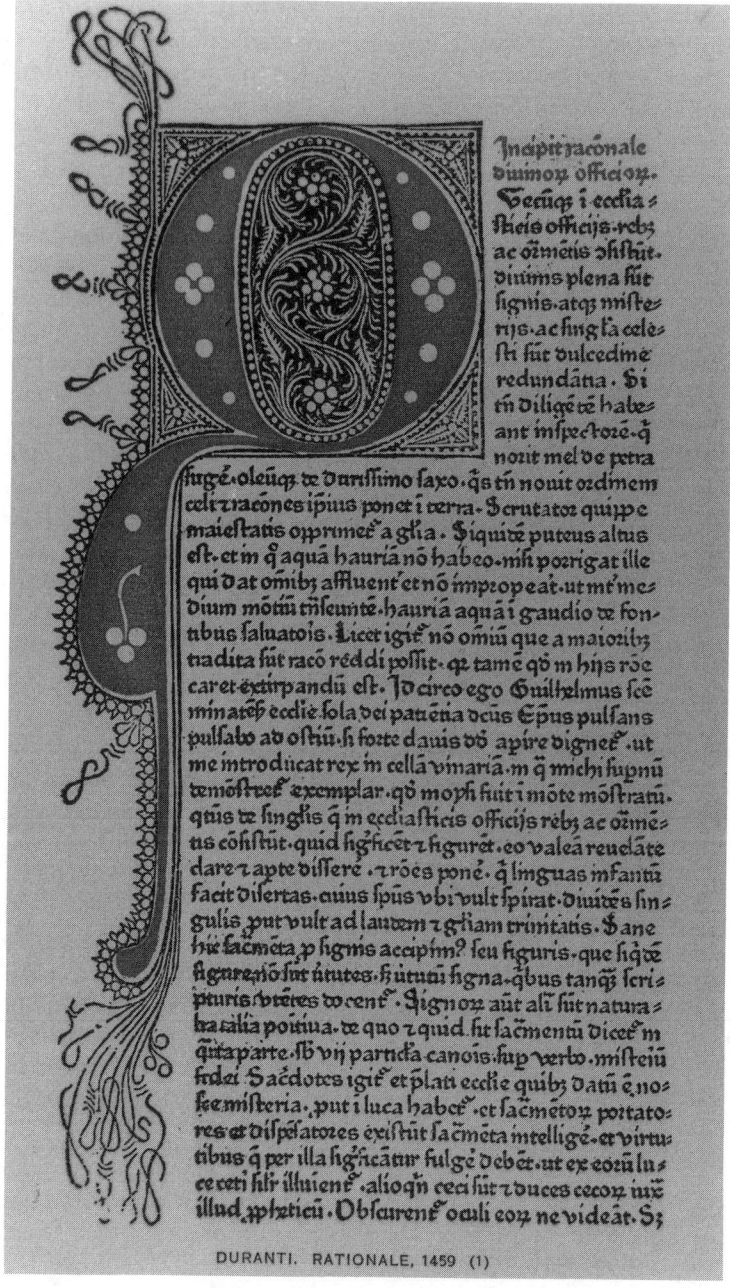

DURANTI. RATIONALE, 1459 (1)

Page from the earliest volume in Thacher's collection of incunabula, Gulielmus Duranti's Rationale divinorum officiorum *(1459)*

The final entry of Thacher's incunabula listed in Frederick W. Ashley's *Catalogue of the John Boyd Thacher Collection of Incunabula* (1915) identifies an item from Portugal, an edition of Abraham Zacuthus's *Tabulae astronomicae* (1496). The collection also includes some previously unrecorded items, such as Cicero's *Epistolae familiares* (Milan: Leonard Pachel, 1495); *Ortulus Rosarum de valle lachrumarium* (Paris: Claude Jaumar, n.d.); Franciscus Niger's *Ars epistolandi* (Paris: Georg

Mittelhaus, 1490); and Nicholaus de Lyra's *Postilla seu exposition litteralis et moralis* (Paris: Jean de Vingle, 26 August 1496), as well as the only known American copies of *Vocabularius ex quo* (Eltville, Germany: Nicolaus Bechtermunze, 1476) and *Breviarium Moguntinense* (Marienthal, 1474), both of which were printed by the Brethren of the Common Life. Provenances include those of Philipp Melanchthon, sixteenth-century German humanist, scholar, and friend of Martin Luther;

William Morris, the writer, collector, and printer; and Harrisse, the bibliographer. The collection also holds thirty-four editions of Ptolemy's *Geographia*–including the 1478 Rome edition of Arnoldus Buckink's *Cosmographiae* that contains the famous map of the world known to Europe just before Columbus's discovery of the New World and four other fifteenth-century editions of *Geographia*.

His collecting was not discriminating, and in many cases the condition of items he collected left much to be desired. Thacher remarked that, in the hope of obtaining from booksellers some specimens of presses not represented in his collection, he ordered incunabula in lots sight unseen.

Emma Thacher deposited her husband's collection of incunabula in the Library of Congress in 1910, and in the *Report of the Librarian of Congress* for that year Herbert Putnam assessed the significance of the Thacher incunabula by comparing them to those comprising the collection of General Hawkins at its location

in the Annemary Brown Memorial building at Providence, R.I., [where it] is (justly) regarded as offering as excellent an opportunity as could conveniently be found in one place for the study of early printing and the comparison of early presses. The catalogue of it (by Mr. A. W. Pollard) shows about 542 entries (including a few later than A.D. 1500 and therefore not strictly incunabula). A similar catalogue of the Thacher Collection would show about 820 incunabula proper. The Hawkins Collection includes some 80 printers (67 of them represented by 15th century imprints) not in the Thacher Collection; but the Thacher Collection includes over 240 not in the Hawkins Collection. As against 141 *places* represented in the Hawkins Collection, there are 126 represented in the Thacher, as against 49 "first issues" of a first press, 35.

Ashley's catalogue of the Thacher collection of incunabula was arranged by place and printer in order to illustrate chronologically the spread of printing. Upon the death of Emma Thacher in 1927 the collection was bequeathed to the Library of Congress.

In addition to incunabula Thacher's second major collecting interest was Columbiana, a subject in which his interest had been stirred by his service during the World Columbian Exposition of 1893, and he compiled an extensive collection that he used for his research into the exploration and discovery of America. Thacher published two noteworthy books on the subject: *The Continent of America: Its Discovery and Its Baptism* (1896) and the biography, *Christopher Columbus: His Life, His Work, His Remains, as Revealed by Original Printed and Manuscript Records, Together with an Essay on Peter Martyr of Anghera and Bartolomé de las Casas, the First Historians of America* (1903–1904). Historians of the day regarded this latter work as his magnum opus, a lasting achievement of American historiography. In his article "A Bibliographical Romance," published in *The Bibliographer* in 1902, Thacher discusses a nineteenth-century forgery of the quarto Spanish letter of Columbus preserved in the Biblioteca Ambrosiana in Milan.

Among the Columbiana rarities he gathered was the 1516 Genoa polyglot Psalter. This book is important not only for being the first polyglot Psalter but also for containing the first biographical account of Columbus. Perhaps the most outstanding piece of Columbiana in his collection is the so-called Sneyd Codex or Trevisan manuscript compiled in Venice in 1503 and containing the account of Columbus's second voyage. This work includes letters written in 1501 and 1502 and transmitting the seven books of "La Navigation de Lolochut facta par Portugalesi 1501," as well as letters written by Angelo Trevisan, Columbus's friend who transcribed Peter Martyr's text describing Columbus's voyages before they were published. Thacher also acquired the 1494 Columbus letter with eight fanciful woodcut illustrations printed in Basel. Another important Columbiana item was Thacher's copy of Martinus Hylacomylus's *Cosmographiae introductio cum quibusdam geometriae ac astronomiae principiis ad eam rem necessariis* (St. Dié, France: Walter Lud, 1507) in which Hylacomylus suggests that the newly discovered continent be named after Amerigo Vespucci. Harrisse had purchased this copy in Rome, and it is believed to have been the Vatican copy.

Thacher's great interests in history and politics may have led him to collect American and foreign autographs. In collecting these items Thacher participated in a collecting habit common in the nineteenth century, when the number and quality of autograph collections soared. Many popular American and European autograph materials were readily available, and with auction prices remaining low throughout the nineteenth and early twentieth centuries, major collections were amassed. Thacher built immense collections of these materials, and like other major collectors of his day he regarded his autograph collections as the most interesting of all his holdings. In 1907 he remarked that he had 41,000 pieces and had two librarians working in his house to catalogue them. Thacher is traditionally ranked among the outstanding autograph collectors of the later nineteenth and earlier twentieth centuries, a member of a group that includes John S. H. Fogg, Elliott Danforth, James Lenox, John Hale, Joshua J. Cohen, Henry E. Huntington, and John Pierpont Morgan. As Victor Hugo Paltsits of the New York Public Library remarks, "In the variety and extensiveness, and quality, of his manuscripts, [Thacher] had no peer in the United States in the nineteenth century."

The bulk of Thacher's autograph collections was sold at auction after his death. The Anderson Gallery (New York) Thacher sales began on 30 October 1913 and continued for almost ten years. A study of the sales catalogues reveals the breadth and diversity of his collecting, which was typical of the great manuscript collectors of the late nineteenth century. According to the introduction to the 30–31 October 1913 auction catalogue, "The collection of books and letters of historical interest relating to North America from the earliest times to the close of the Civil War, formed by the late Hon. John Boyd Thacher of Albany, has been known for years as one of the greatest collections of this country." Thacher is described as a longtime discriminating collector who amassed a collection that is not only voluminous but also one of his high quality and with many remarkable rarities. "The exceptionally fine condition of most of the letters will appeal strongly to collectors," the introduction continues. "The early period at which Mr. Thacher began collecting enabled him to secure not only fine letters but letters in fine condition."

The catalogue lists sets of autographs of the Dutch governors of New Netherlands from Peter Minuit to Peter Stuyvesant; governors from the English Conquest (1664) to the American Revolution; colonial governors of America, generals and famous soldiers of Queen Anne's War and the French and Indian War; early French explorers in New France or Canada; members of the Colonial, Provincial, Stamp Act, and Continental Congresses; famous early divines and notable figures; and all the signers of the Declaration of Independence. Among the rarities are letters and documents signed by major French explorers such as Philippe de Chabot, Comte de Charni, whose protection and support of Jacques Cartier's 1534–1535 voyage resulted in the discovery of the Saint Lawrence River, and a 1693 document signed by Louis de Baude, Comte de Frontenac, perhaps the most important figure to represent the crown of France in early America. Another document, the original deed for the purchase of Rensselaerswyck Manor from the Native Americans, bears the rare signature of Minuit, who purchased Manhattan

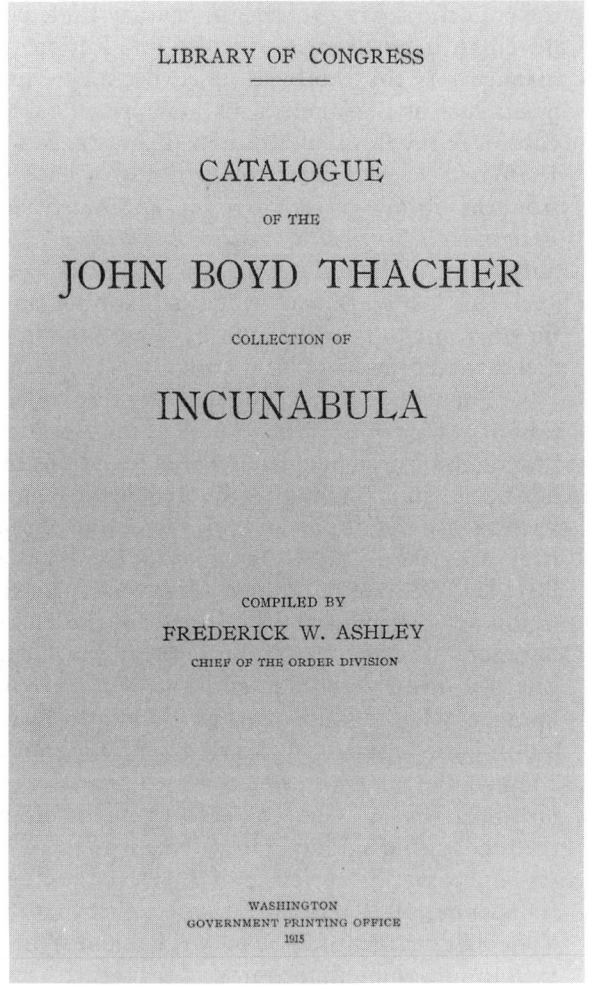

LIBRARY OF CONGRESS
—
CATALOGUE
OF THE
JOHN BOYD THACHER
COLLECTION OF
INCUNABULA

COMPILED BY
FREDERICK W. ASHLEY
CHIEF OF THE ORDER DIVISION

WASHINGTON
GOVERNMENT PRINTING OFFICE
1915

Catalogue for the portion of Thacher's collection that his widow deposited at the Library of Congress in 1910 and willed to that institution in 1927

Island from them (1630). Dated 1 April 1647, another document signed by Miles Standish, who arrived on the *Mayflower,* certifies the choice of Gov. William Bradford and Asst. Gov. John Browne as representatives of Massachusetts in the Congress of the New England Confederation. Two other documents are a deed of sale dated 7 November 1728 and signed by William Bradford, the first printer in Philadelphia and New York, and the first publication of the Declaration of Independence, a folio broadside printed by John Dunlap.

Later sales catalogues present items with literary as well as other historically prominent autographs: a rare manuscript of Nathaniel Hawthorne; a commentary by Edgar Allan Poe on "The Raven"; music manuscripts of Johann Sebastian Bach, Ludwig van Beethoven, Gaetano Donizetti, Richard Wagner, and Carl Maria von Weber; and a letter from Lucretia Borgia. Also in the collection was a thirteenth-century Bible believed to have been Petrarch's. In addition to manuscripts the catalogues also list major imprints such as Benjamin Franklin imprints; a first edition of the Book of Mormon (Palmyra, N.Y., 1830); a Sebastien Gryphius printing of Cicero from the library of Jean Grolier; and *Klagte van Eenige Leeden der Nederduytse Hervormd Kerk,* a 1725 imprint by William Bradford and John Peter Zenger. This last work was Zenger's first book and the only one to bear the imprint of both the first and second printers of New York.

Thacher possessed an especially fine collection of autographs of the signers of the Declaration of Independence. His set was based on the one he bought from Edward Everett Sprague, his friend since childhood and the son of one of the first American collectors of autographs, the Rev. Dr. William B. Sprague. This was a presentation set collected and inscribed by the elder Sprague, "A New Year's Present for My Dear Boy, Edward Everett Sprague, 1861." Reverend Sprague, who lived for years at Woodlawn Plantation, the estate of Martha Washington's adopted daughter, while he collected and worked on the papers of George Washington, is often credited with originating the idea of collecting a set of autographs of signers of the Declaration of Independence. Thacher developed a set that included a document fully handwritten and signed by Button Gwinnett, the rarest of the signers, and a lease signed by Thomas Lynch, whose signature is almost as rare as is Gwinnett's.

Many of Thacher's important European autographs and his collection on the French Revolution were presented to the Library of Congress. Of the two autograph collections, the one on the French Revolution is by far the larger and more focused. Autographs associated with this epoch were popular among collectors, and important specimens were available in good quantity. Thacher started this collection most earnestly during his later years, and the 1889 centennial of the French Revolution, which was celebrated worldwide, may have inspired him to buy many items in this subject and to write a history of the Revolution. The event and the celebration of it may have appealed to this politician who worked for democratic reforms and on celebratory committees throughout his career.

Referring to this collection of French Revolution autographs, Walter Benjamin states in his *Collector,* "I do not believe that its equal can be found even in France." Thacher acquired materials for it through American and European dealers, from whom he bought individual items and entire collections of French Revolution autographs. He and his wife had long spent parts of most years in Europe, and, gathering materials for this project in person, the two traveled throughout France to build this French Revolution collection. Emma Thacher annotated most of the wrappers holding the autographs.

Thacher loaned parts of this collection of autographs to exhibitions in the United States and, according to Benjamin, sent it on extensive loan for exhibition in Paris. For a 1905 exhibit at the Lenox branch of the New York Public Library, Thacher published a catalogue in which he outlined his collection and suggested his motives for collecting and exhibiting it:

> The present exhibition of autographs is an attempt to teach the outlines of history, and particularly of the French Revolution, by means of holographic illustration. The writing of a man, it is held, is the most perfect relic he leaves behind him. Something physical, as well as intellectual and moral, belonging to his personality, has gone into the material substance carrying his writing.

More than the content or the research value of the manuscript, the almost magical, spiritual link with the figure who had handled the paper was the motive for his ardent collecting of autographs. In exhibiting these artifacts of major historical events and personalities, Thacher had pedagogical goals, and he considered those same spiritual forces to be efficacious both in teaching history through exhibits and in illustrating the histories he published.

Thacher's collection on the French Revolution in the Library of Congress is still organized chronologically, from the times of the philosophes such as Charles-Louis de Secondat, Baron de la Brède et de Montesquieu; Voltaire; and Jean-Jacques Rousseau to the Empire of Napoleon Bonaparte. The autograph papers illuminate all the major events and personalities of these times in letters, documents, and some portraits signed by figures such as Montesquieu; Voltaire; Rousseau; Ninon de Lenclos; Madame Louise-Florence-Pétronille de la Live d'Epinay; Comte George-Louis Leclerc de Buffon; Jean Le Rond d'Alembert; Baron Paul-Henri-Dietrich d'Holbach; Denis Diderot; Jacques Necker; Pierre-Augustin Caron de Beaumarchais; Charles-Joseph Panckoucke; René-François-Armand Prudhomme; Camille Desmoulins; Louis XVI; Marie Antoinette; Yolande-Martine-Gabrielle de Polastron, Madame de Polignac; Alessandro di Conte Cagliostro; l'Abbé Emmanuel-Joseph Sièyes; Mirabeau; Thomas Paine; Chrétien-Guillaume de Lamoignon de Malesherbes; Maximilien-François-Marie-Isidore de Robespierre; Saint-Just; Rouget de Lisle; Jean-Paul Marat; Charlotte Corday; Marie-Jean-Antoine-Nicolas de Caritat, Marquis de Condorcet; André-Marie de Chénier; Napoleon; Viscount Paul-François-Jean-Nicolas de Barras; and Charles-Maurice de Talleyrand-Périgord, Prince de Bénévent.

Thacher's interests also included many others whose signatures are no less powerful in evoking the spirit and events of the time. Among them were Claude Antoine Gabriel, Duc de Choiseul, the officer who abandoned his post at Pont-de-Somme-Vesle and was thereby blamed for the failure of the plans for the royal family to escape; Charles Henri Sanson, the public executioner during the Reign of Terror; Joseph-Ignace Guillotin, physician, founder of the Academy of Medicine, and the inventor of the infamous machine of execution by which he was himself eventually killed; Charles Simon Catel, author of hymns for the revolutionary fetes; Antoine-François Momoro, the printer and engraver who in 1791 devised the motto *liberté, égalité, fraternité;* and Anne-Josèphe Théroigne de Méricourt, who on 5 October 1789 led a mob of women dressed like Amazons from Paris to Versailles and then escorted the king to Paris the following day.

A major curiosity of the collection is a signed letter from Danton, then president of the Convention, to Marie Antoinette. The letter is dated 4 August 1793, two days after her transfer from the Temple to the Conciergerie. The letter says (in translation):

To Marie Antoinette, the former Queen of France, at the Conciergerie.
   Citizeness, you will place over your door these words—Unity, Indivisibility of the Republic—Liberty, Equality, Fraternity or Death. Signed, Danton.

It is uncertain whether Danton meant to warn or to mock the queen. The letter had been kept in the hands of the same family since 1816, when a member had received it directly from Louis XVIII. In 1903 Thacher acquired the letter through an English dealer who was working in Paris and negotiated the sale with its owner, Baron de Lartigues.

Thacher complemented his collection of autographs of figures from the French Revolution with an extensive research library. He had set himself the goal of writing an illustrated history of the Revolution based on the personalities of its participants, much as he had written of Columbus and the European discovery of the Americas. Containing both materials from the period under study and interpretive materials from later years, his working library is clearly that of a scholar of his time. Thacher collected runs of contemporary official publications and journals, many pamphlets, and much of the authoritative nineteenth- and early-twentieth-century book and periodical literature published on the Revolution. Few of the printed materials of this collection are truly rare.

Thacher had begun to write his history of the Revolution when he died in 1909. In 1921 Emma Thacher deposited at the Library of Congress his entire collection of materials on the French Revolution, a collection containing 1,581 volumes, 1,600 pieces of autograph material, and miscellaneous items such as unbound periodicals, maps, plans, prints, and broadsides.

Thacher's collection of European autographs was apparently one that he gathered for the pleasure of collecting and not with any intent to write another history, for it is less focused than his collection on the French Revolution. He collected autographs representing nearly every European royal and noble family. The earliest document in this European autograph collection was signed in 1374 by the French king Charles V and includes signatures as modern as that of Giuseppe Mazzini, the nineteenth-century Italian statesman. Among its items are pieces associated with figures as evocative as Frederick the Great, Lorenzo de' Medici, Aldus Manutius, Vittoria Colonna, Queen Isabella of Castille, Jane Seymour, Oliver Cromwell, most of the popes, most Napoleonic notables, Maximilian I, and Queen Caroline. The collection includes many rare signatures, such as those of the French kings Francis II and Charles IX as well as some historically significant documents. Letters from Francis II, also signed by his wife Mary Stuart, Queen of France and Scotland, address the troubles of Scotland; a letter from Elizabeth I to Catherine de' Médicis discusses the safety of Mary, who was being held prisoner by Elizabeth. The collection contains approximately thirteen hundred pieces and helps illustrate why Thacher was known as one of the more renowned collectors of foreign autographs in the United States during his time.

After Thacher's death his wife, who had actively shared in his collecting, deposited four collections at the Library of Congress. In 1910 she deposited those of incunabula and Columbiana; in 1915, the European autographs; and in 1921, the material relating to the French Revolution.

Herbert Putnam, the librarian of Congress, hailed each deposit as an opportunity for the library to use the materials for exhibit and research services as well as to preserve them until Emma Thacher decided what was to be their final disposition. In 1927 she died and in her will relinquished title to all four collections to the Library of Congress. Putnam celebrated the gift as a major "manifestation of the patriotism of American scholarship" and an act consistent with Thacher's long record of public service. Emma Thacher's gift of what became the John Boyd Thacher Collection to the Library of Congress significantly affected the history of that institution.

Since its founding in 1800 the Library of Congress had always recognized the concept of rarity in its book collections and had acquired rare and special items, as well as collections such as the Peter Force Library (1867) and the Joseph Meredith Toner collection (1882). Although the library had no separate rare-book division, it attempted to segregate rare items from its general research or congressional collections. When the library moved from the Capitol to its new building in 1897, the rare-books collection was of sufficient size to place it under the supervision of the superintendent of the Main Reading Room by moving it from the office of the librarian of Congress. The collection grew through additions from the general collections, donations, and purchases, but it remained ancillary to the general collections.

The acquisition of the John Boyd Thacher Collection marked a turning point, for when Emma Thacher bequeathed this collection—so rich in incunabula, Columbiana, manuscripts, and works relating to the French Revolution—the collections were deemed of sufficient size that the library named a curator of rare books and dedicated an architecturally splendid Rare Book Reading Room with an adjoining section of locked stacks. It also began planning for an addition to the library, which would include a rare-book reading room and a large vault area. This wing of the building opened in 1934, and the rare book collections of the Library of Congress thus came of age through the John Boyd Thacher Collection: Emma Thacher's donation highlighted the importance of a national rare-book collection.

References:

Frederick W. Ashley, *Catalogue of the John Boyd Thacher Collection of Incunabula* (Washington, D.C.: U.S. Government Printing Office, 1915);

Walter R. Benjamin, "The French Revolution," *The Collector*, 18 (1905): 62–63;

Edith Brinkman, "John Boyd Thacher," *Papers of the Bibliographical Society of America*, 14 (1920): 33–37;

The Collection of John Boyd Thacher in the Library of Congress, 3 volumes (Washington, D.C.: U.S. Government Printing Office, 1931);

Frederick R. Goff, "John Boyd Thacher," in *Grolier 75: A Biographical Retrospective to Celebrate the Seventy-Fifth Anniversary of the Grolier Club in New York*, edited by R. W. G. Vail and others (New York: Grolier Club, 1959), pp. 38–41;

Victor Hugo Paltsits, "An Analysis of the Auction Sales of The John Boyd Thacher Collection–1913–1922," *Autograph Collectors' Journal*, 3 (1951): 30–31;

Paltsits, "The Honorable John Boyd Thacher," *New York History*, 32 (1951): 18–32;

Report of the Librarian of Congress (Washington, D.C.: Library of Congress, 1910), pp. 23–24;

Report of the Librarian of Congress (Washington, D.C.: Library of Congress, 1915), p. 69;

Report of the Librarian of Congress (Washington, D.C.: Library of Congress, 1916), pp. 115–118;

Report of the Librarian of Congress (Washington, D.C.: Library of Congress, 1921), pp. 26–27, 41;

Report of the Librarian of Congress (Washington, D.C.: Library of Congress, 1927), pp. 1–2, 25–29, 78–79;

"The Thacher Collection," *The Collector*, 41 (1927): 441;

"The Thacher Sale," *The Collector*, 27 (1913): 13–14;

Peter Van Wingen, "The Incunabula Collections of the Library of Congress," *Rare Books and Manuscripts Librarianship*, 4 (1989): 85–100.

Isaiah Thomas
(30 January 1750 – 4 April 1831)

Harold N. Boyer
Florence County Library

See also the Thomas entries in *DLB 43: American Newspaper Journalists, 1690–1872; DLB 49: American Literary Publishing Houses, 1638–1899;* and *DLB 73: American Magazine Journalists, 1741–1850.*

BOOKS: *An Oration: Delivered in Free-Masons-Hall, Lancaster, Commonwealth of Massachusetts, on Thursday, the Twenty-Fourth of June, 1779 (A. L. 5779) to the Right Worshipful Master, Worshipful Wardens and Members, Etc. of Trinity Lodge* (Worcester, Mass., 1781);

A Specimen of Isaiah Thomas's Printing Types. Being as Large and Complete an Assortment as Is to Be Met with in Any One Printing-Office in America. Chiefly Manufactured by That Great Artist, William Caslon, Esq. of London (Worcester, Mass.: Printed by Isaiah Thomas, 1785);

New American Spelling Book: or The Child's Easy Introduction to Spelling and Reading the English Tongue. To Which is Added, an Entire New, Plain and Comprehensive English Grammar. Also, the Shorter Catechism, by the Assembly of Divines. The Whole Adapted to the Capacities of Young Children; Rendering the Use of a Primer Unnecessary (Worcester, Mass.: Printed and sold by Isaiah Thomas, 1785);

Catalogue of Books to Be Sold by Isaiah Thomas, at His Bookstore in Worcester, Massachusetts. Consisting of Many Celebrated Authors in History, Voyages, Travels, Geography, Antiquities, Philosophy, Novels, Miscellanies, Divinity, Physick, Surgery, Anatomy, Arts, Sciences, Husbandry, Architecture, Navigation, Mathematics, Law, Periodical Publications, Poetry, Plays, Musick, Etc. Etc. (Worcester, Mass.: Printed by Isaiah Thomas, 1787);

Literary Proposal. Proposal of Isaiah Thomas and Company, for Publishing by Subscription, a New Periodical Work, to be Entitled, The Massachusetts Magazine: or, Monthly Museum of Knowledge and Rational Entertainment (Boston: Printed by Isaiah Thomas, 1788);

Catalogue of Books to Be Sold by Isaiah Thomas, at His Bookstore in Worcester, Massachusetts. Consisting of

Isaiah Thomas

History, Voyages, Travels, Geography, Antiquities, Philosophy, Novels, Miscellanies, Divinity, Physick, Surgery, Anatomy, Arts, Sciences, Husbandry, Architecture, Navigation, Mathematics, Law, Periodical Publications, Poetry, Plays, Musick, Etc. Etc. (Worcester, Mass.: Printed by Isaiah Thomas & Leonard Worcester, 1792);

Thomas and Andrew's Catalogue of Books, for Sale, Wholesale and Retail, at Their Book and Stationary Store, Faust's Statue, No. 45 Newbury Street, Boston. Consisting of a Very Extensive Collection of the Latest and Most Approved Authors, in Divinity,

Law, Physick, Surgery, Chemistry, History, Biography, Voyages, Travels, Miscellanies, Novels, Poetry, Musick, Arts and Sciences, Philosophy, Navigation, Astronomy, Geography, Architecture, Trade and Commerce, Mathematicks, Bookkeeping, Etc. Etc. To All Which Large Additions are Constantly Making (Boston: Thomas & Andrews, 1793);

The Massachusetts Compiler of Theoretical and Practical Elements of Sacred Vocal Music (Boston: Isaiah Thomas & Ebenezer T. Andrews, 1795);

Catalogue of Books to Be Sold by Thomas, Son & Thomas, at Their Bookstore, in Worcester, Massachusetts: Consisting of History, Voyages, Travels, Geography, Antiquities, Philosophy, Novels, Miscellanies, Divinity, Physic, Surgery, Anatomy, Arts, Sciences, Husbandry, Architecture, Navigation, Mathematicks, Law, Periodical Publications, Poetry, Plays, Music, Etc. Etc. Etc. (Worcester, Mass.: Thomas, Son & Thomas, 1796);

Isaiah Thomas's Catalogue of English, Scotch, Irish and American Books for Sale, at the Worcester Bookstore. Consisting of History, Voyages, Travels, Geography, Antiquities, Philosophy, Novels, Miscellanies, Divinity, Physic, Surgery, Anatomy, Arts, Sciences, Husbandry, Architecture, Navigation, Mathematicks, Law, Periodical Publications, Poetry, Plays, Music, Etc. Etc. (Worcester, Mass.: Printed by Isaiah Thomas, 1801);

Eccentric Biography: or Memoirs of Remarkable Female Characters, Ancient and Modern (Worcester, Mass.: Printed by I. Thomas Jr., 1804);

The History of Printing in America. With a Biography of Printers, and an Account of Newspapers. To Which is Prefixed a Concise View of the Discovery and Progress of the Art in Other Parts of the World, 2 volumes (Worcester, Mass.: From the press of Isaiah Thomas Jr., Isaac Sturtevant, printer, 1810); second edition, with "The Author's Corrections and Additions, and a Catalogue of American Publications Previous to the Revolution of 1776" (Albany, N.Y.: Printed by J. Munsell for the American Antiquarian Society, 1874);

An Address to the Most Worshipful Grand Lodge of Massachusetts, at the Close of the Constitutional Term of His Presiding as Grand Master, A.L. 5805 (Boston: J. Eliot Jr., 1811);

Communication from the President of the American Antiquarian Society to the Members, October 24th, 1814. (Published by Order of the Society.) Together with the Laws of the Society, as Revised (Worcester, Mass.: Printed by W. Manning, 1815);

A Catalogue of Publications in What is Now the United States Prior to the Revolution of 1775-6 (Albany, N.Y.: J. Munsell, 1874);

Catalogue of Standard Trotting Stallions and Mares (Manchester, 1886);

The Diary of Isaiah Thomas, 1805–1828, edited by Benjamin Thomas Hill, 2 volumes (Worcester, Mass.: American Antiquarian Society, 1909);

Extracts from the Diaries and Accounts of Isaiah Thomas from the Year 1782 to 1804 and His Diary for 1808, edited by Charles L. Nichols (Worcester, Mass.: American Antiquarian Society, 1916);

Three Autobiographical Fragments (Worcester, Mass.: American Antiquarian Society, 1962).

OTHER: *Laus Deo! The Worcester Collection of Sacred Harmony,* edited by Thomas (Worcester, Mass.: Printed by Isaiah Thomas, 1786);

The Perpetual Laws of the Commonwealth of Massachusetts from the Establishment of Its Constitution to the First Session of the General Court, A.D. 1788, edited by Thomas (Worcester, Mass.: Printed by Isaiah Thomas, 1788);

William Perry, *The Only Sure Guide to the English Tongue; or New Pronouncing Spelling Book. Upon the Same Plan as Perry's Royal Standard English Dictionary . . . To Which Is Added, A Grammar of the English Language; and a Select Number of Moral Tales and Fables . . . With an Appendix . . . By W. Perry, 11th Worcester ed. . . . Carefully Rev. by Perry's Royal Standard English Dictionary, By Isaiah Thomas . . . ,* revised by Thomas (Worcester, Mass.: Printed by I. Thomas Jr., 1789);

The Perpetual Laws of the Commonwealth of Massachusetts, from the Establishment of Its Constitution to the Second Session of the General Court, in 1798, edited by Thomas (Worcester, Mass.: Printed by Isaiah Thomas, 1799);

The Perpetual Laws of the Commonwealth of Massachusetts, from the Establishment of Its Constitution, in the Year 1780, to February, 1807 . . . with the Constitutions of the Unites States, and of the Commonwealth, Prefixed. To Which is Added, an Appendix, Containing Acts and Clauses of Acts, from the Laws of the Late Colony, Province and State of Massachusetts, Which Either Are Unrevised or Respect the Title of Real Estate . . . (Boston: I. Thomas and E. T. Andrews, 1807).

Isaiah Thomas achieved a national reputation as a printer, author, magazine publisher, and bibliophile. As a printer of newspapers, magazines, pamphlets, and books his career encompassed both the traditional manual printing methods and the new technology of power presses and mass-produced publications. He printed the *Massachusetts Spy,* an im-

Zechariah Fowle's press, on which Thomas learned to print

portant publication supporting colonial rights during the Revolutionary War. His *History of Printing in America* in 1810 was the first comprehensive chronicle of the press in America and is still of recognized value. His founding of the American Antiquarian Society in 1812 preserved one of the finest collections of early American imprints.

The youngest of five children, Thomas was born to Moses Thomas and Fidelity Grant Thomas on 30 January 1750 in Boston, Massachusetts. His grandfather Peter Thomas was a merchant, while his father worked as a schoolteacher, farmer, trader, and storekeeper—all without success. Moses Thomas died in North Carolina in 1752, leaving his widow in dire financial straits with three children to support.

In 1756 Isaiah Thomas was apprenticed to printer Zechariah Fowle of Boston. This apprenticeship bound Thomas to Fowle until 1769 and provided for Thomas to be taught to read, write, and calculate. None of these provisions was honored, but Thomas educated himself by using a dictionary, the Bible, and various publications printed at the shop. While working for Fowle, Thomas did, however, learn a great deal about salesmanship that would benefit him later in his own business ventures.

Two printers left lasting impressions upon Thomas during his apprenticeship. Samuel Draper became Fowle's partner in 1758 and worked with Fowle until 1763. Thomas taught himself to spell us-

Prospectus for Thomas's first magazine

ing *The Youth's Instructor in the English Tongue,* which was printed by Fowle and Draper. Thomas was assuming more responsibility in Fowle's shop by the early 1760s and produced the first work under his own imprint: *The New Book of Knowledge, Shewing the Effects of the Planets and Other Astronomical Constellations; with the Strange Events That Befall Men, Women and Children Born under Them.* Gamaliel Rogers was the second printer to influence Thomas at this time. Thomas often went to Rogers for advice and discussion of printing. Rogers, who was an old man when Thomas knew him, had published the *American Magazine* in 1743. Talks with Rogers may have influenced Thomas's decision to publish magazines later in his career. Thomas remembered with respect both Draper and Rogers.

By 1765 Thomas realized that he had learned all he could under Fowle and decided to go to London to become a master printer. Fowle and Thomas were also experiencing difficulty in executing the stipulations of Thomas's apprenticeship due to Fowle's lack of business acumen and Thomas's concern about printing quality. Consequently, Thomas sailed for Halifax, Nova Scotia, in September 1765 to arrange passage to London.

Thomas did not take passage to London but was hired to help print the *Halifax Gazette*. Since neither the printer nor the editor was interested in this newspaper, Thomas saw a chance to put into practice some of his own ideas about newspaper printing. At this time the Stamp Act went into effect in the colonies, and Thomas included in the newspaper material opposing this act. This decision represented Thomas's first act of resistance to England's colonial policy. As a result of these activities, however, Thomas was fired in March 1766. He left Halifax for Portsmouth, New Hampshire, where he worked for Daniel and Robert Fowle, Zechariah's brother and nephew, respectively, and for Ezekiel Russell and Thomas Furber. Thomas returned to Boston for a short second association with Zechariah Fowle before leaving for London by way of Charleston, South Carolina.

In London, Thomas worked for Robert Wells until the spring of 1770. Wells also ran a bookshop that provided Thomas with his first serious introduction to the book trade, with obvious implications for his future. On 25 December 1769 Thomas married Mary Dill.

In May 1770 Thomas and his wife returned to Boston to establish a partnership with Zechariah Fowle. This association gave Thomas the wherewithal to begin printing the *Massachusetts Spy,* which he began publishing on 7 August 1770. Political issues dominated the contents of the newspaper. Although Thomas promised impartiality in his newspaper, it soon became controversial as a partisan political organ supporting the patriot cause. By March 1771 the *Spy* was being printed as a weekly, four-page folio; that became its standard format.

The printing of the *Spy* brought Thomas recognition, not all of which he welcomed; but this newspaper and the printing in 1771 of the first of his annual almanacs, *The Massachusetts Calendar* (later to become *Thomas's New-England Almanack* in 1775), led to invitations to set up partnerships in other communities. An example is his partnership with Henry W. Tinges, a former apprentice, to print the *Essex Journal* in Newburyport, Massachusetts.

With the printing of *The Royal American Magazine, or Universal Repository of Instruction and Amusement* in January 1774, Thomas embarked upon a magazine-publishing career that included the publishing of three magazines. The *Royal American* was an effort to produce a literary magazine with miscellaneous subjects. Of interest and unusual for the time were the question-and-answer column titled "Directory of Love" and the inclusion of music. The magazine also included sufficient political articles to give it a distinctively patriot stance.

Thomas suspended publication of the *Royal American* in July 1774 due to the British blockade of Boston, but Joseph Greenleaf resumed publication of the magazine in September. The blockade also adversely affected the printing of the *Massachusetts Spy*. It became involved with resistance to royal authority by reporting events and meetings from other colonies, the activities of the Continental Congress, and the Massachusetts Provincial Congress.

The blockade and personal threats to Thomas necessitated his moving in March 1775 both his family and press out of Boston to Worcester, Massachusetts. This relocation began his long association with this town, which became his home. His anti-British activities at this time encompassed more than printing patriot articles. On 18 April 1775 Thomas rode with Paul Revere warning citizens of British troops moving on Concord, Massachusetts, and he joined the militia at Lexington on 19 April 1775.

With the *Spy* moved to Worcester and Boston blockaded, paper, ink, and supplies were hard to obtain. Nevertheless, the *Spy* was the first publication printed in any inland town of Massachusetts. On 15 November 1775 Postmaster General Benjamin Franklin appointed Thomas postmaster for Worcester, and he retained this post until 1802.

The war years were a period of turmoil for Thomas both personally and professionally. His first child was stillborn in 1770, and his daughter Mary Ann was born on 27 March 1772. Isaiah Jr. was born on 5 September 1773. He stopped living with his wife in 1775 after she traveled to Newburyport in the company of a British officer. Thomas filed for divorce on grounds of adultery, and a divorce was granted on 27 May 1777.

Thomas resumed full-time management of the *Spy* in June 1778 in Worcester and on 26 May 1779 married his cousin, the former Mary Thomas Fowle. (Her father, William, was a brother of Moses Thomas.) Her husband had died a soldier in 1776. When they married, she was thirty, and Thomas was twenty-nine. Thomas was drafted for the army in 1780, but he chose to exercise his right to send a replacement. He sent his apprentice Benjamin Russell, who served six months. After his service Russell returned to Thomas's printing office.

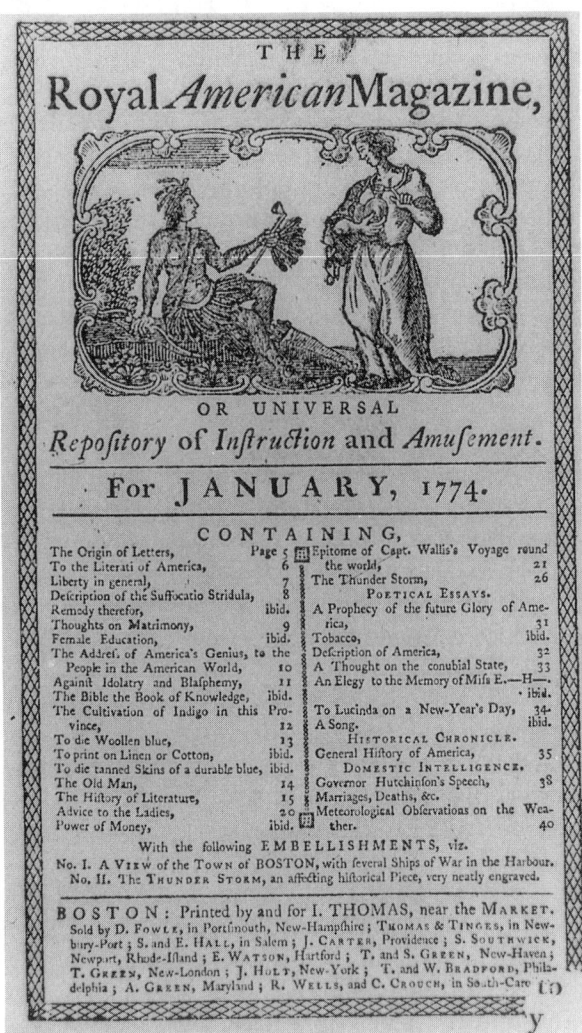

First issue of the magazine Thomas founded "to convey to posterity the labours of the learned"

Financially, 1785 was a turning point for Thomas. The *Spy* made money for him after the war, and he used it to advertise his other publications; these also brought financial success. At this time Thomas was thirty-six and an excellent printer with a successful, growing business. He succeeded in Worcester where there had previously been no presses.

The fifteen years between 1781 and 1795 saw many publications from Thomas's presses. They took the form of almanacs, broadsides, pamphlets, and books. An example of a broadside was the 1781 publication of *The Amorous Sailor's Letter to His Sweetheart. And the Jolly Orange Woman.* Two booklets on the Shakers appeared in 1782 while *The Psalter; or Psalms of David, with the Proverbs of Solomon, and Christ's Sermon on the Mount* was printed in 1784. This collection was intended for juvenile readers.

Almanacs were always best-sellers for Thomas. The war interrupted publication from 1776 to

1778, but Thomas's almanac ran continuously from 1779 to 1820, first as *Thomas's Massachusetts, New Hampshire and Connecticut Almanac* from 1779 to 1781; then as *Thomas's Massachusetts, Connecticut, Rhode-island, Newhampshire and Vermont Almanac* from 1782 to 1798, and *Isaiah Thomas's . . . Almanac* from 1799 to 1803. From 1804, the almanac was published under his son's name as *Isaiah Thomas Junior's . . . Almanac.* These almanacs included the usual astronomical information while the 1784 almanac reprinted the "Preliminary Articles of Peace" and "Substance of the Constitution of Massachusetts" to increase its appeal.

Reprinting of works gave Thomas the opportunity to bring Continental literary and standard texts to his American readers. Examples were *Fanny or The Happy Penitent* by François-Thomas Baculard D'Arnaud and two juvenile titles, *The Beauty and The Monster, A Comedy* by the Countess de Genlis and *Hagar in the Desert.* All were translated from the French and reprinted in 1785.

Reprinting was also profitable for Thomas. Two English works he reprinted were extremely successful. *The Only Sure Guide to the English Tongue: or, New Pronouncing Spelling Book* came off his press in 1785. This was the eighth edition by William Perry, which Thomas copied to create the first Worcester edition. It would go through fourteen Thomas editions and sell more than three hundred thousand copies in the next twenty years. In 1788 Thomas printed the first American edition of Perry's *Royal Standard English Dictionary,* which was copied from the fourth British edition. This work went through four Worcester editions for a total of fifty-four thousand copies.

Of interest to historians of the press is Thomas's *A Specimen of Isaiah Thomas's Printing Types,* printed in 1785. This fifty-page work displayed all the typefaces and sizes owned by Thomas at this time. Thomas states that "£2000 sterling and upwards, were added to this Specimen, in types from Fry's, Caslon's and Wilson's Foundries, between 1785 and 1784 [*sic*]. A great addition, and a great variety of Types were added to the following after 1785. When complete the Printing materials were estimated at Nine Thousand Dollars." This work also displays mathematical, algebraic, and astronomical characters, Greek and Hebrew font, and some examples of type ornaments.

One of the most significant printing efforts by Thomas was his juvenile titles. Altogether, he printed 66 juvenile titles and 119 editions. He began printing children's books in 1779, the same year he started selling imported copies of John Newbery chapbooks and titles such as *The History of Little Goody*

Two-Shoes and Daniel Defoe's *Robinson Crusoe*. He printed the first American edition of *Mother Goose's Melody* in 1786 and became the most significant printer of children's books of his time. He did not, however, consider his juvenile works an important part of his lifetime work, although they did make money for him. When he gave his personal collection of his imprints to the newly established American Antiquarian Society, he did not include any of his juvenile imprints.

The early 1790s saw Thomas expand his activities by starting new partnerships with their attendant diverse printing and financial transactions. He also built his own paper mill near Worcester in 1793 and employed 150 workers in his Worcester shop by the mid 1790s. He became involved in Masonic activities in Massachusetts. He was chosen First Grand Master of the Morning Star Lodge of Worcester in 1793 and by 1803 was the Most Worshipful Grand Master of the Grand Lodge of Massachusetts.

Thomas retired from active involvement in his diverse business activities in 1802. By this time he possessed many printing offices, bookshops, and paper mills. He still remained quite active. While retired he looked after his business interests through partners and managers. He was instrumental in establishing the first bank in Worcester in 1803 or 1804 and served as one of its directors for eleven years. In 1805 he organized a turnpike from Worcester to Boston and served as a director of the Worcester Turnpike Corporation. He donated land in Worcester for the construction of a charity house and courthouse building. For the latter building he laid the cornerstone and supervised construction.

Thomas's contributions to early American bibliography are his publication of his *The History of Printing in America* in 1810, his personal library of early American imprints, and the formation of the American Antiquarian Society in 1812. These accomplishments mark Thomas as a significant early American bibliophile.

Work on *The History of Printing in America* commenced with an entry in his diary for April 1808 stating that he had begun " writing a sketch of the origin and progress of printing." Over the years Thomas had been gathering materials on printing in America. He was concerned about preserving the historical record of early America.

Thomas had two purposes in mind when he published his history of printing. The first was to collect and preserve materials to illustrate such a history, and the second was to show the influence that the press had in promoting freedom and the American Revolution. This was not to be an exhaus-

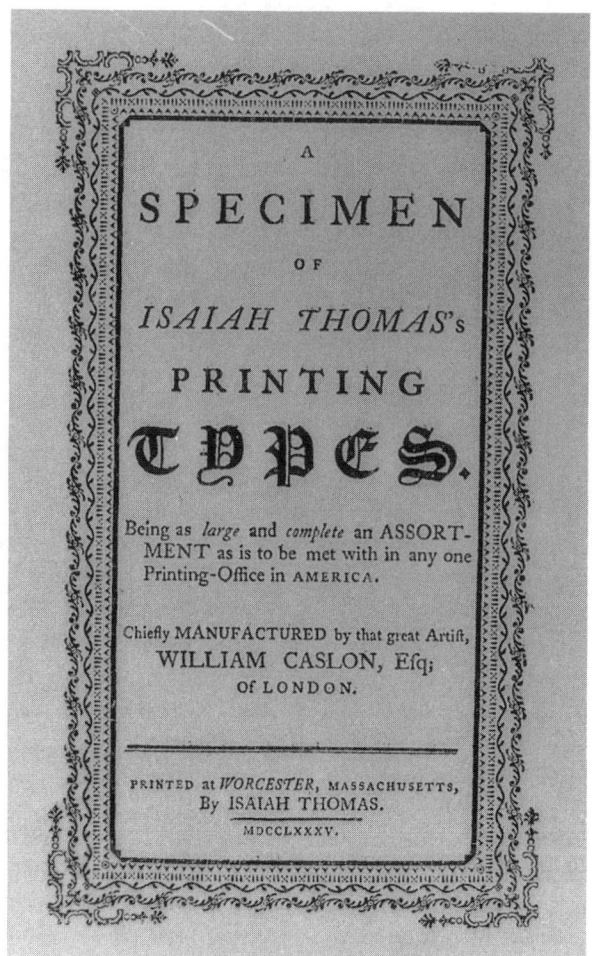

Title page for the book Thomas compiled to illustrate the great variety of his typefaces

tive history of printing but a narrative history of the beginnings of printing in America. Thomas achieved his goal by using selected newspapers, magazines, and pamphlets together with lists of early American books. He also included biographical information about early American printers. His extensive correspondence with American printers over the years provided insight and an understanding of the printing trade as it evolved during his lifetime. These activities and resources provided the historical material for this book. The book was published in two octavo volumes in 1810 with the entire cost of publication being borne by Thomas.

Thomas's history lacks documentation and coordination of subjects. It is also repetitious and marked by omissions and inaccuracies that have been corrected by new research; Thomas's opinions of fellow printers, moreover, were biased by personal experience. Despite these concerns, *The History of Printing in America* remains a work of exceptional value both as history and literature. Its most com-

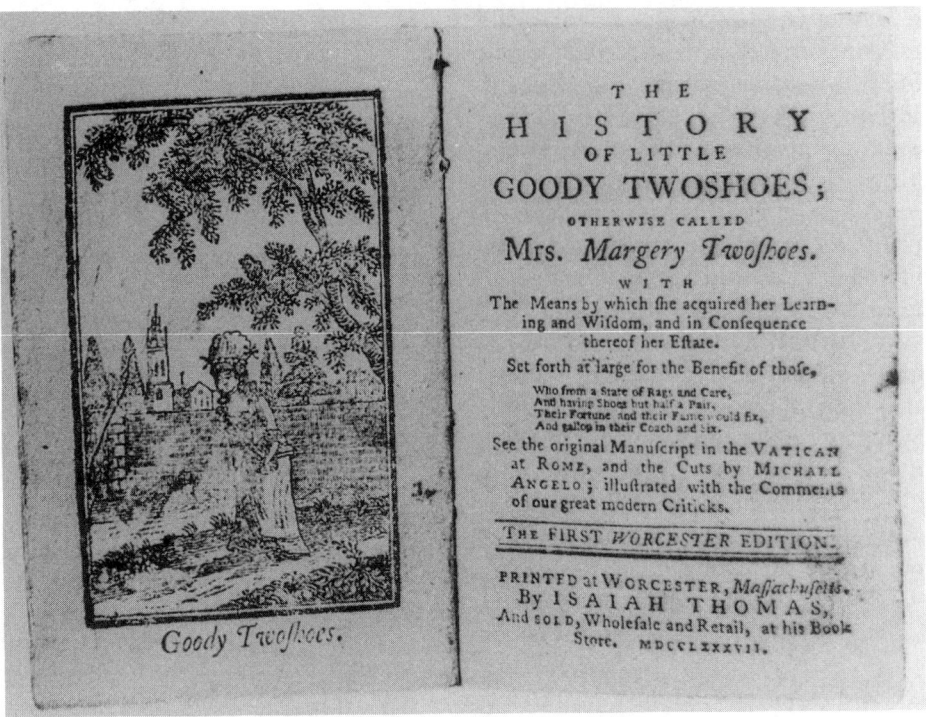

Frontispiece and title page for Thomas's first printing of a popular British children's book

plete chapters deal with printing in Massachusetts, Pennsylvania, and South Carolina, where Thomas had personal contact and firsthand knowledge of events. While the historian of today might criticize Thomas's opinions of fellow printers, these vignettes give the book its particular flavor. Reprinted in 1874 by the American Antiquarian Society with Thomas's added notes and revisions, *The History of Printing in America* stood for more than 150 years as the standard work on the history of printing in early America.

Thomas began collecting materials for his personal library early in his career, and as he became financially secure, his library grew. With his personal estate worth approximately $170,000 in 1811, Thomas became concerned with two problems—finding more material on early American printing and deciding what to do with the growing collection housed in his Worcester residence. In both 1808 and 1811 he enlarged his house and available shelving to accommodate this personal library.

In March 1812 he produced a catalogue of his library that took three months to complete and ran to 217 pages. It divided the collection into seventeen sections: ancient books printed before 1700, modern books printed after 1700, Bibles, dictionaries, books in Indian languages, Masonic works, works on physic and surgery, printing, sermons, tracts, trials, books printed by Thomas and his companies, peri-

odical works, orations, church music, pamphlets, and books printed by Isaiah Thomas Jr.

Books printed by Thomas and by others for him were bound in full calf in a uniform style with his bookplate in each volume. This bookplate was designed and executed by Paul Revere. By 1812 Thomas's personal library was valued at $5,000 and included three thousand volumes.

Some of the variety and richness of Thomas's library are illustrated by titles such as a miniature duodecimo volume titled *Tom Thumb's Play-Book*, which was printed by Thomas in 1762 for Andrew Barclay. It included alphabetical lines, scripture, catechism, and prayers. Some books printed before 1700 are the *Massachusetts Laws* of 1660, 1672, and 1692; William Hubbard's *Indian Wars* with Foster's maps, printed in 1677; Nathaniel Morton's *New-England's Memoriall,* 1688; and *Erasmus on the Psalms,* Venice, 1476. Bibles were included in this library in more than thirty languages and in nonpareil, royal quarto, octavo, and folio editions. A broadside titled "The Lawyer's Pedigree" was set in type by Thomas at the age of six when he was a young apprentice.

This library also included editions of juvenile works such as the first American edition of *Mother Goose's Melody* (1786), music books, English grammar and science textbooks, and copies of more than nine hundred books in original and later editions that Thomas printed.

The founding of the American Antiquarian Society was a natural outgrowth of his *History of Printing in America* and his concern for the preservation of early American history. His reasons for the founding of the society were varied and reflected his democratic outlook. Thomas wanted this society to preserve the materials that were read, used, and produced by ordinary American citizens. At this time Europeans displayed a condescending attitude toward all things American in general and belles lettres in particular. Thomas resented this attitude and saw no place in America where American materials were being collected and preserved. His society would establish such a place.

He first discussed this idea in January 1812 with his friends the Reverend Dr. Aaron Bancroft and Dr. Oliver Fiske. His personal collection of early American imprints, newspapers, magazines, and pamphlets provided the core collection for the society, for he believed that it had value and if properly preserved would serve both the citizens of Worcester and the nation.

In October 1812 a petition was presented to the Massachusetts General Court to incorporate the American Antiquarian Society "to contribute to the advancement of the arts and sciences, and . . . to assist the researches of the future historians of our country." The society was incorporated on 22 October 1812, and the first meeting was held on 19 November 1812 in Boston, with Thomas elected president. He served in this capacity until his death in 1831.

Thomas gave to the society his personal library, but he kept the library in his home for the next eight years until the first Antiquarian Hall was built in Worcester in 1820. He donated the lot for the building and contributed $10,000 toward its construction. The dedication ceremony was held on 24 August 1820.

The role of the society reflected Thomas's belief that access to knowledge was a crucial part of the democratic ideal. He felt that the collection should be open to all. Here one could find opportunities and sources for self-improvement and knowledge.

These views were also reflected in the materials to be collected for the society. Books of every description dealing with the Western Hemisphere were to be collected, as were pamphlets, magazines, newspapers both retrospective and current, manuscripts, maps, charts, prints, broadsides, and the graphic arts. The society as a library was different from other libraries of the day because it was secular, was nonacademic, and provided for the concerns of the common man. An indication of the significance of the society is that among its members were many famous men such as Thomas Jefferson, Daniel Webster, Francis Parkman, and Andrew Jackson.

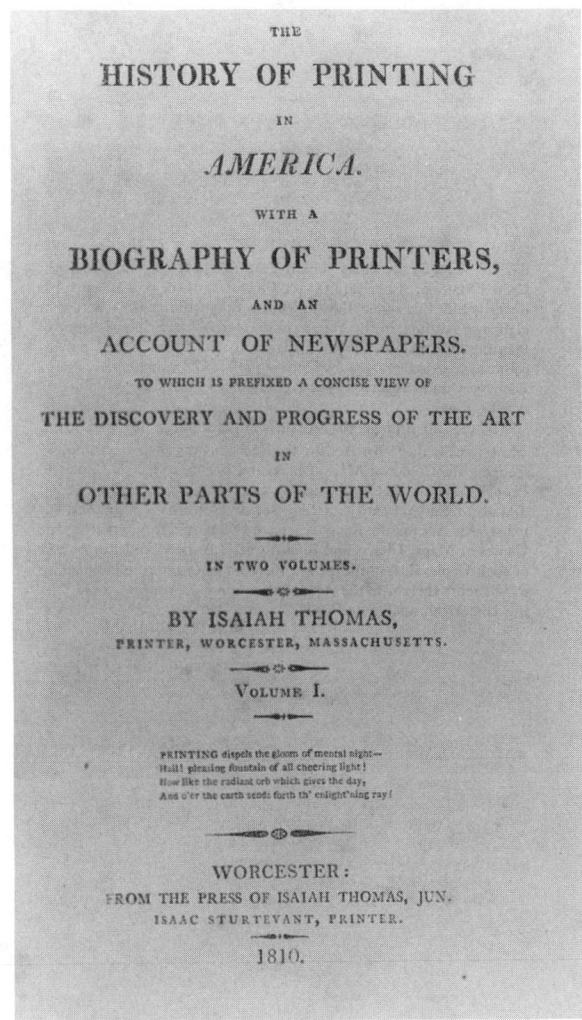

Title page for Thomas's most significant book, for which he drew on his personal contacts with printers throughout the country

In addition to donating his personal collection to the society Thomas purchased the twelve hundred volumes of the Mather library in 1814 and donated them to the society. This collection originally belonged to Increase, Cotton, and Samuel Mather. He also made contributions to other libraries. In 1818 he gave fourteen bound volumes of the *Massachusetts Spy* to the American Philosophical Society in Philadelphia, a further fourteen each to the New York Historical Society and the American Academy of Arts and Sciences, and thirteen to the Massachusetts Historical Society. Dartmouth College was the recipient of books worth $654 in 1819, and Allegheny College in Pennsylvania received a pair of globes and books valued at $550 in 1820.

While Thomas was engaging in philanthropy and bibliophily during these years, his personal life was far from tranquil. His second wife died on 16 No-

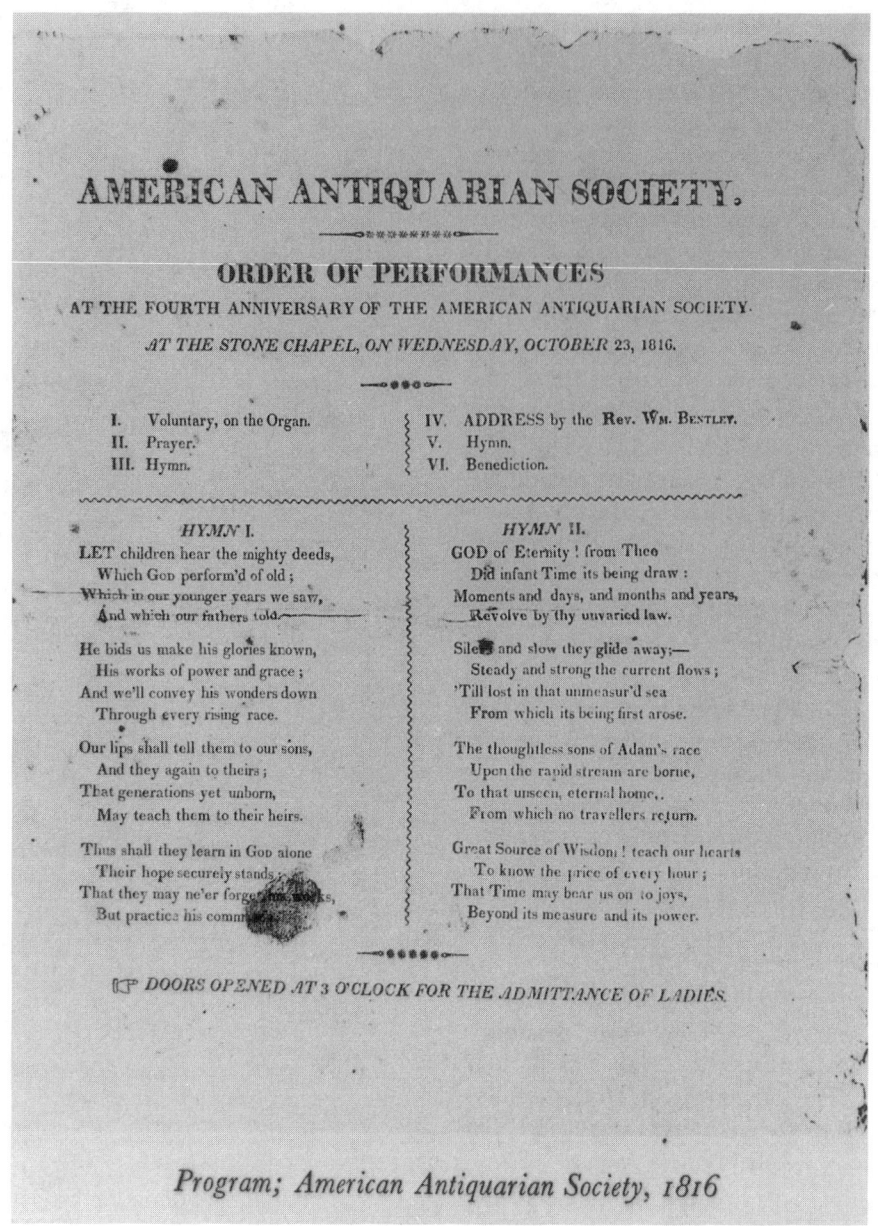

Program; American Antiquarian Society, 1816

Program for a meeting of the American Antiquarian Society, which Thomas founded. He left
his collection of early American publications, including his own, to the society's library in
Worcester, Massachusetts.

vember 1818, and on 25 June 1819 his son died at the age of forty-five. Thomas married for a third time on 10 August 1819 to Rebecca Armstrong. She was sixty-two and Thomas's second wife's cousin and housekeeper. This marriage failed, and the couple separated in May 1822. She died in October 1828.

By 1820 Thomas was blind in one eye and frequently ill. He spent the remainder of the decade disposing of his businesses and landholdings while enjoying the acclaim surrounding an honored printer, historian, and philanthropist. He received honorary

degrees from Dartmouth College in 1814 and Allegheny College in 1818. He was elected to the Massachusetts and New York historical societies, the Philadelphia Typographical Society, and the American Philosophical Society; he was made an honorary member of the American Academy of Arts and Sciences after the publication of his history of printing. Thomas died in Worcester on 4 April 1831.

The significance of Isaiah Thomas lies in his roles as printer, philanthropist, and bibliophile. Benjamin Franklin called Thomas "the Baskerville of America," referring to John Baskerville, the English writing master, type designer, and printer. This was high praise coming from the man most often held in comparison to Thomas. As a printer Thomas accomplished many firsts. His *Royal American Magazine,* using some political illustrations by Paul Revere, was the first American magazine to be amply illustrated. The printing company of Thomas and Andrews was, in its day, the largest in America. Thomas printed in 1789 William Hill Brown's *The Power of Sympathy,* the first American novel. He printed more titles and numbers of copies than any other printer in colonial and early America. More than nine hundred titles came off Thomas's presses. His business acumen is evidenced by his keeping his 1797 edition of the Bible set in type, resulting in a low-cost Bible for mass production.

These examples illustrate the range and complexity of this self-educated man. Brissot de Warville, a European traveler who visited Worcester, wrote in his book *New Travels in the United States, Performed in 1788* that Thomas was "the Diderot of the United States," referring to Denis Diderot, the French philosopher and encyclopedist.

As philanthropist Thomas contributed time, money, and real estate to many projects. He was involved in the development of a bank, a turnpike, and a courthouse, and as one of the original 150 incorporators who took shares at $300 each, he helped found the Boston Athenaeum on 18 June 1807. His extensive memberships in organizations such as the Order of Masons, Boston and Worcester fire societies, Worcester Associate Circulating Library, the Massachusetts Humane Society, and the Auxiliary Bible Society of Worcester County attest to his philanthropic nature.

Thomas's bibliophily is best revealed in his founding of the American Antiquarian Society in 1812 and his book donations to other institutions. His lifelong book collecting in the field of early Americana and donation of his personal library of three thousand volumes to the society insured that it would become one of the primary repositories for early American imprints as it is to this day.

Bibliographies:

American Antiquarian Society, *A Catalogue of Books in the Library of the American Antiquarian Society* (Worcester, Massachusetts: Printed by H. J. Howland, 1836);

Charles L. Nichols, *Bibliography of Worcester: A List of Books, Pamphlets, Newspapers and Broadsides, Printed in the Town of Worcester, Massachusetts, from 1775 to 1848. With Historical and Explanatory Notes* (Worcester, Mass.: Privately printed, 1899);

Dartmouth College, *The Isaiah Thomas Donation, Library of Dartmouth College. Presented by Isaiah Thomas, Esq., A.D. 1819, in His Donation of 470 Volumes* (Hanover, N. H., 1949).

Biographies:

Charles L. Nichols, *Isaiah Thomas: Printer, Writer and Collector* (Boston: The Club of Odd Volumes, 1912);

Annie Russell Marble, *From 'Prentice to Patron* (New York: Appleton-Century, 1935);

Clifford K. Shipton, *Isaiah Thomas: Printer, Patriot and Philanthropist* (Rochester, N.Y.: Leo Hart, 1948).

References:

Frank Roe Batchelder, "Isaiah Thomas, the Patriot Printer," *New England Magazine,* new series 25 (November 1901): 284–305;

David D. Hall, "On Native Ground: From the History of Printing to the History of the Book," *Proceedings of the American Antiquarian Society,* 93, no. 2 (1983): 313–336;

Luther Livingston, "An American Publisher of a Hundred Years Ago," *Bookman,* 11 (August 1900): 530–534;

Marcus A. McCorison, "Isaiah Thomas, the American Antiquarian Society and the Future," *Proceedings of the American Antiquarian Society,* 91, no. 1 (1981): 27–37;

Charles A. Nichols, "The Portraits of Isaiah Thomas with Some Notes upon His Descendants," *Proceedings of the American Antiquarian Society,* new series 30 (October 1920): 251–277;

John Roger Osterholm, "The Literary Career of Isaiah Thomas, 1749–1831," dissertation, University of Massachusetts, 1978;

Clifford K. Shipton, "America's First Research Library," *Library Journal,* 74 (15 January 1949): 89–90;

Madeleine B. Stern, "Saint-Pierre in America: Joseph Nancrede and Isaiah Thomas," *Papers of the Bibliographic Society of America,* 68, no. 3 (1974): 312–325;

John T. Winterich, "Early American Books and Printing," *Publishers' Weekly,* 124 (15 July 1933): 174–176;

Hollis Roger Yarrington, "Isaiah Thomas, Printer," dissertation, University of Maryland, 1970.

Papers:

Isaiah Thomas's diaries, business papers, correspondence, and a complete collection of his works are housed at the American Antiquarian Society, Worcester, Massachusetts.

Otto H. F. Vollbehr

(27 April 1872? – 1945 or 1946)

Kurt S. Maier
Library of Congress

BOOKS: *Introduction to a Collection of Book Illustrations in the Possession of Dr. Otto H. F. Vollbehr* (N.p., 1928);

Memorandum, 11 numbers (Washington, D.C. & Los Angeles, 1931–1936).

Otto H. F. Vollbehr was an expert on fifteenth-century books and medieval manuscripts; he amassed a collection of such items in a short time, only to sell them just as quickly. In the years between the world wars he was one of the most prominent rare-book and manuscript dealers in Europe and the United States; stories about his treasures appeared in the press on both sides of the Atlantic. He spoke six languages and had entrée to the homes of the wealthy and famous. His two greatest sales were to the Henry E. Huntington Library and Art Gallery and to the Library of Congress.

Vollbehr promoted an aura of mystery about himself that still enshrouds him today. One of the few sources of information about him, an account of his life in the *Nation's Capital Magazine* in 1931, has the effusiveness of an interview with a movie star. The article says that Otto Heinrich Friederich Vollbehr was born in the German port city of Kiel on 27 April 1872, but an abstract from the files of the U.S. Bureau of Immigration and Naturalization cites his year of birth as 1869, and this is also the year that is cited in the Library of Congress Catalogue. His father, Emil, was a merchant; his mother's name was Caroline. Vollbehr studied at the Universities of Kiel, Marburg, and Berlin, receiving a degree in chemistry from Berlin in 1897. On his graduation, Vollbehr told the interviewer, his father gave him ten thousand gold marks and sent him on a trip around the world that lasted for three years. Although Germany was the undisputed center for chemical research before World War I, Vollbehr's father wanted him to survey the advances in chemistry in the countries he visited. Vollbehr's itinerary took him to France, Egypt, India, China, Japan, and Hawaii, where a fellow German, Claus Spreckels, a

sugar refiner, introduced him to commodities trading.

Vollbehr arrived in San Francisco in 1898. There he was introduced to Adolph Sutro by Sutro's daughter, whom he had met in Japan. The German-born Sutro had become a millionaire in America as a mining engineer and had served as mayor of San Francisco. Half of his two-hundred-thousand-volume library would survive the fire of 1906; the books are now in the city library. Vollbehr remembered Sutro's advice:

> If you ever adopt a hobby . . . do not collect stamps as many are doing today, but bring together a fine collection of rare books. Specialize in a certain type of rare books. Do this always with a view to preserving something worthwhile for posterity. Let humanity play a large part in your hobby. No matter what it costs you in experience and money and time, you will never regret it; because, when you have done this, you will be able to pass out of the picture with the feeling that, while journeying through this life, you did at least one constructive thing that was also fine and noble.

While Vollbehr was in California, the state was gripped by the Alaska gold-rush fever. Vollbehr set out to make his fortune in the Klondike but got only as far as Victoria, British Columbia, before poor health forced him to turn back. He decided to harden his body by traveling on horseback from Washington state to Mexico—no mean feat since his route took him through Yosemite and Death Valley. In Mexico he received a telegram from the Nobel dynamite-manufacturing firm offering him a position as sales representative in the Orient. Vollbehr traveled to Chicago to accept the job.

Before going to the Orient he went home to Germany. There he met and married Elsbeth Kurtz, known to her friends as Lu, the daughter of the director of the Berlin zoo; she would make a name for herself as a novelist under the name El Vollbehr. The couple made their home in Berlin. It is not known how long Vollbehr worked in China and Japan, but he was soon back in Germany, working as an independent

Otto H. F. Vollbehr (Courtesy of Library of Congress)

chemist. By 1914 he was chairman of the board of a large chemical enterprise, and he accumulated a fortune in the munitions industry. Vollbehr's contributions to the German Empire included the invention of optical instruments that were important for the war effort.

After World War I Vollbehr was paralyzed on his left side when a train he was taking from Brussels to Paris derailed in a tunnel. He spent months in hospitals and was advised by his neurologist to quit the demanding life of business and look for a less-stressful, sedentary vocation. As it turned out, in retirement Vollbehr was more active than ever; this activity, perhaps, led to his recovery from his paralysis.

Following Sutro's advice about book collecting, Vollbehr began to purchase incunabula—books printed in the fifteenth century—and manuscripts. In Constantinople (today Istanbul, Turkey) he purchased a collection of incunabula cheaply and picked up priceless Islamic manuscripts in the bazaars; later he would present the manuscripts as a gift to the sultan of Turkey. The years following World War I were auspicious for book collectors in Europe: government and private libraries, burdened by war debts and taxes, were in desperate need of money. In his travels about the Continent Vollbehr targeted monasteries as the chief source of rare items: they were most likely to have medie-val manuscripts and books dating from the infancy of printing, and they always needed money.

Vollbehr had caught the collector's fever. In an interview in the *New York Evening Post* (26 August 1926) he described his state of mind when he was on the trail of books he had to have:

> The nervous interest is too great . . . and I cannot stand the strain. Often I hear of some fine book that I want to add to my collection, and I cannot sleep for night after night because I think about it so hard. How to get money for it—what books to offer in exchange for it, whether to stop wanting it, or get it at any price—all that keeps me too nervous. You cannot understand.

Between 1924 and 1926 Vollbehr sold 2,385 incunabula to the Henry E. Huntington Library in San Marino, California, for $1.2 million. The first sale consisted of 392 items; it included 30 medical works, among them Johannes Mesue's *Opera medicinalia* (Naples: Conradus Goldenmund, 1478), Mohammad Rhasis's *Liber ad Almansorem* (Milan: Leonardus Pachel and Uldericus Scinzenzler, 1481), and Giovanni Michael Savonarola's *Practica medicinae* (Venice: Printed by Bonetus Locatellus for Octaviaus Scotus, 1497). Among the 136 incunabula printed in Spain were Alphonsus de Cartagena's *Doctrinal de los caualleros* (Burgos: Friedrich Biel, 1487), Antonius Nebrissensis's *Gramatica castellana* (Salamanca, 1492), and Giovanni

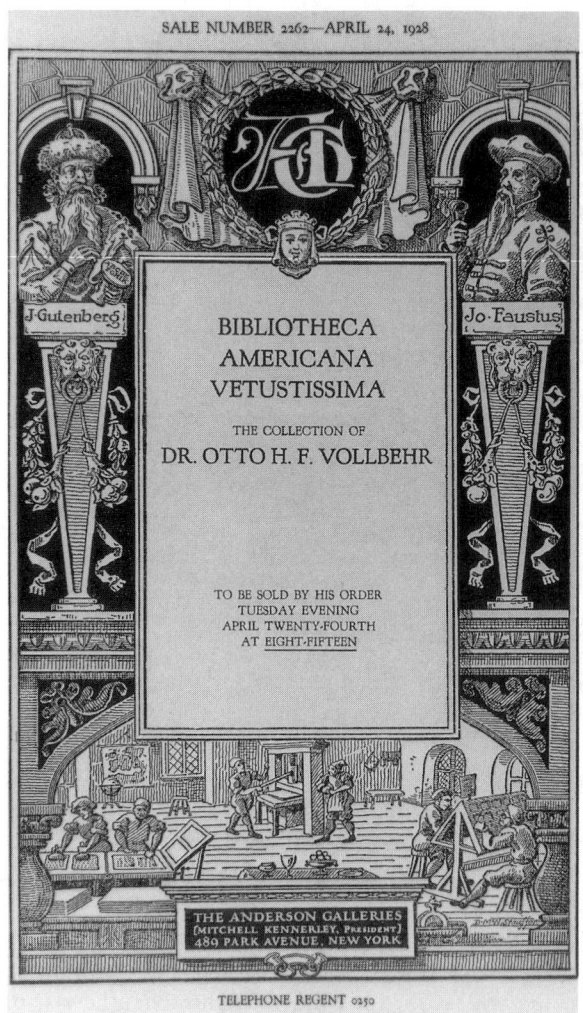

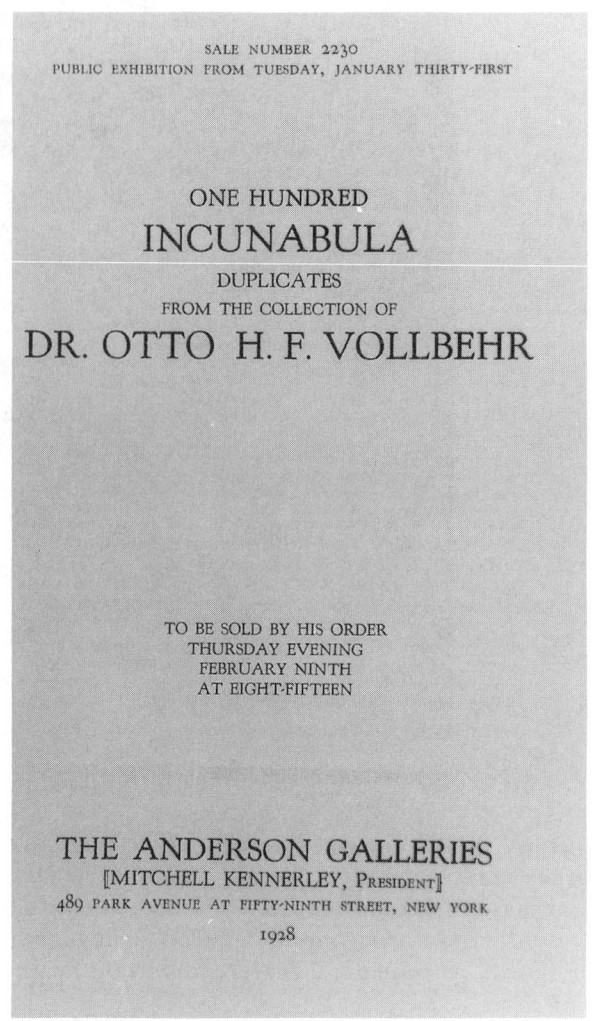

Catalogues for two sales of items from Vollbehr's collection, both held in 1928

Boccaccio's *Las Mujeres ilustres* (Saragossa: Paul Hurus, 1494). *Processionarium ordinis praedicatorum* (Seville: M. Ungut and S. Polonus, 1494) was the first Spanish book with printed musical notations. Also included in the sale were Ludolphus de Saxonia's *Vita Christi* (Lisbon: V. Fernandez and N. de Saxonia, 1495), the first illustrated work, and the *Missale Bracarense (Braga)* (Lisbon: N. de Saxonia, 1498), the first missal, printed in Portugal.

In June 1926 Vollbehr attended the Twenty-eighth International Eucharistic Congress in Chicago. He came with a letter of introduction from Pope Pius XI, the former librarian and vice prefect of the Vatican Library, who had suggested that Vollbehr exhibit his books and manuscripts at the congress. Vollbehr brought steamer trunks full of his choicest wares, including a facsimile of a Gutenberg Bible (1455); he explained that he had an original in Europe but that prohibitive insurance rates prevented him from bringing it to America. Hoping to sell his collection to George

William Cardinal Mundelein of Chicago, who wanted to establish a theological library at the Saint Mary-of-the-Lake Seminary in Mundelein, Illinois, he presented the cardinal with gifts of ancient papal documents. He also sent a locked trunk to the cardinal's residence and, in the presence of newspaper reporters, unlocked it and brought forth rare books. He hoped that the publicity stunt would encourage wealthy benefactors to aid the cardinal's project, but no assistance was forthcoming.

Vollbehr took his exhibition on a tour of American cities, displaying his books and manuscripts at libraries and similar institutions. In New York City an exhibition of books and manuscripts at the National Arts Club included fifty-five different Bibles, fifty editions of works of Saint Augustine, and thirty editions of works of Saint Jerome. The event was marred by the theft of an *Officium mortuorum* (book of prayers for the dead), a fifteenth-century manuscript with illuminations by Attavante degli Attavanti valued at $20,000; it was returned by a lawyer acting as an intermediary.

The final exhibit of Vollbehr's traveling books was at the Library of Congress. The institution's librarian, Herbert Putnam, gave a luncheon on 20 April 1928 to celebrate the opening of the exhibit; the guests included the German ambassador, the chairman of the Library Committee of the House of Representatives, and the undersecretary of state. Vollbehr announced that he and his wife were presenting to the library a collection of 10,800 leaves bearing printers' and publishers' marks from the fifteenth to the nineteenth centuries. Each leaf consisted of a colophon or title page mounted on cardboard. Among the artists who had executed the woodcuts were Lucas Cranach, Hans Holbein, and Hans Baldung. Vollbehr went on to say that he would like to present the library with a Gutenberg Bible and three thousand incunabula, were he in a position to do so, and he called on an American benefactor to step forth and make a pledge. There were no volunteers. He then offered to donate half of his collection if a donor would pay for the rest; again, there was no response. On this note the luncheon ended, and the exhibit opened.

Vollbehr's collection drew large crowds wherever it was shown, and the Library of Congress exhibit was no exception. One of the works that attracted special attention was a Chinese block book in three volumes titled *Huang Hou Ch'uan Shan Shu* (Chinese Book of Exhortation to Virtue). Printed on 9 March 1405 at the command of Empress Jen-hsiao of the Ming Dynasty and including a preface by the ruler, it precedes the earliest printed European block book by a generation. Vollbehr had purchased the book in Spain. Other items at the exhibit included Albrecht von Eyb's *Ob einem Manne sei zuzune men ein ehelich Weib oder nicht* (Nuremberg: A. Korberger, 1472), an amusing German book on the advantages and disadvantages of matrimony; Friedrich Riederer's *Spiegel der wahren Rhetorik* (Freiburg im Breisgau: F. Riederer, 1493), the first book to be printed by its own author; Richardus de Bury's *Philobiblon sive amore librorum* (Cologne: [Printer of Augustinus, "de Fide"] 1473), the earliest work on book collecting and the love of books, by the most-celebrated book collector of the fourteenth century; Girolamo Savonarola's *Predica dell'arte del bene morire* (Florence: Bartolommeo di Libri, after 2 November 1496), a famous sermon by the Florentine reformer who was burned at the stake; Apicius's *De re coquinaria* (Venice: B. Venetus, de Vitalibus, circa 1500), one of the earliest cookbooks; and Paulus de Sancta Maria's *Scrutinium scripturarum* (Strasbourg: Johann Mentelin, 1470), an anti-Jewish tract that was bound in tanned human skin and written by a Jew who had converted to Christianity.

The bookplate for Vollbehr's collection of incunabula

On the occasion of the Carl Schurz Centennial in 1929 Vollbehr presented the Library of Congress with twenty thousand woodcuts and engravings from books printed between the fifteenth and eighteenth centuries. Putnam wanted Vollbehr's three thousand incunabula and Gutenberg Bible, but he did not think Congress would approve the purchase: by then the country was in the grip of the Great Depression, and rare books were not high on the list of national priorities. Vollbehr was desperate to find a buyer; he asked the Philadelphia rare-book dealer Dr. A. S. W. Rosenbach to approach Julius Rosenwald, the founder of Sears, Roebuck and Company, and his son Lessing J. Rosenwald, about purchasing the collection; Vollbehr was willing to accept $900,000 for two thousand volumes and $400,000 for the Bible. The Rosenwalds declined, and it appeared that the books would be returned to Europe and sold off in lots.

At this juncture Rep. Ross Alexander Collins of Mississippi read about the plight of the Vollbehr collection. He gave a ringing speech in the House on 7 February 1930 that was reprinted throughout the country. Pierce Butler of Chicago's Newberry Library and other rare-book experts testified at hearings of the Committee on the Library, and newspaper editorials called for Congress to pass the Collins Bill. The bill passed on 3 July 1930, and in a few weeks trunks and crates filled with incunabula arrived at the library. These acquisitions made the Library of Congress a major research center for fifteenth-century books.

The Gutenberg Bible, however, was missing; Vollbehr had only made a down payment on it and had never owned it outright as he had led others to believe. Putnam had to travel to Austria for negotiations with the Benedictine abbey in Saint Paul, Carinthia, which owned the Bible. The three-volume Bible arrived at the Library of Congress in August 1930. While some forty-nine copies of the Gutenberg Bible on paper and parchment have survived, there are only three perfect parchment copies: one in the British Library, another in the Bibliothèque Nationale in Paris, and the Vollbehr copy in the Library of Congress.

Vollbehr received $1.5 million from the Library of Congress, but he did not have the money for long. Of the 3,255 rare books he sold to the library, 2,200 were mortgaged to a businessman in New York to whom Vollbehr owed $300,000. A bank in Frankfurt am Main had a $500,000 lien against him, and he owed $150,000 to a firm of custom brokers in New York. He was also sued by a lawyer who claimed a commission on the Library of Congress sale. Vollbehr won the case, but after he paid off his creditors he did not have much to show for his efforts.

Represented in Vollbehr's collection were 635 printing presses from 96 towns, an amazing number indicative of the rapid spread of printing in the fifty years following Gutenberg's invention. Aside from classics such as the works of Homer, Cicero, Horace, and Livy, there were 49 works on astronomy; 51 works on natural sciences; more than 50 law books, including Justinian's *Institutes* and the Spanish law code, *Las siete partidas* (Seville: Ungut and Polona, 1491); 159 books on medicine; 34 books on geography and cosmography; and 22 works of orientalia. In addition to Johann Fust and Peter Schoeffer, who took over Gutenberg's printing shop in Mainz, there were printers from Strasbourg, Augsburg, Nuremberg, and Cologne, along with printing shops in Spain, France, Switzerland, and the Low Countries; Conrad Sweynheim and Arnold Pannartz, the proto-printers of Italy; and Aldus Manutius of Venice. While the preponderance of the works were in Greek and Latin, there were also titles in Hebrew, German, Italian, Spanish, French, English, Slavonic, and Chinese. Outstanding among works of Americana was a letter from Christopher Columbus announcing his discovery of what would become America, printed in Basel by Jacobus Wolff de Pforzheim on 15 February 1493; the work also

contained six woodcuts depicting the New World. In all there were twenty works on America out of a total of thirty-two known to have been printed before 1501.

Vollbehr made a unique contribution in giving insight into the popular reading habits of the fifteenth century. In comparison with the classical works in his collection, which are mostly in pristine condition, the books on agriculture, astronomy, chess, cookery, history, matrimony, military science, travel, magic, temperance, and war have been well used. As the bibliographer Alfred W. Pollard once remarked, a large proportion of surviving fifteenth-century books are in suspiciously clean condition.

On 5 July 1932 Vollbehr sold another collection of Americana at auction in Metuchen, New Jersey. Among the 125 items was the *Cosmographicus liber Petri Apiani mathematici studiose* (Landshut: D. J. Weyssenburger, 1524); Petrus Apianus designed one of the earliest maps bearing the name America. The book includes the statement (in Latin): "America, which is now called the fourth part of the world, took its name from Americus Vespuccio, who discovered it; and is called an island for the reason that it is surrounded by water." Also up for auction was *Tractado contra el mal serpentino* (Seville: Domenico de Robertis, 1539), a comprehensive discussion of syphilis and its cure written by Ruy Díaz de Isla, who was in charge of the Lisbon hospital for more than ten years and was considered an authority on the disease. The book includes the comment:

> It appeared and was observed in Spain in the year of our Lord 1493 in the city of Barcelona, which city was infected and consequently whole Europe and all parts of the Universe known and accessible. This disease had its origin on the island today called Espanola, as has been ascertained by a large and sure experience. And as this island had been found by the admiral Christopher Columbus, we have now a constant intercourse with its people.

The most important item on the block was a xylographic first independently printed map of the world, produced between 1475 and 1482 in southern Germany. Showing Jerusalem at the center of the world and depicting cannibals and dwarves, it is a typical specimen of fabulous medieval geography.

In 1936 Vollbehr sold another collection of 1,036 volumes; again most of the proceeds went to creditors. More than seven hundred volumes were bought by Israel Perlstein, a rare-book dealer in New York City, who submitted them to the Library of Congress for appraisal; the books were judged to be in poor condition and overpriced. Perlstein sold

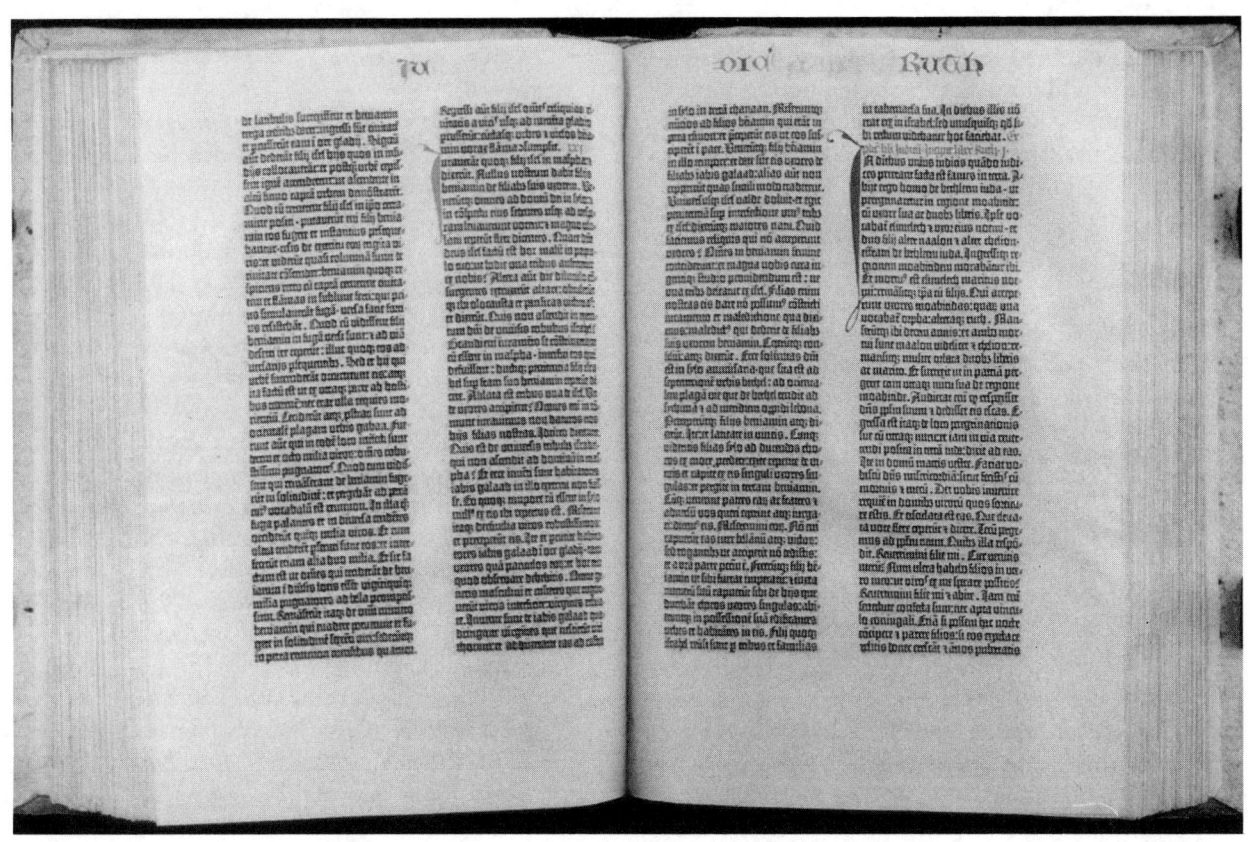

The Gutenberg Bible secured by the Library of Congress with Vollbehr's assistance. It is one of the three perfect vellum copies known (photograph by Michael Freeman and Jonathan Wallen).

them to Gimbel's department store in Manhattan, where they were finally disposed of at knockdown prices.

Vollbehr crossed the Atlantic ten times between 1932 and 1938. In Washington he resided at a luxury hotel near the White House and visited with members of Theodore Roosevelt's family. Although he was away from home for long periods, he stayed in touch with events in Germany. Believing that the American press did not understand the aspirations of the Third Reich, he tried to set the record straight in a series of eleven privately published pamphlets titled *Memorandum* (1931–1936) that he distributed to his American friends. He cited the harsh terms Germany had received under the Versailles Treaty and supported the National Socialist call for German territorial expansion. On 29 December 1934 he was summoned to appear before the House Un-American Activities Committee. He was subjected to hours of intensive questioning and had to defend himself against the charge that he was a paid propagandist of the German government. He was asked to clarify entries in his passport; he was also asked where he had obtained the mailing list for his pamphlets (some names had come from Representative Collins's office files); and he was pressed to explain his sending of copies of the Nazi journal *Der Stürmer* to Americans. Vollbehr admitted that he had failed to follow the advice of the German ambassador not to meddle in American politics and claimed that he intended to become an American citizen. In fact, however, he could never bring himself to renounce the fatherland.

An article in the *Saturday Review of Literature* (18 May 1940) attacked Vollbehr for gouging the American people when he sold his collection to the Library of Congress. The article embarrassed Librarian of Congress Archibald MacLeish and soured his friendship with William Rose Benét, who was an editor of the magazine.

Vollbehr returned to Germany before the outbreak of World War II. He lost his beloved books in the bombing of Berlin. After the war he worked briefly as a library consultant and made plans for another incunabula collection. After he died in Baden-Baden in 1945 or 1946, his widow had to apply for public assistance. The Vollbehrs had a daughter, Irene, who may have settled in Texas after the war.

Had Vollbehr not persisted in his efforts to sell his collection to the Library of Congress, the Gutenberg Bible would have been sold to another buyer, and his incunabula would have been dispersed. He wanted his finest treasures to be housed in the greatest library of the nation he considered a second home.

References:

Frederick W. Ashley, *"A Look Back": The Story of the Vollbehr Collection of Incunabula, Delivered before the Eleventh Annual Conference on Printing Education at a Session in the Coolidge Auditorium of the Library of Congress, Washington, D.C., Monday Evening, June 27, 1932,* second revised edition (Lexington, Va.: Journalism Laboratory, Washington and Lee University, 1934);

Bibliotheca Americana Vetustissima: The Collection of Dr. Otto H. F. Vollbehr, to Be Sold by His Order . . . April Twenty-fourth, sale no. 2262 (New York: Anderson Galleries, 1928);

A Catalogue, Dr. Otto Vollbehr Collection of Americana Vetustissima on Display in the Nash Typographic Library in Sansome Street, San Francisco, from the Eighteenth to the Twenty-ninth of November, 1935 (San Francisco: Printed by J. H. Nash, 1935);

Ross Alexander Collins, *The Vollbehr Collection of Incunabula: Speech of Hon. Ross A. Collins of Mississippi in the House of Representatives, February 7, 1930* (Washington, D.C.: U.S. Government Printing Office, 1930);

Edwin Emerson, *Incunabulum Incunabulorum: The Gutenberg Bible on Vellum in the Vollbehr Collection. An Authentic Story of the Choicest Book of Christendom Told Anew* (New York: Tudor Press, 1928);

One Hundred Incunabula, Duplicates from the Collection of Dr. Otto H. F. Vollbehr: To Be Sold by His Order Thursday Evening, February Ninth, at Eight-fifteen, sale no. 2230 (New York: Anderson Galleries, 1928);

Burton Rascoe, "Uncle Sam Has a Book," *Saturday Review of Literature,* 22 (18 May 1940): 3–4, 14–16;

Herbert Reichner, *Die Gutenberg-Bibel der Sammlung Vollbehr: Schicksale des kostbaren Buches* (Vienna: Jahoda & Siegel, 1927);

E. Paul Saunders, "Dr. Vollbehr Puts 'Incunabula' into American Public's Vocabulary," *The Nation's Capital Magazine* (May 1931): 13–14, 40–44;

Ernst Schulz, *Inkunabelsammlungen und ihr wissenschaftliche Wert: Bemerkungen zur Sammlung Vollbehr* (Munich, 1927);

U.S. Congress, House of Representatives, *Investigation of Nazi Propaganda Activities and Investigation of Certain Other Propaganda Activities: Public Hearings Before the Special Committee on Un-American Activities. 73rd Congress. 2nd Session Hearings No. 73–D.C.–6. Part II, held Nov. 30, 1934 in New York City, N.Y.* (Washington, D.C.: U.S. Government Printing Office, 1935), pp. 703–727;

U.S. Library of Congress, *Loan Exhibition of Incunabula from the Vollbehr Collection: Books Printed before 1501 A.D. and Manuscripts of the Fifteenth Century Selected from the Private Library of Dr. Otto H. F. Vollbehr, Berlin, Germany. Spring, 1928* (Washington, D.C.: U.S. Government Printing Office, 1928);

U.S. Library of Congress, *Loan Exhibition of a Selection of Printers' and Publishers' Marks from the Otto H. F. Vollbehr Collection (Berlin) Fifteenth to the Nineteenth Century: Spring, 1928* (Washington, D.C.: U.S. Government Printing Office, 1928);

George Parker Winship, *The Vollbehr Incunabula at the National Arts Club of New York from August 23 to September 30 MCMXXVI* (New York: Pynson Printers, 1926).

Papers:

The Library of Congress and the Henry E. Huntington Library have correspondence with Otto H. F. Vollbehr on file.

Stephen H. Wakeman
(1859 – 4 January 1924)

Timothy D. Pyatt
University of North Carolina at Chapel Hill

A defining moment in the collecting of nineteenth-century American authors came on 28–29 April 1924, when the personal collection of the late Stephen H. Wakeman was auctioned by the American Art Association. Wakeman had spent twenty years focusing his collecting efforts on nine previously neglected American authors: William Cullen Bryant, Ralph Waldo Emerson, Nathaniel Hawthorne, Oliver Wendell Holmes, Henry Wadsworth Longfellow, James Russell Lowell, Edgar Allan Poe, Henry David Thoreau, and John Greenleaf Whittier. While considered giants of literature and highly collectible today, these authors did not have the same prominence in the early twentieth century. The attention generated by the sale, combined with the record prices received for Poe and Hawthorne items, attracted bibliophiles to this newly charted genre. Wakeman's approach to collecting was also influential, as he sought books in their original bindings in an age when it was customary to have publishers' bindings removed and the works rebound.

Stephen Herrick Wakeman was born in 1859 in New York City to John and Caroline Wakeman. He was educated at the Friends Seminary and then entered into his father's wholesale produce firm, John Wakeman and Company, Beans and Peas. He married Alice L. James of Poughkeepsie on 7 April 1885; they had three children. Wakeman ran the store founded by his father until he retired in 1904.

Wakeman began collecting nineteenth-century American literature in 1900; prior to that time he had collected art, including Japanese works. His acumen and shrewdness as a collector of literature were soon recognized by dealers and fellow collectors, and he was elected to membership in the Grolier Club, America's preeminent book-collecting society, on 4 April 1905. Wakeman returned the compliment by donating to the club a portrait of Hawthorne painted in May 1850 by Cephas Giovanni Thompson. The painting, which Wakeman had acquired from Hawthorne's son, Julian, was hung in the Grolier Club lobby.

Stephen H. Wakeman

The greatest influence on Wakeman's book collecting was the American literature dealer Patrick K. Foley, whose book *American Authors: 1795–1895* (1897) he used as his collecting guide. He steered away from the tastes of the day; for example, instead of having his books rebound in morocco he kept them in their original publishers' boards. He collected works in their first and subsequent editions and in all possible variants, including translations and periodical appearances; he also collected pamphlets, leaflets, and broadsides. He particularly sought association copies, autographs, and manuscripts.

While Foley served as his primary dealer and guide, Wakeman also dealt frequently with Charles E. Goodspeed of Boston and George D. Smith and Luther S. Livingston of New York. He purchased several Hawthorne items from Julian Hawthorne, including the copy of *Twice-Told Tales* (Boston: American Stationers, 1837) that the author had inscribed to Sophia Peabody to celebrate their betrothal.

Wakeman also did business with the bookseller George S. Hellman, who approached him in 1909, after they had attended the sale of the library of the recently deceased bibliophile Jacob C. Chamberlain, and suggested that Wakeman's collection should be preserved for posterity at the Morgan Library rather than scattered in a public auction. Wakeman thought about the proposal for a few weeks, finally deciding that he would consider selling 263 manuscripts he had collected between 1900 and 1909 but that he wanted to keep his first editions and association copies. He insisted that the manuscripts be offered only to John Pierpont Morgan, saying that he "wouldn't accept fifty thousand dollars more for them from anyone else." Negotiations were difficult; at one point Wakeman withdrew the collection from consideration, but the sale was finally concluded for $165,000.

For this sum Morgan secured the manuscripts for Hawthorne's *The Blithedale Romance* (published in 1852) and *Dr. Grimshawe's Secret* (posthumously published in 1882) and the surviving portion of *The Scarlet Letter* (published in 1850)–Hawthorne had destroyed most of the manuscript; Hawthorne letters and diaries; Poe's "Tamerlane" (published in 1827) and his unfinished dramatic poem "Politian"; thirty-nine volumes of Thoreau's journals, still in the wooden box Thoreau had made for them; more than sixty manuscripts of Whittier's prose and poetry; and several Longfellow poems, including "The Children's Hour," a favorite of Morgan's. It may be the manuscript of "The Children's Hour" that convinced Morgan to purchase the collection from Wakeman.

Wakeman died at his brownstone house at 68 West Fifty-second Street on 4 January 1924. He was buried in Sharon, Connecticut, where he and his family spent their summers. On 19 March the American Art Association held a sale of important oil paintings by American and European artists; included were works that Wakeman had owned.

On 6 April 1924 a story in *The New York Times* carried the headline "Wakeman's Library on Sale April 28: Collection of 1,600 Volumes Devoted to First Editions of American Authors." The article noted that Wakeman's library was "said to be richer in rarities and association volumes than any other library in America."

The auction catalogue was prepared by Arthur Swann, director of the American Art Association's Department of Books and Prints. Swann's work, with its detailed descriptions and notes, has become a basic reference work for collectors of American literature. Apart from its valuable bibliographical details, it reproduces many of the notes that Wakeman laid into his books. For example, regarding lot 162, Emerson's *Letter from the Rev. R. W. Emerson to the Second Church and Society* (Boston, 1832), Wakeman wrote, "This little book is so scarce that few collectors have even heard of it, and I know of but two other copies. It is the first Emerson publication." The work, accompanied by an autograph letter signed by Emerson, brought $410. Another Emerson item was lot 206, one of two known copies of a broadside of a congratulatory letter from Emerson to Walt Whitman on the publication of Whitman's *Leaves of Grass* in 1855. Wakeman wrote of it, "This is the rarest of all the Emerson items. Only two examples are known–the other Mr. Foley informs me is in a Whitman collection. Whitman had the letter printed for his private use." It sold for $230. The notes often reveal how Wakeman acquired an item: lot 391, an autograph manuscript dated 23 February 1893 that was probably one of Holmes's last poems, included a letter from Goodspeed to Wakeman noting the purchase date, 27 April 1917.

The auction was conducted by Otto Bernet and Hiram H. Parke in four sessions spanning two days. The first session, with 320 lots, started at 2:30 on Monday afternoon, 28 April. Lots 1 through 155, comprising about 175 volumes, consisted of works by Bryant. Lots 156 through 260, comprising about 150 volumes, consisted of Emerson materials. Among the treasures here was a presentation copy of Emerson's *Representative Men, Seven Lectures* (Boston: Phillips, Sampson, 1850) bearing the inscription "Henry D. Thoreau from R. W. Emerson, 30th December, 1849." It was purchased by William T. H. Howe of Cincinnati for $470. Lot 196, Emerson's *Nature; Addresses and Lectures* (Boston and Cambridge, Mass.: J. Munroe, 1849), was a presentation copy to Hawthorne; it sold for $570. Lots 261 through 439 were works by Hawthorne; some of these were sold in the evening session of 28 April, which began at 8:15 and included lots 321 through 637. Following the Hawthorne items came about 225 volumes by Holmes in lots 440 through 621. Lot 503 was the extremely rare privately printed copy of Holmes's *Lecture* (Boston, 1863), with a letter by Holmes stating that he had printed only six copies; in 1924 Wakeman's was the only copy known to exist. It brought $570. The majority of the Longfellow lots, 620 through 800, were sold on the afternoon of Tuesday, 29 April. Lot 654, Longfellow's *Poems on Slavery* (Cambridge, Mass.: J. Owen,

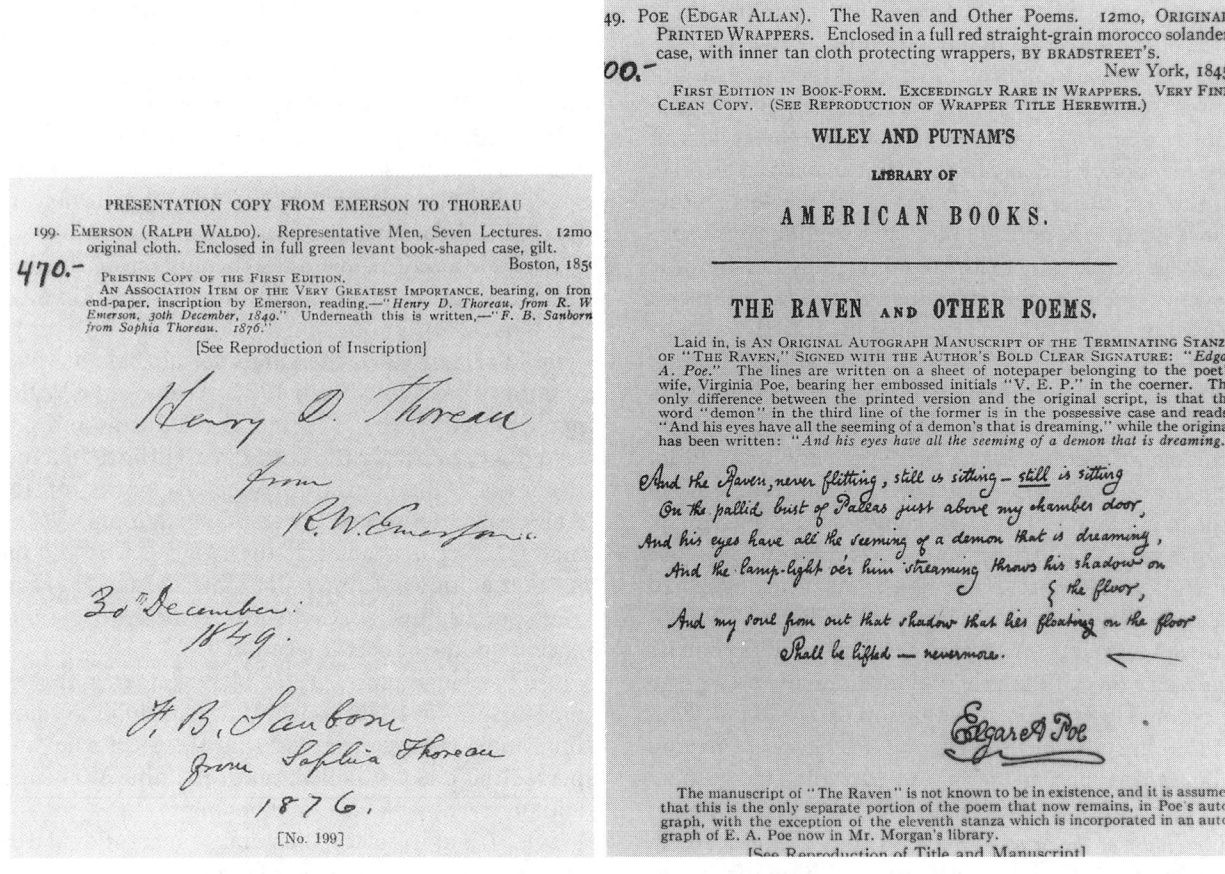

Priced entries in the catalogue for the sale of Wakeman's collection at the American Art Association, New York, 28–29 April 1924.
William T. H. Howe bought Emerson's Representative Men, and Dr. A. S. W. Rosenbach purchased Poe's The Raven
and Other Poems.

1842), uncut and in original wrappers, bore the inscription "N. Hawthorne from the Author"; it sold for $330. The afternoon session also disposed of Lowell's works (lots 801 through 930, comprising about 175 volumes) and much of the Poe material (lots 931 through 971). Lot 809, which brought $4,300, included the complete short run of Lowell's *The Pioneer: A Literary and Critical Magazine* (Boston: James Stringer, 1843), uncut and in original wrappers. Included with the three issues was an original Lowell letter and an autograph Poe manuscript. For $800 the Chicago bookseller Walter M. Hill secured a presentation copy of Lowell's extremely rare *Commemoration Ode* (Cambridge, Mass., 1865), delivered at Harvard to honor the school's graduates who had died in the Civil War.

The final session of the sale began on Tuesday evening at 8:15. The remaining Poe items were dispersed, along with the works of Thoreau (lots 972 through 1,075, comprising about 100 volumes) and Whittier (lots 1,076 through 1,279, consisting of

more than 250 volumes). The final lot was *Catalogues of Collections of Works by American Authors* (New York and Jamaica, 1901–1909). The 1,280 lots of the sale brought a total of $67,586.

A presentation copy of the first edition of Poe's *The Raven and Other Poems* (New York: Wiley and Putnam, 1845) was purchased by Hill for $4,200 on Howe's behalf. Hill also paid $1,000 for Poe's prospectus for "The Stylus," with an autograph note. The Philadelphia bookseller A. S. W. Rosenbach spent $10,900 on Poe items, paying $3,400 for Poe's copy of *Tales of the Grotesque and Arabesque* (Philadelphia: Lea and Blanchard, 1840), with the author's manuscript revisions. For $2,900 he secured a first edition of *The Raven and Other Poems* with an autograph manuscript of the last verse of "The Raven" laid in. He paid $2,600 for another presentation copy of the same work and $2,000 for Poe's copy of *Eureka: A Prose Poem* (New York: Putnam, 1848) with manuscript annotations. Rosenbach's fellow Philadelphia dealer George Grasberger paid $2,900 for a presentation copy of the first edition of Poe's *Al Aaraaf, Tamerlane and Minor Poems* (Baltimore: Hatch and Dunning, 1829).

Howe, acting through Hill, was the single largest purchaser at the Wakeman sale. At one point his bidding prompted Grasberger to call out, "What do you use for money in Cincinnati?" The managing director of the American Book Company, Howe was among those astute enough to take American literature seriously as a collecting field. He successfully bid on some seventy-five lots, concentrating most of his efforts on Hawthorne. Most notable among his Hawthorne purchases was *Fanshawe* (Boston: Marsh and Capen, 1828), Hawthorne's first book, for $1,025; item 264 in the sale catalogue, it had cost Wakeman $450. The catalogue describes it as "one of the very finest (if not the finest) copies in existence." At the Jerome Kern sale in January 1929 a lesser copy would bring $4,750. Howe paid $1,000 for the betrothal copy of *Twice-Told Tales* that had cost Wakeman $450. Wakeman had paid $150 for Hawthorne's pocket diary for 1859; Howe secured it for $425. The diary contains entries for every day of the year and includes an entry documenting Hawthorne's completion of *The Marble Faun* (1860) in Italy. For the copy of *The Scarlet Letter* that Hawthorne had presented to his wife, Howe paid $400; it had cost Wakeman $100. For a first edition of *The House of the Seven Gables* (Boston: Ticknor, Reed, and Fields, 1851), similarly inscribed from the author to his wife, Howe paid $240; this work, too, had cost Wakeman $100. Other Howe purchases included Hawthorne's presentation copies of the first editions of *The Blithedale Romance* (Boston: Ticknor, Reed, and Fields, 1852) and *Our Old Home* (Boston: Ticknor and Fields, 1863) to William Ellery Channing for $120 and $210, respectively; Una Hawthorne's copy of her father's campaign biography of Franklin Pierce (Boston: Ticknor, Reed and Fields, 1852) for $80; and thirteen books from Hawthorne's library.

Howe also purchased twenty-one Bryant items, nine Emerson titles, eleven lots from the Holmes portion of the sale, two lots by Longfellow, and six by Lowell. He acquired the copies of the first edition of *A Week on the Concord and Merrimac Rivers* (Boston: Munroe / New York: Putnam, 1849) that Thoreau had presented to Bryant, Channing, and Hawthorne, paying $250, $160, and $625, respectively, and the manuscript for the first chapter of the work for $590.

The auction included items other than books and manuscripts: a stencil used by Hawthorne at the Salem Custom House (lot 296) was sold to Goodspeed for $20. Lot 1,075 was Thoreau's bookcase; Wakeman had acquired it from Goodspeed, who had purchased it from Adams Tolman. Tolman's father had been curator of the Concord Historical Society and was a noted collector of Thoreau association pieces. The five-shelf bookcase, forty-three inches high and stained with a mahogany finish, sold for $37.50. On 8–9 May 1924 portions of the Wakeman library not related to his favorite nine American authors were sold at the American Art Association, along with books from the library of George B. Woodward.

Four auctions brought the collecting of nineteenth-century American authors to prominence: the Charles B. Foote sale of 1895, the William H. Arnold sale of 1901, the Chamberlain sale of 1909, and the Wakeman sale of 1924. Arnold, like Wakeman, prized copies in original condition and collected works by eight of the same authors (excluding Poe). Chamberlain collected works of ten Americans, the same nine as Wakeman plus Washington Irving. At each sale the value of first and important editions of Emerson, Hawthorne, Thoreau, and Longfellow rose, firmly establishing those authors in the collector's canon.

The biographical sketch of Wakeman in the volume *Grolier 75* (1959), celebrating the club's seventy-fifth anniversary, observed that the 1924 sale "dispersed the greatest collection of the nine Wakeman authors ever assembled; and, owing to the inexorable gravitation of irreplaceable items to institutional treasure rooms in the years that followed, no comparable collection . . . could ever be formed again." Stephen H. Wakeman left an important legacy, both in what and how he collected. His books now enrich private collections and public institutions—most notably New York's Pierpont Morgan Library, which secured so many of his manuscripts.

References:

Barton Currie, *Fishers of Books* (Boston: Little, Brown, 1931), pp. 273–315;

George S. Hellman, *Lanes of Memory* (New York: Knopf, 1927);

John S. Van E. Kohn, "Stephen Herrick Wakeman," in *Grolier 75: A Biographical Retrospective to Celebrate the Seventy-fifth Anniversary of the Grolier Club in New York,* edited by R. W. G. Vail (New York: Grolier Club, 1959), pp. 95–99;

Arthur Swann, *The Stephen H. Wakeman Collection of Books of Nineteenth Century American Writers, the Property of Mrs. Alice L. Wakeman; First Editions, Inscribed Presentation and Personal Copies, Original Manuscripts and Letters of Nine American Authors: Bryant, Emerson, Hawthorne, Holmes, Longfellow, Lowell, Poe, Thoreau, Whittier* (New York: American Art Association, 1924).

Stephen B. Weeks

(2 February 1865 – 3 May 1918)

Robert G. Anthony Jr.

University of North Carolina at Chapel Hill

BOOKS: *The Press of North Carolina in the Eighteenth Century. With Biographical Sketches of Printers, an Account of the Manufacture of Paper, and a Bibliography of the Issues* (Brooklyn: Historical Printing Club, 1891);

The Religious Development in the Province of North Carolina (Baltimore: Johns Hopkins University Press, 1892);

Church and State in North Carolina (Baltimore: Johns Hopkins University Press, 1893);

A Bibliography of the Historical Literature of North Carolina (Cambridge, Mass.: Library of Harvard University, 1895);

"The University of North Carolina in the Civil War." An Address Delivered at the Centennial Celebration of the Opening of the Institution, June 5th, 1895 (Richmond: W. E. Jones, 1896);

Southern Quakers and Slavery: A Study in Institutional History (Baltimore: Johns Hopkins University Press, 1896);

The Weeks Collection of Caroliniana (Raleigh: E. M. Uzzell, 1907);

History of Public School Education in Arkansas (Washington, D.C.: Government Printing Office, 1912);

History of Public School Education in Alabama (Washington, D.C.: Government Printing Office, 1915);

History of Public School Education in Delaware (Washington, D.C.: Government Printing Office, 1917);

History of Public School Education in Arizona (Washington, D.C.: Government Printing Office, 1918).

OTHER: *Register of Members of the Philanthropic Society, Instituted in the University of North Carolina, August 1st, 1795,* third edition, revised, edited by Weeks (Raleigh: Edwards, Broughton, 1886);

"The Lost Colony of Roanoke; Its Fate and Survival," *Papers of the American Historical Association,* 5 (1891): 439–480;

"General Joseph Martin and the War of the Revolution in the West," in *Annual Report of the Ameri-*

can Historical Association for the Year 1893 (Washington, D.C., 1894), pp. 401–477;

"Libraries and Literature in North Carolina in the Eighteenth Century. A Complement and Supplement to 'The Press of North Carolina in the Eighteenth Century,'" in *Annual Report of the American Historical Association for the Year 1895* (Washington, D.C., 1896), pp. 169–267;

"The Beginnings of the Common School System in the South; or Calvin Henderson Wiley and the Organization of the Common Schools of North Carolina," in U.S. Bureau of Education, *Report of the Commissioner of Education for*

1896–97 (Washington, D.C.: Government Printing Office, 1898), pp. 1379–1474;

"Confederate Text-Books, A Preliminary Bibliography," in U.S. Bureau of Education, *Report of the Commissioner of Education for 1898–99* (Washington, D.C.: Government Printing Office, 1900), pp. 1139–1155;

Biographical History of North Carolina, from Colonial Times to the Present, 8 volumes; volumes 1–6 edited by Samuel A'Court Ashe, volume 7 edited by Weeks and Ashe, volume 8 edited by Weeks, Ashe, and Charles L. Van Noppen (Greensboro, N.C.: Van Noppen, 1905–1917)–includes 21 biographical sketches by Weeks;

Index to the Colonial and State Records of North Carolina, Covering Volumes I–XXV, 4 volumes, compiled and edited by Weeks (Goldsboro, N.C.: Nash Brothers, 1909–1914)–volume 4 includes "Historical Review of The Colonial and State Records of North Carolina," by Weeks.

SELECTED PERIODICAL PUBLICATIONS–UNCOLLECTED: "First Libraries in North Carolina," *Trinity Archive,* 5 (October 1891): 10–20;

"A Bibliography of North Carolina's Historical Literature," *Southern Educator,* 2 (February 1892): 1–4; (March 1892): 5–8; (April 1892): 9–12; (July 1892): 13–16; (August 1892): 17–20;

"The Renaissance: A Plea for the Trinity College Library," *Trinity Archive,* 5 (February 1892): 181–185;

"The History of Negro Suffrage in the South," *Political Science Quarterly,* 9 (December 1894): 671–703;

"On the Promotion of Historical Studies in the South," *Publications of the Southern History Association,* 1 (January 1897): 13–34;

"Anti-Slavery Sentiment in the South; with Unpublished Letters from John Stuart Mill and Mrs. Stowe," *Publications of the Southern History Association,* 2 (April 1898): 87–130;

"Literary Estimate and Bibliography of Richard Malcolm Johnston," by Weeks and Edmund C. Stedman, bibliography by Weeks, *Publications of the Southern History Association,* 2 (October 1898): 315–327;

"The Spaniards in the South and Southwest," *Publications of the Southern History Association,* 6 (May 1902): 241–252;

"Expansion of the Old Southwest," *Publications of the Southern History Association,* 7 (September 1903): 369–377;

Prospectus of Weeks's proposed *Bibliography of North Carolina, Publications of the Southern History Association,* 9 (July 1905): 252–254;

"The Pre-Revolutionary Printers of North Carolina: Davis, Steuart, and Boyd," *North Carolina Booklet,* 15 (October 1915): 104–121.

When asked to recount the history of his remarkable North Caroliniana collection, Stephen Beauregard Weeks likened his bibliophily to a childhood game. When smooth wood ends had fallen from the local wheelwright's workbench, Weeks recalled, he had rushed to seize them, prizing these scraps as though they were gems. For more than three decades the adult Weeks experienced similar delight in gathering publications related to his native state. By the time of his death at the age of fifty-three he had built a collection of nearly ten thousand items, a remarkable accomplishment for a man who was never wealthy. Well trained in modern historical methodology, he published extensively on southern history and bibliography, particularly of North Carolina. Often his research was seminal, such as his work on southern Quakers and on intellectual life in early North Carolina.

Weeks was born on 2 February 1865 in Pasquotank County, North Carolina, to James Elliott Weeks and Mary Louisa Mullen Weeks. The families of both parents had been long established in North Carolina, his father's English ancestors as early as 1727 and his mother's Huguenot family sometime prior to 1732. His father died when Stephen was eighteen months old. After his mother's death two years later he was reared by his paternal aunt, Mary, and her husband, Robertson Jackson.

Weeks attended local schools until the age of fifteen, when he entered Horner School at Henderson, one of the best preparatory schools in the state. In 1882 he enrolled at the University of North Carolina at Chapel Hill, where he excelled. In 1884 he won the medal for scholarship in Greek. Two years later, in 1886, he received an A.B. degree and graduated with second-highest honors.

It was during these years at Chapel Hill that Weeks became devoted to the world of books and scholarship. He began writing for publication, beginning in April 1886 with the first installment of his "Biographical Sketches of the Confederate Dead of the University of North Carolina" series in the *University of North Carolina Magazine.* The sketches would continue for eighteen more issues. He also revised the *Register of Members of the Philanthropic Society, Instituted in the University of North Carolina, August 1st, 1795* (1886).

Weeks remained at the university for two years of postgraduate studies, receiving the master of arts degree in English in 1887. The following year he was awarded the doctor of philosophy degree, the first given by the Department of English and only the fourth by the university. His dissertation was titled "The Maid of France: Schiller versus Shakespeare." Shortly after completing his studies, on 12 June 1888 Weeks married Mary Lee Martin of Chapel Hill, the daughter of the Reverend Joseph Bonaparte Martin, a Methodist minister, and the granddaughter of Gen. Joseph Martin, a prominent French and Indian War soldier and Indian agent. Weeks would subsequently publish several articles about the general. The marriage did not last long, however. Mary Martin Weeks died on 19 May 1891, leaving her husband with their two children, only one of whom, Robertson Jackson Weeks, lived to adulthood.

In the fall of 1888 Weeks began three years of additional study on a scholarship at Johns Hopkins University in Baltimore. Although also taking courses in English language, political science, and political economy, Weeks quickly realized that his true interest was history. He became fascinated by the teachings of Herbert Baxter Adams, who had imported German seminar methods to Johns Hopkins and who argued for the writing of "objective" and "scientific" history. In 1891 Weeks completed another dissertation, "The Religious Development in the Province of North Carolina," and was awarded his second doctor of philosophy degree, this one in history. The following year the Johns Hopkins Press published that dissertation.

During his years of graduate study in Chapel Hill and Baltimore, Weeks had engaged in wide-ranging research on southern history and especially on North Carolina. Eager to share his findings, he successfully submitted articles to a variety of scholarly journals, newspapers, and university periodicals. His interests were quite diverse, including religion, politics, dueling, the pirate Blackbeard, the governors of the Roanoke Island colony, drama, early libraries, newspapers, presidential electors, and the North Carolina Historical Society.

In 1891, when Trinity College, a small Methodist institution in Randolph County in the Carolina Piedmont, offered him a position teaching history and political science, he eagerly accepted. By the time of his arrival, however, the college had decided to organize a separate history department, and Weeks was selected to serve as its chair. This appointment made Weeks the first professor in a southern college who taught only history.

Arriving at Trinity in September, the young professor immediately directed his energies to improving the meager library. In February 1892 the *Trinity Archive,* the student magazine, presented "with great pleasure" an appeal by Weeks titled

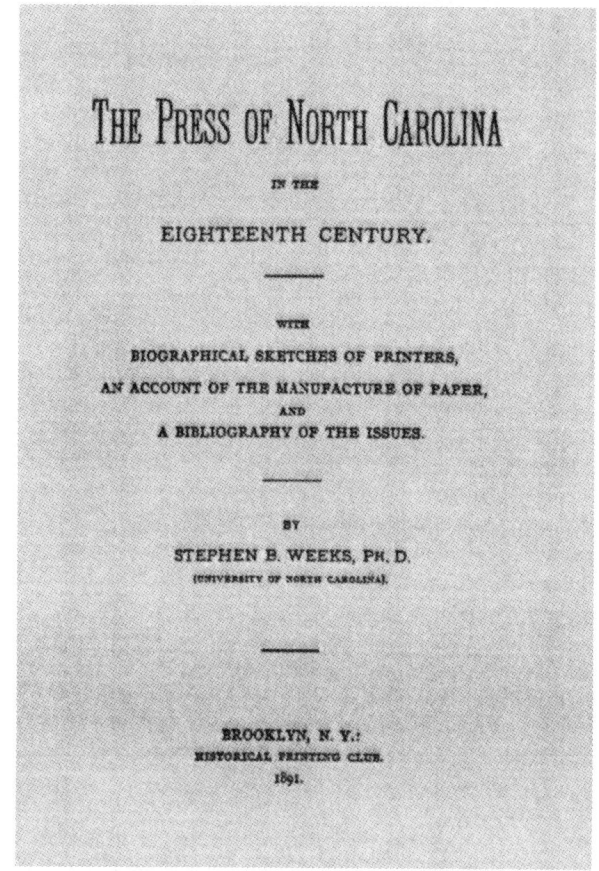

Title page for Weeks's history of printing in his native state

"The Renaissance: A Plea for the Trinity College Library." Weeks's essay had earlier been published by prominent Methodist papers across the state. In it he urged support for improving the library:

> We are very much in need of books of all kinds. We need especially books on history, and most of all do we need the materials for history. . . . to all such friends we appeal to-day and beg their patriotic assistance in getting together here the sources of history for the use of students who desire to do original work in that field. . . . We wish to devote ourselves to original work in the field of Southern history.

Weeks called for "missionaries" to solicit books, pamphlets, manuscripts, maps, pictures and portraits, catalogues, newspapers, and city and town official reports. He urged every Methodist—indeed, every citizen of the state—to view this as an opportunity to join in "building, developing, and strengthening North Carolina and the South." Weeks had displayed the zeal of the bibliophile prior to his arrival at Trinity. His personal collection of North Caroliniana, already at three hundred titles, was impressive and probably the largest in existence. But, with

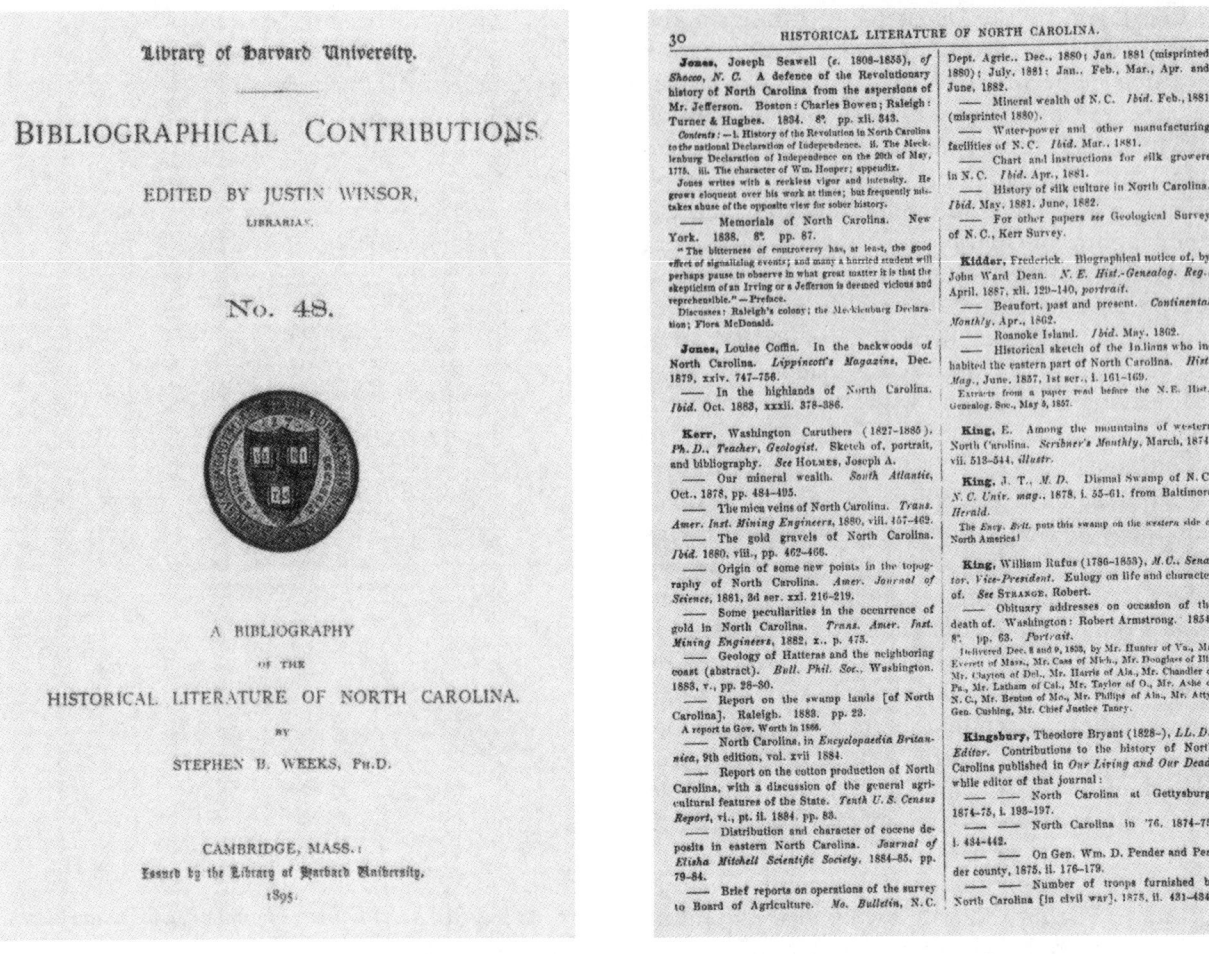

Title page and page from a preliminary version of Weeks's efforts to record every work printed in North Carolina

his Trinity appeal, he embarked on a life of proselytizing and sharing his passion with the world.

On 4 April 1892 Weeks organized the Trinity College Historical Society with an initial membership of fifty students. The first purpose enumerated in the constitution of the society was "to collect, arrange and preserve a library of books, pamphlets, maps, charts, manuscripts, papers, paintings, statuary and other materials illustrative of the history of North Carolina and the South." Additional goals were the encouragement of historical research in primary sources and the promotion of lectures and publications on southern history. Students were encouraged to take a prominent part in the activities of the society, which Weeks saw as a supplement to their class work. In his view upperclassmen should begin conducting in-depth research in original local history sources and should develop theses based on their findings.

Although the ambitious young professor envisioned the society members publishing outstanding papers on southern history, he did not remain at

Trinity long enough to see that accomplished. During his second year with the college it relocated to Durham, where with more-promising prospects for growth and development it eventually evolved into Duke University. A bitter dispute between the president and several faculty members, however, divided the campus. Weeks was among those who distrusted the president. He was further frustrated by the delinquence of the college in paying his salary. In May 1893 he joined several other faculty members in resigning.

Weeks returned to the Trinity community in Randolph County and there married Sallie Mangum Leach on 28 June 1893. As he had done in his previous marriage, Weeks conducted research on and published several articles about his wife's family. Financial pressures on the couple were somewhat relieved when Trinity College finally paid Weeks part of his overdue salary. For the rest of the summer he traveled, studied, and, whenever possible, added to his collection of North Caroliniana. In the fall he accepted a fellowship offered by Johns

Hopkins University and returned to Baltimore for further studies in history.

At the conclusion of the 1893–1894 academic year Weeks accepted a position as specialist in educational history with the United States Bureau of Education in Washington, D.C., where he could continue his research and publishing. He served as associate editor of the annual reports of the commissioner and frequently as editor for other Bureau publications. Included among his works appearing in Bureau publications were "The Beginnings of the Common School System in the South" (1898), and "Confederate Text-Books, A Preliminary Bibliography" (1900).

Weeks's reputation as a scholar grew. In addition to sharing the results of his research through articles in academic and popular periodicals, he accepted frequent invitations to speak on various southern and North Carolina history topics. On 5 June 1895 he delivered an address, "The University of North Carolina during the Civil War," at the centennial celebration of the opening of the college. In 1895 the Library of Harvard University published his *Bibliography of the Historical Literature of North Carolina* as number 48 in its Bibliographical Contributions series. Although the bibliography was well received, Weeks asserted in the preface that it was "nothing more than a preliminary catalogue to serve as a basis for future work." He would continue to gather citations for a more extensive bibliography for the remainder of his life.

Weeks thought existing southern historical organizations focused too much—some even exclusively—on the Civil War. He joined with almost one hundred other historians, civic leaders, college professors, and others in issuing a call for a meeting at Columbian University (now George Washington University) on 24 April 1896 to form a new organization. The resulting Southern History Association was established to encourage original research and scholarly discussions, publish significant work, and promote the collection of historical materials. Weeks called the meeting to order and presided until a permanent chair was elected. He was also named to the five-member publications committee of the association. From 1897 to 1907 he contributed articles as well as his strong editing skills to the quarterly, later bimonthly, *Publications of the Southern History Association*. Among his articles were "On the Promotion of Historical Studies in the South" (January 1897), "Anti-Slavery Sentiment in the South; with Unpublished Letters from John Stuart Mill and Mrs. Stowe" (April 1898), "Literary Estimate and Bibliography of Richard Malcolm Johnston" (October 1898, with Edmund C. Stedman),

THE WEEKS COLLECTION

OF

CAROLINIANA

BY

STEPHEN B. WEEKS

RALEIGH
E. M. Uzzell & Co., Printers and Binders
1907

Title page for Weeks's account of his book-collecting activities, written for the North Carolina Historical Commission

"The Spaniards in the South and Southwest" (May 1902), and "Expansion of the Old Southwest" (September 1903).

Weeks's interest in the history of the American Southwest reflected a dramatic change in his own life. Health problems forced him to seek employment in a climate different from that of Washington, and he successfully requested a transfer to the Indian School Service of the U.S. Department of the Interior. From the fall of 1899 until 1903 he served as principal teacher and, briefly, as assistant superintendent at a Santa Fe, New Mexico, school for Indians. In July 1903 he received appointment as superintendent of a school on the Apache Indian reservation at San Carlos, Arizona, a position he held until 1907.

Although Weeks conducted some research and published several articles on the Southwest, North Carolina remained his passion. He continued to submit articles on history to the *Publications of the Southern History Association* and other publishers. He begged friends, authors, and book dealers back in the East to send him copies of new North

Caroliniana. From San Carlos he published a four-page list (also included in *Publications of the Southern History Association,* September 1905) of books, journals, almanacs, government documents, and other publications he wished to add to his ever-growing collection. In 1895 Weeks owned copies of 863 of the 1,491 titles included in his *Bibliography of the Historical Literature of North Carolina.* By 1900 he owned roughly 1,200. He also had a substantial collection of nonhistorical titles.

One of Weeks's goals was to expand his historical bibliography to include nonhistorical titles. In a prospectus printed in the July 1905 *Publications of the Southern History Association* Weeks declared:

> It will include every known book, pamphlet or magazine article of importance dealing with the State or any part of the same, or with the career of North Carolinians; all literary work of North Carolinians regardless of its character and a list of the monthly and other periodical magazines published in the State.

Although Weeks continued to make progress with his collecting, bibliographies, and historical research, his work for the Indian School Service was less satisfying. On 1 March 1905 Weeks wrote to his friend George S. Wills:

> I realize and know that I am not an administrator. I am not an educator. I am not a teacher. I am a scholar and investigator and that is all. When you have said that you have touched the core of my career.

The refusal of Weeks's wife to live in the Southwest, even in nearby Santa Fe when he was in New Mexico, added to his despondency.

While in the Southwest, Weeks contributed essays on historically significant North Carolinians to the *Biographical History of North Carolina, from Colonial Times to the Present,* a series published by Charles L. Van Noppen in Greensboro, North Carolina. Van Noppen was impressed with Weeks's work in the first six volumes and in 1907 offered him a position as coeditor with Samuel A. Ashe for future volumes. Weeks eagerly and gratefully accepted. He moved to Greensboro, and his wife and children settled in nearby Trinity, her home before marriage.

Finally back in his beloved North Carolina among supportive friends and family, Weeks pushed on with what is arguably his most important publication, a combined index to the ten-volume *Colonial Records of North Carolina* (1886–1890) and the sixteen-volume *State Records of North Carolina*

(1895–1907). Weeks had been commissioned in 1895 to prepare the index and over the years had diligently compiled entries upon receipt of each new volume. In a 3 July 1898 letter to Walter Clark, Weeks reported that he had finished indexing the first thirteen volumes and was well into the fourteenth. He guessed that it would take two to three months simply to alphabetize the cards he had made. Historian H. G. Jones has estimated that Weeks prepared three hundred thousand index cards for the first fifteen volumes alone. The first index volume was not published until 1909; the fourth and final appeared in 1914. Weeks also prepared a separate 239-page index to the Census of 1790 for North Carolina, which made up volume twenty-five in the combined series.

In 1909 Weeks accepted a position as principal teacher in a public school at Trinity in Randolph County and was at last able to reestablish a single household with his wife and children. Two years later, in 1911, the Weeks family moved back to Washington, D.C., where Weeks rejoined the Bureau of Education as historian. He continued to write on North Carolina history and also published significant works on other topics. For example, he produced histories of education in Arkansas (1912), Alabama (1915), Delaware (1917), and Arizona (1918).

Throughout his adult life, whether in the Tar Heel State, the Southwest, or Washington, Weeks sought to add to his personal collection of North Caroliniana. In *The Weeks Collection of Caroliniana* (1907), an account of his bibliophily prepared for the North Carolina Historical Commission, Weeks describes the depth of his passion:

> My purpose in making this Collection has been manyfold. I wished to make first of all a working Collection of Caroliniana for my own use in my North Carolina studies in general and for use in compiling my Bibliography of North Carolina. . . . But do not think it has come for the asking. I have had to pay a price: much study, continued alertness, and great reading. During the last years, 1903, 1904, and 1905, I have read by actual count 71,289 pages of book catalogues, mostly of old or second-hand books; or an average of 23,763 pages per year; and this is not above the average for the last fifteen years.

As early as 1887 Weeks had planned to compile a bibliography of North Caroliniana. In 1895 he had seen his *Bibliography of the Historical Literature of North Carolina* published, and over the years he had also compiled several smaller, specialized bibliographies. But the comprehensive work, the bibliography that included every North Carolina book, pamphlet, and journal article on all subjects, remained to be done. In 1913 the North Carolina Historical Commission offered Weeks the opportunity to fill that void.

On 18 December of that year the Commission agreed to publish Weeks's ambitious bibliography provided that he include in it not only the titles in his own library but also any unique titles found in the State Library at Raleigh and in several important college and private libraries. In a 20 December 1913 letter Commission Secretary R. D. W. Connor offered Weeks $250 for examining these additional libraries, plus actual expenses. On 26 December, Weeks replied, happily accepting the terms and proposing that he also be authorized to examine the holdings of the Harvard University Library, New York Historical Society, New York Public Library, and other out-of-state collections. He reported that his own collection now numbered seventy-eight hundred titles; he expected it soon to reach ten thousand.

Even while working full-time for the Bureau of Education and continuing to publish historical articles, Weeks searched for elusive titles and prepared citations for his bibliography. Once again, however, he developed significant health problems. In late 1917 he suffered a mild stroke. Over the next several months his health declined further, and on 3 May 1918 he died.

Weeks's death did not mean the end of the collection he had so lovingly developed for more than three decades. In early 1918, aware of his declining health, Weeks decided to sell his collection. He appointed Van Noppen as his agent and encouraged him to approach the University of North Carolina at Chapel Hill about purchasing the Weeks Caroliniana. He remembered that in 1911–1912 Louis Round Wilson, university librarian, had expressed an interest in the collection if Weeks should ever wish to sell it. Wilson recognized that the Weeks Collection would add important materials to the collection of North Caroliniana already at the university.

Van Noppen, an alumnus of the university, quickly conveyed Weeks's offer and price, $25,000, to campus officials. He also waived his $1,000 commission. The university requested, and in March 1918 was granted, a six-month option so as to have time to get trustee approval for the purchase and to secure the necessary funds. After Weeks's death in May his family continued the discussions with the university. Wilson realized that several titles in the Weeks Collection duplicated those already held by the university. He suggested a price of $15,000. Eventually the parties compromised at $20,000, and

Bookplate for the items in Weeks's collection, which the university purchased after his death in 1918

more than nine thousand items were added to the North Carolina Collection of the university.

The Weeks Collection complemented well the holdings of the university, comprising many rare items and important depth in periodicals. Weeks had carefully built his collection for most of his life, intending it to be the foundation for his long-planned comprehensive bibliography. Just a few months after his death, however, his other dream—the development of a permanent, comprehensive North Caroliniana collection—was accomplished at his alma mater. The North Carolina Collection at Chapel Hill, enriched by the Weeks addition, serves as an ever-growing monument to him.

Bibliography:

William S. Powell, *Stephen Beauregard Weeks, 1865–1918: A Preliminary Bibliography* (Chapel Hill: North Carolina Collection, University of North Carolina, 1965).

References:

H. G. Jones, "Stephen Beauregard Weeks: North Carolina's First 'Professional' Historian," *North Carolina Historical Review,* 42 (Autumn 1965): 410–423;

Thomas Merritt Pittman, "Stephen Beauregard Weeks," in *Biographical History of North Carolina,* volume 5, edited by Samuel A'Court Ashe (Greensboro, N.C.: Van Noppen, 1906), pp. 432–441;

Nannie M. Tilley, *The Trinity College Historical Society, 1892–1941* (Durham, N.C.: Duke University Press, 1941);

Louis Round Wilson, "The Acquisition of the Stephen B. Weeks Collection of Caroliniana," *North Carolina Historical Review,* 42 (Autumn 1965): 424–429.

Papers:

The Southern Historical Collection at the University of North Carolina at Chapel Hill Library has a collection of Weeks papers. Materials gathered by Weeks in preparation for his comprehensive North Caroliniana bibliography (facsimiles of title pages, clippings from booksellers' catalogues, printed bibliographies, and file drawers of index slips) are in the North Carolina Collection at Chapel Hill. Small collections of correspondence, publication drafts, and other materials related to Weeks are also located at Duke University in Durham, N.C.; Johns Hopkins University in Baltimore; and the North Carolina State Archives at Raleigh.

Donald Goddard Wing

(20 August 1904 – 8 October 1972)

William Baker
Northern Illinois University

BOOKS: *Short-Title Catalogue of Books Printed in England, Scotland, Ireland, Wales and British America And of English Books Printed in Other Countries 1641–1700,* 3 volumes (New York: Columbia University for The Index Society 1945–1951); second edition, revised and enlarged, volume 1: A1–E2926 (New York: Modern Language Association, 1972); volume 2: E2927–O1000, revised and edited by Timothy J. Crist with the assistance of Janice M. Hansel, Phebe A. Kirkham, Jeri S. Smith, and others (New York: Modern Language Association, 1982); volume 3: P1–Z28, revised and edited by John J. Morrison, Carolyn W. Nelson, Matthew Seccombe, Mark E. English, and Harold E. Selesky (New York: Modern Language Association, 1988); second edition, newly revised and enlarged, volume 1: A1–E2926L, revised and edited by Morrison, Nelson, and Seccombe (New York: Modern Language Association, 1994);

A Gallery of Ghosts: Books Published Between 1641–1700 Not Found in the Short-Title Catalogue (New York: Index Committee of the Modern Language Association, 1967).

SELECTED PERIODICAL PUBLICATIONS–UNCOLLECTED: "The Making of the *Short-Title Catalogue, 1641–1700,*" *Papers of the Bibliographical Society of America,* 45 (1951): 59–69, republished in *The Bibliographical Society of America 1904–79: A Retrospective Collection* (Charlottesville: Published for the Bibliographical Society of America by the University Press of Virginia, 1980), pp. 241–251;

"Wing on Wing," *Yale Library Gazette,* 44 (July 1969): 3–7.

In the span of forty-two years Donald Goddard Wing successfully engaged in two pursuits. From 1928 until retirement in 1970 he was a librarian at Yale University. From 1932 until his death in

Donald Goddard Wing

1971 he was engaged in creating, compiling, and revising the great work of enumerative bibliography by which he will be remembered, the *Short-Title Catalogue of English Books, 1641–1700 (STC)*. This project was complemented by his work at Yale and with its holdings. Wing's genius synthesized the needs of the institution for which he worked with his creation of an indispensable bibliographical tool.

Born to Frank and Edith Smith Wing in Anthol, Massachusetts, Donald Wing attended public schools and entered Yale University, graduating in 1926. In "The Making of the *Short Title Catalogue, 1641–1700*" Wing spoke about his childhood: "Sometime about the age of ten I started a notebook alphabetically arranged by actors and actresses of all their movie parts. The first notebook was soon filled, thanks to regular purchases of at least three monthly magazines. It was simple to get a larger notebook and fun to copy it all over leaving room for additions–for at least six months. This complete recopying went on at least four times until either I began to grow up or went to college or rightly or wrongly thought my self too busy. It was fun, and so is an STC." In an interview with Wing publish in the 12 August 1972 issue of *The New York Times*, Michael T. Kaufman quotes Wing as saying "When I graduated from Yale in 1926, all the seniors were asked what they dreamed of doing, an d I said I wanted to read second-hand book catalogues."

After graduating from Yale, Wing studied at Trinity College, Cambridge (1926–1927), and then went to Harvard University, where he earned his master's degree in English in 1928. He then returned to Yale and received his Ph.D. in 1932 for a dissertation on "The Origins of the Comedy of Humor." He married Charlotte Farquhar in Sunday Spring, Maryland, on 28 June, 1930. The Wings had two children, Robert and Cathya.

During a period of unprecedented library acquisition and expansion at Yale, Wing started out in the library order department in 1928, became an assistant reference librarian in 1930 and later served as head of accessions (1939–1945), associate librarian (1945–1965), and associate librarian for collections of the libraries (1966–1970). In the words of his colleague Herman W. Liebert, Wing "helped to make Yale's library greater for more than forty years." In 1967–1968 Wing was the first Yale librarian to be awarded a sabbatical.

One of Wing's early professional tasks as an assistant librarian at Yale was to move the miscellaneous collections of early books into what was then the new Sterling Memorial Library building. As he explained in "The Making of the *Short-Title Catalogue, 1641-1700*," "In 1933 when Yale had been in its new library building for three years, a last attempt to recover all books at Yale in 1742 was to be made. The manuscript catalogue was more complete than the printed version of the following year, but there was still too many unidentified entries." Consequently Wing's first task was to determine exactly what books the university possessed, and he proceeded to make random searches in the stacks.

In the early 1930s, the Sterling Library acquired the library of Falconer Madan, one of the foremost Oxford bibliographers of the early years of the twentieth century, who had collected seventeenth-century books printed in Oxford. Madan's printed catalogue covered books printed through 1680, but left a twenty-year gap. No bibliographical tool for the post–1640 period existed, and a supplement to A. W. Pollard and G. R. Redgrave's *Short-Title Catalogue, 1475–1640* (1926) was clearly a practical necessity. Wing persuaded his superiors to allow him to create a card catalogue of late-seventeenth-century imprints while working at the public reference librarian's desk, a job Wing described as "mostly directing people to the men's room."

In 1935 Wing received a Guggenheim Fellowship to search British libraries for post-1640 books. When he sailed for Great Britain he had thirty-six shoe boxes full of slips. When he returned to America in late 1937 he had fifty-one shoe boxes full of annotated 3"x 5" slips of paper. According to John J. Morrison's preface to the second edition of the Wing *STC*, "On each was written the author, short title, imprint, edition statement, format, number of pages, and other distinguishing features of a 1641–1700 publication." Wing supplemented personal inspection by reading printed library catalogues and book-dealers' catalogues. In England in 1936 and 1937 Wing inspected the Thomason Tracts in the North Library of the British Museum. These tracts, pamphlets, books, newspapers, and manuscripts relating to the English Civil War, the period of the Commonwealth, and the Restoration had been collected by George Thomason, a Scottish bookseller in London during the years 1641–1661. The collection, which was bought by George III in 1762 and presented to the British Museum, includes at least twenty-two thousand books, pamphlets, and sheets. The problems in describing them had ensured that A. W. Pollard and G. R. Redgrave's *STC* did not extent beyond 1640. Working in the British Museum, Wing examined twenty volumes an hour, each composed of about twenty tracts, and he read the British Museum catalogue, sending for all volumes he had not previously seen. He then went to Oxford and to Cambridge, where, he later wrote, he was "able to include . . . college libraries–at Oxford getting locked into Magdalen and Balliol, and at Cambridge listing Magdalene and Trinity." During the Christmas vacation he went to Scottish libraries and in the spring he managed to see some French and Dutch collections.

Wing returned to the Sterling to work and to his slips. By August 1940 more than half the A–E

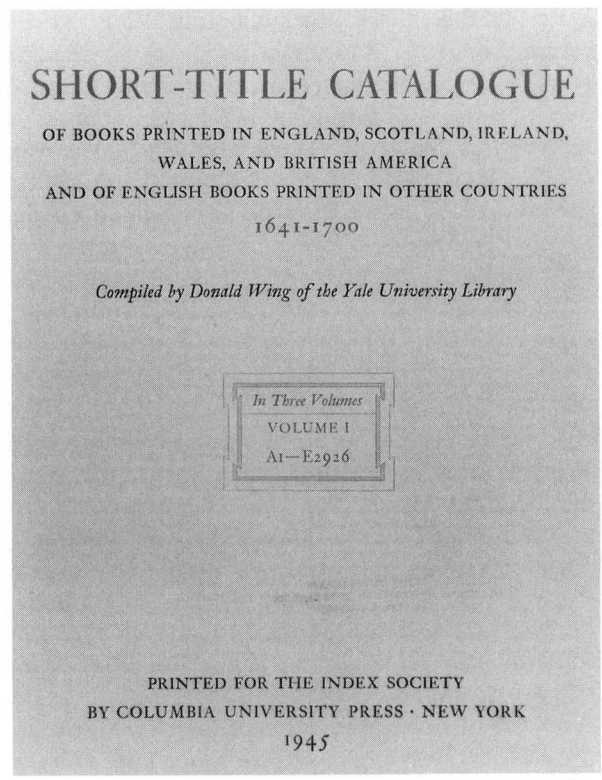

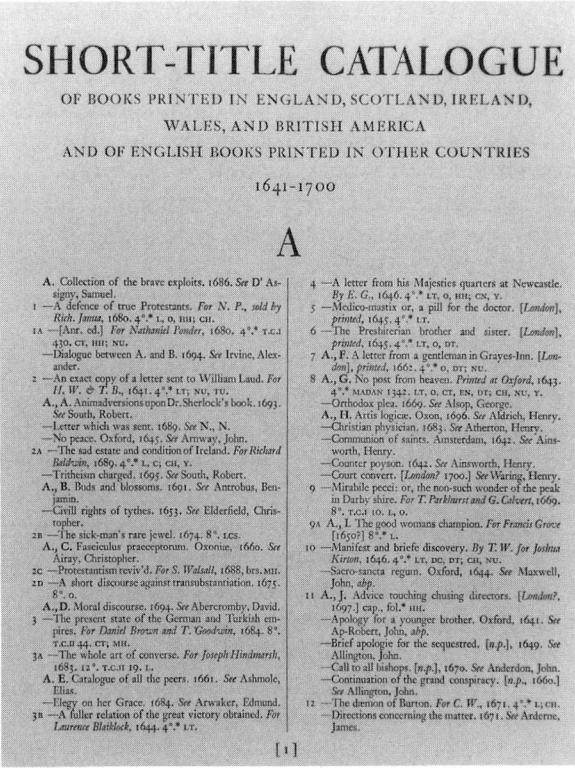

Title page and opening page from Wing's enumerative bibliography of seventeenth-century English books published after the period covered in A. W. Pollard and G. R. Redgrave's Short-Title Catalogue *for the years 1475–1640*

slips had been converted into typescript. Then, according to John J. Morrison and Carolyn W. Nelson's preface to the first volume of the revised *STC,* a prospectus for a three-volume *STC* for 1641–1700 was published. This catalogue represented only what Wing had been able to inspect and the titles he had gathered from printed catalogues. Morrison and Nelson explain, that to broaden the scope of the catalogue, by mid December 1940, Wing had sent carbon copies of the typescript for volume one to Harvard University, the Huntington Library, and the Folger Library, and at all three a section of the typescript was read against their holdings. As word of Wing's project spread, other libraries checked copies of the typescript or the galleys against their holdings as well. Wing also developed a network through correspondence with libraries, booksellers, dealers, collectors and scholars throughout the English-speaking word. His aim was to find every book, pamphlet, and broadside published in English in the last sixty years of the seventeenth century. As Wing told Kaufman, "A man might be a fool to start something like this but he'd be a bigger fool to think he ever finished." Wing's pursuit of items published in 1641–1700, recorded on slips of paper filed in rows of shoe boxes, continued until his death.

Before Wing began his labors, finding books published between 1641 and 1700 in English was exceedingly difficult. Indeed, how little work had been done toward listing the books published during this period may be seen in F. C. Francis's edition of *The Bibliographical Society 1892–1942: Studies in Retrospect* (1949), which includes essays on early printed books, English books before 1640, eighteenth-century and nineteenth-century books but not on books of the period Wing covered. These books were little studied, and with the notable exceptions of Falconer Madan and a few others, little collected. Until the publication of Wing's bibliography, acquisition and collecting was concentrated in more fashionable areas such as incunabula, Shakespeare, and the nineteenth century. Wing's project aroused interest in books of the late seventeenth century. The obituary for Wing in *AB Bookmans Weekly* (16 October 1972) exclaimed that Wing would always have "a special place in the world of books," partly for his *STC* but especially for his help to "antiquarian book dealers who are everlastingly in his debt." Indeed Wing's bibliographical research coincided with a surge of purchasing activity at Yale, led by Wing, who was head of acquisitions. His chosen period includes major authors and a host of minor ones, and it encompasses critical moments in English history:

the Civil War, the Cromwellian period, the Restoration, and of course the development of the American colonies. Wing established the bibliographical record by title, date and location for John Milton, John Dryden, William Shakespeare, and others. His search for their works, as well as everything else published in English between 1640 and 1700, created a flurry of bookselling and book searches to satisfy Wing's demand for material.

Volume one of Wing's *STC,* covering items A1–E2926, was published in 1945, followed by volume two (E2927–O1000) in 1945 and volume three (P1–Z28) in 1951. Wing's main preoccupation was the compilation and subsequent revision of this bibliographical reference. During the 1950s and 1960s information on items published during the 1641–1700 period poured into his Yale office, eventually filling a seventy-drawer card catalogue. Wing's *A Gallery of Ghosts* (1967) is an attempt to locate more than five thousand titles that Wing found listed in bibliographies and booksellers' or auction catalogue but had not seen. The titles that were located were then added to the revised Wing *STC.* The original edition became an important in-house working tool. For instance, the British Museum created Wing files, and interleaved copies of the Wing *STC* recorded their holdings for in-house purposes. Annotated copies of the Wing *STC* were sent across the Atlantic from England to Yale. The revised edition of volume one (A1–E2926) was published shortly before Wing's death, and was followed by revised and enlarged editions of the second and third volumes in 1982 and 1988 respectively. The newly revised and enlarged second edition of volume one was published in 1994.

Wing did the spade work for subsequent revisions of his book. He was an enumerative rather than an analytical or descriptive bibliographer, structuring his entries by recording author, short title, imprint, date, format (4° for quarto, 8° for octavo, or 12° for twelvemo, for example) rather than precise measurement, and locations by abbreviation (for instance, L for British Library, O for the Bodleian, Y for Yale). Wing's bibliography, as Timothy J. Crist's preface to the second edition of volume 2 indicates, "*is not a census of copies* but only a guide to inform scholars where a given entry may conveniently be consulted."

Like other works of pioneering scholarship, the first and revised Wing *STCs* have their limitations, which reviewers have pointed out. For instance, B. J. McMullin wrote in a 1978 review for *The Papers of the Bibliographical Society of America* (*PBSA*) that "*Wing* is essentially a record of holdings of institutions in the British Isles and the United States. Of the 327 location symbols in Wing 189 represent the former, 118 the latter. . . . Australia and New Zealand are not represented at all." Subsequent revisions of the Wing *STC* have attempted to remedy this deficiency. The *Times Literary Supplement* (*TLS*) review of Wing's revision of volume one (26 January 1973) notes that the abbreviated entries have inherent defects. The first Wing is littered with abbreviations such as "anr.ed" (another edition) or "var" (variant) without distinguishing printings, issues, states, or editions—information that is crucially important to the careful descriptive bibliographer.

In his preface to the revision of volume one, Wing wrote, "In the four decades of work which culminate in this new edition I have discovered no substitute for seeing each book before including it in these pages," but this ideal was not possible in reality, and Wing did not always work from the books themselves, and consequently made errors. The *TLS* review of this volume is not alone in finding "The rearrangement of the numeration . . . one of the most disturbing features of the new edition of the *STC.*" Reviewing the revision of a later volume, Theodore Hofman wrote in *The Library* (December 1994), "to accommodate the corrections and new material, Wing made the disastrous decision to cancel and alter entry numbers seemingly oblivious to the fact that the old Wing numbers had become indispensable to the world of cataloguing and scholarship." Furthermore, Hofman added, "the other fundamental problem with Wing is the shortness of the short titles," and the *TLS* reviewer was disturbed to find "no statement of the extent to which the entries" in Wing's *A Gallery of Ghosts* had been incorporated in the 1973 revision; thus, the reviewer asserts that "the revision is far from comprehensive, and additions are haphazard while the concealment of so many changes in unnoted renumeration is, at the very least, disconcerting and inconvenient."

Yet as Hofman noted, "at once the first edition of Wing became the *vade mecum* of acquisitions libraries and the antiquarian book trade." The conclusion of the 1973 *TLS* review, which calls the Wing *STC* "an indispensable tool of scholarship," is percipient in a way the reviewer may not have expected: "Clearly the *Short Title Catalogue* was in need of revision, but it must be doubted whether one man could (or should) have undertaken the task alone . . . . if 'Wing' is ever revised again it is to be hoped that strongly guided cooperative effort will be employed on the task." The 1994 revised edition of volume one of Wing has two editors and an assistant editor listed on its title page. Its list of acknowledgments extends to more than seven double-columned pages.

The *TLS* reviewer probably could not have foreseen the extent to which computerization would come to the aid of bibliography. Wing died in 1972, just as his revised first volume went to press; and he left the second in proof. Unlike these first two volumes of the second edition, volume three is not set with hot-metal Bembo type. It is computer typeset. Since then an editorial team, collaborative projects, and the creation a continuous online Wing *STC* make possible continual revision, expansion and modification of the database. Findings can be included right away rather than being saved for the next printed edition. The original Wing *STC* is an enumerative bibliography of the age of print, the card catalogue, and the individual scholar. The revised Wing employs the new technologies. Significantly, its chronological successor, the Eighteenth-Century Short-Title Catalogue (ESTC), is available only online and in CD-ROM form. These forms were not available to great bibliographers and editors such as Alfred William Pollard (1859-1944) and Gilbert R. Redgrave (1844-1941)and Wing.

Major tributes to Wing's accomplishment are found in the subsequent supplementary works spawned by his *STC*. Among the works Wing inspired is *Early English Books, 1641–1700: A Cumulative Index to Units. 1–60 of the Microfilm Collection* (9 volumes, 1990), an author, title, subject, and reel-position, Wing-number index to the titles in a microfilm collection of works listed by Wing. Others include A. F. Alison and V. F. Goldsmith's *Titles of English Books (and of Foreign Books Printed in England): An Alphabetical Finding-List by Title of Books Published Under the Authors Name, Pseudonym or Initials. Vol. 2: 1641–1700* (1977), Paul G. Morrison's *Index of Printers, Publishers and Booksellers in Donald Wing's Short-Title Catalogue* (1955), and Hilda L. Smith and Susan Cardinale's *Women and the Literature of the Seventeenth Century: An Annotated Bibliography based on Wing's Short-Title Catalogue* (1990), which includes some items that eluded Wing.

Donald Wing's name has become nearly synonymous with a period of literature. For literary scholars 1641–1700 is the Wing period. As Wing himself said, "When booksellers offer Wing-period books I don't want to wonder which period." Writing on "Wing's *STC*" in *The Book Collector* (Autumn 1974), another great bibliographer, A. N. L. Munby, commented, "Whatever its defects, our indebtedness to Wing remains, and his name must be enrolled alongside those of [Ludwig] Hain [the compiler of a basic reference tool on incunabula], [Joseph] Sabin, Palau [a family that compiled of the most extensive bibliography of Spanish-language materials] and a handful of other giants who have performed single-handed prodigies in the field of enumerative bibliography."

Yet Wing's interests were not confined to the 1641–1700 period. As his colleague Liebert points out, Wing "assiduously collected, and also read, Henry James, Ronald Firbank, Marcel Proust, Edith Wharton, Ezra Pound, Ellen Glasgow, E. M. Forster, Andre Gidé, and all the Sitwells." Many of these books and other special association copies that belonged to Wing have been given by his widow to the Yale University Library. Perhaps the best tribute to Wing is this elaborate rondeau by Liebert:

> "In Wing" as if engraved on stone
> A title, long perhaps unknown,
> Compared to it, how fatuous thus.
> The twelve-inch screen, the microphone!
> The row of shoe-boxes has grown,
> Slip after slip, so copious
> That sixty years of books are shown.
>   In Wing.

Papers:
Correspondence relating to Wing's *STC* is in the Donald Wing Correspondence Archive, Yale University Library.

John M. Wing

(7 April 1844 – 4 March 1917)

Robert Williams
University of Chicago Press

BOOKS: *The Great Union Stock Yards of Chicago* (Chicago: Religio-Philosophical Publishing Association, 1865; revised, 1866);

The Great Chicago Lake Tunnel (Chicago: Jack Wing, 1866; revised, 1867);

History of the Great Chicago Lake Tunnel (Chicago: Jack Wing, 1868);

Chicago Illustrated, 2 volumes (Chicago: J. M. Wing, 1872–1873);

Rebuilt Chicago (Chicago: J. M. Wing, 1873);

The Merchants and Manufacturers of Chicago (Chicago: J. M. Wing, 1873);

Wing's Illustrated Travelers' and Visitors' Hand-Book to the City of Chicago (Chicago: J. M. Wing, 1874);

The Tunnels and Water System of Chicago (Chicago: J. M. Wing, 1874);

Illustrations of Greater Chicago (Chicago: J. M. Wing, 1875);

7 Days in Chicago (Chicago: J. M. Wing, 1877);

Family Trees and Genealogy: Wing Family of America (Chicago: Old Corner Library, 1903).

CATALOGUE: *Dictionary Catalogue of the History of Printing, from the John M. Wing Foundation in the Newberry Library* (Boston: G. K. Hall, 1961; supplement, 1970; second supplement, 1981).

SELECTED PERIODICAL PUBLICATION–
UNCOLLECTED: "A Great Wing Library," *Owl,* 1, no. 10 (1900).

John M. Wing, 1866 (courtesy of the John M. Wing Foundation, The Newberry Library)

If John M. Wing is known at all in the world of book collecting and bibliography it is more from the foundation that bears his name at the Newberry Library in Chicago than from his book collection. The John M. Wing Foundation is arguably one of the best collections on the history of printing in the world. Not only does it comprise both primary and secondary sources on the history of printing, but it also contains significant materials on typography, paper making, bookbinding, book illustration, and calligraphy. In short, this collection of more than forty thousand items is a repository of virtually all aspects of the book.

Wing left his entire personal library and nearly $250,000 to the Newberry Library; his will stipulated that the foundation was to use only the interest from his bequest to purchase books "which treat of, relate to, illustrate, exemplify, or depict, either wholly or in part, either directly or indirectly . . . The History and Development of the Arts of Printing, Engraving, and Book-Illustration from the date of the introduction into Europe of the art of printing with movable metal type [and the] Bibliography . . . of printed books." In addition to purchases in these areas part of the interest was to be used for the sal-

344

ary of a full-time curator of the foundation. The library, however, was obliged to maintain the collection at its own expense, none of the bequest being earmarked for any other purposes than those stated in Wing's will. With this endowment the Newberry Library was to become the first American research library with a major collection of the history of printing.

Accounts of Wing's life have been based mainly on two short articles: a 1900 autobiographical sketch published in the family's genealogical journal, the *Owl,* and a 1917 obituary by George S. Seymour printed in the same journal. One of these pieces is partly fanciful and the other contains several inaccuracies.

Born on 7 April 1844 in Fernwood, New York, John Mansir Wing was the first child of Mansir Wing, a blacksmith and sometime farmer, and his second wife, the widow Susan Mace Curtis. Mansir had four children by his first wife and two by his second. John was the second youngest in the household, with a sister three years younger and half-siblings ranging in age from eight to twelve years older than he. He spent the first twelve years of his life in Holmesville, a small town seven and one-half miles from Pulaski, in western New York. Around the age of twelve his family moved to a farm just outside of Pulaski where he spent the next five years. These years at Pulaski were important for Wing as it was there that he received his formal education and first learned the skill of typesetting.

Wing's autobiography begins with a charming fib about a twelve-year-old boy who, while digging potatoes in a field, was lured away by the siren song of the circus. Years later a stranger appeared and bought that field. The stranger, of course, was the prosperous John M. Wing. Wing, however, did more than dig potatoes outside Pulaski. He kept detailed diaries from 1858 to 1866, and it is possible to reconstruct a more credible biography of his early life from these sources.

Wing had a solid basic education (from 1855? to 1860) received at the Pulaski academy, where he studied rhetoric, composition, Latin, and arithmetic, among other subjects. He belonged to a local literary society that met weekly and whose members read their own essays and poems. These exercises would stand Wing in good stead as he made his way in the world of publishing. It was only in order to earn money for his school tuition (his family, tenant farmers at the time, apparently could not afford it) that Wing took a job as a printer's devil at the Pulaski *Democrat* from April to July 1860. In May his first published work, a poem called "The Man Within," appeared in the newspaper, and while he

had no inkling at the time, these two experiences were to shape his professional life. In November, Wing received his teacher's certificate and began teaching school the following month. At this point his goal in life was to be a schoolteacher, but, as Wing would put it, the fates would have it otherwise.

After his three-month teaching contract ended and he could find no other teaching jobs, Wing moved to Oswego, New York, in March 1861. He got a job as a local reporter and typesetter on the *Oswego Times* but was let go the day after the Civil War began. Two days later Wing found a job as a clerk in a local bookstore. The position was ideal for a youngster whose great passions were writing and reading.

Wing had not, however, given up hope of teaching, and in August he returned to study at the nearby Mexico Academy. His interest in forming a library was first manifested around this time, when he had fifty bookplates printed up reading "Jno. M. Wing Library No.__." School turned out to be an economic hardship on Wing, and he left after one term and returned to Holmesville, where he continued to write, publish his poetry in the *Democrat,* and read. After finishing Charles Dickens's *Pickwick Papers* (1836–1837) he wrote in his diary, "Hope that someday I shall be able to own all of Dickens' works and have me a *noble* Library."

He did not get another teaching job until February 1862, and that lasted only a month. Finally, shortly after his eighteenth birthday, he began working as an apprentice typesetter and printer on the *Black River Herald* in Booneville, New York. He was a prodigious worker, setting about six thousand characters of six-point type six mornings a week. He continued to publish his own poetry and prose both in the Pulaski *Democrat* and the *Black River Herald,* and he added reporting to his literary skills. Wing even set some of his own articles without copy directly from his head to his composing stick.

At the end of the year Wing quit the *Black River Herald* to take a job as typesetter on the *Roman Citizen* in Rome, New York. He continued to write for the Pulaski *Democrat* as the "Oneida County Correspondent" and publish his poetry and editorials in the *Citizen.* Within a year Wing was made a journeyman printer and added proofreading to his skills and the *Utica Telegraph* to the newspapers for which he wrote. He was developing into a professional journalist and in January 1864 began working as proofreader and reporter on the *Utica Herald.* Despite frequent twelve-to eighteen-hour workdays at the *Herald* Wing continued to contribute articles to the *Citizen* as well as the *Black River Herald.* In December

Wing's first bookplate (courtesy of the John M. Wing Foundation, The Newberry Library)

1864 Wing seriously considered buying his own newspaper in Little Falls, New York, but backed out of the deal at the last moment.

Wing had made something of a local name for himself, and he accepted a job offer as a reporter for the *Oswego Commercial Advertiser* in mid January of 1865. He worked there for the next four months. Ironically, Wing was fired from his job at the *Advertiser* a few weeks after the end of the Civil War, as he had been fired from the *Oswego Times* at the war's beginning. He had just turned twenty-one.

Perhaps because he had exhausted the newspaper possibilities of his immediate area, Wing decided to travel. While working for the *Advertiser* he had been given a complimentary pass on the Northern Transport Company, whose steamships traveled between Ogdensburg, New York, and Chicago. On 30 May 1865 he set off for the west although Chicago was not his immediate destination. His ship stopped in Cleveland and Detroit, and Wing visited newspapers in both cities, unsuccessfully looking for a job. From Detroit he took the train to Chicago, where he arrived on the afternoon of 4 June.

Wing immediately started looking for newspaper work in the city and called on three major city papers the day he arrived. There were no positions open, but the *Chicago Tribune* gave him a trial assignment as a music critic. His first publication there was a review of *Norma,* performed by the Italian Opera at Chicago's new opera house. Wing, who was somewhat musical and who had attended concerts and minstrel shows in New York, found it a tough assignment. He recalled that he "paid the closest attention to the plot, and the singing, but never saw an opera of the kind before, and was not able to judge at all." Still, he wrote a review, and after considerable editing, it was printed two days after he arrived in Chicago. The *Tribune* did not, however, hire him. He was more successful at the *Times,* where he wrote

several freelance articles and used his own initiative covering local news. In less than a week he was hired there, and within two weeks his salary was doubled. Wing rose rapidly at the *Times,* becoming temporary assistant city news editor five weeks later.

He also began to pick up "rare old books." He does not name the books he purchased at an "old bookstore" in Chicago, but these acquisitions mark the beginning of Wing's antiquarian book collection. All were purchased because of their age, and a few were in French, a language he could not read. He considered them good investments since he was certain they were worth much more than what he paid for them. He also added several nineteenth-century works to his growing library. All were poetry, and all but one were by British authors who were particular favorites of Wing. By August he proudly reported in his diary that his library had grown to "about 60 volumes collected since I came to Chicago."

Jack Wing, as he now styled himself, was as prolific a reporter as he had been a typesetter. His articles for the *Times* ranged from reporting commencement exercises at the University of Notre Dame to the booming growth of Chicago to executions. He spent his free time attending theater and opera in "the great metropolis of the west," as he called Chicago. He was assigned to cover the state fairs of Illinois, Wisconsin, and Michigan, a task he did not particularly relish as he hated the country. He found these assignments lucrative, however, in that he would pick up an extra five dollars or ten dollars by including a "puff" in his article for some local enterprise at the fair.

In November he took a two-week vacation back to New York State and on his return found his position at the *Times* had been taken by another reporter. Angry, he planned to quit the *Times* but could not find a job on any other newspaper. By way of making something on which to live, Wing conceived of writing a pamphlet on the about-to-be-opened Union Stock Yards. He financed this publication by taking large advance orders for it and selling advertisements in the pamphlet as well as including the ever-lucrative puffs. In the midst of his preparations he was hired by the *Chicago Republican.* The pamphlet was printed in December 1865 and proved so successful that he published a second, slightly revised edition of it a month later in January 1866. Both editions of *The Great Union Stock Yards of Chicago* bear the imprint of the "Religio-Philosophical Publishing Association."

Three weeks after he started work at the *Republican* Wing was fired over his refusal to accept ten dollars worth of nickels as part of his weekly salary. No doubt feeling fairly competent about his newspaper skills, he visited a couple of local country newspapers with an eye toward buying or becoming a partner in one of them. He settled on the Waukegan *Gazette,* and by the end of January he was its co-owner, but he found country living and country news insipid and within a week wanted out. Finally, in March his partner agreed to return all but $100 of Wing's $1,000 deposit. Wing seems to have experienced a rather severe emotional trauma from this venture (he had suicidal thoughts and a rash over his entire body); he returned to New York State for most of March but returned to the Midwest before the month was out.

Many of Wing's major professional decisions had taken place around his birthday, and on 7 April 1866 he bought a ticket on a Mississippi steamer to New Orleans. Leaving Saint Louis on 10 April, he arrived in the Crescent City a week later. His quest for work as a newspaperman there was a total failure, and five days later he boarded another ship heading upriver. On board he met the owner of the *Boston Journal,* Maj. Charles O. Rogers. This encounter proved to be important a few years later.

Back in Saint Louis, Wing formed a partnership with three other men to create Sheffield, Wing and Company, a newspaper advertising company. The business did not prosper despite the company's efforts at securing accounts. During the summer and fall of 1866 Wing traveled extensively in the Midwest trying to sign up advertisers, but his only financially successful venture was a daily advertising paper issued for a Chicago fair in September 1866. By the end of October, Wing and his partners dissolved their business, and Wing went back east for a series of visits with family and friends.

In November he returned to Chicago for his second stay in the city. He had several money-making plans, but the only one he realized was another pamphlet. More ambitious than the piece on the Union Stock Yards, *The Great Chicago Lake Tunnel* was longer and contained electrotype illustrations purchased from Frank Leslie's *Weekly.* It also had significantly more advertisers than his first pamphlet, and it was the first publication to bear his own imprint, "Published by Jack Wing." Like the Union Stock Yards pamphlet it was quite successful, and a second, slightly revised edition appeared in 1867 with even more advertisers. Knowing a good thing when he saw it, Wing pub-

Wing's later bookplate (courtesy of the John M. Wing Foundation, The Newberry Library)

lished yet another book on the subject, the *History of the Great Chicago Lake Tunnel* (1868).

The diaries end in 1866, and only a few letters written in 1868 by Wing to his sister Anna give any information on his later activities. His meeting with C. O. Rogers on the Mississippi undoubtedly led to his return east to Boston in 1868, from where he traveled to Europe as the overseas correspondent for the *Boston Journal,* writing travel articles under the pseudonym Gwin. He was accompanied by Rogers's seventeen-year-old son, Charles, an asthmatic, and the two of them took a grand tour of the Continent, traveling from New York in March and visiting England, France, Switzerland, Italy, Austria, and Germany before returning to the United States in August. Rogers likely promised to hire Wing as the managing editor on the *Journal* after his European trip, but

Rogers died before he could do so. Once again Wing returned to Chicago, where he established J. M. Wing and Company, Publishers, in 1869.

Sometime before his first European trip Wing had bought land in Chicago that had doubled in value by the time he returned. His real estate success may have suggested his next publishing venture, for the year he came back to the city he began to publish a monthly magazine on Chicago real estate, buildings, and general city improvements. *The Land Owner,* like his pamphlet on the Union Stock Yards, was part news, part advertisements, and part puff. This magazine was successful, and Wing prospered.

On 8 October 1871 the city was struck by fire, the great Chicago fire, which destroyed most of the city including Wing's publishing house on the corner of Dearborn and Monroe Street. There is a story (probably apocryphal) that Wing took the first available train to New York, where he loaded his empty suitcases with type, returned to Chicago, and printed the next issue the month following the fire. Although Wing was never the printer of *The Land Owner,* he may have gone east to replace the type lost while his printer looked for a new press.

In addition to publishing *The Land Owner* Wing published and authored other short books of puffery and Chicago boosterism in the 1870s, such as his *Rebuilt Chicago* (1873). By 1877 he seems to have tired of *The Land Owner,* for it ceased publication without explanation. The monthly had proved profitable (Wing was reported to have made as much as $35,000 a year from it), and he had started another monthly, *The Western Brewer,* in 1876. Like *The Land Owner, The Western Brewer* contained considerable advertising as well as information on crops, brewery production, and other news pertaining to beermaking. In conjunction with this periodical he also published an annual, *Wing's Brewers' Hand-Book of the United States and Canada* (1877–1884, 1886). *The Western Brewer* ceased publication in 1887; the following year Wing retired before his forty-fourth birthday.

After 1888 Wing returned to Europe, visiting London and Naples, where he apparently bought books. In addition to his business, the great Chicago fire had destroyed his early library. The survival of a few prefire items—including his diaries—in Wing's library must have been the result of his depositing some books with his family on trips to New York. He brought his parents and sister Anna to Chicago in 1873, and with them must have come some of his books.

Little has survived regarding how Wing built up his library of over forty-one hundred books.

Each book contains a bookplate bearing the family coat of arms and the words "The Old Corner Library" (the name given to the three rooms in his house where he kept his library). While a number is stamped on each bookplate, it was clearly just a way of counting the total number of books in the library. For instance, the diaries carry the numbers 2579 to 2587, but they follow numbers found in books published in the 1890s and 1900s and precede some published in the same decades. A survey of Wing's books by the stamped numbers shows they were not grouped by subject, date, or even size. Unlike some of his contemporaries, Wing does not seem to have had a catalogue made of his library, and he seems always to have kept it in a totally idiosyncratic order of his own devising.

In his autobiographical essay Wing claims (with some exaggeration or prior to an actual count) to have five thousand volumes, including examples of works printed by the leading figures of early typography: Aldus Manutius, the Elzivieres, Christophe Plantin, and Johann Froben. He does not mention any incunabula, so the four that came to the Newberry after his death must have been purchased after this article appeared. As one looks through the Wing library deposited at the Newberry, however, no clear collecting pattern emerges. The Elzivieres, Plantin, and Aldines are there, but they are not particularly distinguished copies. The bulk of the library consists of considerable sets of the works of nineteenth-century authors (primarily British), reference books and encyclopedias, travel writing, poetry, European, British and American history, military history, "curiosa" (including several books on phallic worship), books on comparative religion, early (but not first) editions of well-known authors (Henry Fielding, Miguel de Cervantes, Boccaccio, Sir Walter Scott, Voltaire, Edward Bulwer-Lytton), biographies, and a few seventeenth-century atlases. If there is a single preference, it is for illustrated books, especially eighteenth- and nineteenth-century editions heavily illustrated with metal or wood engravings. In short, Wing's library can best be described as a typical nineteenth-century gentleman's library, but his interest in illustration led him further, to create unique books for his library—he was especially fond of adding extra illustrations to his books.

In 1769 James Granger published his *Biographical History of England* with blank leaves to accomodate portraits and other illustrations that purchasers might want to add, and so began the practice that most modern bibliophiles (and almost all bibliographers) deplore. Wing probably started extra-illustrating books around the turn of

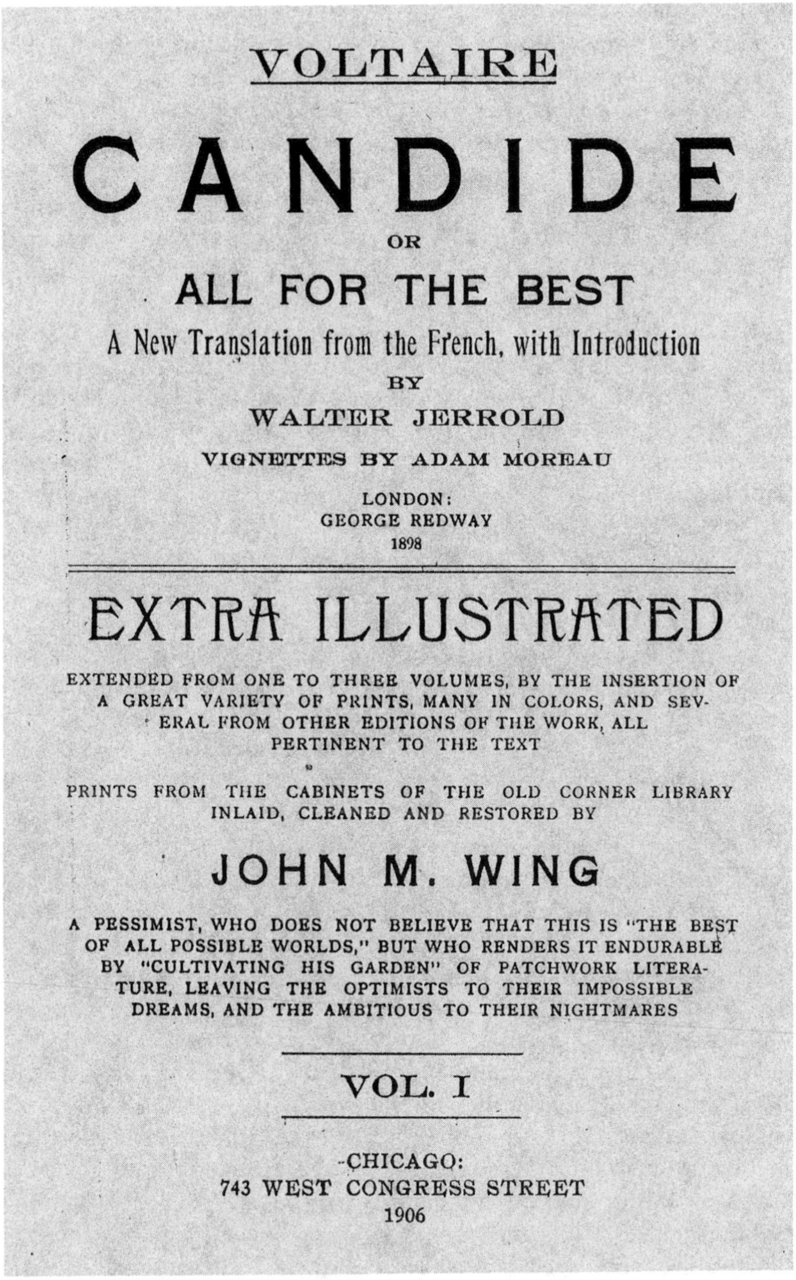

VOLTAIRE

CANDIDE

OR

ALL FOR THE BEST

A New Translation from the French, with Introduction

BY

WALTER JERROLD

VIGNETTES BY ADAM MOREAU

LONDON:
GEORGE REDWAY
1898

EXTRA ILLUSTRATED

EXTENDED FROM ONE TO THREE VOLUMES, BY THE INSERTION OF
A GREAT VARIETY OF PRINTS, MANY IN COLORS, AND SEV-
ERAL FROM OTHER EDITIONS OF THE WORK, ALL
PERTINENT TO THE TEXT

PRINTS FROM THE CABINETS OF THE OLD CORNER LIBRARY
INLAID, CLEANED AND RESTORED BY

JOHN M. WING

A PESSIMIST, WHO DOES NOT BELIEVE THAT THIS IS "THE BEST
OF ALL POSSIBLE WORLDS," BUT WHO RENDERS IT ENDURABLE
BY "CULTIVATING HIS GARDEN" OF PATCHWORK LITERA-
TURE, LEAVING THE OPTIMISTS TO THEIR IMPOSSIBLE
DREAMS, AND THE AMBITIOUS TO THEIR NIGHTMARES

VOL. I

CHICAGO:
743 WEST CONGRESS STREET
1906

*Added title page in one of the books that Wing extra-illustrated with engravings from
his collection (courtesy of the John M. Wing Foundation,
The Newberry Library)*

the century as an occupation of his early retirement. In his library is a copy of Daniel M. Tredwell's *A Monograph on Privately-Illustrated Books: A Plea for Bibliomania* (1881), published in Brooklyn, New York. This copy, inscribed by the author, was previously owned in 1891 by Walter R. Benjamin (a turn-of-the-century New York autograph dealer and publisher of *The Collector*). Tredwell gives suggestions for what kind of books to extra-illustrate as well as very practical instructions on how to add the illustrations. Comparing Tredwell's instructions with Wing's extra-illustrated books shows that Wing followed these guidelines. Tredwell cautions against destroying books of greater value to illustrate those of lesser worth, and in this Wing also adhered. He collected loose prints in vast quantities (on one occasion buying five hundred engravings in a single lot from an English dealer), and although he was particularly fond of metal engravings, he was not above adding photographs or cheap, colored magazine lithographs if the picture was relevant to the content of the book he was expanding.

Each extra-illustrated book contained a specially printed or manuscript title page, often with a whimsical description of Wing. A typical example can be found in *England Displayed* (London, 1769) with a note in Wing's hand: "This Book was Extra Illustrated by John M. Wing, bachelor by the Grace of God, at the Old Corner Library, 743 West Congress St., Chicago, during the year 1899, for his pleasure and as a labor of love for Old England, where he spent many happy days, and met with many adventures."

Aldus Manutius: The First Editor (an undated magazine article expanded to a thick folio volume in 1905) includes the statement: "John M. Wing. Erstwhile Printer, Editor, Publisher, who, approaching the end of a life of turmoil, and not having found in all the world, after traversing many climes, anything worth the trouble, HAS BECOME Philosopher, Paper-splitter and Paster of Literary Patch-work, to employ his leisure and ease his spleen withal, preferring this princely diversion to contact with fools and jackals."

Wing also occasionally prepared books as presents. In a scrapbook from 1903 there are two title pages for extra-illustrated books prepared as gifts. One, to Alexander J. Rudolph of the Newberry Library, was for *A Biographical and Critical Dictionary of Painters, Engravers, Sculptors, and Architects . . .* (New York, 1853). Wing had taken this single-volume work and expanded it to twelve profusely illustrated volumes. It was not uncommon for him to do so, as some volumes include more than one thousand extra illustrations. Once Wing had prepared his volumes by cutting windows in large sheets of paper and carefully pasting text or illustration therein, the books were hand bound in half or quarter leather, often by the binder of the Newberry Library.

Wing's extra-illustrating activity seemed more dependent on the happy coming together of illustrations and appropriate text than any systematic plan of creating a coherent library; it was primarily a hobby. Wing, who frequently traveled back east and to Europe during his retirement, often purchased his books and prints from English and New York dealers, or so the few surviving sales receipts indicate. It is unlikely that Wing looked upon himself as a "bibliophile" in a serious way. He never joined the Caxton Club of Chicago (founded in 1895) or any other book-collectors club. He did belong to the American Bookplate Society and compiled a substantial scrapbook of bookplates, but there was no apparent plan in his collecting in this area either.

The origins of Wing's connection with the Newberry Library are somewhat vague. In his autobiographical essay he states that he has willed his books to the Newberry Library to form a special section "to be known as the 'John M. Wing Foundation of the Newberry Library,'" but he does not describe the nature of the foundation. The earliest correspondence between Wing and the library is a letter dated 8 November 1899 from E. W. Blatchford, thanking Wing for a copy of his *Tunnels and Water Systems of Chicago* (1874). Following this note there is no surviving correspondence between the Newberry and Wing until 1912 when the secretary to the library writes to acknowledge Wing's desire to deposit his books in the library. Despite this hiatus of thirteen years Wing was probably in contact with the library from its earliest days (it was founded in 1887). In a scrapbook of newspaper clippings Wing compiled beginning in 1899 there are several articles on the construction and opening of the library. This collection also contains many cuttings about book collectors and library benefactors. It seems clear from this scrapbook and Wing's 1900 announcement that he had the Newberry in mind as the final resting place of his library practically from the date of the library's creation. The letter from Blatchford suggests Wing was personally acquainted with the library staff and may have discussed his donation with them well before putting anything in writing.

The idea of establishing a foundation on the history of printing may not, however, have been entirely Wing's idea. Pierce Butler, the first custodian of the Wing Foundation, wrote in an article published in 1921 in *The Papers of the Bibliographical Society of America* that a trustee of the library, Horace H. Martin, "had long cherished the idea of a purely typographical collection . . . and the Wing Foundation thus owes its establishment and organization very largely to his interest." Joel Samuels, in his 1973 master's thesis on the John M. Wing Foundation, suggests that W. N. C. Carleton, the Newberry librarian from 1909 to 1920, may have played a part in directing Wing to set up a foundation on the history of printing. Wing's background would have disposed him to the idea, even if his personal book collection did not especially reflect such an interest. This decision was undoubtedly made only in the last years of his life since there is no reference to it in the 1900 essay.

Three wills—in 1913, 1914, and 1915—were drawn up giving specific provisions for the creation of the Wing Foundation. Wing probably sold or moved from his home on West Congress Street around the time of the first will as his entire library was placed in a room specially fitted out for it in the Newberry in September 1913. The library also became his mailing address, and he had stationery printed with his name and the Newberry Library's address. There Wing continued his pastime of extra-illustration, and the library even bound up the results in their bindery. He lived out of hotels during this time, and on the first Friday in March 1917 he "caught a chill" in the library. At 1:30 A.M. the following Monday he died of pneumonia in his room at the Auditorium Hotel.

References:

Pierce Butler, "A Typographic Library," *Papers of the Bibliographic Society of America,* 15, part 2 (1921): 73–78;

Joel L. Samuels, "The John M. Wing Foundation on the History of Printing at the Newberry Library," *Library Quarterly,* 58, no. 2 (1988): 164–189;

George S. Seymour, "Obituary of John M. Wing," *Owl,* 18, no. 2 (1917): 1651–1655;

George B. Utley, *Handbook of The Newberry Library* (Chicago: The Newberry Library, 1933), pp. 61–70;

James Wells, "The John Wing Foundation of the Newberry Library," *Book Collector* (Summer 1959): 156–162;

Wells, "The Wing Foundation," *Print,* 7 (March 1953): 157–162.

Papers:

The Newberry Library holds all of John M. Wing's surviving books and papers—including his unpublished diaries, his scrapbooks, and scattered notes, sometimes written by him on a flyleaf or printed in his extra-illustrated books.

Lawrence C. Wroth
(14 January 1884 – 25 December 1970)

Carolyn Smith
Johns Hopkins University

BOOKS: *Parson Weems: A Biographical and Critical Study* (Baltimore: Eichelberger, 1911);

A Description of Federal Public Documents (White Plains, N.Y.: H. W. Wilson, 1915);

A History of Printing in Colonial Maryland, 1686–1776 (Baltimore: Published by the Typothetae of Baltimore, 1922);

The John Carter Brown Library: Report to the Corporation of Brown University, 34 volumes (Providence, R.I.: John Carter Brown Library, 1924–1957);

Abel Buell of Connecticut, Silversmith, Type Founder & Engraver (New Haven: Yale University Press for the Acorn Club of Connecticut, 1926; second edition, revised, Middletown, Conn.: Wesleyan University Press, 1958);

William Parks, Printer and Journalist of England and Colonial America; With a List of the Issues of his Several Presses and a Facsimile of the Earliest Virginia Imprint Known to be in Existence (Richmond, Va.: William Parks Club, 1926);

Acts of French Royal Administration Concerning Canada, Guiana, the West Indies and Louisiana, Prior to 1791, compiled by Wroth and Gertrude L. Annan (New York: New York Public Library, 1930);

The Colonial Printer (New York: Grolier Club, 1931; second edition, revised and enlarged, Portland, Maine: Southworth-Anthoensen Press, 1938);

An American Bookshelf, 1755 (Philadelphia: University of Pennsylvania Press, 1934);

The John Carter Brown Library in Brown University (Providence, R.I.: Privately printed, 1936);

The Way of a Ship: An Essay on the Literature of Navigation Science (Portland, Maine: Southworth-Anthoensen Press, 1937);

Roger Williams: Marshall Woods Lecture, in Sayles Hall, October 26, 1936 (Providence, R.I.: Brown University, 1937);

Some Reflections on the Book Arts in Early Mexico (Cambridge, Mass.: Department of Printing and Graphic Arts, Harvard College Library, 1945);

Lawrence C. Wroth (courtesy of Brown University Library)

The First Century of the John Carter Brown Library: A History with a Guide to the Collections (Providence, R.I.: Associates of the John Carter Brown Library, 1946);

Some American Contributions to the Art of Navigation, 1519–1802 (Providence, R.I.: Associates of the John Carter Brown Library, 1947);

Typographical Heritage: Selected Essays (Portland, Maine: Anthoensen Press for the Typophiles, 1949);

The Walpole Society: Five Decades (N.p.: Walpole Society, 1960);

The Voyages of Giovanni da Verrazzano, 1524–1528 (New Haven: Yale University Press for the Pierpont Morgan Library, 1970);

Benjamin Franklin, Printer at Work (New York: Privately printed, 1974).

OTHER: "Churches and Religious Organizations in Baltimore," in *Baltimore its History and its People,* edited by Clayton Coleman Hall (New York: Lewis Historical Publishing, 1912), pp. 678–694;

War Record of Battery A, Maryland Field Artillery, compiled by Wroth (Baltimore: Barton-Gillet, 1923);

"The First Work with American Types," in *Bibliographical Essays, A Tribute to Wilberforce Eames,* edited by Wroth, George Parker Winship, and Randolph G. Adams (Cambridge, Mass.: Printed at the Harvard University Press for the Subscribers, 1924), pp. 128–142;

A List of Titles of Books on Printing and Allied Arts and Crafts Contained in the Collections of the Peabody Institute and the Enoch Pratt Free Library of Baltimore City, compiled by Wroth and Louis H. Dielman, introduction by Wroth (Baltimore: Ottmar Mergenthaler School of Printing, 1926);

"North America (English-Speaking)," in *Printing, a Short History of the Art,* edited by R. A. Peddie (London: Grafton, 1927), pp. 319–373;

Archives of Maryland, volume 45, introduction by Wroth (Baltimore: Maryland Historical Society, 1927);

"The Maryland Colonization Tracts," in *Essays Offered to Herbert Putnam by his Colleagues and Friends on his Thirtieth Anniversary as Librarian of Congress 5 April 1929,* edited by William Warner Bishop and Andrew Keogh (New Haven: Yale University Press, 1929), pp. 539–555;

Bibliotheca Americana: Catalogue of the John Carter Brown Library in Brown University, Providence, Rhode Island, volume 3, compiled by Wroth and the staff of the library (Providence, R.I.: John Carter Brown Library, 1931);

"Mystical Reflections on the Ampersand," in *Diggings From Many Ampersandhogs* (New York: The Typophiles, 1936), pp. 1–12;

"The Eighteenth Century," in *A History of the Printed Book, Being the Third Number of the Dolphin,* edited by Wroth (New York: Limited Editions Club, 1938), pp. 201–232;

Joseph Towne Wheeler, *The Maryland Press, 1777–1790,* introduction by Wroth (Baltimore: Maryland Historical Society, 1938);

"Book Production and Distribution from the Beginning to the War between the States," in *The*

Book in America: A History of the Making, the Selling, and the Collecting of Books in the U.S., edited by Wroth, Hellmut Lehmann-Haupt and Ruth Shepard Granniss (New York: R. R. Bowker, 1939; revised and enlarged, 1951), pp. 3–111;

"A Historical Study of the Oath of a Free-man," in *The Oath of a Free-Man* (New York: Press of the Woolly Whale, 1939), pp. 3–10;

Rutherford Goodwin, *The William Parks Paper Mill at Williamsburg,* foreword by Wroth (Lexington, Va.: Journalism Laboratory Press, Washington and Lee University, 1939);

"The Cambridge Press," in *Bookmen's Holiday. Notes and Studies Written and Gathered in Tribute to Harry Miller Lydenberg,* edited by Deoch Fulton (New York: New York Public Library, 1943), pp. 498–524;

"Evans' American Bibliography, A Matrix of Histories," in *American Bibliography, 1639–1729, by Charles Evans, Illustrated with Fifty-Nine Original Leaves from Early American Books. . . .* (Boston: C. E. Goodspeed, 1943), pp. vii–xiii;

"Good Booksellers Make Good Libraries," in *To Dr. R.: Essays Here Collected and Published in Honor of the Seventieth Birthday of Dr. A .S. W. Rosenbach, July 22, 1946,* compiled by Percy E. Lawler (Philadelphia, 1946), pp. 263–272;

"The Validity of Antiquarianism," in *Addresses Delivered at a Convocation Held in Yale University, 18–19 October, 1946* (New Haven, 1947), pp. 27–32;

George Leland Miner, *Angell's Lane: The History of a Little Street in Providence,* introduction by Wroth (Providence, R.I.: Akerman-Standard Press, 1948);

In Retrospect, 1923–1949. An Exhibition Commemorating Twenty-six Years of Service to the John Carter Brown Library by Lawrence C. Wroth, Librarian, compiled by Wroth and the staff of the library (Providence, R.I., 1949);

"Early Americana," in *Standards of Bibliographical Description,* by Curt F. Bühler and James G. McManaway (Philadelphia: University of Pennsylvania Press, 1949), pp. 93–120;

"A Tribute to the Library and its First Director," in *The First Quarter Century of the Pierpont Morgan Library: A Retrospective Exhibition in Honor of Belle da Costa Greene* (New York, 1949), pp. 9–29;

Elizabeth Baer, *Seventeenth Century Maryland: A Bibliography,* introduction by Wroth (Baltimore: John Work Garrett Library, 1949);

The Colonial Scene, 1602–1800. A Catalogue of Books Exhibited at the John Carter Brown Library in the Spring of 1949, Augmented by Related Titles from the Library of the American Antiquarian Society, ed-

ited by Wroth and compiled by the staffs of
the two libraries (Worcester: American Antiquarian Society for the Associates of the John
Carter Brown Library, 1950);

"The Thomas Johnston Maps of the Kennebeck
Purchase," in *In Tribute to Fred Anthoensen, Master Printer* (Portland, Maine, 1952), pp. 77–107;

"The Pierpont Morgan Library and the Historian,"
in *Studies in Art and Literature for Belle da Costa
Greene,* edited by Dorothy Miner (Princeton:
Princeton University Press, 1954), pp. 10–22.

SELECTED PERIODICAL PUBLICATIONS–
UNCOLLECTED: "The Wickedest Book in the
World," *Dial,* 46 (16 May 1909): 315–318;

"Francis Scott Key as a Churchman," *Maryland Historical Magazine,* 4 (June 1909): 154–170;

"The Story of Thomas Cresap, a Maryland Pioneer," *Maryland Historical Magazine,* 9 (March
1914): 1–37;

"The First Sixty Years of the Church of England in
Maryland," *Maryland Historical Magazine,* 11
(March 1916): 1–41;

"William Goddard and Some of His Friends," *Rhode
Island Historical Society Collections,* 17 (April
1924): 33–46;

"Some Early French Guiana Tracts, an Addition to
the Bibliography of El Dorado," *Proceedings of
the American Antiquarian Society,* new series 35
(April 1925): 28–45;

"Recent Bibliographical Work in America," *Library,*
fourth series 9 (June 1928): 59–85;

"The Indian Treaty as Literature," *Yale Review,* 17
(July 1928): 749–766;

"Poe's Baltimore," *Johns Hopkins Alumni Magazine,* 17
(June 1929): 299–312;

"James Sterling: Poet, Priest and Prophet of Empire," *Proceedings of the American Antiquarian Society,* new series 41 (April 1931): 25–76;

"Juan Ortiz and the Beginnings of Wood Engraving
in America," *Colophon,* 3, no. 12 (December
1932);

"Formats and Sizes," *Dolphin, A Journal of the Making
of Books,* 1 (1933): 81–95;

"The Maryland Muse by Ebenezer Cooke. A Facsimile with an Introduction by Lawrence C.
Wroth," *Proceedings of the American Antiquarian
Society,* new series 44 (October 1934):
267–335;

"The St. Mary's City Press, a New Chronology of
American Printing," *Colophon,* new series 1, no.
3 (1936): 333–357;

"Career in Books," *Johns Hopkins Alumni Magazine,*
26 (April 1938): 81–86;

"The Bibliographical Way," *Colophon,* new series 3,
no. 2 (1938): 225–237;

"Toward a Rare Book Policy in the Library of Congress," *Library of Congress Quarterly Journal of
Current Acquisitions,* 1 (September 1943): 3–11;

"The Early Cartography of the Pacific," *Papers of the
Bibliographical Society of America,* 38 (1944):
87–268;

"American Woodcuts and Engravings, 1670–1800.
Catalogue of an Exhibition Arranged in the
John Carter Brown Library for the Meeting of
the Walpole Society, October 26, 1945," compiled by Wroth and Marion W. Adams, *Walpole Society Note Book* (1945): 49–86;

"The Chief End of Book Madness," *Library of Congress Quarterly Journal of Current Acquisitions,* 3
(October 1945): 69–77;

"Joshua Fisher's 'Chart of Delaware Bay and
River,'" *Pennsylvania Magazine of History and Biography,* 74 (January 1950): 90–109;

"An Unknown Champlain Map of 1616," *Imago
Mundi,* 11 (1954): 85–94;

"Lathrop Colgate Harper: A Happy Memory," *Papers of the Bibliographical Society of America,* 52
(1958): 161–172;

"Alonso de Ovalle's Large Map of Chile," *Imago
Mundi,* 14 (1959): 90–95.

In a dual career as author and librarian, Lawrence C. Wroth interpreted American history
through bibliography. His publications ranged from
the definitive *Colonial Printer* (1931) to newspaper articles, and he drew the material for much of his writing from his study and development of a major collection, the John Carter Brown Library in Providence, Rhode Island.

Lawrence Counselman Wroth was born in
Baltimore on 14 January 1884, one of three sons of
the Reverend Peregrine Wroth, an Episcopal minister, and Mary Augusta Counselman Wroth. The
Wroths were descended from a family of early settlers in Kent County on the eastern shore of Maryland, and Lawrence's great-grandfather, another
Peregrine Wroth, tried his hand at poetry and wrote
his memoirs. An interest in history and literature
thus seems to have run in the family.

As a child Wroth loved to read and was especially attracted to the romance of history. After attending public schools and a private preparatory
school in Baltimore, he entered Johns Hopkins University, with scholarship assistance, and took the
historical-political course of study. He joined a fraternity, where he made a permanent friendship with
a graduate student in German, Leonard L. Mackall,

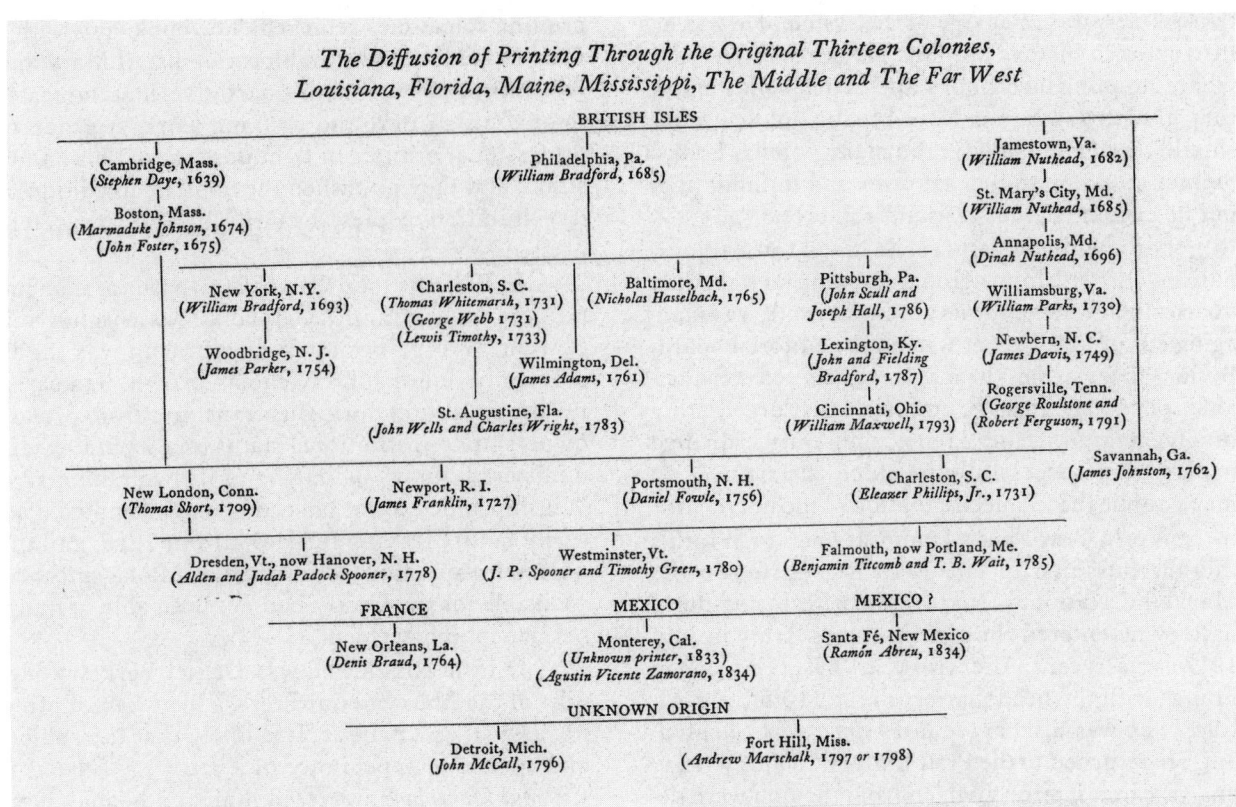

The Diffusion of Printing Through the Original Thirteen Colonies,
Louisiana, Florida, Maine, Mississippi, The Middle and The Far West

BRITISH ISLES

Cambridge, Mass.
(*Stephen Daye*, 1639)

Boston, Mass.
(*Marmaduke Johnson*, 1674)
(*John Foster*, 1675)

Philadelphia, Pa.
(*William Bradford*, 1685)

Jamestown, Va.
(*William Nuthead*, 1682)

St. Mary's City, Md.
(*William Nuthead*, 1685)

Annapolis, Md.
(*Dinah Nuthead*, 1696)

New York, N.Y.
(*William Bradford*, 1693)

Charleston, S.C.
(*Thomas Whitemarsh*, 1731)
(*George Webb* 1731)
(*Lewis Timothy*, 1733)

Baltimore, Md.
(*Nicholas Hasselbach*, 1765)

Pittsburgh, Pa.
(*John Scull and Joseph Hall*, 1786)

Williamsburg, Va.
(*William Parks*, 1730)

Woodbridge, N. J.
(*James Parker*, 1754)

Wilmington, Del.
(*James Adams*, 1761)

Lexington, Ky.
(*John and Fielding Bradford*, 1787)

Newbern, N. C.
(*James Davis*, 1749)

St. Augustine, Fla.
(*John Wells and Charles Wright*, 1783)

Cincinnati, Ohio
(*William Maxwell*, 1793)

Rogersville, Tenn.
(*George Roulstone and Robert Ferguson*, 1791)

New London, Conn.
(*Thomas Short*, 1709)

Newport, R. I.
(*James Franklin*, 1727)

Portsmouth, N. H.
(*Daniel Fowle*, 1756)

Charleston, S. C.
(*Eleazer Phillips, Jr.*, 1731)

Savannah, Ga.
(*James Johnston*, 1762)

Dresden, Vt., now Hanover, N. H.
(*Alden and Judah Padock Spooner*, 1778)

Westminster, Vt.
(*J. P. Spooner and Timothy Green*, 1780)

Falmouth, now Portland, Me.
(*Benjamin Titcomb and T. B. Wait*, 1785)

FRANCE

MEXICO

MEXICO ?

New Orleans, La.
(*Denis Braud*, 1764)

Monterey, Cal.
(*Unknown printer*, 1833)
(*Agustin Vicente Zamorano*, 1834)

Santa Fé, New Mexico
(*Ramón Abreu*, 1834)

UNKNOWN ORIGIN

Detroit, Mich.
(*John McCall*, 1796)

Fort Hill, Miss.
(*Andrew Marschalk*, 1797 or 1798)

Wroth's chart of early American printers, from the revised edition (1938) of his The Colonial Printer

who had a sophisticated interest in books and introduced Wroth to bibliography.

Wroth graduated with an A.B. in 1905. He wanted to write, but did not know what his direction would be. The magazine *Country Life in America* had accepted his articles on country house sanitation and window construction when, in the fall of 1905, he had an opportunity for a regular occupation. The librarian of the Maryland Episcopal Diocesan Library died unexpectedly, and Wroth, probably through his father's influence, was appointed to fill the vacancy.

The library, in Baltimore next door to the residence of the Episcopal bishop of Maryland, was an important collection of more than thirty thousand volumes, many rare and others for circulation. Besides theology, it was strong in history, particularly the history of the American colonies. There were early imprints, from incunabula to the work of Benjamin Franklin, and an extensive collection of American historical manuscripts. The staff consisted of the librarian and a part-time janitor.

One of Wroth's responsibilities was to promote the use of the library, because neither its resources nor its easy accessibility were well known. Sometimes he gave talks to church groups, and he put notices about the books in the *Maryland Churchman,* the monthly newspaper of the diocese. By 1908 Wroth was editing the paper and publishing historical articles, based on the collections of the library, in scholarly periodicals. His first book, *Parson Weems, a Biographical and Critical Study,* appeared over the imprint of a Baltimore bookseller in 1911. This study of American clergyman, bookseller, and biographer Mason Locke Weems has many of the characteristics of Wroth's best later work: a painstaking use of sources, a graceful and attractive style, and attention to the human interest of his story. Wroth, weighing the evidence, believed there may have been truth in Weems's account of young George Washington chopping down the cherry tree.

In spite of steady efforts, Wroth never succeeded in convincing clergy and laity that they should increase their use of the Diocesan Library. Early in 1912 he resigned from the library and the *Maryland Churchman* to become assistant librarian of the Enoch Pratt Free Library in Baltimore, a general library providing services to a large urban population.

At the Pratt Library the collection was mostly circulating, and Wroth's responsibilities were with the branches. A scholarly librarian, Bernard Christian Steiner, was in charge of the system. He was an instructor in history at Johns Hopkins University, where he published books and articles on the history of Maryland; he believed that a public library should teach and not have too many popular books. Steiner could be somewhat dour and intimidating, but he encouraged his assistant's interests.

For a while Wroth was inclined toward journalism. In 1912 Johns Hopkins began to publish a quarterly magazine for its alumni. Wroth was managing editor and Steiner was on the editorial board. Besides news stories the magazine devoted considerable space to aggressive editorials that urged more involvement of faculty in the community, ridiculed hazing, and successfully prodded the trustees to make public the financial situation of the university.

World War I put a temporary end to Wroth's literary pursuits. In late 1915 he enlisted in the Maryland National Guard, and with his artillery battery he entered the United States Army in July 1917 as a sergeant. After two years of service, one in France with the headquarters of the 110th Field Artillery, he was discharged in 1919 as a first lieutenant. He returned to the Pratt Library and his writing and research interests, which from then on were devoted to the history of the book.

William Parks, who opened a shop in Annapolis in 1726, had long been considered the first Maryland printer, because the documentary and physical evidence of his predecessors' work was so scanty that it had escaped notice. The publication, beginning in 1883, of the *Archives of Maryland* made an important source available; using these records, Wroth was the first to notice that the Assembly of the Province had paid William Nuthead, a printer of St. Mary's City, for his services in 1686. Nuthead was followed as public printer by his widow, Dinah; Thomas Reading succeeded her; and John Peter Zenger also printed in Maryland before the arrival of Parks. Wroth published his discoveries in 1922 in *A History of Printing in Colonial Maryland, 1686–1776,* which has not been superseded as a basic text.

Wroth did much more than extend the history of Maryland printing back for forty years. Using a wide range of sources in Maryland, other states, and England, he wrote a history of the colony through the printed record created there. He shows what was printed and why—laws, jobbing work, newspapers, and belles lettres—and how the printers dealt with the politics and business conditions of their times. When enough evidence is available he draws vivid portraits of the craftsmen, and, although a sympathetic observer, he is sometimes critical of their work. He notes bad proofreading and bad equipment, but admires the clear and dignified

printing sometimes achieved. The book ends with a detailed bibliography and location list of Maryland imprints to 1776. Wroth's narrative communicates the pleasure of groundbreaking work. A group of professional printers in Baltimore shared his enthusiasm, and they published the book in an edition of five hundred copies, beautifully and accurately printed.

In 1922 the John Carter Brown Library, an important collection of Americana, was without a librarian. George Parker Winship, who was the librarian of donor John Nicholas Brown, had cared for the collection during its transition from private ownership to institutional status as a separately administered library belonging to Brown University. Winship added to the collection and promoted it actively before leaving for Harvard in 1915, and the university-appointed Committee of Management responsible for the library had not been able to find a permanent replacement.

On the committee was Daniel Berkeley Updike of the Merrymount Press, a historian of printing as well as a printer. It is likely that the subject and attractive appearance of *A History of Printing in Colonial Maryland* impressed him, and he may have influenced the committee to offer the position of librarian to Wroth. In 1923 Wroth moved to Providence.

The John Carter Brown Library was somewhat smaller than the Episcopal Diocesan Library of Maryland, but more focused. Wroth had assistants for his work, and the Committee of Management took a serious interest. The collection, begun by John Carter Brown in the 1840s and continued by his son John Nicholas Brown, was devoted to sources for the history of the Western Hemisphere, from the classical works that influenced the earliest explorers through eighteenth-century publications. As Wroth learned about the resources of the library, he began to develop them. From 1924 he wrote the annual *Report to the Corporation of Brown University* submitted by the committee, describing the growing numbers of readers, the ways in which their needs brought out different aspects of the collection, and the books added. Wroth's *Reports* are essays on the collection, particularly effective in their discussion of individual books as they relate to the whole.

Wroth was a hardheaded researcher, but he refers often to the "adventure" of book collecting. The books he discovered in the library, or added to it, ranged from obvious high spots to works which could be appreciated best with imagination and sympathy. On one occasion he acquired two important and rare maps for the library on the same day: the Robert Thorne map of the world to complete the library's copy of Richard Hakluyt's *Divers Voyages Touching the Discouerie of America*. . . . (London: Printed by Thomas Dawson for Thomas Woodcocke, 1582); and the Wright-Molyneux map, first to use the Mercator projection, in a perfect set of the revised three-volume edition of Hakluyt's *Principal Navigations, Voiages, Traffiques and Discoueries of the English Nation*. . . . (London: Printed by George Bishop, Ralph Newberie and Robert Barker, 1598–1600).

These items were monuments of cartography, significant from their first appearance; but Wroth also found interest in more routine records of the past. At the John Carter Brown Library he first became acquainted with the "Indian Treaties," transcripts of the speeches at meetings of Native Americans and colonists, with the Native American speeches in literal translation. Wroth recognized that they were not only a moving evocation of a world coming to an end, but a distinct form of literature: sometimes humorous, sometimes poetic, and much more vivid than ordinary eighteenth-century English prose.

Wroth continued with his research on North American printing, and in 1931 the Grolier Club published *The Colonial Printer*. In this book, which besides his history of Maryland printing is his best-known achievement, Wroth introduces the earliest printers on the Eastern Seaboard; answers, in an easily understandable way, all the basic questions about the printing trade in the colonies; and makes clear the printer's place in his community and his time. Wroth describes the techniques of printing and the making of its necessary equipment, from presses and type to ink and paper. He tells how industries manufacturing these necessities developed in the colonies, so that by the end of the eighteenth century printers no longer were dependent on imports to do their work. He explains how the economics of the time affected labor relations and even the format of books; discusses the aesthetic qualities of the books and their bindings; and, finally, analyzes the many different kinds of printed work. The first edition was handsomely printed for the Grolier Club by the Merrymount Press. Whenever possible, Wroth was actively concerned with the appearance of his publications.

Brown University gave Wroth the degree of D. Litt. in 1932 and appointed him Research Professor of American History, "an honorable post without duties or emolument," as he remarked in a letter of 15 June 1932 to his friend Mackall. Although Wroth did not teach, he advised Brown students with bibliographic interests, one of whom, Joseph Towne Wheeler, later published a history and bibli-

Second edition in Latin (1493) of a letter by Christopher Columbus describing the New World, an item Wroth helped to acquire for the Library of Congress

ography of Maryland printing which extended Wroth's history to 1790.

In Providence Wroth, who never learned to drive, always lived within walking distance of the John Carter Brown Library. On 27 December 1930 he married Barbara Pease, a schoolteacher. He was active in the community, particularly with the Providence Athenaeum, a subscription library for families, and he held a position on the Advisory Council of the Rhode Island School for the Deaf.

Beyond Providence and the university, Wroth was a member of the Bibliographical Society of America and served as its president from 1931 to 1933. The Bibliographical Society of London made him an Honorary Secretary for America; in this post he was involved with matters of membership and publications, until his lack of time made it necessary for him to resign. As a Rosenbach Fellow in Bibliography he gave three lectures which the University of Pennsylvania Press published in 1934 as *An American Bookshelf, 1755*. Through the collecting activities of

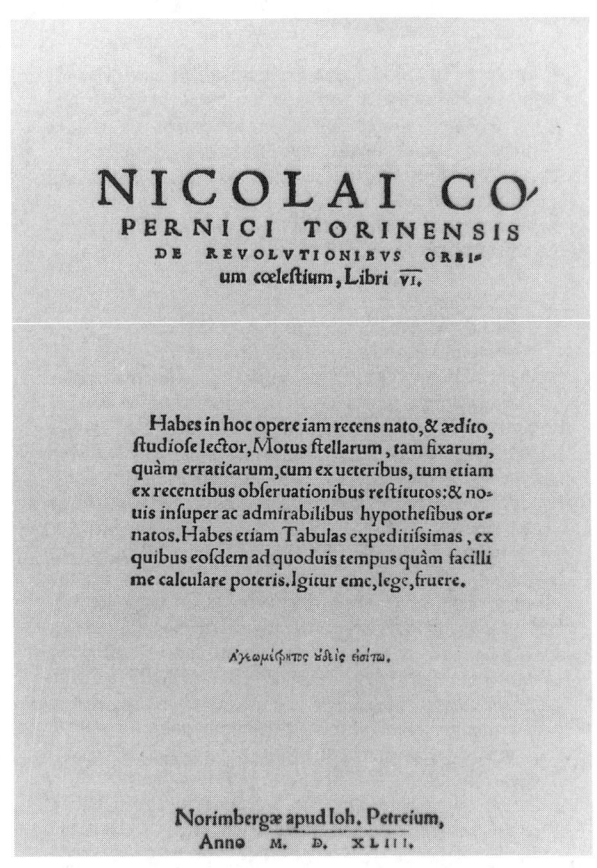

Title page for the first edition of a work by Copernicus that Wroth acquired for the Library of Congress

an imaginary Mr. Loveday, who accumulates all the American publications of his time in politics, religion, science, and literature, Wroth illustrates the intellectual activity of the generation before the Revolution. *An American Bookshelf* supplements *The Colonial Printer,* expanding its chapters on the product of the press.

A third important book appeared in 1937. *The Way of a Ship: An Essay on the Literature of Navigation Science* originated in an exhibition of books on navigation at the John Carter Brown Library. It is a charmingly written work showing how the technical literature of the sea, and the mapmaker's art, developed from the craft of navigation.

Wroth was a conscious stylist and a lover of formal English; he wrote without affectation and with absolute clarity. He excelled at explaining matters, such as printing procedures, that can seem bewildering to those who are not familiar with them. His best writing has a smooth flow and elegant finish, and he has the gift of meeting his reader directly and almost personally. Although good with people, Wroth was reserved with those he did not know

well, and only his readers and close friends noticed his quiet, dry humor and his warmth.

The biographer Catherine Drinker Bowen, who admired *An American Bookshelf,* came to Providence especially to meet Wroth. From the book she had formed the impression of a courtly, glamorous personality, straight from the eighteenth century. She found a rather stocky gentleman with glasses, a kind but infrequent smile, and not much to say. He gave her some "Indian Treaties" to read and disappeared about his work, returning later to take her to lunch, which was a pleasant occasion but not memorable.

Wroth's articles usually appeared in specialist journals, and his books were published in small editions; but he gained a wider readership when Leonard Mackall, who edited the "Notes for Bibliophiles" column in the Sunday "Books" section of the *New York Herald Tribune,* sometimes asked him to write for it. In 1937 Mackall died, and the *Tribune* invited Wroth to take over the column. The Committee of Management at the John Carter Brown Library agreed to his outside activities, which reflected well on the library. Under Wroth's editorship "Notes" appeared biweekly from 1937 to 1947, when it was discontinued. Usually Wroth provided the copy, although, as Mackall had done, he invited contributions from others. He reported and commented on news interesting to book professionals and serious amateurs. While he corresponded with readers and replied thoughtfully to their suggestions, he avoided controversy. The column was sometimes like a dialogue between the editor and interested people, and a public beyond the active book world followed it.

In 1938 Wroth was appointed a consultant to the Pierpont Morgan Library to help its director, Belle da Costa Greene. At first he visited New York once a month. With the newspaper work this post was time-consuming, but Wroth now had three sons to educate and needed the extra income. Wroth and Greene had a pleasant, informal relationship and enjoyed working together. His responsibilities were never exactly defined. Greene asked for his suggestions on whatever she was concerned about: exhibits and a program of publications; the color and weight of paper for invitations and posters; even staffing decisions. Wroth was tactful with the staff, who had confidence in him. He seems to have been less involved with purchases, although this was his greatest expertise.

Thomas R. Adams, who succeeded him at the John Carter Brown Library, noted that Wroth increased its holdings by fifty-five hundred books. Wroth studied the collection, compared it with others and with bibliographies in the areas it covered, and always knew what it needed. He usually went beyond his budget and once remarked before a talk he gave on his collection-building that its subtitle should be "A Quarter Century in the Red." The library never lacked a book because it could not pay immediately. Wroth had excellent relationships with booksellers, who often waited a long time for their money. On some occasions Wroth sought help in the community for major acquisitions.

Two dealers from whom he bought frequently were Lathrop C. Harper and A. S. W. Rosenbach. In 1939 Rosenbach bought the Herschel V. Jones collection of Americana, intending to break it up for individual sales. Wroth knew such an acquisition opportunity would not occur again. He had no book funds left for the year but hurried to New York and picked out the books most important for the collection of the library, including unique items on the Spanish Southwest. Brown alumni and other friends of the library contributed the money necessary for the purchase—more than $30,000.

Archibald MacLeish, the Librarian of Congress, asked Wroth to take charge of its rare books in 1943. For lack of time he was unable to do so but accepted the position of consultant for the acquisition of rare books. The Library of Congress had begun to administer its rare books separately only sixteen years before and was still analyzing the collection and searching for a definite policy and direction. When Wroth assumed his new position, the acting chief of the Rare Book Division was Frederick Goff, a Brown graduate whom Wroth had recommended to the Library of Congress in 1940. Greene and Wroth were old friends, but the relationship of Wroth and Goff was more like that of teacher and pupil. Wroth drew up a policy for developing the rare collections. He believed purchases should be divided between Americana and the general field of the history of ideas. He never thought of rare books as totally distinct from the other library collections, but rather as supplementing them. He believed the library should build on strength and anticipate the future needs of researchers. Wroth's definition of rarity was simple: the esteem in which a book was held, combined with its scarcity.

As consultant Wroth visited Washington several times a year, for two or three days at a time, and he and Goff were always in close touch about purchases. They both made selections and managed to avoid conflict when their libraries were interested in similar items. Beyond the Rare Book Division Wroth gave advice to other departments when they requested it, and he was chairman of the committee on the catalogue of Thomas Jefferson's library. He

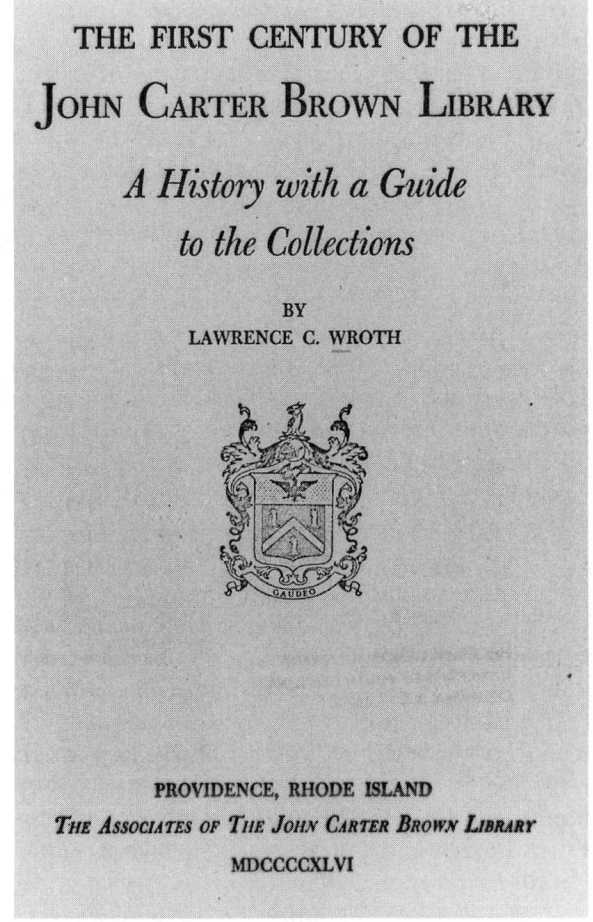

THE FIRST CENTURY OF THE

JOHN CARTER BROWN LIBRARY

A History with a Guide to the Collections

BY
LAWRENCE C. WROTH

PROVIDENCE, RHODE ISLAND
THE ASSOCIATES OF THE JOHN CARTER BROWN LIBRARY
MDCCCCXLVI

Wroth's history of the John Carter Brown Library, where he worked for more than thirty years

sometimes visited potential donors outside Washington; on one occasion he saw a donor in New York, worked at the Pierpont Morgan Library, and gave a talk on the same day. With visits to dealers, as well, Wroth was on the road more often than he liked; he remarked in a letter to a friend that he felt his age most when he traveled, even before he set out.

A group of friends of Wroth and the John Carter Brown Library, among them the Horace Walpole collector Wilmarth S. Lewis and Clarence S. Brigham of the American Antiquarian Society, formed the Associates of the John Carter Brown Library in 1944. The Associates sponsored exhibitions and publications and provided funds for purchases. Their annual meetings became important events in the book world, and Wroth invited the Associates and other visitors to his home after the sessions.

In the late 1940s Wroth was at the peak of his reputation and began to receive honors. The American Institute of Graphic Arts gave him its gold medal in 1948, and in 1951 Goff edited a Festschrift in his honor. Wroth retired from the Library of Congress in 1954 at the mandatory age of seventy but continued to work at the John Carter Brown Library for three more years. In 1957 the Bibliographical Society of London, calling him the "dean of American bibliographers," awarded him its gold medal, an honor given only once before to an American.

As librarian emeritus, Wroth stayed at the John Carter Brown Library for seven years after his successor, Thomas R. Adams, arrived. He was general editor of Brown's bicentennial publications and pursued his interest in cartography. After he gave up his office in the library he continued to make frequent visits, for he had a new publication under way that grew into a major project.

Wroth never left his consultancy at the Pierpont Morgan Library, and Frederick Adams, Greene's successor, asked him to prepare an edition of the library's Cèllere Codex, a manuscript account of Giovanni da Verrazzano's voyage of exploration to the East Coast of North America in 1524. The manuscript was written by a scribe and had annotations which were possibly in the hand of the explorer himself. The edition of the Codex grew into a full-scale book on Verrazzano, which occupied Wroth nearly to the end of his life.

Verrazzano, like others before him, was hoping to find a passage to Asia when he sailed west in 1524. Instead he was the first European to see and describe the North American coast from the Carolinas to Newfoundland. Wroth made an exhaustive study of all the available sources to place Verrazzano, his 1524 voyage, and his later voyages in their proper context. Researching and writing the book went slowly.

As Wroth grew older he could walk the four blocks downhill from his house on Meeting Street to the John Carter Brown Library on the university campus, but returning uphill was too much for him, and a staff member from the library drove him home after he had finished his research for the day. Wroth also found it trying that he had less control over the production of this book than any of his earlier ones, and he was not comfortable working with an editor.

The Voyages of Giovanni da Verrazzano, 1524–1528 was published in October 1970. It is an impressive work of scholarship. The book does not have quite the easy style of his earlier work, but it is on a much larger scale. Wroth presents evidence, then draws the story from it. Always a bookman, he is particularly effective as he shows what printed information Verrazzano would have had before he sailed, and how his voyage increased the knowledge of explorers who came after him. Less than three months after the book was published, Wroth died, on Christmas Day 1970. His work on Verrazzano seems to have supported him toward the end of his life.

Wroth had an important place in the book world of his time, and his influence is lasting. He left the John Carter Brown Library stronger in resources and better known than he found it, and he helped to set the collecting direction of the Library of Congress in rare books. As a writer he made an original and permanent contribution to the history of the book in America. His writing has the qualities he admired in Peter Kalm's eighteenth-century *Travels into North America . . . ,* which Wroth described in his 1946 *Report.* It is "rich in fact, in careful observation, and in thoughtful interpretation."

Bibliography:

Marion W. Adams and Jeannette D. Black, comps., "A List of Published Writings of Lawrence C. Wroth to December 31, 1950," in *Essays Honoring Lawrence C. Wroth,* edited by Frederick R. Goff (Portland, Maine: Anthoensen Press, 1951), pp. 485–504.

References:

Thomas R. Adams, *Lawrence Counselman Wroth, 1884–1970: The Memorial Minute Read Before the Faculty of Brown University 9 February, 1971; and a Handlist of an Exhibition of his Writing in the John Carter Brown Library of Brown University* (Providence, R.I., 1971);

Catherine Drinker Bowen, *Adventures of a Biographer* (Boston: Little, Brown, 1959), pp. 126–129;

William Matheson, "Seeking the Rare, the Important, the Valuable: the Rare Book Division," *Quarterly Journal of the Library of Congress,* 30 (1973): 211–227;

Bradford Fuller Swan, "Lawrence Counselman Wroth," *Proceedings of the American Antiquarian Society,* new series 81 (1971): 37–39.

Papers:

Papers of Lawrence Wroth are in the John Carter Brown Library, Providence, Rhode Island. Some of his correspondence with Leonard Mackall is in Special Collections, Milton S. Eisenhower Library, Johns Hopkins University.

Books for Further Reading

Ahearn, Allen. *Book Collecting: A Comprehensive Guide.* New York: Putnam, 1989.

Barlow, William P. Jr. *Book Collecting: Personal Rewards and Public Benefits.* Washington, D.C.: Library of Congress, 1984.

Bernard, Philippa, ed., with Leo Bernard and Angus O'Neill. *Antiquarian Books: A Companion for Booksellers, Librarians and Collectors.* Philadelphia: University of Pennsylvania Press, 1994.

Block, Andrew. *The Book Collector's Vade Mecum.* London: Dennis Archer, 1932.

Blumenthal, Walter Hart. *Bookmen's Bedlam: An Olio of Literary Oddities.* New Brunswick, N.J.: Rutgers University Press, 1955.

Booth, Richard, ed., *The Country Life Book of Book Collecting.* London: Country Life Books, 1976.

Bowers, Fredson. *Bibliography and Textual Criticism.* Oxford: Clarendon Press, 1964.

Bowers. *Textual & Literary Criticism.* Cambridge: Cambridge University Press, 1959.

Boynton, Henry Walcott. *Annals of American Bookselling, 1638–1850.* New York: Wiley, 1932; republished, with an introduction by Joseph Rosenblum, New Castle, Del.: Oak Knoll Books, 1991.

Brewer, Reginald. *The Delightful Diversion: The Whys and Wherefores of Book Collecting.* New York: Macmillan, 1935.

Brook, G. L. *Books and Book-Collecting.* London: Deutsch, 1980.

Brotherhead, William. *Forty Years Among the Old Booksellers in Philadelphia.* Philadelphia: Brotherhead, 1891.

Burton, John Hill. *The Book Hunter.* Edinburgh: Blackwood, 1862.

Cannon, Carl L. *American Book Collectors and Collecting from Colonial Times to the Present.* New York: Wilson, 1941.

Carter, John. *ABC for Book Collectors.* New York: Knopf, 1951; sixth edition, with corrections and additions by Nicolas Barker, New York & London: Granada, 1980.

Carter. *Books and Book-Collectors.* Cleveland: World, 1957.

Carter. *Taste & Technique in Book Collecting: A Study of Recent Developments in Great Britain and the United States.* Cambridge: Cambridge University Press, 1948; republished, with an epilogue, London: Private Libraries Association, 1970.

Davis, Richard Beale. *A Colonial Southern Bookshelf: Reading in the Eighteenth Century.* Athens: University of Georgia Press, 1979.

Davis. *Intellectual Life in Jefferson's Virginia 1790–1830.* Knoxville: University of Tennessee Press, 1964.

Dickinson, Donald C. *Dictionary of American Book Collectors.* New York: Greenwood Press, 1986.

Dunbar, Maurice. *Books and Collectors.* Los Altos, Cal.: Book Nest, 1980.

Ettinghausen, Maurice L. *Rare Books and Royal Collectors: Memoirs of an Antiquarian Bookseller.* New York: Simon & Schuster, 1966.

Everitt, Charles P. *Adventures of a Treasure Hunter.* Boston: Little, Brown, 1951.

Farmer, Bernard J. *The Gentle Art of Book-Collecting.* London: Thorson's Publishers, 1950.

Farnham, Luther. *A Glance at Private Libraries.* Boston: Press of Crocker and Brewster, 1855; reprinted, with an introduction and annotated index by Roger E. Stoddard, Weston, Mass.: M & S Press, 1991.

Gaskell, Philip. *A New Introduction to Bibliography.* Oxford: Clarendon Press, 1972.

Goodrum, Charles A. *Treasures of the Library of Congress.* Revised and expanded edition, New York: Abrams, 1991.

Greetham, D. C. *Textual Scholarship: An Introduction.* New York & London: Garland, 1992.

Greg, W. W. *Collected Papers.* Oxford: Clarendon Press, 1966.

Iacone, Salvatore J. *The Pleasures of Book Collecting.* New York: Harper & Row, 1976.

Jackson, Holbrook. *The Anatomy of Bibliomania,* 2 volumes. London: Soncino Press, 1930–1931.

Joline, Adrian H. *The Diversions of a Book-Lover.* New York & London: Harper, 1903.

Landon, Richard G., ed. *Book Selling and Book Buying: Aspects of the Nineteenth Century British and North American Book Trade.* Chicago: American Library Association, 1978.

Lehmann-Haupt, Hellmut. *The Book in America: A History of the Making, the Selling, and the Collecting of Books in the United States.* New York: Bowker, 1939.

Lewis, Roy Harley. *Antiquarian Books: An Insider's Account.* New York: Arco, 1978.

Littlefield, George Emery. *Early Boston Booksellers, 1642–1711.* Boston: Club of Odd Volumes, 1900.

Malclès, Louise Noelle. *Bibliography,* translated by Theodore Christian Hines. New York: Scarecrow Press, 1961.

Matthews, Jack. *Collecting Rare Books for Pleasure and Profit.* New York: Putnam, 1977.

McKerrow, Ronald B. *An Introduction to Bibliography for Literary Students.* Oxford: Clarendon Press, 1927.

Morley, Christopher. *Ex Libris Carissimis.* Philadelphia: University of Pennsylvania Press, 1932.

Muir, Percy H. *Book-Collecting as a Hobby: In a Series of Letters to Everyman.* London: Gramol, 1944.

Muir, *Book-Collecting: More Letters to Everyman.* London: Cassell, 1949.

Oliphant, Dave, and Robin Bradford, eds. *New Directions in Textual Studies.* Austin: Harry Ransom Humanities Research Center, University of Texas at Austin, 1990.

Pearson, Edmund Lester. *Books in Black or Red.* New York: Macmillan, 1923.

Peters, Jean, ed. *Book Collecting: A Modern Guide*. New York: Bowker, 1977.

Rees-Mogg, William. *How To Buy Rare Books: A Practical Guide to the Antiquarian Book Market*. Oxford: Phaidon Christie's, 1985.

Rogers, Horatio. *Private Libraries of Providence, with a Preliminary Essay on the Love of Books*. Providence: Sidney S. Rider, 1878.

Savage, Ernest Albert. *The Story of Libraries and Book-Collecting*. London: Routledge, 1909.

Schneider, Georg. *Theory and History of Bibliography,* translated by Ralph Robert Shaw. New York: Columbia University Press, 1934.

Sowerby, E. Millicent. *Rare People and Rare Books*. London: Constable, 1967.

Stern, Madeleine B. *Antiquarian Bookselling in the United States: A History from the Origins to the 1940s*. Westport, Conn.: Greenwood Press, 1985.

Stern. *Books and Book People in 19th-Century America*. New York: Bowker, 1978.

Stillwell, Margaret. *Incunabula and Americana, 1450–1800*. New York: Columbia University Press, 1931.

Storm, Colton, and Howard Peckham. *Invitation to Book Collecting, Its Pleasures and Practices, with Kindred Discussions of Manuscripts, Maps, and Prints*. New York: Bowker, 1947.

Tanselle, G. Thomas. *A Rationale of Textual Criticism*. Philadelphia: University of Pennsylvania Press, 1989.

Tanselle. *Textual Criticism Since Greg: A Chronicle, 1950–1985*. Charlottesville: University Press of Virginia, 1987.

Targ, William, ed. *Bouillabaisse for Bibliophiles: A Treasury of Bookish Lore, Wit & Wisdom, Tales, Poetry & Narratives & Certain Curious Studies of Interest to Bookmen & Collectors*. Cleveland: World, 1955.

Targ, ed. *Carrousel for Bibliophiles*. New York: Philip C. Duschnes, 1947.

Thomas, Alan G. *Great Books and Book Collectors*. London: Weidenfeld & Nicolson, 1975.

Towner, Wesley, and Stephen Varble. *The Elegant Auctioneers*. New York: Hill & Wang, 1970.

Williams, William Proctor, and Craig S. Abbott. *An Introduction to Bibliographical and Textual Studies*. New York: Modern Language Association of America, 1985.

Willoughby, Edwin Eliott. *The Uses of Bibliography to the Students of Literature and History*. Hamden, Conn.: Shoe String Press, 1957.

Wilson, Robert A. *Modern Book Collecting*. New York: Knopf, 1980.

Winterich, John T. *A Primer of Book Collecting*. New York: Greenberg, 1926; third edition, revised by Winterich and David A. Randall, New York: Crown, 1966.

Wynne, James. *Private Libraries of New York*. New York: E. French, 1860.

Contributors

Robert G. Anthony Jr..*University of North Carolina at Chapel Hill*
Carol Armbruster ....*Library of Congress*
William Baker...*Northern Illinois University*
Edmund Berkeley Jr..*University of Virginia Library*
Francis J. Bosha..*Kawamura Gakuen Woman's University*
Harold N. Boyer ....*Florence County Library*
Matthew J. Bruccoli ....*University of South Carolina*
Beth E. Clausen...*University of Northern Iowa Library*
Robert Coale ....*The Newberry Library*
Jud H. Copeland ....*Emporia State University*
Robert Hauptman..*St. Cloud State University*
Kevin J. Hayes..*University of Central Oklahoma*
Karen Nelson Hoyle..*University of Minnesota*
Dean H. Keller..*Kent State University*
Harlan Kessel...*The Book Club of California*
David Klappholz...*Stevens Institute of Technology*
Michael E. D. Koenig...*Dominican University*
William H. Loos ....*Buffalo and Erie County Public Library*
Kurt S. Maier ....*Library of Congress*
Marcus A. McCorison...*Worcester, Massachusetts*
Robert A. McCown ....*University of Iowa*
Eileen L. McGrath...*University of North Carolina at Chapel Hill*
Karen Nipps ....*Library Company of Philadelphia*
Richard W. Oram ....*University of Texas at Austin*
Judith A. Overmier ....*University of Oklahoma*
John Pollack ....*University of Pennsylvania*
Timothy D. Pyatt ....*University of North Carolina at Chapel Hill*
Richard Raleigh...*St. Thomas University*
Ruth Rosenberg...*City University of New York*
Joseph Rosenblum ....*University of North Carolina at Greensboro*
Alison M. Scott...*Bowling Green State University*
Carolyn Smith ....*Johns Hopkins University*
Jeanne Somers ....*Kent State University*
Theodore Spahn..*Rosary College*
Madeleine B. Stern ....*Leona Rostenberg and Madeleine Stern—Rare Books*
Larry E. Sullivan ....*City University of New York*
Thomas M. Verich ....*University of Mississippi*
Robert Williams..*University of Chicago Press*
Peter M. Van Wingen................*Rare Book and Special Collections Division, Library of Congress*

Cumulative Index

Dictionary of Literary Biography, Volumes 1-187
Dictionary of Literary Biography Yearbook, 1980-1996
Dictionary of Literary Biography Documentary Series, Volumes 1-16

Cumulative Index

DLB before number: *Dictionary of Literary Biography*, Volumes 1-187
Y before number: *Dictionary of Literary Biography Yearbook*, 1980-1996
DS before number: *Dictionary of Literary Biography Documentary Series*, Volumes 1-16

A

D

Cumulative Index

O

Q

R

S